A HISTORY OF THE BEMBA

A History of the Bemba

Political growth and change in
north-eastern Zambia before 1900

Andrew D. Roberts

THE UNIVERSITY OF WISCONSIN PRESS

Published 1973
In North America by
The University of Wisconsin Press
Box 1379, Madison, Wisconsin 53701

Elsewhere by
Longman Group Limited
London

First printing 1973

ISBN 0-299-06450-6, LC 73-5813
Printed in Great Britain

To my mother,
and in memory of my father

Information I got from some people when set
against information I got from others always
revealed contradictions. But by dint of much
work and thought I consider that what follows
is not far from the truth.

ANTONIO GAMITTO on the Bemba, in 1832:
King Kazembe (tr. Cunnison), II, p. 159

Contents

Preface   xv

Acknowledgements   xix

Introduction   xxiii

1   *SOURCES*   1
Literary sources   2
Oral traditions
     The social basis   12
     Perspectives of the past   22
     Effects of modern social change   28
     Assessing the evidence   31

2   *THE ORIGINS OF BEMBA CHIEFTAINSHIP*   38
The Legend of Migration   39
General Commentary   43
Topography   50
Chronology   56
Early inhabitants of Bembaland   65

3   *THE EIGHTEENTH CENTURY*   77
The earlier Chitimukulus   78
Councillors and royal chiefs   79
Political relations   88

4   *THE GROWTH OF BEMBA POWER, c.* 1770–*c.* 1860   94

The reigns of Mukuuka and Chiliamafwa, *c.* 1770–*c.* 1820   94

    The foundation of the Ituna chiefdom   94

    The foundation of the Makasa chieftainship   98

    Chileshye Chepela and Susula Chinchinta   100

The reign of Chinchinta (*c.* 1820–?1827)   102

The reign of Chileshye (?1827–*c.* 1860)   104

    Ituna   104

    The Bemba and the Bisa   107

    The coming of the Ngoni   119

5   *THE REIGN OF CHITAPANKWA,* early 1860s–1883   125

The accession of Chitapankwa   127

The southeast: Ichinga and the Bisa   132

The southwest: Mwamba II, the Lungu and the Bisa   139

The north: the Ngoni, the Mambwe and the Lungu   142

The northwest: the Tabwa and Swahili   151

The south: Nkolemfumu and Chikwanda II   160

6   *POLITICS AND TRADE*   164

Bemba politics in about 1880   164

Trade   182

    Local exchanges   183

    Long-distance trade   189

Political effects of long-distance trade   198

7 *THE REIGN OF SAMPA*, 1884–96   215

Internal conflicts   217

European approaches, 1883–93   229

The Arabs and Swahili   236

Mporokoso and Ponde   241

The White Fathers, the Mambwe and Makasa   246

8 *EUROPEAN OCCUPATION*, 1896–9   255

The BSAC initiative, 1895–6   255

Mwamba and the White Fathers, 1896–7   259

Mwamba, the BSAC, and the eastern frontier, 1897   269

The last phase, 1898–9   276

Aftermath   284

9 *CONCLUSIONS*   293

Appendices   327

1 Tables (a) Outline Chronology   328

        (b) Bemba chiefs, showing areas occupied and
            former rulers   338

        (c) Census figures for Bemba country, early twentieth
            century; Note on labour migration   342

2 Supplementary Notes   344

3 The Bemba and the Ngoni   363

4 Select Historical Texts   377

5 List of Informants   384

6 List of Written Sources   390

Index   401

Illustrations

1 Kalungu river *facing page* xxxii

2 *Citemene* garden (chief Mubanga's area, 1969) xxxii

3 Mwalule, the burial grove of senior Bemba chiefs xxxiii

4 Staff owned by chief Mwamba, said to represent Chilimbulu 30

5 *Kabilo* Mulewa Chimfwembe, wearing head-dress of feathers
from the weaver-bird 30

6 *Ilamfya*, or war-charm 31

7 *Lunkumbi:* wooden slit signal drum, owned by the Bwile
chief Puta 190

8 Salt marsh at Chibwa, near Mpika, September 1969 190

9 *Mondo:* wooden slit signal drum, played by its owner,
Shimwalule 191

10 Bwile salt-makers' camp near Puta, on Lake Mweru 191

11 Chief Mwamba VI Musenga 222

12 Police guard outside the post office at Abercorn in 1893 223

13 The *malaila* war-dance, Chitimukulu's village, 1933 223

Tables

1 Lists of Chitimukulus: a comparison 59

2 Comparative lists of dynasties in north-eastern Zambia 62–3

3 Provenance of early Chitimukulus 89

Maps

1 Central Africa north of the Zambezi   xxv
2 Sites mentioned in the Bemba migration legend   41
3 Lubemba   81
4 Bembaland in the early nineteenth century   86
5 East-central Africa in the earlier nineteenth century   108
6 Bemba and Bisa, to 1860   112
7 Bemba and Ngoni, to 1860   120
8 Bemba expansion in the nineteenth century   126
9 The eastern borders   133
10 The southwest   140
11 The northeast   144
12 The northwest   156
13 The south   161
14 Bemba chiefdoms in 1883   175
15 Local trade in north-eastern Zambia   185
16 North-eastern Zambia in the 1890s   224
17 Bemba chiefdoms, c. 1905   290
18 Ngonde and Kamanga   355

Figures

1   Legendary origin of Bemba chieftainship   40

2   Nkweto and Mumena   83

3   Chileshye Mukulu and Mutale Mukulu   85

4   Bemba royal succession, earlier nineteenth century   101

5   Mukupa Kaoma   106

6   Bisa chiefs of Lubumbu   114

7   Bemba chieftainships, c. 1860   122

8   Bemba royal succession, later nineteenth century   130

9   Chimbola and Chandaweyaya   132

10   Katongo/Chewe   135

11   Makasa   147

12   Tafuna   149

13   Nsama   154

14   Bemba chieftainships, early 1883   176

15   Cross-cousin marriage of Bemba royals (i) males   178

16   Cross-cousin marriage of Bemba royals (ii) females   179

17   Bemba royal chieftainships, twentieth century   321

Preface

This book is a study of the pre-colonial history of the Bemba, a
Bantu-speaking agricultural people who live in the woodland of north-
eastern Zambia. In the later years of the last century, their powerful
and warlike chiefs compelled the attention of missionaries and explorers, such as David Livingstone, and officials, such as Sir Harry
Johnston, who sought to suppress the slave trade and 'open up' the
African interior to European trade and occupation. In 1898 the Bemba
submitted to British rule and in due course became one of the main
groups of people to furnish labour for the mines of central and southern
Africa. The scale of this labour migration aroused the concern of
administrators and others impressed by the effects of modern economic
change on African life. Partly for this reason, the economy and social
organisation of the Bemba have been the subject of numerous studies,
notably by Dr Audrey Richards.

The present work, however, is the first attempt to discuss Bemba
history at any length. Owing mainly to their central position in the
African interior, the Bemba were visited by few literate travellers before
they came under colonial rule: the first were Monteiro and Gamitto, in
1831. Much of this book therefore is based largely on the oral traditions
of the Bemba and their neighbours. Synthetic accounts of some of these
were compiled by early officials and missionaries, but I recorded many
traditions verbatim in the course of field research in 1964–5.

The character of these traditions has necessarily affected the scope
of this book. Among the Bemba, it is primarily the institution of
chieftainship which has given rise to both the need and the means for
transmitting stories about the past. (This point is elaborated in chapter
1, where I discuss in detail the sources for this study.) Bemba history,
as it can be reconstructed today, is not so much the history of Bemba
society in general as the history of Bemba chiefs. Furthermore even
the traditions about chieftainships do not provide much reliable

information for any period before the earlier nineteenth century. Traditions about the foundation of Bemba chieftainship take the form of a more or less mythical legend of migration; this calls for analysis of a rather special kind, which I attempt in chapter 2. The greater part of this book consists of an account of Bemba dynastic conflict and territorial conquest during the nineteenth century; and two chapters are devoted to the fifteen years before the imposition of colonial rule, for which period the literary evidence is relatively abundant.

These topics, however, are less restricted than they might at first appear. In the first place, the very fact that Bemba chiefs fought over much of north-eastern Zambia during the nineteenth century means that a study of Bemba history necessarily involves study of neighbouring peoples with whom they came into conflict. As a result, this book embodies a good deal of research into the histories of the Bisa, Tabwa, Lungu and Mambwe. None of these peoples had received any systematic attention from historians, and only the last two had been studied at all extensively by a social anthropologist.

In the second place, Bemba political history is of considerable comparative interest to students of political change in pre-colonial Africa—a subject which has recently attracted attention from both historians and social anthropologists. This book traces the emergence, in a thinly populated part of the central African woodland, of a polity primarily organised on the basis of matrilineal kinship which achieved a degree of territorial extent and internal cohesion unusual in this region and for this kind of polity. In chapter 6 I give a description of the Bemba polity at the height of its power, in about 1880, and I try to show in what ways it had profited both from a particular geographical setting and from a particular historical process—the penetration of central Africa by traders from East Africa in ivory, slaves and copper. In the last chapter, I consider Bemba political development in the context of pre-colonial polities elsewhere in Africa. The Bemba example serves to show that an understanding of African political organisation calls both for an anthropologist's appreciation of factors making for equilibrium and repetitive change, and for the historian's appreciation of factors making for irregular, non-recurrent change.

Finally, a study of Bemba reactions to the intrusion of European empire-builders may claim to have some value as a contribution to recent discussion of reactions to such intrusion elsewhere in Africa. Research into the history of Africa both before and during the colonial period has had the effect of underlining the crucial importance, in many cases, of the manner in which different societies came under

European rule. The full significance of this process can, of course, only be understood in the light of later developments, both during and after the colonial period. For two reasons, I have not myself pursued this study of Bemba history into the twentieth century. There was the practical difficulty that such an enterprise would have encroached considerably on the limited time available for research in Zambia. And there was also an important theoretical point. Pre-colonial Bemba politics were largely a matter of dynastic conflict, played out in terms of conquest and raiding as well as intrigue. The imposition of colonial rule, by bringing fighting to an end, meant an abrupt and radical change in the environment of Bemba politics, quite apart from the fact that the Bemba were now part of a huge labour reserve for European mines. Thus the pre-colonial history of the Bemba forms a fairly self-contained field of investigation, in which their reaction to white intrusion can be seen primarily as a climax to, and commentary upon, their earlier political development. Most fortunately, however, this approach has now been complemented by the researches of a Zambian scholar, Dr Henry Meebelo, who has surveyed the imposition of colonial rule in Bemba country as prelude to a study of African reactions to Europeans and European rule in north-eastern Zambia (Northern Rhodesia) up to 1939.[1]

The presentation of the material in this book may call for some explanation. Its subject involves the consideration of geography, genealogy, sociology and historical epistemology of a more or less complex and unfamiliar kind. I have tried to clarify geography and genealogy by means of maps, figures and tables, and I provide in the introduction a short account of the environment and social institutions of the Bemba. The epistemology is less easily dealt with. Although this history should sufficiently demonstrate—if the point still needs making —that meaningful history can be written from oral traditions, such evidence does present special problems of assessment and interpretation, and the historian should expose them to the reader. In the interests of clarity, however, I have tried as far as possible not to interrupt narrative or analysis with discussion of conflicting or inadequate evidence. In consequence, some of the footnotes are inevitably rather long, though the longest have been banished to appendices at the end of the book. To give some idea of the kind of oral evidence used in this book, the appendices include a few short texts of historical traditions. Further texts recorded by me will be published in due course.

[1] Henry S. Meebelo, *Reaction to Colonialism,* Institute for African Studies, University of Zambia, Lusaka—Manchester University Press 1971

NOTE ON SPELLING

For all proper names, I adopt English spelling. All other words from African languages are given in italics and spelled according to the practice of the International African Institute. Thus, the *c* in *icalo* is pronounced 'ch' as in 'chair'. The phonetic symbol *ŋ* is pronounced like the 'ng' in 'longing'. Pre-prefixes are omitted.

Acknowledgements

This book is a much revised version of a Ph.D. thesis accepted by the University of Wisconsin in 1966. From 1961 to 1965 I held a Carnegie Fellowship in the Program in Comparative Tropical History at that University, and my researches in Britain and Central Africa were further assisted by travel grants made by the Program. I should like to thank the University of Wisconsin, and in particular Professor Philip Curtin, for thus enabling me to collect material for the thesis. I am further obliged to the Anglo-American Corporation (Zambia) for a generous grant towards travel expenses at a critical stage in fieldwork. Throughout my stay in Zambia from February 1964 to July 1965 I was affiliated to the then Rhodes–Livingstone Institute for Social Research, Lusaka. From 1965 to 1966, while writing the thesis, I held a Junior Research Fellowship in the School of African and Asian Studies at the University of Sussex. I am grateful to the University, and especially to Professor D. A. Low, for this invaluable support. My tenure of a research fellowship at the University of Zambia from 1968 to 1971 afforded me time to prepare this book for publication.

My work on the thesis was supervised throughout by Professor Jan Vansina, of the University of Wisconsin. I am deeply indebted to him, both for the example of his own work and for his patient guidance and encouragement. Professor Low also gave helpful advice, and a number of other scholars provided much stimulus. In particular, I wish to thank Dr Audrey Richards and Professor Ian Cunnison for the illumination I have gained from their writings and for the interest they have shown in my work. I have also profited from conversations with Dr Bruce Kapferer, and from the criticisms and suggestions of Miss Ann Tweedie, Professor Jaap van Velsen and Dr Richard Werbner. Whatever inadequacies or misconceptions remain are due to my own wilfulness or myopia.

For access to written sources, I must first thank the Rev. P. B.

Mushindo, of the United Church of Zambia, for enabling me to consult his most valuable history of the Bemba before publication.[1] Dr Richards generously allowed me to make use of her fieldnotes, while Mr Medard Kasese lent me records of his own interviews among the Bisa. Father Joseph Hering, formerly of Chilubula Mission (White Fathers), lent me his typescript history of the Bemba, based on notes by the late Fr E. Labrecque; this was of very great assistance, since the larger part of Labrecque's history was not published until 1968. The Generalate of the White Fathers in Rome kindly allowed me to consult the Society's archives there in July 1968; I am also indebted to the custodians of archives and libraries in London, Edinburgh, Oxford, Lusaka, Livingstone and Salisbury, Rhodesia.

Several people smoothed my path while in the field. Mr Simon Kapwepwe, at that time Minister of Foreign Affairs in the nascent Republic of Zambia, was kind enough to introduce me to the Bemba paramount chief, Chitimukulu, and to local officials of the United National Independence Party. Mr Friday Mwango Musunka worked for much of the time as my interpreter and scribe, and I am most grateful to him for his assistance: this study rests in no small degree on his labours. I should also like to record my thanks to at least some of those whose hospitality and company I enjoyed in Bembaland: Mr and Mrs John Alder, Dr Derek Braithwaite, Mr and Mrs C. M. Chipungu, the late Sir Stewart Gore-Browne, Miss Elizabeth Hodgkin, Mr and Mrs William Mackenzie, the late Mr James Makumba, Mr and Mrs Edward Sefuke, and the missionaries of the White Fathers, especially at Mulilansolo, Mambwe, Mbala and Serenje.

My largest debt, however, is to all those Zambians who made a traveller welcome in their homes and villages, and ungrudgingly cooperated in the often laborious task of setting down their history. To mention names here would be invidious, but by naming my informants in footnotes I have provided some indication of my indebtedness. I hope very much that this book, based so largely on their efforts, may encourage a younger generation of Zambians to look back into their past: in such an endeavour, an outsider can only make a beginning.

A. D. R.

---

[1] Mr Mushindo died in December 1972; it is sad that he should not have lived to see his history finally in print.

We are grateful to the following for permission to reproduce copyright material:

Cambridge University Press for the tables, 'Lists of Chitimukulus: a comparison' and 'Comparative lists of dynasties in north-eastern Zambia' both from *Journal of African History*, 11, ii (1970), pp. 224–5 and 237–8 respectively.

The cover design is based on an original photograph by Dr A. I. Richards of a wall-decoration made for the Bemba girls' initiation ceremony (*cisungu*).

Introduction

In chapter 1 I examine in detail the literary and oral sources for the study of Bemba history. Before doing so, however, it may be helpful to indicate how I approached the subject: to describe the relevant academic literature that was available when I embarked on research; to summarise the economic and social background to Bemba history and to give some account of my methods of fieldwork.

By 1960, there was a body of literature on the peoples of northern and eastern Zambia which was remarkable both in quantity and quality. The Bemba themselves were the first people in Central Africa to be studied by a professional anthropologist, Dr Audrey Richards: her researches into Bemba economy and society, between 1930 and 1934, are embodied in two books[1] and numerous papers. Over the next ten years or so, the ethnography of the Bemba was substantially augmented by the work of W. V. Brelsford, an administrative official.[2] In the years after 1945, the Rhodes–Livingstone Institute initiated a number of major studies by social anthropologists in northern and eastern Northern Rhodesia. One of these, indeed, is largely presented in the form of history: Barnes's study of political change among the Ngoni of Mpezeni since the later nineteenth century.[3] Two other studies dealt with neighbours of the Bemba: Watson's account of the Mambwe[4] and Cunnison's account of the

[1] Audrey I. Richards, *Land, Labour and Diet in Northern Rhodesia*, London 1939 (references to second edition, 1961); *Chisungu*, London 1956

[2] The fullest bibliography for the Bemba is in Ruth Jones, *Bibliography for South-East Central Africa and Madagascar*, International African Institute, London, 1961.

[3] J. A. Barnes, *Politics in a Changing Society: a Political History of the Fort Jameson Ngoni*, Cape Town 1954; reprinted Manchester 1967. One of the first publications of the Institute was also a historical study: Godfrey Wilson, *The Constitution of Ngonde*, Rhodes–Livingstone Paper 2, Livingstone 1939.

[4] W. Watson, *Tribal Cohesion in a Money Economy*, Manchester 1958. Watson's researches on the Lungu of Chief Tafuna are as yet unpublished.

Lunda kingdom of Kazembe, on the lower Luapula. Cunnison's work is of special interest to the historian, partly because he made a pioneering study of the role of history in Luapula society, and partly because his analysis of Kazembe's kingdom furnishes many illuminating points of comparison with Bemba politics and history.[5] Furthermore, the Institute sponsored the first attempt by a professional historian, Lewis H. Gann, to examine the African background to European intrusion in central Africa: in this respect, Gann's work represented a great advance on the work of writers such as Hanna who had been wholly preoccupied with European policy and action.[6]

But little of the work bearing specifically on the Bemba was concerned with history. To be sure, there were various accounts of Bemba myths and legends,[7] and of the Bemba system of chieftainship. Brelsford's account of the latter topic stimulated Gluckman to make an arresting, if not wholly convincing, analysis of the history of succession to the Bemba paramountcy.[8] In 1960-1, Richards touched on the subject of Bemba attitudes to history and elaborated her earlier descriptions of Bemba political structure.[9] Miss Ann Tweedie, while engaged in a socio-economic study of the Bemba, drew attention to certain problems in early Bemba history, and most recently Werbner has reassessed Bemba political organisation on the basis of published and archival sources.[10] But in 1963 the history of the Bemba had not yet received anything like the close attention accorded to Bemba social and economic life in the present century.

[5] Ian G. Cunnison, *History on the Luapula*, Rhodes–Livingstone Paper 21, Cape Town 1951; *The Luapula Peoples of Northern Rhodesia*, Manchester 1959. The only published report on research among the Bisa is by Bruce Kapferer, *Co-operation, Leadership and Village Structure*, Zambian Paper 1, Manchester and Lusaka 1967; this concerns ten villages around Lake Baka-Baka in the chiefdom of Kopa

[6] Lewis H. Gann, 'The End of the Slave Trade in British Central Africa, 1889–1912', *RLJ*, 1954, 16, pp. 27–51; *The Birth of a Plural Society*, Manchester 1958; A. J. Hanna, *The Beginnings of Nyasaland and North-Eastern Rhodesia, 1859–95*, Oxford 1956, written some years before Gann's studies

[7] See below, pp. 9–10.

[8] W. V. Brelsford, *The Succession of Bemba Chiefs*, Lusaka 1944; Max Gluckman, 'Succession and Civil War among the Bemba', *RLJ*, 1954, 16, pp. 6–25

[9] A. I. Richards, 'Social Mechanisms for the Transfer of Political Rights in some African Tribes', *JRAI*, 1960, 90, ii, pp. 175–90; 'African Kings and their Royal Relatives', *JRAI*, 1961, 91, ii, pp. 135–50

[10] Ann Tweedie, 'Towards a History of the Bemba from Oral Tradition', *The Zambesian Past*, eds E. T. Stokes and R. Brown, Manchester 1966, pp. 197–225; Richard P. Werbner, 'Federal Administration, Rank, and Civil Strife among Bemba Royals and Nobles', *Africa*, 1967, 37, i, pp. 22–48

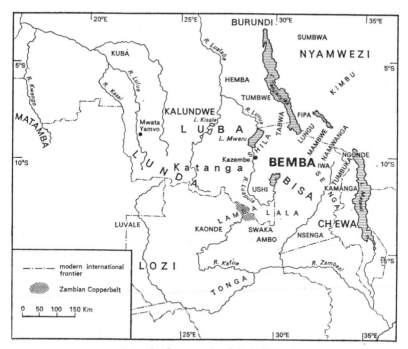

1 Central Africa north of the Zambezi

From what was already known, the pre-colonial history of the Bemba promised to be of interest for various reasons. The Bemba past evidently comprised processes of growth and change which were related to some of the main currents in central African history. The Bemba belong to a large group of peoples in north-eastern and north-western Zambia who trace their origins to the Luba and Lunda states of the upper Congo basin, in what became Katanga (now Shaba) province in Zaïre. Bemba history is part of a major historical phenomenon: the development of chieftainship in a large and culturally fairly homogeneous region of central Africa. (A summary of the very patchy and often unreliable evidence for this process had long since been compiled by Verhulpen; the subject has recently been critically reviewed by Vansina.)[11] A study of Bemba history could thus be of much more than merely local interest: it could contribute, if only in a small way, to an understanding of one of the most important phases in the pre-colonial history of central Africa. Moreover, by the end of the

[11] E. Verhulpen, *Baluba et Balubaïsés*, Antwerp 1936; Jan Vansina, *Kingdoms of the Savanna*, Madison 1966

last century, the Bemba had formed an extensive and relatively unified political system, in which a number of chiefs were subordinated to a single paramount. Such a system is *prima facie* likely to preserve a longer memory of the past in oral traditions than small-scale political systems, for concepts of time are limited by social horizons and the number and variety of interlinked groups of whose several pasts history must take account. A study of pre-colonial history was thus likely to be more feasible among the Bemba than among, for example, the relatively amorphous small communities of the Plateau Tonga.[12]

Indeed, a question of obvious historical importance was raised by the very extent and cohesion of the Bemba political system, for this was in fact exceptional: in north-eastern Zambia, only the Lunda kingdom of Kazembe, on the Luapula, compared in scale with that of the Bemba. One factor in the growth of Bemba power was evidently their association with the East African trade in ivory and slaves. In this respect, the Bemba resembled the Ganda, Nyamwezi and other peoples in the African interior whose scale of political organisation expanded rapidly as a result of contact with long-distance trade in the nineteenth century. Yet although the Bemba (unlike the Ganda and Nyamwezi) excluded European missions until near the very end, they eventually submitted to European rule after no more than piecemeal military resistance. This fact alone indicated the need to elucidate the interplay in Bemba history between external forces for change and those arising from the local environment and social institutions.

THE ECONOMIC AND SOCIAL BACKGROUND

I have noted that there is a considerable body of expert writing on the Bemba: indeed, without this support it would hardly have been possible to undertake a specifically historical study. There is thus no need here for a detailed examination of the economic and social background to Bemba history. It may nonetheless be appropriate to mention briefly certain customs and institutions of special relevance to the present study.

The Bemba live in what is now the Northern Province of Zambia, and Kasama, the provincial headquarters, is in the centre of Bemba country. Kasama is also the headquarters of a district; the other district headquarters in Bemba country are Mpika, Chinsali, Mporokoso and

---

[12] Cf. Elizabeth Colson, 'The Plateau Tonga of Northern Rhodesia', eds E. Colson and M. Gluckman, *Seven Tribes of British Central Africa*, London 1951, p. 100 and note 2

Luwingu. Unlike many so-called 'tribes', the Bemba can be fairly precisely defined, as those people who consider themselves subjects of Chitimukulu, the Bemba paramount chief.[13] Thus defined, the Bemba rural population in 1963 numbered about 250,000.[14] Their villages, most of which comprise between 100 and 300 people, are scattered over about 22,000 square miles on the wooded plateau between the Luapula river and the abrupt escarpment of the Luangwa valley. This plateau lies at over 4,000 feet above sea level, and daytime temperatures range between 50° and 90° F. The rainfall, which is concentrated in one rainy season between November and April, is plentiful, and the *brachystegia* woodland is intersected by 'dambos', wide grassy corridors formed by streams and rivers. Here and there, on the banks of streams, are remnants of high evergreen forest, survivals from an earlier, wetter climate.

Nowadays, many Bemba earn a living on the mines of the Copperbelt and send money home to relatives in Bembaland. But the local economy is still one of subsistence: there is no significant cash crop. There is little trade or exchange except near the few small towns, missions and fishing villages. The Bemba do not, generally speaking, keep cattle, since tsetse fly is widespread and pasture scarce. Ironwork, woodcarving and basketwork are of the simplest, and weaving is unknown, though bark cloth was made and worn in the old days.

Thus agriculture is the chief economic activity in Bembaland. The staple crop is finger-millet (*eleusine corecana*), though kaffircorn (*sorghum* spp.) and maize are also grown. Cassava (manioc) is now widely planted; groundnuts are common and sweet potatoes are occasionally grown. In general the soil is poor and ill-suited to simple hoe-cultivation; instead, it has compelled the adoption of *citemene*, a form of slash-and-burn agriculture.[15] Every year, between June and

[13] Cf. Richards, *Land, Labour and Diet*, 23, and below, p. 20. 'Bemba' is often also used to refer to those peoples of north-eastern Zambia who speak languages broadly similar to that of the Bemba proper.

[14] This figure was obtained by superimposing a map of Bemba chiefdoms on a distribution map based on the first census of African population in Northern Rhodesia, in 1963: George Kay, *Maps of the Distribution and Density of African Population in Zambia*, University of Zambia Institute for Social Research, Communication 2, Lusaka 1967. The figure (which obviously excludes Bemba living in towns on the line of rail) roughly agrees with the result of correlating the figures for population by districts in 1963 with the proportion of Bemba in each district indicated in the reports of local officials earlier this century: cf. *Second Report of the May/June 1963 Census of Africans*, Lusaka 1964, 39, and Appendix 1 (c).

[15] Cf. W. Allan, *The African Husbandman*, Edinburgh 1965, p. 70. The most thorough study of Bemba agriculture in relation to the local ecology is by C. G. Trapnell, *The Soils, Vegetation and Agriculture of North-Eastern Rhodesia*, Lusaka 1953.

November, the men of a household make a clearing in the woodland in which to plant a new crop of millet. They lop the branches of trees in the surrounding areas; their women collect the branches and stack them up all over the clearing. In October, at the end of the dry season, the branches are fired, leaving a bed of ash in which the seed is broadcast after the first rains have softened up the ground. The crop is harvested in April and May, and stored in granaries: it is ground into a white flour and eaten in the form of *bwali*, a polenta-like dumpling, with a relish of meat, fish or greens. Beer is also made from the millet grains. For most families, there is an annual period of shortage, if not actual famine, during the later part of the rainy season (January to March) before the new crop is ready for harvest. The old gardens are used for subsidiary crops, but after a few years they are exhausted. As time goes on, the trees over a large area surrounding a village will have lost their branches. Eventually the gardens and the uncut woodland will be too far away from the village for convenience, and the chief or headman will move the village to a new site, leaving the denuded woodland to regenerate.

The Bemba, like most of the neighbouring peoples (Bisa, Lala, Tabwa, Chishinga, southern Lungu), observe matrilineal descent, and this is the basis of their social and political organisation. Headmen, priests and chiefs all succeed to titles, and these pass from brother to brother and then to sisters' sons. Positional succession is practised: that is to say, the successor to a position inherits not only his predecessor's title, insignia, rights and duties, but also his social and political relationships. The identification of titleholder and title is so complete that he may be thought of as assuming the identities as well as the position of his predecessors. Thus the paramount chief, Chitimukulu, is not only Musenga or Kanyanta, or whatever his personal name may be; he is also Chileshye, Chitimuluba and other famous chiefs of bygone days. In some cases, the relationships between hereditary positions may be fixed regardless of the actual relationships of their holders at any given moment. It might be that originally a chief created a title for one of his sons. Thereafter, all the holders of that title would be 'sons' of that chief, regardless of the current ties of kin between the two incumbents. This extension of positional succession is known as 'perpetual kinship'. It is in fact less common among the Bemba than among the Mambwe or the peoples of the lower Luapula.[16] It usually takes the form, among

[16] Positional succession has been described for the Bemba by A. I. Richards, 'Some Types of Family Structure amongst the Central Bantu', *African Systems of Kinship and Marriage*, eds A. R. Radcliffe-Brown and D. Forde, London 1950,

the Bemba, of linking 'father' and 'son', whereas the matriliny which normally determines succession gives rise to few perpetual relationships other than the 'mothers of chiefs' (*banamfumu*) who are usually real mothers of chiefs as well.

Over thirty clans are represented in Bembaland, named after animals and other natural phenomena. These clans are not strictly exogamous and are not significant as units of social organisation. Inter-clan joking relationships are observed, but clans do not cooperate within themselves on any large scale, nor are they associated, for the most part, with particular areas: it would seem that there has long been much movement of matrilineages among villages throughout Bembaland. Indeed, matrilineages are in general of limited importance as corporate groups. This is partly due to the economic necessity for moving village sites, which gives frequent opportunities for breaking away from a headman to set up a new village. It is also due to the common practice of uxorilocal marriage, which means that a husband sets up house among his in-laws rather than his own matrikin. In many respects, the bilateral group known as a *lupwa*, which comprises both agnatic kin and affines as well as matrikin, is more important than the lineage group. The size of a matrilineal group, as a recognised body of living people, is thus liable to be determined by residential patterns as well as by descent. In practice, lineages are seldom reckoned more than two or three generations back from the oldest living members. The concept of lineage is fluid, and lineages are not sharply identified and defined in terms of depth of descent from given ancestresses.[17]

The one clan with political significance is the *bena ŋandu*, the 'people of the crocodile'. This is the royal clan, to whom is reserved succession to many chieftainships. In the present century, most of the senior chieftainships, such as Chitimukulu, Mwamba, Nkula and Nkolemfumu, have been held by members of a shallow lineage within the royal clan. Depending on their genealogical seniority, and their personal qualities, these men have been promoted from the lesser to the greater chieftainships, culminating in that of Chitimukulu, as occupants of these positions die off or are themselves promoted. A few chieftainships, such as Nkweto, Mwaba and Chimbola, are held by *bena ŋandu* whose lineages are remote from the present dominant line. Others are

---

pp. 207–51. Perpetual kinship among the Luapula peoples is described by Cunnison in 'Perpetual Kinship: a political institution of the Luapula Peoples', *RLJ*, 1956, 20, pp. 28–48.

[17] Cf. Richards, 'Some Types of Family Structure', pp. 223–30; 'The Bemba of North-Eastern Rhodesia' in Colson and Gluckman, *Seven Tribes*, p. 176.

held by 'sons' of chiefs; these men are the real sons of *bena ŋandu* chiefs, living or dead, and succeed to positions of 'perpetual sonship' in relation to a chieftainship held at some time by their fathers. Thus Makasa is the 'son' of Chitimukulu and any individual Makasa is usually the son of some Chitimukulu, but not necessarily the present one. Finally, there are a number of *bena ŋandu* headmen living in the Bemba heartland, such as Chileshye Mukulu and Chewe Kalubila. They are now distant from the present royal line, and unlike Chimbola or Nkweto they have never been recognised as chiefs by Government, though their forebears were chiefs in pre-colonial times.

Each Bemba chief, including Chitimukulu, governs a named territory (*calo*), bounded by hills and streams. Thus Chitimukulu has Lubemba, Nkula has Ichinga, Mwamba has Ituna, and so forth. From every village within his area, a chief formerly had the right to levy tribute (in labour, food, beer and a share in game) and military service. He controlled the hunting of elephant and the trading of ivory. On a wide range of subjects he heard disputes between his people and gave judgement; offences against the chief himself might lead to severe punishment, such as death or mutilation. The dignity and mystique of chieftainship was affirmed by a number of rituals, more or less elaborate according to the status of the chief. In the case of Chitimukulu, these rituals were extremely involved, and there is no doubt that Chitimukulu was, and is, a 'divine king' in the sense that his office is believed to carry with it supernatural control over the life and welfare of the land and people. To maintain the power of the kingship, Chitimukulu must observe numerous taboos and ritual duties, and if he fails in these the kingship itself suffers, and the people with it. In this sense, as has been pointed out, it is the kingship and not the king who is 'divine'. To a lesser extent, other senior chiefs of the royal clan are also invested with this 'divinity'.[18]

The powers of a Bemba chief were extensive, and there were few institutional checks upon it. Subordination is deeply ingrained in Bemba society, and it is not too much to say that *mucinshi* (respect, deference, propriety) is, like the very similar *kitiibwa* of the Ganda, one of those essentially untranslatable key words which characterise a whole society.[19] But a chief's authority was limited by virtue of the

[18] Cf. A. I. Richards, 'Keeping the King Divine', *Proceedings of the Royal Anthropological Institute*, 1968, pp. 23–35

[19] Cf. E. E. Evans-Pritchard, *Social Anthropology*, London 1951, p. 80; A. I. Richards, 'Traditional Values and Current Political Behaviour', *The King's Men*, ed. L. A. Fallers, London 1964, p. 301.

very fact that he, or rather his office, was divine. He was only the earthly vessel, so to speak, for the abiding principle of chieftainship, by which in turn the strength of the land was maintained. And the maintenance of royal ritual, and hence a major share in control over the distribution of chiefly authority, was (and is) vested in a large group of priests. These men, mostly known as *bakabilo*, form the nucleus of Chitimukulu's circle of councillors, and they have their own villages in the neighbourhood of the capital. They are themselves members of non-royal clans and in fact are ineligible for any chieftainship. But they determine chiefly succession, and they compel the attention of Chitimukulu and other chiefs because they are the source of chiefly legitimacy. To this extent, they can be said to represent both the principle of chieftainship and the Bemba people against the failings of any particular Bemba chief.

FIELDWORK METHODS

In order to record historical traditions among the Bemba, I travelled extensively over Bemba country in 1964–5, seeking out people who were in one way or another qualified to talk about the past. I discuss in chapter 1 the various sources of Bemba traditions; here I wish only to give some indication of my methods while working in the field. I spent a total of more than three months at the capital, Chitimukulu's village, visiting surrounding villages in the Bemba heartland, for such villages are among the oldest in Bemba country. I also spent some weeks at the village of Chief Mwamba, and spent lesser periods visiting twelve of the sixteen other chiefdoms recognised by Government. In addition, I visited chiefs of the Bisa, Iwa, Mambwe, Lungu, Tabwa and Chishinga—peoples whose histories have at one time or another been involved with that of the Bemba.[20]

At the start of my fieldwork, I spent three weeks learning the rudiments of the Bemba language (*ciBemba*), and thereafter improved my acquaintance with it in the course of my work. I never became fluent, and I relied much of the time on the services of an interpreter. Fortunately, this man was well connected in Bemba terms, being a son of a daughter of chief Mwamba, the second most important Bemba chief. I was in any case sufficiently familiar with the language to exercise control over the process of translation. I collected information partly through question-and-answer interviews and partly by tape-recording

[20] In October 1969 I carried out a few more interviews in Bembaland and also visited the Shila and Bwile on the eastern shores of Lake Mweru.

narratives. These were transcribed by my assistant and translated by both of us together; this was usually done as soon as possible, in order to enable me to return to informants and elucidate obscurities, check doubtful points and generally gain further information appropriate to the text.

I arrived in Bembaland in April 1964, a few months after the Central African Federation was dissolved. The Bemba had long been prominent in the opposition to Federation which was organised by the United National Independence Party (UNIP). With the end of Federation, however, the way was open for Northern Rhodesia to attain independence as Zambia, and this took place in October 1964. By the time I began fieldwork, the political atmosphere in Bemba country, which had been extremely tense and hostile to Europeans, had relaxed considerably. The fighting, in July 1964, between the UNIP Government and the Lumpa Church of Alice Lenshina, in Chinsali and Mpika districts, did not seriously interfere with my research. I found the local UNIP officials friendly and welcoming, and the people in general, wherever I went, were eager to provide hospitality and help me pursue my enquiries. Only on two or three occasions did a potential informant decline to discuss history. In establishing contacts, the tape-recorder proved to be a help rather than a hindrance: most people appreciated the value of having an accurate record of what they had said and enjoyed the opportunity to check it for themselves.

At this time and place there was, of course, no question of my pretending to any authority, even had I wished it. If I wanted to meet a potential informant, I arranged a mutually convenient rendezvous, which frequently meant spending whole days visiting villages to give notice of my wish to return on another occasion. The villages of Bemba chiefs are all now accessible by roads or motorable tracks (and a motorcar is essential for studying a political system which is territorially as extensive as that of the Bemba). But much travelling must still be done by bicycle, on foot, or by dugout canoe, and not only to reach villages but to visit sites of historical interest which are now deserted. My researches inevitably cost my guides and informants considerable time and effort, and I made presents of beer, tea, sugar, cloth and other 'luxuries' that were commensurate with their social standing. I only made cash payments for specific services, such as ferrying, or else, very rarely, as part of a leavetaking present following a long period of interviews with one informant.

Finally, a few remarks are needed on various aspects of the presentation of this study. It is incumbent upon the historian to cite his sources,

1 Kalungu river. Kapasa's village is on the far bank

2 *Citemene* garden (chief Mubanga's area, 1969). Branches stacked for burning

3 Mwalule, the burial grove of senior Bemba chiefs. The keeper, Shimwalule, is standing beside the relic hut of his own ancestors; the bones are those of a sacrificial hippopotamus

whether these are written documents or oral testimonies. Wherever possible, therefore, I name the informants whose statements I have drawn upon as evidence about the Bemba past. Such references take two forms. The first are to tape-recordings to be filed, together with transcriptions and English translations, at the University of Zambia, the School of Oriental and African Studies, London, and the Archives of Traditional Music, Bloomington, Indiana. Such a reference might run: Milambo, T4; this refers to the informant, Milambo, and one of the numbered tape-recordings listed against his name in the index to the collection. (There are also occasional references to numbered notes on recorded texts.) The second type of reference to informants simply gives a date (day, month, year) after the informant's name: these refer to my own notes of interviews. Details of informants, such as their political and social status, and their own authority for the information they gave, are set out in Appendix 5. Abbreviations for literary sources are listed in the bibliography.

My use of certain terms may also call for explanation. 'Plateau' refers to the 'great plateau' of north-eastern Zambia, between the Luapula and Luangwa valleys. 'Chief' normally refers to a man who, either in the present or in the past, has held some or all of the attributes of Bemba chieftainship as I have summarised them, though in a few cases a 'chief' can only be distinguished from a headman by the fact that he has rights over more than one village. 'Lineage' is not used in any precise sense. Bemba society is not organised on the basis of lineages, and the closest Bemba equivalent is *ŋanda*, the ordinary word for 'house', which can also refer to the matrilineal descendants of any given woman over a span of not more than four generations or so. In this book I use 'lineage' without any special connotation of time-depth, though I occasionally use 'branch' or 'line' to refer to relatively shallow lineages within a relatively deeper lineage; in such cases, the context should make the distinction sufficiently clear. I normally use kinship terms, such as father, brother, etc., in their usual English sense of own father, own brother. Where they are used in a classificatory sense, or in reference to links of perpetual kinship, corresponding to Bemba usage of the equivalent Bemba terms, I signify this by the use of quotation marks: 'father', 'brother'.

I use the word 'polity' in preference to 'state' as a means of referring to the Bemba political system. It seems to me that the use of 'state' in this context would beg too many questions concerning the proper definition of 'state', a thorny subject. 'Polity', by comparison, is a conveniently neutral word. 'Kingdom' might do equally well, but it raises the question, in relation to peoples other than the Bemba, of what in fact kingship, as opposed to chieftainship, consists in. Besides, 'kingdom' and 'kingship' denote territory and system respectively, whereas 'polity' denotes both. The Bemba themselves have no special word for the status of Chitimukulu, the senior chief; he is an *mfumu* (chief), though various honorific modes of address are more properly used before him than before other chiefs. I conform to usual practice in referring to Chitimukulu as a paramount chief, though I have occasionally found it convenient to use the adjective 'royal' in reference to him and his position. References to holders of the Chitimukulu title are asterisked where the reference is to such men at the time they were Chitimukulu. Thus Chileshye* refers to the Chitimukulu of that name during the period of his reign; Chileshye, to the same man before he became Chitimukulu.

Chapter 1

Sources

The sources for writing the history of Africa, and particularly the African interior, are multifarious, uneven and often hard of access. If we look for 'certainties', we shall often be baffled and frustrated; it is sometimes possible to do no more than indicate probabilities. In writing on the history of an African people, it is therefore appropriate to begin with a more detailed account of the sources available for study than might be necessary in a more conventional historical enquiry.

The principal sources for the study of pre-colonial Bemba history are the oral traditions of the Bemba themselves. The Bemba made few and late contacts with the world of letters, and we thus have few eyewitness testimonies for events earlier than the lifetime of the oldest men alive today. The use of oral traditions as historical sources has been discussed by several scholars.[1] It is generally allowed by most historians and anthropologists conversant with Africa that oral tradition, if critically used, is potentially a valuable source of information about the African past. There is no need here to make a formal apologia for writing history on the basis of oral traditions. But, just as the historian must specify his documentary sources and take note of the circumstances in which they were written, so too, in extending his reach to oral traditions, he must specify his informants and show how their testimony may be evaluated as evidence about the past.

In this chapter, then, I discuss both documentary and oral sources for the study of Bemba history. The literary sources are of two kinds. First, there are the eyewitness records of travellers in and around Bemba country in the course of the nineteenth century. Second, there are the written records, almost all made during the present century, of the oral testimonies and traditions of the Bemba and their neighbours. From these records I pass on to a consideration of such testimonies and

[1] See, for example, Jan Vansina, *De la Tradition Orale*, Tervuren 1961, tr. by H. M. Wright as *Oral Tradition*, London 1965; and several articles in the *JAH*.

traditions as I encountered them in the field in 1964–5, outlining the different types of historical tradition among the Bemba and the bases of tradition in Bemba society.

LITERARY SOURCES

The first known reference to the Bemba occurs in the accounts of the Portuguese expedition, led by Lacerda, from Mozambique to Kazembe's in 1798. This expedition, which followed an African trade route, did not directly encounter any Bemba, and the reports mention them only in passing. Nonetheless, they illuminate Bemba history in so far as they indicate the extent of Bemba territory at that time and provide information on the Bisa and the Lunda kingdom of Kazembe on the Luapula.[2] Between 1802 and 1811 two *pombeiros* (half-caste traders) travelled from Angola to the lower Zambezi via Kazembe's and followed much the same route as Lacerda's party; their report does not mention the Bemba at all, but again some useful information on the surrounding area is provided.[3] In 1831 the Portuguese in Mozambique despatched a second expedition to Kazembe. This took a broadly similar route, but by this time the Bemba were pushing southwards and the expedition met several Bemba chiefs and headmen. Gamitto, the second-in-command, kept a journal which is a pioneering achievement in ethnography; for the history of east-central Africa, it is a source of the first importance.[4] In the 1860s, the senior Bemba chiefs were visited by the Swahili trader Tippu Tip, whose autobiography, dictated in Zanzibar in 1901, refers briefly to these exploits of his youth.[5] In 1867–8 David Livingstone passed through Bembaland in the

[2] The best edition of Lacerda's own diary of his journey is in F. J. de Lacerda e Almeida, *Diários de Viagem*, ed. S. B. de Holanda, Bibliotheca popular brasileira, 18, Rio de Janeiro 1944, pp. 183–261. The continuation of his diary, by Fr Pinto, was reprinted in F. J. M. de Lacerda e Almeida, *Travessia da Africa*, Lisbon 1936, pp. 251–377. This text, and the version of Lacerda's diary in *Travessia*, originally appeared in the *Annaes maritimos e coloniaes* Lisbon 1844, 4, whence they were translated by Richard Burton (R. F. Burton, *The Lands of Cazembe*, London 1873, pp. 50–164).

[3] (P. J. Baptista), 'Exploraçoes dos Portuguezes no interior d'Africa meridional', *Annaes maritimos e coloniaes*, 1843, 3, v, pp. 162–90, 223–40, 278–97, 423–39, 493–506. A translation, by B. A. Beadle, was published in Burton, *The Lands of Cazembe*, pp. 167–244. There is a partial French translation, with commentary: A. Verbeken and M. Walraet, *La Première Traversée de Katanga*, Brussels 1953.

[4] A. C. P. Gamitto, *O Muata Kazembe*, Lisbon 1854; this has been translated by Ian Cunnison as *King Kazembe*, Lisbon 1960.

[5] Tippu Tip, *Maisha ya Hamed bin Muhammed el Murjebi yaani Tippu Tip* (Swahili text, tr. by W. H. Whiteley), Nairobi 1966. This is a reprint of an edition

course of his last expedition, and he travelled around the northern and western borders of Bembaland in 1872, shortly before his death near the swamps of Lake Bangweulu in the following year. Livingstone was the first European to visit Chitimukulu, the Bemba paramount. His journals, with those of Gamitto, are the most important literary source for the early history of north-eastern Zambia.[6] Both works are valuable not only for their descriptions but for the help they provide in dating events recounted in Bemba tradition. Also valuable in this respect is the account by Victor Giraud, a French naval officer, of his journey through Bemba country in 1883: this provides the fullest picture we have of the impact of long-distance trade upon the Bemba.[7]

By the time Giraud visited Chitimukulu, European missionaries had begun to settle in the country north and east of the Bemba. In 1879 the engineer James Stewart set out from the Free Church of Scotland mission at Livingstonia, on Lake Malawi, and made the first European crossing from the head of Lake Malawi to Lake Tanganyika. Stewart passed well to the north of Bemba country, and his report refers only briefly to Bemba activities,[8] but his route was soon followed by a growing traffic of European caravans as Scots, English and later French missionaries, set up stations around the borders of Bemba country. These left a considerable, if uneven, literature, from which much information may be gained concerning the peoples, such as the Lungu and Mambwe, among whom the missionaries first worked, and rather less, though often useful, material concerning the Bemba. The reports and correspondence of members of the London Missionary Society (LMS) are preserved in the Society's archives; in addition, a few LMS men published material bearing on the Bemba.[9] The archives of the Free Church of Scotland missions, now in the National Library,

first published as a Supplement to the *Journal of the East African Swahili Committee*, 1958–9; the Swahili text was first published by H. Brode in 1902–3.

[6] David Livingstone, *The Last Journals of David Livingstone*, ed. H. Waller, London 1874. There are occasional discrepancies between this text and Livingstone's original notebooks in the Livingstone Memorial museum at Blantyre, Scotland (of which there are photocopies in the National Library of Scotland (NLS)). I take note of these discrepancies where necessary.

[7] Victor Giraud, *Les Lacs de l'Afrique Equatoriale*, Paris 1890

[8] James Stewart, C.E., 'Lake Nyasa and the water route to the lake region of Africa', *PRGS*, 1887, n.s. 3, pp. 257–74; the original MS is Stewart to Smith, NLS 7904, 31 October 1879.

[9] E. C. Hore, *Tanganyika*, London 1892; James B. Wolf (ed.), *Missionary to Tanganyika* [Hore] London 1971; A. J. Swann, *Fighting the Slavehunters in Central Africa*, London 1910; W. T. [Thomas] in *British Central Africa Gazette (BCAG)*, 12 October 1894

Edinburgh, contain references to the Bemba in correspondence from their missions at the eastern end of the Malawi–Tanganyika road. I was unable to consult the few early records of the African Lakes Company, which handled European traffic between Lakes Malawi and Tanganyika, but two of its staff left memoirs.[10] The French White Fathers arrived somewhat later in the area, but they were the first mission to gain a foothold in Bemba country, and their efforts to do so may be traced in the diaries of their earliest stations, Mambwe and Kayambi. These are now lodged in the archives of the diocese of Mbala (formerly Abercorn); in 1968 I consulted copies of them in the archives of the White Fathers' Generalate, Rome. The greater part of these diaries, for the period 1892–8, was printed, usually verbatim, in the Society's *Chroniques Trimestrielles*, which also contain an important account by Bishop Dupont of a journey through Bemba country in 1897.[11] I have found no record by Dupont of his still more important visit to chief Mwamba in October 1898, but he evidently kept a private diary at the time, which was used by his official biographer.[12]

Besides these missionary sources, there are reports by other travellers in and around Bemba country. In 1889 Captain Emile Trivier, retained by the French journal *La Gironde*, came east from the Congo to Lake Tanganyika and so down the missionary road to Lake Malawi: his little-known book gives some account of Mambwe politics at the time.[13] In 1893 Hermann von Wissmann, the Imperial Commissioner for German East Africa, routed a Bemba army near the south end of Lake Tanganyika: an account of this engagement by a Swahili N.C.O., Selim bin Abakari, was recorded by Carl Velten, interpreter to the governor of German East Africa,[14] while Wissmann's own despatch

[10] F. L. M. Moir, 'The Eastern Route to Central Africa', *Scottish Geographical Magazine*, 1885, 1, pp. 95–112; *After Livingstone: An African Trade Romance*, London 1923; L. Monteith Fotheringham, *Adventures in Nyassaland: A Two Years' Struggle with Arab Slave-Dealers in Central Africa*, London 1891

[11] J. Dupont, 'Voyage de cinq semaines dans l'Ubemba', *CT*, April 1898, 79, pp. 246–58

[12] H. Pineau, *Evêque-Roi des Brigands: Monseigneur Dupont*, Paris 1937; further editions were published in Montreal in 1944, 1949 and 1960, and I refer to the last of these. This work forms the basis for a short account of the White Fathers' penetration of Bembaland by Fr W. F. Rea, S.J., 'The Bemba's White Chief', Historical Association of Rhodesia and Nyasaland, Local series 13, Salisbury 1964, mimeo.

[13] E. Trivier, *Mon Voyage au Continent Noir*, Paris and Bordeaux 1891

[14] Selim bin Abakari, 'Safari yangu ya Nyassa', in C. Velten (ed.), *Safari za Wasuaheli* (Göttingen 1901), 50–105; there is a German translation in C. Velten, *Schilderungen der Suaheli* (Göttingen 1901).

was also published.[15] In 1894 the American journalist E. J. Glave travelled round the southern borders of Bemba country and observed the conflict between Swahili and Belgians west of Lake Tanganyika.[16] From 1895 to 1898 the sportsman Poulett Weatherley lived more or less continuously in the country between Lakes Tanganyika and Mweru and was in touch with two outlying Bemba chiefs.[17] In 1897 the French sportsman Edouard Foà made a brief excursion into north-eastern Bembaland on his way from Lake Malawi to the Congo.[18] In the same year a prospector, Hugo Genthe, paid a visit to the southern Bemba chief Chikwanda, on his way from Fort Jameson to Livingstone's grave.[19]

We also have a few firsthand African reports on north-eastern Zambia in the late nineteenth century. Three of these come from Swahili traders. There is a brief description of the Bemba by an anonymous trader who evidently visited them in the 1880s, though this is of little value.[20] Much more interesting are the recollections of Selemani bin Mwenye Chande, who travelled through Lungu, Tabwa, Chishinga and Bemba country in 1891 and a few years later described this expedition to Velten.[21] Among the Tabwa, northwest of the Bemba, there was a colony of Swahili: one of these, Abdullah ibn Suliman, had been in the area at intervals since 1867 and he remained there until his death in 1916. In about 1905 the history of Abdullah and his colleagues was recorded by a British official from Kawambwa, and this greatly illuminates the complicated relations between the Swahili, Tabwa and Bemba in the later nineteenth century.[22] Specially valuable

[15] H. von Wissmann, despatch from Kituta, 14 July 1893, in *Deutsches Kolonialblatt*, 1893, 4, pp. 492–3; for further details, see below, p. 234.

[16] E. J. Glave, *Century Magazine*, New York 1896, 52, pp. 589–606, 765–81, 918–33; and letter in *BCAG*, 1 January 1897

[17] Letters from Poulett Weatherley in *BCAG*, 1895–9; and MS letter to H. H. Johnston (see bibliography for full citations)

[18] E. Foà, *La Traversée de l'Afrique*, Paris 1900, pp. 114–27

[19] H. Genthe, 'Livingstone's Grave', *BCAG*, 5 February 1898

[20] 'Beschreibung von Usango, Ruemba und andern Reichen im südwestlichen Theile von Deutsch-Ostafrika', *Suaheli-Schriftstücke*, ed. and tr. C. G. Büttner, Stuttgart and Berlin 1892, pp. 91–102 (Swahili text and German translation). The Swahili text was reprinted in H. P. Blok, *A Swahili Anthology*, Leiden 1948, pp. 33–9.

[21] Sleman bin Mwenyi Tshande, 'Safari yangu ya barra Afrika', in Velten, *Safari za Wasuaheli*, pp. 1–49. There is a German translation in Velten, *Schilderungen der Suaheli*; the text and English translation of Selemani's narrative in Lyndon Harries, *Swahili Prose Texts*, London and Nairobi 1965, is incomplete and poorly edited.

[22] 'Abdullah ibn Suliman', Kawambwa District Notebook (DNB), II, pp.

as eyewitness impressions of Bemba life at this period are the reminiscences of headman Bwembya, recorded by Audrey Richards in the 1930s.[23]

The major documentary source for Bemba history in the last decade of the nineteenth century consists of the records of the first British consuls and administrators in the area. From 1886 there was a British consul, subordinate to the consul in Mozambique, stationed at Karonga at the north end of Lake Malawi. In 1891 'British Central Africa' (approximately the territory now known as Malawi) became a British protectorate; the commissioner carried responsibilities for expanding administration westwards, but in 1895 these were taken over by the British South Africa Company, whose officials brought the Bemba under British rule in 1898. The records of British officials bearing on the Bemba are to be found in the Public Record Office, London; the National Archives of Zambia, Lusaka; the National Archives of Rhodesia, Salisbury; and the library of Rhodes House, Oxford.[24] Several officials also published articles which include observations on the Bemba in the 1890s.[25]

In order to form a picture of Bemba society at the period when it came under British rule, the historian naturally turns to the records of the first officials to administer the Bemba. Unfortunately, these are very incomplete, particularly the records for Kasama district, which comprises the central area of Bemba country and most of the senior chiefdoms. This is presumably because Government offices at Kasama were burned down in November 1918 by an overzealous Irish sergeant who had been instructed only to burn military stores before the arrival of the German General von Lettow-Vorbeck.[26] Nonetheless, the

---

81–97 (National Archives of Zambia (NAZ), KSG 3/1). This text has been published and annotated: Andrew Roberts, 'The History of Abdullah ibn Suliman', *ASR*, December 1967, 4, pp. 241–70.

[23] A. I. Richards, 'The Story of Bwembya', *Ten Africans*, ed M. Perham, London 1936, pp. 17–40

[24] Some of these reports have been published, though the editing leaves much to be desired: 'Alfred Sharpe's Travels in the Northern Province and Katanga [1890–1]', *NRJ*, 1957, 3, iii, pp. 210–19 (from FO 84/2114); T. W. Baxter, 'Slave-Raiders in North-Eastern Rhodesia [1896–7]', *NRJ*, 1950, 1, i, pp. 7–17 (from NAZ/NE/A1/1/1–2).

[25] See below, chapters 7 and 8.

[26] Anon. [W. V. Brelsford], 'Jack Merry', *NRJ*, June 1951, 1, iii, p. 74. At the time, Hector Croad, the District Commissioner, Kasama, supposed that the offices had been blown up by Lettow-Vorbeck (D. C. Kasama to Administrator, 14 November 1918, cited in *British South Africa Company: Annual Report on Northern Rhodesia, 1918–19*, 2). Lettow-Vorbeck, however, assumed that public

archives of the British South African Company's administration and its successor (from 1924), the Northern Rhodesia Government, do preserve some valuable evidence for the historian of pre-colonial Bembaland. They form an important source for the second type of literary evidence I have distinguished: written records of oral testimony.

First of all, there is the evidence given by witnesses in official enquiries into disputes over boundaries or chiefly succession. Obviously, these are not wholly ideal occasions for obtaining dispassionate testimonies, but they do involve recourse to history, and the very urgency of the occasion sometimes stimulates more detailed accounts than would otherwise be available. Second, there are the notes made by officials about local history and custom. These are mostly contained in the District Notebooks. Their quality is very uneven, and the informants are seldom named, but in several cases they represent the earliest written records of oral tradition or memory, made before modern changes had begun seriously to affect the preservation of tradition. Of special value is the account of 'Awemba History as I have heard it' made in about 1900 by Robert Young; this is the earliest substantial written record of Bemba history and the dynasty of Chitimukulu.[27] Young was a man of limited education, but he showed a more active interest in Bemba history than most of his more polished successors. It is not clear where he obtained his information. The history is dated at Mirongo, the station he had just opened on the eastern border of Bemba country, but he had already been to ancient parts of Bemba country on both sides of the Chambeshi river.

Young's history has never been published, but it became the source, direct or indirect, for several published king-lists and histories of the Bemba. W. G. Robertson, an LMS missionary who had worked only briefly among the Bemba (near the border-chief Mporokoso), published a brief and most unreliable history in 1904 which explicitly acknowledged its debt to Young.[28] The next account of Bemba history came from a prospector, George Pirie, in 1905–6. His account was

buildings in Kasama had been looted by local people just before the Germans arrived: P. von Lettow-Vorbeck, *My Reminiscences of East Africa*, London n.d. (1920), p. 314.

[27] Chinsali DNB, I, pp. 232–9 (NAZ/KTQ 2/1/1). A few garbled details appear in Foà, *Traversée*, p. 116; these presumably derive from his visit to the White Fathers at Kayambi in 1897.

[28] W. G. Robertson, *An Introductory Handbook to the Language of the Bemba People*, London 1904; the historical introduction was reprinted as 'Kasembe and the Bemba Nation', *JAS*, 1903–4, 3, pp. 183–93.

gathered from various sources, but principally 'from personal observation and the experience of others who have done a good deal towards the pacification and development of the country'.[29] Comparison quickly shows that Pirie's main source was Young. Pirie or Robertson seem in turn to have been the source for the account of Bemba history published in 1914 by another official, Coxhead.[30] Finally, the influence of Young's history may be traced in Verhulpen's *Baluba et Balubaïsés*, a compilation on the history of chieftainships in Katanga and Northern Rhodesia.[31] Verhulpen's source for most of his remarks on the Bemba was either Robertson (whom he acknowledges) or Pirie (whom he does not). His list of Chitimukulus repeats that of Young exactly, except in spelling and with the omission of one name towards the end.

Various other historical records by officials may also be noted. In 1910, E. B. H. Goodall compiled a comprehensive genealogy of royal chiefs, including chiefs' sons, though this only goes back three generations before 1900.[32] This is the source for the genealogies later published by Richards and Brelsford.[33] In 1911 Gouldsbury and Sheane, two officials well acquainted with the Bemba, published *The Great Plateau of Northern Rhodesia*; this, like their articles on Bemba topics, represents a serious, if amateurish, essay in ethnography. The main source for their brief account of Bemba history was the first chief Shimumbi (died *c.* 1906), though they were also conversant with Young's history.[34] W. V. Brelsford, who served as an official in Bemba country between 1934 and 1945, has published many studies of the Bemba, including three which bear particularly on Bemba history.[35] Brelsford's main sources were Young's history and Goodall's genealogy, though his own notes, gathered mostly in Chinsali district, added a good deal to the published

[29] G. Pirie, 'North-Eastern Rhodesia: its peoples and products', part I, *JAS*, 1905-6, 5, pp. 130-47. Pirie worked for Tanganyika Concessions in Katanga: A. Verbeken, *Msiri Roi du Garenganze*, Brussels 1956, p. 58.

[30] J. C. C. Coxhead, *The Native Tribes of North-eastern Rhodesia*, Occasional Paper of the Royal Anthropological Institute, London 1914

[31] E. Verhulpen, *Baluba et Balubaïsés*, Antwerp 1936

[32] E. B. H. Goodall, 'Tree of the House of the Wemba Chiefs', NAZ/KSZ 4/1

[33] A. I. Richards, 'The Political System of the Bemba Tribe, North-eastern Rhodesia', *African Political Systems*, eds M. Fortes and E. E. Evans-Pritchard, London 1940, p. 102; W. V. Brelsford, *The Succession of Bemba Chiefs*, Lusaka 1944 (references are to the second edition of 1948), pp. 49-50

[34] C. Gouldsbury and H. Sheane, *The Great Plateau of Northern Rhodesia*, London 1911, p. 31

[35] W. V. Brelsford, *The Succession of Bemba Chiefs*; *Aspects of Bemba Chieftainship*, Rhodes–Livingstone Communication 2, Livingstone 1944; 'Shimwalule— A Study of a Bemba Chief and Priest', *African Studies*, 1942, 1, iii, pp. 207-23

accounts. There is some material concerning Bemba–Bisa relations in the somewhat disjointed notes on Bisa history compiled by F. M. Thomas, formerly an official in Bisa country; these are based on traditions from the Bisa chieftainship of Kopa (formerly Mwansabamba).[36]

Besides the records of tradition made by administrative officials, there are those made by missionaries of the White Fathers. The most important of these is the history of the Bemba, from their origins up to the present century, compiled by Fr E. Labrecque some time before 1930. The first part of this history, based on Bemba traditions of migration and settlement, was published in 1933; it was mainly derived from a catechist (Dismas Musobandesa) whose father was a royal councillor, Kangwa *wa mpumpa*.[37] The complete text of Labrecque's history appeared only in 1968.[38] His colleague Fr J. van Sambeek had long since produced the first comprehensive Bemba history in the vernacular, a school reader published in 1932 at Chilubula mission, near Kasama.[39] A later vernacular history, by Fr F. Tanguy, relies heavily on Labrecque, though Tanguy also consulted a catechist who himself became a royal councillor: this was Joseph Muma, who now holds the title Chikunga.[40] There are several points on which my Bemba informants disagreed with these histories by the White Fathers, but Labrecque's complete text is useful in that it relates several episodes in Bemba history which are now hardly remembered, if at all. More recently, Fr L. Oger has compiled a vernacular history of the Makasa chieftainship, derived from informants in Makasa's chiefdom.[41]

The White Fathers also published vernacular histories of certain peoples whose histories are related to that of the Bemba. There is a

[36] F. M. Thomas, *Historical Notes on the Bisa Tribe, Northern Rhodesia*, Rhodes–Livingstone Communication 8, Lusaka 1958

[37] E. Labrecque, 'La Tribu des Babemba, I; les origines des Babemba', *Anthropos*, 1933, 28, pp. 633–48 (cited hereafter as 'Tribu')

[38] E. Labrecque, 'Les Origines des Babemba de la Rhodésie du Nord (Zambia)', *Annali del Pontificio Museo Missionario Etnologico*, 1968, 32, pp. 249–329 (cited hereafter as 'Origines'). The account of early Bemba history in this varies slightly from that published in 1933, which I cite only for information omitted from the 1968 version. For the identification of Labrecque's informant on early history, see Labrecque, 'Origines', p. 263.

[39] White Fathers, *Ifyabukaya: Fourth Bemba Reader*, Chilubula n.d. (?1932)

[40] F. Tanguy, *Imilandu ya Babemba*, London 1948 (my references are to the second edition of 1963)

[41] L. Oger, 'Calo ca Mpanda; Calo ca kwa Makasa', mimeo. at White Fathers, Kasama, and in the Library of the University of Zambia. There is also a translation by Miss Ann Tweedie at the latter place, and my references are to this.

history of the Mukulu chieftainship of Chungu, written by 'African elders' who were assisted by Fr Labrecque.[42] More important, there is the history of the Lunda kingdom of Kazembe, on the Luapula. This was compiled by Kazembe XIV and various Lunda notables in 1942; this too was edited by Labrecque. A French version was published in 1949[43] and the vernacular (Bemba) version followed in 1951.[44] An annotated English translation of this version appeared in 1963.[45]

There is as yet only one history of the Bemba written by a Bemba: this is by the Rev. P. B. Mushindo, a minister of the United Church of Zambia.[46] Mushindo's father was a nephew of a senior royal councillor, Chitikafula, and as a child Mushindo lived in and near the royal capital. From 1906 to 1910 he lived with his maternal grandmother near the country of her late husband, Kabundi, who had held the Mwaba chieftainship near Chinsali. Since then, Mushindo has spent most of his life at nearby Lubwa. He has thus been able to learn much history in the oldest parts of Bemba country. Finally, we may note that Stephen Mpashi, a leading Bemba author, gathered some oral tradition with which to introduce his brief account of the White Fathers' arrival in Bemba country.[47]

All these records of oral tradition are more or less deficient in two important respects. They do not make it clear what the writer, or editor, has interpolated by way of comment, explanation or correction, and what was originally told him by his informants.[48] And they seldom indicate in any detail who the informants were, let alone which passages are derived from which informant. Thus none of these texts

[42] African Elders (assisted by Fr Labrecque), *History of the Bena Ŋoma (Ba-Chungu wa Mukulu)*, London 1949

[43] E. Labrecque, 'Histoire des Mwata Kazembe Chefs Lunda du Luapula', *Lovania*, 1949, 16, pp. 9–33; 1949, 17, pp. 21–48; 1951, 18, pp. 18–67

[44] Kazembe XIV, *Ifikolwe Fyandi na Bantu Bandi*, London 1951

[45] I. G. Cunnison (ed. and tr.), *Historical Traditions of the eastern Lunda*, Central Bantu Historical Texts II: Rhodes–Livingstone Communication 23, Lusaka 1961. My references are to this version.

[46] P. B. Mushindo, *A short history of the Bemba*, Lusaka, in press; I refer to numbered sections. There is a Fragment (8″ × 6″) of MS by an African in Bemba, dealing with Bemba History, 64 pages, among the manuscripts left by the Rev. R. D. MacMinn: this is almost certainly by Mushindo, who was MacMinn's assistant for many years. C. M. Doke, 'The Linguistic Work and Manuscripts of R. D. MacMinn', *African Studies*, 1959, 18, iv, p. 188.

[47] S. A. Mpashi, *Abapatili bafika ku Lubemba*, Cape Town 1956; Lusaka 1966, 1968

[48] This point is specially relevant to the texts edited by Labrecque: the Lunda history, for example, seems occasionally to reflect Labrecque's knowledge of Bemba traditions as well as of European exploration.

present an actual oral tradition, that is, history as it has been handed down by word of mouth to a given informant or body of informants. It is therefore not easy to make a critical assessment of their relative reliability or bias as evidence about what happened in the past. I have drawn on them to some extent in the present study because they do help to corroborate or amplify the evidence provided by my own informants, but these shortcomings must be borne in mind. Moreover, these compilations contain a number of inconsistencies which are perhaps as much the result of attempts to 'tidy up' Bemba tradition as reflections of contradictory evidence. For example, Tanguy provides a genealogy purporting to represent the descent of the Chitimukulu dynasty *ab initio*, but this leaves out most of the Chitimukulus named in Tanguy's own narrative.[49]

It should also be noted that these sources give a number of dates for events in Bemba history which are either demonstrably wrong or else unsupported by any evidence. Robertson's dates seem to be conjectures based on the erroneous assumption that the Bemba did not settle in their present country until around 1800. His date of 1853 for the expulsion of Chitimukulu Susula Chinchinta* seems to be the basis for Labrecque's date of 'about 1852' and Brelsford's 'about 1850' for this event.[50] Brelsford's other dates for the reigns of Chitimukulu Chileshye*, Bwembya* and Chitapankwa* are evidently derived, along with his dates for the Mwamba chieftainship, from *Ifyabukaya*, where it is also said that Chileshye* was born in 1783 and succeeded in 1810.[51] These dates are mostly repeated in Tanguy's *Imilandu ya Babemba*. None of them are documented: at best, they are no more than more or less intelligent guesses. As for Verhulpen's chronology of Chitimukulu, this is of no value.[52] He gives three dates for which he claims the authority of a written source; the only correct one is that for the death of 'Mutali' (sc. Chitapankwa*), that is, 1883. Verhulpen correctly says that 'Mwamba' died in 1898, but this chief was not Chitimukulu. The date 1868 for the death of 'Chireshia' (sc. Chileshye*) is obviously wrong, as Livingstone attests that Chitapankwa* was Chitimukulu in 1867 and 1872.[53] And Verhulpen's dates for

[49] Tanguy, *Imilandu*, pp. 44, 20–1

[50] Robertson, *Introductory Handbook*, p. xx; Labrecque, 'Origines', p. 292; Brelsford, *Succession*, p. 5

[51] Brelsford, *ibid.*, pp. 5–6; White Fathers, *Ifyabukaya*, pp. 39–40, 43. The date of 1887 for the death of Chitapankwa has been widely repeated since; it is thus perhaps worth noting that the correct date, 1883, was given by a White Fathers source first published in 1937: Pineau, *Evêque-Roi*, p. 125.

[52] Verhulpen, *Baluba*, Annexe II   [53] *Last Journals*, I, pp. 184–95; II, p. 248

Chileshye's* predecessors (his list is derived from Young's, as I have noted) are simply reckoned by allotting each one a reign of sixteen years: this seems to be a quite arbitrary estimate.

ORAL TRADITIONS

The social basis

I now turn to an account of my own informants and their relationship to Bemba social and political structure. Among the Bemba, as in any society, memory of the past is contingent upon 'social mechanisms'[54] for transmitting memory from one generation to the next, and these in turn depend on the role which memory of past events plays in the life of the society as a whole. Strictly speaking, there are no traditions of Bemba history as such; there are only histories of various groups and positions in Bemba society.[55] These histories are handed down because they have social and political significance, not so much for the Bemba in general, as for certain Bemba families. Thus, to find out what the Bemba may have done in the past, one must consult a great many different people all over the country.

The most important social institution among the Bemba, other than the family, is chieftainship. It is above all this institution which generates and perpetuates historical traditions. Since my main preoccupation was with political history, I sought out informants connected in one way or another with the hierarchy of chieftainships, in an attempt to record the histories of each Bemba chieftainship. And since so much of Bemba history has involved the surrounding peoples, I also visited chiefs of the Bisa, Iwa, Mambwe, Lungu, Tabwa and Chishinga.[56] By collating such evidence, I was able to form some idea of how the Bemba political system had evolved, at least during the century or so before colonial rule.

The Bemba do not have any officials whose special duty it is to remember and transmit tribal and chiefly history: strictly speaking, there are no professional historians, in the sense in which these are found in Rwanda, the Yoruba states, or among the Wolof.[57] However,

[54] I borrow the term from Dr A. I. Richards: cf. her 'Social Mechanisms', which discusses at some length the bearers of royal tradition among the Bemba.

[55] This point is made for the Luapula peoples by Ian Cunnison: cf. *History on the Luapula*, pp. 3–6.

[56] Chieftainship is an important institution among all these peoples. It should be noted, however, that an important potential source of tradition among the Bisa would be those families whose forebears were traders; I did not have time to locate such families. [57] Cf. Vansina, *De la Tradition Orale*, pp. 32–3

the Bemba do have, in the priest–councillors (*bakabilo*) of Chitimukulu and the senior chiefs, groups of men whose business it is to be experts on most aspects of chieftainship—ritual, government and the choice of successors. These subjects involve recourse to history, since practice is based on precedent. Each chieftainship, and each title of office associated with it, has its own body of traditions regarding its function-ing (its rights and duties) and its history (its genealogy and list of ancestors, and some record of what these men did). These traditions are 'owned' by each title and transmitted by those among whom that title is inherited. They are not necessarily transmitted directly and exclusively from one titleholder to his successor. Bemba succession indicates a number of possible heirs, and among a number of brothers and nephews it is not possible to say who will succeed, for no decision is taken until after a titleholder's death. And, as Richards observes, where knowledge is power, it is not readily shared or transmitted to men eligible for positions of authority. The *bakabilo* learn their ritual duties only after they succeed to office. It may be that these are learned from the sons of a predecessor (i.e. men who had never been eligible for succession).[58] I have been told that a new *kabilo* learns his duties from his colleagues, but this is probably a recent development.[59] It is, after all, crucial to the prestige and indispensability of a title that the knowledge pertinent to that title be jealously guarded by its holders. Not all tradition, however, is equally arcane, and explicitly historical knowledge—the names and doings of past chiefs and an-cestors—is transmitted with rather less reserve than the secrets of royal ritual. These are subjects about which it is proper that a titleholder instruct his potential heirs. And a good deal of history can (or could) be learned from the talk of his elders by any young man who has ears to hear. Many of my informants named as their principal authority a brother of their mother or maternal grandmother, a man who had often, but not always, held the title himself.

History, of course, is not only embodied in 'documents'—whether these are scrolls of parchment or stories told around an evening fire. It is encapsulated in the behaviour and physical environment of human societies. Bemba awareness of the past is reinforced by their sense of its perpetuation in the present, in people, positions and places. Various forms of 'perpetual behaviour', re-enacting or referring to events relating different social positions, recall to present incumbents the historical origin of these relationships.[60] And memory of individual

---

[58] 'Social Mechanisms', p. 186   [59] Katenda, 31 May 1965. See below, p. 30.
[60] Cf. Brelsford's accounts of the burials of Chitimukulu Kanyanta and Nkweto

chiefs is kept alive in a number of ways. Most important, perhaps, for the Bemba themselves are the personal relics (*babenye*) of chiefs—their bows, spears and stools. Possession of his predecessor's relics is essential to a chief's legitimacy. Relics, however, are guarded in special huts, in the greatest secrecy; they are not accessible to outsiders, nor is it prudent to make detailed enquiries about them. Hence it is not clear how far they act as mnemonic devices by which successive chiefs may be identified, though it is clear that the Bemba, who lack a tradition of woodcarving, do not commemorate their chiefs in images.[61] Royal graves have often been used in Africa as valuable testimony to past chiefs: but among the Bemba the royal burial groves, like the royal relic huts, are places of the greatest secrecy, and are not open to investigation.

Chiefs are, however, remembered in less occult ways. Some are remembered by the sites (*fibolya*) of their villages; especially well known are the sites of certain Chitimukulus and chiefs in Ituna, and those occupied by the first chiefs on their migration from the Congo. At such sites certain *bakabilo* or other priests are charged with keeping in repair a spirit-house (*lufuba*), offering token presents of food and beer, and making prayers to the dead chief.[62] Such attentions are usually prompted by the need to obtain the favour of chiefly ancestors at critical points in the annual economic cycle. Indeed, there are special rituals associated with such events as the first tree-lopping, and it is proper on such occasions to invoke the blessing of all the chiefs thought to have occupied the area, since they are believed still to exercise power over the fertility of the land, livestock and people.[63] Finally, chiefs are remembered in triumph-songs (*malaila*) and praise-poems (*mishikakulo*). These are composed in a flamboyant style, characterised more by poetic images than by the citation of actual incidents. Their value to the historian is further limited by the fact that they are not always exclusively associated with one chief. The words of songs are frequently changed, even though the old melodies are retained. Several people can sing these melodies, but the words usually deal with the chiefs of today and the hazards of modern life. Moreover, the archaic language (called

Mwaba for the way this extended series of rituals calls into play roles sanctioned by history and evokes the historical associations of sites in Bembaland: *Aspects*, pp. 26–37; 'Shimwalule', pp. 213–20; also a journalist's account of the burial of Chitimukulu Musungu in 1966, *Times of Zambia*, 25 July 1966

[61] See below, Appendix 2, Note A.

[62] Richards, *Land, Labour and Diet*, pp. 239–40, 357

[63] *Ibid.*, pp. 363, 369–70; cf. *ibid.*, pp. 234–5; Richards, 'Social Mechanisms', p. 183

by the Bemba 'Chiluba') of the praise-poems is difficult for even Bemba to understand, and an informant may be unwilling or unable to give a version in Bemba. But such archaisms may perhaps afford some clue to the more distant Bemba past.[64]

History serves to reinforce the mystique of chieftainship, and thus its power. It accounts for the origins of chieftainship and illustrates the power and majesty of individual chiefs in the old days. But the history to be learned at the courts of Bemba chiefs is no mere panegyric. The senior *bakabilo* are no mere servants of Chitimukulu but are themselves the hereditary holders of historic titles, some as old as the Chitimukulu-ship itself. Since they are essential to the maintenance of chieftainship, through their control of chiefly appointments and their responsibility for chiefly rituals, they have an ambivalent relationship to the chiefs. In their capacity as village headmen, they are politically subordinate to Chitimukulu, and they are excluded from chiefly office, yet while they derive their prestige from their association with the institution of chieftainship, they are very conscious that they are in a real sense the source of chiefly legitimacy. Thus they speak with a certain independence of mind. They represent chieftainship; at the same time they are critics of the holders of chieftainship. This is most true of the *bakabilo* of Chitimukulu, for these are concerned with not only the paramountcy, but all the more important chieftainships. It is less true of the councillors of other chiefs, for their authority is very much less, though it is still of a similar kind, in that they hold hereditary positions and have control in matters of succession and ritual over a chief's subordinates— lesser chiefs and headmen—as well as being responsible for local shrines.

The term *bakabilo* is a convenient means of referring to the various kinds of hereditary priests and/or councillors associated with Bemba chieftainship. This is not, however, a strictly accurate use, and in any case there are nearly eighty such titles in Lubemba, the Bemba heartland, varying considerably in antiquity and importance. It is thus necessary to describe more exactly these various offices.

First of all, there are the senior *bakabilo* of Chitimukulu, those who determine the most crucial issues, such as the royal succession. These men are known as the *bashilubemba*, the fathers, or elders, of Lubemba. There are six of these—Chimba, Chitikafula, Kapukuma, Katenda, Munuca, Nkolemambwe—and each has an important role in the rituals of installing and burying Chitimukulu. Chimba, in fact, stands somewhat apart from the other *bashilubemba*. He acts as regent during the

---

[64] I collected texts of some *imishikakulo* and have submitted them for comment to students of the Bemba and Luba languages.

lengthy burial rites of Chitimukulu; this office was performed by the first Chimba, who was a half-brother of the first Chitimukulu. Hence Chimba claims to be a chief and is quick to correct the misapprehension that he is simply one of the *bakabilo*. He claims to be a *mwina ŋandu*, a member of the royal clan, though his matrilineage belongs to the Mushroom clan (*bena bowa*).

There are a number of other *bakabilo* who are charged with important ritual functions: Chishika, Chikutwe, Chipasha, Kabwa, Kamenge, Kasenge, Lumpombwe, Mulewa Chimfwembe, Mulombelwa, Mwana Bwalya. Of these, Mulombelwa and Chipasha are the senior *bakabilo* of the house of Katongo (*ŋanda ya kwa Katongo*), that is, the thirty-three councillors said to have accompanied a Chitimukulu who came to Lubemba from Ichinga, east of the Chambeshi. There are the eight pall-bearers (*bena tembwe*) who carry the dead Chitimukulu to the burial grove at Mwalule. There are also a few *bakabilo* whose titles are evidently of great antiquity but who do not have any ritual duties though they recall the origin of their title in various acts of perpetual behaviour. Such are Sompe, Mumba ŋombe, Chikunga, Kangwa *wa mpumpa*. One further class of hereditary official are the *bamukabenye*, the wives of the relics; these are women (who must be celibate) who clean and maintain the houses in which the relics are kept.

Finally, there are the two royal undertakers (*bafingo*). One of these, Kakwela, guards the forest of Bwalya Chabala, near the Kalungu river, where the lesser royal chiefs and the mothers of chiefs are buried. Mwalule, the principal royal burial grove, is situated east of the Chambeshi river. Its guardian, Shimwalule, is thus clearly distinguished from all the other royal officials, who live west of the Chambeshi, in Lubemba. Indeed, Shimwalule is not strictly Bemba, since the original Shimwalule was a Bisa: from one point of view he represents the authority of the autochthones against the Bemba settlers. Moreover, unlike the *bakabilo* in Lubemba, Shimwalule is not only a village headman but exercises a measure of political authority over other headmen nearby. He has himself a number of hereditary *bakabilo*, and he claims to have received tribute from the most senior Bemba chiefs, though he never sent any himself.[65]

Other chiefs besides Chitimukulu retain hereditary officials, though none on a comparable scale. Since few of the other chieftainships are more than a century old, the status and duties of these officials are often not nearly so well defined as among the *bakabilo* of Chitimukulu. Nkolemfumu, which is among the oldest of the subordinate chieftain-

[65] Shimwalule, 18 May 1965; cf. Brelsford, 'Shimwalule', p. 209

ships, has at least six hereditary officials (including the councillor Shimulamba, one of my principal informants). But Mwamba, a more recent chieftainship, though much more important politically than Nkolemfumu, has only three hereditary officials: a councillor, Milambo (also one of my main informants), Muchilingwa, guardian of the graves of Mwamba's sons, and Mwika, the *mukabenye*.

Besides the various officials attached to chieftainships, there are several other headmen whose titles are of particular historical interest. There are those headmen, mostly resident in Lubemba, who belong to the royal clan and whose ancestors were chiefs, though their lineages are now excluded from chiefly succession. One of them, Chileshye Mukulu, was a particularly helpful informant. There are various priests (*bashimapepo*) who tend the shrines and pray to the spirits known as *ngulu*: these spirits are associated with striking natural features, such as rocks and waterfalls, and are usually spoken of as *bashamfumu*, great chiefs, though in few cases are these names remembered as figures in stories about the Bemba past.[66]

Bemba society, on the whole, is and was economically relatively undifferentiated. Elephant-tracking, in pursuit of ivory, was a specialised occupation requiring magical as well as more mundane skills. A few foreign traders—Swahili and Yeke—settled among the Bemba in the late nineteenth century: some of their descendants are now village headmen. But the only groups which today claim particular and localised economic interests within the pre-colonial economy are the few fishing villages near the Chambeshi, such as Mulilo or Mulema.[67] Apart from these places, there has always been more than enough room on the thinly populated plateau for the Bemba to move around without having to change their mode of life. There is not, for example, the attachment to specific areas which is characteristic of the Luapula valley with its fish-stocked lagoons, and this is a point to which I shall return. In general, we may say that among the Bemba history is not shaped by economic as opposed to political interests. The situation may well be different among the Bisa, who long had a reputation as traders. It may be that there are families who could bear witness to the importance of their forebears as traders and travellers, but it is not even clear whether such families are still prominent today.

---

[66] Cf. Richards, *Land, Labour and Diet*, pp. 241, 358; Cunnison, *Luapula Peoples*, pp. 222–3; J. H. West Sheane, 'Some Aspects of Awemba Religion', *JRAI*, 1906, 36, p. 151; Fr L. Etienne, 'Indigenous Customs observed among the Bemba' (MS tr. Ian Cunnison, University of Zambia Library), pp. 109–11

[67] Cf. Richards, *Land, Labour and Diet*, p. 341; Brelsford, *Aspects*, pp. 15–18

In the old days, there were several minstrels (*ŋomba*) to be found at the capitals of the more important Bemba chiefs.[68] The last at Chitimu-kulu's, Chishaleshale, died some years ago, and I encountered Bemba minstrels only at the border chief Mporokoso's. But there are still a few old men, of no special social importance, whose memories reach back to pre-colonial days. I met two such old men—one of them severely mutilated as a result of some youthful misdemeanour—and heard of a few others.

There are among the Bemba no clan heads or priests such as may be found among the neighbouring Mambwe.[69] Clans are not sufficiently localised to promote much sense of corporate identity, and if they ever functioned in Bembaland as discrete social units they have long ceased to do so. There are clan praises and a few stories about how clan names originated, but no special places of origin seem to be remembered, in contrast to the Luapula peoples.[70] Except for the royal clan, the only stories about people as clan members are those which explain inter-clan joking relationships.[71] Clans are indeed associated with certain *fikolwe* (ancestors), but these are only the most eminent members of their clans, such as *bakabilo*, and clan members in different parts of the country often acknowledge different *fikolwe*.[72] Thus it is scarcely possible to speak of clan histories among the Bemba.

The social basis of oral traditions among the Bemba is thus primarily to be sought in the institution of chieftainship. The affairs regarding which the Bemba look to history for guidance and inspiration are the affairs of chiefs: the stories which the Bemba tell about the past concern the rivalries and achievements of chieftainships rather than of non-chiefly lineages, clans, or specialist economic groups. It is above all the chiefs who provide, in their own offices and in those of their priests and councillors, the institutions through which memory of the past may be transmitted from one generation to another. And since

[68] Cf. Richards, 'Bwembya', pp. 27–8

[69] Cf. Watson, *Tribal Cohesion*, pp. 139–43

[70] Cunnison, *Luapula Peoples*, pp. 70–1. Whiteley evidently has the Luapula clans in mind when he remarks on the Bemba-speaking peoples in general that 'Clan centres, in the sense of original villages of occupation, are remembered . . .' (*The Bemba and Related Peoples of Northern Rhodesia*, London 1951, p. 15); his source may be Gouldsbury and Sheane, *Great Plateau*, p. 95.

[71] A. I. Richards, 'Reciprocal Clan Relationships among the Bemba of North-ern Rhodesia', *Man*, 1937, 37, p. 222

[72] A. I. Richards, 'The Bemba of North-Eastern Rhodesia', Colson and Gluck-man, *Seven Tribes*, p. 178. Watson's term 'doyen' for *fikolwe* among the Mambwe is equally apt for those of the Bemba.

Bemba society consists of a hierarchy of chieftainships acknowledging the paramountcy of a single chief, Chitimukulu, Bemba traditions reach some way back into the past, far enough indeed to provide accounts of how these various chieftainships arose, and how they came by their present relationships with one another. This is most clearly shown by Bemba genealogies. The genealogy of the royal chiefs is traced back at least six generations from the present, whereas commoner families—even those of *bakabilo*—can seldom trace their ancestors back more than three generations from the present. Genealogies do not underpin Bemba social structure as they do in a society organised round patterns of lineage segmentation, such as the Tiv.[73] For the Bemba, it is only the royal genealogy which is needed to comprehend the means by which the political order is maintained.

Bemba history, then, is above all the history of Bemba chieftainship and the doings of the royal clan, the *bena ŋandu*. Yet although such history serves to affirm and reinforce the power and prestige of a ruling group, it is nevertheless accepted by the Bemba at large as being in an important sense their own history. The coming of the first Bemba chiefs and their retinue is widely told as a story of 'where the Bemba came from' and how the tribe came into being; there is no other account of Bemba origins. The glory of the *bena ŋandu* is something in which all Bemba can share and derive a sense of communal pride. The *bena ŋandu* are Bemba, and Bemba alone,[74] whereas some other neighbouring chiefly clans (the *bena ŋoma* of the Mukulu and Chishinga, or the *bazimba* of the Lungu and Tabwa) are found among more than one tribe. Besides, no other chiefly clan in the region has gained such power for its tribe as the *bena ŋandu*. Furthermore, as we have seen, the values of chieftainship (which is the prerogative of the *bena ŋandu*) are principally affirmed and maintained by men who are not *bena ŋandu* at all. The *bakabilo* and *bafingo* of Chitimukulu have an interest, not so much in the ruling elite for its own sake, as in the offices which are reserved to it. As guardians of chieftainship and final arbiters of a man's personal and ritual fitness to rule, the *bakabilo* can be said to represent the Bemba as a people, not indeed against the *bena ŋandu* in general, but certainly against individual chiefs who appear unworthy of their office. Significantly, the *bashilubemba*—the senior *bakabilo*—like to speak of themselves simply as *ifwe baBemba*, 'we the Bemba'.[75]

---

[73] Laura Bohannan, 'A Genealogical Charter', *Africa*, 1952, 22, iv, pp. 301–15
[74] There are *bena ŋandu* among the Shila, on the lower Luapula and Lake Mweru, but these claim to have come from Bembaland: see below, p. 61, and Appendix 2, Note D (p. 348).   [75] Cf. Richards, 'Political System', p. 108

The Bemba are in fact politically homogeneous, to the extent that social groups are not sharply differentiated in point of political authority and power. The only group so differentiated—the *bena ŋandu*—is not counterposed against the rest of Bemba society as a whole. Although they are a ruling group, they are not an exclusive, conquering elite; so far from being an intrusive, alien minority, like most such elites, they seem to have been part of a cultural majority which settled in the area over a prolonged period of time and absorbed or expelled remnants of earlier peoples. There are, to be sure, various non-Bemba elements which have not been wholly assimilated. There are scattered groups of 'Sukuma'—people of Fipa origin—on the Muchinga escarpment, east of Bemba country; there are probably others closer to the Bemba heartland. And at least in those parts of Bemba country which were conquered during the nineteenth century, there are recognised non-Bemba—Mambwe, Lungu or Bisa—who are acknowledged as *bene calo*, owners of the land, in that chthonic powers reside in their ancestors and not those of the intruding Bemba.[76] The fact that they are remembered as the autochthones serves to perpetuate the memory of Bemba conquest and thus gives depth and colour to local history. Yet the difference between the Bemba and such 'owners of the land' is not of great political, social or economic import. For one thing, such ownership is primarily of religious or ritual significance. It may be necessary for a great chief such as Mwamba to make offerings to the ancestors of some Bisa headman; such men may have been chiefs who in their day ruled over large areas of Mwamba's present country, and they still have power to affect its fertility and prosperity. But such areas are not now of any distinctive economic or political consequence; they do not now form social, economic or political entities. Not only is there little economic differentiation in Bembaland; there is little social differentiation. Most of the peoples who have come under Bemba rule—Lungu, Tabwa, Mukulu, Bisa—closely resemble the Bemba in their social customs. Not only are they all matrilineal; most of them belong to a common network of clans. Intermarriage between the Bemba and their subject peoples has been frequent,[77] and as a

---

[76] Cf. Richards, *Land, Labour and Diet*, p. 249, n. 3. Shimwalule is thus himself an 'owner of the land'.

[77] In about 1905, well before labour migration had begun significantly to affect the pattern of Bemba marriage, the Collector at Abercorn noted that the Bemba intermarried freely with Bisa, Tabwa, Chishinga, Unga, Lunda, and the Malaila Lungu (of chief Mukupa Kaoma). Marriages with the northern Lungu (of chief Tafuna), Senga, Ushi and Mambwe (this last a patrilineal people) were dis-

result the latter have seldom survived as discrete groups. Unless a non-Bemba family is associated with a particular conquered or displaced chief, its consciousness of being Bisa or Lungu rather than Bemba is likely to fade, for there are few factors other than actual descent to bring out the distinction.[78]

The Bemba polity, in fact, is not a conquest state, and this affects the role and nature of history as the Bemba tell it. In this respect, the Bemba may be contrasted with the neighbouring Lunda kingdom of Kazembe, where the Lunda dominate a congeries of peoples belonging to various other groups and tribes.[79] The non-Lunda subjects of Kazembe belong not only to the kingdom athwart the Luapula but also to some group—a tribe or clan—many of whom live outside the kingdom, under another political authority. Indeed, the Lunda themselves belong to such a group, for there are several Lunda-ruled kingdoms west of the Luapula, around the various headwaters of the Congo. Fractions of all these groups have settled at different periods along the Luapula valley. At one stage in this process the Lunda came from the west and subordinated the peoples of the valley and the surrounding areas to their rule—the rule of an intrusive elite, culturally distinct in certain respects (such as their patrilineal descent) from their subjects. The subject groups, now coordinated in a single polity through a common principle of hierarchy, the kingship of Kazembe, proceeded to seek honour and influence in terms of their relationship with this kingship. Thus the unity afforded by the kingship also served to perpetuate the diversity of the kingdom, for the kingship and its reflected glory became a stimulus to competition and rivalry. And in this context of social and political heterogeneity it was the more important for the dominant interest-group, the Lunda, and in particular the kingship of Kazembe, to emphasise its unique authority and distinctiveness. Yet this political differentiation might not have persisted were it not also rooted in the local economy. Just because life on the Luapula, with its plentiful fish and cassava, has long attracted immigrants from the less bountiful plateau to the east, there has been

approved of but not unknown. (H. C. Marshall, 'The Awemba . . .', Livingstone Museum (LM) G 69/5/6)

[78] Cf. Richards, *Land, Labour and Diet*, p. 156, n. 2. Richards observes of the Bisa in chief Nkula's area that 'Slight differences in religious and magic rites practised in this area seemed to be the only distinguishing marks'. I do not have adequate evidence of the extent to which non-Bemba villages have in fact been 'assimilated', but see below, pp. 99–100, 110, n. 86, 148, n. 98.

[79] This paragraph is based on Cunnison's analysis of Kazembe's kingdom, as set out in *Luapula Peoples, History on the Luapula*, and elsewhere.

keen competition for space to fish and hunt in the enclosed valley floor. Rights to land use and occupation are thus an important element in local politics, and their assertion reinforces the strong sense of geographical and historical identity characteristic of the various Luapula peoples. This differentiation is expressed in, and so strengthened by, the histories told on the Luapula. They are charters of land use, social prestige and political rights. History on the Luapula thus comprises a wide range of separate histories linked by varying attachments to a common area—the Luapula valley, and a common institution—the kingship of Kazembe. In this way, history permeates and cements the society, and, as Cunnison observed, conversation at public gatherings quickly takes a historical turn.[80]

Among the Bemba, by contrast, history is of less consequence. To be sure, the telling of history has a number of social roles and is prompted in different areas and among different groups throughout Bembaland. Yet there are among the Bemba neither of the pressures which above all motivate history on the Luapula: the attachment to the land, and the supremacy of an exclusive class of alien conquerors. It is fair to say that the Bemba do not see themselves as creatures of history to the extent that the Luapula peoples do. History provides the rationale for the state of Kazembe in that it both serves to unify it under the kingship and to distinguish its component parts. The Bemba, lacking such tensions between rulers and ruled, and among the ruled, have the less need for history. With the Bemba, the tensions are, rather, to be found among the rulers. Interest in, and knowledge of, history may be characteristic of a chiefly family and its retainers; it is not strikingly characteristic of Bemba society as a whole.

Perspectives of the past

All the same, the Bemba view of the past, the shape which they give to their own historical narratives, closely resembles that of the Luapula peoples. Cunnison noted that his informants were usually aware of the past as a chronological sequence of known periods as far back as 'the time of the Arabs' (the mid-nineteenth century). Before this

> there is a large gap of over a hundred years to '*Kazembe talaisa*'—the time before Kazembe came. A few may use the names of reigning Kazembes back to Keleka (Kazembe IV, 1805–50) but only a few will do so with a true appreciation of the order in which they reigned.[81]

---

[80] *Luapula Peoples*, pp. 230–1; *History on the Luapula*, p. 1   [81] *Ibid.*, p. 31

Richards has noted the same pattern in Bemba traditions, and she points out that it is common for 'historical charters' to fall into three parts: an explanation of how a ruling group established itself; a vague memory of rulers succeeding one another; and accounts of the more recent past, in which real people, real events and real genealogies are remembered.[82] In the historian's view, as Jones observes, 'there is a beginning and an end but no middle . . . The main problem is to reconstruct this middle section.'[83] Such a hiatus is common, just because it arises from the very nature and function of oral traditions.

Among the Bemba, as among the Luapula peoples, there are, broadly speaking, two kinds of history. There are the *res gestae* of chiefs and other notables who were known to, or remembered by, the fathers and grandfathers of old men alive today, and there is the story—the most widely known part of Bemba history—which relates how the Bemba chiefs came from the Congo and how, after many adventures, they settled in their present country. This latter story is the nearest approximation the Bemba have to a 'tribal' history. All subsequent history is about individual chiefs and chieftainships, the content of which varies from one part of the country to another. It is noteworthy that the 'tribal' history, the story of chiefly migration, is markedly more mythical in style: it abounds in clichés common to other such migration legends. Some of these may be based on real incidents; others involve miraculous and supernatural effects which, to the sophisticated mind, clearly distinguish this story from other kinds of Bemba history.[84] This mythical character consorts with the social function of the story as a charter of Bemba occupation and a general explanation of the origins of Bemba society.[85] It establishes who the Bemba are, how they came to live in their present country, and how Bemba chieftainship began. As Nadel observes of the Kede myth of origin, it 'anchors the existing system in a dim past, which, by its very remoteness and its

---

[82] 'Social Mechanisms', pp. 178, 182; cf. H. Kuper, *An African Aristocracy* (Swazi), London 1947, p. 8; Bohannan, 'Genealogical Charter', p. 313. For a similar hiatus in Greek views of history cf. M. I. Finley, 'Myth, Memory and History', *Listener*, 23 and 30 September 1965

[83] G. I. Jones, 'Time and Oral Tradition with special reference to Eastern Nigeria', *JAH*, 1965, 6, ii, p. 153

[84] Cunnison suggests that for the (unsophisticated) African there is no such distinction: 'Mythological, and possible, old histories and new histories, are received with the same degree of credulity' (*History on the Luapula*, p. 21). Nonetheless, he himself shows that there is a difference in the way they are regarded, in so far as they are told in different ways.

[85] See below, pp. 46-7.

supernatural and sacred associations, endows the present with an immensely convincing validity'.[86] The Bemba usually tell this story as a self-contained narrative, and in style it resembles lineage histories on the Luapula, which conclude with the apportionment of land to a lineage. Since then, said Cunnison's informants, 'we have just been living here'. More history is known, of course: the deeds of 'personally remembered ancestors', but 'events so related are not incorporated into lineage history'.[87] Read 'tribe' for 'lineage', and these remarks are also apposite to the Bemba.

The second type of Bemba history is projected back from the present; it corresponds to the Luapula histories of 'personally remembered ancestors'. It is not so much the history of the Bemba, or even of the *bena ŋandu*, as the history of different chiefs and titles. Thus the perspective, as well as the content, of such history naturally varies from one place or person to another. For different informants, different periods and episodes in the Bemba past are significant.[88] Those associated with the older chieftainships and titles will tend to have a more extended view of the past than can usually be found in more recent positions. Yet whether this is in fact so will partly depend on whether there are a number of significant topics to be remembered, thus promoting the sense of a prolonged lapse of time. For example, the founding of a chieftainship in Ituna is obviously more significant at Mwamba's (the chief in Ituna) than at Nkula's, and there is correspondingly a keener sense at Mwamba's of this and associated events constituting a 'period' in a chronological sequence, although Nkula is the older chieftainship. Again, there are a number of headmen whose ancestors were once eligible for succession to the senior chieftainships. They might reasonably be expected to know more than the present line of chiefs about the period before this line gained ascendancy. In this way, two such headmen, Chileshye Mukulu in Lubemba and Mbutuka in Ichinga, were valuable informants on the earlier history of the Chitimukulu and Nkula chieftainships respectively.

But even where a number of related events or successors to an office are remembered, there may be little sense of a temporal sequence linking them in a unique pattern. The events and persons may be placed in a more or less timeless past which tends to be assimilated to

---

[86] S. F. Nadel, 'The Kede: a riverain state in Northern Nigeria', eds Fortes and Evans-Pritchard, *African Political Systems*, p. 190

[87] Ian Cunnison, 'History and Genealogies in a Conquest State', *American Anthropologist*, 1957, 59, i, p. 27

[88] Cf. Cunnison, *History on the Luapula*, pp. 29–32

the beginning of Bemba history—the coming of the chiefs. Several informants spoke as though Mukulumpe, the putative ancestor of the Bemba royals, was a senior contemporary of quite recent chiefs, such as Chitapankwa* (who died in 1883).[89] Such 'telescoping' is encouraged by the related customs of positional succession and perpetual kinship, devices by which the incumbent of a title identifies himself with any and all of his predecessors and their social and political relationships.[90] In this way an informant may speak of the remote past as though it were only yesterday, indeed as if it were today and he himself was taking part in the events described; yet in another context, on another occasion, he may indicate that he is well aware of the lapse of generations. Chronology is further confused by the common tendency to credit the activities of different people to one well-known representative figure. Not only are all Chitimukulus 'Chitimukulu'; all Swahili may be 'Tipu Tipu' (Tippu Tip) and all European explorers 'Livingstone'.[91]

There is, then, considerable variation in the time-perspective of Bemba histories. To write an account of the Bemba past as a connected sequence of events, it is thus necessary to take these different histories and piece them together where they appear to overlap and complement each other. As a result, it is possible to see the Bemba past in a longer and more comprehensive perspective than any one informant can achieve. But even then we are left with an evident gap or hiatus between the period of Bemba origins, with the arrival of the first chiefs, and the limits to which the Bemba can trace back the histories of particular titles in a more or less connected sequence. It is clear that such a gap is real and not illusory, since there is a striking discrepancy between the large number of Chitimukulus named by several informants and the fact that few of these are comprised within a coherent genealogy placing them in a time-sequence. Moreover, it is reasonable

---

[89] E.g. Chimbola, T1: 'When we came from Mukulumpe we found the country with our friends, but our friends remained in Ituna: that is where Chitapankwa and Malama *wa kwiswa ŋombe* [Mwamba II] remained.' Cf. Brelsford, 'Shimwalule', p. 210, for a similarly telescoped genealogy. A priest for the Bisa chief Chinkumba said that the latter was driven out by the Bemba when they came from the Congo (Kabwela, 10 May 1965), though it is clear that this expulsion in fact took place in the later nineteenth century (see below, p. 138).

[90] Cunnison, 'Perpetual Kinship'

[91] The same difficulty, of course, occurs in written sources. Gouldsbury and Sheane (*Great Plateau*, p. 21) and E. H. Lane-Poole (*Native Tribes of the Eastern Province of Northern Rhodesia*, London 1949, p. 9) refer to Livingstone in contexts which make it clear that Giraud and Joseph Thomson respectively are meant.

to assume an interval of a few decades at least in order to account for the emergence of various chieftainships and titles not accounted for in the legend of origin but said to have been in existence before the period at which memory of the past as a time-sequence falters. It is thus worth looking a little closer at the reasons for this hiatus.

The principal means by which the Bemba conceive of time as a sequence of periods or phases is the genealogy. Time is not counted off in years, decades and centuries; in so far as it is measured at all beyond the annual cycle of the seasons, it is measured in terms of the human life-cycle. It may be divided up into vague periods such as 'before the Europeans came' or 'in the time of Chitapankwa', but it is only genealogy which provides a means of assessing the distance of such periods from the present. Thus, in so far as they provide an indication of time-depth, Bemba historical narratives are conditioned by the genealogical grasp of the informant. Few commoners, even the senior *bakabilo*, now trace their own genealogies back more than three generations, even though they may remember quite a long list of predecessors. And even the longest genealogies, showing the descent of Chitimukulu, are not traced back more than six or seven genera- tions from the present, i.e. to Chiliamafwa* or Mukuuka*. For the time before this, there is a general agreed genealogy setting out the relations of the founding chiefs: this is incorporated in the legend of migration. Thereafter, several names of Chitimukulus are remembered, but they are mentioned in no consistent order. For some, praise-names are quoted, but few are associated with stories, and these few are mostly picturesque anecdotes or clichés. There is no attempt to maintain a comprehensive genealogy, however telescoped, that would link all the remembered Chitimukulus in a single pattern of descent.[92] Richards has remarked that Bemba chiefs are able to claim descent from the first Chitimukulu.[93] They make the claim; they are bound to; they do not feel obliged to provide a supporting genealogy. 'The first ancestors are remembered very accurately and their sacred relics are kept. The ensuing vagueness in the chain seems to be of no account.'[94] Indeed, as Richards has more recently observed, 'it would be difficult to speak of a real line of descent'.[95]

Few informants, then, could offer either genealogy or narrative to span the presumed interval between Chilufya*, the first Chitimukulu

[92] That is, among the royal councillors. I did obtain a comprehensive, tele- scoped genealogy from a royal headman (Chileshye Mukulu), but this was only elicited by asking questions.   [93] 'Political System', p. 100
[94] *Ibid.*   [95] 'Social Mechanisms', p. 182

to rule in Bembaland, and Chinchinta* or Chileshye*, three to four generations from the present. This hiatus does not seem to be simply the result of latter-day forgetfulness; it occurs in the first written record of Bemba history, made by Young in 1898. After narrating the settlement of the Bemba at the end of their migration, Young continues, 'The Ba-Luba, now known as the WA-Wemba [Bemba], appear to have lived peacefully until Chinchinta 13th Kitimkulu, appeared.'[96] Similarly, a literate Bemba historian, Mushindo, writes, 'There must have been many wars in the reigns of Chilufya's early successors, but we have little knowledge of events until the reign of Chileshye.'[97] One may suggest two reasons for this hiatus. First, in the period before Mukuuka*, royal succession appears to have followed no very clear pattern. Several different lineages competed for the paramountcy and as a result the relationships of successive Chitimukulus were frequently rather remote, thus confusing the genealogical record.[98] Later, Chileshye* switched the succession from the senior to the junior branch of the lineage to which Mukuuka* had belonged. This junior branch is the origin of the present ruling lineage; present-day interest in chiefly descent is thus largely confined to Chileshye* and his successors, for this is virtually all that is needed to explain the present configuration of Bemba chieftainships. One might suppose that it was important to show a relationship between Chileshye* and his predecessors in order to demonstrate Chileshye's* legitimacy. (In fact, two informants could trace the succession as far back as Mukuuka*.) But this is not now a live issue.

In any case, genealogy does not serve a major role as a charter for political office: such a charter is, rather, to be found in the doctrine of positional succession.[99] The theory that a chief inherits not only the position of his predecessors but also, in some sense, their identities as well, tends to reduce the importance of tracing the actual patterns of succession through each individual predecessor, even though, for ritual purposes, it may be important to remember their names. One might hope to be able to supplement and check the royal genealogy by invoking the genealogies of other titles which claim a relationship with it, such as the royals now excluded from succession, or certain *bakabilo* whose ancestors are said to have been sons of 'Chitimukulu'. But these genealogies are not long enough to act as an effective check on the royal genealogy, and in any case, just because of the importance of

---

[96] Chinsali DNB, I, p. 233   [97] Mushindo, *History*, s. 35
[98] This probability was noted by Richards, 'Social Mechanisms', p. 189, n. 8.
[99] *Ibid.*, p. 182

positional succession, claims to a relationship with a given Chitimukulu seldom mention the personal or praise-names of the chief in question; a titleholder was and is a son or nephew of Chitimukulu, and that is enough.

Effects of modern social change

In the foregoing discussion I have sought to characterise Bemba traditions and Bemba views of history in terms of the social background. But under the impact of colonial rule, Bemba society underwent changes which considerably affected Bemba awareness of the past. The Bemba became labour migrants, spending periods of several years in the towns of the Northern Rhodesian Copperbelt, Katanga or Southern Rhodesia.[100] And those men who may succeed to hereditary titles are not less likely than others to seek work abroad, for as I have noted they are not selected, let alone trained for office, before the incumbent's death. Thus almost all my informants had been away to work. Those few who had returned to Bembaland by 1930 or so were mostly fairly well informed about the past, for they still had an opportunity to learn from old men who had lived most of their adult lives under the old regime. But informants who were younger, or who had simply spent longer away from home, tended to have a noticeably less certain grasp of history. Work in the towns has diminished the opportunities for hearing talk about the past in the setting where that past is most real. It has also, of course, introduced the Bemba to a whole new range of ideas and experiences: there are many things to talk about nowadays besides history.

Again, a comparison with the Luapula peoples of Kazembe is appropriate. These have not become labour migrants on anything like the scale of the Bemba.[101] The Luapula valley, with its thriving fish-trade,[102] has provided a cash income, as well as a living, for many of its peoples, and it has retained a powerful hold on those who did go away to seek their fortunes in the towns. And the attractions of its material advantages are but part of the whole way of life represented by the

[100] Before World War II, many Bemba also went to sisal plantations and the Lupa goldfields in Tanganyika. Between 1928 and 1957 between 40% and 65% of the taxable male population was absent from Bembaland (Chinsali DNB, I, p. 180; cf. Richards, *Land, Labour and Diet*, p. 23).

[101] In 1949 the official figure was 23% of taxable males (Cunnison, *Luapula Peoples*, p. 28). This presumably refers only to Kazembe's kingdom.

[102] For some years after 1960 this suffered severely from the fall in value of the Congolese franc.

kingship; the traditions of the kingdom continue to arouse interest and satisfy ambitions despite modern political and economic change.[103] Among the Bemba, chieftainship also continues to command respect and stimulate local pride.[104] But in many ways Bemba country has been further impoverished, rather than enriched, by the modern economy, and unlike the Luapula valley it offers little or no scope for returning migrants to enjoy the advantages of life on the Copperbelt in their native surroundings. In particular, circumstances have undermined the means by which the dignity of chieftainship is maintained. Until 1950 or so the payments made to chiefs by Government, in lieu of former tribute rights, were quite inadequate to sustain the considerable burden of gifts and food by which chiefs used to reward the services of priests and councillors.[105] Largely as a result of this, much chiefly ritual fell into abeyance, and with it many of the occasions whereby history is retold or re-enacted. Chitimukulu Musungu*, who by the time he died in 1965 received a salary of over £1,000 p.a., did have the wherewithal to provide such rewards. But he was very little concerned with ritual matters and saw no point in paying the *bakabilo* when he could use his income as a source of further profit through trade. The *bakabilo*, in consequence, did not visit the capital more often than they could help, and freely expressed their lack of respect for Chitimukulu. Some tension between them is inevitable, as I have shown, but the disaffection with Musungu* was peculiarly bitter.

In these circumstances, the *bakabilo* nowadays are a much less fertile source of historical tradition than one might at first suppose them to be. Indeed, as Richards has observed, 'If historic traditions disappear in this area it will be due, at least in part, to the fact that the owners of the histories were not paid.'[106] It is true that at all times and places the alien enquirer is likely to encounter suspicion and reserve when

[103] *Luapula Peoples*, pp. 25, 28–9

[104] Between 1944 and 1946 the death of Chitimukulu Kanyanta and the choice of his successor were matters of considerable concern among Bemba on the Copperbelt and in Katanga: cf. NAZ/Sec/Nat 184–5; Brelsford, *Succession*, p. 25. See *Times of Zambia*, 31 October 1969 and 6 November 1969, for reactions to the death of Chitimukulu Musenga in 1969; also Appendix 2, Note N.

[105] A. I. Richards, 'Tribal Government in Transition', Supplement to the *JRAS*, 1935, 34. In the 1930s Chitimukulu received £60 p.a. (*Land, Labour and Diet*, p. 25); in 1962, £1,233. In 1916–17 Nkula received £12; in 1962 £672 (files at Chinsali district headquarters). By the early 1950s, the more senior *bakabilo* were entitled to allowances of between £5 and £35 p.a.; but during my stay in Bembaland they were complaining that these were not forthcoming.

[106] 'Social Mechanisms', p. 186

questioning old men about the past. 'We are just boys,' say the grizzled veterans, 'we know nothing.'[107] But today at least it is clear that this is not always simply a delaying tactic, gaining time in which to assess the enquirer's *bona fides*. A few remarks on some of the *bakabilo* may serve to indicate the situation in which I worked, where work histories as well as titles were important evidence for assessing an informant's value as an authority on the past.[108] Only five of the twenty-odd *bakabilo* whom I interviewed had succeeded to their titles before 1946, when the late Chitimukulu succeeded, and only two of these, Katenda and Nkolemambwe, are among the *bashilubemba*, the king-makers. Significantly, these two were, of the *bakabilo*, among my most useful informants. Chimba, who succeeded in 1943, was of some assistance, but the other three *bashilubemba*, Munuca, Chitikafula and Kapukuma, were all comparatively young men, appointed since 1959 after several years spent mostly in the towns. It is possible that such men do in fact know more than they appear to, but understandably they refer the enquirer to men of greater experience in the traditional setting. I gathered that these three *bashilubemba* were dependent upon their senior colleagues for learning their ritual duties. If, in the past, each *kabilo* kept his knowledge of traditional ritual to himself and his family, this may no longer be practicable.

The only *kabilo* who was able to provide me with a substantial narrative of Bemba history in the nineteenth century was Chikunga, and his expertise owes something, perhaps much, to his experience as a catechist for the White Fathers: the coherence of his account as a chronological sequence was facilitated by his ability to make notes and sort out his knowledge before recording it. How far Chikunga was indebted to the White Fathers and how far Fr Tanguy was indebted to Chikunga is not very clear.[109] But it is likely that anyone under the age of fifty or so has gained most of his knowledge of Bemba history directly or indirectly from the White Fathers' vernacular readers. Most

---

[107] Cf. Cunnison, *History on the Luapula*, p. 21. In 1859 John Kirk noted in the middle Shire valley, south of Lake Malawi: 'They are shy as to their traditions. They say the elders all died when they were young so they don't know them, but it is just as we would be if a German or any foreign individual were to come to a country village and ask for the fairy and ghost stories' (R. Foskett (ed.), *The Zambesi Journal and Letters of Dr. John Kirk*, Edinburgh 1965, p. 174).

[108] Details of my informants are set out in Appendix 5

[109] This could to some extent be worked out by comparing Chikunga's texts, Tanguy's *Imilandu*, *Ifyabukaya*, and Labrecque's history. I have not made any such detailed collation, though important variations are noted when I draw upon these sources.

4 Staff owned by chief Mwamba, said to represent Chilimbulu. The seated figure is about 20 cm high. Photograph: Zambia Information Services

5 *Kabilo* Mulewa Chimfwembe, wearing head-dress of feathers from the weaver-bird

6 *Ilamfya*, or war-charm. An iron bell is suspended from a roan antelope horn
(50 cm) mounted on a basket, draped with skins containing charms. This
swivelled on an iron rod to indicate the direction in which an attack should
be launched. Also shown is an iron-bladed executioner's knife. Courtesy of
the Royal Scottish Museum, Edinburgh

of my informants were older than this and were illiterate, yet even among them it may be possible to trace the influence of traditions other than those of their own families or chieftainships, as a result of the circulation of such composite histories.

Assessing the evidence

By way of concluding this survey of Bemba traditions it may be appropriate to suggest in what ways it might usefully be supplemented and how far Bemba tradition is susceptible to critical assessment as historical evidence. The present study has sought to achieve breadth of coverage over the whole scene of Bemba history, rather than to examine in depth the roots and sources of Bemba tradition. I have not, for example, attempted a close study of the social role of history in the life of any one Bemba community—a village or group of villages. To do this would undoubtedly illuminate the extent to which history is a living concern to the Bemba nowadays; it would also illuminate the way in which awareness of the past is perpetuated. It is one thing for informants to impart their knowledge of traditions to the student at prearranged meetings; it may be quite another thing to hear the same informants discoursing for the benefit of their own people rather than for an outsider. Ideally, the student should endeavour to record tradition as it is articulated in the course of social and political events. Such an exercise would help to reveal how traditions are transmitted from one generation to another. In my enquiries I sought to discover from whom my informants had learned their history, in order to show how far this history could be associated with a particular social position and how well placed my informant was for learning it. But study through observation rather than interview could give a much clearer indication of the character of oral traditions; it could show how far they really represented the peculiar and exclusive property of certain individuals, how far they were susceptible to addition and alteration from sources other than those individuals, and in what ways they were liable to distortion and variation as a result of special social interests.

It is, of course, doubtful whether such an enterprise is really feasible in modern conditions: in contemporary Bembaland, as in many other parts of Africa, social life has changed so much that the student must wait long, and sometimes in vain, to see anything like the full range of historical consciousness reveal itself in the life of a community. Even in the most favourable circumstances, some of the most important and revealing processes in a large-scale political system happen only two or three times in a lifetime. (Our knowledge of African political systems has been restricted by the inevitable fact that a fieldworker is seldom lucky enough to witness, for example, the burial or installation of a king or paramount chief.)[110] And as I have noted, the occasions which prompt recourse to history are much reduced in modern Bembaland, while the absence of half the men from the villages seriously affects the transmission of traditions. Nonetheless, it could still be of interest to enquire how the modes of transmitting tradition are affected by modern changes, an enquiry which would obviously have to include communities on the Copperbelt as well as in Bembaland.[111]

A full account of Bemba oral tradition would also include a more comprehensive survey than I have attempted of the different sources for tradition in the structure of Bemba society. The present study is almost wholly derived from what may be called official histories, the traditions of chiefly titles. It could profitably be supplemented by the traditions of non-chiefly groups and positions. It is true that, in a relatively homogeneous society such as the Bemba, a dependence on official history is less likely to be misleading than in a more rigidly stratified society, such as old Rwanda, where Vansina has pointed out the dangers of relying only on the histories of the Tutsi monarchy.[112] All the same, research among the older-established commoner villages would enable one to trace in some detail the movement of Bemba families throughout the course of a long history of conquest and migration. It would facilitate a study of how Bemba chiefs occupied new areas and assimilated under their rule peoples of other tribes. It would also illuminate the means by which chiefs recruited and cemented political support through contracting marriages into the families of their subordinates.[113] Furthermore, such research might also elicit links between local traditions and the numerous names of chiefs and headmen recorded by early travellers through Bemba country. There

---

[110] I left the field in 1965; it was only in 1966 that Chitimukulu Musungu was buried and his successor, Musenga, installed.

[111] I asked one senior *kabilo*, who had recently returned from a long sojourn on the Copperbelt, if he could tell me the story of where the Bemba chiefs came from. He replied, 'We heard on the radio that they came from the Congo.'

[112] J. Vansina, *L'évolution du royaume rwanda des origines à 1900*, Brussels 1962.

[113] It is significant that Katwamba, one of my few informants from a non-official commoner lineage, was comparatively well informed about history: not only does this lineage (that of headman Mulilo) belong to a close-knit fishing group on the Chambeshi (see above, p. 17); its sense of historical identity is reinforced by its belief in descent from Chilufya, son of an unnamed Chitimukulu (Katwamba, T1).

are, for example, several such names mentioned by Gamitto which I cannot as yet identify with positions or families now known in Bemba country.[114] But to attempt such a comprehensive survey of traditions, even within a single chiefdom, would be a considerable undertaking. In the time available, I judged it advisable to concentrate on the outlines of political history as they were to be elicited from the political structure.

For the same reason, I devoted less time than I might have done to seeking out and interviewing certain other potentially valuable informants. I interviewed some of the priests responsible for the sites of *ngulu* spirits, and those said to have been occupied by long-distant chiefs. But a detailed tour of the sites with the responsible priests could well elicit more information than I was able to obtain, since I had not time to visit more than a dozen or so, and there are many more. This procedure could also throw light on those lineages in the royal clan no longer eligible for succession to chieftainship. Some of these are still well known, especially those who retain villages in Lubemba and preserve their old titles. But others seem to be almost lost to view, for example the old royal lineages in the country of Nkolemfumu. The priest Nsanda, who prays to a local spirit called Chinyanduba,[115] and perhaps to others, might well be able to throw some light on the earlier history of the area. I am also conscious of not having interviewed any descendants of ivory-hunters. Finally, there are those few old men who grew up in pre-European days. They are clearly of quite special value as eyewitnesses, even though they may not know any particular traditions. The difficulty is to locate them, and then track them down, in a large and sparsely populated country, if they do not live at a chief's village and hold no salient political or social position themselves. More than once, after interviewing titled informants at a chief's village, I have been told that I should really consult some old man living far from the road; the information has come too late, and I have been obliged to move on to prearranged meetings elsewhere. It must in any case be recognised that the time is long past when one could reasonably hope to obtain much firsthand oral information about Africa before 1900.

[114] One major difficulty is that travellers might record either the personal name of a headman or his title, or even confuse one of these with the name given to the site of his village. Thus a thorough attempt at identification (which could be very useful for dating purposes) would involve obtaining lists and genealogies, and the location of remembered village sites, all along and around the travellers' routes. It is doubtful whether the results would be commensurate with the labour and time expended, unless the effort was shared.

[115] Shimulamba, T1. See below, p. 85, for the early history of Nkolemfumu.

It remains to discuss how far Bemba traditions can be used as reliable evidence as to what happened in the past: how far they are susceptible to bias and distortion, and in what ways it is possible to estimate this; and how far they may be checked against other kinds of sources. Some of the answers to such questions will have been suggested by the foregoing survey of the sources for Bemba history. For the nineteenth century, and in particular the last decade, Bemba traditions and those of their neighbours may be compared with the written records left by European travellers. These last, of course, are no more to be accepted uncritically than African versions of the past,[116] but they have a special corroborative value in that they are for the most part eyewitness testimonies, and the dates they provide afford a means for checking the indications of time-depth implicit in Bemba genealogies. And it may be said here that in the few cases where such comparisons are possible, the genealogies are shown to be quite accurate records of time-depth in respect of the particular names involved.[117] It is also possible to compare Bemba traditions with those of their neighbours, such as the Bisa or Lungu.[118] Furthermore, it is possible to compare and complement the traditions emanating from different titles and areas in Bemba country. As we have seen, the Bemba political system is such that there are likely to be a number of informants with varying perspectives of a history which, more or less, concerns them all—the history of Chitimukulu. At the same time, the information obtainable in different chieftainships does not simply provide the material for a number of different histories: such histories are related and overlap, contributing to a larger history, that of the whole Bemba polity.

Divergencies and contradictions between different informants can thus be partly accounted for in terms of the perspectives and interests consequent upon their social and political status. It is, to be sure, not always easy to adduce reasons for preferring one version to another as evidence about past events. Sometimes it may be possible to show clearly that one is more likely than another to be biased, for example when an informant has an obvious interest in asserting the prestige of a now unimportant title. Frequently, I have, in the absence of more explicit indications, preferred a version which seems to

[116] Cf. G. I. Jones, 'European and African Tradition on the Rio Real', *JAH*, 1963, 4, iii, pp. 391–402; C. M. N. White, 'The Ethnohistory of the Upper Zambezi', *African Studies*, 1962, 21, i, esp. pp. 20–5

[117] Cf. below, pp. 96, 113, 115, for genealogies of Bemba and Bena Mukulu chiefs supported by inferences from Portuguese sources.

[118] For such corroboration, see below, pp. 117–18 (Bisa and Bemba), 97, 107, 143 (Lungu and Bemba).

accord best with accounts of other, related events from other sources and with the general pattern of events as it is indicated by a number of sources. In such cases, I have cited and sometimes quoted conflicting versions. But it can be said that on the whole disagreements are relatively unimportant regarding what happened, in the sense of the broad outlines of Bemba history. Differences most commonly arise in describing the way in which events occurred and the reasons given for significant developments, and in this Bemba historians are at one with historians everywhere. I found a large measure of concurrence among my informants, and I have taken this concurrence as an assurance of a fairly high degree of probability that the traditions are substantially 'true'.

Vansina has persuasively argued that, where there are efficient methods of transmitting traditions and they are recited in a more or less formal manner, it should be possible to apply to them the same kind of 'higher criticism' that is applied to literary documents. One could then work out genealogies of traditions, showing how they were diffused through different sections of society and acquired distinctive features in the process.[119] I am, however, doubtful whether Bemba traditions are susceptible to such sophisticated analysis, since they are told informally, without any fixed, regular patterns which would lend themselves to purely formal criticism. The nearest form to a fixed recitation which the Bemba have is the *mushikakulo*, the praise-poem, and as I have noted these are of limited historical value. Moreover, such criticism is only likely to be valid where there are a large number of versions bearing on common themes, both from different social positions and from any one social position. I think it unlikely that more intensive research could produce more than one or two histories comparable in breadth and detail to those given by my principal informants. Besides, the means of transmitting traditions have, as I have noted, been so far affected by modern social change that it is no longer safe to assume that the history given by or about a titleholder necessarily represents the tradition proper to that title.

Elsewhere in Africa, references to eclipses in oral traditions have proved an invaluable aid to the establishment of absolute chronology. As yet, however, there appear to be no references to eclipses in the traditions of the Bemba and their neighbours. Over the past 350 years, four total eclipses, in 1619, 1676, 1701 and 1840, have traversed the area 29°–33°E and 8°–12°S. Those of 1619 and 1676 passed well to the north and south respectively of the Bemba heartland and their penumbrae

[119] *De la Tradition Orale*, pp. 101–10

might well not have been visible as they occurred during the rainy season. That of 1701 passed well to the north of Bemba country but in the dry season. One might have expected the eclipse of 1840 to have made some impression on the Bemba as it passed from west to east along the northern border of Lubemba soon after sunrise on an August day.[120] An annular eclipse traversed southern and western Bembaland in 1879, during the rainy season;[121] this probably occasioned little or no alarm.[122]

The main body of Bemba traditions does not extend back in time beyond about 1800. For the earlier period, of which the oral accounts are either fragmentary or legendary, there is, so far at least, no documentary evidence. It may be that the archives of the Portuguese in Mozambique contain material relevant to the history of north-eastern Zambia in the eighteenth century, but it is improbable that they could throw much light on developments as far north of the Zambezi as Bemba country.[123] A little more, perhaps, may be hoped for from archaeology. Several sites visible today are remembered as places where the ancestors of Bemba chiefs supposedly stayed in the course of migration over the plateau from the Congo; others are associated with early chiefs such as the first Chitimukulus, Katongo and Nkole; while at least one site may have been occupied by a pre-Chitimukulu chief.[124] I have myself made a superficial survey of some such sites,[125] but they would probably repay more expert investigation. As yet, north-eastern Zambia is not nearly so well known to Iron Age archaeologists as is southern Zambia. It is, however, unlikely to yield so rich a record. Phillipson notes that the relatively infertile woodland in the northeast is less suitable than the country further south for the prolonged occupation of single village sites. 'Frequent moving of settlements, still a

[120] The eclipses referred to are those of 7 November 1619, 5 December 1676, 4 August 1701 and 27 August 1840: Richard Gray, 'Eclipse Maps', *JAH*, 1965, 6, iii, pp. 258, 260.

[121] Eclipse of 22 January 1879; annular eclipses had also traversed the larger area here defined on 4 December 1611 and 2 December 1850: Richard Gray, 'Annular Eclipse Maps', *JAH*, 1968, 9, i, pp. 155-7.

[122] Compare Cameron's accounts of annular eclipses seen in Lungu country and near Bihé, Angola, in 1874 and 1875: V. L. Cameron, *Across Africa*, London 1877, I, p. 282; II, p. 192.

[123] There may yet, however, be more relevant material for the nineteenth century than has so far come to light: there was an expedition to Kazembe under João Vicente da Cruz in 1814 (Gamitto, *King Kazembe*, II, p. 11) and perhaps another in 1853 (see below, p. 191, n. 2).

[124] See below, p. 70.

[125] A copy has been deposited at the Livingstone Museum, Zambia.

feature of the area today, would be represented in the archaeological record by very thin occupation scatters which, in the absence of modern large-scale farming, are likely to remain undiscovered.'[126]

There can at least be little doubt that the study of the earlier phases of Bemba history would gain considerably from a comparative approach to the evidence of social and cultural anthropology.Where, as on this plateau, contiguous societies show a number of associated similarities in their social structure and culture, history as well as geography suggests itself as a mode of explanation for such similarities and attendant divergencies. A critical comparison of the Bemba and their neighbours, both in Zambia and in Zaïre, could well throw light, if only in the form of suggestive hypotheses, on the process whereby tribes, clans, and chieftainships were differentiated and gained more or less authority. Much evidence necessary for such study (especially on political institutions) remains to be collected, but the climate among social anthropologists is more favourable than it once was to making historical inferences from ethnographic evidence.[127] And the Bemba, as one group in a large cluster of peoples related to each other in respect of culture and social structure, are well placed to benefit from this climatic change.

[126] D. W. Phillipson, 'The Early Iron Age in Zambia', *JAH*, 1968, 9, ii, p. 198. See also below, p. 66.

[127] Cf. Jan Vansina, 'The Use of Ethnographic Data as sources for history', *Emerging Themes of African History*, ed. T. O. Ranger, Nairobi 1968, pp. 97–124; Mary Douglas, 'Matriliny and Pawnship in Central Africa', *Africa*, 1964, 34, iv, pp. 301–13; Max Gluckman and Fred Eggan, Introduction to *Political Systems and the Distribution of Power*, A. S. A. Monographs 2, London 1965, p. xxxii; and below, p. 294.

Chapter 2

The origins of Bemba chieftainship

In this chapter I discuss the evidence for the beginnings of Bemba history: that is to say, for the foundation of the chieftainship of Chitimukulu. The main evidence on this subject is a legend of migration, typical of its kind. I collected several versions of this legend, all very similar; for the purposes of this discussion, it is enough to consider a synthetic, abbreviated account which includes the main features.[1] I shall then indicate how much the migration legend contributes to our understanding of what may have 'really happened' by setting it in the context of our present knowledge of earlier Central African history. In particular, I consider where the founding chiefs may have come from; when they may have arrived; and whom they found on arrival in Bembaland. Since so much of the evidence is inconclusive and much of the discussion tentative, it may be helpful to summarise, in chronological order, the arguments of this chapter; it must, however, be stressed that this summary presents not only ascertainable facts but also mere probabilities.

Like other parts of north-eastern Zambia, Bemba country was inhabited at one time by Late Stone Age hunters and gatherers; the last of these seem to have disappeared some centuries ago. It is likely that since the first few centuries of the Christian era the woodlands of north-eastern Zambia and Katanga have been inhabited by Iron Age cultivators speaking Bantu languages. It is possible that for many centuries small groups settled in north-eastern Zambia in the course

[1] Versions of the migration legend are included in the recorded texts of Chileshye Mukulu, Milambo, Shimulamba, Chikunga, Makwaya and Chibingo, and in histories by Young, Mushindo and Labrecque. Some of the differences between these versions might well be significant for an analysis of their symbolic, rather than historical, content; but for historical purposes the principal variations are those between these Bemba traditions and the migration legends of neighbouring peoples such as the Lunda, Bisa, Mambwe or Lala: see below, pp. 53, 55, 61, 64.

38

of south-eastward movements from Katanga. In the course of time, chieftainships came into being, and as different groups developed a growing sense of corporate identity they acquired 'tribal' names. One group, to the northeast of Lake Bangweulu, became known as Bemba; they were matrilineal, and were probably related in some way to the north-eastern Luba, or Hemba; they practised *citemene* cultivation, and had a chief called *mulopwe*. Their neighbours included a few groups of cattle-keeping people of East African origin or affinities.

It is probable that in the course of the seventeenth century a number of groups entered north-eastern Zambia from the country west of the Luapula river and established chieftainships. One such group seems to have come from western Luba country, perhaps from the state of Kalundwe. These people left as a result of some dispute, perhaps connected with civil wars in Kalundwe. Among the migrants were members of the Crocodile clan (*bena ŋandu*); these were descended from chiefs, and perhaps from Lunda conquerors of Kalundwe. Eventually a group of *bena ŋandu* and their followers settled on the Kalungu river and established a new chieftainship called Chitimukulu. The newcomers either subdued or expelled the earlier inhabitants, but they adopted the name Bemba, which henceforward identified those who acknowledged the authority of Chitimukulu.

THE LEGEND OF MIGRATION

The Bemba account for their origins by telling the following story.

In a country called Luba or Kola there was a chief called Mukulumpe. He had a number of sons by different wives, but one day he heard of a woman, with ears as large as an elephant's, who said she came from the sky and belonged to the crocodile clan. Mukulumpe married this woman, who was called Mumbi Mukasa, and by her had three sons, Katongo, Chiti and Nkole, and a daughter, Chilufya Mulenga. Chiefly descent in Luba went from father to son, and as Mumbi Mukasa was of divine origin her sons were the first in line to succeed their father Mukulumpe. But these impetuous young men built a great tower, which fell down and killed many people. Mukulumpe was furious; he put out Katongo's eyes and banished Chiti and Nkole. Later, Mukulumpe appeared to relent and called back the exiles. He had in fact dug a game-pit on the path, meaning to trap and kill them as they re-entered the capital. But Katongo, though blind, warned his brothers of the danger by tapping out a message on the talking-drum. (The code is still known today.) Mukulumpe, discomfited to see his sons alive and well, punished them by making them sweep the royal courtyard. This of course offended their dignity, as it was meant to. Again, there was trouble. (Some versions say that the sons interfered with their father's younger wives.)[2] Chiti and Nkole now left the kingdom for good, taking with them their half-brothers Chimba, Kapasa, and Kazembe, and a number of retainers who later became councillors in Bembaland.

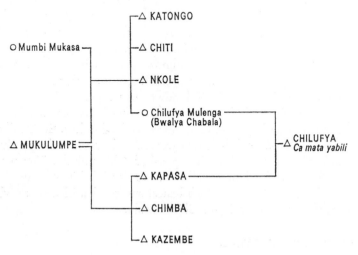

Fig. 1 Legendary origin of Bemba chieftainship.

The refugees fled east—some carrying seeds in their hair—until they came to the middle reaches of the Luapula river. They were ferried across by Matanda, a chief of the Bena Mukulo on the east bank. Here the fugitives paused, and the leaders realised that in their haste they had left behind not only their blind brother Katongo but also their sister, Chilufya Mulenga,[3] whom Mukulumpe had shut up in a doorless house. So they despatched their half-brother Kapasa with a few retainers to go back and abduct Chilufya. This was ingeniously effected, but on the way to the Luapula Kapasa seduced Chilufya. When Chiti learned that Chilufya was pregnant, he discovered that Kapasa was to blame and disowned him.

Meanwhile, the migrants had fallen in with a white magician, Luchele Ŋanga.[4] On their arrival at the Luapula, Kazembe had decided

[2] Cf. Gouldsbury and Sheane, *Great Plateau*, p. 30; Labrecque, 'Origines', p. 252   [3] Some sources, e.g. Mushindo, call her Bwalya Chabala.

[4] *Ŋanga* = doctor or diviner

to settle there, but Nkole and Chiti were uncertain where to go next
Luchele Ŋanga conjured up a fish from a mortar, which was taken as
an omen that they should continue eastwards. So they moved on round
the north of Lake Bangweulu and over the plateau to the Chambeshi
river, which they crossed near the Safwa rapids. At the Luchindashi
river, there was a quarrel between two women, which ended in part
of the group staying behind; these were the *bena ŋona* (Mushroom
clan), the royal clan of the Bisa people. The other migrants continued
southwards and came across the Lala, who asked for a chief and were
given a man called Kankomba. The migrants then turned eastwards
to the Luangwa valley and encountered among the Senga (or Nsenga)
a chief called Mwase. Mwase's wife, Chilimbulu, was very beautiful,
and her stomach was adorned with elegant cicatrisations. Chiti greatly
desired Chilimbulu, and one day he contrived to seduce her while
Mwase was out hunting. Mwase returned, however, to find the
guilty pair *in flagrante delicto*; the two chiefs fought, and Chiti was
grazed by a poisoned arrow. He soon died, and Nkole with
his followers sorrowfully bore his corpse away with them, turning

2 Sites mentioned in the Bemba migration legend

northwards in search of a suitable grove in which to bury Chiti.[5]

At this juncture, the migrants met Luchele Ŋanga once again, who before continuing his journey to the east directed them to a majestic grove called Mwalule, or Milemba. Here they found a woman, Chimbala; they also found another visitor, a Bisa headman called Kabotwe, who had come to trade but was also paying court to Chimbala. Chimbala gave Chiti's people permission to bury their leader in the grove, and then they got her to marry Kabotwe, thus ensuring her ritual competence to purify those who buried Chiti. Kabotwe became the keeper of the grove, taking from it his title Shimwalule, and thereafter his matrilineal descendants succeeded to this title. Before Chiti's burial, Nkole had sent out a party to seize cattle from the Fipa chief 'Pilula' in order to provide an ox-hide shroud. He now despatched a party to avenge Chiti's death by killing Mwase and Chilimbulu. This was done, and their bodies burned at Mwalule. But the smoke from the fire choked Nkole, who also died, and he too had to be buried at Mwalule.

The migrants from Kola had adopted a rule of matrilineal succession, and the successor to Chiti and Nkole was a son of their sister Chilufya Mulenga, perhaps by her incestuous liaison with Kapasa.[6] This boy, who was also called Chilufya, was as yet too young to rule as chief, so Chiti's half-brother, Chimba, took charge of the bows of Chiti and Nkole. The migrants left Mulambalala, their site near Mwalule, and crossed the Chambeshi further north. Kapasa, however, was in disgrace, and he settled on his own in Bulombwa, driving out the Iwa chief Kafwimbi and his herds of cattle. As the others travelled westward up the Kalungu river, two men, Kabwa and Chikunga, came upon a dead crocodile rotting on the riverbank. Since the chiefs, as children of Mumbi Mukasa, were of the Crocodile clan (*bena ŋandu*), this was taken to be a good omen. The migrants decided to make their capital, *Ŋwena* (the modern word for crocodile), on the Kalungu, and they settled in the surrounding country. The few groups of people who lived in the area were called Sukuma, Musukwa, Kalelelya and Ngalagansa; they were either killed or driven away by the Bemba, as the immigrants were now called.

In due course, Chilufya* grew up, and Chimba handed over the bows of Chilufya's* uncles Nkole and Chiti. Chilufya* thus gained the praise-name *ca mata yabili* (of the two bows), but though he kept the

---

[5] Chief Mwamba possesses a hardwood staff carved with figures which are identified with Chilimbulu and Mwase: see Appendix 2, Note A, and Plate III.

[6] Labrecque says the boy's father was Kapasa ('Origines', 265); Mushindo says he was one Pokili (*History*, s. 15). My informants were not clear on this point.

bow of Chiti he insisted that Chimba keep the bow of Nkole. So Chimba kept this bow and founded his own village at Chatindubwi, a few miles north of the Kalungu. Thereafter, the Bemba became many: new villages and chieftainships were founded, and many chiefs succeeded Chilufya*, each taking the name of the original leader, Chiti *mukulu* (Chiti the great).

GENERAL COMMENTARY

This legend is clearly a rather special kind of historical tradition. It is not simply a record, however distorted or fragmentary, of the doings of dead men in whom particular groups among the living have some special interest. The migration legend of the Bemba is indeed a 'mythical charter' which serves a communal and not merely sectional interest. Its manifest concern is to account for the origins of Bemba chieftainship by tracing a putative ancestry for its founders, by explaining where they came from, and by associating them with the names of some of the first *bakabilo*. By thus accounting for its origins, the legend justifies the Bemba political order. It establishes that the *bena ŋandu* have a divine right to be rulers, and it shows how they came to rule where they do. The claims are strengthened by the mingling of elements from the world of experience and the world of the supernatural. The local details lend force to the argument by placing the story firmly within a familiar environment of known groups and places. The status of the *bena ŋandu* is enhanced by displaying their first achievements not simply in a vacuum but as the central feature of the early history of the whole region known to the Bemba. At the same time, the miraculous and supernatural elements in the story invest the protagonists with a special power and prestige: they are shown to belong to a vanished world of gods and heroes.

It is thus a delicate task to make use of this legend as evidence as to what may have actually happened in the past. It is necessary, at the very least, to distinguish those features which are essentially mythical in character, whether or not they have any basis in past events. And we must recall that, for the Bemba, there is no other story of 'tribal' origins. The legend about the founders of the Chitimukuluship is also accepted as an explanation of how the Bemba tribe came into being, since all Bemba are subjects of Chitimukulu. Inasmuch as the migration legend is thus a charter for Bemba society as well as for their ruling group, we might well expect it to have a relatively high mythical content. It is obviously much more difficult, with or without writing, to preserve the history of a large group as such than to preserve that of a relatively small group such as the founders of a dynasty. And the important characteristics of a society, such as its kinship system and economy, are not easily susceptible to historical explanation. Besides, the people themselves are primarily concerned, in tracing their origins, to stress moral norms through an imaginative vision of the past. For them, this is history because it must be history: no other version would have the same relevance to the world as they see it.[7]

Much in the Bemba legend of migration is very clearly material for the student of myth and social structure rather than the historian. Certain features are especially arresting and familiar: the oppressive father, the rebellious sons (perhaps competing for their father's wives), the royal incest. There are resemblances here to the myths invoked by Freud to explain the origins of 'human society' in terms of his psychoanalytic theory. It is of course notorious that in *Totem and Taboo* Freud grossly overreached himself, but one social anthropologist has recently noted the special relevance of Freud's argument to matrilineal societies.[8] Indeed De Heusch has specifically acknowledged the importance of the Bemba legend of migration as a charter for a matrilineal society. The abduction of Chilufya Mulenga dramatises the limited rights of a father over his children in such a society, while the special value it sets upon brother–sister relations is illustrated by Chiti's punishment of Kapasa, after the latter's incest with Chilufya. De Heusch also observes that the legend may be evidence, albeit compressed, of an actual change of descent among patrilineal invaders of a matrilineal society.[9] One might go further and interpret the story of brother–sister incest as a means of providing Chitimukulu with descent both in the female line from the goddess Mumbi Makasa and in the male line from the 'Luba' king Mukulumpe.[10] On the other hand, we must note that other

[7] These points are banal for social anthropologists, but they are too seldom acknowledged in historical studies. Cf. Cunnison, *History on the Luapula*, pp. 11–22; J. S. Boston, 'Oral Tradition and the History of Igala', *JAH*, 1969, 10, i, pp. 29–43; Aylward Shorter, 'Religious Values in Kimbu Historical Charters', *Africa*, 1969, 39, iii, pp. 227–37; T. O. Beidelman, 'Myth, Legend and Oral History: a Kaguru Traditional Text', *Anthropos*, 1970, 65, pp. 74–97; E. E. Evans-Pritchard, *The Azande*, Oxford 1971, pp. 414–35.

[8] Robin Fox, 'Totem and Taboo Reconsidered', *The Structural Study of Myth and Totemism*, ed. E. R. Leach, London 1967, pp. 161–77

[9] Luc de Heusch, *Essais sur le symbolisme de l'inceste royal en Afrique*, Brussels 1958, pp. 146–50; and see below, pp. 54, 74.

[10] Cross-cousin marriage would also have secured such bilateral descent, but just because it is in fact a Bemba norm it would have had a less didactic impact than the story of incest and its retribution.

matrilineal dynasties also explain their descent systems by stories of a change from patrilineal descent;[11] such stories may well have no grounding in distinct historical events. Besides, many features of the Bemba legend are clichés which recur again and again in the traditions of other peoples in central Africa: such clichés are the falling tower, the concealed pit, the menial work, the seeds carried in the hair, the benevolent figure of Luchele, and the incest itself.[12] Any full analysis of the Bemba legend of origin would have to take into account not only Bemba social institutions and Bemba folklore in general, but also similar legends throughout Central Africa.

To acknowledge the mythical element in an oral tradition is not, of course, to deny it all value as evidence for past events.[13] The Bemba legend of migration describes a journey from a particular region—the Luba country west of the Luapula river—to the banks of the Kalungu river, between Lake Bangweulu and the Luangwa valley. And there is every reason to suppose that there have indeed been population movements into north-eastern Zambia along this general line of approach. This is suggested by the broad linguistic and cultural resemblances of the Bemba, and many of their neighbours, to the Luba and Lunda peoples of Katanga. Moreover, there are many other Zambian groups, such as the Bisa, Ushi, Lala and Lamba, who also have traditions of origin in 'Luba'. But having conceded this, we must consider whether the Bemba legend is evidence for any particular type of population movement, and if so, where exactly it originated, and at what period it took place.

As we have seen, the migration story is related by Bemba people in general as an explanation of 'where the Bemba came from'. For the Bemba, as for many other African peoples, the tribes of today have always existed: an explanation of how they came into being can only be given in terms of an explanation as to how they came to their present country from somewhere else. Such an attitude may be both adequate and inevitable in pre-literate societies whose view of the past is based as much on aetiology—inference from the present—as on actual testimony to past events. Yet this naïve conception of 'tribal

[11] For example among the Kuba, and also the Atié of the Ivory Coast: for the latter, see Denise Paulme, 'Première approche des Atié', *Cahiers d'études africaines*, 1966, 6, p. 88. (I owe this reference to Professor J. Vansina.)

[12] See Appendix 2, Note B (p. 346).

[13] The interpenetration of myth and history in the Old Testament is acknowledged by Edmund Leach in 'The Legitimacy of Solomon', reprinted in his *Genesis as Myth and other Essays*, London 1969, pp. 42–3, 53–4, 114. See also Finley, 'Myth, Memory and History'.

history' has been unthinkingly perpetuated by all too many modern writers. So far from existing from time immemorial, the ethnic groupings now known as 'tribes' are, like any other social groups, the result of specific changes, some of them quite recent.[14]

We should not, therefore, assume that the Bemba legend of migration is evidence of any large-scale movement of population. Migration, after all, can take place in a variety of ways. The march of an organised horde is spectacular but rather uncommon, and it would have been most unlikely in the dense woodland of the upper Congo basin. It is much more probable that the present populations of these regions have been formed through a prolonged process of growth and recurrent migration lasting many centuries: indeed, there is some evidence to this effect.[15] Migration from Luba and Lunda country into north-eastern Zambia plainly has taken place, but the significant groups were most probably no more than clan-sections.[16] Here and there, some of these groups achieved pre-eminence, perhaps through conquest, perhaps through successful raiding, perhaps through association with established ruling groups in the Congo. Because of the largely uniform habitat, and a general similarity in cultural background, such larger groupings as came about under a dominant clan of chiefs might achieve a sense of communal or 'tribal' identity, in which the various histories of the different groups were merged in or subordinated to that of the ruling group.

The Bemba, in fact, seem to illustrate these points rather well. The main purpose of their migration legend is clearly to explain the origins of Bemba chieftainship: it narrates the adventures of a quite specific group—the founders of the royal dynasty and their few followers. In so far as the legend can be accepted as evidence for actual historical events, it is evidence for the arrival of a particular group from Luba country and their establishment of a new chieftainship among the existing inhabitants of Bemba country. The intruders' legend of origin came in the course of time to be accepted by their subjects as the history of all Bemba, since both rulers and subjects formed a fairly homogeneous society which derived its identity as a 'tribe' from a

[14] Cf. Vansina, *Kingdoms of the Savanna*, pp. 14–18; Andrew Roberts (ed.), *Tanzania before 1900*, Nairobi 1968, ii; R. J. Apthorpe, 'Problems of African History: the Nsenga of Northern Rhodesia', *RLJ*, 1960, 28, pp. 47–67

[15] See below, pp. 66–7.

[16] Cf. Vansina, *Kingdoms*, p. 88; Gouldsbury and Sheane, *Great Plateau*, p. 31. C. M. N. White makes the same point for the peoples of north-western Zambia: 'Clan, Chieftainship and Slavery in Luvale Political Organisation', *Africa*, 1957, 27, 1957, i, p. 60.

common subordination to Chitimukulu.[17] It may well be that the adoption of the legend as an explanation of tribal origin accounts for the fact that, whatever else it may be, it clearly is a mythical charter for a matrilineal society. And the status of the legend as a tribal charter would also account for the large element of aetiology in it: the explanation, for example, of the origin of Kazembe's kingdom and of other chieftainships.[18]

We may therefore treat the Bemba legend of migration as evidence of a kind for the establishment of the Chitimukulu dynasty by a fairly small group of people from somewhere to the west of the Luapula river. This much, however, could in any case be inferred from the ethnographic evidence. It remains to discover how far the various incidents related in the legend can be regarded as events that happened to real people at particular times and places. In approaching this problem, I shall first look more closely at certain general features of the legend itself; I shall then consider whether its historical content may be illuminated through comparison with other oral traditions in central Africa.

There is a marked contrast in the legend between the fairly specific geographical detail of the later part, describing the journey east of the Luapula, with the geographical vagueness of the earlier part. And as soon as we attempt to distinguish the obviously mythical elements in the legend, we see that these are concentrated in the earlier part, in the account of the departure from 'Luba' and the journey as far east as the Luapula. We might conclude that the lack of any precise indication as to where the migrants began their journey reflects the fact that the legend had been adopted as an explanation of 'tribal' as well as dynastic origins: since the former are likely, in reality, to be more diverse, they are unlikely to be represented very exactly in any shared tradition. But it also seems probable that the lack of detail about Luba country in the legend is due to the fact that the Bemba have maintained no links with this part of the world. For the migrants in the story, it was the country to the east that was strange and new. For the Bemba story-teller, this country is familiar ground; it is the country west of the Luapula which is unknown, and hence an apt setting for symbolic fantasy. It is significant that the incest which supposedly gave rise to the new dynasty is said to have taken place shortly before the migrants committed themselves to continuing eastwards from the Luapula. For it is usual in myths and fairy tales that only incest or some other forbidden act makes possible an emergence from a state of naïve

[17] See above, p. 19.   [18] See below, pp. 53, 64.

irresponsibility into a mature awareness of life's complexities and problems.[19] The crossing of the Luapula represents a transition from a fabulous primeval simplicity to the world of actual experience: the river marks a frontier between the unknown and the known.

As raiders and conquerors, the Bemba have long been acquainted with the whole expanse of plateau between the Luapula and Luangwa rivers. But the country further west was always remote and alien to them, partly because it was dominated by Kazembe's own kingdom. There is no evidence that the Bemba ever maintained any links with any kingdom or chiefdom in Luba country. To this extent, indeed, we may well believe that Bemba chieftainship originated in discord of some kind, even if the legend describes this in a form that is highly stylised and remote from literal accuracy. If there was some sort of rebellion and secession, the dissident chiefs would hardly have remained in touch with the original dynasty. In the same way, it is not surprising that in the recorded traditions of the Luba and western Lunda there is, as we shall see, no clear mention of the departure of chiefs identifiable with those of the Bemba.

The Bemba legend of migration may usefully be contrasted with the eastern Lunda story of how the kingdom of Kazembe was founded on the Luapula. This story relates that Kazembe's kingdom was set up on the initiative of the western Lunda king, Mwata Yamvo, and the subsequent history of Kazembe attests that this historic relationship was maintained by regular contacts between the two rulers. The historical traditions of the eastern Lunda deal from the outset with places and positions which are still known, and they can be corroborated both by the traditions of Mwata Yamvo's Lunda and by the testimony of early European visitors to Kazembe. Furthermore, the eastern Lunda traditions of origin are not, like those of the Bemba, the shared traditions of a whole society. They are the traditions of a discrete ruling group, whose various subject peoples have their own traditions of origin. Kazembe's kingdom did not form a single community, to be explained by reference to a common origin; there was thus no motive for eastern Lunda tradition to take a generalised and mythological form.[20]

If the Bemba migration legend says little about the country and people west of the Luapula, it is fairly specific about events and places

[19] Cf. Robert Donington, *Wagner's 'Ring' and its Symbols*, London 1969, (second ed.), pp. 105–7; also Leach, *Genesis as Myth*, pp. 10–11, on unnatural acts as means of mediation between different worlds.

[20] See above, pp. 20–2.

east of that river. The migrants from 'Kola' are believed to have crossed the Luapula at a particular place, near Chief Matanda's.[21] Kazembe then left them to found his own kingdom lower down the river. The migrants moved on eastwards, to the north and east of Lake Bangweulu. They provided the Lala with a chief, and after they crossed the Chambeshi the ancestors of Bisa chiefs split off. The main body continued eastwards as far as the Luangwa, where there was trouble with a Senga or Nsenga chief called Mwase; they then turned north, found a burial place for their chiefs at Mwalule, and raided the 'Fipa' to obtain an ox-hide shroud. Finally, the migrants settled in Lubemba, though one of their number, in disgrace, obtained country by expelling an Iwa chief.

Such details, concerning peoples and places with whom the Bemba are more or less familiar, have an air of verisimilitude: it might seem that their migration legend is at least evidence for an actual journey east of the Luapula, even if it tells us little about events further west. On closer reflection, however, the legend itself does not appear to warrant such a conclusion. It is likely that the story of 'Bemba' wanderings east of the Luapula is no less mythical in character than the account of their flight from 'Kola'. The fact that this later part of the legend deals with recognisable peoples and places merely indicates that the myth has taken on a new purpose. It is now concerned to place the origins of Bemba chieftainship securely in relation to neighbouring peoples and chieftainships. The aetiology has become more narrow in focus, but it remains aetiology.

The migration, as related in the legend, very roughly describes two great arcs across the plateau between the Luapula and Luangwa. This route approximates more or less to the furthest limits of Bemba activity throughout their pre-colonial history. The various peoples said to have been encountered on the way—the Lala, Senga, Iwa and Fipa—were all subject to Bemba raiding, especially in the later nineteenth century. It therefore seems likely that, in narrating the progress of the migrants across the plateau, the legend is simply asserting that Bemba movements within this region, and Bemba predominance therein, are intrinsic to Bemba chieftainship.[22] Other oral traditions suggest that in fact the Bemba polity grew from very small beginnings,[23] but the legend of migration serves to give the Bemba imperial

---

[21] For further details see Appendix 2, Note C (p. 347).

[22] I have been encouraged in this interpretation by Beidelman's analysis of legends of clan movements among the Kaguru of Tanzania: see his 'Myth, Legend and Oral History', p. 90.　　　　　　[23] See below, ch. 3.

tradition the stamp of high antiquity. This interpretation appears the more plausible when we consider the circumstances in which other groups of people are referred to in the legend. The seniority of Bemba chieftainship is asserted in respect of Kazembe, the Bisa chiefs, and Lala chiefs. Bemba military superiority is asserted in relation to the Senga, the Iwa and the Fipa.

Thus, whatever else it may be, the legend of migration east of the Luapula is a fairly comprehensive statement of Bemba attitudes towards their neighbours, which clearly reflects the known history of Bemba expansion. As such, it can hardly be accepted on its own as evidence for a particular sequence of actual historical events. Its historical content can only be demonstrated through comparison with evidence from other sources. I therefore consider now whether the traditions of other peoples in central Africa seem to throw any light on early Bemba history.

TOPOGRAPHY

The Bemba usually refer to their place of origin as 'Kola', sometimes as 'Luba' or 'Buluba', and occasionally as 'Lunde'. 'Koola' is the name of the heartland of Mwata Yamvo, the emperor of the western Lunda.[24] One Bemba informant, Chileshye Mukulu, said on being questioned that the chief in Kola was called Singa.[25] Mwata Yamvo (whose relation to Singa was not known) went to go and live in Luba. Singa's son Kapopo lived between the Lulua and Kasai rivers. (This region, it may be noted, is that of Mwata Yamvo's kingdom.) Kapopo's son, Mukulumpe, rebelled and ran away to Luba, where his sons in

---

[24] Y. Struyf, 'Kahemba...', *Zaire*, 1948, 2, iv, p. 360. It has often been assumed by Europeans that 'Kola' is simply a version of 'Angola' (see, e.g., Lacerda in Burton, *Cazembe*, 41), but this is unlikely since both the chiefdom of Ngola and the eponymous Portuguese colony of Angola lay well to the west of Mwata Yamvo's.

[25] This might conceivably be an echo from the state of Matamba, west of the river Kwango, which was ruled in the seventeenth century by the famous queen Nzinga, and whose subjects, the Ginga, later travelled as caravan porters to the upper Kasai (Vansina, *Kingdoms*, p. 203). According to Labrecque ('Origines', p. 269), the relics of Chitimukulu include small statues which he guessed might have been the work of Capuchins, who were indeed active in Matamba in the later seventeenth century. There is, however, more reason to believe that these objects came from Kazembe's in the late nineteenth century; they were possibly the work of early missionaries in Katanga (Chitikafula, 1 April 1933, 28 June 1934: A. I. Richards, fieldnotes).

turn rebelled against him.[26] Another informant, Chimba, also said that
Mukulumpe's father was Kapopo (Kapopo *lapwa*), and this was
supported by Chikunga in so far as he gave 'Kapopo lapwa' as a name
for Mukulumpe: this might well be a patronymic.[27] But none of these
names, to my knowledge, can be identified in Luba or Lunda traditions; *mukulumpe* is simply a Luba word meaning 'old' or 'great' and
also 'elder' or 'headman'.[28] Some Bemba informants were inclined to
associate or even identify Mukulumpe with Mwata Yamvo, but this
probably reflects no more than a vague awareness of Kazembe's origin
at Mwata Yamvo's, and an assimilation of this into Bemba tradition,
which as we have seen has its own version of Kazembe's origin.[29]
There is a tradition at Mwata Yamvo's about the departure of one
Kabemba, but this is evidently Kazembe, for Kabemba is said to have
gone east to the Luapula and introduced manioc; 'Kabemba y devint
le grand chef Lunda.'[30] The name 'Kabemba' would naturally arise
from the adoption by Kazembe's Lunda of Bemba speech and some
Bemba customs.

Thus it seems impossible to say with any confidence whether the
Bemba chiefs are of Luba or Lunda origin. One good reason for this
uncertainty is the very fact that the two areas are closely connected:
the dynasty of Mwata Yamvo traces its origin to the marriage of a
Lunda princess, Lweeji, with a Luba hunter, Chibinda Ilunga.[31]
Vansina has accordingly made light of this uncertainty about Bemba
origins. He cites the praise-poem quoted by Labrecque which says of
the Bemba leader Nkole, 'You extend Lunda country, you are a true
Luba chief.'[32] Vansina suggests that this supports the theory that the
Bemba came from Luba with the founders of the Lunda dynasty and
then moved on east from the Lunda kingdom. But this theory pro-
visionally assumes that the story of Chibinda Ilunga and Lweeji can

[26] Chileshye Mukulu, 15 April 1965. It is, however, doubtful whether his
knowledge of the local topography is derived from oral tradition: he visited the
Kasai region in 1923 as a labour recruiter.
[27] Chimba, T1, n. 1; Chikunga, T1.
[28] E. van Avermaet, *Dictionnaire Kiluba-Français*, Tervuren 1954, pp. 304–5
[29] Labrecque ('Origines', p. 251) says that Mwata Yamvo was a son of Mukulumpe, but I never heard this from my informants.
[30] Struyf, 'Kahemba', p. 359; cf. Vansina, *Kingdoms*, p. 276, n. 29
[31] Cf. V. W. Turner, 'A Lunda Love Story and its Consequences' (translated
excerpts from the work of Dias de Carvalho, cited below), *RLJ*, 1955, 19, pp.
1–26; see also Marie-Louise Bastin, 'Tshibinda Ilunga: à propos d'une statuette de
chasseur ramenée par Otto H. Schütt en 1880', *Baessler-Archiv*, n.f. 1965, 13, ii,
pp. 501–45; and *idem, Tshibinda Ilunga: héros civilisateur*, Brussels 1966.
[32] Vansina, *Kingdoms*, p. 88; Labrecque, 'Tribu', p. 642

be taken as referring to an actual event, and is not simply the dramatisation of a more lengthy process. Moreover, it rests on an identification between Lunda and Bemba tradition for which there seems to be no evidence.

Vansina, following Verhulpen, identifies the Bemba with people sent eastwards by Chibinda Ilunga. According to Lunda tradition, as recorded at Mwata Yamvo's by Carvalho in 1887, these included some of Chibinda's companions from Luba.[33] But elsewhere, in a more detailed account, Carvalho says that it was not Chibinda but the fourth chief to succeed him, Mwata Yamvo Naweeji, who sent out this expedition.[34] And in any case Verhulpen's identification of the Bemba with migrants from the Lunda kingdom is unsound. It is based on the mere assumption that 'Chiti' was 'Kazembe Mushidi', who according to Verhulpen was sent out by Mwata Yamvo along with 'Kazembe *mu Nkinde*' (whom Verhulpen identifies as the first Kazembe of the eastern, Luapula, Lunda).[35] Verhulpen gives no reason for this identification of Chiti beyond saying vaguely that it is based on a comparison of Mwata Yamvo's traditions with those 'du pays des Babemba'. 'Kazembe Mushidi' is mentioned in none of the published accounts of Bemba history, nor by any of my informants; nor, among the accounts of Lunda history, is he mentioned by Pogge or Carvalho.[36] Duysters' version does mention a Kazembe Mushidi, who went south across the upper Zambezi and sent tribute to Mwata Yamvo until the latter was defeated by the Chokwe in 1885.[37] On the strength of this, Verhulpen declares that Mwata Yamvo maintained contact with the successors of Chiti up to 1885.[38] But nowhere does Duysters provide any evidence that Kazembe Mushidi might have been Chiti. On the contrary, the history of Kazembe's Lunda on the Luapula confirms and adds to

[33] H. Dias de Carvalho, *Ethnographia a historia tradicional dos Povos da Lunda*, Lisbon 1890, p. 91. The Lunda of Kazembe also mention the Luba migrants, saying that they were given hard work by Chibinda Ilunga, so fled east across the Luapula (Cunnison, *Historical Traditions*, p. 7). Vansina thinks these might be the Bemba migrants (*Kingdoms*, p. 276), but it is not at all clear that they can be identified with any particular group. Quite possibly this passage is a modern accretion, influenced by the editor of Kazembe's history, Fr Labrecque, who in his own article on Bemba origins had traced the Bemba to the Lunda kingdom (Labrecque, 'Origines', p. 251).

[34] Carvalho, *Ethnographia*, p. 541   [35] Verhulpen, *Baluba*, pp. 152–3

[36] P. Pogge, *Im Reich des Mwata Jamvo*, Berlin 1880, pp. 225–6; Carvalho, *Ethnographia*, pp. 91, 527, 541

[37] L. Duysters, 'Histoire des Aluunda', *Problèmes de l'Afrique Centrale*, 1958, 20, p. 86. The manuscript version of this paper was used by Verhulpen.

[38] Verhulpen, *Baluba*, p. 153

Duysters' version: they say that Mushidi, a follower of Chinyanta (father of Kazembe I of the Luapula), was sent by Mwata Yamvo, along with Nshinde (presumably the Kazembe *mu Nkinde* of Mwata Yamvo's tradition) and Kanongesha to rule the Kaonde and Luvale in what is now north-western Zambia.[39]

It is certainly clear enough that the migration described in the Bemba legend was distinct from that of Kazembe's Lunda to the Luapula. Bemba tradition, as we have seen, presents Kazembe as a half-brother of Chiti who stayed on the Luapula while Chiti went on eastwards. Kazembe's history provides a highly circumstantial account of Kazembe's departure from Mwata Yamvo's which nowhere mentions the Bemba chiefs. According to this history, Kazembe first encountered the Bemba in the shape of the Shila, a tribe whose chiefs ruled on the Luapula when Kazembe's Lunda arrived; the Shila chief Nkuba says that his ancestor was a Bemba immigrant from the east.[40] The Lunda account seems more plausible than that of the Bemba, not only because it is more prosaic but because it accords with the relative lengths of the king-lists of Kazembe and Chitimukulu, and with the considerable differences between the kingships of Kazembe and Chitimukulu. The institutions and general court culture of the latter show a much more distant resemblance to the kingship of Mwata Yamvo. Probably the Bemba story about Kazembe simply expresses, in the idiom of kinship, the mutual, if qualified, respect and goodwill which the Bemba and Lunda, as the strongest powers in the area, have usually felt towards each other, along with an awareness that both chieftainships originated in the west.[41] Besides, Bemba culture has been

[39] Cunnison, *Historical Traditions*, p. 29. It is not at all clear that this is a genuinely independent tradition: Fr Labrecque, the editor of the original text, may have interpolated his own knowledge of western Lunda tradition. The only other reference to a chief who could be identified with Duysters' Kazembe Mushidi seems to be the 'Mushili' mentioned in Lozi traditions as the name of a chief somewhere around the Zambezi/Congo watershed: cf. Vansina, *Kingdoms*, p. 177 and p. 288, n. 11. *Mushidi* or *umushili* means 'earth' or 'soil' in the languages of the region, and it may well have been a short-lived praise-name. In the earlier nineteenth century, Kazembe on the Luapula was called 'Luchenda' or 'Panchenda' after the site (Nshinda) of his capital in 1798 (Livingstone, *Last Journals*, I, p. 264; R. F. Burton, *The Lake Regions of Central Africa*, London 1860, II, p. 148). In any case, the titles of chieftainships are known to change on occasion in this region, certainly among the Bemba and Bisa.

[40] Cunnison, *Luapula Peoples*, pp. 37–8; cf. also his *Historical Traditions*, p. 53

[41] It was a discussion on history in about 1930 between the Lunda court and a deputation from Chitimukulu which prompted Kazembe IX, in 1942, to arrange for a compilation of Lunda traditions to be written down (Cunnison, *Historical Traditions*, p. ii).

influenced to some extent by that of Kazembe's Lunda: it is well
known, for instance, that in the last century Bemba chiefs patronised
minstrels from Kazembe, and some of the praises which they composed
are still remembered.[42]

It is nonetheless very possible that Bemba origins are to be sought in
both Luba and Lunda history. We have already seen that one informant,
Chileshye Mukulu, considered that 'Mukulumpe' ran away to 'Luba'
from his father Kapopo, who lived in the region of Mwata Yamvo's
kingdom. This may only be a recent gloss on the migration legend
rather than a genuine historical tradition; on the other hand, it does
appear to gain some support from the traditions of the Luba state of
Kalundwe (whose chief is called Mutombo Mukulu). According to
Verhulpen, Kalundwe was taken over by *bena ɲandu* from Lunda,
perhaps in the sixteenth century. There was a period of civil war
between these Lunda and two earlier ruling lineages, one of which was
also Lunda.[43] Perhaps these *bena ɲandu* may be identified with those
who constitute the Bemba royal clan; and perhaps the departure of
Chiti and Nkole corresponds to an episode in these civil wars. Such a
theory would account for the mixture of Luba and Lunda elements in
Bemba court culture.[44] It would also, as Roland points out, accord
with the apparent shift from patriliny which that tradition records,
since the *bena ɲandu* are said by the Luba to have introduced patriliny to
Kalundwe.[45] But such a hypothesis needs to be tested against properly
recorded Luba and Lunda traditions, and also against a comparison of
other cultural evidence.[46]

So far, we have seen that, even after comparison with the traditions

[42] If the Bemba affect to resent what they see as Kazembe's pretensions of
grandeur, this is just because they are, inevitably, impressed by his sense of style. I
have heard one senior Bemba chief, Nkula, addressed as 'Mwata'—a style proper
only to Kazembe. I have also heard, in a praise for a Bemba chief, the words,
'We are here in the chief's village, in the village of Mwata Kazembe' (Nkamba,
T1). This was a praise for Mwamba III Mubanga Chipoya, who had Lunda at his
court and also had carved umbrellas from Kazembe's country (Richards, 'Bwembya', p. 23).

[43] Verhulpen, *Baluba*, pp. 235–6. Perhaps one or other of these Lunda groups
may be identified with the 'Caembe Muculo' who according to Carvalho
(*Ethnographia*, p. 527) founded a state near Mutombo Mukulu.

[44] Lunda words in the Bemba vocabulary of politics include those for capital
(*musumba*), village-section (*citente*), section-leader (*cilolo*).

[45] H. Roland, 'Résumé de l'histoire ancienne de Katanga', *Problèmes sociaux
congolais*, 1963, 61, p. 17, n. 1; but cf. above, pp. 44–5.

[46] Since this book was written, M. Bruno Mavar (F. Crine) has produced a
study of the western Lunda, but it has not been available to me.

available from the Lunda and Luba, the Bemba legend of migration
yields only the most general sort of historical information. We have
also seen that in the narrative of events east of the Luapula one important element is clearly no more than aetiology: the reference to
Kazembe. Comparison with the traditions of other neighbours of the
Bemba suggests that this is also true of references to them. The Bemba
claim to have provided the Lala with a new chief, Kankomba.
Kankomba is indeed a praise-name used by various Lala chieftainships,
but Lala traditions of origin do not refer to the Bemba and clearly
concern a distinct process of migration from Luba country.[47] Bisa
traditions, by contrast, do appear to lend some support to the Bemba
legend. The Bisa chieftainships of Kopa (formerly Mwansabamba),
Kabanda, Mungulube and Matipa all trace descent from an ancestor
called 'Mukulumpe' or 'Mukulumpwe'.[48] It is noteworthy that none
of these Bisa groups appear to have any stories telling how their own
chiefs came west from the Congo; their origin is simply explained
in terms of fission from the Bemba. But the very lack of any independent and more circumstantial migration legend among the Bisa suggests
that their account of chiefly origins is also no more than an aetiological
explanation, arising from more recent historical relations between
Bemba and Bisa. Finally, we should note here that there does not seem
to be any independent corroboration of the Bemba story concerning
their encounter with the Senga (or Nsenga) chief Mwase. 'Mwase'
was indeed the name of an early holder of the Chifunda chieftainship
among the Senga,[49] while a Chewa chief Mwase is said to have come
at one time from the chiefdom of Mwase wa Kasungu to the lower
Rukusi valley east of the Luangwa.[50] But there appears to be no further
independent evidence from either Senga, Chewa or Nsenga sources to
support the Bemba story.[51]

[47] J. T. Munday, 'Kankomba', *Central Bantu Historical Texts*, I, Rhodes–
Livingstone Communication 22, Lusaka 1961. Another aetiological invention
would seem to be the story that Luchele Ŋanga went away to the east to found
Ngonde chieftainship (Shimulamba, T1, n. 14; Vansina, *Kingdoms*, p. 89).

[48] Mungulube, T1; Munsoma, T1

[49] Personal communication from Professor H. W. Langworthy

[50] Lane-Poole, *Native Tribes of the Eastern Province*, pp. 28–32. Gamitto found
a 'Mwase' on the nearby Rukusushi river in 1831 (*King Kazembe*, I, p. 125). A
Mwase wa Minga is said to have been left on the Luangwa by the Mwase who
settled at Lundazi (H. W. Langworthy, personal communication)

[51] H. W. Langworthy, personal communication; Apthorpe, 'Problems of
Political History', The Nsenga live far to the south of the Senga, and Bemba
informants who called Mwase an Nsenga chief were probably contributing a gloss
of their own, or of the White Fathers, whose histories refer in another context to

One further source for checking on Bemba stories of migration east of the Luapula might be the sites which are said to have been occupied by the migrants on their journey eastwards. At least ten such sites seem to be remembered: two between the Luapula and Lake Bangweulu; two or three near the river Luena; one near the Chambeshi; one or two near the Luangwa; and three in the neighbourhood of Mwalule.[52] The only one I have visited is one of the latter group, Mulambalala; this was certainly a sizeable village, though a cursory inspection revealed no clue as to its age. It may be that a close examination of such sites, and of local traditions concerning them, might yield evidence in support of the Bemba legend; but it is also possible that the legend mentions some, if not all, of these sites simply in order to provide an explanation for them.

From this examination of the Bemba migration legend, we are obliged to conclude that, while it plainly has the character of a myth, it includes few elements which can also be accepted as historical fact. It is simply not possible at present to determine whether any one group of people actually did once cross the Luapula, wander across the plateau to the Luangwa, and make Mwalule their royal burial grove before finally settling on the Kalungu river. To judge both from the preceding discussion and from what is known of other traditions of migration it seems very probable that in so far as the Bemba legend does describe historical events it compresses a more or less prolonged process of migration and settlement into a single dramatic story, which has been elaborated with various aetiological details to form a 'tribal' myth.

CHRONOLOGY

Since the actual historical content of the Bemba migration legend remains so uncertain, it would clearly be inadvisable to use it as evidence for estimating the antiquity of Bemba chieftainship.[53] Whatever chronological inferences may be made concerning the early history of other peoples in the region, we are scarcely justified in extending these to Bemba history simply on the basis of the Bemba migration legend.

'Nsenga' where 'Senga' is clearly meant (Labrecque, 'Origines', p. 311; *Ifya bukaya* p. 107; Tanguy, *Imilandu*, p. 71; cf. below, p. 375.

[52] Cf. Labrecque, 'Origines', pp. 255–60; 'Tribu', pp. 636–41; Tanguy, *Imilandu*, pp. 11–15; Chileshye Mukulu, T1

[53] Here and elsewhere in this chapter much of the material has been presented in Andrew Roberts, 'Chronology of the Bemba', *JAH*, 1970, 11, ii, pp. 221–40.

Verhulpen considered that a *terminus post quem* for the beginnings of Bemba chieftainship could be derived from dates proposed for events in the early history of the western Lunda.[54] Several attempts have been made, with the aid of Portuguese records from Angola, to date the marriage between Chibinda Ilunga and Lweeji.[55] But it is now clear that this 'Lunda love story' is a 'mythical charter' which refers, not to historical events, but to processes which may have spanned several centuries.[56] In any case, there is, as we have seen, no good reason to follow Verhulpen in associating Bemba migration with any of the Lunda migrations mentioned in Lunda traditions. Nor can the historian of the Bemba make use of the meagre clues in Portuguese records about the antiquity of Lala and Chewa chieftainships. It has been suggested that 'Kankomba' existed as a chiefly title among the Lala by the early seventeenth century,[57] while there was evidently a Chewa chief called Mwase in the Kasungu area by 1624.[58] But we have already seen that there is no good reason to accept Bemba references to these titles at face value.

Since the Bemba migration legend offers no sound basis for chronological inferences, we must turn to the evidence of genealogies and king-lists among the Bemba and their neighbours. As we saw in chapter 1, there is no continuous genealogy for the Chitimukulu chieftainship, and no other Bemba genealogy provides an alternative indication of maximum time-depth. There is thus no indication in Bemba tradition as to how many generations have elapsed since the time of, say, Chilufya* *ca mata yabili*. The most we can say is that Mukuuka* lived four generations before 1900 (that is, four generations before that of Chitapankwa*, Sampa* and Makumba*), and apparently there were many Chitimukulus before Mukuuka*. Thus for present purposes it is of no great moment to estimate a reliable average interval between generations of Bemba royals. For the century or so before 1900, for which we have detailed information on the pattern of succession, it

[54] *Baluba*, p. 135

[55] D. B. Birmingham, 'The Date and Significance of the Mbangala Invasion of Angola', *JAH*, 1965, 6, ii, pp. 143–52; J. Vansina, 'More on the Invasions of Kongo and Angola by the Jaga and the Lunda', *JAH*, 1966, 7, iii, pp. 421–9.

[56] Joseph C. Miller, 'The Imbangala and the Chronology of Early Central African History', *JAH*, 1972, 13, iv, 549–74

[57] D. P. Abraham, review of Munday, 'Kankomba', in *Africa*, 1962, 32, pp. 182–3

[58] In 1624 Luis Mariano, a Portuguese Jesuit travelling in the area, heard of a chief called 'Massi': cf. C. Beccari, *Rerum Aethiopicarum* . . . , Rome 1912, pp. 113–14. I owe this information to Professor E. A. Alpers.

would seem appropriate—and not a mere rule-of-thumb guess—to apply the familiar generational interval of thirty years not only to Bemba chieftainships but to other matrilineal dynasties in the area.[59] But for earlier periods an informed guess is neither possible nor, indeed, of much use.

Bemba genealogies, then, are of little if any relevance for the chronology of Bemba origins. A better indication of time-depth is provided by the number of remembered Chitimukulus. On this there is admittedly no agreement among the various sources. The following figures refer to Chitimukulus up to and including Sampa* (died 1896). Young listed seventeen; Fr Guillemé (in 1902) listed eighteen, only ten of which appear in Young's list. In 1924 Lloyd, an official, took down twenty-nine names before an 'Assembly of the Babemba' (probably a meeting of *bakabilo*): four of these are not cited elsewhere, while seven others are given by other sources but not by Young.[60] Labrecque's history lists twenty-nine Chitimukulus up to 1896: of these, two are given by no other source except Labrecque's own earlier article on Bemba origins. Tanguy lists twenty-three names; and Mushindo lists twenty-eight names, only two of which are mentioned by no other source. As for my informants, Chikunga gave twenty-three names, while Chileshye Mukulu gave twenty-six names. I am fairly sure that this latter list at least is genuinely independent of the literary sources. I had hoped for a check on such king-lists from Shimwalule. In the past, each Shimwalule who buried a Chitimukulu was supposed to be replaced.[61] One might thus expect a list of each Chitimukulu with the corresponding Shimwalule, or else at least infer that the number of remembered Shimwalules would be a rough guide to the number of Chitimukulus. But at Shimwalule's I could only obtain the names of four Chitimukulus, and four Shimwalules, earlier than Susula*, and Brelsford fared little better around 1940.[62]

Of all the names mentioned in these lists, it is evident that some are only praise-names or secondary personal names, such as patronymics. In table 1 which compares these various lists, I have indicated such instances where I recognised them. It is possible that many more of

---

[59] See Roberts, 'Chronology of the Bemba', pp. 235–6.

[60] Guillemé, 'List of Bemba Kings' (tr. P. Cookson), Kasama DNB I, p. 403; Lloyd, 'List of the Chitimukulus' (June 1924), *ibid.*, pp. 413–14

[61] Brelsford says that Shimwalule was supposed to be actually killed by his successor ('Shimwalule', p. 210); such a custom, especially in the sylvan setting of Mwalule, would curiously resemble that of Frazer's murderous kings in the sacred wood beside Lake Nemi.

[62] Shimwalule, 18 May 1965; Brelsford, 'Shimwalule', p. 210

Table 1. LISTS OF CHITIMUKULUS: A COMPARISON

	Chileshye Mukulu	Chikunga	Tanguy	Labrecque 1968	Labrecque 1933	Guillemé	Mushindo	Young	Lloyd	Goodall	Coxhead
Chiti *muluba*	√	√	√	√	√	.	√	√	√	√	1
Nkole	√	√	√	√	√	√	√	.	√	.	2
Chilufya *ca mata yabili*	√	√	√	√	√	.	√	.	.	.	
Mulenga Pokili	√	√	√	√	√	√	√	.	√	.	
Kanabesa	√	√	√	√	.	√	√	.	.	√	
Chibamba Manshi	√	√	√	√	√	√	√	.	√	.	
Chisoka *ca bakata, nshiwile*	√	√	√	√	√	√	3	√	√	4	√
Chishisa	√	.	.	√	√	.	.	.	√		
Kapampa *mubanshi*	√	√	√	√	√	.	.	.	√		
Kasansu	√	√	√	√	√	.	√	.	√		
Kayula *milyango*	√	√	√	√	√	√	√	√	√	√	.
Chibengele *ukupile fyulu*	√	√	√	√	√	√	√	√	√		
Chifunda *ca busoshi*	√	√	√	√	√	.	√	.	√		
Lwipa *cacila mabyalwe*	√	.	.	√	√	√	√	.	√		
Mutale *wa munkobwe*	√	.	.	√	√	5	√	6	√	√	.
Salala *bana bonke*	√	√	√	√	√	√	√	√	√	√	√
Kabemba *na bantu*	√	√	√	√	√						
Chimanga	.	.	.	.	.	√	√	√	√	.	√
Chimpolonge	√	.	.	7	7	√	√	√	√	√	.
Kafula	.	.	.	.	√	.	.	.	.	.	.
Kalilunga *mutwalo*	.	.	.	√	.						
Chimfwembe	.	.	.	.	.	.	√	.	.	.	.
Kasonde	.	.	.	.	.	.	√	.	√	.	.
Chimfungwa	.	.	.	.	.	.	.	.	√	8	.
Munuka											
wankalwe	.	.	.	.	.	.	.	.	√	.	.
chipinula	.	.	.	.	.	.	.	.	√	.	.
Chisona	.	.	.	.	.	.	.	.	√	.	.
Ndubwila	.	.	.	√	9	.	.	.	√	.	.
Ntamba Lukuta (10)	.	.	.	√	√	.	.	.	.	.	.
Chipasha *wa makani* (11)	.	√	√	√	√	.	.	.	.	.	.
Sekwila	.	.	.	.	.	.	√	.	.	.	.
Chimba *nsoka*	.	.	.	.	.	.	.	√	.	12	.
Kapolyo *mukulu*	.	.	.	.	.	.	√	.	.	.	.
Katongo *ncilamalilo*	√	√	√	√	√	√	√	√	√	√	.
Mukuuka *wa malekano*	√	√	√	√	.	√	√	.	.	.	
Chiliamafwa	√	√	√	.	.	√	√	√	√	.	
Susula Chinchinta	√	√	√	√	.	.	√	√	√	√	√
Chileshye *cepela*	√	√	√	√	.	√	√	√	√	√	
Bwembya	√	√	√	√	.	.	√	√	√	√	
Chitapankwa (d. 1883)	√	√	√	√	.	√	√	√	√	√	√
Sampa *kapalakashya* (d. 1896)	√	√	√	√	.	√	√	√	√	√	√

Table continued overleaf

Table 1 (cont.)

1 Called Chileshye.	7 Given as praise for Katongo.
2 Named, but not as Chitimukulu.	8 Given as praise for Chiliamafwa.
3 Called Nshiwile.	9 Given as praise for Chishisa.
4 Given as praise for Kayula.	10 A common praise-name.
5 Mutale wa Nimbo.	11 Name of early Ituna chief.
6 Mutale wa Chisoka.	12 Given as praise for Chisoka.

Praises are quoted after the names of Chitimukulus with whom they are generally associated. Tick–signs indicate references to Chitimukulus.

Ifyabukaya (White Fathers, 1932, 35–9) lists the names given by Labrecque, except for Kafula, Chibengele and Ntamba Lukuta.

---

these names are in fact simply praise-names. In Burundi, Vansina has been able to show by a comparison with the royal graves that despite the thirty names known for Rundi kings there were only six rulers before 1900.[63] Unfortunately, no such test is possible among the Bemba.[64] But I think it unlikely that their lists are quite so misleading as the Rundi ones: most of the names were given as those of different individuals by several independent sources. For some, their individuality is attested by praise-names which are associated specifically with one personal name rather than another, and of course the identities of the later names are well established by narrative traditions and genealogies. The Bisa apparently say that the Bemba 'often quote as chiefs the names of claimants'.[65] This may well account for names which only occur in one or two lists, but it is less likely to invalidate names given by several independent sources.

We may conclude, then, that a provisional estimate of twenty-five Chitimukulus up to 1896 is not excessive. It remains to estimate the average length of their reigns. This is clearly affected by the practice of adelphic succession, which makes for the succession of a series of men of relatively advanced years. Reign-lengths are thus inherently likely to be fairly short. For the period between 1883 and 1965 the average was 13·66 years. Under British rule, of course, there were no succession wars, but the general pattern of succession as it evolved during the nineteenth century was not strikingly altered by colonial rule. However, in the absence of a continuous genealogy the pattern of royal succession before about 1800 is not clear. There are said to have been many succession wars,[66] and reign-lengths may well have been, on average, quite short. In the circumstances, it is probably advisable to reckon from an average reign-length of ten years at most. If there were

[63] J. Vansina, 'Notes sur l'histoire de Burundi', *Aequatoria*, 1961, 24, i, p. 3
[64] See above, p. 14.   [65] Thomas, *Bisa*, p. 4
[66] Chikunga, T1; cf. further discussion of this period in ch. 3.

twenty-five Chitimukulus before 1900 this suggests that the dynasty has been established on the Kalungu since the middle years of the seventeenth century.

The traditions of other peoples in north-eastern Zambia appear to provide some support for a *terminus ante quem* of about 1700 for the establishment of the Chitimukulu dynasty in Bembaland. We have already seen that there is no mention of the Bemba in Lunda traditions of Kazembe's settlement and early conquests on the Luapula. It is therefore apparent that any migration by founders of Bemba chieftainship is likely to have crossed the Luapula before the Lunda arrival there, which may be roughly dated to about 1740.[67] And traditions from the Shila peoples on the lower Luapula suggest that in fact the Chitimukulu dynasty was established in Bembaland well before this date. The Shila chief Nkuba, who is himself a *mwina ŋandu*, claims that his ancestor was originally a Bemba royal, who settled on the Luapula after quarrelling with Chitimukulu.[68] Nkuba was evidently established on the Luapula when the Lunda first arrived, and he had probably been there since about 1700, for the fourth Nkuba was killed by the Lunda soon after the accession of Kazembe III, which probably took place in about 1760.[69] According to the tradition of another Shila chieftainship, Mununga, Nkuba lived on the Bemba plateau, and left it, shortly *before* the arrival of Chitimuluba's followers,[70] but in either case the inference is that the Chitimukuluship was established no later than about 1700. It should, however, be noted that such Shila stories may themselves be no more than aetiological explanations.[71] The Bemba, for their part, appear to know nothing of Shila history.

[67] Ian Cunnison, 'The Reigns of the Kazembes', *NRJ*, 1956, 3, ii, p. 132, based on Fr Pinto's remark that the Lunda arrived on the Luapula about sixty years before Lacerda's expedition thither in 1798, to which Pinto was chaplain (Pinto, in Lacerda, *Travessia*, pp. 290–1; Burton, *Cazembe*, p. 126).

[68] Cunnison, *Luapula Peoples*, p. 37; cf. D. Crawford, *Back to the Long Grass*, London n.d. (?1924), pp. 128–9, 254

[69] Cunnison: 'Reigns', pp. 132–3; *Luapula Peoples*, p. 40; *Historical Traditions*, p. 56

[70] Chisanga, T1. Labrecque presumably relies on Shila traditions when stating that some of the original inhabitants of Bemba country fled to Lake Mweru ('Origines', p. 263).

[71] The earliest reference to Nkuba's story is by Crawford, who apparently heard it in 1897. Thus it may only have been a response to the settlement of some Bemba, a few years earlier, to the north of Kazembe's capital (see Crawford, *loc. cit.*, and below, p. 223 and n. 41. Some time in the 1940s, as a manœuvre in Luapula politics, Nkuba reaffirmed his supposed link with the Bemba by taking tribute to Chitimukulu (Cunnison, *Luapula Peoples*, p. 49, n. 2).

Table 2. COMPARATIVE LISTS OF DYNASTIES IN N.E. ZAMBIA (List 1)
Chiefs grouped by generations and dated by death: see JAH 11, ii (1970), 239

Bemba		Bisa		Chishinga	Mukulu	Tabwa	Lungu			
Chitimukulu	Other Bemba	Mwansabamba	Matipa	Mushyota	Chungu	Nsama	Mukupa Kaoma	Kaoma	Tafuna	Died
			'Mukulumpe'							1630
'Mukulumpe'		'Mukulumpwe'								1660
Chiti Nkole		Mwansabamba I								1690
Chilufya			(Chonso) Chota							1720
(Many names telescoped)		M. Buzembe	Chingandu Mukosha	Chikula Mayembe						1750
			Chinyimba Mwape Kalenga Chama							
Mukuka	Chitundu we Tuna	Mwaba Chintu		Mambwe						1780
Chiliamafwa	Mubanga Kashampupo	Malama	Yombwe Kabamba	?Chikumbi	Chibwe I	Makungu	Kambole			1810
Susula Chinchinta		Mwaba Chalwe	Mumpuku Nkalamo	Kaunda Kamina	Chimpulumba (Chibwe II) Kakomwe	Kabobole ante 1841	Kaoma	Chikoko		1840
Chileshye Bwembya	Chikwanda I Mutale (Mwamba I)	Chibesa Museba Mwaba Nkandu Chiti	Muma 1883 (Matipa I)	M.wa mikolo	Mushinka Mushitu Kunda	Chipili Chipioka c. 1870?	Kamambwe	Ngoolwe Kafumbo Chungu 1870?		1870
Chitapankwa 1883 Sampa 1896 Makumba 1911	Chileshye (Mwamba II) 1883 Shimumbi I 1906?	Mwape 1890? (Kopa I)	Kabamba (Matipa II) 1897	Kaminda Chama Mambwe 1903	Kapopo 1904/11	Katandula 1873? Kafwimbi ante 1883 Chimutwe	Chisunkumya	Shikansa Kabwe	Kakungu 1905?	

Died	Kazembe	Chitimukulu	Nsokolo	(Nkansi) Iwaachi (Lyangalile)	(Milansi)	Died
					Ntatakwa	1690
1700			Changala		Sulandasi	1720
	Nganda Bilonda c. 1740?	(Many names telescoped)				
1740			Sichilundu		Ntaseka	1750
	Kanyembo c. 1760?	Mukuuka	Sipa Kupombwe	Msili Ndasia		
1780					Chamkaango	1780
				Ntinda Mkolokombe Suumba Mwaana Nsia Sangu		
	Lukwesa 1804/5	Chiliamafwa	Mwimbwe Kwizya	Nandi wa Kukutango		1810
1820			Funda Kuchipoka N.wa Chisenga			
	Keleka c. 1845? Kapumba	Susula Chinchinta (deposed 1826/7?)		Ntinda Kwasinganwa	Nguwa Mwaana Nyekenti	1840
	Chinyanta 1862?	Chileshye c. 1860?	Mutala	Nchinga Chileengwi		
	Muonga 1872	Bwembya	Musanya	Suumba Kalonga Sangu		
				Suumba Kasuumba ('Pilula') (fl. 1880)		
1860	Chinkonkole		Malamba	Nandi Kapuufi 1891		1870
	Lukwesa 1886? Kanyembo 1904	Chitapankwa 1883	Chitambi Kakamyalile 1907	Suumba Ntinda Kiteta	Yulamaasi (fl. 1890) 1898/9	
		Sampa 1896 Makumba 1911	Mwesimupiya 1929	Nandi Msuulwa 1898 Kapele	Nti Kifata	
1900	Mwonga 1919 Chinyanta 1935					1900

The remaining possible clues to early Bemba chronology are to be found in the traditions of various peoples who are mentioned in the Bemba migration legend. As I have noted, this is hardly a secure basis for chronological inference. Nonetheless, it is worth noting the evidence that certain chieftainships among neighbours of the Bemba have been established for at least seven generations before 1900, that is since some time around 1700. The Iwa chieftainship of Kafwimbi traces descent eight generations before 1900 to one Mukulika, who was driven out of Bulombwa by the Bemba; Bemba traditions, as we have seen, place this event in the period when the Bemba chiefs first settled on the Kalungu.[72] It is not at all clear whether the Chitimukulu title preceded the foundation of Bisa chieftainships—as both Bemba and Bisa believe—but the comprehensive genealogy of Mwansabamba, as recorded by Thomas, spans seven generations before 1900, while the history of the Matipa chieftainship indicates a span of at least seven, and perhaps nine, generations before 1900.[73] It is also worth noting that one genealogy of the Mambwe paramount Nsokolo places his ancestor Changala seven generations before 1900,[74] though the Mambwe tradition that Changala came from 'Kola' with the Bemba chiefs is probably no more than aetiology.[75]

Thus, regardless of possible early connections between Bemba and other chieftainships, there is good reason to suppose that at least the older chiefly dynasties now established in north-eastern Zambia were founded by about 1700. And if this is true of Bisa, Iwa or Mambwe chieftainships, it is certainly just as likely to be true of Bemba chieftain-

[72] P. M. Simtala, 'History of Kafwimbi' (MS); Isoka DNB I, p. 192; cf. above, p. 42. But according to Mr John Willis (Grinnell College, Iowa), the related Namwanga dynasty traces twelve generations from 1900 back to Musyani, whom the Iwa say was a son of Mukulika; the Namwanga also say that Musyani's son was killed in a fight with the Bemba (Beverley Brock, 'The Central Corridor Area', paper for SOAS Conference on African Chronology and Genealogies, 1966). Labrecque reports a Bemba story that the men of Chitimukulu despatched one Mukoma to subdue the Namwanga ('Origines', p. 263). This is plainly aetiology: the first Namwanga chief to take the title of Mukoma ruled when the Ngoni arrived, in about 1840 (John Willis, as reported by Brock, 'Central Corridor Area'; cf. M. Wilson, *Peoples of the Nyasa–Tanganyika Corridor*, Cape Town 1958, p. 66).   [73] Thomas, *Bisa*; Munsoma, T1–2.

[74] Aaron Sichivula and Zombe Nsokolo, 13 June 1965. This adds two generations, between Changala and Nsokolo I, to the genealogy in Watson, *Tribal Cohesion*, p. 144. But both are probably more or less telescoped: see below.

[75] Aaron Sichivula, T2; cf. Watson, *Tribal Cohesion*, p. 13; Labrecque, 'Origines', p. 264. Aaron says that the Bemba started from Musokantanda (a deputy of Mwata Yamvo), but he is a much travelled man and this detail is probably an accretion. See also below, pp. 72–3.

ship; if there is little evidence to show that it is older than these other chieftainships, there is certainly none to suggest that it is more recent. The sceptical social anthropologist might object that any rough agreement in depth of chiefly genealogies may reflect, not historical actuality, but structural necessity. But the agreement is only very approximate and is not demonstrably based on any structural pressures common to each chieftainship in question. That some genealogies in this region are systematically retained at a constant depth has been shown by Cunnison, for commoner lineages on the Luapula, and by Watson, among the Mambwe.[76] Watson indeed argues that the Mambwe royal genealogy is influenced by the political structure, in which all the various royal titles are linked by ties of perpetual kinship in a manner analogous to Luapula lineages; but such a system is not found among the Bemba and Bisa. In any case, I have only been concerned to use the genealogies as they stand as approximate indications of minimum time-depth; the probability that they are more or less telescoped does not affect the present argument.

EARLY INHABITANTS OF BEMBALAND

There is one remaining feature of the Bemba legend of migration which merits discussion: its reference to people found by the followers of Chiti and Nkole at the time they settled in Bemba country. There are no references, either in this legend or in other forms of Bemba tradition, to people who could be identified with the Late Stone Age people known to have inhabited sites near the heart of Bemba country, such as Mwela rocks near Kasama. The archaeological record attests that Late Stone Age cultures persisted in central Africa long after the arrival of Early Iron Age peoples early in the first millennium A.D., and in parts of central and eastern Zambia Late Stone Age groups survived until comparatively recent times. At Nakapapula, in Serenje District, a Late Stone Age industry probably continued until about the middle of the second millennium A.D., and this lends support to Lala traditions of finding small-statured people in the area.[77] At Mwela rocks, as at Nakapapula, Early Iron Age pottery has been found among Late Stone Age artefacts,[78] but it would seem that the makers of the latter were

[76] Cunnison, 'History and Genealogies in a Conquest State', pp. 22–3; Watson, *Tribal Cohesion*, pp. 147, 150

[77] D. W. Phillipson, 'The Prehistoric Sequence at Nakapapula Rockshelter, Zambia', *Proceedings of the Prehistoric Society*, 1969, 35, p. 200

[78] Sheryl F. Miller, 'Contacts between the Later Stone Age and the Early Iron Age in Southern Central Africa', *Azania*, 1969, 4, p. 84

displaced or absorbed somewhat earlier than their counterparts further south, in view of the silence of Bemba traditions regarding people of this kind.

As for the Early Iron Age groups in north-eastern Zambia, it might at first appear that there has been a significant measure of cultural and physical continuity between them and the majority of Bemba-speaking peoples today. It has been argued that the Bemba and Luba languages, more than any others, resemble 'proto-Bantu', the putative common ancestor of the Bantu languages; that therefore the regions in which Bemba and Luba are spoken were the scene of the initial stages in the main thrust of expansion by Bantu speakers; and that this process was contingent upon food-production and the use of iron.[79] Such arguments for prolonged linguistic continuity in the central African woodland have been reinforced by physiological evidence from the Luba.[80] They receive further support from archaeological evidence which strongly suggests a north-western origin for the Early Iron Age inhabitants of north-eastern Zambia. Such people are known to have lived near Kalambo Falls from about the fourth or fifth century A.D., while Early Iron Age pottery has also been recovered from sites further west, around the south end of Lake Tanganyika, and from Samfya on Lake Bangweulu. As yet, no Early Iron Age occupation sites have been found in Bemba country, but this may be only because the environment does not favour the prolonged occupation of single sites.[81] The Early Iron Age pottery at Mwela rocks would seem to have been imported by Late Stone Age people, but the schematic paintings there are almost certainly the work of Early Iron Age people.[82] It is thus not inconceivable that Bemba traditions of the 'Musukwa' cultivating mounds on

[79] Malcolm Guthrie, 'Some developments in the prehistory of the Bantu languages', *JAH*, 1962, 3, ii, pp. 273–82; but see also the cautionary remarks by W. M. Mann, 'Internal Relationships of the Bantu Languages: Prospects for Topological Research', *Language and History in Africa*, ed. D. Dalby, London 1970, pp. 133–45; and Christopher Ehret, 'Bantu Origins and History: Critique and Interpretation', *Transafrican Journal of History*, 1971, 2, i.

[80] Biological analysis indicates that the Luba of Katanga 'may be regarded as relatively little modified descendants' of the original physical stock of Bantu speakers: J. Hiernaux, 'Bantu Expansion: the evidence from physical anthropology confronted with linguistic and archaeological evidence', *JAH*, 1968, 9, iv, p. 508. For a comprehensive discussion of the varied evidence for Bantu expansion, see Roland Oliver and Brian M. Fagan, 'The Emergence of Bantu Africa' in the *Cambridge History of Africa*, Cambridge, in press, II.

[81] Phillipson, 'Early Iron Age', pp. 197–200, 208–10

[82] D. W. Phillipson, *Prehistoric Rock Paintings and Engravings of Zambia*, Livingstone 1972

riverbanks[83] represent some dim memory of riverain groups descended from Early Iron Age peoples who had originally occupied the region at an early stage in the main phase of Bantu expansion.[84]

It is, however, probable that the present physical stock and culture of the Bemba owe more to a somewhat later phase in Iron Age population movements. For the most recent research indicates that much modern pottery in central, north-eastern, and eastern Zambia belongs to the same basic tradition as pottery from this region which has been dated to the early part of the second millennium A.D. and which is markedly different from Early Iron Age pottery. There appear, for example, to be important features in common between sherds of this period from Kalambo and Nakapapula and contemporary pottery styles in these areas.[85] Thus it would seem very likely that in north-eastern, as in southern, Zambia the early part of the second millennium witnessed the intrusion of new groups, probably from the general direction of Katanga (Shaba), and that such intrusion was large enough in scale to leave its mark on so basic a cultural trait as pot-making.

There is, then, some reason to trace the 'origins of the Bemba', in the sense of ancestors of the main body of present-day Bemba, to a process of settlement in regions south and east of the Luapula as much as a thousand years ago. But if pottery provides some slight indications of broad cultural identities and continuities, we must look to oral traditions for clues about early forms of social and political organisation. And such meagre clues as they provide suggest that the main phase of settlement in north-eastern Zambia, and the formation of discrete social or political units, such as chiefdoms, were relatively gradual and prolonged processes, involving migration and interaction among many different groups of culturally akin people in the woodlands of the upper Congo basin. It is probable that for a long time the main principle of differentiation between such groups was membership of a clan or clan-section.[86] It is asserted in several oral traditions in

[83] Chipasha, 19 November 1964; Chandaweyaya, 26 November 1964; and cf. Labrecque, 'Tribu', p. 644, n. 4. As Mushindo points out (*History*, s. 29), there are people called Sukwa in the hill country on the lower reaches of the Songwe river, at the north-western corner of Lake Malawi (cf. Wilson, *Peoples of the Nyasa-Tanganyika Corridor*, p. 9 and map). Some informants called such early inhabitants of Bembaland *bashimatongwa*, but this only means 'autochthones' (Katenda, 6 June 1964; Chibwe, 2 September 1964); cf. the Namwanga *amatongwe*.   [84] Cf. Phillipson, 'Early Iron Age', p. 210

[85] D. W. Phillipson, 'Iron Age Archaeology and History in Zambia', *JAH* in press; for the dating of the later Kalambo pottery see B. M. Fagan, 'Radiocarbon Dates for Sub-Saharan Africa: V', JAH, 1967, 8, iii, pp. 522–3.

[86] Cf. above, p. 46

the region that clans preceded tribes and chieftainships,[87] and the relative antiquity of clans is further indicated by the widespread diffusion of sections of the same named clans from the Lualaba in the west to the Luangwa in the east.[88] There are now no real clan histories as such,[89] but this may be due to the very fact that for most practical purposes affiliation on the basis of clan membership has tended to decline with the establishment and growth of territorial chieftainships:[90] the only surviving clan histories are those of ruling clans. As for the introduction of chieftainship in Bemba country, it is at least clear that this preceded the establishment of the present dynasties. Bemba traditions indicate that the founders of Bemba chieftainship encountered people on the plateau whose leaders at least were also kin to the Luba. Bemba informants spoke of a Musukwa chief called Mulopwe Kalelelya, while Labrecque and Mushindo agree that before the arrival of Chiti's followers the original Bemba lived in Bembaland under a chief called Mulopwe.[91] *Mulopwe*, or *Mulohwe*, is the universal Luba word for chief, so we may infer that well before the present dynasty of Bemba chiefs was founded traditions of chieftainship had been introduced in the course of movements between Luba and Bemba country.

Since the Luba region is itself of great extent, it is worth considering whether there are any grounds for associating such pre-Chitimukulu chiefs or people with one group of Luba rather than another. Historical traditions do not appear to provide any evidence on this point, though the question might be illuminated by linguistic, cultural and perhaps archaeological comparisons. It is at least reasonable on linguistic grounds to suppose that the name Bemba was indeed adopted, and not introduced, by the founders of the Chitimukuluship.[92] It is not, however, possible to make any particular historical inferences from the name.[93] There are indeed people to the north of Lake Mweru who have

[87] Cf. Cunnison, *Luapula Peoples*, pp. 35, 37, 48–9; Watson, *Tribal Cohesion*, p. 137   [88] Cunnison, *Luapula Peoples*, pp. 62, 158

[89] *Ibid.*, pp. 47–8; and cf. above, p. 18. Richards says that among the Bemba 'clans are ranked in some kind of precedence, according to the order in which their ancestors are thought to have arrived in the country from the west' (*Chisungu*, p. 38; cf. 'Political System of the Bemba Tribe', p. 94). I have no evidence on this point.   [90] Cf. Cunnison, *Luapula Peoples*, pp. 81–2

[91] Chileshye Mukulu, T2; Chiwele, 14 July 1964; Labrecque, 'Origines', p. 263; Mushindo, *History*, s. 29. Mushindo says that Mulopwe and Kalelelya were different people (*ibid.*). See also below, p. 70.

[92] Personal communication from Mr W. M. Mann, SOAS, London

[93] There is a word, *bemba*, meaning a stretch of water, usually a lake or a broad reach in a river. The Bemba sometimes derive their name from this word; Mr

been known as Bemba; but although this name may possibly derive
from the Bemba of Chitimukulu there is no reason to suppose the
opposite.[94] Nor is it possible to connect the Bemba on purely ono-
mastic grounds with the Hemba, or north-eastern Luba.[95] Nonetheless, the fact that the Hemba are among the few matrilineal groups of
Luba-speaking peoples does suggest that, as a people, the matrilineal
Bemba of north-eastern Zambia are more closely related to them, and
to the north-eastern Luba in general, than to the patrilineal Luba
further west, beyond the Lualaba, from whom Bemba chieftainship
as we know it may derive.[96]

Few traces, however, of 'proto-Bemba' remain in Bemba traditions
today.[97] It is possible that ancestors of Nkuba, the *mwina ɲandu* chief
of the Shila on the Luapula, lived in Bembaland before the arrival of
bena ɲandu from the west.[98] Bemba traditions do not appear to throw
light on this point, but Chewe Kalubila, who is today a *mwina ɲandu*
headman in Lubemba, claims that his own ancestor came from Luba
before 'Chitimukulu', and he was supported in this by Chikunga.[99]
Chewe Kalubila is the only *mwina ɲandu* headman explicitly to make a
claim of this kind for his own title. A few Bemba informants stated
independently that certain *bena ɲandu*, Chimbola, Chileshye Mukulu
and Mutale Mukulu, preceded the main migration of *bena ɲandu*,
from the Congo.[100] But none of these titleholders make any such claim
themselves. It seems very likely that with regard to these three titles
there has been a confusion in some minds between the original conquests of the earliest Chitimukulus and the process, which took place
during the nineteenth century, by which these particular *bena ɲandu*

Mann tells me that on tonal criteria a connection is plausible between *bemba* and
ulúbémbá (the Bemba country). He points out, however, that the latter is tonally
distinct from *abábembá* (the Bemba people) and that these two words should
therefore, however surprisingly, be treated as unrelated.

[94] See Appendix 2, Note D (p. 348).

[95] The Bemba *p* corresponds to *h* in Luba/Hemba (and also, e.g. in Lunda,
Sukuma and Nyamwezi), but Mr Mann tells me that there is no reason to suppose
any similar correspondence between the Bemba *b* and *h* elsewhere (cf. White
Fathers, *Ifyabukaya*, pp. 8–9).

[96] See above, p. 54. Mushindo says that the original Bemba tribe 'came from
the north' (*History*, s. 29).

[97] See above, p. 42.

[98] Mushindo (*loc. cit.*) says that the Shila are the first-known inhabitants of
Bembaland.

[99] Chewe Kalubila, 9 June 1964; Chikunga, 28 July 1964

[100] Katenda, 25 November 1964; Chimpamba, 30 May 1964; Nkweto, T1.
Nkweto and Chimpamba added the names of Mfungo and Mumena.

titles were excluded from succession to the paramountcy and in most cases deprived of the territorial rights of chiefs. The dynastic manipulations of Chileshye* and Chitapankwa* do appear to exist, for several informants, on the same chronological plane as the original foundation and expansion of the Chitimukuluship.[101]

At all events, Chewe Kalubila's is the only Bemba *ŋandu* title which is definitely associated with specific clues that its history is distinct from those of other *bena ŋandu*. *Kalubila mipunda* means 'a small person lost in the crowd',[102] and Chewe says that this nickname was given to his ancestor by the Bemba of Chitimukulu. There is a tradition at Chewe Kalubila's that there was once a chieftainship with the title Kanabesa: this was related to the Chewe title, and Chewe could succeed as Kanabesa.[103] The site of Kanabesa's capital, Umuonga, is situated beside the river Bwambi, a few miles from Chewe's village and only fifteen miles or so west of Ŋwena, the first site of the Chitimukulus on the Kalungu. One of the two chiefs said to have lived at Umuonga was called Mwengu *wa tipwa*; the other was called Kaleya, and there may be a connection with the 'Musukwa' Kalelelya.[104]

There is also the possibility that certain pre-Chitimukulu chiefs are remembered, even if only unwittingly, in the names of various spirits associated with specific places in the older parts of Bembaland. Many such names were given by Kamima, a priest in western Lubemba; his list included Kalelelya. Kamima spoke of such spirits as *bashamfumu*, great chiefs, though there is no certainty that they were all once actual human beings. Of Mwela, who lives in Mwela rocks near Kasama, Kamima said that he appeared to the Bemba in dreams after they arrived, giving advice on hunting and warning them of natural

---

[101] See above, p. 25, n. 1, for such telescoping in Chimba's own tradition. It is probably a memory of comparatively recent eminence which prompts Chileshye Mukulu to claim, 'we are the oldest in this country' (T2), and Chimbola, 'I alone am the owner of this Lubemba'.

[102] White Fathers, *Bemba–English Dictionary*, London 1954, p. 224

[103] Chewe Kalubila, 9–10 June 1964; 15 July 1964; Chiwele, 14 July 1964. See also Ann Tweedie's discussion of this tradition in 'Towards a History of the Bemba', pp. 215–16. Labrecque says that Kanabesa came from 'Kalubila' but lists him as a Chitimukulu ('Origines', p. 269, and see p. 89, n. 3).

[104] Umuonga (named after the *muonga* tree on the site) is about 400 yards round and partly ringed by a ditch, now very shallow. A few decorated sherds from the surface were deposited at the Livingstone Museum, Zambia, in 1965, but they were probably recent debris. The site seems to be kept free of undergrowth, and spirit huts for Kaleya and Kanabesa are occasionally erected by Chewe. Across the Bwambi river there is another old site, Nkolekache, next to the burial grove for Chewe's lineage.

disasters. Mwela, and perhaps certain other spirits named by Kamima, such as Changa *wa musase* and Mulenga, can possess people, and neither this phenomenon nor the apparition of spirits in dreams is confined to any one locality in the case of any particular spirit. But these spirits are said to live among rocks or at the sources of streams, and they are honoured with prayers and presents at these places.[105] Sheane considered that spirits such as these, or Chishimba, at a waterfall near Kasama, are the spirits of very ancient chiefs: he observed that true nature spirits are absent among the neighbouring peoples.[106] The Bemba often refer to 'haunted' rocks and waterfalls as *ngulu*, and Cunnison notes that on the Luapula people know of *ngulu* on the eastern plateau: they are 'natural objects considered to be the abodes of nature spirits'. 'It is not held that they are in fact the spirits of deceased persons', but they are sometimes called the 'real' 'owners of the land'.[107] It is worth remarking that the Luba around Lake Kisale believe that the spirits of early heroes reside in springs, caves and rocks. Such places are called *bavidye*, as are the priests through whom the spirits speak. These heroes appear to be Luba, but it is also said that the early inhabitants, the Kalanga, who lacked kings, revered spirits called *vidye* in trees and rocks.[108] There is certainly scope for further investigation of such spirits in Bemba country. It may be significant that Kamima's spirits were all located near the Ituna–Lubemba border; I did not hear of any such spirits being associated with sites within the more central parts of Lubemba, where the *bakabilo* as well as Chitimukulu have their villages. Perhaps the growth and maintenance of rituals concerning Chitimukulu have involved the suppression of earlier cults.[109]

This discussion, inconclusive though it is, suggests that it is possible to make some very general inferences about the population of what is now Bembaland during the period—the seventeenth century—when it was settled by the people remembered as followers of Chiti and

[105] Kamima, T1; 6 October 1964

[106] Sheane, 'Aspects of Awemba Religion', p. 151

[107] Cunnison, *Luapula Peoples*, pp. 222–3

[108] W. F. P. Burton, *Luba Religion and Magic in Custom and Belief*, Tervuren 1961, p. 50. In the Rukwa valley, in Ufipa, there is a grove sacred to the spirit of Nkulu, a chief who long resisted the invading Twaachi chiefs (R. G. Willis, 'Changes in Mystical Concepts and Practices among the Fipa', *Ethnology*, 1968, 7, ii, p. 140).

[109] One *kabilo* specifically denied that there were any *ngulu* in Lubemba (Mulewa Chimfwembe, 3 June 1965). For further discussion see Douglas Werner, 'Some Developments in Bemba Religious History', *Journal of Religion in Africa*, 1971, 4, i, pp. 1–24.

Nkole. Such earlier inhabitants included people who spoke a language similar to modern Bemba, who were the physical ancestors of most Bemba today, and who were themselves probably known as Bemba. Such 'proto-Bemba' were probably matrilineal, and they had chiefs of some sort, some of whom were *bena ŋandu*. In general, they were culturally akin to the Luba, in particular perhaps the north-eastern Luba (Hemba). In one important respect, however, they probably differed from the Luba, in that they are likely to have practised *citemene*. This system of preparing millet gardens is not characteristic of Luba peoples; on the other hand, it is clearly of some antiquity in north-eastern Zambia. The Bemba do not claim to have introduced *citemene*; on the contrary, some informants believed that the Bemba learned *citemene* from peoples already in the region, such as the Lungu, Mambwe and Iwa.[110] These informants mean by 'Bemba' the Bemba of Chitimukulu rather than any putative 'proto-Bemba' but in this as in some other contexts we may perhaps suppose that the history of the dynasty has subsumed and replaced the history of the people at large: that in fact *citemene* gardens have been made in Bemba country since well before the coming of Chiti and Nkole.[111]

There is some evidence in Bemba traditions that the followers of Chiti and Nkole found parts of Bembaland occupied not only by 'proto-Bemba' but also by groups of cattle-keeping people of East African origin or affinities. As we have seen, the Bemba claim that when Kapasa settled in Bulombwa he drove out the Iwa chief Kafwimbi with his cattle, and this is confirmed by the Iwa.[112] The Kafwimbi chieftainship probably derives from the west, but both the professed origins and elements of the culture of the Iwa people link them to the Namwanga, Mambwe and perhaps Fipa further north.[113] The Bemba in fact speak of finding Mambwe, in particular the ancestors of the Mambwe chief Chindo; Chindo was the leader of the Mambwe

[110] Milambo, 12 April 1965; Chileshye Mukulu, 15 April 1965; Mubanga, 20 May 1965. Trapnell notes such traditions and considers that they are borne out by the differences between Bemba *citemene* and the forms practised by their neighbours. He also notes that while kaffir-corn, the crop of chief ritual importance among the Bemba, may persist as 'a heritage from the Congo', it was probably at one time much more widely grown on at least the southern part of the plateau, perhaps by hoe-cultivation (Trapnell, *Soils*, pp. 35, 45).

[111] Labrecque says of Kanabesa, whom he lists among early Chitimukulus, that he 'taught the people *citemene*' ('Origines', p. 269). But Kanabesa was probably the name of a chieftainship among the 'proto-Bemba' (see above, p. 70), while it is not certain that there was any Chitimukulu of this name (see below, p. 89).

[112] Chileshye Mukulu, T2; Simtala, 'History of Kafwimbi' (MS); cf. Labrecque 'Origines', p. 264   [113] Wilson, *Nyasa–Tanganyika Corridor*, pp. 19–28

before the dynasty of Nsokolo was established, and Mambwe commoners, among whom Chindo is counted, plausibly trace their
origins to the north-east.[114] And it appears that people related to those
now known as Fipa used to inhabit Bembaland. Several accounts of
Bemba tradition say that the Bemba encountered the 'Sukuma'.[115] In
1798, Lacerda observed that the 'Mussucumas' were 'a tribe mixed in
small numbers with the Muizas' between the Chambeshi and Lubansenshi rivers.[116] Remnants of Sukuma were noted elsewhere by the
British administration,[117] and I gathered that there are still Sukuma
villages in the Muchinga hills, though I was unable to visit any of them.
'Sukuma' is also the name of those people 'who now inhabit the central
region of Ufipa and regard themselves as the original inhabitants of the
country'.[118] Thus when the Bemba say that they raided the Fipa
in order to obtain an ox-hide with which to bury Chiti at Mwalule,
they probably refer, not to a long-distance raid into what is now Ufipa,
but to a local raid on 'Sukuma' not far from Mwalule.[119]

According to some informants, the early inhabitants of Bembaland
included the Ngalagansa. These may have been subjects of Mulopwe
Kalelelya,[120] but one informant called the cattle-keepers in Bulombwa
'Ngalagansa'.[121] There may conceivably be some connection with the
Galagansa or western Nyamwezi, who certainly kept cattle until
the later nineteenth century.[122] It is at any rate likely that the identity of
names accounts for the tradition, reported by Labrecque, that some of
the original Bemba, expelled by Chiti's followers, went to live near
Tabora;[123] this is clearly an aetiological explanation for the Nyamwezi who came to Bembaland in the last century from Katanga, where
they were known as Yeke or Galagansa.[124]

[114] Chileshye Mukulu, T2; Brelsford, 'Shimwalule', p. 209; Watson, *Tribal Cohesion*, pp. 13–14
[115] Shimulamba, T1, n. 16; Labrecque, 'Tribu', p. 644; Brelsford, *Aspects*, p. 2
[116] Lacerda, *Diários*, p. 250 (Burton, *Cazembe*, p. 94)
[117] Chinsali DNB I, p. 110 (note of 1907); Mpika Tour Report no. 8, 1952, NAZ/NA/1/1/1
[118] R. G. Willis, *The Fipa and Related Peoples of South-West Tanzania*, London 1966, xii, n. 21. These Sukuma were noted by several Europeans in the 1890s.
[119] See also below, p. 78. Shimulamba says that the people of Bulombwa dug mounds as well as keeping cattle: the Fipa sow their crops in mounds of compost (Willis, *Fipa*, p. 23).   [120] Chisanga, T1   [121] Shimulamba, T1
[122] Andrew Roberts, 'Nyamwezi Trade', *Pre-colonial African Trade*, eds R. Gray and D. Birmingham, London 1970, p. 58
[123] Labrecque, 'Origines', p. 263
[124] Livingstone, *Last Journals*, I, pp. 276, 279. Whiteley says, 'There is still a small group of Bemba near Tabora' (*Bemba and Related Peoples*, p. 8), but from

It is probable that people such as the Sukuma were no more than small outlying groups of pastoral societies which were mainly concentrated in the grasslands to the north of the plateau. There are few herds of cattle today in the woodland which covers the plateau: this tree cover, and the game which used to be much more widespread than it now is, would always have harboured tsetse fly.[125] But tsetse may not have been quite so widespread in the past,[126] and it is worth noting that even today cattle are kept in the Bulombwa area north of Mwalule, both on a modern ranch and by Bemba villagers.

Since so little is known of the earlier inhabitants of Bembaland, one cannot say much about the relationship between them and the new chieftainship of Chitimukulu. If they were in fact mostly matrilineal people affiliated to the north-eastern Luba, it may be that the new-comers, derived (as it seems) from the patrilineal western Luba, changed their mode of descent as they intermarried with the earlier Lubans.[127] As we have seen, the Bemba legend of migration tells a story of such a change of descent in the chieftainship, though it should not necessarily be taken at face value.[128] It is very likely, as Mushindo claims, that the newcomers took over the language of the earlier 'Luban' inhabitants;[129] they may also have preserved their own form of Chiluba as an arcane language of chieftainship, such as survives in praise-poems.[130] But there is no evidence that those of the earlier inhabitants who were not expelled by the people of Chitimukulu retained any special social and political identity: the impression is that chiefs and people joined to form a common Bemba tribe, unlike the Lunda on the Luapula.

There is some reason to suppose that the Bemba of Chitimukulu were from the first dependent on their neighbours for their ironwork,

my own enquiries in Tabora district in 1967 I gathered that almost anyone from northern Zambia is known there as 'Bemba', and that such migrants are of quite recent origin.

[125] Allan notes that the prevalence of tsetse in this area may be due to intrinsic soil poverty, which has prevented population densities reaching the level necessary to alter the environment, and the distribution of game, to the detriment of the fly (Allan, *African Husbandman*, p. 211).

[126] The transformation of open grasslands to tree savannas has been recorded in parts of Uganda, Rwanda and Burundi: Frank Lambrecht, 'Aspects of Evolution and Ecology of Tsetse Flies . . .', *JAH*, 1964, 5, i, pp. 16, 20.

[127] This is conjectured by Verhulpen, *Baluba*, p. 119.

[128] See above, pp. 44–5. The genealogy of the chiefs of Milansi in Ufipa displays a shift from patriliny after the third ruler; the founder of the dynasty is said to have come from the southwest and would thus have had Luba affiliations (Willis, *Fipa*, pp. 18, 20).   [129] Mushindo, *History*, s. 30   [130] Cf. above, p. 14

as they certainly were in the last century. It is noteworthy that some Bemba traditions specifically mention that some pre-Chitimukulu groups were ironworkers.[131] The Bemba themselves have no traditions of smelting iron, but this skill is characteristic of the Iwa and Namwanga (whose founder-chief is said to have been a smith), the Mambwe, the Fipa and the Lungu.[132] In eastern Bembaland, the 'Sukuma' were known as smiths in the last century.[133] Some Bemba informants spoke of early inhabitants of Bembaland as *bashimalungu*, meaning ironsmelters, and it is probable that the Lungu owe their name to this craft.[134]

There is some evidence that the royal burial ritual of the Bemba was influenced by people with East African affiliations. It is remarkable that the Bemba, who have no traditions of pastoralism, should use cattle in some of their solemn rituals.[135] In particular, they wrap a dead chief in a cowskin, and Bemba traditions relate that Chiti's followers raided the 'Fipa' to obtain a cowskin with which to bury Chiti. As we have seen, this should not be interpreted literally,[136] but Vansina may well be right to infer from the story that the Bemba borrowed elements of royal burial ritual from an 'East African type of kingdom'.[137] The ox- or cowskin shroud for a dead chief is widespread in western and northern Tanzania and in most of the interlacustrine kingdoms,[138] whereas it does not appear to occur in the Luba–Lunda areas.[139]

[131] Mushindo, *History*, s. 29; Labrecque, 'Origines', p. 264; Chileshye Mukulu, 15 April 1965   [132] Willis, *Fipa*, pp. 25–6, 33, 38, 51; and below, pp. 184, 186.

[133] Kabwela, 10 May 1965; Chiwelewele, 29 April 1965; 'Human Geography of Chinsali District', 1932, NAZ/Sec/Nat 398

[134] Katenda, 25 November 1964; Willis, *Fipa*, p. 40; cf. the *walongo* ironsmelters to the south of Lake Victoria (Roberts, 'Nyamwezi Trade', p. 45)

[135] Richards, *Land, Labour and Diet*, p. 360; Katenda, 7 September 1964. Chitimukulu and Mwamba had a few cattle in 1867, but these were exceptional, and even so were clearly not 'royal herds' such as Kazembe keeps (Livingstone, *Last Journals*, I, pp. 181, 186; Cunnison, *Luapula Peoples*, p. 201).

[136] See above, p. 73; also below, p. 78. The Fipa chiefs are indeed all buried in cowskins (Willis, *Fipa*, p. 30); but their first ancestors probably all arrived in Ufipa after the first Bemba chiefs reached Bemba country. The Milansi chieftainship (which in any case traces its origin to the west) dates back to about 1700. The other two Fipa chieftainships may well derive from the inter-lacustrine region of East Africa, but they were not founded before about the middle of the eighteenth century (R. G. Willis, 'The Fipa', in Roberts, *Tanzania before 1900*, pp. 83–6).

[137] Vansina, *Kingdoms of the Savanna*, p. 89

[138] Many examples are given in Tor Irstam, *The King of Ganda*, Stockholm 1944, pp. 131–5. Burton reported the custom among the Nyamwezi (*Lake Regions*, II, pp. 25–6; see also below, p. 76, n. 144).

[139] Cf. H. Baumann, *Lunda*, Berlin 1935, pp. 136–8, for southern Chokwe and Lunda of Mwata Yamvo; Burton, *Luba Religion*, pp. 19–20, 41; T. Theuws, 'Naître et Mourir dans le rituel Luba', *Zaïre*, 1960, 14, pp. 163–4

On the other hand, it is found in several chiefdoms neighbouring the Bemba which also claim an origin in 'Luba': among the Bisa,[140] Chishinga, Tabwa, Lungu and Mambwe (of whom only the last two are even partly pastoral).[141] Yet neither this nor other features of Bemba chiefly burial are found among the pastoral Iwa and Namwanga, whose common ancestor is said to have come from 'Kola' or Bisa country.[142] Nor does it seem to occur among the Nyiha and Safwa, or the pastoral Nyakyusa, north-east of the Bemba.[143] A proper evaluation of this question would of course involve a consideration of other associated traits in Bemba royal ritual—such as the desiccation of the chief's corpse or the use of special burial groves or caves. The conjunction of these traits would indeed seem to be an East African rather than a Congolese phenomenon,[144] but a systematic survey is needed if we are to do more than speculate on this aspect of the history of chieftainship in eastern and central Africa.

[140] The burial rites of the Bisa chief Matipa were fully described in 1936 by C. H. J. Rawsthorne (Luwingu DNB I, pp. 1–5). It should be noted that not only was the corpse of Matipa preserved in an ox-hide covering; like those of senior Bemba chiefs, it could not be buried until certain crops had been both sown and harvested.

[141] Fieldnotes, 1965; Watson, *Tribal Cohesion*, p. 138

[142] Simtala, 'History of Kafwimbi' (MS); J. A. Chisholm, 'Manners and Customs of the Winamwanga and Wiwa', *JAS* 1909–10, 9, pp. 377–9

[143] M. Wilson, *Communal Rituals of the Nyakyusa*, London 1959, pp. 64–5; E. Kootz-Kretschmer, *Die Safwa*, Berlin 1926–9, I, p. 308

[144] The prolonged burial rites of the Rwanda and Rundi kings resemble those of Chitimukulu in several respects: cf. M. d'Hertefelt and A. Coupez, *La Royauté Sacrée de l'Ancien Rwanda*, Tervuren 1964, pp. 199, 205–9; J.-P. Chrêtien, 'Les tombeaux des *bami* du Burundi', *Cahiers d'études africaines*, 1970, 10, i, pp. 61–5. The combination of ox-hide shroud, desiccation and burial cave is reported for the Vinza, east of Ujiji, while further south several Tongwe chiefdoms practised desiccation, wrapping the corpse in a sheepskin, and burial in groves (Kigoma District Book, National Archives of Tanzania).

Chapter 3

The eighteenth century

The Bemba legend of migration usually concludes with the coming of age of Chilufya* *ca mata yabili* and his inheritance from Chiti, leader of the migration from 'Kola'.[1] This is enough to show how the Chitimukulu chieftainship was established on the Kalungu river; all subsequent history is but an aftermath to this key event. Little is known of Chilufya's* reign, and still less of the reigns of most of his successors until towards the end of the eighteenth century. As we have seen in chapter 1, this ignorance is not accidental; it is due to the fact that the period following the establishment of Chitimukulu has long ceased to have much relevance for Bemba political organisation. For most Bemba, the most important features of this period are the actual names of the early Chitimukulus, and even the memory of these becomes confused when no narrative is remembered by which their identity and relationships could be more securely woven into a common pattern.

Nonetheless, the fact that for the Bemba in general these early Chitimukulus belong to a 'middle period' of tradition, with little contemporary significance, does not in itself mean that nothing valuable can be learned about this period. It is, after all, a 'middle period' only in the perspective of the Chitimukuluship. Other positions were founded in the course of this period, and from their point of view the beginnings of history are to be sought in the reigns of early Chitimukulus, whether or not these are actually known by name. Alternatively, some people may claim to belong to the same lineages as certain Chitimukulus and so have special reason to remember something of them. However little may be known about this 'middle period', it involves the histories, not of any one group or title, but of a number of different components of a growing political system. By piecing together what is known about their early histories, it is possible to form some impressions which may

[1] See above, p. 43.

77

serve as a baseline for studying the more demonstrable developments of the nineteenth century.

These impressions may be summarised briefly. After the Chitimukulu chieftainship had been established, subordinate hereditary titles were created. Some of these were for priest-councillors (*bakabilo*) who were assigned villages near the capital; others were for members of the royal clan, the *bena ŋandu*. Around a small central domain, under Chitimukulu himself, territorial chiefdoms were assigned to *bena ŋandu* and became hereditary in separate lineages. The Chitimukuluship, however, was not monopolised by any one lineage. Instead, all the various *bena ŋandu* lineages competed for succession to the paramountcy. This was partly, no doubt, because the paramount, by virtue of his seniority, exerted a unique ritual authority over all Bemba country: his position was worth competing for. If a lineage which already held a chiefdom gained control of the Chitimukuluship, this clearly increased its political and economic resources considerably, if only for one reign. At the same time, the very fact of such competition served to hold together the various subordinate chiefdoms which otherwise were virtually autonomous. This, together with the limited extent and compactness of Bemba territory throughout the eighteenth century, probably explains why the Bemba polity held together, unlike the numerous chiefdoms of the much more widespread Bisa.

THE EARLIER CHITIMUKULUS

It is usually said that Chilufya* was followed by Mulenga Pokili*. Mulenga* may have been a brother of Chilufya*, and there is a story that he refused to pay homage to Chilufya*, throwing his tribute into the Kalungu river.[2] When Mulenga* became Chitimukulu, a Bemba warrior called Chubili routed the 'Balangashi' and the 'Fipa' of one Pilula, who had come to avenge the raid in which the Bemba stole cattle for Chiti's burial.[3] But the name Pilula here can be no more than a cliché for any 'Fipa' leader: *Pilula Ufipa* (who reunited Ufipa) is the praise-name of Suumba Kasuumba, a chief of Lyangalile who lived in the late nineteenth century.[4] And in any case it is fairly clear that these 'Fipa' of 'Pilula' were not the subjects of Fipa chiefs but were Sukuma who may have lived well to the south of the present Ufipa.[5]

---

[2] Milambo, T1. Labrecque tells the story of Mulenga, a younger brother of Salala ('Tribu', p. 647). [3] Chikunga, T3; Labrecque, 'Origines', pp. 265–6
[4] I owe the explanation of 'Pilula' to Dr R. G. Willis; cf. Willis, *Fipa*, p. 19; and below, p. 149. [5] See above, p. 73.

The reign of Chibengele* was remembered for the manufacture of arrows, spears and axes.[6] Chibamba Manshi and Chisoka are remembered as rivals for the Chitimukuluship. The *bakabilo* decided that they should fight in single combat. Chisoka was thrown to the ground, but refused to give in, saying, 'I am not defeated; I only touched the ground': hence his praise-names *nshiwile, napyatapofye*.[7] Chibamba* won, but was succeeded on his death by Chisoka*. It is said that Chisoka* then took revenge on the *bakabilo* by getting all the young men to kill their fathers. But a large snake settled on Chisoka's* neck one day and no one could remove it (hence his name *cisoka cabakata*, 'the snake caught him'). The snake was finally enticed away by an old man, Mpombo, who had been hidden by his son, and Chisoka* duly relented of his anger.[8] When Chisoka died, he was succeeded by Chishisa*, who had also been a rival of Chibamba's*.

Labrecque says that after the death of a Chitimukulu called 'Ntamba Lukuta'[9] a royal called Shula Malindi, struggling for support in a bid for the Chitimukuluship, drove out a group of Mambwe and killed some of their leaders in Lubemba, but was himself killed by his Bemba rivals. (The place where he died is remembered, and Kamima makes offerings there.)[10] Kapampa* was a leper, and was buried near the village of the *kabilo* Munuca, for he would have defiled the royal burial grove at Mwalule. Kasansu* did not reign long. Apart from these few details, virtually nothing is known of the activities of Chitimukulus between Chilufya* and Mukuuka*.

COUNCILLORS AND ROYAL CHIEFS

Rather more insight into early Bemba history may be obtained from the histories of subordinate positions. Villages and hereditary titles were granted by Chitimukulus to their matrilineal relatives, sons and

[6] Labrecque, 'Origines', p. 266

[7] *Ibid.*, pp. 267-8; Chikunga, T3; Chileshye Mukulu, T1, T8. The same story was told of Chilufya and Nsenshi, sons of an unnamed Chitimukulu: Chilufya won and founded the lineage of Mulilo, a village near the Chambeshi (Katwamba, T1).

[8] Chileshye Mukulu, T8; Chitichipalo, 16 September 1964; see also below, p. 89. This story is also told, as a legend of origin, by the Bena Mukulu, west of Lake Bangweulu: cf. Cunnison, *Luapula Peoples*, p. 48; African Elders, *History of the Bena Ŋoma*, pp. 10–17.

[9] This seems to be only a praise-name: cf. Kabwa, T2; White Fathers, *Bemba Dictionary*, see under *ntamba*. After Zambia became independent, *Ntamba lukuta* was used in the vernacular press as an honorific for the President.

[10] Labrecque, 'Origines', p. 267; Chikunga, T3; Kamima, T1

companions. Villages were also assigned to the senior *bakabilo*, clustered on either side of the Kalungu river, east and west of Ŋwena, the first royal capital. This process cannot be reconstructed in any detail. The names of Mwangata, Kabwa, Kapukuma, Mumba Ŋombe, Sompe and Katenda are usually mentioned in the story of migration from 'Kola'. But there seems to be, curiously, no such legendary background for the titles of Chitikafula and Munuca who, with Katenda, are considered the most senior *bakabilo*. Katenda, Lumpombwe, Nsenshi and Kalemba are perpetual 'sons' of Chitimukulu; the last two are said to have become pall-bearers for Chitimukulu because they touched the corpse of their father Chiti: an act of ritual defilement which prevented their becoming chiefs.[11] 'At Mwata Yamvo's we were all chiefs,' said Katenda; 'then they made us councillors.'[12] But such stories seldom give a personal name—other than 'Chiti' or 'Chitimuluba'—to Chitimukulu. The creation of new titles, associated with new duties of decreasing importance, was presumably a continuous process, as successive Chitimukulus dispensed honours to their sons (debarred from becoming chiefs) and favourites. It would seem likely that there is a rough correspondence between the age of titles among most *bakabilo* and the distance of their villages from Ŋwena.[13] And certain *bakabilo* are associated specifically with the relics of one chief, Katongo, who probably lived in the later eighteenth century.[14] But the reasons for this association remain obscure.

Titles were also conferred by Chitimukulu upon *bena ŋandu*. Within present-day Lubemba, there are seven *ŋandu* headmen: Mulenga wa Chibungu, Nkweto wa Chisungu, Mumena, Chewe Kalubila, Chileshye Mukulu, Mutale Mukulu, and a former 'mother' (*namfumu*) of Chitimukulu, Chandaweyaya. The last three titles are related to the Chimbola chieftainship, now situated on the northern border of Lubemba. Those of Mumena and Chewe Kalubila seem to be related,

[11] Nkolemambwe, 3 September 1964; Mulenga wa Chibungu, 12 September 1964. Mushindo quotes this story for Pumbwe as well as Nsenshi and Kalemba (*History*, s. 20); Chimbola quotes it for Lumpombwe (9 September 1964). In India, castes sometimes explain decline from a supposedly higher ranking in the past with stories of ritual defilement through an action carried out for the best of reasons.

[12] Katenda, 17 September 1964. Perhaps these stories are connected with the putative shift in chiefly descent from patriliny to matriliny: the implication is that at one time Chitimukulu's sons could have become chiefs but were then debarred for a while.

[13] See map 3. One of the *bakabilo* most distant from Ŋwena is Lumpombwe, for whom there is other evidence suggesting a relatively recent foundation for his title: see below, p. 301. [14] See below, p. 91.

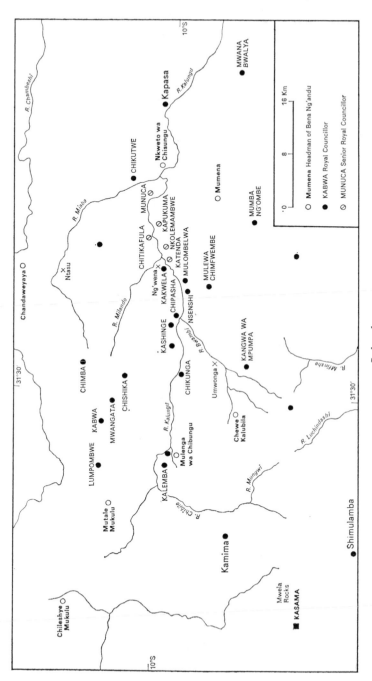

3 Lubemba

respectively, to the Nkweto and Mwaba titles east of the Chambeshi. We have seen that of these *bena ŋandu* Chewe Kalubila probably represents a line of chiefs who preceded Chitimukulu. We have also seen that this is said of other *bena ŋandu*, such as Chimbola, and that this is probably due to a telescoping in Bemba historical perspectives. Of these various *ŋandu* titles, the present holders of those in Lubemba say that their predecessors had some authority in pre-colonial times over a number of villages—villages which had most probably split off at different times from that of the titleholder. Thus the area under Chitimukulu's direct control would have excluded much of what is now Lubemba, though it may briefly have extended further west than it now does.[15] These *bena ŋandu* appear, in fact, to have been chiefs, with a few hereditary officials of their own, and they were honoured with at least some of the observances proper to chiefs of royal blood.[16] If their territories were small, this was simply a corollary of their antiquity. I have not, however, been able to work out in any detail what these territories were. The relevant informants were not all able even to make claims to former territory with much precision, while during the first decade of British administration many villages were amalgamated and several such small chieftainships 'abolished'.[17]

These *ŋandu* titles have their own stories of origin, though otherwise little or nothing is known of their histories until two or three generations ago. The title of Mulenga wa Chibungu is said to derive from the first holder, Mulenga Pokili, uncle of the Chitimukulu (name unknown) who created the title and assigned Mulenga his country beside the Chibungu stream. Curiously, the present Mulenga does not agree with the traditions that Mulenga Pokili was a Chitimukulu. But, as perpetual mother's brother to Chitimukulu, Mulenga is accorded special honour at the capital. He does not, like other people, lie down to greet Chitimukulu; instead, Chitimukulu puts out a cowskin for Mulenga to sit on and claps his hands in greeting to show respect for his

[15] See below, p. 95.

[16] For example, Chileshye Mukulu, Mutale Mukulu, Mumena and Nkweto wa Chisungu are all desiccated before burial (Mwangata, 12 July 1957, A. I. Richards, fieldnotes).

[17] Not all these *bena ŋandu* headmen are mentioned in the list, dated 1906, of village amalgamations in Kasama District (Kasama DNB, II, pp. 173 ff.). Some of these headmen, such as Mumena and Chewe Kalubila, were appointed parish heads when a system grouping villages into parishes was introduced in 1949. But in the absence of adequate documentary evidence, it would require considerable field research in depth to map in any detail the political geography of Lubemba at the end of the last century.

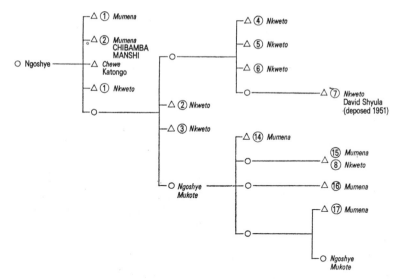

Fig. 2 Nkweto and Mumena. From Nkweto 8, 17 May 1965, 19 May 1965.
(Mumenas numbered following list by Mumena 17, 20 July 1964)

'uncle'. Mulenga has his own burial grove on the Chibungu stream, and his undertaker, Chimpa Kalemba, has a headdress of red lourie feathers like some of Chitimukulu's own *bakabilo*. Before 1900, there were seven villages under Mulenga, including those of two *bakabilo*.[18]

The first Mumena was a 'brother' of Chitimukulu (?Chilufya*) who, after Chitimukulu settled at Ŋwena, crossed the Kalungu to the country of Kasembo, where Mumena now lives.[19] The present Nkweto says that Nkweto I Kayula was a 'younger brother' (*mwaice*) of Mumena, who summoned him from Kola. Nkweto settled in Chilinda to wait (*kulinda*) before succeeding his 'brother' as Mumena. Such at least is the story told by the present Nkweto, but I did not check it with Mumena and it may well be suspect.[20]

[18] Mulenga wa Chibungu, 5 September 1964, 4 June 1965; Luchembe (at Mulenga's), 12 September 1964.   [19] Mumena, 20 July 1964; T1.
[20] Nkweto, T1 (see Appendix 4/i). The Nkweto in office in 1965 had succeeded from Mumena in 1951 after the previous Nkweto had been removed by Government. He was still regarded locally as an intruder and had an obvious need to stress the affinity of the two titles. The genealogy given by Nkweto indicates that the two titles began to diverge in different lineages only two generations ago, but there is evidently some telescoping since Nkweto I is placed at only three genera-tions from the present. Mushindo only says that Nkweto was chosen to look after the country near Mwalule after the burial of Chiti (*History*, s. 26). Nkweto's *kabilo*, Makwaya (T1), says that Nkweto I Kayula was a nephew of Nkole.

It is more certain that there is a link between Mwaba wa Nkulungwe, on the left bank of the Chambeshi, and Chewe Kalubila, in Lubemba. Mwaba said that Kapolyo Mfumu, the *namfumu* of Chewe Kalubila, was a 'sister' of Chitimukulu.[21] One day, a son of Chitimukulu killed a son of Kapolyo; in her grief, she left Lubemba with her two surviving sons and settled across the Chambeshi, being granted country by the Bisa headman Chinkalanga (who now lives to the south of Mwaba). One of Kapolyo's sons, Chintu *wa nsalu*, became Mwaba I.[22] The legendary connection between Mwaba and Chewe Kalubila is acknowledged in the tradition (to which both villages testified) that Chewe may succeed as Mwaba. This of course reverses the historic relationship, which makes Mwaba junior to Chewe; perhaps this is because the Mwaba chiefdom, founded well beyond the Bemba heartland, became more extensive than that of Chewe. At all events, Mwaba now calls Chewe his younger brother.

The Chimbola title belongs to a lineage which occupied Iyaya, to the north of the Kalungu;[23] Chimbola's perpetual mother or *namfumu* was called Chanda, and she had her own village near the Chambeshi; she also, at one time or another, ruled over four other villages. In the nineteenth century, a rival Chanda was appointed, so that the original Chanda became known as Chandaweyaya: it will be convenient to refer to her throughout by this name. She still keeps some state: she has four priests, an undertaker and other hereditary officials.[24] Besides Chimbola, Chanda had another perpetual son, Mutale Mukulu, who ruled over Katumba, further west. It is not clear just how old these titles are, nor how they came to be connected, but by the beginning of the nineteenth century members of the same lineage appear to have succeeded to both the Chimbola and Mutale Mukulu titles.[25]

---

[21] Brelsford says this was Chibamba Manshi* (*Succession*, p. 38); but see below, pp. 88–9.

[22] Mwaba, T1. The name of Kapolyo Mfumu has not survived: the present title of Mwaba's *namfumu* is Mubelamfumu.

[23] It was in the later nineteenth century that Chimbola occupied his present country, Matengele (see below, p. 132). It may be that this move partly accounts for the brevity of Chimbola's genealogy: the first remembered name, Chimbola *wa museshi*, is spoken of as a contemporary of Chitimukulu Chileshye, who displaced the Chimbola line from the paramountcy (Chimbola, T2; Chibwe, 9 September 1964).

[24] Chandaweyaya, T1; 23 September 1964. See below, pp. 131–2.

[25] See below, pp. 101–2. Today, Chandaweyaya calls Chandampala, a *namfumu* in the lineage of Mutale Mukulu, her 'young sister'. Unfortunately, Mutale Mukulu was unwilling to discuss history with me, despite a quite unsolicited

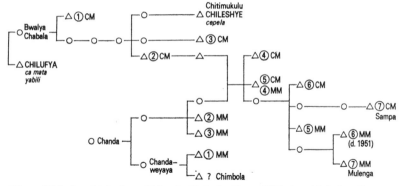

Fig. 3 Chileshye Mukulu and Mutale Mukulu. From Chileshye Mukulu 7 Sampa, 18 September 1964 (Chitimukulus in capitals)

The title of Chileshye Mukulu can now trace kinship with those of Chimbola and Mutale Mukulu, but apparently it had a distinct origin. The present holder said that in the early days of Bemba history, soon after the arrival of the chiefs from Luba, a *mwina ŋandu*, Chileshye, lived at Katonga, near the confluence of the Kalungu and Chambeshi. As the population increased, Chitimukulu (unnamed) sent Chileshye to govern his present country between the Lumpombwe and Lukupa rivers. Chileshye acquired the praise *wa nyimbo* (mine) from the iron ore near the Lupungu stream in this area. Formerly, there were a number of villages subordinate to Chileshye Mukulu, but only one of these villages is now extant. The chieftainship of Chileshye Mukulu, in the sense of authority over a number of villages in one territory, was said to have been ended shortly after 1902.[26]

The Nkolemfumu title is derived from Nkole, a 'brother' of Nkole and Chiti. This junior relative of the first chiefs did not continue to the Kalungu river with the other migrants but settled to the west, in Miti. He was known as Nkole *wa mapembwe*, since he is credited with introducing the digging of ditches around villages. Only one successor to Nkole before Chisala (Mubanga Chipoya, who ruled as Nkolemfumu from the 1870s to 1883) is now remembered at Nkolemfumu's: this is Mwalula.[27] But the early history of this chieftainship has

attempt by Chileshye Mukulu to bring him to such a discussion. Hence my information on this important title is very inadequate.

[26] Chileshye Mukulu, 18 September 1964, 28 November 1964; the chiefdom was 'abolished' by Cookson, who was District Commissioner, Kasama, from 1902 to 1909.

[27] Nkolemfumu and Shimulamba, 10 December 1964; and see below, p. 105, n. 64. Another early chief in Miti, Chisanga, is remembered by Milambo, at

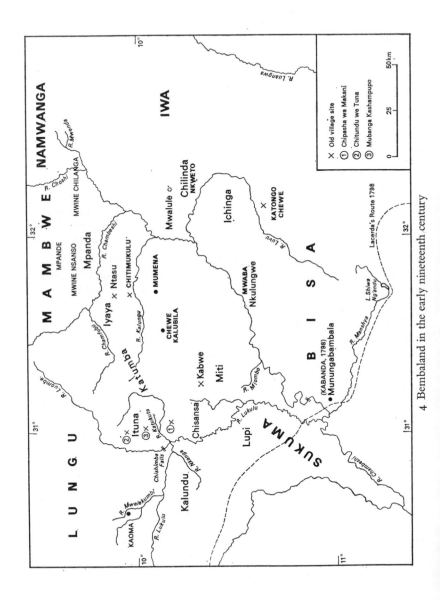

4 Bembaland in the early nineteenth century

obviously been obscured by dynastic changes during the last century. There are probably *bena ŋandu* in Miti who know rather more about the early history of the chiefdom than is known either by the lineage which has ruled it in recent times or by its leading councillor, Shimulamba. The first Nkolemfumu is said to have occupied at least part of what is now the chiefdom of Ituna,[28] and it is likely that much of both areas was under a single chief for many years, as also in more recent times.[29] Throughout the eighteenth century the western border of Miti, along the Lukulu river, was also the western limit of Bemba power: in 1798 the country west of the Lukulu was occupied by Bisa and 'Sukuma'.[30]

East of the Chambeshi, between the chiefdoms under Mwaba and Nkweto, lay the chiefdom of Ichinga. This was much smaller in the eighteenth century than it later became (largely as a result of annexing the country of the neighbouring Bisa chief Mungulube).[31] The title of the chieftainship in Ichinga is now Nkula, but it was originally known as Katongo and later as Chewe. Its early history, like that of Nkolemfumu, has been obscured by more recent developments, but I obtained some account of its origins from representatives of the lineage which formerly succeeded to it. Two such informants, Sewuka

Mwamba's: cf. below, p. 105. Mwalula occupied a site at the source of the Lupambwe stream (a tributary of the Miombo river), where Nkole *wa mapembwe* had died (Nkolemfumu, 10 December 1964).

[28] Milambo (6 October 1964) and Nkolemfumu (10 December 1964) said that Nkole *wa mapembwe* lived at a site near the Miongolo stream, in what is now Ituna. Brelsford says of 'the old Nkolemfumu' that 'his sway stretched across [the Chambeshi] into part of what is now Nkula's country', and that this eastern area was given by Chitapankwa to his brother Sampa (*Succession*, 28). This seems doubtful, since the left bank of the Chambeshi opposite Nkolemfumu's country was all under the Bisa chiefs Kabanda and Mungulube until Chitapankwa's reign (Kabanda, T1; Mungulube, 11 May 1965; and see below, pp. 133, 160). Perhaps Brelsford's story arose from confusion with Sampa's subsequent occupation of Bisa country west of the river Mwaleshi (see below, p. 136).

[29] Mushindo says that Ituna, west of the Chibile stream, was taken from a Lungu chief, Nkanka, by Mulenga Pokili; he gave it to his mother, Bwalya Chabala, who, however, preferred to settle in Miti (which had been under another Lungu chief, Kambi) (Mushindo, *History*, s. 37).

[30] Lacerda, *Diários*, p. 250 (Burton, *Cazembe*, p. 94); and cf. below, p. 110. From his route maps (reproduced in *Travessia*) and his journal, it may be deduced that Lacerda passed Shiwa Ŋandu and travelled west along the river Manshya before striking north to 'the powerful Morungabambara' (*Diários*, p. 247; Burton, *Cazembe*, p. 92), crossing the Chambeshi a little way below the Safwa rapids: he encountered no Bemba throughout his journey. Munungabambala was the name of a village site, and perhaps a praise name, for an early holder of the Bisa chieftainship of Kabanda (Kabanda, 18 October 1964; Kapeso Chipe, T1).

[31] See below, p. 138.

and Mbutuka, said independently that the Katongo of this title was the blind brother of Chiti and Nkole, who followed his brothers from 'Kola' and settled on the Luvu river while the rest of the expedition went on to Mwalule.[32] I return to the early history of this title in the following section.

POLITICAL RELATIONS

The relationship between these chieftainships and Chitimukulu is for the most part not at all clear. Little can be said about the procedure for appointing and installing these subordinate chiefs in the early days. The power of selection evidently rested within the various lineages, since the titles appear to have been retained within these lineages, but this cannot be conclusively demonstrated in genealogies. Nor can one say which titleholders went to the capital for investiture, or were invested at their own villages by the *bakabilo* of Chitimukulu. Chiefs and headmen in what is now Lubemba were probably always under obligation to provide the capital with food and beer, labour and military service in time of war.[33] But from the chiefs further afield, and across the Chambeshi, there may have been no regular collection or submission of tribute. At the same time, one should not overlook the influence that may have been exercised east of the Chambeshi by Shimwalule, by way of maintaining crucial links with Lubemba and representing the ritual and historical unity of the Bemba.[34]

Furthermore, it appears that the various *bena ŋandu* chiefs were linked together in so far as they competed for succession to the Chitimukuluship. Informants say that in the old days there were many succession wars, and that Chitimukulus were chosen from many lineages within the royal clan.[35] But it does seem possible to associate certain early Chitimukulus with the lineages of different chieftainships. The evidence is very incomplete, but there is broad agreement that, of the Chitimukulus who followed Chilufya*, up to and including Mukuuka*, four came from Iyaya, four (including Chisoka*) from Katumba (the country of Mutale Mukulu), one had been Mumena (Chibamba Manshi*) and one had been Katongo, in Ichinga

[32] Sewuka and Mbutuka, 14 May 1965. Brelsford (*Aspects*, p. 39) tells a similar story, and chief Mwamba (9 October 1964) also identified Katongo I in this way.

[33] Cf. Mushindo, *History*, s. 31.

[34] Chibingo, one of Shimwalule's *bakabilo*, declared that Mwalule was the only truly Bemba country: all the great chiefdoms are characterised by conquered tribes—Lubemba is Mambwe, Ituna is Lungu, Ichinga is Bisa (18 May 1965).

[35] Chikunga, T1; Chileshye Mukulu, T5; Milambo, 29 September 1964

Table 3. PROVENANCE OF EARLY CHITIMUKULUS

Title and area of provenance	Name	Sources*
Chimbola (*Iyaya*)	Kabemba	CM (from Katonga)
	Chibengele	CM, M
	Chifunda	CM, CY
	Kayula	M, MN, CK (CM:Katumba; S: Ichinga)
	Chiliamafwa	CM, CY, M
Mutale Mukulu (*Katumba*)	Salala	CM, LT (M,K:Chimbola)
	Mutale	CM, M
	Chisoka	CM, C, N (K: Nkulungwe)
	Mukuuka	M (CM: Chileshye Mukulu)
	Chinchinta	CM, KW, CB
Mumena (*Kasembo*)	Chibamba Manshi	CM, N, K (M: Nkulungwe)
Chewe Kalubila	Chishisa	CM
Mwaba (*Nkulungwe*)	Kanabesa	CK, M, G (LO:Kalubila; CM: Iyaya)
	Kapampa	CM
	Kasansu	M, K (CM:Chilinda)
	Lwipa	M (CM:Mulenga wa Chibungu)
Katongo (*Ichinga*)	Chimpolonge	M, MB, K (CM: Chileshye Mukulu)
	Katongo	CK, M, K, CM, LO

* Sources abbreviated thus:

C: Chitichipalo, 16.ix.64
CB: Chibwe, 8.vi.65
CK: Chikunga, 11.ix.64
CM: Chileshye Mukulu, 25.vii.64, 18.ix.64; T5
CY: Chandaweyaya, 23.ix.64
G: Goodall, 'Tree'
K: Katwamba, 22.vii.64

KW: Kakwela, 27.viii.64
LO: Labrecque, 'Origines'
LT: Labrecque, 'Tribu'
M: Mushindo, *History*, s. 34
MB: Mbutuka, 14.v.65
MN: Mumena, 20.vii.64
N: Makwaya (Nkweto's), 16.v.65
S: Sewuka, 14.v.65

(Katongo*).[36] Thus the famous fight between Chibamba Manshi* and Chisoka* was probably a fight between different lineages, those of Mumena and Mutale Mukulu.[37] Certain other Chitimukulus are connected by some informants with the titles of Mwaba, Chewe Kalubila, Mulenga wa Chibungu and Nkweto wa Chisungu, but few of these links are confirmed by present holders of these titles. 'Kanabesa' is frequently named as a Chitimukulu who came from Nkulungwe. We have noted that 'Kanabesa' is said to have been the name of a chieftainship, older than that of Chitimukulu, to which Chewe Kalubila could succeed; and that Mwaba, the chief in Nkulungwe, is linked with Chewe Kalubila. It may be that there was indeed a Chitimukulu who was called 'Kanabesa' because of his association with Chewe and Mwaba.[38]

In the absence of any comprehensive genealogy for the early Chitimukulus, there is no means of establishing in what order they all reigned. It is agreed that Chisoka* succeeded Chibamba*, and that Chishisa* succeeded Chisoka*, but otherwise the Chitimukulus between Mulenga Pokili* and Katongo* are listed in no special order. There does, however, seem to be good reason to place Katongo* relatively late, perhaps immediately before Mukuuka*. (There is general agreement on the order of succession after Mukuuka*.) Katongo was the title of the chief in Ichinga, and it may be that Chitimukulu Katongo* is to be identified with one or other holder of the Katongo title, such as Chimpolonge or Kasansu; alternatively, there may have been two or three Katongos who at different times became Chitimukulu.[39] At all events, there is some agreement that after 'Katongo' became Chitimukulu, his sister's son Kamponge, who was also called Chewe, was about to take over the chieftainship when he was challenged by Katongo's son Masaye. This man wished a brother of Kamponge to succeed, but Kamponge defeated his opponents. He

[36] I set out such associations, as they were made by different informants, in table 3.   [37] See above, p. 79.

[38] It certainly seems that he would have come from Mwaba (Nkulungwe) rather than Chewe, for there is a story that, for lack of a suitable candidate among the *bena ŋandu* who came with Chiti and Nkole, the *bakabilo* on one occasion sought a new Chitimukulu from the sons of Kapolyo Mfumu, when she had settled in Nkulungwe. She refused, saying that she could not spare any of her sons (Chewe Kalubila, 9 June 1964; Brelsford, *Succession*, p. 38; Mushindo, *History*, s. 44; see also Tweedie, 'Towards a History of the Bemba', p. 217, for a different opinion on Kanabesa).

[39] Village sites are remembered near the Luvu river in Ichinga for both Katongo and Chimpolonge, but they may well have been the same person.

took the name Nkula (*kukula*, to pull) because Masaye, in trying to obtain the chiefly relics, had dragged Kamponge out of a hut by the leg.[40] According to Mushindo, this man, Kamponge Chewe Nkula, did not die until some time after the death of Chileshye*, which was probably around 1860.[41] Thus Kamponge was probably not born much before 1780. Mushindo says that after Katongo's departure for Lubemba 'there was no chief in Ichinga for a very long time'.[42] Hence Kamponge may have been too young to succeed immediately, and Katongo may have gone to Lubemba soon after 1780. Such a chronology is certainly compatible with the genealogy of this royal lineage.[43] It may thus not be mere accident that Katongo is placed immediately before Mukuuka* in Chileshye Mukulu's list of Chiti-mukulus;[44] as will be shown in the next chapter, Mukuuka* probably reigned in the last years of the eighteenth century.

Since we know so little about the order in which Chitimukulus reigned, it is not possible to discern the patterns of competition between different lineages of the *bena ŋandu*. We cannot say, for example, whether one lineage, such as that in Katumba, held on to the Chiti-mukuluship for several reigns in succession, whether there was a system of rotation between different lineages,[45] or whether there was an unchecked struggle for power on the death of every Chitimukulu. We can only see that Chisoka*, from the lineage in Katumba, obtained the paramountcy after it had been held by a Mumena, Chibamba*; and that after it was held by Katongo*, from Ichinga, it apparently reverted to Mukuuka*, who came from Katumba. If my relative dating of Katongo* is correct, we can discern the significant fact that at this stage—perhaps well over a century since the foundation of the Chiti-mukuluship—it was both possible and worthwhile for a member of a royal lineage east of the Chambeshi to become Chitimukulu. It may be that geographical and genealogical distance explains why Katongo (according to some informants)[46] brought his ancestors' relics with him to Lubemba and appointed special *bakabilo* to look after them.

---

[40] Brelsford, *Aspects*, p. 40; Mushindo, *History*, s. 44; Sewuka and Mbutuka, 14 May 1965

[41] Mushindo, *History*, s. 59. For the dating of Chileshye's reign, see below, pp. 104, 123.

[42] Mushindo, *History*, s. 44   [43] See below, p. 135.

[44] Chileshye Mukulu, T1. Miss Ann Tweedie, following a slightly different line of reasoning, has suggested that Katongo ruled as Chitimukulu around the middle of the eighteenth century ('Towards a History of the Bemba', p. 212).

[45] As in the Luba state of Kalundwe (Verhulpen, *Baluba*, pp. 287–8)

[46] For example, Katenda, 25 November 1964

On the other hand, the two most senior of these *bakabilo* say that Katongo was a younger brother of some Chitimukulu and was sent *from* Lubemba to govern Ichinga; they disagree as to whether Katongo later succeeded as Chitimukulu.[47] If these *bakabilo* are right, this unnamed Chitimukulu might have been seeking to regain a measure of influence over a chieftainship east of the Chambeshi whose incumbents had become increasingly remote genealogically and politically.

What does seem clear is that the subordinate chieftainships remained in the control of distinct lineages. A few pairs of chieftainships were linked together: Chewe Kalubila with Mwaba, Mutale Mukulu with Chimbola, Mumena with Nkweto. It may be that men sometimes succeeded from one of these positions to the position thus linked to it. But with these possible exceptions, it does not seem that there was any succession from one subordinate chieftainship to another. Moreover, a man who had held a chiefly title, or who was closely related to a chief, might then become Chitimukulu; but he was not thereby enabled to assign other subordinate chieftainships to his own close kin. It may be, as I have noted, that there is a hint of such a development in connection with the Katongo title, and as we shall see this was to become a dominant theme in the nineteenth century. But it is obvious that the whole system of chiefly succession in pre-1800 Bembaland was rather different from the system which has operated during the last hundred years. Correspondingly, the political system was rather different, for the holders of subordinate chieftainships were only remotely related to each other and might well be very remotely related to Chitimukulu. We may well suppose that some at least of these chieftainships were more or less autonomous, and were held together largely by a common awareness of vague affinity with Chitimukulu, which gave rise to competition for the royal succession, and a common acknowledgement of the overriding ritual powers of his *bakabilo*. But we should also note that the extent of Bemba territory, so far as can be judged, was even by 1800 very limited: perhaps no more than 5,000 square miles, about one-fifth of the area under Bemba chiefs by 1900. Within this relatively small and compact territory the establish-

[47] Mulombelwa, 1 September 1964; Chipasha, 15 September 1964. I should note that these two *bakabilo* were in general much less informative about Katongo than my informants in Ichinga. Robertson says, 'The Chitimukulu was always succeeded by a nephew—member of the Chewe [?Katongo] family, and nominated by the ruling Chewe, and vice-versa' (*Introductory Handbook*, p. xv). This is presumably derived from Young's report that Chinchinta 'was a nephew of Chewe and made Kitimkulu by him' (Chinsali DNB I, p. 233), but there is no other evidence to support even this one example (see below, pp. 102, 122).

ment and maintenance of a single paramountcy was much more feasible than, for example, in the very much larger area occupied by Bisa chiefs. Indeed, it is likely that in the later eighteenth century one or two Bisa chieftainships each exercised an independent authority at least as extensive as that of Chitimukulu.[48]

[48] See below, pp. 108–9.

Chapter 4

The growth of Bemba power
c. 1770–c. 1860

With the accession of Chitimukulu Mukuuka* *wa malekano*, Bemba history begins to emerge from obscurity. There is, from this point, general agreement on the royal genealogy among those few informants who spoke with any assurance on the period. Both genealogies and narrative traditions, together with the traditions of neighbouring peoples and the evidence of the first European visitors to the region, enable us to discern a continuous and coherent pattern of events in Bemba history from the later part of the eighteenth century.

This improvement in the quantity and quality of the oral evidence largely reflects the nature of the political changes which began to take place among the Bemba around the end of the eighteenth century. The genealogical record becomes clear because the Chitimukuluship came to be occupied, not by a succession of members of competing royal lineages, but by members of only one relatively shallow lineage. Moreover, this lineage began to take over chiefdoms which had formerly been held by other lineages, while it also placed its own members or agnatic kin in newly conquered territories. And the very fact that the nineteenth century was a period of large-scale territorial expansion in some respects favoured the preservation of historical traditions. On the one hand, expansion led to the creation of several new chiefdoms whose origins at least it has been important to remember. On the other hand, territorial expansion brought the Bemba into increasingly frequent contact and collision with neighbouring peoples who have preserved their own traditions concerning Bemba conquests and campaigns.

THE REIGNS OF MUKUUKA* AND CHILIAMAFWA* (*c.* 1770–*c.* 1820)

The foundation of the Ituna chiefdom
Chitimukulu Mukuuka* belonged to the lineage of Iyaya, which controlled the chiefdom of Katumba, under Mutale Mukulu, and the

lesser title Chimbola. The chief development for which the reign of Mukuuka* is remembered is the founding of a chieftainship in Ituna, to the west of Lubemba. This is noteworthy as the first known instance of the creation of new chiefdoms for close relatives of Chitimukulu which is a main feature of later Bemba history. The earlier Bemba 'chiefs' (they were probably only headmen, but known as chiefs like all *bena ŋandu*) said to have lived in Ituna are Chikuku Mwela and Chipasha wa Makani.[1] The relationship of these two men to Mukuuka* is not very clear; perhaps they were his mother's brothers. It is possible that Ituna represented a quite recent addition to Bemba territory, rather than forming a long-established part of Lubemba.[2] At all events, there are two traditions that Mukuuka's* praise-name *wa malekano* ('of the separation') refers to his dividing Lubemba and giving the western part, Ituna, to his own brother, Chitundu.[3] Evidently Mukuuka* sought (as others, perhaps, had tried and failed) to build up and retain power for his own lineage. It may also be that the creation of a new chieftainship in Ituna, a border area, was partly a defence measure: it was about this time, according to their genealogies, that the first Leopard clan chiefs of the Lungu and Tabwa came from the western shores of Lake Tanganyika and settled to the north and west of the Bemba.[4]

Mukuuka* was succeeded as Chitimukulu by his sister's son Chiliamafwa*: this is the earliest known case of succession to the paramountcy passing to so close a relative. Chitundu was succeeded as chief of Ituna by Mubanga Kashampupo, a brother of Chiliamafwa*.[5] These two appointments strikingly testify to the growing concentration of power within a single shallow royal lineage. Mubanga is said to have come 'from Nkolemfumu' before succeeding in Ituna,[6] though whether he

[1] Milambo, T1. Chipasha was named after his village Makani, on the Milenge stream, a few miles west of the modern Kasama.

[2] But see above, p. 87, n. 29.

[3] Chikunga, T3; Chileshye Mukulu, T3. Chief Mwamba (9 October 1964) said that Chipasha wa Makani was a 'brother' of Chitundu, but it is not clear that they were actual siblings. The site of one of Chitundu's villages is remembered, some miles to the north of Makani, and a shrine for him is kept in repair.

Ituna may originally have been part of Miti country, under Nkolemfumu (see above, p. 87), but in any case Miti and Ituna have in more recent times been combined on occasion under a single chief (see below, pp. 105, 160, 220).

[4] See below, pp. 106, 149, 154.

[5] Milambo, who in 1964–5 was the leading authority on traditions in Ituna, insisted that Mubanga preceded Chitundu. But this is at variance with two independent traditions (Chikunga, T3; Chileshye Mukulu, T3) which also indicate, as Milambo does not, the relationship between Chitimukulu and the early chiefs of Ituna.   [6] Chileshye Mukulu, T3

was actually Nkolemfumu is not clear; nor is it clear whether he was chief over both Miti and Ituna. It is, however, possible to provide an approximate date for Mubanga's rule in Ituna. Calculation from the royal genealogy places him at the end of the eighteenth century, and this is supported by inferences from Lunda history. Fr Pinto, chaplain to Lacerda's expedition, recorded that in 1799 Kazembe III moved his capital to Mofwe.[7] The Lunda history indicates that this happened not long after the Bemba chief Mwamba blocked the roads into Bemba-land against Kazembe.[8] By 'Mwamba' we may here understand 'chief in Ituna', as the Mwamba title seems to be of more recent origin.[9] The Lunda history refers to this 'Mwamba' as Mubanga,[10] so it is evident that Mubanga was ruling in Ituna before 1799. Mubanga's rule in Ituna is generally spoken of by the Bemba as being contemporary with the reign of Chiliamafwa*, which may, for this and other reasons to be explained below, be placed *c.* 1790–*c.* 1820.

As chief of Ituna, Mubanga's principal concerns were the new Lungu chiefdom under Mukupa Kaoma and the rapidly expanding empire of Kazembe. Kazembe III Lukwesa Ilunga (*c.* 1760–1804/5) obtained tribute from the Tabwa and Lungu on his north-eastern borders. He then marched eastward to raid the Mambwe for cattle, but Mubanga sent messengers to meet him at the borders of Bemba country. According to Lunda traditions,

> When the Lunda arrived there they found people waiting for them peaceably, and they rolled on their backs in homage to him, and said: 'We are sent by the great Mubanga with the message: "Go and meet my uncle [sc. Kazembe] for I have heard he is coming with troops to fight the Mambwe and the Nsenga; but he should not come and destroy my country." ' Mwata Ilunga told them: 'Very well, I have heard your words; he should block all the paths leading into his country.' When Mwamba [sc. Mubanga] heard this, he sent people to bar all the roads and kill men across paths leading into his land. Mwata Ilunga avoided all the paths on which he found the bodies of men.[11]

[7] Lacerda, *Travessia*, p. 326 (Burton, *Cazembe*, p. 139). This would place the event rather late in the reign of Kazembe III (he died in 1804/5), whereas Lunda history as compiled by Labrecque indicates that it happened in the earlier part of his reign (Cunnison, *Historical Traditions*, p. 53).

[8] *Ibid.*, 49, 53; see below.   [9] See below, p. 105.

[10] Cunnison, *Historical Traditions*, p. 49; we must, however, note the possibility of interpolation by Labrecque from his knowledge of Bemba history.

[11] Cunnison, *Historical Traditions*, p. 49

When Kazembe returned home from this expedition, he found that Mubanga had sent him presents of a woman and child and cattle; in return, Kazembe sent Mubanga a gun and a keg of gunpowder.[12] There appear not to be any Bemba traditions concerning these events, but in view of the Lunda evidence we need not accept at face value Lacerda's report in 1798 that the Bemba and Sukuma were 'mortal enemies to, never sparing, the Cazembe's people'.[13] This may well refer, not to the Lunda themselves, but to peoples such as the Lungu who had recently been laid under tribute by Kazembe.

This conjecture is supported by traditions about early relations between the Bemba of Ituna and the neighbouring Lungu of Mukupa Kaoma, who at this period occupied much country to the east of their present borders.[14] Mubanga or Chiliamfwa* is said to have made a treaty with Kaoma, the second ruler in the dynasty, whose genealogy indicates that Kaoma could well have lived some time around 1800.[15] Gifts were exchanged, and royal princesses.[16] It may be that this was the occasion for the marriage between Mulenga Mwimba, a son of Mubanga Kashampupo, and Mwimba Nsangwa, a junior relative of Kaoma.[17] But the Lungu soon became involved in a quarrel between Munkonge and Mulenga Mwimba, sons of Mubanga Kashampupo by different wives. Munkonge lived in Kalundu, west of the Lukulu river, in country taken recently from the Bisa.[18] But he was jealous of his brother Mulenga, who had been specially favoured by their father and had been put in charge of a small area further south, Chisansa.[19]

[12] *Ibid.*, p. 51

[13] Burton, *Cazembe*, p. 99 (Lacerda, *Diários*, p. 255)

[14] Mukupa Kaoma's own village was on one or other branch of the Mwelekumbi river, about twenty miles east of his present village, and the burial grove for early Mukupa Kaomas is on the Mwelekumbi (Labrecque, 'Origines', p. 292; Kasama DNB II, p. 50; Molo Makungo, 2 July 1965).

[15] See below, p. 106. The Lungu confirm the story of a treaty but say Kaoma made it with Chitundu (Molo Makungo, 2 July 1965). Labrecque says the Lungu chief was Tafuna, but locates him in Malaila country, which is that of Mukupa Kaoma ('Origines', p. 290). Tafuna's Lungu live further north, around the south-eastern corner of Lake Tanganyika: see below, p. 148.

[16] Labrecque, 'Origines', p. 290; Chileshye Mukulu, T5, n. 24

[17] Nshilika Mwenya, T1. He said that Mwimba Nsangwa was a niece (*mwipwa*) of Kaoma; this could only mean that they belonged to the same matrilineage. Yet he also said that Mwimba Nsangwa was a *mwina mbao* (Otter clan), though Kaoma, as a Lungu royal, belonged to the *zimba* (Leopard) clan.

[18] Chief Munkonge, 5 December 1964; and see below, p. 110. Munkonge I's village was near the Nkanga stream.

[19] This was on the left bank of the Lukulu river, near its confluence with the Kampandwe stream (Milambo, 2 October 1964). Mulenga was succeeded here by

In the course of this quarrel, Munkonge was killed; his sons then got help from Kaoma and killed Mulenga, whose wife, Lukonde Mwaba, was captured by Kaoma. Mubanga, who had evidently been unable or unwilling to stop the war, invoked his treaty with Kaoma, who then returned Lukonde (who was also Mubanga's niece).[20] A Bemba–Lungu border was then agreed upon; it evidently followed the Luombe river.[21]

The foundation of the Makasa chieftainship

It was probably in Chiliamafwa's* reign that a further critical innovation took place in the expansion and strengthening of Bemba chieftainship. Chiliamafwa* was apparently the father of Kalulu, first holder of the Makasa title in the chiefdom of Mpanda, to the north of Lubemba.[22] This was the first known appointment of any consequence of a son of an *ŋandu* chief to a territorial chieftainship—a practice that was to become increasingly important in the course of the nineteenth century.[23] Mpanda was henceforward the preserve of sons of Chitimukulu, who thereby exerted a greater control both over appointments and over the submission of tribute than he enjoyed over subordinate *bena ŋandu*.

The establishment of Makasa I in Mpanda represents perhaps the earliest phase of Bemba conquests in the nineteenth century. Until 1800 or so, the Mambwe had continued to occupy country immediately to the north of the Bemba capital, and they were probably subject to no more than occasional raids for cattle.[24] One informant at Chandaweyaya's, near the northern border of Lubemba, said that a Mambwe chief called Ntachimbwa ('I am not surrendered to', that is, 'I take no prisoners') occupied the village site known as Ntasu, only ten miles from the Kalungu river and Chitimukulu's present village.[25] This testimony seems to be supported by the fact that pottery found at Bwalya, a son of Chileshye who later became Makasa III (Labrecque, 'Origines', p. 292). Chisutula, another son of Mubanga, lived on the Luombe and was guardian of the shrine at Chishimba Falls (*ibid.*; Chisutula, 1 October 1964).

[20] Chileshye Mukulu, T5 and notes; cf. Chikunga, T3; Milambo, T1; Labrecque, 'Origines', pp. 291–2. See also Appendix 2, Note K.

[21] Labrecque, 'Origines', p. 292

[22] There is some uncertainty about the first Makasas: see Appendix 2, Note E.

[23] See chapters 5 and 6 for further discussion of this development.

[24] Chimbola (9 September 1964) said, however, that long ago a son of Chimbola, Chikasa Mulungu, ruled Mpanda; there were people there who used their teeth to make bark-cloth—a common cliché about the 'Musukwa' (cf. Labrecque, 'Origines', p. 263; Mushindo, *History*, s. 29; Oger 'Mpanda', 1).

[25] Sampa Kalambwe, 26 November 1964

Ntasu, both on the surface and embedded in the ditch walls, is not in any known Bemba style.[26] Oger, the historian of Mpanda, says that Ntachimbwa lived at 'Ntabu'; he was chief of a Mambwe group known as Nkondo who were defeated by the Bemba in the time of Chiliamafwa*.[27] I could learn no more about Ntachimbwa during a brief visit to Nsokolo, the Mambwe paramount, but the Mambwe acknowledge that the Bemba killed the southern Mambwe chief Mpande II, who evidently lived in the earlier nineteenth century.[28]

The results of Bemba conquest in Mpanda were somewhat unusual. The patrilineal and semi-pastoral Mambwe and Namwanga differ far more from the Bemba than do the Bisa and other peoples to the south and west who were also conquered by the Bemba. They were thus less easily assimilated into a uniform pattern of Bemba authority and custom. In part of Mpanda there remain to this day distinct non-Bemba villages under Makasa. To the east, there is one small group of Namwanga villages, whose headmen are known as 'owners of the land', implying that they are the first known inhabitants. They live east of the Choshi river, and thus beyond Makasa's borders, but it is said that the senior headman, Mwine Chilanga, used to rule on both sides of the Choshi.[29] Oger reports that Mwine Chilanga and Makasa formerly received equal tribute in fish from the Mwenda river, and that Makasa confirmed, as a formality, Mwine Chilanga's appointment.[30] In the middle of Mpanda are the Nkondo or *bashimpili* (people

[26] The decorated sherds are much more varied and elaborate than Bemba pottery, and they elicited surprise and admiration from Bemba informants. (A selection of these sherds has been deposited at the Livingstone Museum, Zambia.) Most appear to be very generally related to pottery styles of peoples north and northwest of Lake Malawi, though a few somewhat resemble the Kisii-type sherds excavated at Mbande Hill, near Karonga (K. R. Robinson, 'A Preliminary Report on the recent archaeology of Ngonde, Northern Malawi', *JAH*, 1966, 7, ii, pp. 169–88).

There are still hardwood (*mubanga*) stakes lying by the ditch at Ntasu, which is still several feet deep: this indicates relatively recent occupation. Some informants say that Ntasu was reoccupied by Sampa, i.e. in the later nineteenth century; if so, he must have had foreign craftsmen in the village (Kakwela, T1; Chimbola, 8 June 1965, Makofi, 9 June 1965; Kakwela also named another site for Sampa on the Miaba river and perhaps there has been confusion between this and Ntasu).

[27] Oger, 'Mpanda', I, 11–12. Mushindo says that Chiliamafwa killed Ntachimbwa, a Mambwe chief; he says that the Nkondo were people who came from the north and were conquered by the Bemba who were antecedent to Chitimukulu (*History*, s. 29, 35).

[28] Watson, *Tribal Cohesion*, p. 149   [29] Makofi, 9 June 1965

[30] Oger, 'Mpanda', 9–10. Mwine Chilanga has a special relationship with another intruding chief, Kafwimbi of the Iwa (Isoka DNB, II, p. 2).

of the hills). Here there are at least six Mambwe villages of long standing, whose headmen are appointed by one Mwine Nsanso. (The first holder of this title appears to have been a Fipa, who fled to Mpanda after some trouble arising out of a poison ordeal.) When the Bemba invaded Mpanda, Mwine Nsanso promptly submitted and was made a councillor of Makasa.[31] The western part of Mpanda appears to have been left by Makasa I under a Mambwe headman, Kavwinta, whose sister he married. Those members of Kavwinta's clan, the Silwamba, who accepted Bemba rule 'changed and became Bemba under a new name of the Nsofu (Elephant) clan'.[32] Makasa I also assigned a small area within Mpanda to his son Fwangila.[33]

Chileshye Chepela and Susula Chinchinta

The reign of Chiliamafwa* witnessed the rise to prominence of a young man who was to achieve great fame as Chitimukulu. This was Chileshye Chepela, who seems to have been a favourite of Chiliamafwa* and was related to him through both parents: Chileshye was the son of Chiliamafwa's* niece Lukonde Mwaba and of Mulenga Mwimba, son of Chiliamafwa's* brother Mubanga Kashampupo, the chief of Ituna. Chileshye had been born with a stunted arm,[34] and this had caused his mother Lukonde Mwaba to abandon him. Chileshye was rescued by Mwimba Nsangwa, the first wife of his father Mulenga Mwimba; and she brought him up in Chisansa together with her own son Kabwibwi.[35] When Mwimba Nsangwa and Mulenga Mwimba were killed by the sons of Munkonge, Chileshye left Chisansa and went eastward with his full brother Mutale to the neighbouring chiefdom of Miti, where they stayed with chief Nkolemfumu. Here they got involved in a quarrel with a son of Nkolemfumu, and as a result they left Miti and went to Lubemba.[36] Some time later, Chileshye paid a visit to Kazembe's court, probably at Chiliamafwa's* request, and obtained ingredients for a war-charm (*ilamfya*).[37] According to one

[31] Oger, 'Mpanda', 5–8, 11, 13, 20. Mwine Nsanso has a special role in the tree-cutting ceremonies: he shows Makasa where to make a new garden every year. When a new Makasa succeeds, Mwine Nsanso comes to greet him with criticism and exhortation (*ibid.*, 6–7).

[32] H. E. Silanda, 'Enslavement of Grandmother Mary', LM/IV D 19, pp. 1–3

[33] Oger, 'Mpanda', 12; cf. Brelsford, *Aspects*, p. 8

[34] Hence his nickname *cepela* (from *kucepa*, to be small, to be lacking)

[35] Nshilika Mwenya, T1; Chileshye Mukulu, T1 (see Appendix 4/ii); Labrecque, 'Origines', pp. 290–1   [36] Shimulamba, T1; Milambo, T1

[37] Chikunga, 11 September 1964; cf. Tanguy, *Imilandu*, p. 26. There is some confusion about this episode: see Appendix 2, Note F (p. 351).

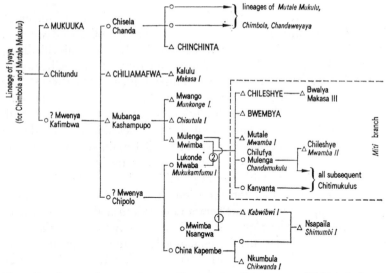

Fig. 4 Bemba royal succession, earlier nineteenth century. (Chitimukulus in capitals)

informant, Chiliamafwa* bequeathed his country to Chileshye and Mutale;[38] but no chief really has, or had, power to do this, and another informant relates that when Chiliamafwa* died the *bakabilo* thought of choosing Mutale Mukulu Mulenga to succeed him. The relationship between Chiliamafwa* and this Mutale Mukulu was not known to my informants, but Chiliamafwa*, as a nephew of Mukuuka*, belonged to the lineage of Chandaweyaya, to which the Mutale Mukulu title also belongs.[39]

For some reason which is not clear, the *bakabilo* then turned against Mutale Mukulu and instead appointed Susula Chinchinta.[40] This man was probably Chiliamafwa's* sister's son;[41] the choice before the *bakabilo* may, as often, have lain between an older candidate of the same generation as the deceased but relatively remote genealogically,

[38] Milambo, T1

[39] Chileshye Mukulu, T1; Mutale Mukulu Mulenga was addressed as 'grandfather' (*shikulu*) by Chileshye Chepela, but this seems to have been no more than its normal usage as a term of respect.

[40] Chileshye Mukulu T1: his story of Chileshye's accession is given in Appendix 4/ii (p. 381).

[41] Chikunga, T3; Chileshye Mukulu, 25 July 1964. Young says that Chinchinta 'was a nephew of Chewe and made Kitimkulu by him' (Chinsali DNB I, p. 231), but no other source supports this: see below, p. 121. Labrecque ('Origines', p. 271) says that Chinchinta was a nephew of Mulenga Mwimba, but this is impossible if 'nephew' is taken in its Bemba meaning of 'sister's son'.

and a much more closely related but younger candidate. Chinchinta*
is certainly commonly associated with the lineage of Chandaweyaya.
Three informants said he came 'from' Mutale Mukulu or his chiefdom,
Katumba.[42] A fourth said Chinchinta* came from the river Chamfubu,
near what was then the northern frontier with the Mambwe.[43] The
present Chimbola thought that Chinchinta* may actually have held the
Chimbola title, and one of his priests identified Chinchinta* with
Chimbola *wa museshi*.[44] The Chimbola title is certainly associated with
that of Chandaweyaya, but it is not at all certain that Chinchinta*
actually held it, especially as Chimbola was unable to state Chinchinta's* relationship with any other Chitimukulus.[45] The important
point, however, is that the accession of Chinchinta was the third
successive appointment to the paramountcy from within the lineage of
Chandaweyaya. The right of this lineage to monopolise the royal
succession was being firmly established; future arguments would
revolve round the question of which branches within this lineage
remained eligible for the succession.

THE REIGN OF CHINCHINTA*, c. 1820–?1827

Having preferred Chinchinta* to Mutale Mukulu, the *bakabilo* soon
had reason to regret their choice. It is said that when people were slow
in coming to work in his fields, Chinchinta* would send men out to
burn down their granaries.[46] Mutale Mukulu Mulenga was once
again asked to succeed, but he now refused, partly out of pique, but
also because Chinchinta* was his nephew, and an uncle could not be
expected to succeed his nephew.[47] Instead, Mutale recommended

---

[42] Chileshye Mukulu, T2; Kakwela, 27 August 1964; Chibwe, 8 June 1965

[43] Chikunga, 11 September 1964. It may be that Chinchinta, before his accession, was attacked by Kazembe III Lukwesa Ilunga; the Lunda list 'Chinchinta'
among various Mambwe chiefs whom they say Lukwesa defeated (Cunnison,
Historical Traditions, pp. 49–50).

[44] Chimbola, 8 June 1965; Chibwe, 9 September 1964.

[45] Thus when Brelsford (*Succession*, p. 5) and, following him, Gluckman ('Succession and Civil War', pp. 1–12) identify Chinchinta with Chimbola, they may
well only be right in so far as Chinchinta came from the lineage within which the
Chimbola title was hereditary.

[46] Chileshye Mukulu, T1; cf. Tanguy, *Imilandu*, p. 26. At Chandaweyaya's
(23 September 1964) I was told that Chinchinta's failing was simply that he was a
leper; this is a handicap usually ascribed in traditions (e.g. Chikunga) to an earlier
Chitimukulu, Kapampa Mubanshi.

[47] Chileshye Mukulu, T1; in view of the uncertainty about Chinchinta's
relationship with other chiefs, these terms are not necessarily to be taken literally.

Chileshye Chepela. One informant said that Chileshye was still at Kazembe's when Chiliamafwa* died. The *bakabilo* sent out one of their number, Lumpombwe (said by some to have been a son of Chiliamafwa*) to fetch Chileshye. Another informant said that Chileshye, with his brother Mutale, cajoled Lumpombwe into persuading his colleagues to replace Chinchinta;[48] there is also a story of how Chileshye and Mutale impressed another *kabilo*, Mwangata, with their generosity and got him to canvass for Chileshye at the capital.[49]

We can perhaps discern in this situation rather more than a dispute over the individual merits of Chinchinta* and Chileshye. Each man represented different branches of the dominant royal lineage, and each of these branches was associated with certain areas. Chinchinta* and other descendants of Chiliamafwa's* elder sister lived, or had lived, in northern Bembaland, in Katumba and Iyaya, while Chiliamafwa's* own son Makasa also lived on the northern borders, in Mpanda. The descendants of Chiliamafwa's* younger brother and sister lived in western Bembaland. Mubanga Kashampupo ruled Ituna, while his sons, Munkonge, Chisutula and Mulenga Mwimba, lived, or had lived, nearby. Mubanga's younger sister appears to have had no sons, but the elder sons of her daughter Lukonde Mwaba were Mutale and Chileshye, who had grown up in Chisansa with Mulenga Mwimba before moving to Miti for a time.[50] It is thus very likely that Chileshye was able to count on support from Mubanga Kashampupo and other relatives to the south of Ituna, and that this was an important consideration for some *bakabilo*.

It is in any case probable that Chileshye obtained Bisa support before attempting a coup. He is known to have occupied several sites in the southern part of Lubemba after leaving Miti, and two informants said that Chileshye defeated the Bisa of Kabanda, south of the Chambeshi river.[51] Some writers claim that Chileshye became rich by trading in ivory or slaves;[52] this seems doubtful, but my principal informants

---

[48] Chikunga, 11 September 1964; Milambo, T1; Nshilika Mwenya, T1. The latter implies that Chileshye rebelled because Chinchinta was on good terms with Chileshye's mother, who had abandoned him as a baby.   [49] Shimulamba, T1

[50] Milambo stresses that when Chileshye and Mutale had to leave Miti, they did *not* go to Mutale Mukulu in Katumba, or to Chileshye Mukulu.

[51] Milambo, T1; Shimulamba, T1. Labrecque ('Origines', p. 296) says that Chileshye occupied Chinama, near the present Mpika, before becoming Chitimukulu, but this is not confirmed by any other source.

[52] Brelsford says that Chileshye's people became rich from ivory obtained in Kabanda's country (*Succession*, p. 5). Labrecque says that Chileshye attracted a large following by exchanging Bisa slaves for guns and cloth from Arab traders

agreed that in one way or another Chileshye got help from Kabanda.[53] Chileshye then arranged with certain *bakabilo* that when he attacked Chinchinta* at the capital he would meet only a pretence at resistance. So it turned out; the *bakabilo* allowed Chileshye to take the capital, and Chinchinta* fled.[54] He took refuge with the Mambwe chief Nsokolo, in whose country he soon died.[55]

The date of Chileshye's* accession may be placed not long before 1830. By this date he seems to have sent Chikwanda I to rule the Bisa in Chinama.[56] And if it is true that he was involved in fighting with the Bisa before his accession, as both Labrecque and my informants claim, this may well have been the war between Bemba and Bisa which Gamitto says began in 1826.[57] Moreover, Gamitto noted, while in the same area, that 'Locusts are a plague which have been the scourge of East Africa since 1827'.[58] It may not be wholly fanciful to associate this with a story that Chileshye's* people were afflicted with locusts after they had driven away Chinchinta*.[59] If we place Chileshye's* accession in about 1827, that of Chinchinta* can be placed no more than a few years earlier, perhaps between 1820 and 1825: the traditions suggest that the people did not put up with him for very long.[60]

THE REIGN OF CHILESHYE, ?1827–c. 1860

Ituna
It appears that Mubanga Kashampupo, chief of Ituna, died shortly after

from the Bisa chief Kambwili ('Origines', pp. 272, 296, 325). It is possible that by this time the Bemba had access to trade goods from the coast, but there is no other evidence that Arabs or other coastal traders frequented the country south of Bembaland until the 1860s (see chapter 6). The first Kambwili was indeed a host to Arab traders on the middle Luangwa, but it is unlikely that he settled there and opened trade with them before the 1880s (cf. Lane-Poole, *Native Tribes of the Eastern Province*, p. 32; Livingstone, *Last Journals*, I, pp. 156–87). Perhaps, however, Labrecque's 'Arabs' were really Bisa: see below, p. 192, n. 120.

[53] Milambo, T1; Shimulamba, T1; cf. Labrecque, 'Origines', p. 272. One account of Bisa traditions says that it was the first holder of the Kabinga chieftainship (in Mpuki, south of Kabanda's) who helped to defeat Chinchinta (Simon Vibeti, 'History of the Bisa' (MS), pp. 38–40).

[54] Milambo, T1; Shimulamba, T1; cf. Labrecque, 'Origines', p. 272. The story current at Chimbola's gives a rather different account of how the *Miti* branch displaced that of Chimbola: see Appendix 2, Note G (p. 352).

[55] Chinchinta's death outside Bembaland presented Chileshye with a problem: see Appendix 2, Note H (p. 353).   [56] See below, pp. 113–14.

[57] Gamitto, *King Kazembe*, II, p. 161   [58] *Ibid.*, I, p. 175

[59] Labrecque, 'Origines', p. 274; note (by Robert Young?) in Chinsali DNB I, p. 253   [60] For example, Chikunga, 11 September 1964

Chileshye's* accession.[61] He was succeeded by Chileshye's* brother Mutale *wa kabwe*. Mutale was the first chief of Ituna to take the title Mwamba. The story goes that one Mutale Mukulu, a son of Chanda-weyaya, killed the Mambwe chief Mwamba (a title which is still extant among the Mambwe) and assumed his title. But this new 'Mwamba' was mad: he attacked his brothers and sacked his mother's village. When Mutale *wa kabwe* heard of this, he came to the aid of Chandaweyaya and killed 'Mwamba' Mutale Mukulu. Chandaweyaya then gave the name Mwamba to Mutale *wa kabwe*.[62]

It is clear that Chileshye* followed up his displacement of Chin-chinta* with attempts to gain as much power as possible for his own *arriviste* branch of the royal lineage. We have already seen that Ituna passed, on the death of Mubanga Kashampupo, to Mutale *wa kabwe*, who was likewise brother to Chitimukulu at the time of his appointment. But Chileshye* also brought Miti, the chiefdom lying to the south of Ituna, under the control of Mwamba I Mutale. Nkolemfumu, the chief of Miti, died shortly before Chileshye's* accession.[63] Milambo says that this Nkolemfumu was Chisanga, an 'uncle' of Chileshye and Mutale, but there is no more detailed evidence to suggest that Chisanga was in fact at all closely related to them.[64] In any case, when Nkolem-fumu Chisanga died, no successor was found until Chileshye* had become Chitimukulu. Brelsford says that since Chileshye's* younger brother, Bwembya, was a 'fool', Chileshye* 'brought all the *babenye* relics and gave them to the care of Mwamba [Mutale *wa kabwe*] who also took over most of the area [Miti]'.[65] Milambo confirms that Mwamba I Mutale ruled Miti as well as Ituna, and his village, Kabwe, was within the present borders of Miti.[66] Whatever chiefs had

[61] Shimulamba, T1, n. 34

[62] Milambo, 30 September 1964; Mushindo, *History*, s. 36; the latter locates the incident in the reign of Chiliamafwa, i.e. when Mubanga Kashampupo was still chief of Ituna. Chileshye Mukulu (25 July 1964) told much the same story, but with reference to Malama, i.e., Mwamba II Chileshye Kapalaula.

[63] Milambo, T1; Brelsford, *Succession*, p. 28

[64] Though we must note that Mubanga Kashampupo is said to have come 'from Nkolemfumu's' (see above, p. 95). It was said at Nkolemfumu's in 1957 that when Chileshye succeeded, Miti was ruled by Mupundu, successor to Mwalula (A. I. Richards, fieldnotes, 7 September 1957), but Shimulamba (10 December 1964) gave Mwalula Mpundu as the name of one man and did not make it clear when he ruled.

[65] Brelsford, *Succession*, p. 28. Some such story is perhaps the basis for the report (dated 1924) that before Mutale *wa kabwe* took over Ituna the area was under Mwalula, also a brother of Chileshye (Kasama DNB I, pp. 412–13): Mwalula is the name of an early chief in Miti (see above, n. 64).

[66] Milambo, 9 October 1964, 30 September 1964

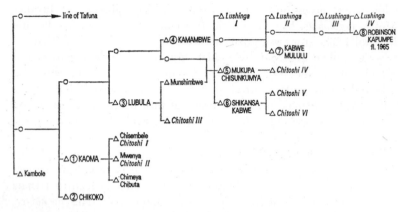

Fig. 5 Mukupa Kaoma. From table by Mukupa Kaoma 8, dated 1964.

previously ruled there, Miti was henceforward ruled by scions of Chileshye's* lineage, i.e. descendants of his mother Lukonde Mwaba, whether or not these also ruled Ituna simultaneously. It is generally assumed that it was from this episode that the matrilineal descendants of Lukonde Mwaba came to be known as the *Miti* branch of the *bena ŋandu*.[67]

On his western border, Mwamba I Mutale had to assert his control of Ituna in face of an attack by the Lungu of Mukupa Kaoma. Kaoma, their second chief, had made peace with Mubanga Kashampupo, chief of Ituna (?died *c.* 1830),[68] but war broke out again between Kaoma's successor, Chikoko, and Mubanga's successor, Mwamba I Mutale *wa kabwe*. Chikoko was reviled by his subjects as a weakling, in contrast to Kaoma, who had despite his pacific rule been known as a strong man. So when a fight started between Lungu and Bemba children on the Luombe river, which formed the Lungu–Bemba border, Chikoko was goaded into attacking Mwamba I by Kaoma's sons, Chisembele (who had held the minor title of Chitoshi) and Mwenya.[69] The Lungu crossed the Luombe in force and invaded Ituna, determined to

[67] Cf. Mushindo, *History*, s. 37. I do not know when the *ŋanda ya Miti* (house of Miti) came to be so called; perhaps only after Chisansa, where Chileshye *cepela* had grown up, was incorporated in Miti (see below, p. 160, n. 3). The association would be more obvious if Chileshye was in fact the nephew of an Nkolemfumu.

[68] See above, pp. 104–5.

[69] Chileshye Mukulu, 25 July 1964; Labrecque, 'Origines', p. 292; cf. Tanguy, *Imilandu*, p. 29

occupy it.[70] Bwalya, a son of Chileshye*,[71] raised the alarm among the Bemba from his village on the Katukuta stream; both Mwamba I and Chileshye* sent soldiers, and there was a fierce battle on the Katukuta. Finally, the Lungu fled back in disarray across the Luombe and their chief, Chikoko, was killed.[72]

The Bemba and the Bisa

Up to the time of Chileshye's* accession, the Bemba polity had not expanded much beyond the borders of the oldest chiefdoms: Mpanda, in the northeast, seems to have been the only notable acquisition in the early nineteenth century. In terms both of direct control over territory and indirect control through tribute and raiding, the most powerful ruler in north-eastern Zambia at this time was not Chitimukulu but the Lunda king, Kazembe. By the later eighteenth century, Kazembe's capital on the Luapula had become the meeting-point of trade routes which spanned the continent. The western route ran through the copper country of Katanga to Kazembe's suzerain Mwata Yamvo, and thence ultimately to Portuguese Angola. The eastern route reached the east coast through the countries of the Bisa, south of the Bemba, and the Yao, to the east of Lake Malawi.[73] Bisa traders were active on this eastern route, but Kazembe exercised a measure of tributary control over several of the Bisa chiefs along it; he also dominated some of the chiefs further north. In the course of Chileshye's* reign, however, this extensive sphere of influence was mostly lost by Kazembe. Large parts of Bisa country were invaded by Bemba chiefs, and though they failed to retain their original conquests, Kazembe did not intervene: the way

[70] Labrecque ('Origines', p. 293) and Chileshye Mukulu (25 July 1964) say the Lungu took their women, who brought their mortars and grindstones; this may well be a mere cliché.

[71] Bwalya (later Makasa III) also lived at some time in Chisansa, further south (see above, p. 97, n. 19).

[72] Milambo, T7; Chileshye Mukulu, 25 July 1964. Labrecque indicates that Chikoko was killed in his village, where he had stayed behind, dead drunk ('Origines', p. 294). Chileshye Mukulu says that his own predecessor killed Chikoko; Milambo only says that the warrior called himself *natoba* ('I have destroyed him'). The Lungu of Mukupa Kaoma tell the whole story in much the same way (Molo Makungo, T2). They (and Milambo) omit the incident on the Luombe river but add that Mwamba was displeased at Chikoko's death and sent his own undertakers to bury him. An account by an early official, Cookson, gives a different *casus belli*: he says that Mukupa Kaoma (?Chikoko) committed adultery with wives of Mwamba and Chitimukulu when these women were visiting friends at Mukupa Kaoma's (Kasama DNB II, p. 50).

[73] For further discussion of this trade see below, pp. 189–91.

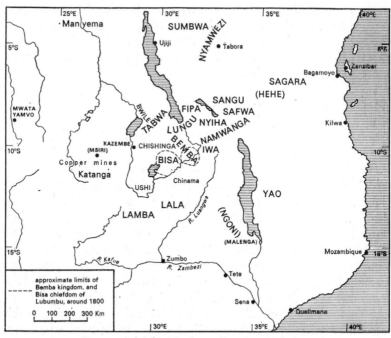

5 East-central Africa in the earlier nineteenth century

remained open for a second, and more successful, phase of Bemba expansion.

The Bisa, in whose country the Bemba made their most substantial challenge to Kazembe's power, were governed by no single system of chiefdoms, however loosely organised. The leading Bisa chiefs all belonged to the *bena ŋona* (Mushroom clan), but their lineages have long been distinct and seem for the most part to have been independent of each other. At one time Mwansabamba (the chief in Chinama) exercised some form of overlordship over the Bisa chiefs in Lubumbu, northwest of Lake Bangweulu: he confirmed the appointment of the fourth, fifth and sixth rulers there.[74] But by the end of the eighteenth century the Lubumbu chiefs were probably rather more important than Mwansabamba: their dynasty not only ruled Lubumbu but had subordinates located in a great arc from Kalundu and Lupi, in the east, to Isansa, under chief Chama, in the west.[75] In the later eighteenth

[74] Munsoma, T1; cf. Livingstone: 'Moanzabamba was the founder of the Babisa tribe' (*Last Journals*, II, p. 281).

[75] Munsoma, T1. Lacerda visited Chama 'Mouro Achinto' in 1798 (Lacerda, *Diários*, p. 255; Burton, *Cazembe*, p. 99). The Chama title was reserved for

century, Kalenga, the sixth chief of Lubumbu, moved his capital from Chilubi island, in Lake Bangweulu, to a site on the mainland called Mwala, near the Lukutu river.[76] Kalenga appointed one Chilando Chipala to rule over Masonde, in the northwest, and this chief appears to have had one or more successors known as Chinyimba.[77] In the eastern part of Bisa country, near the Muchinga escarpment of the Luangwa valley, chief Mukungule seems to have enjoyed considerable authority in the later eighteenth century, but by 1831 his former subordinate chiefs were said to be independent.[78]

This relative disunity of the Bisa no doubt explains in part why they ultimately lost so much territory to Bemba chiefs. Yet by about 1800 the Lubumbu chiefs appear to have dominated an area comparable to that under Chitimukulu at that date. Bisa weakness was perhaps mainly due to the manner of Bisa involvement in the long-distance trade from Kazembe's, from which the Bisa appear to have derived relatively little profit. It is not yet clear how far Bisa chiefs may themselves have participated in this trade. It would, however, appear that in the early nineteenth century the trade was dominated by Kazembe, and that Bisa ivory traders were responsible to him rather than to their own chiefs.[79] And several chiefs in the western part of Bisa country became tributary to Kazembe. The history of the Lunda claims that in the reign of Kazembe III (died 1804/5) the Lunda border governor Mwinempanda ruled 'the Chishinga, and the Bisa of Chinyimba, Chipako, Chilando and as far as the Chambeshi river'.[80] This is borne out by the early Portuguese travellers: Gamitto heard in 1831 that Kazembe III 'had extended the limits of his empire . . . to the river

matrilineal relatives of the chief of Lubumbu, and the seventh ruler there, Chama, had succeeded from the Chama chieftainship (Munsoma, T1; see also below, p. 115).

[76] The location of Mwala is given on a map of the Luena Division of about 1906, in Luena DNB II.

[77] Munsoma, T1–2. For Chinyimba, cf. Thomas, *Bisa*, p. 17, and below, p. 114. I do not know whether there was any connection between this chieftainship and Chinyimba, the fourth ruler of Lubumbu.

[78] 'At one time the [Bisa] nation was united under a supreme chief called Mukungule, to whom all the Bisa rendered vassalage; but in the later periods of his existence obedience to him was only nominal and each Mambo, having become independent, governed his own dominion. . . .' (Gamitto, *King Kazembe*, I, p. 202)

[79] Lacerda, *Travessia*, pp. 155, 387; *Diários*, p. 250 (Burton, *Cazembe*, pp. 37, 57, 94)

[80] Cunnison, *Historical Traditions*, p. 63. This Chilando was probably the Chishinga chief (a *mwina ŋoma*); cf. Kawambwa DNB III, p. 246.

Chambeshi', while in 1798 Lacerda had noted that whereas Mukungule was independent, some of the 'Sukuma' west of the Chambeshi were subject to Kazembe.[81] In the early nineteenth century the Lunda conducted campaigns against the Chishinga, the Mukulu of Chungu, and Bisa in Lubumbu.[82] Kazembe III is said to have subdued a group of Tabwa on his northern marches; he obtained tribute from them and from the southern Lungu; he raided the northern Lungu for cattle; and in 1831 Kazembe IV received tribute from a Lungu chief, probably Mukupa Kaoma.[83]

It is, however, doubtful whether Kazembe actually governed such eastern tributaries; he does not even appear to have posted agents at their courts. Lacerda had gathered in 1798 that the Bemba and Sukuma were enemies both of 'Kazembe's people' and of the Bisa, but Kazembe does not appear to have provided the latter with any military assistance; on the contrary, Kazembe III was on good terms with the western Bemba chief Mubanga Kashampupo.[84] It might be supposed that both Kazembe III and IV would have been anxious to resist by all means any threat to their control of the trade route to the east; on the other hand, the latter may by 1830 or so have begun to look more hopefully at the new routes further north, operated by coastal traders but beyond the reach of the Portuguese.[85] At all events, Bemba pressure on the Bisa and southern Lungu found these people enervated rather than fortified by their association with Kazembe. Bemba expansion to the south and west provoked no direct conflict between Bemba and Lunda, and indeed the absence of such conflict is one of the more remarkable features of the history of the plateau in the nineteenth century.

Although the Bemba were known by 1798 to be enemies of the Bisa, the first remembered Bemba encroachment on Bisa territory probably took place rather later, towards the end of Chiliamafwa's* reign. Munkonge I Mwango, son of Mubanga Kashampupo, wrested Kalundu from the minor Bisa chief Muma Chalwe;[86] this probably

[81] Gamitto, *King Kazembe*, II, p. 109; Lacerda, *Diários*, pp. 241–3, 250 (Burton, *Cazembe*, pp. 88–9, 94)

[82] Cunnison, *Historical Traditions*, pp. 62, 69; Luwingu DNB I, p. 122; African Elders, *History of the Bena Ŋoma*, pp. 37–43; Munsoma, T1. One or other of these campaigns delayed a group of half-caste *pombeiros* at Kazembe's from 1806 to 1810: Baptista, 'Exploraçoes', p. 226 (Burton, *Cazembe*, p. 191).

[83] Cunnison, *Historical Traditions*, pp. 49–50; Colle, *Baluba*, I, p. 53; Watson, *Tribal Cohesion*, p. 149, n. 3; Gamitto, *King Kazembe*, II, p. 35

[84] See above, p. 97.   [85] See below, pp. 193–4.

[86] See above, p. 97. The Bemba still make offerings to the spirit of Muma Chalwe at the grove where he is said to have died (Munkonge, 5 December 1964). Munkonge's village at this time was near the Nkanga stream.

marked the first Bemba advance west of the Lukulu river. As we have seen, Chileshye Chepela may have defeated Kabanda, a Bisa chief south of the Chambeshi, in the course of his rebellion against Chinchinta*, which took place in about 1827.[87] And once he had become Chitimukulu, Chileshye* assigned Lupi, west of the Lukulu and south of Ituna, to his half-brother Kabwibwi. Kabwibwi supplanted the former Bisa chief,[88] and the new chieftainship continued in Kabwibwi's matrilineage (which was of Lungu, not Bemba, origin).[89]

The first major Bemba advances into Bisa country, from the Muchinga hills in the east to the Chimpili hills in the west, can be precisely dated from the journal of Antonio Gamitto, who with Monteiro traversed the area on his way to and from Kazembe's in 1831–2. As the Portuguese descended the western slopes of the Muchinga, they saw

> many human remains which, we were told, were those of Bemba and Bisa killed in various fights. The Bisa here submitted to his conqueror and still lives with his wife and children, not migrating on account of his great age.

This Bisa headman, Chintu Kapenda, said that

> the land has not been cultivated for two years; he said that in the time of the Bisa there were many villages here, as also in the hills, and both hills and plain had been cultivated. Since that time it had been, as we see it, peopled only with skeletons, for it was here that the Bisa had gathered for their final and strongest resistance; but in the last series of fights, in which the Bemba lost many men, the Bisa succumbed.[90]

Many Bisa migrated eastwards across the Luangwa and settled among the Chewa.[91]

The Portuguese found Chinama firmly under Bemba rule. The then Mwansabamba, Mwaba Mwelwa, had fled into the Muchinga hills.[92]

[87] See above, p. 104.

[88] This was perhaps Nkaka Kasela (Munsoma, T1), though according to Nshilika Mwenya (T1) the original rulers were two Bisa women, Chanda *upapwa* and Mumbi Munkusa. Brelsford says that Lupi was 'cut from country held by Mwamba' (*Aspects*, p. 8).

[89] See above, pp. 97, 100; Nshilika Mwenya, T1; Kasama DNB III, p. 32; and cf. Brelsford, *Succession*, p. 44.

[90] Gamitto, *King Kazembe*, I, 164, 166

[91] *Ibid.*, I, p. 55. Some had done so by 1798, seeking more fertile land (Burton, *Cazembe*, pp. 78, 93).

[92] Thomas, *Bisa*, pp. 40–1; though this confused record of Bisa traditions anachronistically juxtaposes the first Bemba invasions with those of 'Yeke'.

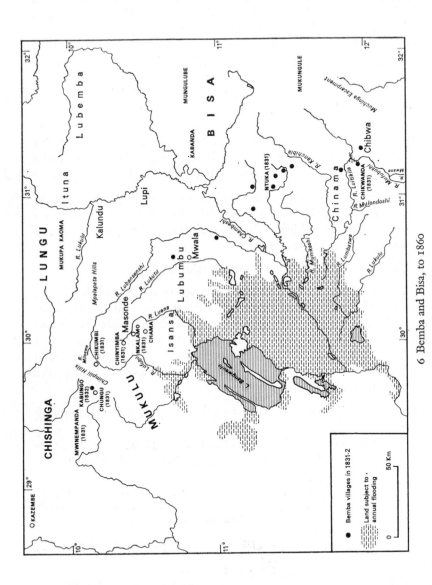

6 Bemba and Bisa, to 1860

Instead, the Portuguese paid a road toll to Mwenya, sister of the intruding Bemba chief, Simukamba. His village, surrounded by a half-finished stockade, was situated between the Mufubushi stream and the Luitikila river.[93] It is clear that 'Simukamba' was in fact Nkumbula, sons of a younger sister of the mother of Chileshye*, who according to both Bemba and Bisa traditions sent Nkumbula to rule in Chinama after a Bemba expedition had subdued the Bisa there.[94] Nkumbula was evidently the first chief to be called Chikwanda, a title which has been held by subsequent chiefs of Chinama. The name 'Simukamba' does not seem to be recognised in the area today, but 'Shilukamba' was a praise-name for Chikwanda I Nkumbula,[95] and the Bemba royal genealogy supports the inference that he flourished around 1830.

Gamitto was naturally much concerned at the encroachment of the Bemba upon a trade route which the Portuguese hoped to open to their own trade, and he made enquiries among both Bisa and Bemba about the origins of their war.

It was in 1826 that the war between the two tribes started, and it originated in a raid which the Bemba made upon neighbouring Bisa. The latter took vengeance: but the Bemba joined in great force, fell upon the Bisa, took and destroyed the first villages, killed anyone they met, and in the plunder they found cloth, beads, etc. Attracted by these spoils, and encouraged by their initial victory, and knowing that the Bisa, as traders, had good cloth, they came in greater numbers and began to invade; and because at first on the frontier they met with little resistance, they carried on and conquered the country, destroying whatever they encountered. The Bisa meanwhile, who were unprepared, retired until they managed to concentrate their forces and began to resist. But by now the conquerors had become exceedingly strong, so that the Bisa were destroyed in many battles, and the remainder, unable to resist, left their vast territory completely abandoned to the conquerors, and

[93] Gamitto, *King Kazembe*, I, pp. 168–9. Gamitto calls the stream 'Mufutushe'.
[94] Chief Nkula, 24 August 1957 (A. I. Richards, fieldnotes); Mushindo, *History*, s. 48; Labrecque, 'Origines', p. 296; Thomas, *Bisa*, p. 40. I suggest below (p. 180) why Chinama was not given to any closer relative of Chileshye.
[95] Labrecque, 'Origines', p. 296; Brelsford, *Succession*, pp. 32, 39 (following Goodall); Nkula, 24 August 1957 (A. I. Richards, fieldnotes; Shimakasa Chitolo, 29 June 1965. My informants at Chikwanda's were uncertain about this identification. They said that *shilukamba* meant 'fierce', but in view of the later history of Chikwanda I the name probably derives from *lukamba*, 'conceit' (see below, p. 117).

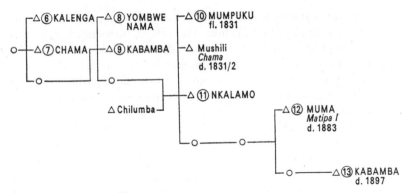

Fig. 6 Bisa chiefs of Lubumbu. From Chota Mwila (holder of the Bukunkwe title in Lubumbu), as recorded by Mr Medard Kasese; see also Munsoma, T1.

this is now in Bemba hands right up to the Muchinga hills which, perhaps because they do not consider there is much in them, they have not entered.[96]

At Chintu Kapenda's some Bemba specifically told the Portuguese that

the Bisa had always much good cloth since they were close to the Europeans, and when the Bemba wanted to go and sell ivory they would not let them pass, and this was the main reason for the war, and it would not finish until they reached the Luangwa.[97]

It may also be presumed that, in a region where salt was very scarce, the Chibwa salt marsh around the Luitikila–Mufubushi confluence was a scarcely less powerful inducement to Bemba conquest: Chikwanda I had built his village immediately to the south of it.[98]

As the Portuguese continued to the northwest in October 1831, they found Bemba headmen as far west as the Chambeshi river; one of them, Ntuka, felt strong enough to dispense with a stockade round his village. Beyond the Chambeshi, the Portuguese encountered Bisa chiefs and headmen until they reached the territory of Mwinempanda on Kazembe's borders; but these had also suffered from Bemba attacks and nine months later there were two Bemba headmen between the Chambeshi and the Lukutu river.[99] Many Bisa in these parts were in

[96] Gamitto, *King Kazembe*, II, p. 161

[97] *Ibid.*, I, p. 165. For the impact of the Bemba on this trade route, see below, pp. 191–2.

[98] Gamitto described the salt-making on his return from Kazembe's: *King Kazembe*, II, p. 132. See also below, pp. 187, 359.

[99] Gamitto, *King Kazembe*, I, pp. 171, 176; II, pp. 136–7, 139–40, 142–4

hiding from the Bemba, living on wild fruits and fish: in Gamitto's words,

> The land we are in shows many traces of great population. We are
> told that in these parts there were many battles between Bemba and
> Bisa, and when the Bemba were victorious they destroyed every-
> thing. There are now only the remains of ruined cassava gardens.[100]

After crossing Lubumbu, the Portuguese reached the village of Chama, chief of Isansa, and further on they met his brother Nkalamo.[101] (We may infer from this that the chief of Lubumbu at this time was their elder brother Mumpuku, since both Chama and Nkalamo were living far from the known capital sites of Lubumbu chiefs.)[102] Beyond Nkal-amo, the Portuguese came to the village of Chinyimba, chief of Masonde: this was

> encircled by a strong stockade, and the Bisa say that they are still
> prepared to resist as they have done so up to today. Outside the
> stockade is a trench, and they consider themselves well fortified.[103]

But on his return in the following year, Gamitto recorded that Chiny-imba's village, among others, was in ruins, and it is likely that Chiny-imba had fled to the northeast.[104] Gamitto did not this time mention Chama at all, and he had probably been killed in the interval. It is said in Lubumbu that Chama Mushili Chilumba was due to succeed Mumpuku as chief when he was killed by Bemba (led by Kamfwa) on the Miloswe stream in Isansa. Nkalamo was then installed as chief of Lubumbu, but on Chilubi Island, far from the Bemba.[105]

[100] *Ibid.*, I, pp. 182, 188

[101] The Chama whom Gamitto met was called 'Masile Chilumba' (*ibid.*, I, p. 183); he can therefore be identified with Mushili, who according to Munsoma (T1) was, with Mumpuku and Nkalamo, a son of one Chilumba.

[102] Cf. above, p. 109; Munsoma, T2.

[103] Gamitto, *King Kazembe*, I, p. 188. On his outward journey, Gamitto called the chief northwest of Nkalamo 'Cheuhimbe'. Cunnison suggests that 'Chif-wembe is meant' (*ibid.*, I, p. 188, n. 1), but almost certainly the name was really Chinyimba. It was evidently in this same area, which corresponds to Masonde, that Gamitto on his return journey found the ruined stockade of 'Chilando Chinyimba', 'which we had passed on our way to Kazembe' (*ibid.*, II, p. 135), though there is no previous mention of this name. Chilando, we know, was the name of the first Bisa chief in Masonde (see above, p. 109). The 'Chinimba Cam-peze' met by Lacerda in 1798 was evidently much further east (Lacerda, *Diários*, p. 250; Burton, *Cazembe*, p. 94).

[104] Gamitto, *King Kazembe*, II, p. 135, see below, p. 141.

[105] Munsoma, T2

West of Chinyimba's, in the Chimpili hills, Gamitto came in 1831 to the 'Bisa' chief Chikumbi; he remarked that 'The people here are Bisa but they pride themselves on having the manners and customs of the Lunda.'[106] He then reached the stockaded village of the 'Bisa' 'Kankoma', who 'said he was subordinate to the Mwata Kazembe, but he was now under threat of invasion from Bemba'.[107] This 'Kankoma' is clearly the Kakomwe whose village was taken over a few months later by a Bemba headman called Kabungo, and we know that Kakomwe was a holder of the Mukulu chieftainship of Chungu.[108] On his return, in July 1832, Gamitto remarked that the Chimpili hills 'serve today as the boundary between the domains of the Mwata Kazembe and the Bemba'. He exchanged presents of cloth for food with Kabungo, 'the Bemba conqueror', and

> found him sitting on a wooden stool like a Marave Shite [stool], with some thirty Bemba around him. The village is enclosed inside a stockade some two hundred yards in diameter, for it is circular and contains about forty huts.[109]

Gamitto does not indicate Kabungo's relationship to other Bemba chiefs, but he had already observed that the Bemba whom he encountered on the outward journey 'still owe obedience to their own Mambo [Chitimukulu]'.[110]

It appears that both in the countries near Kazembe's borders and in Chinama the Bemba failed to hold their first conquests. In the west, permanent Bemba occupation and overrule was established only in the 1860s, following campaigns against the Lungu of Mukupa Kaoma as well as the Bisa. Kabungo, for example, is not remembered as a per-

---

[106] Gamitto, *King Kazembe*, I, p. 191. Chikumbi was in fact a chief of the Bena Mukulu (Kawambwa DNB II, p. 179), while people in this area today are known as Bena Chishinga.

[107] Gamitto, *King Kazembe*, I, p. 192

[108] *Ibid.*, II, pp. 131–3; African Elders, *History of the Bena Ɖoma*, pp. 45, 73. The genealogy supports this dating for Kakomwe. Chungu was a title subordinate to that of Chibwe at this time. Kakomwe is said by the Mukulu to have lived first at 'Nchinda-Bulungu', and then at Chisuku in Chimpili; he is said to have died soon after moving there (*ibid.*, p. 45). This might be a meiosis for death at Bemba hands, but Gamitto specifies that 'Kankoma' (Kakomwe) had been very old when he saw him in 1831 (*King Kazembe*, I, p. 192). In 1873 Livingstone found the then Chungu living well to the south of the Chimpili hills (*Last Journals*, II, p. 263).

[109] Gamitto, *King Kazembe*, II, p. 132. Kabungo was greatly amused by the antics of the donkey used by the Portuguese.

[110] *Ibid.*, II, p. 110

sonal name for any holder of the Bemba chieftainships now near the Chimpili hills: Chipalo and Muchereka. Bemba traditions strongly suggest that these, together with Tungati and Shimumbi, were not established until long after 1832. In that case, Kabungo was probably killed or forced to withdraw from the Chimpili, and such a setback could account for present ignorance about him.[111]

Control over Lubumbu continued to be disputed by Bemba and Bisa for many years. By about 1840,[112] Nkalamo had been succeeded as chief of Lubumbu by Muma, the first chief to hold the title Matipa. Nkalamo, as we have seen, had lived on Chilubi island for fear of Bemba attacks. Matipa I Muma appears to have reoccupied Mwala, on the mainland, but he was attacked there by Mwamba I and fled to Nsumbu Island.[113] It was perhaps at this time that Bemba raiders killed all Matipa's children.[114] After the death of Mwamba I, in the late 1850s, Matipa I reoccupied Lubumbu, thus prompting a new war with the Bemba.[115]

Further south, in Chinama, the Bemba lost control some time around 1850.[116] Their first chief there, Chikwanda I, estranged himself from his senior relatives and then fell victim to a rebellion by his Bisa subjects. We know that Chikwanda I took tribute to Chitimukulu in 1832,[117] but he evidently asserted the right, as a territorial chief, to receive all tribute due from residents of his territory before forwarding any to more senior chiefs. This right, however, was defied by one Shikatundu, a 'slave' of Mwamba who had come south with Chikwanda and had settled near the Munikashi river, well to the north-west

---

[111] Milambo (9 October 1964) mentions an early chief in Ituna called Kabungo Kabwa, evidently in the same generation as Chiliamafwa. At Nkolemfumu's, I was told that Kabungo in Ituna was in the same generation as Chileshye. In 1966 the then chief Chipalo said that Kabungo was indeed one of the first Bemba chiefs in Luwingu district. But 'the small tribes like the Lungu and Tabwa have their organised chieftainships and therefore some of the Bemba representatives have long been wiped out'. (I owe this report to Mr Felix Chipalo, son of Chief Chipalo: letter of 4 May 1966.)

[112] This very tentative date is based firstly on the assumption that Nkalamo had become chief after 1832 (see above, p. 115), and secondly on the estimate of a British official that Matipa I ruled for fifty years—implying at least that he ruled for a long time before his death in 1883 (Luwingu DNB II, p. 161; Giraud, *Lacs*, p. 284).

[113] Sheane, 'Wemba Warpaths', p. 22

[114] Munsoma, T1; he says that after this disaster Matipa fled to Mwansabamba but then returned and settled at Katenta.   [115] See below, pp. 140–1

[116] See below, p. 119   [117] Gamitto, *King Kazembe*, II, p. 148

of Chibwa. Shikatundu sent tribute to Mwamba,[118] and also angered Chikwanda by refusing to help him fight against Chileshye* and Mwamba I.[119] So Chikwanda killed Shikatundu and thus provoked Chileshye* into declaring, 'You are separate from us now.' Chikwanda moved further south and persuaded many Bisa to reoccupy Chinama and Kasenga, while many of his own Bemba following withdrew to the north. When the Bisa saw that Chikwanda was the only Bemba chief left, they turned against him.[120] According to Bemba sources, a Bisa warrior came to Chikwanda's village, on the Mwane river, early one morning, performed a dance as if to honour him, and then treacherously stabbed him; according to the Bisa, Chikwanda was killed after fleeing from a battlefield.[121]

Among the few Bemba who had remained with Chikwanda I was his nephew, Shimumbi Nsapaila Nkumbula.[122] He now withdrew northwards to the Luitikila and sent for help from the Bemba heartland. Meanwhile, a new Mwansabamba, Nkandu Chiti, had established himself in western Chinama.[123] When Chileshye* sent his sister's son Malama to succeed Chikwanda, Mwansabamba opposed him, and Malama was forced to retreat north across the Chambeshi. Thereafter, as Mushindo concedes, Chinama 'for long lacked a Bemba governor'.[124] The chiefly insignia of Chikwanda—his stool and bow—were rescued, but by Shimumbi, who kept them for himself.[125] As a nephew of the late Chikwanda, Shimumbi was presumably angered at Chileshye's* attempt to transfer the title to one of his own nephews, and thus to the rising *Miti* lineage. Such conflict would account for the stories that Shimumbi—who was also a son of Chileshye's*

---

[118] Luchembe's evidence in Nkuka-Chikwanda dispute, 1918 (NAZ/ZA/1/ 9/27/6/1; hereafter cited as '1918 evidence')

[119] Mushindo, *History*, s. 48   [120] Luchembe, 1918 evidence

[121] Labrecque, 'Origines', pp. 296–7; Milambo, T10; Thomas, *Bisa*, p. 43

[122] Shimakasa Chitolo, 29 June 1965; Goodall, 'Tree'. Shimumbi I Nsapaila died in about 1905 (Luena DNB I, p. 62); his age had been estimated as over ninety (Gouldsbury and Sheane, *Great Plateau*, p. 22), but this may well be an exaggeration. As a military commander of some kind, he was presumably at least twenty, and perhaps a good deal older, when Chikwanda I died. Hence we may suggest that this happened some time between about 1840 and about 1850; other considerations point to the later rather than the earlier date (see below).

[123] Thomas, *Bisa*, pp. 43–4: Nkandu Chiti built his first villages on the Lumbatwa, and between the Luitikila and Mulondoshi rivers.

[124] Thomas, *Bisa*, p. 44; Mushindo, *History*, s. 50. Malama (also called Chileshye Kapalaula) later became Mwamba II.

[125] Milambo, T10; Shimakasa Chitolo, 26 June 1965. Brelsford is clearly mistaken in saying that Bwembya gave them to Chikwanda II (*Succession*, p. 32).

foster-brother Kabwibwi I—quarrelled with Chitimukulu and eventually fled to Lubumbu.[126]

The coming of the Ngoni

The failure of the Bemba to retain Chinama was probably due largely to a preoccupation with the Ngoni. During their northward advance from the Zambezi to Ufipa, in the late 1830s, these warrior herdsmen seem to have bypassed Bemba country. But after the death of their leader Zwangendaba, in about 1845, the Ngoni dispersed from Ufipa under several leaders. Some time around 1850 one Ngoni group, under Mpezeni and Mperembe, moved down the eastern borders of Bemba country, and this prompted Makasa I to assert himself in Nkweto's country, Chilinda. He sent one of his wives to supervise it, but she soon had to call on Makasa for help against the Ngoni. Makasa came with his son Changala I and fought the Ngoni at Chisenga, but both chiefs were killed.[127] Mpezeni then moved on southwards out of Bemba country, but Mperembe led a band of Ngoni across the Chambeshi into Lubemba. They attacked Chileshye's* capital, Kasansama, and though rebuffed there they continued to fight their way westwards through Lubemba, burning two or three villages. The Ngoni entered Ituna but avoided Mwamba's capital and turned south. In due course, they recrossed the Chambeshi and passed through Ichingo, the country of the Bisa chief Kabanda. They eventually settled on his eastern border, near the confluence of the Manshya and Mwaleshi rivers.[128]

Here the Ngoni built a village called Chibungu, from which they raided far and wide. Kabanda himself is said to have held off the Ngoni with guns provided by the Bemba, but to the northeast Ngoni raiders laid waste the country of the Bisa chief Mungulube,[129] and they attacked the Bemba of Nkula, Mwaba and Shimwalule. Mwaba

---

[126] Gouldsbury and Sheane, *Great Plateau*, p. 31; Nshilika Mwenya, T1. It is clear that Shimumbi originally lived in his father's country, Lupi, but the sequence of his later movements is obscure. The Bena Mukulu say that Shimumbi fled to Lubumbu to escape Mwamba's wrath, after being 'framed' by a diviner in Ituna (African Elders, *History of the Bena Ŋoma*, pp. 68–70).

[127] This and the following paragraph are largely based on Mushindo, *History*, s. 53–5. For a detailed discussion of the sources for Bemba–Ngoni history and chronology, see Appendix 3.

[128] Labrecque says that on their way out of Lubemba the Ngoni put to flight Shimumbi Nsapaila; if true, this suggests that he had been restored to favour, at least temporarily ('Origines', p. 302); cf. above, p. 118.

[129] See below, p. 133.

7 Bemba and Ngoni, to 1860

managed to hold the Ngoni at bay, but further north they put Shim-walule to flight and burned his village.[130] The chief of Ichinga, Nkula/ Chewe Kamponge, had retreated eastwards to the Fitondo stream, in Chilinda, but Masaye (son of the previous Chewe) fell upon the Ngoni

---

[130] 'They failed to burn the ancient sacred house of the Bemba chiefs and that led them to expect failure in the war with the Bemba' (Mushindo, *History*, s. 55).

and killed many of them.[131] According to Mushindo, this induced the Ngoni to leave their base at Chibungu and settle elsewhere, but before they did so they had terrorised much country further south. They raided Chinama and the northern Lala, and they finally broke up the Bisa trade route to Kazembe's.[132] It is clear that by this time—the years around 1860—the Bemba had abandoned Chinama, for there is no evidence that they clashed with Ngoni in that area.[133] The chief of Chinama, Mwansabamba Nkandu Chiti, continued to live there throughout the 1860s and the earlier 1870s, though never far from the Bangweulu swamps.[134] But it was not until late in the reign of Chile-shye's* successor Chitapankwa,* long after the Ngoni had withdrawn from the plateau, that Chinama was subjected once more to Bemba rule.

The advent of the Ngoni may have prevented Chileshye* from regaining Chinama, but it provided him with opportunities to extend his influence east of the Chambeshi. After Makasa I had been killed by the Ngoni in Chilinda, Chileshye* summoned various chiefs and councillors to discuss the appointment of a new Makasa. The choice seems to have fallen upon Chansa *wa mbala*, a brother of the late Makasa. But he too was killed by the Ngoni, and he was succeeded by Bwalya, a son of Chileshye* who is said to have governed both Mpanda and Chilinda, and to have resided in both areas. Nkweto appears to have fled from Chilinda after the Ngoni victory, and it was probably Bwalya who was ordered by Chileshye* to guard Chilinda and the eastern borders against the Ngoni.[135] Nkweto evidently returned after a time and was allowed to retain part of Chilinda, but in the north-eastern part of the chiefdom he was henceforth acknow-ledged only as a priest (*shimapepo*), with ritual rather than administra-tive powers.[136]

Chileshye* also challenged the other ancient *yandu* chieftainship

[131] Both Kamponge and Masaye must have been well advanced in years by this time: see above, p. 91.

[132] Luchembe, 1918 evidence; see below, pp. 192–3.

[133] It is thus difficult to accept Thomas' assertion that 'the Bisa had suffered from the Ngoni for two or three years before the latter had come into contact with the Bemba'; in any case, he admits that 'the traditions concerning the Ngoni are most confusing' (*Bisa*, p. 41).

[134] During this period, he occupied villages between the Lukulu and Muni-kashi rivers: cf. Thomas, *Bisa*, pp. 43–8; Livingstone, *Last Journals*, II, p. 297.

[135] Oger, 'Mpanda', 12, 22; Mushindo, *History*, s. 51; and see Appendix 2, Note E. Labrecque says that Nkweto fled from Chilinda to escape the wrath of a man whose daughter he had taken to wife without giving appropriate presents ('Origines', p. 299).

[136] Mubanga, 20 May 1965

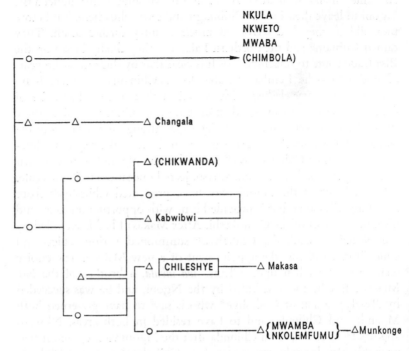

Fig. 7 Bemba chieftainships, *c.* 1860. (*Bena Ŋandu* chiefs in capitals)

east of the Chambeshi, that of Nkula/Chewe. The details of this conflict are obscure, but it is agreed that there was fighting between
Chileshye* and Nkula/Chewe Kamponge. Milambo says that the
latter attacked Chileshye*, while Mushindo says that the fighting was
provoked by a son of Chinchinta*, Nsunge, who had settled in
Ichinga and married there a runaway wife of Chileshye*. Chewe's
life was spared, but many of his people fled eastwards to the Kamanga.[137]

The date of this episode, even in relative terms, is not at all clear.
It is possible that it was this conflict with Chileshye* which accounted
for Chewe's absence from Ichinga when it was invaded by the Ngoni

[137] Milambo, T1; Mushindo, *History*, s. 45; and see Appendix 2, Note J.
Informants in Ichinga from the Chewe lineage did not mention any quarrel
between Chileshye and Chewe. A very garbled account is given by Young
(Chinsali DNB I, pp. 232–4); this is followed by Pirie, 'North-Eastern Rhodesia',
pp. 136–7, and Gouldsbury and Sheane, *Great Plateau*, p. 29. Chileshye's conflict
with Chewe is possibly to be identified with the 'rebellion' against Chileshye
which is mentioned in the history of Kazembe's Lunda: see Appendix 2, Note K.

from Chibungu.[138] It is at any rate likely that this conflict took place during the period—in the 1850s—when eastern Bembaland was threatened by the Ngoni. For Chewe had made an agreement with Mwamba I Mutale whereby, when either man died, the other would take care of his children. When Chileshye* obliged Mwamba to fight Chewe, Mwamba 'fell ill with guilt', and he hoped to revive his spirits by a war against the Iwa of Kafwimbi.[139] Chileshye* joined Mwamba on this campaign, which was to punish Kafwimbi for having given aid to the Ngoni. But Mwamba died on the Mansenke river before reaching Kafwimbi's. So Chileshye* returned to the capital and had Mwamba buried at Mwalule.[140] Chileshye's* only surviving brother, Bwembya, was physically, and perhaps mentally, handicapped, so Mwamba I Mutale was succeeded in Ituna by his eldest sister's eldest son, Malama Chileshye Kapalaula. Within a year, in about 1860, Chileshye* himself was dead.[141]

In the last years of Chileshye's* reign, the growth of Bemba power had been sharply interrupted. Their far-reaching campaigns among the Bisa to the south and southwest had failed to establish permanent Bemba overrule. In the 1830s the Bemba had held sway over the north-eastern plateau from the Luangwa valley to the northern shores of Lake Bangweulu, and they seemed to rival the Lunda kingdom of Kazembe. But when Chileshye* died the borders of effective Bemba control were not much more extensive than at his accession. Makasa's chiefdom, Mpanda, had been conquered well before that, early in the nineteenth century, and the only other new territory still in Bemba hands at Chileshye's* death were the small areas of Kalundu and Lupi,

[138] See above, p. 120.

[139] Mushindo, *History*, s. 52

[140] Tanguy, *Imilandu*, p. 39; cf. Labrecque, 'Origines', p. 285. Mushindo (*loc. cit.*) says Mwamba I was buried in the grove of Bwalya Chabala for lesser *ŋandu* chiefs.

[141] Tanguy, *Imilandu*, p. 41, following *Ifyabukaya*, p. 39. These sources do not explain their date of 1859 for the death of Mwamba I, but it fits well enough with the chronology suggested here for the death of Chikwanda I and the movements of the Ngoni. And there are good grounds for supposing that Chileshye died in about 1860. Makasa VI Mulenga, probably his youngest son, died in 1930 (Oger, 'Mpanda', 35; Labrecque, 'Origines', p. 286): this suggests that Chileshye did not die much before 1860. We know from Livingstone that by 1867 Chitapankwa was Chitimukulu, and according to all traditions Chileshye's immediate successor, Bwembya, ruled only a short time. Thus Chileshye may be presumed to have ruled from about 1827 to about 1860, which agrees with reports that he lived 'many years' (*Ifyabukaya*, p. 39) and that he had a long reign (Mushindo, *History*, s. 56).

west of the Lukulu river. And meanwhile the Bemba heartland was menaced by Ngoni warriors encamped south of the Chambeshi; they had fought their way right through the middle of Lubemba and now raided around its southern and eastern borders.

Thus the early successes of Chileshye's* reign seemed to be overshadowed by more recent setbacks. Yet there is also evidence that Chileshye* had managed to further those internal changes making for greater royal control which had been set in train around the beginning of the century. His brother Mutale had succeeded as chief of Ituna, and had then taken over Miti from the old royal lineage of Nkolemfumu. Mutale had himself been succeeded as Mwamba by his nephew Malama. Across the Chambeshi, Chileshye* had harassed the old royal lineage of Chewe/Nkula, while his perpetual son Makasa had taken over much of Chilinda from another remote royal line, that of Nkweto. Thus the *Miti* lineage had maintained and extended its influence at the expense of other branches of the royal clan. Far more than at the beginning of the century, Bemba power was concentrated in a small group of closely related royals and their agnatic kin. This was to provide a most effective basis for the spectacular expansion of Bemba power in the later nineteenth century.

Chapter 5

The reign of Chitapankwa*
(early 1860s–1883)

The great period of Bemba expansion, which largely created the modern political map of Bembaland, was the quarter-century following the death of Chileshye*. For most of this period, the Bemba were ruled by Chileshye's* nephew Chitapankwa*, who with his own brother Mwamba II pursued with conspicuous success the expansion and concentration of power which had been initiated by earlier rulers. By the end of Chitapankwa's* reign, the *Miti* lineage had gained control over almost all the older chieftainships, while both Chitapankwa* and Mwamba II distributed new conquests among their own sons and close matrikin. And these conquests were extensive. They encompassed those Bisa territories to the south and west which had been gained and then lost in Chileshye's* reign; more Bisa country to the southeast; further encroachments on the Mambwe and Lungu; and part of Tabwa country in the far northwest. It is not possible to determine just how far all this territory was systematically administered and exploited by Bemba chiefs, but it would seem that the extent of Bemba rule increased between two and three times during Chitapankwa's* reign.

This dramatic expansion was encouraged and facilitated by important new developments in the history of east-central Africa. Up to the middle of the nineteenth century, it is likely that geography was the decisive factor in Bemba conquest. Bemba country was poor, but this very fact predisposed the Bemba to prey upon their neighbours: the extension of Bemba rule was probably the outgrowth of a long history of raiding. The central position of the Bemba on the plateau gave them access to the varied resources of their neighbours: to cloth, ironwork, cattle and grain in the north, and to salt and fish in the south and southwest.[1] Bemba imperialism, like other imperialisms, may have

---

[1] Patterns of production and local trade are discussed below, pp. 183–9.

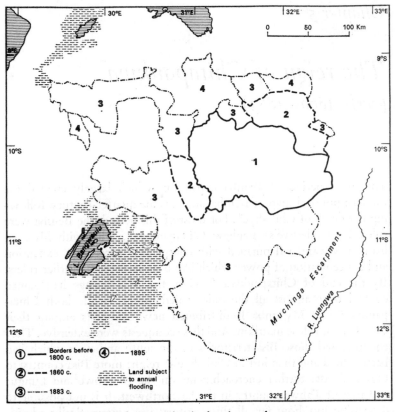

8 Bemba expansion in the nineteenth century

arisen in part from the desire to obtain a surer access to economic assets than periodic raids or trading could provide. Certainly the Bemba, inasmuch as they depended on raids to supplement the meagre resources of their homeland, were more orientated towards warfare and military skills than their more industrious and pacific neighbours. And the central position of the Bemba on the plateau was plainly a strategic as well as an economic advantage. In 1832, Gamitto reported that 'the Bemba . . . are today powerful and feared by all for their fierceness which their territorial position helps them to exercise'.[2] The Bemba had plenty of room to expand while other peoples were driven back into environments which, if not necessarily hostile to human occupation, compelled a more specialised mode of life or made rapid combination difficult: such areas were the Luangwa valley,

[2] Gamitto, *King Kazembe*, II, p. 193

beneath the great Muchinga escarpment, and the swamps of Lake Bangweulu.

From the middle years of the century, however, the external relations of the Bemba began to be shaped by two new factors: the irruption of the Ngoni and the advent of long-distance traders from East Africa. The settlement of Ngoni warriors on the borders of Bemba country challenged Bemba aspirations to hegemony over the north-eastern plateau. In combating the Ngoni menace, the Bemba supplanted them as masters of much country around the borders of Bembaland: as so often, a 'defensive' war gave free rein to aggression. Among the Bisa to the southeast, Ngoni devastation paved the way for subsequent Bemba invasion. By then, the Ngoni had moved north into Mambwe country, and Bemba pressure upon them there led not only to Ngoni withdrawal from the plateau but to Bemba conquest of their Mambwe allies and subjects. Meanwhile, Bemba chiefs had been drawn into the ivory trade of East Africa. Although the long-distance trade of the Bisa had helped to provoke the first wave of Bemba conquests to the southeast, in the 1820s, it was only from the 1860s that the Bemba themselves engaged in such trade to any important degree. The advent of Arabs, Swahili and Nyamwezi seeking ivory, and later slaves, provided new incentives for raiding and conquest; it also enabled Bemba chiefs to increase their military power. It is doubtful whether access to firearms significantly increased Bemba firepower until after Chitapankwa's* death, but it is clear that the ivory trade improved the ability of chiefs to recruit support through the distribution of material wealth among their followers.[3]

THE ACCESSION OF CHITAPANKWA*

When Chileshye* died, in about 1860, he was succeeded by his brother Bwembya*. Bwembya* could not speak properly, and was probably feeble-minded,[4] but this does not seem to have provoked dispute at the time of his accession. We have seen that Chileshye's* other brother, Mutale, had recently been succeeded as Mwamba by their sister's son

---

[3] See below, pp. 189–209.

[4] It is said that when Bwembya's mother, Lukonde Mwaba, was captured by the Lungu (see above, p. 98) she was forced to carry on her head a basket containing the newly severed heads of Bemba opponents of Munkonge, notably that of her own husband (Bwembya's father), Mulenga Mwimba. As the blood dripped down her back, it was licked up by the infant Bwembya, whom she carried on her back. It was this which caused Bwembya's speech impediment (Shimulamba, T1; Chikunga, T3; cf. Labrecque, 'Origines', p. 292).

Malama Chileshye Kapalaula, in preference to Bwembya. Brelsford observes, 'It is difficult to understand why Bwembya should have been allowed to take the Paramountcy when he was not considered to become Mwamba. The spiritual status of the Paramountcy may indicate why even a fool should be given it.'[5] Evidently a distinction was made between removing unworthy holders of this title and actually precluding them from succeeding to it. The former procedure simply accelerates the operation of rules of succession; the latter may be said to interfere with them.[6] It is said that on Chileshye's* death his own son Makasa III brought a tusk to Mwamba II, saying he wished Mwamba to become Chitimukulu, but Mwamba refused and pointed instead to Bwembya.[7]

There was no hesitation about removing Bwembya* as soon as his infirmity proved a positive liability. For the Bemba faced a grave external threat. In recent years, Ngoni based on Chibungu, just beyond the southern borders of Bembaland, had raided both the Bisa and the eastern Bemba. And shortly before or after Bwembya's* accession these Ngoni moved north once more. They marched through Ituna into Lungu country, where they built up a new power-base and impeded Bemba access to their northern raiding-grounds.[8] If the Ngoni menace was to be dealt with, it was clearly necessary to have an alert and resolute Chitimukulu.

Bwembya's* foremost critic was his nephew (and Mwamba II's brother), Mutale Chitapankwa, who was evidently a pugnacious and ambitious young man.[9] Chitapankwa had once made war on Chileshye* and sought help against him from the Lungu of Tafuna, but they insulted him, so he went back and made his peace with Chileshye*.[10] Chileshye* gave Chitapankwa his daughter Kafula in marriage and assigned him a village on the Mabula stream,[11] but he does not seem to

[5] Brelsford, *Succession*, p. 5

[6] Gluckman cites a similar case among the Zulu: their king Mpande upheld the law in finding against one of his favourites but then tried to nullify the verdict by wiping out the successful litigant and his family (M. Gluckman, *Analysis of a Social Situation in Modern Zululand*, Rhodes–Livingstone Paper no. 28, Manchester 1958, p. 34, n. 2).

[7] Nkula, 21 October 1924, in 1924 succession dispute (enclosure in Mporokoso DNB, hereafter cited as 'Willis Enquiry').

[8] See Appendix 3, and below, p. 143.

[9] Chitapankwa was a praise-name, from *kutapa* and *nkwa*: 'he who seizes slabs of bark' (cf. Labrecque, 'Origines', p. 278).

[10] Milambo, T15; 30 September 1964

[11] Goodall, 'Tree' (it is not clear when Chitapankwa married Kafula); Milambo, T15

have given him any further appointment. Thus by the time of Bwembya's accession Chitapankwa would have been impatient to obtain
any chieftainship. The *bakabilo* agreed that Bwembya* should be
replaced, but they first called on Chitapankwa's eldest brother,
Mwamba II, to succeed as Chitimukulu. Mwamba, however, said that
he was very well satisfied with his own post and wished Chitapankwa
to succeed instead.[12] It has been said that Mwamba disapproved of the
whole business, and that Chandamukulu (presumably the last of the old
lineage, in Iyaya) told Mwamba not to succeed or he would die.[13]
Fears of supernatural retribution may also have been reinforced by
economic considerations: Mwamba may already have begun trading
with East Africans whose trade route to Kazembe's passed near his
north-western borders, and he may have reckoned that as Chitimukulu
he would be less well placed for such trade, and the power to be derived
from it.[14]

To secure the removal of Bwembya*, Chitapankwa and his supporters employed a stratagem. A young man called Mutale Sichansa,
son of a sister of Chitapankwa and Chileshye Kapalaula, was despatched to Bwembya's* house, while Bwembya's* attention was
distracted by a dance performed by Chitapankwa.[15] Mutale Sichansa
managed to lay hands on Bwembya's* *babenye*—his spears and bow—
and handed them over to Chitapankwa, who was then installed as
Chitimukulu. Bwembya went away to a Mambwe village, on the
Kafika stream, and died there.[16] Chitapankwa* may well have met with
opposition from his equally fierce brother Sampa. There is one tradition that Sampa had already fought Bwembya* and prevented Makasa
from paying homage to him. To safeguard his own position, Chitapankwa* had to fight and defeat Sampa, and in due course he sent
him across the Chambeshi to Ichinga, no doubt to put him at a safe
distance from the capital.[17]

It is noteworthy that the events leading to Chitapankwa's* accession

---

[12] Milambo, T1; Shimulamba, T1; Chileshye Mukulu, T1
[13] Evidence by Mwamba IV Kanyanta and Makasa (VI) in Willis Enquiry,
1924   [14] Cf. below, pp. 193–4.
[15] Chileshye Mukulu, 15 April 1965
[16] Milambo, T1; Shimulamba, T1, n. 42. Chitapankwa appears to have married
Kasuba, formerly the senior wife of Chileshye (Goodall, 'Tree'); this would have
implied that Chitapankwa saw himself as succeeding directly to Chileshye, since
an essential part of Bemba succession is inheritance of the predecessor's senior wife.
But it may also have involved Chitapankwa in marrying his own mother-in-law,
since Kasuba is said to have been the mother of his wife Kafula (*ibid.*).
[17] Mwamba IV Kanyanta, 20 October 1924: Willis Enquiry

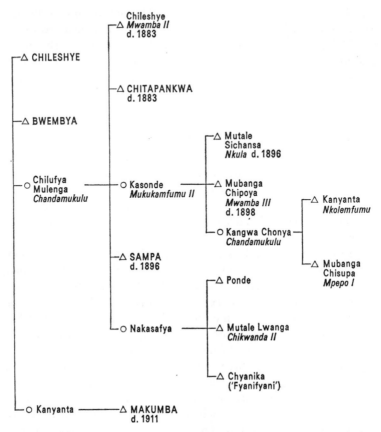

Fig. 8 Bemba royal succession, later nineteenth century. (Chitimukulus in capitals)

do not appear to have involved any members of the senior royal line displaced by Chileshye*: that is, Chimbola and other descendants of Chandaweyaya. They do not appear to have contested the succession of either Bwembya* or Chitapankwa*. Once the latter was installed, the victory of the junior line, of Lukonde Mwaba, seemed assured. Nonetheless, the displaced line might vent their anger, if not in life, then from the grave, and eventually a modus vivendi was reached in which the historic importance of Chandaweyaya and Chimbola was acknowledged. To trace how this came about, it is necessary to go back to the reign of Chileshye*.

When Chileshye* succeeded, he does not seem to have disturbed the succession, or the territories in Iyaya, of either Chandamukulu (Chandaweyaya) or Chimbola. But his mother Lukonde Mwaba became known as *Mukukamfumu*: this is the only other female title among the *bena ŋandu*, and it is associated with Kabumba, an area south of the Kalungu river. Lukonde Mwaba is the first known holder of this title, so we may assume that it was created for her in order to increase the prestige of the *Miti* line. (It is not clear whether she actually went to live in Kabumba.)[18] Some time later, Chitapankwa* took the country of Chibundu, between the Lukulu and the Chambeshi, from the Bisa chief Kabanda. He gave Chibundu to his mother, Chilufya Mulenga.[19] Then Chandamukulu (? Nalumya 'Chanda *wa mwefu*') died in Iyaya, and Chitapankwa* seized the opportunity to try to obtain the title for the *Miti* line. He sent his mother to Iyaya, and the inheritance ceremony was under way when a lion broke into the village and seized one of Chilufya's slaves.[20] This was regarded as a bad omen; it seemed that Chimbola, the (absent?) owner of the country was angry, so Chilufya returned to Chibundu. She was given the title Chandamukulu, but the Iyaya line were allowed to summon Chifunda, a sister of the deceased Chandamukulu, and give her the title Chanda *weyaya*.[21] This title is honorary: Chandaweyaya is allowed the dignity of a *namfumu* ('mother of chiefs'), but she cannot bear chiefs. Indeed, a crucial condition was attached to the title, that the holder be celibate.[22] Not surprisingly, the people of Iyaya continue to call this *namfumu* Chandamukulu, and refer to the *Miti* titleholder merely as 'Chanda wa Chibundu'.

Meanwhile, Chimbola *wa museshi* had died, and had been succeeded

[18] Milambo (1 October 1964) said that Mukukamfumu (? sc. Mandechanda) was given a village in this area by Chitimukulu Ponde (1918–22).

[19] Milambo (30 September 1964; 1 October 1964) said that Chibundu was occupied by Lukonde Mwaba, in the time of Chileshye, and that Chilufya Mulenga grew up there. I follow here the versions of Chandamukulu (13 August 1964) and Chinga *wa labwalabwa*, a priest for the displaced Bisa (13 December 1964). Milambo says that Chilufya became Chandamukulu in the reign of Chileshye; Chimbola (8 June 1965) says she succeeded in the reign of Sampa.

[20] It is said at Kabanda's that Kabanda gave Chibundu to the Bemba in return for an ivory tusk, as he already had a big country and couldn't properly look after this area across the Chambeshi (Kabanda, 13 December 1964).

[21] Chandaweyaya, T1; 23 September 1964; 30 November 1964; Chibwe, T1. Chifunda had gone to the Mambwe chief Nsokolo with her uncle (but perpetual son) Chinchinta, when he was expelled from the Chitimukuluship.

[22] Brelsford (*Succession*, p. 13) says that Chandaweyaya must be past child-bearing age: I gathered that, as with the *bamukabenye* (female keepers of relic-houses), the point was simply that the holder must live alone. In practice, of course, this comes to the same thing: in 1965 Chandaweyaya said she could have succeeded thirty years earlier if she had been willing to leave her husband then. She did so only in 1958, and she was a venerable old lady in 1965.)

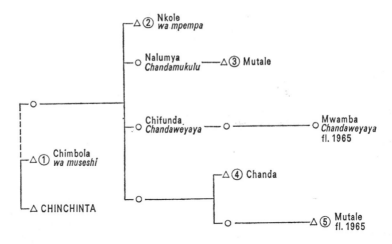

Fig. 9 Chimbola and Chandaweyaya. From Chimbola 5, 9 September 1964, and Chandaweyaya Mwamba, 23 September 1964.

by Nkole *wa mpempa*. (It is not clear where Nkole was living at this time.) After Chitapankwa's* death (in 1883). Nkole *wa mpempa* was suspected of having had him poisoned. Nkole (or his grandson Mulemfwe)[23] was made to undergo a poison ordeal. But Nkole survived, and the people of Chitimukulu (the *bakabilo?*), ashamed of their mistake, said, 'We are sorry. He belongs to our family. It is best to live at peace with him.' They decided that an elephant would be meagre compensation, so they gave Chimbola an area called Matengele, which had been occupied by Chilangwa, a son of Makasa, after the latter had taken it from the Mambwe of Mvula.[24]

THE SOUTHEAST: ICHINGA AND THE BISA

The chief problem facing Chitapankwa* during the early years of his reign, in the middle 1860s, was the Ngoni settlement in Lungu, and

[23] Chimbola, 8 June 1965
[24] Chibwe, T1 and 9 September 1964; Chibwe and Chimbola, 8 June 1965; Oger, 'Mpanda', 29. Chibwe also traced the remorse of the *Miti* lineage to Chilufya Mulenga's inauspicious attempt to settle in Iyaya. Brelsford incorrectly says that Chimbola was given an area on the 'Weyaya stream' (*Succession*, p. 13); in fact, he left Iyaya to go to Matengele. It was presumably after Chimbola settled in Matengele that Mfungo, a junior member of his lineage, occupied Makalandu, further to the west (Abercorn DNB I, p. 5; Brelsford, *Succession*, p. 37; *Aspects*, p. 10). Chilangwa later moved into Mambwe country north of Mpanda (see below, p. 247).

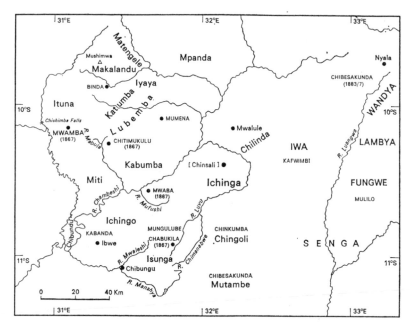

9 The eastern borders

later in Mambwe country. But for the time being he deferred any serious attempt to dislodge them. Instead, he turned his attention to those parts of Bemba and Bisa country south of the Chambeshi which had been raided by the Ngoni during their sojourn at Chibungu, on the Manshya. The Bemba seem first to have occupied Isunga, the country of the Bisa chief Mungulube, who had earlier been driven out by Ngoni and sought refuge among the Senga.[25] Early in 1867, on his way west from the Luangwa valley, Livingstone found a 'deputy of Chitapangwa' lording it over a Bisa headman, Chabukila, in what may have been Mungulube's former capital, near the upper Luvu river.[26]

[25] E. Munday to H. G. Willis, 25 April 1930, Chinsali DNB IV/Q; D.C. Chinsali to D.C. Mpika, 2 June 1939, Chinsali DNB III/D. The Bemba allowed Mungulube to return, but only to placate the local ancestral spirits (*ibid.*, and Brelsford, *Aspects*, p. 6). Mungulube's borders ran along the Mufushi, Lumpene, Chimanabwe and Manshya rivers; the Bisa blame the British for the loss of his territory (Mungulube, 11 May 1965 and T1; Kabanda, T1).

[26] The village was called 'Lisunga' (Livingstone, *Last Journals*, I, pp. 174–5), and Mungulube has usually lived close to the upper Luvu. The neighbouring Bisa chief Chibesakunda has a perpetual son called Chabukila, but the name is not uncommon.

Soon after this occupation of Isunga, Chitapankwa* intervened in the affairs of Ichinga, the Bemba chiefdom lower down the Luvu. Some years before, Chileshye* had quarrelled with the chief there, Nkula/Chewe Kamponge,[27] and Chitapankwa* was now prompted to replace the old royal lineage in Ichinga with his own close kin. Kamponge died soon after Chileshye*, and a great dispute broke out over the succession.[28] Chikabala, a holder of the minor *ŋandu* title Kabungo and probably a nephew of Kamponge, claimed the Nkula title but was suspected of having killed Kamponge. An appeal was made to Chitapankwa*, who at this stage does not seem to have been over-anxious to meddle with the succession. He recommended Chimfwembe, another nephew of Kamponge, and Chimfwembe duly succeeded. But he died soon afterwards; again foul play was suspected, and one faction again asked Chitapankwa* to make an appointment. Meanwhile, another faction (led by Nsunge, a son of Chimfwembe) approached Mwaba, the chief in nearby Nkulungwe, and invited him to succeed. This infuriated Chitapankwa*, who had already been irritated by Mwaba's pretensions.[29] Chitapankwa* set off for Ichinga himself, and summoned Mwaba to a meeting. Forewarned of death by his diviners, Mwaba went, and was killed in an ambush near the site of the modern Chinsali, not earlier than January 1867.[30] Chitapankwa* then attacked Nsunge, but without success.

Kabungo had again laid claim to the Nkula title, but again his claim was rejected. None of Chimfwembe's nephews were thought fit to rule, so Chitapankwa* installed as regent his daughter Mande Namusenge. Mande employed many elephant hunters (for by this time East African ivory traders were active in the region), and one day a hunter discovered Chimfwembe's body and regalia. Mande had him reburied at Mwalule[31] and took over his relics. Those who had offended Chita-

[27] See above, p. 121.

[28] This paragraph is based on Mushindo, *History*, s. 59–60. In 1924, Mporokoso stated that Chileshye drove out the original Nkula, so that there was no Nkula until Chitapankwa appointed Sampa (Willis Enquiry). But Mushindo, who has lived for many years in Ichinga, would seem to be a better authority.

[29] Milambo, June 1964

[30] In that month, Livingstone visited Mwaba (*Last Journals*, I, p. 179) and the Bemba traditions indicate that after Chitapankwa killed Mwaba Kabundi there was some interruption of the succession (see below, p. 135). It has also been said that it was not Chitapankwa but Sampa who killed Mwaba (Chief Nkula, 24 August 1957: A. I. Richards, fieldnotes).

[31] This is a significant detail, as it implies that it was not normal practice for chiefs in Ichinga to be buried at Mwalule, though all the evidence suggests that they were.

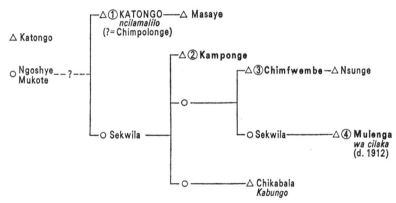

Fig. 10 Katongo/Chewe. Composite genealogy based on Mushindo, Sewuka and Mutashya.

pankwa* by inviting Mwaba to succeed fled from Ichinga, along with Kapeya, a nephew of Mwaba, and Kabungo. They went to the upper reaches of the Luangwa valley, to Nyala and the hills in Fungwe country.[32] Two of Chimfwembe's nephews, Mulenga *wa cilaka* and Chabatama, also fled through Senga country to Nyala.[33] Such refugees were noted by Europeans in the far northeast in 1887 and 1897.[34]

After killing Mwaba, Chitapankwa* seems to have installed a new Mwaba of his own choosing, his sister's son Mutale Sichansa. A son of Chileshye*, Mukwikile, may also have spent a short time in Nku-lungwe.[35] But the succession soon reverted to Mwaba's own family, for Mutale left Nkulungwe to take over Ichinga.[36] Understandably, there is no tradition at Mwaba's of such an interruption in the succession, though one informant there said that his mother's mother's father Mwaba Kabundi was indeed killed at Chinsali by Chitapankwa*.[37]

Some time after Mande settled in Ichinga, Chitapankwa* sent his brother Sampa to relieve her there. By all accounts, Sampa was a prickly and stubborn character; he may already have disputed

---

[32] Mushindo, *History*, s. 60

[33] Mbutuka, 14 May 1965; Mpyana Bwalya, T1; Chinsali DNB I, pp. 230, 233

[34] By 1887 a Bemba chief called 'Tituna' had settled in Wandia country, where the Livingstonia mission established a station called Chirenji: the Wandia chief 'Mweniwanda' relied on Tituna for support against raids by other Bemba (Bain to Laws, 2 June 1887, NLS 7890). The name Tituna does not seem to be recognised in Ichinga today, but it is fairly clear that this is a reference to one of the refugees from Ichinga. The same migration may also account for the two Bemba villages noted in Lambya and Fungwe country in 1897 (*Aurora*, 1 December 1897, 1 February 1898). [35] See below, p. 138.

[36] Brelsford, *Succession*, p. 38   [37] Kapasa Matumbo, T1

Chitapankwa's* accession; and in any case he soon fell out with Mande and her husband, Chipala Nkungulu.[38] When Chitapankwa* heard of the trouble between Sampa and Mande, he made ready to fight Sampa, who thereupon moved out of Ichinga to a site in Bisa country on the Mwaleshi river. Sampa's other brother, Mwamba II Chileshye Kapalaula, gave Sampa a small area near Chishimba Falls, but Sampa complained that there was no game or fish, and he returned to the Mwaleshi. But by this time the area was occupied by Sampa's brother-in-law Chonya. Sampa fought Chonya, and blinded him; to escape Chitapankwa's* wrath he fled further west, to Ibwe, in the country of the Bisa chief Kabanda. Here Sampa remained until Chitapankwa's* death in October 1883.[39]

To replace Sampa in Ichinga, Chitapankwa* sent his sister's son Mutale Sichansa, giving him his daughter Mande in marriage and telling him to help her against the Ngoni.[40] This suggests that Mutale had become Nkula by 1870;[41] moreover, the Bemba were visited in 1869 or 1870 by the Arab trader Tippu Tip, who before going on westwards to Katanga traded with 'Mwamba, Kitimkaro and Shanza, chiefs of Ruemba. These were the three most important.'[42] Tippu Tip bought ten loads of ivory from 'Shanza' and though he does not make it clear where 'Shanza' was at the time, we may assume that 'Shanza' was Mutale Sichansa, who as Nkula might well be considered one of the most important Bemba chiefs.

As chief of Ichinga, Mutale Sichansa was indeed well placed for trading in ivory, for he was well within striking distance of the

[38] The story goes that Sampa took offence when Mande brought him a buck without its head (Mushindo, *History*, s. 61). Bush (in Brelsford, *Aspects*, p. 43) tells the same story, though he says that Sampa had only been sent to 'help' Mande: perhaps the quarrel had something to do with Sampa exceeding his mandate from Chitapankwa. Sampa's nephew, Kanyanta, said in 1924 that Chitapankwa drove Sampa away after the latter had fought with Mande's husband (Willis Enquiry).

[39] Mushindo, *History*, s. 61–3; Shimulamba, T1, n. 43. Brelsford says that an area east of the Chambeshi, which had formerly belonged to Nkolemfumu, was transferred by Chitapankwa to Sampa when the latter went to Ichinga (*Succession*, p. 28). I am disinclined to accept this (cf. above, p. 87, n. 28). Nkolemfumu Mubanga occupied part of Kabanda's country, but probably not until about 1870 (see below, p. 160). I was unable to obtain any coherent account of these events from my informants, though it was agreed that Sampa lived at Ibwe.

[40] R. P. Bush, in Brelsford, *Aspects*, p. 44

[41] At about that time the Bemba drove the Ngoni off the plateau (see below, p. 145). I do not, however, know where the Ngoni mentioned here were based; they are perhaps more likely to have come from Mbelwa or Mpezeni east of the Luangwa, than from Mperembe in Mambwe country.

[42] Tippu Tip, *Maisha*, p. 47

elephant herds in the Luangwa valley. And Ichinga, on the borders of Senga and Bisa country, also proved a convenient base for slave-raiding. In May 1883 the French explorer Giraud reached Ichinga from the northeast, and his description of 'Mkéwé' (Chewe, i.e. Nkula) testifies to Mutale Sichansa's continuing business with foreign traders.

Mkéwé a une quarantaine d'années; gros et gras comme tous les chefs de l'Uemba, qui ne vivent que de pombé, il est vêtu d'un nombre incalculable de bracelets de grosses perles rouges qui lui couvrent la poitrine, les bras et les jambes; au-dessous d'un abdomen rebondi, un morceau d'étoffe également rouge est jeté avec néglig-ence sur ses jambes; la figure est légèrement peinte de même couleur; les yeux, pleins de finesse, sont sournois et faux. Il est assis le dos appuyé à la palissade; une centaine d'indigènes armés d'arcs ou de vieux fusils à pierre font le cercle, accroupis autour de lui. Un orchestre, composé de six tambours et de trois chanteurs, hurle et bougle les louanges du chef sur un mode impossible à rendre.[43]

Giraud found several Nyamwezi traders at Nkula's court; it is clear that Nkula was able to obtain guns, cloth and other imports from them quite independently of Chitapankwa*. Indeed, the Nyamwezi in-formed Giraud that south of the Chambeshi all the chiefs asserted their independence. They said, moreover, that Sampa was at war with Nkula, which bears out the evidence about their relations from oral traditions. Sampa was said to have twice as many guns as Nkula, which he apparently gained by raiding caravans rather than by trading with them.[44]

Nkula seems to have extended his authority south of Ichinga into

[43] Giraud, *Lacs*, p. 238: 'Chewe is in his forties. He is large and fat like all Bemba chiefs, who live only on beer. He is dressed in a multitude of chains of big red glass beads which cover his chest, his arms and his legs. Beneath his ample paunch, a piece of red cloth is casually thrown over his legs. His face is lightly painted in the same colour; his eyes, full of cunning, are shifty and deceitful. He sits with his back resting against the stockade; around him, in a circle, crouch a hundred natives armed with bows or old flintlocks. A band of six drums and three singers roar and bellow the praises of the chief in a musical mode impossible to record.'
The beads worn by Nkula perhaps included the scarlet coral beads listed by Burton; they were known in Swahili as 'town-breakers' because 'the women are mad for them' (*Lake Regions*, II, p. 392).
[44] Giraud, *Lacs*, p. 242. Giraud does not mention the name Sampa, but his 'Marukutu' can easily be identified with Sampa; not only did Marukutu live to the west of 'Mkéwé'; we are later told that he succeeded Chitapankwa as Chiti-mukulu (*Lacs*, p. 532). For trade in Ichinga, see below, pp. 195, 208.

Isunga, the previously conquered chiefdom of Mungulube.[45] And during the 1870s the Bisa chiefdoms east of Ichinga also fell into Bemba hands. Chingoli, the country of Chinkumba, was taken over by Bwalya, a son of Chileshye*. This man had originally been appointed by Chitapankwa* to rule in Mwaba's country, Nkulungwe, at about the same time as Mande took over Ichinga.[46] The people in Nkulungwe brought some complaint against Bwalya (now called Mukwikile), and Chitapankwa* sent him to settle in Ichinga. After a war with the Iwa chief Kafwimbi, Chitapankwa* gave Mukwikile the country of Chinkumba.[47] It is significant that the first Mukwikile was a son, not of the reigning Chitimukulu, but of the deceased Chileshye*. Here, as in the succession to Makasa I,[48] we may discern that, once there were chieftainships open to sons of chiefs, Chitimukulu and Mwamba had to take account of the ambitions of their predecessors' sons. The fact that such chieftainships were considered to stand in a relationship of perpetual kinship to those of Chitimukulu and Mwamba, regardless of the occupants' identities, hindered these senior chiefs from using such posts simply for the advancement of their own offspring. Consequently there was continuing pressure to provide new territories for sons of Chitimukulu.

Meanwhile, Nkula Mutale Sichansa placed his own son Ndakala in charge of Mutambe, the country of Chibesakunda.[49] The circumstances of this conquest are obscure. It may be that Chitapankwa* had attacked and killed Chibesakunda at the request of another Bisa chief, Mukungule:[50] it is also said that Ndakala had 'helped' Chibesakunda and Chinkumba against the Ngoni, and that Ndakala then drove Chibesakunda away to Senga country.[51] The Bisa of Chibesakunda do not explicitly refer to such conflict with the Bemba, but they indicate that Chibesakunda Mwelwa lived far to the northeast of Mutambe, and

[45] This is to be inferred from the fact that no other Bemba chief took over Isunga. There may in any case have been few Bisa left in the area.

[46] See above, p. 135. This Bwalya is to be distinguished from his brother of the same name, who became Makasa III. Brelsford (*Succession*, p. 43) seems to be mistaken in saying that Mukwikile I was a son of Chitapankwa.

[47] Mukwikile I, statement dated 1913 (Chinsali DNB I, p. 261); Mubanga V Mutale (formerly Mukwikile III), T1; Kabwela, 10 May 1965

[48] See above, p. 121.

[49] Labrecque, 'Origines', p. 311; Nkula's statement, 1917 (Chinsali district files), but see also Mushindo, *History*, s. 51

[50] Mushindo, *History*, s. 60

[51] Mbutuka, 14 May 1965; Mukwikile, 22 April 1965. It is probable that Chibesakunda was still in Mutambe in 1867, for Livingstone then noted in his diary 'Matambi o Chabisa Kondo' (NLS 4091/12).

we know from European sources that Chibesakunda was living at the head of the Luangwa valley in 1883 and 1887.[52]

THE SOUTHWEST: MWAMBA II, THE LUNGU AND THE BISA

While Chitapankwa* had consolidated and extended Bemba power east of the Chambeshi in the 1860s, his brother Mwamba II Chileshye had been active in the southwest: during this period, he reconquered those areas north of Lake Bangweulu which had been first invaded by the Bemba in the 1830s. This campaign followed upon a renewal of war with the Lungu of Mukupa Kaoma, whose earlier invasion of Ituna had been repelled by Mwamba I.[53] Soon after his accession, and before Chileshye's* death,[54] Mwamba II set about taking further vengeance on the Lungu by attacking the junior Lungu chief Chitoshi and his brother Chibuta. Against them, Mwamba II sent his son Mutale, who then or later succeeded to the title of Munkonge.[55] Munkonge II Mutale killed Chitoshi and evidently took possession of his country on the Mukanga river.[56] Munkonge thereby extended his territory well to the west of his base in Kalundu (itself taken long since from the Bisa).

[52] Mwelwa (who was succeeded by Longa, Kaluba and Chibesa, who died in 1934: Chinsali DNB II, p. 16) lived for a time at a place called Chishembe and then moved to another village, where he died, near the Fungwe chief Mulilo (Chabukila, T1; 26 April 1965). Chishembe was evidently situated at the head of the Luangwa valley, for Giraud located 'Kiouesa Pounda' in that area in 1883 (*Lacs*, map f.p. 42, pp. 220–1), and in 1887 a missionary at Chirenji mentioned 'Chiwesakunda, a village less than twenty miles from here' (Bain to Laws, 2 June 1887, NLS 7890).

[53] See above, p. 107.   [54] Cf. Milambo, T7

[55] It would seem that this name was now revived for the ruler of Kalundu, after having lapsed for several years: Munkonge I Mwango had been killed in the time of Mubanga Kashampupo (see above, p. 98); and if he had had any immediate successor this would probably have been another son of Mubanga Kashampupo or a son of his successor Mwamba I Mutale *wa kabwe*.

[56] Milambo, T7; Kasama DNB II, p. 50; Munkonge's present village is in this area, while Chitoshi lives far to the west-northwest. Not only Chitoshi I but his brothers Mwenya and Chibuta are remembered as former inhabitants of Kalundu (Munkonge, 7 December 1964). Some time after 1872, Chitoshi (presumably Chitoshi III, a brother of Munshimbwe) fled to the Chishinga chief Mushyota; the Bemba pursued him but were repulsed on the Munena river (Kawambwa DNB II, pp. 180–1: the event is there dated after the death of the Swahili trader 'Pembamoto', which can be dated to shortly after 1872: see below, p. 155, n. 129). But there may be some confusion with the similar story of flight and resistance by the Lungu in Mukulu country: see below, p. 141, n. 61; Mushyota VII, 'History wa Bena Chishinga' (MS)).

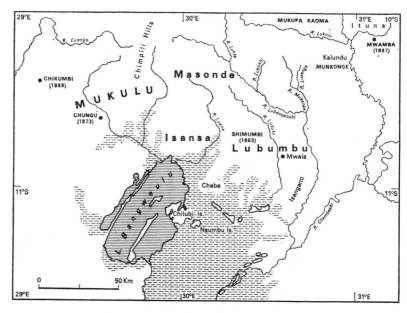

10 The southwest

War with the Lungu drew the Bemba into renewed attacks on Matipa I, the Bisa chief of Lubumbu, for he and the Lungu were allies. Matipa had been forced to withdraw to Lake Bangweulu by Mwamba I,[57] but after the latter's death he drove the Bemba out of Lubumbu, with the aid of magic supplied by the Lungu, and occupied various sites on the mainland: Mungombe, Lwata and Chaba.[58] Meanwhile, Mwamba II had made war upon Mukupa Kaoma III Lubula, who refused to return to Mwamba a wife of his who had fled to Lubula. Mwamba II thus attacked and destroyed Lubula's village on the Lukulu river. Lubula escaped with Mwamba's errant wife and enlisted Matipa's aid. Matipa came north and joined Lubula in a battle with the Bemba on the Lusenga river, but the Bemba won.[59] Lubula

[57] See above, p. 117.

[58] Sheane, 'Wemba Warpaths', p. 23; Munsoma, T1. Sheane says that Matipa reoccupied Mwala, but his informants were probably Bemba and may well have used 'Mwala', a much-occupied site for Lubumbu chiefs, to refer to Matipa's capital, wherever it was. Sheane also says that full details of these wars are recorded in the Luena DNB, but there is no trace of such records in the two volumes now in the National Archives of Zambia. Munsoma's account is obscured by his omission of any reference to actual victories by the Bemba over Matipa.

[59] Sheane, 'Wemba Warpaths', p. 23. His reference to 'Lukutu' can be presumed to be a mistake for 'Lukulu'.

fled west across the Luena river into Isansa, formerly under the Bisa chief Chama.[60] He was evidently pursued by Munkonge II, for the latter occupied Isansa for a time, though in due course it was given by Mwamba II to another of his sons, Tungati.[61] Further north, Mwamba II followed up his defeat of the Lungu by attacking Matipa's subordinate Chinyimba Kabulwe, chief of Masonde. Mwamba occupied Chinyimba's village on the Fipopo stream (a tributary of the Lunte river) and Chinyimba fled south to join Matipa, who had returned to Chaba.[62] Masonde was given to Muchereka, a son of Mwamba I.[63] Further west, the Bemba seized country from Chikumbi, a Mukulu chief; by 1868, Chikumbi had retreated towards the Luongo river, presumably as a result of this invasion.[64] His country was given to Chipalo I Chikulula, who was probably a son of Mwamba II.[65]

Soon after 1870, Mwamba II turned south to punish Matipa for having supported Mukupa Kaoma III in his quarrel with Mwamba.

[60] *Ibid.*; cf. above, p. 115.

[61] Milambo, T9. Some of Lubula's Lungu took refuge in Mukulu country, where they withstood Bemba attacks (African Elders, *History of the Bena Ŋoma*, pp. 67–8).

[62] Munsoma, T1; Labrecque; 'Origines', p. 295; cf. Milambo, T8. Labrecque says that Chinyimba was killed, but this is probably due to exaggeration by Bemba informants. He calls Chinyimba a Lungu chief, but this is doubtless because his village was close to a recent site of Chitoshi's village. Tanguy's report that Mwamba II killed 'Chinyimba Chitoshi' on the Kafipopo, near the Lubushi river (*Imilandu*, p. 34) is probably due to confusion compounded from Labrecque and the story of the death of Chitoshi I, who lived at Fipopo, on the Mukanga stream (see above, p. 139).

[63] Goodall, 'Tree'; Brelsford, *Succession*, p. 43; cf. African Elders, *History of the Bena Ŋoma*, pp. 69–70. According to Shimumbi (29 June 1965), Muchereka himself chased 'Chilando Chipela' to Matipa's; Chilando Chipala was the name of the first Bisa chief in Masonde (see above, p. 109). Bena Mukulu tradition mentions a 'Chilando Chipala' among the Lungu who fled from the Bemba to the Bena Mukulu (African Elders, *History of the Bena Ŋoma*, p. 67; and see above, n. 61).

[64] See above, p. 116; Livingstone, *Last Journals*, I, p. 308; cf. Kawambwa DNB II, p. 179.

[65] Milambo, T9; Labrecque, 'Origines', p. 296; Chikunga, T4. Milambo says that Chipalo succeeded one Chikukula; this is supported by Shimakasa Chitolo (29 June 1965) and perhaps also Goodall ('Tree'), who lists a Chikukula II called Chipalu. Goodall (and thus Brelsford, *Succession*, p. 43) shows this Chipalu as a son of Mwamba I Mutale *wa kabwe*, but he shows Chikukula I Shichitundu as a son of Mwamba II Chileshye Kapalaula; this corresponds with the Chikukula mentioned by Milambo. In 1966 chief Chipalo confirmed that Chipalo I was called Chikukula (Mr Felix Chipalo, letter to the author, 4 May 1966).

By the end of the century, Chipalo had a sub-chief, Kasonka; the first was also a son of Mwamba II (Brelsford, *Succession*, p. 45; cf. Luena DNB I, pp. 82–3).

He expelled Matipa from a village near the lake[66]—presumably Chaba; and Matipa withdrew to the islands.[67] It was probably at about this time that Mwamba II installed, as chief over most of Lubumbu, Shimumbi I Nsapaila, a war-leader under Mwamba and a distant relative, though he may already have been in the area for some time.[68] But Matipa was at odds with his fellow Bisa as well as with the Bemba. He had been turned away from Chilubi Island by another chief, Yombwe, and after an irresolute attempt to seek aid from Mwansabamba, to the southeast, he settled on Nsumbu Island.[69] When Livingstone visited him there in 1873 he gathered that there was rivalry between Matipa and his 'brothers', especially for control over the abundant elephant in the adjacent country.[70] Matipa seems during the 1870s to have expelled Yombwe from Chilubi Island; at all events, Yombwe went to Shimumbi, whose son Kombo-Kombo returned with Yombwe to launch a vain attack on Matipa on Chilubi.[71] In 1883 Matipa died, but his people still occupied Chilubi Island, though many had recently fled from the Bemba.[72]

THE NORTH: THE NGONI, THE MAMBWE AND THE LUNGU

Throughout most of the 1860s there seems to have been little contact between Bemba and Ngoni. The latter seem to have moved north from Chibungu, through Miti and Ituna, into Lungu and Mambwe

[66] Sheane, 'Wemba Warpaths', p. 23; he implies that this happened soon after the Ngoni had finally been defeated by the Bemba (cf. below, p. 145).

[67] Munsoma, T1

[68] Cf. Sheane, 'Wemba Warpaths', p. 23, and above, p. 118. In July 1883 Giraud found Shimumbi I Nsapaila living near Shimumbi's present site, while his son 'Kombo-Kombo' had a small village nearby (*Lacs*, pp. 275–9, and map on p. 220). By the end of the century there were also two minor chiefs in Lubumbu: Kalulu (the first was a parallel cousin of Shimumbi I) and Chibanda (the first was a nephew of Shimumbi I) (Brelsford, *Aspects*, p. 8; *Succession*, p. 32; Goodall, 'Tree'). I do not know when Shimumbi occupied Isangano, southeast of Lubumbu.

[69] Munsoma, T1

[70] Livingstone, *Last Journals*, II, pp. 280, 283

[71] Munsoma, T1; he says Matipa had recruited allies by dispensing cloth and guns obtained from Swahili in exchange for ivory. Sheane ('Wemba Warpaths', p. 23) says that Yombwe and Shimumbi expelled Matipa from Chilubi with great slaughter, but I suspect that this refers either to Yombwe's rebuff of Matipa before the latter moved to Nsumbu, or else to an incident in the 1880s or later (see below, p. 223, n. 40).

[72] Giraud, *Lacs*, p. 284

country without encountering any resistance. The Ngoni then seem to have been preoccupied for some years with the north-western neighbours of the Bemba. Mperembe led one group of Ngoni westwards around the south end of Lake Tanganyika; they were repulsed by the Tabwa of Nsama, some time before 1867, and returned to settle among the Lungu of Tafuna, whom they compelled to work and fight for them.[73] It was perhaps at this stage that Mperembe allied against the Bemba with the Lungu chief Munshimbwe, a son of Mukupa Kaoma III Lubula. Munshimbwe lived near the Luombe river,[74] which still formed the western border of Ituna. The Lungu complained to Mwamba that Munshimbwe had taken all the wives of the previous Mukupa Kaoma, Chikoko.[75] Chitapankwa* then killed Munshimbwe's son Mwaba. Munshimbwe enlisted the help of Mperembe, who may have killed Kamfwa, a son of Makasa III, on his way. The Bemba then fought the Lungu and Ngoni on the Kafubu river, and Munshimbwe was killed.[76] It seems quite possible that this battle took place shortly before Livingstone's visit to the Bemba in 1867: at a village in Ituna, not far north of Mwamba's, he noted that 'a few trophies from Mazitu [Ngoni] are hung up. Chitapangwa had twenty-four skulls ornamenting his stockade . . . it is likely that Mochimhe will be effectually checked'.[77] But if Mperembe did indeed fight in the battle on the Kafubu, he seems to have brought only a small force, for the occasion is not now remembered by the Bemba as a major conflict with the Ngoni.

The decisive series of battles between Bemba and Ngoni began only after the latter had made a camp called Ititini on the Saisi–Chambeshi watershed.[78] From this base, the Ngoni obtained the submission of the nearby Mambwe chief Mpande, probably Mpande V Chitongwa,

[73] Mporokoso DNB I, p. 245; and see Appendix 3. The main Ngoni camp at this stage may have been near the Uningi salt licks south of Mbala: Labrecque says they made a camp called 'Buningi' ('Origines', p. 302). Livingstone indicates that in March 1867 Ngoni were living further west, in the hills south of Mbete (*Last Journals*, I, p. 207).

[74] Cf. Labrecque, 'Origines', pp. 294–5.   [75] Molo Makungo, T2

[76] Labrecque, 'Origines', pp. 294–5; Milambo, T7: these say it was Chitapankwa who killed Munshimbwe, while Molo Makungo (T2) says it was Mwamba. Labrecque says that Mperembe had come from Chibungu, in Bisa country to the south, but his chronology of Ngoni movements is very confused (see Appendix 3). According to Mushindo, the Ngoni killed Kamfwa in Musoa, on their way south from Lubemba (*History*, s. 53).

[77] NLS 4091/21, p. 266. *Mucime* is the usual Bemba term for Ngoni: Waller wrongly transcribed the name as 'Mochimbe' in the *Last Journals*, I, p. 199.

[78] Mushindo, *History*, s. 55; Labrecque, 'Origines', p. 302

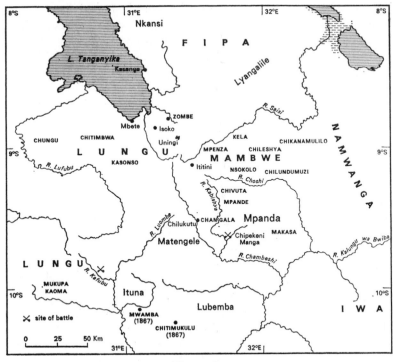

11 The northeast

whose father Musanta had been killed by the Bemba many years before. Mpande welcomed the Ngoni as allies against the Mambwe paramount, Nsokolo, and both Nsokolos VIII Musanya and IX Malamba were killed by the Ngoni, the latter perhaps in 1867.[79] Then Mperembe was provoked into invading Bemba country by the desertion of an Ngoni captain, Mapupo, who fled to Manga, the new village of Makasa III, between the Kabishya and Mombo rivers. Mperembe's Ngoni attacked Manga in vain, but they made a camp nearby.[80] After a fierce battle, Makasa forced the Ngoni to withdraw to

[79] Abercorn DNB I, p. 100; Watson, *Tribal Cohesion*, pp. 149, 153. (My numbering of Nsokolos follows the genealogy given by Aaron Sichivula and Zombe Nsokolo, 13 June 1965.) In November 1867, near Lake Mweru, Livingstone heard that 'Mambwe' was dead, though this might refer to the Chishinga chief Mambwe (*Last Journals*, I, p. 241).

[80] This brief account of the war is based on the narratives by Mushindo (*History*, s. 65–74) and Labrecque ('Origines', pp. 302–11). Both provide much interesting and probably authentic detail: they seem to be independent of each other but are in very close agreement.

Ititini. Makasa was now joined by Chitapankwa*, and both chiefs followed the Ngoni to Ititini, which they partly burned before returning home. It was probably at this stage that Makasa placed his 'son' Changala over that part of Mpanda occupied by the Silwamba, a Mambwe family who had long accepted Bemba rule.[81]

Meanwhile, the Ngoni recruited support from among the Lungu, Mambwe, Namwanga and Iwa. They returned to Manga with a large force and launched a successful attack, in which they killed Mukukamfumu II Kasonde, a sister of Chitapankwa*, and captured her daughter Chimbabantu.[82] Makasa himself fled west to his 'son' Changala's village, Chilukutu, while the Ngoni occupied Manga and built a village of their own, Chipekeni, on the same site. For several months there were no further actions, but Chitapankwa* and Makasa now obtained assistance from Mwamba, Nkula, Munkonge, Shimumbi and several other Bemba chiefs. In about 1870,[83] the combined Bemba force advanced on Chipekeni, aided by a few Swahili armed with guns, and perhaps also by Nsokolo X.[84] After an initial skirmish or two, the Bemba lured a group of Ngoni warriors into a fatal ambush and then stormed Chipekeni. This onslaught finally persuaded the Ngoni to abandon all hope of subduing the Bemba, and Mperembe led his gravely depleted forces away to the northeast, to the Namwanga. For a short while, these allied with the Ngoni, and the refugee Bemba of Chewe, in raiding Bemba villages north of the Chambeshi and the Kalungu wa Bwiba.[85] But within a year of his defeat at Chipekeni, Mperembe continued eastwards, and he eventually settled in Tumbuka country near his brother Mbelwa.[86]

The retreat of the Ngoni opened up a new phase of Bemba expansion to the north, and consolidation on their north-eastern borders.

[81] Silanda, 'Enslavement', p. 3; cf. above, p. 100. This was probably Changala III, who was Makasa III's own son. One of the Silwamba, Mulama son of Kavwinta, fought so well for Makasa against the Ngoni and Mambwe that Makasa made him a military commander (Silanda, 'Enslavement', p. 1).

[82] Chimbabantu was sold to a Fungwe who married her; she was brought back to Bemba country in about 1890, after Swahili traders had brought news of her (Brelsford, *Succession*, p. 13).

[83] For dating, see Appendix 3. Both Mushindo and Labrecque indicate that the actions in Mpanda and at Ititini spanned a period of about eighteen months.

[84] Watson, *Tribal Cohesion*, p. 153: he reports that the Ngoni were also afflicted by an outbreak of smallpox. For the role of firearms in this battle, see below, pp. 203, 205.

[85] No doubt this is why Makasa III built a new village at Bwanga, well to the east of Manga (Oger, 'Mpanda', 27).

[86] Young, Chinsali DNB I, pp. 234–5; cf. Appendix 3

Chitapankwa, Mwamba and Makasa besieged and killed one of the Ngoni's leading local allies, Mpande V Chitongwa. Mpande VI, together with his perpetual son Chivuta, took refuge among the Namwanga.[87] Mpande's people were laid under tribute, especially tribute in cattle, and most of them came under the control of Makasa's 'sons' Changala and Chipukula; the latter settled on the upper reaches of the Choshi river.[88] Soon after the expulsion of Mpande, in 1871 or early 1872, Makasa III Bwalya died.[89] Chitapankwa* contrived to have his own son Chisanga Chipemba installed as Makasa IV, but this appointment flouted the claims of Chileshye's* surviving sons.[90] One of these, Mukuuka Mwilwa, was allowed, perhaps by way of compensation, to take over Makasa's former territory in Chilinda.[91]

During the 1870s, Bemba rule or raiding appears to have oppressed not only the Mambwe of Mpande but also those of their old enemy Nsokolo. For these confessed in 1879 that they 'would welcome Mperembe among them again, as he treated them better than the Bemba do now'.[92] Two years earlier, indeed, a Bemba outpost had been defeated by Nsokolo X Chitambi, aided by the commoner Mambwe chief Chileshya and headman Chilundumuzi.[93] And it was also in 1877 that the senior Namwanga chief, Chikanamulilo, repelled an attack by Chitapankwa* and Makasa IV.[94] But in 1879 Bemba

[87] They caused trouble here: in 1885 Chivuta attempted to seize the senior Namwanga chieftainship (Fotheringham, *Adventures*, p. 17).

[88] Labrecque, 'Origines', pp. 317–18; Oger, 'Mpanda', 12; Abercorn DNB I, pp. 86, 101; cf. Watson, *Tribal Cohesion*, pp. 149, 169; Mushindo, *History*'s. 79. I do not know the identity of this Chipukula; the first was a son of Makasa I Kalulu (Goodall, 'Tree').

[89] Oger indicates that Makasa III died shortly before Chitapankwa's unsuccessful campaign against the Lungu chief Zombe in 1872 (see below, p. 150). He also says that Chitapankwa had Makasa III poisoned ('Mpanda', 29).

[90] Compare the appointments of Mukwikile I and Muchereka I (see above, pp. 138, 141).

[91] Oger, 'Mpanda', 31; cf. Labrecque, 'Origines', p. 318. For the identity of 'Mukuuka' and 'Mwilwa' cf. Mporokoso DNB I, p. 268; Kapoka, T1. Mukuuka Mwilwa was visited by Giraud in 1883 (*Lacs*, pp. 227–30) and in 1887 joined Nkula in an unsuccessful attack on the Iwa: a missionary at Chirenji, among the Wandya, heard of 'The Wawemba who under two chiefs Nchewi and Mwirwa appeared in great force in Wiwa two and a half days west of here'; they were defeated with heavy losses and retreated (Bain to Laws, 6 June 1887, NLS 7890; cf. Kapinda, T1). It is more likely that Mwilwa allied with his neighbour Nkula (the new 'Chewe') than with the refugee Chewe to the northeast of Iwa country.

[92] Stewart, 'Lake Nyasa', p. 268

[93] Abercorn DNB I, p. 101; this action can probably be identified with the Bemba defeat at 'Mambwe' in 1877 reported by Stewart ('Lake Nyasa', p. 267).

[94] *Ibid.*, Oger, 'Mpanda', 29.

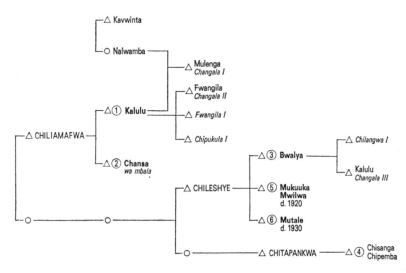

Fig. 11 Makasa. See Appendix 2, Note E.

plundered a Namwanga village, and Chitapankwa* appears soon afterwards to have defeated Chikanamulilo and put him to flight.[95] Following this victory, the southernmost part of Namwanga country, athwart the Kalungu wa Bwiba, was occupied by Mubanga Chele, a brother of Mukuuka Mwilwa.[96] As for the Mambwe, their internal divisions persisted, and the Bemba soon turned them to their own advantage. Chief Kela, a sworn enemy of Nsokolo, made a treaty with Chitimukulu: the latter took to wife the daughter of some Mambwe chief, while Makasa married Malunda, daughter of the Mambwe chief Mpenza, who belonged to the same royal lineage as Kela.[97] This alliance did not last, but the Mambwe failed to unite among themselves, and they suffered sorely from Bemba raids for more than a decade after Chitapankwa's* death. This had two important consequences. First, the Mambwe welcomed the arrival of European missionaries,

95 Stewart, 'Lake Nyasa', p. 267; he says that the Bemba were encouraged to raid the Namwanga by 'Mpunda, Kasang, and Mpanga, chiefs near Livingstonia'.

96 Labrecque, 'Origines', pp. 318–19; though if Young is right there were already Bemba in the area (see above, p. 145). Mubanga Chele and Lombe Shyula (a son of Mwamba I) had probably been in Chilinda since at least 1867: see below, p. 196, n. 146.

97 Abercorn DNB I, p. 101; Watson, *Tribal Cohesion*, p. 172. Milambo (T15) implies that the Bemba were aided by Kela when they defeated Zombe between 1880 and 1883 (see below, p. 151).

whom they saw as potential protectors. Second, it was Makasa, on the Mambwe border, who profited most from Mambwe weakness, and the power of the Makasa chieftainship became a major factor in Bemba reactions to European intrusion.

In the years following his defeat of Mperembe, Chitapankwa* also involved himself in the affairs of the Lungu of Tafuna, around the south-eastern corner of Lake Tanganyika. The Tafuna dynasty, together with that of Mukupa Kaoma and the Tabwa chiefly dynasties, belongs to the matrilineal *zimba* (Leopard) clan. The commoners under Tafuna, however, tend to be patrilineal and have close affinities with the Mambwe to the east, whereas the 'Malaila' Lungu of Mukupa Kaoma are all matrilineal and have far more in common with the Bemba.[98] The two main groups of Lungu have been distinct and independent throughout their brief remembered histories, and there is no record of their collaborating in any common effort against the Bemba. Furthermore, there was much conflict in the later nineteenth century among the Lungu who nominally accepted Tafuna's paramountcy. In the 1860s the minor chief Chungu I became Tafuna III, but he had difficulty in maintaining his position at Isoko, the royal capital, and by 1867 he had moved west to settle on the Lufubu river. Other Lungu chiefs, such as Kasonso, Chitimbwa and Chibwe, seem to have been independent of Tafuna III.[99] Soon afterwards, Tafuna III died, but his successor as holder of the Chungu title was more concerned to protect his own country in the west against Bemba raiders than to move east and claim the Tafuna title.[100] Instead, in about 1870,

---

[98] An early British official remarked, 'The Malaila Alungu are, for all practical purposes, Awemba' (Marshall, 'The Awemba', LM/G69/5/6). Tafuna's Lungu are sometimes referred to as 'Mambwe' or 'Mambwe-Lungu'.

[99] 'Notes on Lungu royal family extracted from notes by J. Gibson Hall' (c. 1905?) in LM/G69/5/7 (these are the source for the narrative in Gouldsbury and Sheane, *Great Plateau*, pp. 33–5); Livingstone, *Last Journals*, I, p. 229. Tippu Tip remembered 'Tafuna' as the name of Chungu's village (*Maisha*, p. 23), but Livingstone does not mention Tafuna at all in describing his two visits to Lungu country, in 1867 and 1872. In about August 1873 Livingstone's party returned through Tafuna's country and apparently gathered that Chungu's 'brothers Kasonso, Chitimbwa, Sombé, and their sister, are all notorious for their reverence for Tafuna' (*Last Journals*, II, p. 333); but all the other evidence would seem to contradict this.

[100] Gibson Hall, 'Notes'. Livingstone's party revisited Chungu's on their way to the coast in 1873, and the chief was then a 'young man'. Waller, the editor of the *Last Journals*, assumed that this was the Chungu who had been Livingstone's host in 1867, but there may well have been some misunderstanding (*Last Journals*, II, p. 333).

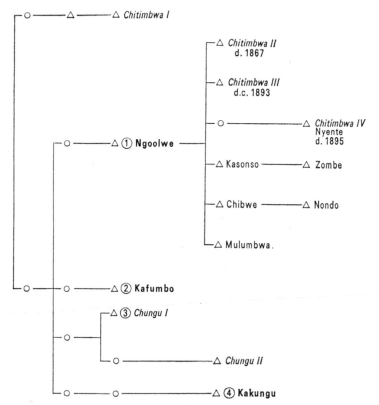

Fig. 12 Tafuna. From Gibson Hall, 'Notes' and table based on this, dated 1934, in Mporokoso DNB, I, 263. (For dates, see page 246 and Livingstone, *Last Journals*, I, 241)

another Lungu royal, Kakungu, obtained help from Tippu Tip and in face of local opposition set himself up at Isoko as Tafuna IV.[101]

It seems clear that from the first Tafuna IV Kakungu was at odds with his Lungu neighbours and looked more to outsiders for support. At all events, it was not Kakungu but his neighbour Zombe, son of a son of Tafuna I, who felt the full force of Bemba invasion. In the middle of 1872, Chitapankwa set out northwards to aid the Fipa chief of Lyangalile, Suumba Kasuumba, against Kapuufi, chief of Nkansi; Suumba had sent ivory to Chitapankwa* in recognition of his defeat

[101] Jones to Thompson, 15 April 1891, LMS/CA/8/3C; Andrew Roberts, 'The History of Abdullah ibn Suliman', *African Social Research*, 1967, 4, p. 253; this indicates that Kakungu's accession occurred just when Tippu Tip returned from the coast on his third expedition into the interior, which was in about 1869 or 1870 (cf. internal evidence from *Maisha*).

of the Ngoni. But while most of the Bemba force went on into Fipa country, Chitapankwa* and his son Makasa IV were provoked by Zombe into attacking his village on the Lucheche river.[102] They underestimated their opponent. Zombe held out under siege; he was eventually relieved by Chitimbwa and Kasonso; and together the Lungu chiefs routed Chitapankwa*.[103] Two months later, in November 1872, Livingstone visited Zombe on his way south from Tabora. He learned that Chitapankwa*

> compelled some Malongwana [Swahili] to join him, while Moamba refused to join him . . . Motoka [Chitapankwa*] plundered a native Arab party of 6 bales of cloth & one load of beads & said if you wish to get the goods back come with me and fight Zombe— the siege lasted 3 months, then Kasonso & Chitimba who are of the same family came & a complete rout ensued—they [the Bemba] left many of their guns & clothing—the Malongwana had previously escaped. It is two months since the rout so we have been prevented by a kind Providence from coming soon enough to fall into the hands of Motoka's immense horde. He was impudent & extortionate before & much more now that success in plundering has emboldened him.[104]

This defeat so shocked Mwamba II that he is said to have threatened rebellion.[105] But eventually—probably between eight and ten years later—Chitapankwa* made amends. The occasion seems to have been provided by Tafuna IV Kakungu, who already leaned more on Bemba than on Lungu support. Some time earlier he had defeated Chitimbwa with the help of Makasa's 'son' Chilangwa, chief of Matengele.[106] By the end of 1879, Bemba raids had forced the people of Mbete, on the lake shore, to flee to the hills.[107] But by 1880 Zombe, further east,

[102] Milambo says that Chitapankwa remembered his poor reception among the Lungu before his accession (T15; 30 September 1964; cf. above, p. 128).

[103] Mushindo, *History*, s. 76; Labrecque, 'Origines', p. 315: the latter says that the Bemba withdrew in such haste that Chitapankwa threw off his royal anklets of glass beads, which hindered his flight. Both accounts call Suumba by part of his praise-name, *Pilula Fipa* (cf. above, p. 78).

[104] Entries for 13 and 14 November 1872 in NLS 4091/15. I quote from Livingstone's own notebook since Waller's printed version omits the important reference to Mwamba and in several minor respects departs from the original wording (cf. *Last Journals*, II, pp. 248–9).

[105] Labrecque, 'Origines', p. 315

[106] Gouldsbury and Sheane, *Great Plateau*, p. 35

[107] Stewart, 'Lake Nyasa', p. 270; cf. J. Thomson, *To the Central African Lakes and Back*, London 1881, I, p. 312; II, p. 211

would seem to have become quite as powerful as Kakungu,[108] and soon afterwards Zombe expelled Kakungu from Isoko. Kakungu then went to the Bemba;[109] Chitapankwa* recruited support from Makasa and Nkula; and in or before 1883 he led a large force back to Zombe's. The Bemba used a decoy with great success and inflicted a crushing defeat; they claim that Zombe was killed and his village razed to the ground.[110] Nonetheless, Kakungu failed to re-establish himself at Isoko; instead, he withdrew northwards to Kasanga.[111] Thereafter, no Tafuna resided at Isoko for many years,[112] and Chitapankwa* left his sister's son Ponde in charge of the country between Isoko and the Luombe river.[113]

THE NORTHWEST: THE TABWA AND SWAHILI

While Chitapankwa* and Makasa extended Bemba power in the 1870s to the north of Lubemba and Mpanda, Mwamba II continued to expand his sphere of influence west of Ituna. This process was in large part a response to the settlement of East African traders in Itabwa. Whereas the Ngoni settlement in Mambwe country had primarily threatened Makasa and Chitapankwa*, Mwamba had probably been more concerned with the growing trade with East Africa, since his borders lay closer to that region between Lakes Tanganyika and Mweru through which traders bound for Kazembe's or Katanga had to pass. Indeed, one reason for Mwamba II's evident reluctance to join in Chitapankwa's* campaigns against Zombe's Lungu may have been a wish to avoid seeming to threaten the traders' route around the southeastern corner of Lake Tanganyika. At the same time, Mwamba II was clearly determined that the Bemba, rather than the East Africans or any other group, should dominate the country north and west of Ituna. The advent of East African colonists in this region considerably affected the stability of the local polities, especially among the Tabwa,

[108] Cf. Hore to Thompson, 8 May 1880, LMS/CA 3/1/D (Wolf, *Missionary to Tanganyika*, p. 120–1)
[109] Jones to Thompson, 15 April 1891, LMS/CA 8/3/C
[110] Mushindo, *History*, s. 77; Labrecque, 'Origines', p. 315–16; Gouldsbury and Sheane, *Great Plateau*, p. 36. For the arguments supporting the chronology given here, see Appendix 2, Note L (p. 357).
[111] Gibson Hall, 'Notes'. It was at Kasanga that Kakungu made a treaty with Johnston in 1889: see below, p. 231.
[112] Gouldsbury and Sheane, *Great Plateau*, p. 35
[113] Mushindo, *History*, s. 77

and Mwamba's expansion to the northwest should perhaps be seen, not simply as a means of enriching himself through tribute, but as an attempt to limit the traders' opportunities for political interference.

The initial steps in this phase of Bemba expansion were prompted, not by the activities of the Tabwa or East Africans, but by the defeat of Munshimbwe, the Lungu chief west of Ituna, in the late 1860s.[114] The Bemba had followed this up by occupying Munshimbwe's country, Maseba, on the west bank of the Luombe river. Maseba was given to Munkonge's brother Mulume *wa nshimba*, who built a village on the Njitwa stream.[115] On taking over Maseba, Mulume gave himself the name *Mporokoso cinga wa labwa labwa*,[116] 'the forgotten potsherd', in allusion to the fact that he was the last of his many brothers to be given any special honour.[117] This name was belied by events. During the 1870s, Mporokoso was drawn into the dynastic quarrels of Nsama's Tabwa, and he exploited these, and the advent of traders from East Africa, to such effect that by the end of the century he was one of the most powerful Bemba chiefs.

The Tabwa chieftainship of Nsama appears to have been founded towards the end of the eighteenth century, following a southward migration along Lake Tanganyika by the chiefly *zimba* (Leopard) clan, from which the Lungu chiefs are also derived. The main group of *bazimba* settled in Itabwa under a chief called Nsama. Somewhat later, one of his subjects, Mulilo, moved north and founded a new chiefdom on the western shore of the lake.[118] The third Nsama, Chipili Chipioka, enjoyed considerable power. He routed a party of Arab traders in 1841–2,[119] and he later defeated an alliance between the Lunda king Kazembe VII Muonga (?1862–72) and the Arab trader Muhammed ibn

[114] See above, p. 143.

[115] Milambo, T7; Chinyumba, 17 April 1965; Njalamimba, T1

[116] This was part of a praise: the full name is given by Chiwale, who also provides an exegesis (J. C. Chiwale, *Royal Praises and Praise Names of the Lunda Kazembe of Northern Rhodesia*, Rhodes–Livingstone Communication 25, Lusaka 1962, pp. 53–4).

[117] His own brothers included Munkonge II, Tungati I and Chipalo I.

[118] Peyala Kapembwa, T1 and 21–23 June 1965; J. Weghsteen, 'Origine et histoire des Watabwa (Haut-Congo)', *Annali Lateranensi*, 1960, 24, pp. 370–1. Weghsteen heard traditions among the Congolese Tabwa (presumably those of Mulilo and another junior chief, Manda) early this century. He suggests that Mulilo broke away during the eighteenth century. From Nsama's genealogy (which may well be telescoped), I infer that the Nsama title was not founded until about 1800. The later history of Mulilo is outlined in C. G. F. Delhaise, 'Chez les Wabemba', *Bull. soc. roy. belge geog.*, 32 (1908), at pp. 273–83

[119] Burton, *Lake Regions*, II, pp. 151–2; Tippu Tip, *Maisha*, p. 17

Saleh.[120] Chipili's brother Lukwesa defeated a party of Ngoni, probably those of Mperembe; Chipili himself wrested territory from Mulilo[121] and established subordinate posts for his sons, Mukula and Katele, and his nephew Kaputa. But in 1867 Chipili overreached himself: he fell out with a caravan led by Tippu Tip. By this time, there were several Arab and Swahili traders encamped between Lake Mweru and the southern end of Lake Tanganyika, and they were able to obtain some support from the neighbouring Lungu. Chipili was soundly defeated by Tippu Tip, and thereafter it was the foreign traders, not Nsama, who were the real power in Tabwa country.[122] Livingstone met Chipili late in 1867. He had already observed that Nsama 'was the Napoleon of these countries';[123] he now reported:

Nsama is an old man, with head and face like those sculptured on the Assyrian monuments. He has been a great conqueror in his time, and with bows and arrows was invincible. He is said to have destroyed many native traders from Tanganyika, but twenty Arab guns made him flee from his own stockade, and caused a great sensation in the country.[124]

Nsama III Chipili died soon after his defeat by Tippu Tip, and it was the ensuing succession dispute which opened the way for Bemba expansion into Itabwa. In about 1869, Chipili's nephew Katandula became Nsama IV,[125] but he was challenged by his mother's sister's son Kafwimbi. When Livingstone passed westwards down the Luangwa valley[126] in December 1872, he visited Kafwimbi, 'an intelligent and pleasant young man, who has been attacked several times by Kitandula, the successor of Nsama of Itawa'.[127] Hitherto,

[120] Livingstone, *Last Journals*, I, p. 297. The Lunda report a victory for Kazembe, but perhaps this was another occasion (Cunnison, *Historical Traditions*, p. 87).

[121] Livingstone, *Last Journals*, I, p. 242 (the printed text gives 'Moriri'; the manuscript, 'Moriro': NLS 4091/13); Peyala Kapembwa, 21–23 June 1965; Tippu Tip, *Maisha*, p. 19

[122] Livingstone, *Last Journals*, I, pp. 207–20; Tippu Tip, *Maisha*, pp. 19–23; Kawambwa DNB II, p. 25; Roberts, 'Abdullah', pp. 250–1. The Tabwa themselves pass over the incident in silence.

[123] Livingstone, *Last Journals*, I, p. 231   [124] *Ibid.*, I, p. 258

[125] Tabwa and Swahili informants disagreed as to whether Katandula had succeeded by the time of Tippu Tip's return to Tabwa country on his way to the Congo in 1869/70 (Peyala Kapembwa, T1; Nsemiwe, T1; cf. Tippu Tip, *Maisha*, p. 47).

[126] The valley, that is, of the Luangwa which flows into the Kalungwishi, not to be confused with the Luangwa which flows into the Zambezi.

[127] Livingstone, *Last Journals*, II, p. 253

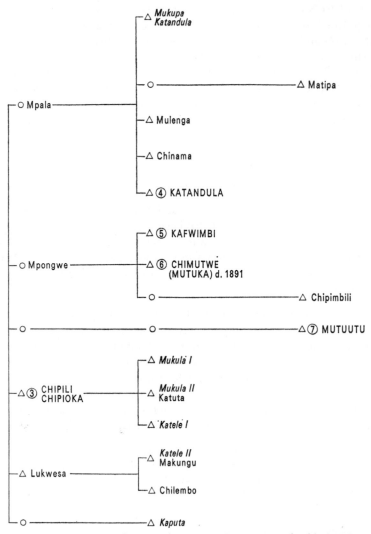

Fig. 13 Nsama. From Peyala Kapembwa, 21–23 June 1965, and table in Mporo-koso DNB I, 260–1 (*c.* 1906).

Katandula had been supported by the foreign traders, who now included Tippu Tip's half-brother 'Kumba Kumba' (Muhammed ibn Masud el-Wardi). But Katandula soon tried to make himself independent of the traders and sought help instead from Chitapankwa*. The latter was dissuaded from complying by his brother Mwamba II,[128] who doubtless attached greater importance to maintaining good relations with the foreign traders in Itabwa.

In about 1873, however, a party of ivory traders under the direction of Kumba Kumba came to blows with the Chishinga chief Mushyota and got the worst of the affray.[129] This encouraged Nsama IV Katandula to seek to expel the Arabs from Tabwa country; indeed, his brothers Chinama and Mulenga, and his nephew Matipa, killed some of Kumba Kumba's men as they fled from Mushyota. Kumba Kumba, whose stockade near Nsama's was now in grave danger, sought to ally with Kafwimbi against Katandula.[130] Two sons of Kafwimbi and a son of Nsama III Chipili, Mukula I Katuta, took refuge with the Arabs.[131] Kafwimbi himself had by this time gone for assistance to the Bemba.[132] Kumba Kumba now sent a messenger (apparently Katuta) to ask for help from Kafwimbi, who in turn asked Mwamba for support. Mwamba held Kafwimbi but despatched seventy men under Katuta. These joined forces with Kumba Kumba's men, and the combined expedition defeated and killed Katandula.[133]

Kafwimbi now left Mwamba's to succeed Katandula as Nsama,[134]

---

[128] Roberts, 'Abdullah', pp. 247, 255

[129] Nsemiwe, T1; Peyala Kapembwa, T1. The Swahili trader Pembamoto was killed, either by the Chishinga (Chief Mushyota, 'History wa Bena Chishinga'; African Elders, *History of the Bena Ŋoma*, pp. 60–1; Cunnison, *Historical Traditions*, p. 92), or by Tabwa warriors serving under Pembamoto (Roberts, 'Abdullah', pp. 257–8). Pembamoto's death took place after that of Kazembe VII Muonga in 1872: cf. *ibid.*, pp. 256, 258; Andrew Roberts, 'Tippu Tip, Livingstone, and the Chronology of Kazembe', *Azania*, 1967, 2, p. 119.

[130] Nsemiwe, T1; Peyala Kapembwa, T1; cf. Roberts, 'Abdullah', p. 258. Chinama may have been a nephew of Katandula (*ibid.*, p. 259).

[131] Roberts, 'Abdullah', p. 258

[132] The Swahili gathered that Kafwimbi 'was in hiding with Chitimukulu' (*ibid.*). My Tabwa informant said that Kafwimbi went to get help from Mwamba against Katandula at the request of his Bemba stepfather Chaisamba, after Kafwimbi's mother Mpongwe had been killed by Katandula (Peyala Kapembwa, 21–23 June 1965). My Swahili informant said that some other Tabwa chiefs had taken refuge with Mwamba (Nsemiwe, T1).

[133] Roberts, 'Abdullah', pp. 258–9; Nsemiwe, T1

[134] Roberts, 'Abdullah', p. 259; but my Tabwa informant claimed that Kafwimbi himself had helped to kill Katandula (Peyala Kapembwa, 21–23 June 1965).

12 The northwest

but he had to contend with Katandula's brothers, Chinama and Mukupa, and with his nephew Matipa.[135] Kafwimbi obtained assistance both from Kumba Kumba and from Mwamba, who sent a force under his son Mporokoso. Thus Kafwimbi, after a fierce siege, killed Chinama and Matipa and established himself as Nsama V.[136] Soon afterwards, and not later than 1876, Kumba Kumba left Itabwa for the east coast.[137]

Having once encouraged the Bemba to enter Itabwa, Nsama V Kafwimbi found it impossible to make them leave. He obtained a daughter of Mwamba II in marriage,[138] but he had to cede to Mwamba an area called Isenga in southern Itabwa. The extent of this area is dis-

[135] Roberts, 'Abdullah', p. 259.

[136] Roberts, 'Abdullah', p. 259; Njalamimba, T1 (see Appendix 4/iii) (p. 382)

[137] Roberts, 'Abdullah', p. 259; Nsemiwe, T1; Tippu Tip, *Maisha*, pp. 79–81; H. M. Stanley, *Through the Dark Continent*, London 1880, p. 386

[138] Peyala Kapembwa, 21–23 June 1965; Milambo, T11; Labrecque', 'Origines' p. 327 (but his account of the Bemba-Tabwa wars is somewhat confused)

puted: the Tabwa insist that the ceded area lay south of the Luangwa river, while the Bemba claim that it included country north of the Luangwa and also an area south of the river Itabu.[139] At all events, the Bemba settled along the Luangwa soon after the defeat of Katandula. Mporokoso left his original chiefdom, Maseba, and built Kashinda village, several miles north of the Luangwa.[140] Mporokoso's brother Sunkutu had already taken country south of the Luangwa from the Lungu of Mukupa Kaoma; he now settled near the Luangwa–Kalungwishi confluence in country taken from the Chishinga chief Chama.[141] And it was probably in the course of this advance to the northwest that the Bemba took Lisunga, north of Maseba across the river Kafubu, from the Lungu chief Mulumbwa (a 'son' of Tafuna).[142] Lisunga was assigned to Mukuuka, a son of Mwamba I, who was also known by his teknonym Shibwalya Kapila.[143]

The position of Nsama V Kafwimbi was far from secure. Katandula's younger brother Mukupa had escaped to the west, where he set up a chieftainship subsequently known as Mukupa Katandula;[144] this was a thorn in the side of Kafwimbi and his successors as Nsama. The various bands led by East African traders, who lacked any recognised overlord, provided further occasions for conflict. Soon after Mporokoso settled near the Luangwa, Kafwimbi was killed, probably on the Lwao river, north of Lake Mweru, by traders allied to Mukupa Katandula.[145] Again, there was a succession dispute in which the

[139] Peyala Kapembwa, 21–23 June 1965; Njalamimba, T1; Mporokoso I (*c.* 1905?), reported by H. Marshall in 'The Awemba', LM/G69/5/6; and cf. Mporokoso DNB I, p. 86

[140] *Ibid.* Maseba seems to have been taken over by Mwamba II himself, but it was later given to a minor chief called Chisangula, who held it as a separate chiefdom until the late 1920s (Kasama DNB II, pp. 39, 134–6; III, p. 32). It was presumably in the 1870s that the Bemba occupied Kasenga, west of Maseba, though this does not seem to have become a separate chiefdom until after 1883 (see below, p. 220).

[141] Mporokoso DNB I, p. 104 (*c.* 1904); Kasama DNB II, p. 51. Milambo (T7), mentions three Chishinga 'chiefs' killed by Sunkutu: Tumbanya, Munkanta, Mulenga. The name Sunkutu may derive from this area: earlier, Kazembe VII Muonga adopted it after taking part of Chishinga country—the exact location is not clear (Cunnison, *Historical Traditions*, p. 69).

[142] Gibson Hall, 'Notes'. Mulumbwa succeeded Chibwe, who in 1867 and 1872 occupied country that later formed part of the Lungu–Bemba border (Livingstone, *Last Journals*, I, p. 201; II, p. 251).

[143] Milambo, 2 October 1964.   [144] Peyala Kapembwa, 21–23 June 1965

[145] There is some uncertainty about the details of this episode. Some sources agree that Kafwimbi was killed fighting a trader, Chandalala, on the Lwao river (Peyala Kapembwa, 21–23 June 1965; D.C. Mporokoso to D.C. Kasama, 29

Bemba intervened. The two claimants were Mukupa's brother Mulenga and Kafwimbi's younger brother Chimutwe (also called Mutuka). Mulenga was supported by a son and nephew of Katandula, and also by Mukula and Katele, sons of Nsama III Chipili.[146] Chimutwe then sought aid from Mporokoso and Sunkutu[147] and went on to Mwamba's, whence he sent an appeal for help to Kumba Kumba at Tabora. Kumba Kumba duly despatched a party under a Swahili trader, Abdullah ibn Suliman, but meanwhile Chimutwe had obtained support from Mporokoso and a combined force of Bemba and Tabwa killed Mulenga.[148] The Bemba also helped Chimutwe to kill two sons of Chungu, the Lungu chief on Mporokoso's north-eastern border,[149] though Chungu II himself later defeated a Bemba–Swahili force and Mporokoso made an alliance with him.[150]

Kakoma, the village of Nsama VI Chimutwe, became the head-quarters of the elephant hunters who had come with Abdullah ibn Suliman. Chimutwe soon had occasion to call on these Swahili: he was expelled from his capital by members of the lineage of Mukupa Katandula and only regained it with Abdullah's aid. A quarrel then arose between Abdullah and Chimutwe, and they resorted to arbitration from Mwamba: a remarkable indication of the extent to which Bemba authority was acknowledged in an area where a few years before it was unknown. (The dispute came before Mwamba and not Mporokoso because Chimutwe had already gone to Mwamba's with a load of ivory, perhaps by way of tribute.) Mwamba, however, refused

October 1937, in Anthropology file in Mporokoso DNB; cf. Milambo, T11). The Swahili now say that Kafwimbi was killed while hunting down defeated rivals (Nsemiwe, T1); their earlier account says that Chandalala was indeed 'an adherent of Katandula's' but that Kafwimbi was killed by the Baluchi trader Hasani ibn Salimu ('Kabunda'), who was based near the mouth of the Lufubu river (Roberts, 'Abdullah', p. 260). Elsewhere, Chandalala is described as a Nyamwezi chief in Bwile country whom Kabunda killed (Kawambwa DNB II, pp. 123–4).

[146] Roberts, 'Abdullah', p. 260; according to this source, Mulenga was backed by the Baluchi trader Kabunda.

[147] Nsemiwe, T1; he says that Chimutwe virtually became a slave to the Bemba.

[148] Roberts, 'Abdullah', p. 260; cf. Milambo, T11

[149] Milambo, T11; he says that it was these men, Mutapa and Kapoma, who killed Kafwimbi. There was a 'Kapoma, son of Chungu' near Mporokoso in 1891 (Velten, *Safari*, p. 34). Livingstone mentions Kapoma as a son of Nsama (*Last Journals*, I, p. 209); either he was mistaken or this was a different Kapoma.

[150] Abercorn DNB I, p. 87; Gouldsbury and Sheane, *Great Plateau*, p. 36; Mather to Thompson, 21 March 1894, LMS/CA 9/2/B. The Lungu relate that Chungu II defeated Nsama, and also Kasengere (a Makua ivory hunter): Gibson Hall, 'Notes'; see below, p. 239.

to listen to the two parties and sent them away; Abdullah then returned to Tabora.[151]

Mwamba II Chileshye Kapalaula died in the first part of 1883,[152] and within a year or so fighting broke out between Mporokoso and Nsama VI Chimutwe. The latter was anxious to regain Isenga from Mporokoso,[153] who for his part had already meant to attack Chimutwe but felt freer to do so after Mwamba II's death.[154] Chimutwe sent for help from Tippu Tip (who was returning from Zanzibar to the Congo by way of Ujiji). Tippu Tip despatched Abdullah ibn Suliman to intervene once more on Chimutwe's side, and Abdullah brought with him a force of Nyamwezi, led by Nsemiwe, a headman from Unyanyembe.[155] Chimutwe allowed Abdullah to build a village on the Kabuta stream, where his heirs have lived ever since.[156] At first, Mporokoso's Bemba repelled an attack launched prematurely by Chimutwe, fifty of whose Swahili auxiliaries were killed.[157] But Chimutwe then offered 'the whole of his country' to Abdullah, who mustered his forces in a stockade. The new Mwamba, Mubanga Chipoya, came to Mporokoso's aid and the two chiefs, with Sunkutu, attacked Abdullah; but they had to retire after heavy losses. The Bemba then withdrew to Mporokoso's village, Kashinda, near the Luangwa, in such haste that they left behind their war-drums and war-charm (*ilamfya*). Mwamba III then sent Abdullah ivory in exchange for salt (presumably from the Tabwa or Bwile)[158] and re-established trading relations with the Swahili.[159] A Tabwa force later tried to expel Mporokoso from Kashinda but was routed.[160]

---

[151] Roberts, 'Abdullah', pp. 260–1   [152] Giraud, *Lacs*, p. 272; cf. below, p. 217.

[153] Peyala Kapembwa, 21–23 June 1965

[154] Roberts, 'Abdullah', p. 261. Labrecque says that Mporokoso suspected the Tabwa of poisoning his sister Chisela, who had been given in marriage to Kafwimbi ('Origines', pp. 327–8).

[155] Roberts, 'Abdullah', p. 260; Nsemiwe, T1. Tippu Tip probably left Zanzibar towards the end of 1883 and crossed Lake Tanganyika in the first quarter of 1884: cf. Tippu Tip, *Maisha*, p. 113; Hore to LMS, 23 April 1884, LMS/CA 5/4/B; Hore, *Tanganyika*, pp. 236, 238; P. Ceulemans, *La Question Arabe et le Congo*, Brussels 1959, p. 65, n. 2.   [156] Roberts, 'Abdullah', p. 261

[157] *Ibid.*, p. 262; Milambo, T11   [158] See below, p. 187.

[159] Roberts, 'Abdullah', pp. 262–3; cf. Peyala Kapembwa, 21–23 June 1965; Njalamimba, T1. This war probably took place some time after Giraud's journey through Itabwa in November 1883: Giraud makes no reference to Abdullah (cf. *Lacs*, p. 420). Mporokoso seems for a time to have retreated from Kashinda to a village, Kakumbi, on the Luangwa (Mporokoso DNB I, p. 86).

[160] Enclosure in D.C. Mporokoso to D.C. Kasama, 29 October 1937 in Anthropology file in Mporokoso DNB; Chinyumba, 17 June 1965

G

This seems to have been the only occasion when Abdullah's men fought the Bemba. It appears that the basic policy of the East Africans was to dominate the Tabwa of Nsama, by exploiting their divisions, while maintaining friendship with the more powerful Bemba. But one result of this policy, with the shifting alliances which it entailed, was that the East Africans gave the Bemba too an opportunity to assert authority in Itabwa. When the Bemba, under whatever provocation, attacked Nsama VI Chimutwe in Abdullah's absence, they challenged the position of the East Africans as the real masters of Nsama's chiefdom, and at this point Bemba expansion clearly had to be checked. Having fought the East Africans and lost, the Bemba seem to have realised that they had more to gain by leaving Nsama's country to them than by taking it over themselves.[161]

THE SOUTH: NKOLEMFUMU AND CHIKWANDA II

During the 1870s, after the Ngoni threat had been removed, both Chitapankwa* and Mwamba II took part in a renewed Bemba thrust southwards, beyond newly-conquered Bisa country south of the Chambeshi into country first occupied by the Bemba in the later 1820s. One feature of this expansion was the re-emergence of the Nkolemfumu chieftainship in Miti. After ousting the old lineage there, Mwamba I had ruled both Ituna and Miti, and Mwamba II inherited both chiefdoms.[162] But some time around 1870 the Nkolemfumu title was revived for Mubanga Chipoya (Chisala), a sister's son and son-in-law of Mwamba II.[163] Mubanga Chipoya had already fought much against the Bisa,[164] and as Nkolemfumu he ruled over both Miti and Bisa territory south of the Chambeshi. His first capital was on the Lualuo river, on the borders of Miti and Ituna, but he then went to live on the Kampemba stream in Ichingo, Kabanda's chiefdom.[165] Since Mubanga's uncle Sampa was also in Ichingo at about this time,[166] it seems clear that Kabanda was now subject to the

[161] Roberts, 'Abdullah', p. 248   [162] See above, pp. 105, 123
[163] Milambo, 2 October 1964. Mubanga had hitherto had charge of Chisansa, a small area in Ituna which had once belonged to Mulenga Mwimba; he now incorporated this in Miti (*ibid.*, cf. above, p. 97). Brelsford says that Mubanga became Nkolemfumu after Sampa's brief occupation of Ichinga, which probably took place in the 1860s (*Succession*, p. 28; and above, p. 136). This agrees with Shimulamba's story that at first Sampa was chosen to be Nkolemfumu but refused, saying, 'I can't succeed from a higher position' (Shimulamba, T1).
[164] Brelsford, *Succession*, p. 28
[165] Shimulamba, T1; Luchembe, 1918 evidence   [166] See above, p. 136.

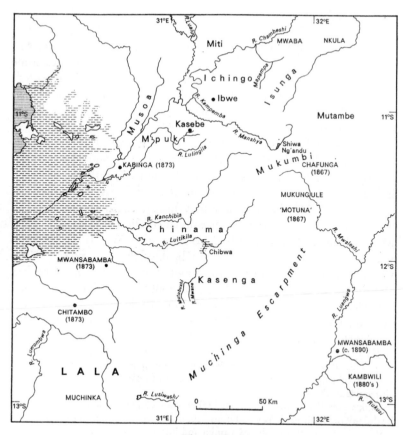

13 The south

Bemba. By 1873, Kabanda's southern neighbour Kabinga had retreated
westwards into the swamps of the lower Chambeshi, and much of his
chiefdom, Mpuki, was taken over by Nkolemfumu Mubanga.[167] And
it was probably Mubanga who directed the Bemba occupation of
Musoa, a small area east of the Lubansenshi river under a Bisa chief,
Mubenshi.[168] In 1883, when Mwamba II died, Nkolemfumu Mubanga
was living at Kasebe, on the Kachili stream in Mpuki, where he obtained much cloth from a Swahili trader, 'Katanga'.[169]

---

[167] Mpika DNB II, p. 215; Livingstone, *Last Journals*, II, p. 289
[168] Thomas, *Bisa*, p. 20, and see below, p. 221. It is possible that Musoa was
occupied by a grandson of Chileshye in the 1850s: see above, p. 143, n. 76).
[169] Shimulamba, T1; Milambo, 1 October 1964; Luchembe, 1918 evidence.
Giraud, in 1883, heard that 'Moincoirémfumu' was south of the Chambeshi; he

Meanwhile, Bemba rule was extended still further south, over the southern part of Mpuki and over Chinama, which the Bisa had regained after killing Chikwanda I in about 1850.[170] Chitapankwa* or Mwamba II appears to have reconquered these territories some time around 1880, and perhaps as late as 1882: in 1883 Giraud reported: 'Le Bisa n'existe plus depuis l'an dernier: Kétimkuru l'a dévoré tout entier, et l'Ubemba s'étend maintenant sur les deux rives du Chambezi jusqu'à l'infini.'[171]

South of the Lulingila river, Chitapankwa* installed his son Shichileshye, with the title Masongo.[172] Chinama was assigned to Mutale Lwanga, son of a sister of Chitapankwa* and Mwamba II, who had hitherto lived on the Mapampa, on Kabanda's eastern border. As Chikwanda II, Mutale Lwanga settled first on the Kanchibia and then on the Luitikila.[173] There were occasional conflicts with the Bisa chief Mwansabamba Mwape Yumba (also known as Kopa I), but he soon withdrew from Chinama to the east bank of the Luangwa.[174] Chikwanda also occupied Kasenga, the country of chief Nkuka, who had already fled to the Luangwa,[175] and it would appear that Chikwanda extended his authority further north, into Mukumbi, at the expense of yet another Bisa chief, Mukungule.[176] Here, as in some other

was feared by the Nyamwezi at Nkula's almost as much as Sampa (*Lacs*, p. 242, and map f. p. 220).   [170] See above, p. 117.

[171] Giraud, *Lacs*, p. 224 ('Since last year, Bisa country has ceased to exist. Chitimukulu has devoured it all, and Bembaland now extends indefinitely on either side of the Chambeshi').

Chikwanda II was unlikely to have taken over Chinama much before 1875 as he did not die until 1916. When Tippu Tip, in reference to events in 1869/70, said that relatives of Chitimukulu, Mwamba and Nkula ('Chansa') were in control of Bisa country, he must have referred to Lubumbu in the west and Isunga or Mutambe in the east rather than to Chinama (*Maisha*, p. 47).

[172] Mpika DNB II, p. 165; cf. L. Molinier, diary, 20 September 1899, *CT*, 1900, 87, p. 433   [173] Luchembe, 1918 evidence; Thomas, *Bisa*, p. 45

[174] *Ibid.*, pp. 48–9; cf. E. H. Lane-Poole, 'The Luangwa Valley in 1918', *NRJ*, 1956, 3, ii, p. 157. Thomas says Mwape Yumba retreated due to Ngoni raids, but these were most destructive in Chinama in the 1860's (see below, p. 192). Kopa III, in 1918, said only that Kopa I was afraid of the Bemba (1918 evidence). After Kopa I's death, Kopa II Lombe moved from the Luangwa to the lower Luitikila, perhaps as late as 1895 (Thomas, *Bisa*, p. 51).

[175] Luchembe and Chinandu, 1918 evidence. Chikwanda later induced Nkuka to return and give him a daughter in marriage (*ibid.*).

[176] In the early 1900s Chikwanda's borders were defined to run along the Manshya, in the north, and the Muchinga watershed, to the east (Mpika DNB II, p. 179). Mukungule's predecessors were buried within this area, in a grove on the Mumbule stream, south of Shiwa Ŋandu (Quarterly Report, April–June 1922, in Chinsali DNB IV/F). Thus in 1961-2, when cattle were sick on Shiwa Ŋandu

parts of Bisa country, the population seems to have been already depleted by Ngoni raiding, and the Bemba seem to have kept Mukumbi as an elephant-hunting reserve.[177] Elsewhere, Chikwanda II gave small areas to junior relatives, and Bisa headmen were mostly replaced by Bemba.[178] Chikwanda levied tribute from the salt-workers of Chinama, and he may also have obtained a regular share of the iron produced by the famous Lala smelters:[179] the Bemba claim that the Lala chief Muchinka, weary of fighting, submitted to Chik-wanda, 'bringing many hoes'.[180] The Lala admit that headman Kasubika, on the Luwombwa river, fled from Bemba attacks,[181] and in about 1884 headman Chitambo left his village to escape Chikwanda's raiders.[182] Chikwanda also seized cattle from the Lala on the Lusiwashi river and raided as far south as the Lunchu river, near the modern Kabwe.[183] He was certainly well placed to push forward the frontiers of raiding in the last years of the century, when the activities of Bemba chiefs further north began to be constrained by European advances.

estate, Mukungule sent Bisa to make offerings to his ancestors (Henry Mulenga, 23 April 1965). In 1866, before reaching 'Motuna' and Chafunga, headmen in Mukumbi, Livingstone was told that they were Bemba, but he did not specify this in recording his visits to them (*Last Journals*, I, pp. 165, 170, 172). He does not mention Mukungule at all.

[177] Chinsali DNB I, p. 127 (tour report *c.* 1900, by R. Young?)

[178] Cf. Mpika DNB I, p. 6; II, p. 181; and below, p. 221.

[179] See below, p. 186.

[180] Chinandu, 1918 evidence; cf. Richards, 'Bwembya', p. 33

[181] Munday, 'Kankomba', p. 33

[182] Glave, 'Journey to the Livingstone Tree', *Century Magazine*, September 1896, p. 776. For Chikwanda II's fearsome reputation among the Lala cf. R. Campbell, 'Garenganze to Blantyre', *GJ*, 1898, 12, p. 613.

[183] Chikwanda III, October 1936 (statement filed in Kasama DNB)

Chapter 6

Politics and trade

The last three chapters have surveyed the history of Bemba dynastic struggles and territorial expansion up to the death of Chitapankwa* in 1883. This account has been narrative rather than analytic; in the present chapter, therefore, I examine the character of Bemba government and the sources of Bemba power. In so doing, I shall pay special attention to the trade of the north-eastern plateau and assess its importance as a factor in Bemba politics. The discussion will focus on conditions in the latter part of Chitapankwa's* reign, partly because there is a certain amount of contemporary literary evidence for this period, but also because the period represents the climacteric of Bemba power in terms of a balance between internal cohesion and territorial extent. Moreover, some analysis of this period is essential for an understanding of the reign of Chitapankwa's* successor Sampa*, which was marked both by major internal conflicts and by the intrusions of Europeans bent on occupying Bemba country. In the first part of this chapter, therefore, I outline the character of the Bemba polity in about 1880. I then sketch the nature and growth of Bemba involvement in local and long-distance trade. Finally, I assess the political effects on the Bemba of long-distance trade.

BEMBA POLITICS IN ABOUT 1880

During the half-century or so before the death of Chitapankwa*, the Bemba polity had greatly increased in territorial extent: this was at least doubled in the twenty or so years after the death of Chileshye*. And the Bemba polity also increased in cohesion, in that it largely came under the control of members of a single shallow lineage within the royal clan. By 1880, there were about twenty Bemba chiefdoms spread over an area of rather more than 20,000 square miles and comprising a scattered population of about 100,000.[1] Nonetheless, it is only in the most general sense that these twenty chiefdoms may be said to have constituted a single political unit. Chitimukulu continued to exercise a unique pre-eminence in the sphere of ritual, but there were no institutions whereby he could exercise political, military or economic control throughout Bembaland. Thus in describing the Bemba political system as it was in about 1880, it is convenient to consider the pattern of government within each chiefdom before examining the links which held them within a larger structure.

The chiefdom (*calo*) was the basic unit of administration, within which a chief dispensed justice and levied tribute and military service.[2] Each chiefdom was marked off from its neighbours by borders defined by natural features, usually streams and rivers, though in recently conquered areas the borders with non-Bemba territory might not be at all certain. A chief might seek to consolidate his power by granting village headmanships to his own relatives,[3] and to some he might delegate authority over other headmen in the chiefdom; but such sub-chiefs ruled only on his behalf, not in their own right. And the chief's own village, the *musumba*, assumed special importance in the later nineteenth century as a refuge for the surrounding area in time of war. Informants assert that there were few villages apart from these capitals; certainly Livingstone and Giraud mention few villages between those of the Bemba chiefs they visited.[4] A chief's capital was a large place,

[1] This figure is almost certainly an underestimate. It is based on an amalgam of estimates for Bemba population by officials in the early decades of the twentieth century: see Appendix 1(c). These estimates are probably considerably below the true figures, due to labour migration and the difficulty of enumeration in such sparsely inhabited country; in any case, there was probably a marked net decline in population following the smallpox epidemic of 1901–3 (as also that of 1883: see below, p. 218, n. 9). The present Bemba population is about 250,000, excluding Bemba on the line of rail (see above, p. xxvii).

[2] My principal informants on aspects of Bemba life and government in the late nineteenth century were Chitichipalo (31 July 1964), Kachasa (26 August 1964), Chipasha (15 September 1964), Milambo (1–2 October 1964, 13 April 1965), Chinyumba (17 June 1965). All but the last were young men by the time of Sampa's death in 1896, but their information may not always be relevant for the reign of Chitapankwa, in view of the great changes in Bemba politics following the latter's death.

[3] Richards noted (*Land, Labour and Diet*, pp. 412–13) in 1934 the percentage of headmanships held by chief's relatives in Ituna (41), Ichinga (33) and Lubemba (19: here, the opportunities were limited by the large number of villages under hereditary councillors).

[4] In 1934 there were only seven villages in Ituna which had had three or more previous holders of the headmanship, and only ten which had had two previous

well fortified by ditches and stockades which are usually still partly visible today. Livingstone found in 1867 that Chitapankwa's* village had a triple stockade, about 1,400 yards round on the outside. In 1883 Giraud found that Chitapankwa's* residence was surrounded by four or five hundred huts, occupying a square kilometre.[5] Thus the total population of his capital may have been rather more than a thousand;[6] this might have represented between 7% and 10% of the total population of Lubemba—a modest but not insignificant proportion.[7] The capitals of at least the major chiefs were divided into sections (*fitente*), each under an elder (*cilolo*) who was appointed by the chief and was directly responsible to him for law and order within his section.[8] In Sampa's* time, Chitimukulu's village had eleven such sections, and there were about the same number in the village of his contemporary Mwamba III Mubanga Chipoya.[9]

Within their chiefdoms, most chiefs enjoyed almost unqualified judicial power, though they normally sought the advice and consent of their *bafilolo*. In general, the justice of Chitimukulu did not extend beyond Lubemba, inasmuch as most chiefs could deal with any case not involving the lèse-majesté of another chief, and there was no system of appeals.[10] Giraud had the impression that Chitapankwa* did not

headmen; in Ichinga, the respective figures were ten and fourteen (Richards, *Land, Labour and Diet*, p. 412).

[5] Livingstone, *Last Journals*, I, p. 184; Giraud, *Lacs*, pp. 253–4. In 1899 Makasa's village was thought to comprise not less than five hundred huts (E. S. Grogan and A. H. Sharp, *From the Cape to Cairo* (London 1900, 79). Ŋwena and Ikula, late-nineteenth-century sites for Chitimukulu and Mwamba, measure roughly 1,000 yards and 800 yards respectively around their outer ditches.

[6] The usual ratio of people to huts is rather more than 2·5:1 (cf. Luena DNB II, for 1907 figures among the western Bemba; also Watson, *Tribal Cohesion*, p. 54, for the Mambwe).

[7] For evidence as to the total population of Lubemba in 1908 and 1926, see Appendix 1 (c). Lubemba, of course, comprises a large number of long-established villages other than the capital. Kazembe's capital was very much larger than Chitimukulu's, even if the estimate of 20,000 made at the end of the century is a gross exaggeration (Sharpe to Hill, 17 September 1899, FO 2/210).

[8] Richards, 'Political System', p. 107; Gouldsbury and Sheane, *Great Plateau*, p. 22

[9] According to my informants. Gouldsbury and Sheane (*ibid.*) say that there were thirty-three *fitente* at Chitimukulu's; Labrecque, thirty or forty ('Origines', p. 301). Headman Bwembya, in old age, boasted that there were 'forty or fifty' divisions in the capital of Mwamba III (1883–98) (Richards, 'Bwembya', p. 21).

[10] C. Gouldsbury, 'Notes on the Customary Law of the Awemba', *JAS*, 1915–16, 15, p. 176; Milambo, 2 October 1964. There were no appeals to Kazembe in the eastern Lunda kingdom (Cunnison, *Luapula Peoples*, p. 182).

trouble to hear cases of theft and murder, and was only concerned to punish those who meddled with his wives.[11] But chiefs reserved to themselves the power of life and death, and summary revenge for murder was punishable by payment of a slave.[12] And there is no doubt that a chief spent a good deal of time hearing disputes. Livingstone gives an attractive picture of Mwamba II sitting in judgement, and his successor is said to have dispensed justice throughout his last illness.[13] Certain powers were restricted to the more senior chiefs, such as the administration of the poison ordeal (*mwavi*) for suspected sorcerers, or punishment by physical mutilation.[14]

Bemba chiefs were notoriously harsh rulers. It is not easy to determine how far justice was perverted or travestied to satisfy a chief's private whim,[15] but throughout Africa the slave trade provided chiefs with an incentive to enslave their own subjects quite arbitrarily. And the severity of Bemba punishment, especially the frequency of mutilation, impressed African as well as European visitors.[16] The Bemba were ruled by despotism no less sanguinary than that of Muteesa or Mwanga, Mirambo or Msiri. But this brutality was not simply due to the personal proclivities of chiefs. We may well suppose that the use of terror as an instrument of policy increased as the scale of government increased: as the opportunities of chiefs expanded, so too did the need to enforce obedience; and Bemba chiefs, like any other men, were undoubtedly debased by the practice of extreme violence. Nonetheless, Giraud was impressed by the relative mildness of Chitapankwa's* rule:

> Au commencement, Kétimkuru, pour assurer son autorité, a dû se montrer excessivement sévère; mais à l'heure présente son prestige

[11] *Lacs*, p. 264

[12] Gouldsbury, 'Customary Law', *JAS*, 1914–15, 14, p. 381. It is said that Chikwanda had to send murder cases to Chitimukulu (Kalesu, 21 April 1965); if so, this was probably true of other junior chiefs, at least within Chitimukulu's sphere of influence (cf. below, pp. 180–1).

[13] *Last Journals*, I, p. 198; Pineau, *Evêque-Roi des Brigands*, p. 187; see also the description of Mwamba III in judgement in Richards, 'Bwembya', p. 24.

[14] Gouldsbury, 'Customary Law', *JAS*, 1915–16, 15, p. 44; Milambo, 2 October 1964. For a general discussion, see A. I. Richards, 'The Conciliar System of the Bemba of Northern Zambia', *Councils in Action*, eds A. I. Richards and Adam Kuper, Cambridge, 1971, pp. 100–29.

[15] Cf. the stories about Bemba chiefs heard by Becker, at Karema on Lake Tanganyika, in 1882 (Jérôme Becker, *La Vie en Afrique*, Paris 1887, II, p. 323).

[16] Cf. the anonymous Swahili report on a visit to the Bemba in Büttner, *Suaheli-Schriftstücke*, pp. 100–1; Giraud, *Lacs*, p. 256; and also the account of Mwamba III's brutal punishments in Richards, 'Bwembya', pp. 28–31.

est trop bien établi pour qu'il ait besoin de l'affirmer par des répressions excessives.[17]

It is in any case likely that an important Bemba chief gave more thought to military campaigns than to dispensing justice. Giraud remarked of Chitapankwa* that 'he appears to be always at war, although his person is by no means martial, and despite the fact that his obesity renders marching difficult'.[18] This is certainly borne out by the historical record.[19] And warfare provided special opportunities for a chief to build up a personal following. Giraud was doubtless misled by appearances in supposing that Chitapankwa* decided matters of war and peace on his own: public approval by the elders was probably given only after private consultation.[20] But we may well believe that a chief exerted more independence of his councillors in warfare than in matters of justice and ritual. He appointed military leaders (*bamushika*) who usually lived in the capital and were often selected from those who in boyhood had served the chief as pages.[21] A few chiefs maintained small groups of hand-picked warriors. Mwamba III had such an elite, the *basole*, which included several of his sons and grandsons. Chitapankwa* is said to have kept a group of warriors in a village of their own under a leader called Kalembe.[22] Sometimes Chitimukulu would work upon the ardour of the young men at his capital in order to sway the more prudent counsels of the older men.[23] But there was no standing army. To mount an expedition of more than two hundred men or so, it was necessary to conscript villagers outside the capital; each campaign was a somewhat ad hoc affair.[24] Apart from the fact

[17] Giraud, *Lacs*, p. 256: 'To begin with, Chitimukulu had to establish his authority by proving his ruthlessness, but by now his position is so secure that he has no need for harsh repression.'

[18] Giraud, as reported in *PRGS*, 1885, n.s. 5, p. 333

[19] Cf. above, pp. 134–5, 143–51.   [20] *Lacs*, p. 263

[21] Chitichipalo, 16 September 1964, cf. Richards, 'Bwembya', 34. It seems that *bamushika* were often associated with particular village-sections.

[22] Personal communication from the Rev. P. B. Mushindo

[23] Sheane, 'Wemba Warpaths', p. 24

[24] In 1893 Sampa and Makasa mounted a force which German observers estimated at five thousand (see below, p. 234). Even if other chiefs sent men, a force of anything like this size would have represented a heavy drain on the able-bodied manpower available to the most powerful Bemba chiefs and could only have been kept in being for a month or two of successful raiding during the dry season. This point is made clear by population figures for the twentieth century, even though some allowance must be made for labour migration: in 1926 the total adult male population of Lubemba was reckoned to be 4,234 (Kasama DNB I, p. 24); in 1914 there were about 3,000 adult Bemba males in Abercorn district—

that the *basole* of Mwamba fought together as a vanguard, there do not
appear to have been regular patterns of assembly, line of march and
deployment, in which leaders and followers had fixed roles and
positions. Bemba society was strongly characterised by military
ambition and achievement, but it could hardly be said to have been
'militarised' in the sense that this was true of Ngoni or Zulu society.[25]

Every chief levied tribute (*mutolo*), in services and in kind, from the
people living in his chiefdom. His authority was at once political,
religious and economic. Not only did he exercise control over his
people's behaviour, he also claimed ultimate ownership of their land
and the fruits thereof, and the right to control their use. These claims
were reinforced by the general belief that chiefs had power to affect
the fertility of the land and its inhabitants, animal and human: through
prayers and ritual observances, chiefs controlled the economic cycle.
It was in this context that Bemba chiefs recruited labour (*mulasa*)
for their own villages and gardens, and also exacted levies of grain,
beer and certain parts of game. Village headmen submitted offerings
of food to their chief after the annual harvest; in addition they were
always liable to sudden emergency demands from their chief, especially
for fresh beer; and they sent people to work in their chief's gardens,
perhaps for a week or two each year.[26] Rights to fish in certain pools
were controlled by the local chief, and fishing villages had specific
tribute obligations.[27] Smiths and other craftsmen paid tribute in their
own products, and people making salt on the Luitikila river each
had to pay one ball of salt to Chikwanda.[28] Each chief claimed a

a very crude guide to the number of people under Makasa and such lesser chiefs as
Changala and Chilangwa (Abercorn DNB I, p. 130). Three weeks was considered
a long time for a campaign: cf. Richards, 'Bwembya', 34.

[25] Cf. Richards, *Land, Labour and Diet*, p. 257. Codrington, who briefly visited
the Bemba in 1899, asserted that 'After the repulse of the Angoni the Awemba,
hitherto not an especially warlike race, formed a military organisation . . .'
(BSAC, *Reports on the Administration of Rhodesia, 1898–1900*, p. 66); but I encountered no confirmation of this, nor of Wissmann's oft-quoted remark (based
only on hearsay) that 'Among the Awemba there exists a perfectly developed
rank, determined by the number of heads of the enemies they have killed' (H. von
Wissmann, *My Second Journey through Equatorial Africa*, London 1891, p. 272).
Besides, this is hardly adequate evidence that the Bemba as a people had any uniform military organisation. They seem rather to have resembled in this respect
the no less martial Lunda of Kazembe: cf. Gamitto, *King Kazembe*, II, pp. 114–15;
Cunnison, *Luapula Peoples*, p. 180.

[26] There is a very thorough discussion of Bemba tribute, and its socio-religious
significance, in Richards, *Land, Labour and Diet*, pp. 251–63.

[27] *Ibid.*, pp. 338–40; Brelsford, *Aspects*, pp. 15–17

[28] For details of this salt industry see Appendix 2, Note M, p. 359.

monopoly of the ivory from elephants killed in his country.[29] Elephant hunting was practised only by special groups led by *fibinda*, trackers with magical powers; and these only worked under the control of the more senior chiefs.[30] Besides such participation in the yield of his own territory, a chief also took a share of his subjects' war-booty; and it was the custom for each subject of Chitapankwa* to give him the first person he captured in a raid.[31]

Such tribute payments were no mere forced levies but expressions of the personal bonds between villagers, headmen and chiefs, and of their beliefs in a mystical relationship between them and the land. There do not appear to have been any tribute collectors, though a chief had messengers to keep him informed of economic conditions. It was taken for granted that a headman would bring due tribute, if only because he needed his chief's blessing on his gardens. In Richards' words, such levies 'formed only one element in the relationship of mutual interdependence between subject and chief by which the commoner, in return for accepting the political authority of his ruler, gained complete security as to his rights of occupying any amount of land he could use'.[32] Besides, the payment of tribute sometimes elicited a direct material reward. People could expect to be fed by their chief while working in his gardens, and it was a chief's business to maintain food reserves against times of scarcity. Beer and meat were needed for councillors and other visitors, while chiefs had to provide for residents of the capital too young or too old to support themselves—boys sent to court as pages, or old men fallen on hard days.[33] Finally, tribute enabled a chief to feed his men on campaigns and so increase by plunder the wealth available for distribution to his

[29] Milambo, 2 October 1964; Richards, *Land, Labour and Diet*, pp. 22, 349; BSAC, *Reports, 1898–1900*, p. 66. Gouldsbury and Sheane, referring to the region in general, say that a chief only took both tusks if they were very small (*Great Plateau*, p. 211), but Marshall had earlier reported that the Lungu chief Tafuna monopolised ivory ('The Awemba', LM/G69/5/6), and Watson says the Mambwe chiefs did so too (*Tribal Cohesion*, p. 36).

[30] Richards, *Land, Labour and Diet*, pp. 348–9; Munkonge, 5 December 1964. There is an account of Bisa *fibinda* in J. E. Hughes, *Eighteen Years on Lake Bangweulu*, London, n.d. (?1933), p. 223; see also Richards, 'Bwembya', p. 32.

[31] According to a Bisa woman who spent three years as a child slave at Chitapankwa's before being sold to an Arab: E. Kootz-Kretschmer, *Die Safwa*, Berlin 1929, II, p. 323

[32] Richards, *Land, Labour and Diet*, pp. 253, 260, 262. The reciprocal character of tribute is emphasised in Mauss' classic study of such 'prestation': cf. M. Mauss, *The Gift*, tr. Ian Cunnison, London 1954, p. 73.

[33] Richards, *Land, Labour and Diet*, pp. 147–8, 261

followers. Generosity was held to be a cardinal virtue in a chief: Livingstone was given an ivory tusk by Chitapankwa* 'because I had sat upon it', while to Giraud Chitapankwa* grandly announced, 'Chitimukulu is a great chief: when he gives, he gives without thought of return'.[34] In fact, it was very much in a chief's interest to attract support by dispensing material favours when there were so few formal institutions of political control.

It will be clear from this brief survey of the rights and duties of Bemba chiefs that they exercised a large measure of autonomy. Although they were all subjects of a common paramount, Chitimukulu, there was no system of centralised administration through which Chitimukulu could exert control throughout Bemba country. Bemba chiefdoms were linked to one another, not primarily through subordination to other institutions of government, but through a complex and flexible network of kinship ties between the chiefs themselves. Nor were the subordinate titles ranked in any formal hierarchy by which their rights and responsibilities might have been defined in relation to the paramountcy and to each other. The power of each Bemba chief, from Chitimukulu downwards, was largely determined by the prevailing constellation of alliances and antagonisms within an expanding and unstable system.

The one basic force for centralisation derived from the mystical nature of chieftainship. Other chiefs might claim to be the owners of their chiefdoms, with mystical powers over their resources, but Chitimukulu was identified not only with his own domain, Lubemba, but with all Bemba country and all Bemba people. In theory, at least, he was invested with a divine kingship over all Bemba: his health and efficacy in ritual could affect them all. The legend of Bemba 'origins' affirmed the seniority of Chitimukulu in point of antiquity, and it was believed that all other Bemba chiefs ultimately derived their authority from their association with Chitimukulu, as the first embodiment of Bemba chieftainship. Thus the *bakabilo* who watched over the royal relics and organised royal rituals could claim to be trustees for the very principle of Bemba chieftainship. They were, in fact, acknowledged as the ultimate source of chiefly legitimacy, inasmuch as claimants to the more important royal chieftainships had to be approved and installed by the *bakabilo* of Chitimukulu. Such ceremonies conferred prestige

---

[34] Livingstone, *Last Journals*, I, p. 186; Giraud, *Lacs*, p. 261. Chitapankwa had of course done very well out of both travellers. Among East African explorers, Thomson showed an unusual appreciation of the subtle etiquette of exchanging 'presents' with chiefs (*Central African Lakes*, I, pp. 236-7).

by the same token that they expressed subordination, and they countered the inclination of subordinate chiefs to arrogate a similar ritual power over their own subordinates. As Richards puts it, 'The senior chief wants to brag that he is so royal that he is installed by Chitimukulu's *bakabilo*; but he wants independence so much that he claims that his counsellors can appoint and instal all his sub-chiefs'.[35] These ceremonies of installation are complemented by those of burial: all royal chiefs seek a final resting-place in the burial groves of Mwalule or Bwalya Chabala.

This ritual authority, however, was effect as well as cause of political structure. The political importance of the *bakabilo*'s role in installing chiefs, for example, depended on the extent to which Chitimukulu could influence their decisions; at the same time, their freedom of action was contingent upon Chitimukulu's standing in relation to his fellow-chiefs. A powerful paramount might on occasion be able to bend the *bakabilo* to his will, while under a weak one their rights over appointments and installations might be flouted by other chiefs. It would probably be vain to search for any established traditions in these matters, especially for the nineteenth century, when the whole political structure was constantly being modified by the creation of new titles and disputes over old ones.[36] So too, a major ritual such as the *lupepo lukalamba*, in which Chitimukulu initiated a cycle of sacrifices throughout Bembaland, could only succeed if he was already assured of his authority: it was undertaken only in time of unusual disaster or when a Chitimukulu was in a relatively powerful position and wanted to demonstrate his strength.[37]

It would thus be rash to invoke the paramount mystical authority of Chitimukulu as being in itself a sufficient reason for the continuing integrity of the Bemba polity. As Werbner has emphasised, the political unity of the Bemba in the later nineteenth century is rather to be explained in terms of the kinship and affinal links which gave their chiefs specific interests in subordination under a common paramount.[38] Nevertheless, before proceeding to examine these ties, we should perhaps question whether they in turn had, in themselves, quite the weight given them in Werbner's analysis. The importance of kinship

---

[35] Richards, 'African Kings', p. 148

[36] Thus Richards' recent account of the ritual links between Bemba chiefdoms should be taken to refer to practices in this century rather than the last (Richards, 'Keeping the King Divine', especially map following p. 24).

[37] *Ibid.*, p. 33; Richards, *Land, Labour and Diet*, p. 361

[38] Werbner, 'Federal Administration', p. 41

in Bemba politics derived partly from its economic base (which is discussed below) and partly from belief in the power of the dead to harm or help the living, especially their own descendants. The fact that by 1880 so many royal Bemba chiefs were descended from common ancestors who had died in the recent past meant of course that they stood in a more or less close relationship to the living paramount and were drawn together in a wide field of competition for hereditary positions. But it also meant that they were more or less closely related to a small number of dead chiefs and other royals who might be expected to favour some living chiefs at the expense of others. Injury to a living parallel cousin, for example, might bring retribution from the spirit of a man who had been mother's brother to both parties. And since there were several dead Chitimukulus among the ancestors of living chiefs, Chitimukulu himself, as principal intercessor to his predecessors, was well placed to affect their influence upon his subordinates. This point, of course, must remain largely conjectural since there is so little specific evidence.[39] But from what is known of both Bemba political history and Bemba beliefs it would not seem too much to claim that the bonds of kinship exerted a special force from beyond the grave.

By 1880, most of Bemba country was ruled by close matrilineal relatives of Chitimukulu and their sons. Chitapankwa* himself was lord over Lubemba, the Bemba heartland. (It is likely that by this time the power of minor royal chiefs near the capital, such as Chileshye Mukulu or Mumena, had been much reduced, though I am not sure whether their small areas were now considered part of Lubemba.)[40] The Mwamba title was held by Chitapankwa's* brother, Chileshye Kapalaula. Mwamba's own area, Ituna, was not exceptionally large, but he held sway over a much wider region through his sons, especially Mporokoso and Munkonge. In Ichinga, the Nkula title was held by Chitapankwa's* nephew Mutale Sichansa. Mutale's brother, Mubanga Chipoya, held the Nkolemfumu title in Miti and ruled Bisa further south. Two more nephews of Chitapankwa* (sons of his younger sister) governed large areas that had been conquered very recently: to the north, Ponde, among the Lungu; in the far south, Mutale Lwanga, who ruled over Bisa as Chikwanda II. Chitapankwa's* own brother,

[39] See, however, p. 261.
[40] See above, p. 82. It is said that many people in the lineages of Chileshye Mukulu and Mutale Mukulu were killed by Chitapankwa or Mwamba III Mubanga Chipoya (A. I. Richards, fieldnotes at Chileshye Mukulu's, 5 September 1957).

Sampa, had no chiefly title but probably dominated Ichingo, the Bisa chiefdom of Kabanda; while Chitapankwa's* parallel cousin Makumba seems to have been no more than a headman in eastern Lubemba.[41] The other male *bena ŋandu* of any consequence were all more distantly related to Chitapankwa*, their common ancestor being three or four generations removed; but of these men, only Shimumbi held an important chieftainship. Chimbola seems at this time to have had no territorial authority beyond perhaps a village or two in Iyaya. Nkweto, whose lineage was very remotely related to that of Chitapankwa*, had lost much of his territory to Makasa and Mukuuka Mwilwa, sons of Chitimukulu. Indeed, of the older *ŋandu* titles, only Mwaba seems to have retained anything like its earlier importance. In relation to other titles, this did not amount to much, and in any case, as we have seen, Mwaba did not escape unscathed from Chitapankwa's* far-reaching ambitions. For the most part, eastern Bembaland was dominated by Chitapankwa's* nephew, Nkula, and his sons, Makasa and Mwilwa.

This distribution of power had been achieved through almost a century of dynastic conflict and manipulation. In two crucial respects, Bemba chiefdoms had been drawn more closely together. On the one hand, many were now ruled by chiefs who, as members of a single shallow matrilineage of *bena ŋandu*, had good claims to succeed to several positions, including the paramountcy. On the other hand, much Bemba country was ruled by sons of Chitimukulu and Mwamba, the two most senior chiefs within this lineage. These sons were not eligible for posts held by *bena ŋandu*, and those who were sons of a reigning chief tended to have a direct interest in their father's continuance in power. Inasmuch as they were not of royal blood, their authority was more qualified than that of *bena ŋandu*. In general, they were not entitled to the same ceremonies and insignia as *bena ŋandu*;[42] they derived their legitimacy not primarily from the *bakabilo* of Chitimukulu but from their perpetual fathers, and for administrative purposes their territories were often adjuncts to those of their fathers.[43]

[41] See below, p. 261.

[42] Though in the course of time the more powerful chiefs developed pretensions to royal usages: cf. Richards, 'Keeping the King Divine', p. 26. Makasa and Munkonge have kept relic-houses for many years, and several Makasas have been buried in an ox-skin, as was Mporokoso I in 1909 (H. C. Dann, *Romance of the Posts in Rhodesia*, London 1940, p. 50). Makasa also came to play a minor role in the burial and accession of Chitimukulu (Brelsford, *Succession*, p. 34).

[43] Richards notes that in general fathers' rights are more pronounced among the Bemba than among the also matrilineal Bisa or Chewa; she quotes this interesting comment by an educated Bemba: 'The father is stronger amongst the Bemba than

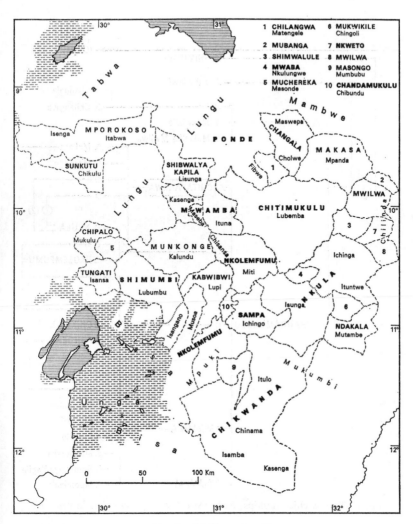

1	CHILANGWA Matengele	6	MUKWIKILE Chingoli
2	MUBANGA	7	NKWETO
3	SHIMWALULE	8	MWILWA
4	MWABA Nkulungwe	9	MASONGO Mumbubu
5	MUCHEREKA Masonde	10	CHANDAMUKULU Chibundu

14 Bemba chiefdoms in 1883

175

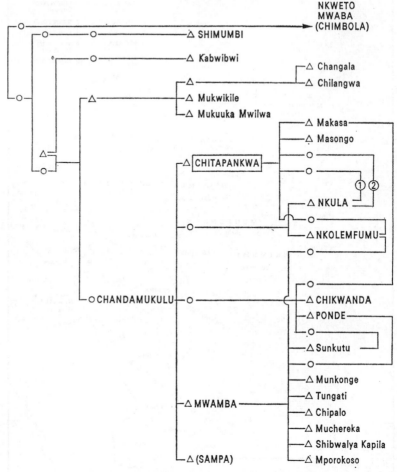

Fig. 14 Bemba chieftainships, early 1883. (*Bena Ŋandu* chiefs in capitals)

To assign a chiefdom to a son was of course no guarantee of obedience, and since the theory of perpetual kinship enabled sons of dead as well as living chiefs to claim such positions, the relationship between a 'son of a chief' and his father' was often not at all close. Yet perpetual kinship between father and son was not lightly ignored. When Sampa*

the Bisa. It is a matter of chieftainship. Members of the crocodile clan always try to get hold of their own sons as well as their sisters' sons' (Richards, 'Some Types of Family Structure', p. 227; see also Kapferer, *Co-operation, Leadership and Village Structure*, p. 27).

declared war on his nephew Nkula, the latter advised Mukwikile (a son of Chileshye*) to keep clear of the fighting 'as you are a son of Mulenda's [Sampa's*] so ought not to fight against him'.[44]

Thus for at least two Bemba chiefs, Chitimukulu and Mwamba, the opportunities for exercising patronage independently of the *bakabilo* had greatly increased. At the same time, new opportunities for other *bena ŋandu* chiefs had been created, in such a way as to focus their energies upon a common path of promotion. Even the few remaining chiefs of distant royal lineages—Nkweto, Mwaba, Shimumbi—served a complementary purpose: now that they were in a minority, they were more likely to value their links with the centre, as a means of countering the ambitions of the perpetual sons and the younger *bena ŋandu*.

It is not enough, however, to consider only the bonds of kinship between Bemba chiefs: affinal links also played an important part in shaping their relationships. In politics, as much as or more than in ordinary social life, position was determined by membership, not simply of a matrilineal descent group, but of a bilateral group, the *lupwa*, composed of relatives on both sides of the family and also of relatives-in-law. Indeed, Richards has remarked that 'the *lupwa* of a ruler is an important unit in the whole political machine'.[45] The *bena ŋandu*, like other dynasties, used marriage as a political device: Richards has specifically noted the importance among Bemba royals of 'carefully arranged cross-cousin marriages'.[46] The relations between a Bemba husband and his parents-in-law involve certain customary rights and duties on both sides, but the former is clearly subordinated to the latter and in the case of marriages by Bemba royals or their children this subordination acquired political significance. As Werbner has pointed out, 'cross-cousin marriages and other marriages of kin allow the constitutional relations between royals to be regulated, through *contracts*, as the relations between superior and subordinate'.[47] It does not seem that affinal links gave rise to perpetual relationships between chieftainships,[48] but such links were certainly more specific and binding than those of descent, and they provided a weighty counterpoint to the royal genealogy.

The evidence for the marriages contracted by *bena ŋandu* during

[44] Mukwikile I (1913), Chinsali DNB I, p. 261
[45] 'Political System', p. 89   [46] 'African Kings', p. 140
[47] 'Federal Administration', p. 41
[48] Richards implies that they did, but she seems rather to have in mind marriages between royal women and commoners, from which the heirs of the latter could derive special prestige ('African Kings', p. 138). See also below, p. 181, n. 4

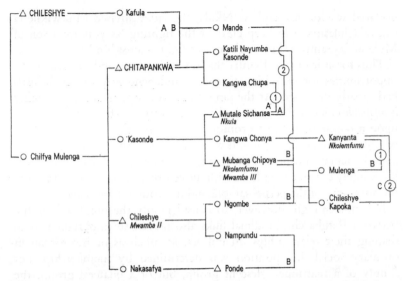

Fig. 15 Cross-cousin marriage of Bemba royals. (i) Male *bena ŋandu* with daughters of *bena ŋandu*. Sources: A, Bush in Brelsford, 'Aspects', 43–4; B, Goodall, 'Tree'; C, Thomas, 'Kanyanta', 477.

the nineteenth century is very incomplete, but several marriages between royal cross-cousins are indicated in figures 15 and 16. Marriage between male *bena ŋandu* and daughters of *bena ŋandu* chiefs was especially important, for this could create direct contractual links between chiefs in office. Nkula Mutale Sichansa became son-in-law to Mwamba II Chileshye Kapalaula, while Nkolemfumu Mubanga Chipoya was son-in-law to both Chitapankwa* and Mwamba II (a reflection, no doubt, of his central position between eastern and western Bembaland). But marriages between female *bena ŋandu* and sons of *bena ŋandu* would also have been a means of seeking alliance and support. Thus, for example, Makasa IV Chipemba was not only a son of Chitapankwa* but a son-in-law of Chitapankwa's* sister Nakasafya, who was the more likely to value this relationship, and her kinship with Chitapankwa*, in that she herself succeeded to neither of the titles for 'mothers of chiefs'. We may thus infer that through Nakasafya, as well as through other channels, Chitapankwa* was able to bring pressure to bear when necessary on Makasa IV. We must also note that Bemba chiefs contracted marriage alliances with neighbouring chiefs, which were also regarded with respect. The Iwa chief Kafwimbi gave one of his daughters in marriage to Chitapankwa*; when a Bemba headman, Lombe Shyula, attacked and killed a son of Kafwimbi, the latter

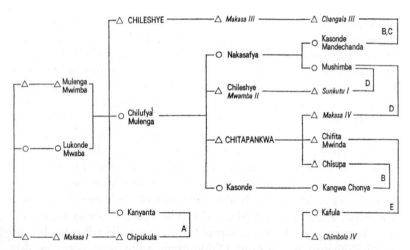

Fig. 16 Cross-cousin marriage of Bemba royals. (ii) Female *bena ŋandu* and sons of *bena ŋandu*. Sources: A, Robertson, *Introductory Handbook*, xxii; B, Goodall, 'Tree'; C, Letort in *CT* 87 (July 1900), 428; D, Mporokoso DNB I, 270; E, Chimbola, 8 June 1965.

complained to his mighty son-in-law, who rebuked Shyula and transferred him.[49]

The overall effect of the changes which took place under Chiliamafwa*, Chileshye* and Chitapankwa* was to diversify the sources of political power and increase the scope for manipulation from the centre, while multiplying the occasions for competition and conflict which hinged upon, and therefore stressed, the diverse relationships between the subordinate chiefs, Mwamba and Chitimukulu.[50] That this was the result of calculation on the part of a few ambitious and far-sighted chiefs is clear enough: the historical record, such as it is, bears witness to a lively tradition of power politics. Unfortunately, we know almost nothing of the discussions and decision-making which took place in specific situations, and we can usually only guess at the motives for particular appointments and manœuvres. Werbner has plausibly suggested that Chitapankwa* deliberately allowed the Mwaba chieftainship to survive as a counterpoise to that of Nkula, even though (or precisely because) Nkula was now a nephew of Chitapankwa*.[51] But it is often not at all clear from the available traditions why particular areas of conquered territory were assigned to one man rather than another. We may reasonably guess why Chinama was

[49] Isoka DNB I, p. 470. For other examples, see above, pp. 100, 147, 156
[50] Cf. Werbner, 'Federal Administration', p. 25   [51] *Ibid.*, p. 44

given in about 1830 to Chikwanda I, a parallel cousin of Chileshye*, rather than to any closer relative. Of Chileshye's* two brothers, Mutale was probably chief in Ituna by this time, while Bwembya was mentally defective; Chileshye's* nephews were probably all too young (they died between 1883 and 1911, and none were especially old when they died); while at this date, so soon after his accession, it is unlikely that any of Chileshye's* sons were old enough to be considered for so important a post. Similar arguments may also hold good for the appointments made about twenty-five years later in country taken from the Lungu of Mukupa Kaoma and the Bisa of Matipa: this was assigned to Shimumbi I, a son of a sister of Chikwanda I, and to several sons of Mwamba. By this time, one of Chileshye's* nephews, Chileshye Kapalaula, was Mwamba. The other nephews may well have been younger than Shimumbi (he was very old when he died in 1907); Chitapankwa* became Chitimukulu a few years later, but this was dictated by genealogy, whereas age and experience might have counted for more in succession to a border area such as Lubumbu. However, such inferences must remain somewhat speculative in the absence of more certain chronological and genealogical information.

It will be apparent from this description of Bemba political relations that by 1880 the Bemba polity, though far more coherent than in 1800, consisted of two major spheres of influence, centred on Chitimukulu and Mwamba. Through conquest, cajolery and conciliation, both chiefs had acquired a direct and more or less specific authority over a number of chiefdoms beyond their own borders. This authority was exercised in various ways: in the appointment and installation of new chiefs; in the collection of tribute; in making war, and in demands for military assistance. Thus Chitapankwa* appointed real or perpetual sons as Makasa, Mukuuka Mwilwa, Mukwikile and Masongo, and at least one son of Makasa, Chilangwa I, was bound to Chitapankwa* as a son-in-law.[52] Giraud reported that Mukuuka Mwilwa, in Chilinda, had orders to send all caravans to Chitimukulu, his perpetual father. Chitapankwa* claimed to receive tribute from Nkula, who as his son-in-law was certainly under a special obligation to him.[53] Chitapankwa* also took a share of the salt levied by Chikwanda on the Luitikila;[54]

[52] Goodall, 'Tree'
[53] Giraud, *Lacs*, pp. 229, 264. Nkula made Giraud give him one of his best guns, but he returned it when Giraud threatened to report him as a robber to Chitapankwa (*ibid.*, p. 244).
[54] Kalesu, 21 April 1965; Milambo, 26 July 1957 (A. I. Richards, fieldnotes); cf. above, p. 169 and Appendix 2, Note M (p. 359).

and he gave Giraud the impression that Shimumbi was 'un de ses fidèles sujets', though it was Mwamba II who had installed Shimumbi.[55] It may be that the various officials who according to Gouldsbury and Sheane enforced the will of Chitimukulu among the Bemba and their neighbours[56] were at least employed to further his interests within the chiefdoms in his own sphere, and among the non-Bemba chiefs on their borders. And Chitapankwa's* exceptional energy enabled him to supervise the military activities of his subordinates, at least in the northeast and southeast. On these borders, it does not seem that Bemba chiefs conducted wars of invasion and conquest independently of Chitapankwa*. He probably exercised little control over border raids, but he occasionally intervened to cut short a minor dispute between Bemba and others.[57]

Mwamba's sphere of influence comprised the chiefdoms under his many sons—Munkonge, Tungati, Chipalo, Sunkutu, Mukuuka (Shibwalya Kapila), Mporokoso; and also that of his nephew and son-in-law Ponde. Mwamba may also have dominated the small chieftainship of Kabwibwi, to the south of Ituna and west of Miti, in which succession was hereditary in a matrilineage of Lungu origin.[58] The position of Nkolemfumu was somewhat equivocal, since Nkolemfumu was son-in-law to both Mwamba and Chitimukulu. It may be no accident that Chitapankwa* sent his son Masongo to country lying between those of Chikwanda and Nkolemfumu.[59] But further west, and along the north-western borders with the Lungu and Tabwa, the influence of Mwamba II predominated. His many sons forwarded tribute to him, and he evidently exercised some control over their relations with non-Bemba neighbours: he appears, for example, to have been a restraining influence upon Mporokoso.[60] Indeed, as we have seen, Mwamba II might also on occasion influence Chitapankwa's* foreign policy,[61] while there is no evidence of Chitapankwa* exerting a similar sway over Mwamba.

---

[55] *Lacs*, p. 262; and above, p. 142. Chitimukulu's claim to appoint Shimumbi II in 1907 does not seem to have been challenged by Mwamba: cf. Luena DNB I, p. 62.

[56] *Great Plateau*, pp. 24–6   [57] See above, p. 179.

[58] See above, pp. 97, 100. Brelsford says that it was the custom for Chitimukulu and Kabwibwi to exchange daughters in marriage (*Succession*, p. 45), but in Lupi I only heard that a former Kabwibwi married a daughter of Kanyanta (Nshilika Mwenya, T1). As a young man, the late Chitimukulu, Musenga, married a sister's daughter of Kabwibwi, who bore him the present chief Tungati Kangwa (Tungati, 23 November 1964).

[59] See above, p. 162.   [60] See above, p. 159.   [61] See above, p. 155.

TRADE

The power of Bemba chiefs, as of other leaders, derived to a large extent from their command of material wealth and their ability to circulate it among their subjects.[62] Bemba country itself had few natural resources: the central, and oldest, areas provided little more than the poor soils, trees and game of the woodland, and the fish of the Chambeshi. But all around the Bemba, along and beyond the edges of the north-eastern plateau, there was considerable variety of terrain and hence of resources. The Bemba were thus peculiarly well placed to gain access to a wide variety of goods: to ironwork and basketwork, to salt and cattle, and to much more fish and ivory.

They obtained such goods by raiding, by levying tribute and by trade. As they themselves had relatively little of their own to offer, it was to be expected that they would seek wealth by raiding rather than trading. But the importance of raiding for the Bemba has perhaps been exaggerated. It is certainly true that the Bemba themselves lay stress on the wealth they got by raiding rather than trade, for this, in their view, reflects much greater glory. In the old days, at least, they took a positive pride in 'cultivating with the spear'. 'When the first Europeans arrived, they asked the Bemba where their gardens were. It is said that the Bemba pointed towards the north, towards the Mambwe.'[63] Raiding was a characteristic feature of Bemba expansion; and precisely because raiding occurred around the expanding borders of Bemba country, it impressed itself very forcibly upon Europeans who began to visit and settle among neighbours of the Bemba in the late nineteenth century. But it is also apparent that Bemba chiefs sometimes sought to stabilise relations with their neighbours by exacting tribute from them, while the very expansion of Bemba-ruled territory enlarged the area within which wealth was acquired by political rather than military means. Moreover, it must be remembered that 'tribute' was not always a one-way process; in the Bemba context, the payment of *mutolo* commonly involved an exchange of goods and/or services between a political superior and inferior, the type and quantity of goods depending on their respective needs and resources, and their relative status and power.

[62] Some of the material which follows has been published in Andrew Roberts, 'Pre-colonial Trade in Zambia', *African Social Research*, 1970, 10, pp. 715–46; see also Christopher St John, 'Kazembe and the Tanganyika-Nyasa Corridor 1800–1890', in Gray and Birmingham, *Pre-Colonial African Trade*, pp. 202–28.

[63] Watson, *Tribal Cohesion*, p. 111, n. 2; cf. Richards, 'Bwembya', p. 23; Foà, *Traversée*, p. 115

Indeed, it is often misleading to attempt to distinguish such exchanges from 'trade'. For the Bemba especially, all economic transactions, including those with professional traders from the east coast, tended to be subordinated to political considerations, and Bemba chiefs sought to monopolise dealings with long-distance traders. In this sense, to be sure, the Bemba were never 'traders' in the sense in which the Bisa or the Nyamwezi were.[64] Nevertheless, it is equally true that in one way or another the Bemba did participate extensively in the exchange of commodities produced in north-eastern Zambia, and that such exchanges, as well as pillage and plunder, were an important source of Bemba power.[65]

Local exchanges

One of the most important items in the pre-colonial trade of north-eastern Zambia, as indeed of all Africa, was iron. This was used to make tools—axes, knives and hoes—and weapons—spears, axes, fish-hooks. The Bemba, whose way of life was based so largely on cutting trees and on warfare, had a considerable need for iron. Yet there seems to have been little workable ore in Bemba country, and the Bemba themselves had no traditions of smelting. Further away, there were several areas where iron was extracted, but the available evidence suggests that these areas were in fact isolated centres and that on the plateau as a whole iron-smelting was not a particularly common activity. (It must of course be remembered that sites of iron extraction might be worked for only a short time before being abandoned.) Iron was indeed a relatively rare commodity in eastern and central Africa until quite recent times; it is clear that in Tanzania the production and use of iron increased markedly during the nineteenth century.[66] One Bemba informant explicitly remarked that iron was scarce among the Bemba in the reign of Chinchinta* (c. 1825), and in 1867 Livingstone noted that the Bisa in 'Lokumbi' (probably subjects of Mukungule in

---

[64] Richards discusses Bemba attitudes to wealth, and compares them with those of the more commercial Bisa (*Land, Labour and Diet*, pp. 211–27).

[65] Gann seems to read too much into his source in asserting that the Bemba 'were unable to engage in trade with their neighbours' ('Slave Trade', p. 34; cf. L. A. Wallace, 'The Nyasa-Tanganyika Plateau', *GJ*, 1889, 13, p. 601). Gamitto noted of the Bemba that 'The instruments which they use are either pillaged or bought from other tribes. They do not indulge in commerce' (*King Kazembe*, II, p. 160); by 'commerce' he presumably meant long-distance trade.

[66] J. E. G. Sutton, 'The Iron Age in East Africa', *The African Iron Age*, ed P. L. Shinnie, London 1971, pp. 179–82; Roberts, 'Nyamwezi Trade', pp. 44–5, 52–3; see also below, p. 209.

Mukumbi) used a wooden hoe for turning over the soil after sowing millet.[67]

The main iron-producers with whom the Bemba associated in the nineteenth century were the Lungu, Mambwe, Iwa, Chishinga and Lala. Of these, the Lungu were probably the most important for the Bemba.[68] Iron was smelted near the Mululwe river and around the watershed between the Luombe and Lufubu rivers.[69] On the south-eastern fringes of this area, Lungu smiths came to settle under Bemba chiefs, to whom they paid tribute in hoes and axes. Some settled in Ituna,[70] while others lived near Chileshye Mukulu, paying tribute to him, Mutale Mukulu and Chitimukulu: two of these Lungu smiths, Mponge and Kamonyo, had their own villages.[71] Further east, a Lungu called Kafusha is said to have built smelting furnaces in Mpanda, perhaps around 1860 or so.[72] The Mambwe were also well known for iron-working: in 1879 Stewart found eight furnaces on one hillside, each capable of smelting nearly half a ton of iron ore.[73] It was perhaps these same furnaces which impressed Giraud five years later on visiting the Mambwe chief Fwambo, who was said to export a great deal of iron.[74] On the eastern borders of Bemba country, iron was smelted in and around Iwa country. The Iwa both smelted and worked iron,[75] but smelting in the last century is also attributed to 'Sukuma', both in Kafwimbi's country and in those of the Bemba sub-chief Musanya and the Bisa chief Chinkumba.[76] The Bisa seem not to have produced iron themselves to any significant extent. Gamitto reported

[67] Shimulamba, T1; Livingstone, *Last Journals*, I, pp. 170–1. See also below, p. 209.

[68] See above, p. 75, for the probable derivation of 'Lungu'.

[69] W. T. [Thomas] in *BCAG*, 12 October 1894; Livingstone, *Last Journals*, I, p. 201. For an account of Lungu ironworking, see H. Johnson, *Night and Morning in Dark Africa*, London 1903, pp. 129–33.

[70] Milambo, 13 April 1965

[71] Chileshye Mukulu, 15 April 1965 (and see above, p. 85); Molo Makungo, 2 July 1965. Lungu immigrants probably worked the few furnaces still to be seen near Chitimukulu's.

[72] Kafusha is said to have arrived in Mpanda in the time of Makasa II Chansa (Oger, 'Mpanda', 11).

[73] Stewart, 'Lake Nyasa', p. 269; cf. Thomson, *Central African Lakes*, I, pp. 303–4

[74] Giraud, *Lacs*, pp. 531–2; cf. L. Decle, *Three Years in Savage Africa*, London 1898, pp. 297–8

[75] Gouldsbury and Sheane, *Great Plateau*, p. 279; Codrington in BSAC, *Reports, 1898–1900*: Giraud, *Lacs*, p. 222

[76] Chiwelewele, 29 April 1965; 'Human Geography of Chinsali District' (1932), NAZ/Sec/Nat 398; Kabwela, 10 May 1965. For these Sukuma see above, p. 73.

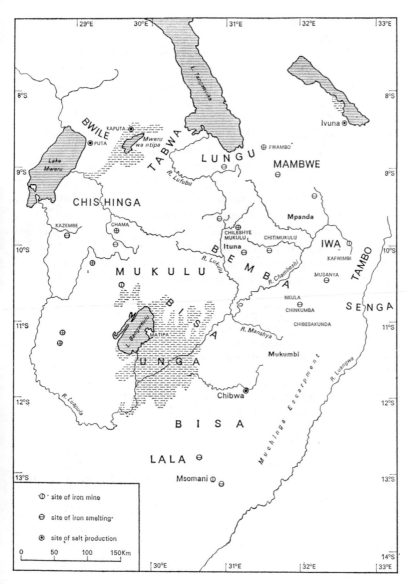

15 Local trade in north-eastern Zambia

that 'minerals were not worked in their lands' and that the Bisa bought the metal goods they needed.[77] This may have been a slight exaggeration: in 1798 there were ruined furnaces near the Manshya river, perhaps in the country of the Bisa chief Kabinga, and in 1867 there were furnaces in the southeast, towards the Muchinga hills; but it is likely that in both places the smelters were Sukuma.[78] The southern Bisa obtained their iron from the Lala, whose output was famous for its quantity and quality;[79] there was a particularly large open mine at Msomani in the country of chief Mailo.[80] The Bemba may not have gained access to Lala ironwork much before the settlement of Chikwanda II in Chinama around 1880; more continuously important for them were the industries to the northwest of Lake Bangweulu. Especially productive were those in the Chishinga chiefdom of Chama, on the eastern borders of Kazembe's kingdom,[81] though iron was also produced among the Bena Mukulu and close to Kazembe's capital.[82]

Salt was also an item of considerable importance in the trade of the plateau. Deposits of salt were few and far between, and Richards

[77] *King Kazembe*, I, p. 205

[78] Lacerda, *Diários*, p. 241 (Burton, *Cazembe*, p. 90); Livingstone, *Last Journals*, I, p. 144; Chiwelewele, 29 April 1965. Iron-smelting in Bisa country is described by a Bisa ex-slave in Margery Perham, *Ten Africans*, London 1936, pp. 85–6, but it is not clear where this took place (the chief was 'Mtisa') or whether the smelters were Bisa.

[79] 'The Ilala are a nation of blacksmiths; all the hoes in this part of the country were made by them' (Glave, 'Livingstone Tree', p. 776; cf. Thomas, *Bisa*, p. 31). For the quality of Lala spears and hoes see below, p. 209, and Mpika annual report, 1905–6, NAZ/KSD 7/1.

[80] J. A. Bancroft, *Mining in Northern Rhodesia*, London 1961, p. 37; D. C., Serenje to Chief Secretary, 24 March 1943, NAZ/Sec/Nat 147; cf. D. W. Phillipson, 'Cewa, Leya and Lala Iron-Smelting Furnaces', *South African Archaeological Bulletin*, 1968, 23, iii, pp. 102–113. The numerous deep pits at Msomani are easily visible today.

[81] G. Quick, 'Notes on Native Iron Industry', enclosure in D. C. Kawambwa to Chief Secretary, 16 February 1943, and R. H. Howard, 'Notes on Making Native Hoes', November 1942, NAZ/Sec/Nat 147; W. V. Brelsford, 'Rituals and Medicines of Chishinga Ironworkers', *Man*, 1949, 49, pp. 27–9; Livingstone, *Last Journals*, II, p. 259. Chaplin describes the process and says that Chishinga hoes were used (presumably by the Chishinga) in making marriage payments: hence the name of a stream, *akamana mpango* ('the stream of bride-wealth') on which one mine was situated (J. H. Chaplin, 'Notes on Traditional Smelting in Northern Rhodesia', *South African Archaeological Bulletin*, 1961, 16, ii, p. 53). In 1905 the Chishinga were said to be the only people who smelted iron in the country north of Lake Bangweulu (Luena DNB I, p. 30).

[82] Livingstone, *Last Journals*, I, pp. 268, 307; II, p. 264; Cunnison, *Luapula Peoples*, p. 19

observes that 'of the special cravings recognized by the Bemba the longing for salt is probably the most pronounced'.[83] Many dambos furnished a saline grass which was burnt to yield a bitter salty ash for immediate and local use,[84] but there were only two areas in the country known to the Bemba where salt was produced in any quantity. There was a great abundance of rich saline grass in Chibwa marsh on the Luitikila river, in Chinama: the ash from this was diluted and filtered into pots, in which the solution was evaporated by boiling; the residue was then left in pots to crystallise in the form of small cakes. Gamitto, in 1832, noted that this salt was relatively pure, though much weaker than mineral salt, and it commanded a high price. Both Bemba and Bisa made salt there in his day,[85] and we learn from later reports that a number of people from the surrounding country came to make salt in September and October, when the dambo had dried up.[86] North of the Bemba, salt was exported from pans at Ivuna, on Lake Rukwa,[87] but it is not clear whether much of this reached the Bemba. More important for their western chiefdoms, at least, were the salt marshes between Lakes Mweru and Mweru wa ntipa, especially near Puta and Kaputa. At these sites, the saline soil yielded a solution from which salt was obtained in much the same way as on the Luitikila. It was mostly worked by the indigenous Tabwa and Bwile, who sold it in standard loads of about twenty-five pounds.[88]

The iron and salt thus produced provided the basis for a not inconsiderable trade among the peoples of north-eastern Zambia. Among the Bemba, iron and salt were circulated partly in the form of tribute payments and the gifts which might be made in return. Chiefs

[83] *Land, Labour and Diet*, p. 55

[84] As on the Lukulu river, south of Mwamba's, in 1883 (Giraud, *Lacs*, p. 274). There are two salt pans at Uningi, six miles south of Mbala (Abercorn), in Lungu country, but the salt attracted game rather than people: cf. F. H. Melland and E. H. Cholmeley, *Through the Heart of Africa*, London 1912, p. 6.

[85] *King Kazembe*, II, p. 148; cf. Hughes, *Eighteen Years*, p. 234

[86] For details see Appendix 2, Note M. Salt was still produced at Chibwa in 1970, though only by a few families living nearby.

[87] St John, 'Kazembe and the Tanganyika-Nyasa Corridor', p. 208

[88] Livingstone, *Last Journals*, I, pp. 243–4; Trivier, *Voyage*, pp. 270–1; *BCAG*, 12 October 1894, 15 March 1897; Johnson, *Night and Morning*, pp. 127–8; R. J. Moore, 'Industry and Trade on the Shores of Lake Mweru', *Africa*, 1937, 10, ii, p. 138. Exports were estimated at 15,000–20,000 lbs in 1898 (Wallace, 'Nyasa-Tanganyika Plateau', p. 616). A load was sold at this period for four yards of calico (H. Croad, 'The Choma Division of the Mweru District', *GJ*, 1898, 11, vi, p. 621). Salt was still produced and sold at Kaputa and Puta in 1969, though only for local use.

sometimes organised expeditions to obtain such goods: in 1883 Nkula received in this way a consignment of salt from Chibwa.[89] But it seems that ordinary Bemba might also obtain iron and salt at source on their own initiative: Bemba chiefs imposed no restrictions, other than the levy of tribute, on the production and exchange of these commodities. Bemba commoners occasionally visited the Lunda (and presumably the less distant Chishinga) to buy hoes; they also went to Chinama for salt.[90] Bisa from Chibesakunda's obtained salt in Chinama and might use it to buy ironwork from the Sukuma under Kafwimbi.[91] The southern Bisa exchanged salt for iron, from the Lala, and both Bemba and Bisa sold salt and iron to the Senga on the upper Luangwa, who in return supplied tobacco, mats and baskets, and also grain and cotton.[92] The Senga and Bisa are said to have woven cloth from their own cotton; the Tambo on the upper Luangwa certainly did;[93] and so did the Lungu, who sometimes paid tribute in it to the Bemba.[94] The usual dress of the Bemba was bark-cloth, and they were well-known for their skill in making it.[95] Bark-cloth was the usual material component of marriage payments,[96] and probably some was also traded to neighbours in less densely wooded areas lacking the appropriate trees.[97] The Unga, in the swamps of Lake Bangweulu, and the Bisa of Matipa exported dried fish, nets, mats and baskets;[98] otter skins were traded all round the north and east of the lake;[99] and the Unga exchanged fish

[89] Giraud, *Lacs*, p. 241. It is possible, but unlikely, that this salt had been brought to Nkula as tribute: see Appendix 2, Note M (pp. 360–1).

[90] Richards, *Land, Labour and Diet*, p. 222

[91] Chiwelewele, 29 April 1965

[92] Mpika annual reports, 1906–7, 1910–11, NAZ/KSD 7/1; M. P. Miracle, 'Aboriginal Trade among the Senga and Nsenga of Northern Rhodesia', *Ethnology*, 1962, I, ii, p. 215

[93] *Ibid.*; Chinsali DNB I, p. 190; *Aurora*, 1 December 1897

[94] Livingstone, *Last Journals*, I, p. 207 (he noted that the Lungu grew a variety from Pernambuco, Brazil); Hore, journal, LMS/CA/J3; Chitichipalo, 31 July 1964

[95] Cf. Codrington in BSAC, *Reports, 1898–1900*, p. 10; and below, p. 207

[96] Richards, *Land, Labour and Diet*, p. 219; Gouldsbury and Sheane, *Great Plateau*, pp. 286–7

[97] The most favoured trees for making bark-cloth were the *mutaba* (*ficus Thonningii*); *ngalati* (*Brachystegia mimosaefolia*); and *muombo* (*B. longifolia*); cf. Gouldsbury and Sheane, *Great Plateau*, p. 287. In 1899 Makasa's village (then a short distance east of the upper Chambeshi) was said to be 'a great centre of the bark-cloth industry' (Grogan and Sharp, *From the Cape to Cairo*, p. 79).

[98] Mpika annual report, 1909–10, NAZ/KSD 7/1; Luena DNB I, 1907, p. 30

[99] Gamitto, *King Kazembe*, II, pp. 193–4; cf. Mpika annual report, 1908–9, NAZ/KSD 7/1

and antelope meat for ironwork from the Bena Mukulu on the northern shores.[100]

Cattle and other livestock were of limited importance to most people on the plateau: they could only be bred in tsetse-free areas, and the only people who kept herds of any size were the Lungu, Mambwe and Iwa. Even among them, cattle were not openly traded, but they changed hands in marriage payments,[101] in the payment of tribute and in raids. Throughout their history, the Bemba had raided the cattle of their northern and eastern neighbours.[102] From time to time, they were able instead to levy tribute in cattle and smaller stock: thus in 1883 Giraud noted that the people around the headwaters of the Luangwa paid an annual tribute to Chitimukulu, as a result of which they had lost most of their cattle, sheep and goats.[103] In 1888 Chitimukulu sent out a small party to collect tribute from Mambwe chiefs in cattle and goats.[104] Even at the height of their power, few Bemba chiefs had much livestock,[105] but they were all the more important as a means of providing spectacular hospitality for followers and subjects.

Long-distance trade

Useful though such local patterns of trade and tribute were to the Bemba and their neighbours, they were in themselves of less political significance than the long-distance trade of the nineteenth century, in which ivory, slaves and copper were exported to other parts of central and eastern Africa and to the east coast.[106] For a hundred years or more, between about 1760 and 1860, it was the Bisa, in association with the Lunda king Kazembe, who dominated the long-distance trade of north-eastern Zambia. But during the later nineteenth century Bisa trade fell into a sharp decline, and it was the Bemba who most successfully

[100] W. V. Brelsford, *Fishermen of the Bangweulu Swamps*, Rhodes-Livingstone Paper 12, Livingstone 1946, pp. 47-8, 120

[101] Watson, *Tribal Cohesion*, pp. 37, 40

[102] In Barotseland, in 1853, Livingstone inferred that lack of salt promoted a craving for meat, which 'is one of the most exciting causes of wars'; D. Livingstone, *Livingstone's Private Journals 1851–1853* ed. I. Schapera, London 1960, p. 177.

[103] Giraud, *Lacs*, p. 221; cf. Codrington, in BSAC, *Reports, 1898–1900*, p. 12

[104] Jones to Thompson, 23 July 1888, 25 September 1888: LMS/CA 7/3/D

[105] Livingstone noted cattle, sheep and goats at Mwaba's, cattle at Chitimukulu's, and goats at Mwamba's (*Last Journals*, I, pp. 181, 186, 197-8); Giraud found no sheep between Chitimukulu's and the Ushi, west of Lake Bangweulu (*Lacs*, p. 308; cf. *ibid.*, p. 335).

[106] For several regional studies see Gray and Birmingham, *Pre-Colonial African Trade*; see also Roberts, 'Pre-colonial Trade in Zambia'.

exploited the advent of traders from the East African coast and interior.

In the course of the eighteenth century, Kazembe's capital on the Luapula became the meeting-point of trade routes which were ultimately linked to both the east and west coasts of Africa. Kazembe's kingdom had indeed been established early in the century in the course of extending trading contacts eastwards from the capital of Mwata Yamvo, the Lunda emperor,[107] whose trading links to the west considerably expanded during the century.[108] Kazembe III Lukwesa (*c.* 1760–1804/5) received from Mwata Yamvo goods which had come from the west coast,[109] and he also extended Lunda power eastwards among the Chishinga and Bisa.[110] This facilitated contacts with traders on the Zambezi and around the south end of Lake Malawi. By 1763, Portuguese traders at Zumbo, at the Zambezi–Luangwa confluence, were buying ivory and copper from Africans who came from the northwest.[111] It is not known whether any of these were Bisa, but the Bisa soon became the main exporters of ivory from north-eastern Zambia, and it is likely that this was due in part to their experience in local trade.[112] For a short time, much ivory from Kazembe's dominions reached the port of Mozambique, and on occasion the Bisa carried ivory to Tete, on the lower Zambezi, and as far as Quelimane, on the east coast. The relationship between Bisa traders and Kazembe is not altogether clear, but it appears that the traders obtained ivory for imported cloth both from him and from their own chiefs, who received ivory from Kazembe in return for their tribute of cloth; the Bisa also exchanged their cloth at Kazembe's for copper from his western dominions.[113]

By the 1790s, the Bisa were trading much less with the Portuguese

[107] The first recorded account of Kazembe's early history is in Baptista, 'Exploraçoes', p. 438 (Burton, *Cazembe*, p. 232).

[108] David Birmingham, *Trade and Conflict in Angola*, Oxford 1966, pp. 148–9, 156–7, 161

[109] Lacerda, *Travessia*, p. 390 (Burton, *Cazembe*, p. 41)

[110] See above, pp. 109–10

[111] Anon, 'Memorias da Costa d'Africa Oriental', in A. A. Andrade, *Relaçoes de Mocambique Settecentista*, Lisbon, 1955, p. 204

[112] See above, p. 188, and compare also the history of Nyamwezi trade (Roberts, 'Nyamwezi Trade', p. 49).

[113] Lacerda, *Travessia*, pp. 385–8, *Diários*, p. 250; Baptista, 'Exploraçoes', pp. 434–5 (Burton, *Cazembe*, pp. 35–9, 95, 228–9). By 1806 some Bisa were taking Kazembe's ivory westwards as far as the Lunda king Kasongo, on the Kwango (Baptista, *loc. cit.*; cf. Birmingham, *Trade and Conflict*, p. 149; also Lacerda, *Travessia*, pp. 396–8; Burton, *Cazembe*, pp. 48–9).

8 Salt marsh at Chibwa, near Mpika, September 1969. The grass has been cut and is being stacked for burning

7 *Lunkumbi*: wooden slit signal drum, owned by the Bwile chief Puta

10 Bwile salt-makers' camp near Puta, on Lake Mweru; filtering baskets in the foreground

9 *Mondo*: wooden slit signal drum, played by its owner, Shinwalule

than with the Yao, east of Lake Malawi: the Yao had formerly traded
much at Mozambique but now exchanged ivory for cloth mainly with
traders from the rapidly growing market of Zanzibar.[114] Kazembe III
was eager nonetheless to establish more regular and more direct
contact with the Portuguese, while the Portuguese also became
increasingly aware of the strategic importance of Kazembe's trade, as a
possible means of establishing links between their colonies in Angola
and Mozambique. Kazembe sent envoys to Tete in 1798 and Lacerda's
expedition reached his capital in the same year. It failed to reach any
sort of agreement with Kazembe, but traders from Sena and Tete
evidently visited him around the turn of the century. Two half-caste
traders from Angola reached Kazembe in 1806 and finally arrived at
Tete in 1810. In 1814, Kazembe IV sent another embassy to Tete and a
Portuguese trader from thereabouts visited him in the same year, but
there seems to have been no further contact for several years. A group
of Portuguese settled at the trade route crossing on the middle Luangwa
in 1827 but were soon withdrawn. In 1830 a caravan from Kazembe's
brought ivory to Tete, and this prompted the expedition led by
Monteiro and Gamitto in 1831-2, but this also failed to find a mutually
acceptable basis for regular commerce and it had no sequel.[115]

One reason why Portuguese interest in Kazembe lapsed after 1832
was probably Gamitto's report that the trade route thither was now
subject to interference by the Bemba, who had occupied much of the
country through which it passed. Gamitto indeed said that the Bemba
had advanced southwards in order to gain access to imported cloth.

[114] Lacerda, *Travessia*, pp. 385-8, *Diários*, p. 250 (Burton, *Cazembe*, pp. 35-9, 95); Gamitto, *King Kazembe*, II, pp. 169-71; E. A. Alpers, 'Malawi and Yao responses to external economic forces, 1505-1798', *East Africa and the Orient: Problems of Cultural Synthesis in Pre-Colonial Times*, eds H. N. Chittick and R. I. Rotberg, forthcoming.

[115] Ian Cunnison, 'Kazembe and the Portuguese', *JAH*, 1961, 2, i, pp. 61-76; also Baptista, 'Exploraçoes', p. 435 (Burton, *Cazembe*, p. 229); Gamitto, *King Kazembe*, II, pp. 11, 124. Cunnison notes that there is a hint of a Portuguese expedition to Kazembe's in 1853 (cf. F. T. Valdez, *Six Years of a Traveller's Life in Western Africa*, London 1861, II, p. 213); and in 1855 an Arab who reached the upper Zambezi by way of Kazembe's told Livingstone that Kazembe's soldiers were drilled by 'a person from Pernambuco' (D. Livingstone, *Livingstone's African Journal, 1853-1856*, ed I. Schapera, London 1963, pp. 297-8). We may also note the following passage: 'In 1853, J. B. Abreu da Silva, and his brother Victoriano Romão J. da Silva, proprietors in Quilimane, went on a trading expedition in search of ivory . . . to the valley of Aroangwa, and as far as the vicinity of Lake Bemba. Robbed by the natives, they, in defence, fought them, and, authorised by the government of Quilimane, subjugated many chiefs' (J. Batalho-Reis, 'The Portuguese in Nyasaland', *Scottish Geographical Magazine*, 1889, 4, p. 261).

Bemba chiefs and headmen certainly made heavy demands on the Portuguese expedition and had firm opinions on the types of cloth and beads they wanted.[116] But it does not appear that the Bemba made any attempt to take over Kazembe's role as a major supplier to the Bisa merchants. This may partly have been because the Bemba lacked aptitude for trade; perhaps more important was the fact that Kazembe could supply copper and malachite as well as ivory. In any case, Bisa continued for several years to export these goods from Kazembe's. In the 1830s and 1840s, at least, they sold ivory to traders from the country to the south and east of Lake Malawi, and occasionally Bisa caravans went on through this region to Kilwa, on the coast.[117]

It was not Bemba but Ngoni raids which proved disastrous for the trade through Bisa country. The assassination of Chikwanda I in about 1850, and the temporary withdrawal of the Bemba from Chinama, had been followed by Ngoni incursions into the area.[118] In 1866, near the south-western corner of Lake Malawi, Livingstone found a chief of 'Bisa origin' called Marenga, who by 1861 had fled from the 'Mazuite of Binda' near the Luangwa;[119] he evidently came from Chinama, for in 1873 Livingstone's party were told by a Bisa at Chitambo's that

all those who used to go on trading expeditions were now dead. In former years Malenga's town, Kutchinyama, was the assembling place of the Wabisa traders, but these had been swept off by the Mazitu [Ngoni]. Such as survived had to exist as best they could among the swamps and inundated districts around the Lake [Bangweulu].[120]

116 Gamitto, *King Kazembe*, I, pp. 100, 161, 171, 177–8. Pacheco, who reopened Zumbo in 1861, reported that the place had once been 'the absolute mistress of the trade of the Nsenga, Bisa and Bemba', but I know of no evidence that the latter traded directly at this date with agents from Zumbo (A. M. Pacheco (tr. C. Millot), 'Voyage de Tête à Zumbo', in P. Guyot, *Voyage au Zambèse*, Paris 1895, 301).

117 Gamitto, *King Kazembe*, I, pp. 203–4; II, pp. 169, 171; J. L. Krapf, *Travels, Researches and Missionary Labours*, London 1860, p. 419; C. Guillain, *Documents sur l'histoire, la géographie et le commerce de l'Afrique Orientale*, Paris, n.d. (1856), II, p. 377; Burton, *Lake Regions*, II, p. 150

118 See above, pp. 119–21.

119 Livingstone, *Last Journals*, I, pp. 112–13; J. P. R. Wallis (ed.), *The Zambezi Expedition of David Livingstone, 1858 to 1863*, London 1956, I, p. 195

120 Livingstone, *Last Journals*, II, p. 302. Perhaps 'Malenga' is to be identified with 'Mulenga' whom Labrecque says led the first 'Arab' traders from the south-east ('Origines', pp. 272, 321); they may have been remembered as Arabs simply because these later supplanted the Bisa as the principal traders of the region.

Chitambo himself, a Lala, informed the travellers that 'I too have travelled, and more than once have been to the Bwani (the coast), before the country on the road was destroyed by the Mazitu'.[121] This route was probably abandoned by about 1860, for there is no clear reference to trade between Kazembe's and the country south of Lake Malawi after 1859, when a caravan of coastal traders passed the south end of the lake on their way back from Kazembe's.[122] And it is very likely that by then Bisa traders had already forsaken Kazembe's, and the trade route thither; it is surely significant that in the 1850s and 1860s Bisa were buying ivory well to the south of this route: among the Lamba, and people still further west;[123] on the middle Zambezi;[124] and among the Chewa and Manganja.[125] By 1866, certainly, the south-eastern route to Kazembe's was defunct.

Even before the Ngoni irruption, however, the trade route south-east from Kazembe's had begun to lose its importance as the major link between Lunda country and the east coast. For during the first half of the nineteenth century a new line of trade was opened up further north: this drew Kazembe into the network by which Arabs and Swahili from the coast, and Nyamwezi from the interior, were rapidly expanding trade between the coast, Lake Tanganyika and the eastern Congo.[126] Kazembe appears to have been visited by people from Ujiji in 1798/9,[127] and certainly by 1831 Swahili traders from the

[121] Livingstone, *Last Journals*, II, p. 302; see also Appendix 3.

[122] Wallis, *Zambezi Expedition*, II, p. 334; Kirk, *Zambezi Journal*, pp. 257, 536–7

[123] A. Silva Porto (ed. G. Sousa Dias), *Silva Porto e a Travessia do Continente Africano*, Lisbon 1938, pp. 108, 113

[124] D. Livingstone, *Missionary Travels and Researches in South Africa*, London 1857, p. 567

[125] D. and C. Livingstone, *Narrative of an Expedition to the Zambesi and its Tributaries*, London 1865, p. 547; Livingstone, *Last Journals*, I, p. 118. Late in 1861 there were traders from the Luapula on the western shore of Lake Malawi, but they appear to have brought their ivory direct from Katanga rather than from Kazembe's (Wallis, *Zambezi Expedition*, I, p. 210; Kirk, *Zambesi Journal*, p. 392).

[126] Cf. Roberts, 'Nyamwezi Trade', pp. 48–57; Ian Cunnison, 'Kazembe and the Arabs to 1870' in Stokes and Brown, *The Zambesian Past*, pp. 226–37

[127] Livingstone, *Last Journals*, I, p. 246. There is no mention of them in the records of Lacerda's expedition, although Pinto noted that Kazembe sat on a couch lined with red cotton brought from the north (Burton, *Cazembe*, p. 113). They are unlikely to have been either Swahili or Arabs, who probably did not reach Lake Tanganyika or the Luapula until somewhat later. They may have been Nyamwezi, but it is doubtful whether the 'Tungalagazas' at Kazembe's in 1806 can be identified with the Galagansa or western Nyamwezi (cf. Roberts, 'Nyamwezi Trade', p. 56).

coast south of Zanzibar had reached his court, though we do not know what route they took.[128] An Arab called Muhammed ibn Saleh may also have been there at the time; he was in any case a member of a large Arab caravan which reached Kazembe's in 1841/2 by way of Ujiji and Lake Tanganyika and was forced to settle at the Lunda capital.[129] In 1844 Said ibn Habib el Afifi left Zanzibar and reached Kazembe's by way of Ujiji; he went on to the Katanga copper mines and Benguela, and met Livingstone on the upper Zambezi in 1853 and 1855.[130] In 1851 two Arabs from Bagamoyo reached Katanga and Benguela by way of Lake Tanganyika and Kazembe's;[131] thereafter, visits to Kazembe's and neighbouring areas by traders from the coast and interior of East Africa became increasingly common.

This development favoured the Bemba at the expense of the Bisa and, ultimately, Kazembe himself. The Bemba were geographically well placed to respond to the southward advance of ivory traders from the *mrima* coast opposite Zanzibar and their bases up-country, such as Tabora. It was indeed these traders who first provided the Bemba with regular access to cotton cloth and other imports from overseas. There is little reason to accept the report that Chileshye Chepela traded with Arabs from the southeast before becoming Chitimukulu (i.e. *c.* 1827);[132] Gamitto gives no hint that there were any Arabs or other men from the coast on the south-eastern route to Kazembe's in or before 1832. On the other hand, there is no reason to doubt the tradition that Chileshye* obtained the body of his predecessor, Chinchinta*, by giving imported cloth to the Mambwe among whom Susula had died.[133] This cloth might have been derived from Gamitto's expedition, but it could well have come (as one informant asserted)[134] from coastal traders: either, perhaps, from the Swahili at Kazembe's in 1831 or from the Arabs who went there in 1841/2. By the 1850s, if not earlier, Bemba country was frequented both by traders from Kazeh

[128] Gamitto, *King Kazembe*, II, pp. 119–20. They were familiar with Mozambique Island and spoke to the Portuguese in the Makua language.

[129] Livingstone, *Last Journals*, I, pp. 287, 294; Burton, *Lake Regions*, II, pp. 151–2; Tippu Tip, *Maisha*, p. 25; Cameron, *Across Africa*, I, p. 242

[130] 'Narrative of an Arab Inhabitant of Zanzibar', *Transactions of the Bombay Geographical Society*, 1860, 15, pp. 146–8; Livingstone, *African Journal*, pp. 13 and n. 2, 297

[131] B. F. F. A. de Castro, 'Notice of a Caravan Journey from the East to the West Coast of Africa' (with comments by W. D. Cooley), *JRGS*, 1854, 24, pp. 267–71

[132] See above, p. 103.

[133] See Appendix 2, Note H (p. 353).

[134] Milambo, T2

(Tabora) and by Bisa traders who took their ivory to Kilwa.[135] Such Bisa evidently reached the east coast by way of country to the north of the Bemba,[136] and in 1857 Bisa were well known in Zanzibar,[137] though they do not seem to have continued long on this northern route.[138] During the 1860s, the Bemba were visited three times by the most famous of all ivory traders, Hamed ibn Muhammed el Murjebi, otherwise known as Tippu Tip. In 1863/4 Tippu Tip went to 'Fipa, Nyamwanga, Ruemba and Urungu where I got a great quantity of ivory'. Tippu returned to the Bemba around the end of 1866 and visited Mwamba's; he found no ivory there but left his half-brother 'Kumba-Kumba' there with fifteen guns.[139] At 'Maraira's place' (the village of Mukupa Kaoma, chief of the 'Malaila' Lungu), Tippu Tip found a trader, Amer ibn Said esh Shaksi, who had first visited the Tabwa in 1841/2, though it is not clear whether Amer had traded in Bemba country since then.[140] After Tippu Tip had defeated Nsama, in 1867, he went back to Bemba country to fetch Kumba Kumba, and they seem to have gone back together to the coast.[141] On his third journey to the region, in 1869/70, Tippu Tip went back to Nsama's and from there visited 'my friends Mwamba, Kitimkaro and Shanza, chiefs of the Bemba'. Tippu obtained thirty loads of ivory from Mwamba, fifteen from Chitimukulu (i.e. Chitapankwa*) and ten from Nkula Mutale Sichansa. Tippu provided each chief with credit in goods to encourage them to lay in further supplies of ivory, and when he proceeded on his way west to Manyema, he left Kumba Kumba in charge of a depot at Nsama's; this was the first step towards a permanent settlement of coastal traders in Itabwa.[142]

[135] J. H. Speke, *What Led to the Discovery of the Source of the Nile*, London 1864, p. 232 n. (and cf. p. 199). Mushindo (*History*, s. 51) says that Makasa I, who was killed by the Ngoni around 1850 (see above, p. 119), received tribute in ivory, which suggests that the northern Bemba valued it for trade by that date.

[136] Cf. Burton, *Lake Regions*, II, p. 149   [137] Burton, *Cazembe*, p. 34n.

[138] In 1889 Wiese reported that Bisa traders in the country of the Chewa chief Mwase wa Kasungu visited Tabora as well as the east coast and Katanga, but it is not clear whether this refers to current or past practice: C. Wiese, 'Expediçao portugueza a M'Pesêne', *Boletim da Sociedade de Geographia de Lisboa*, 1892, 11, p 500.   [139] Tippu Tip, *Maisha*, pp. 13, 17

[140] *Ibid.*, pp. 17, 23; Roberts, 'Abdullah', p. 249; for Amer's earlier adventures see also Burton, *Lake Regions*, II, pp. 149, 228.

[141] Tippu Tip, *Maisha*, 25. At Tabora, in the course of his journey to the coast, Tippu fell in with another Arab, who was taking goods to 'Nyamwanga, Ruemba and Urungu' (*ibid.*, p. 27).

[142] *Ibid.*, pp. 47–9; cf. above, pp. 136, 153–5. Werbner's assertion that Tippu Tip was an 'arbitrary pirate' is based, not on Tippu Tip's own detailed memoirs,

Until the last years of the nineteenth century, the ivory traders' main line of access to Bemba country was Lake Tanganyika and the country lying immediately to the east and west of the lake. This was partly due to the somewhat hazardous convenience of water transport, but primarily to political conditions in East Africa which by 1850 favoured the general use of the Bagamoyo–Tabora–Ujiji route for long-distance trade.[143] This circumstance, and the related growth of traders' colonies between Lakes Tanganyika and Mweru, meant that it was the western Bemba, notably Mwamba and Mporokoso, who were best placed to participate in long-distance trade. Nonetheless, traders occasionally used a more direct route which ran slightly north of east from Bemba country and so favoured Chitimukulu and the eastern chiefs. The main hazard on this approach was war and raiding in the countries of the Hehe and Sangu, but it was used by Tippu Tip in 1863/4.[144] Giraud implies that Arab traders from Kilwa visited Chitimukulu in the 1860s; they would presumably have come round the northern end of Lake Malawi.[145] We know from Livingstone that —somewhat to his surprise—Swahili traders from Bagamoyo visited Chitapankwa* in 1867 by way of the Sangu, Safwa and Nyiha, probably entering Bembaland through Chilinda.[146] Makasa, on the north-eastern borders, is said to have sold ivory and slaves to 'Arabs' by about 1868.[147]

The trade to be had in Bemba country was clearly very profitable. The ivory itself was said to be of specially good quality: Giraud spoke of *'une incomparable finesse de grain'*.[148] And the demand for ivory on the coast rose sharply in the later years of the nineteenth century: between about 1870 and 1890, the average price of ivory at Zanzibar more than

but on the much less reliable summary by Brode, and on Young's somewhat garbled account (Werbner, 'Federal Administration', p. 31).

[143] Cf. Roberts, 'Nyamwezi Trade', p. 50

[144] Tippu Tip, *Maisha*, pp. 13, 17, 27

[145] Giraud, *Lacs*, p. 238

[146] Livingstone, *Last Journals*, I, pp. 186–7: the itinerary from Chitimukulu's was as follows: 1. 'Chasa' (?Kachasa); 2. 'Lombe' (Lombe Shyula, a son of Mutale *wa kabwe*); 3. 'Uchere' (Mubanga Chele, who like Lombe was a deputy of Makasa in or near Chilinda after 1880: see pp. 147, 257); 4. 'Nyamiro' (possibly a reference to Chikanamuliro, who however probably did not become chief of the Namwanga until the late 1870s); 5. 'Zonda' (the Nyiha chief Nzunda); 6. 'Zambi' (a chief in the eastern Songwe valley); 7. 'Lioti' (Lyoto, a Safwa chief); 8. Merere (the Sangu chief Merere I Towelamahamba); 9. 'Kirangabana' (a Nyamwezi chief in Usagara). I am indebted to Mrs Beverley Brock for advice on nos. 4–7.

[147] Mushindo, *History*, s. 65; cf. below, pp. 202–3   [148] *Lacs*, p. 260

doubled.[149] As early as 1879, Joseph Thomson, perhaps indulging a weakness for exaggeration, inferred that over the past twenty years elephant had practically disappeared in the country between Lake Tanganyika and the coast.[150] At all events, in 1883, a trader called Aley at Chitimukulu's reckoned that his net profit often came to sixty per cent of his total outlay, and he could buy ivory from the Bemba for a fifth of its price at the coast.[151] I have no detailed information as to where the Bemba hunted elephant, but at least up to the 1880s elephant were plentiful in southern Lubemba, around the south end of Lake Tanganyika, to the northeast of Lake Bangweulu, and in the upper Luangwa basin, while they were always abundant in the middle Luangwa valley and around Mweru wa ntipa.[152]

The Bemba sold slaves as well as ivory. It had been the quest for ivory which had brought traders from the coast thus far into the interior, but as elsewhere in Africa the ivory trade stimulated a trade in slaves. These were sought, not only for export overseas from the market at Kilwa,[153] but also for the households and plantations of traders settled in the interior. And in the countries south of Lake Tanganyika slaves were sometimes needed to carry ivory to the coast, since the region was less frequented by professional porters than the trade route between the coast and Ujiji.[154] Bemba chiefs, for their part, were ready enough to supply slaves in exchange for goods. Among the Bemba, as among their neighbours, domestic slavery was of minor social or economic importance. People might become slaves in Bemba households as a legal punishment, as compensation for irreparable damage or injury, or after being captured in battle.[155] But Bemba country was too poor to encourage chiefs to take prisoners simply to

[149] In 1868 prices for the best ivory at Zanzibar varied between 50 and 80 dollars per frasila (35 lb.); in 1880, between 80 and 111 dollars; in 1887, between 116 and 141 dollars; in 1893, between 120 and 180 dollars (N. R. Bennett, *Studies in East African History*, Boston 1963, p. 89).

[150] *Central African Lakes*, II, pp. 17, 285–6

[151] Giraud, *Lacs*, p. 260; he also describes the business of buying ivory in these regions (*ibid.*, pp. 378–9).

[152] Livingstone, *Last Journals*, I, pp. 184, 206; Giraud, *Lacs*, pp. 235, 253, 266, 278; Carson, journal (April 1886), p. 69, LMS/CA/J 3; Trivier, *Voyage*, p. 270

[153] In 1873 the Sultan of Zanzibar, under British pressure, closed the slave market there and prohibited the export of slaves from the mainland. But though the slave trade at Kilwa was 'negligible' in 1880, it revived in the later 1880s and early 1890s: cf. F. Renault, *Lavigerie, l'Esclavage Africain et l'Europe*, Paris 1971, I, pp. 285, 342, 346–8; and below, p. 225.

[154] See Roberts, 'Nyamwezi Trade', pp. 58–61.

[155] Richards, *Land, Labour and Diet*, pp. 144–5

reinforce their own population, in the manner of the Lozi or Ngoni.[156] It is not clear when the Bemba began to sell, and to hunt for, slaves in any quantity. The traders whom Livingstone met at Chitimukulu's were said by him to be 'slavers', but he gives no other evidence of slave-trading in Bemba country, and he reported that the 'Arabs' among the Tabwa and Lungu bought slaves only when ivory seemed unobtainable.[157] In 1881, however, many slaves from 'Ou-Emba' were seen in Tabora, and in 1884 some 'Bemba' slaves were ransomed in Bagamoyo.[158] The trader Aley had himself been captured by the Bemba: he had been taken to Zanzibar and had since become a trading agent for his employer. In 1883 he had been three years at Chitapankwa's* capital; he had his own quarter there and a few Zanzibari under him worked as craftsmen on their own account. Giraud found that Aley had amassed two hundred tusks, and as he had long since dismissed his porters, he had just bought two hundred Bisa to carry the tusks to the coast.[159]

POLITICAL EFFECTS OF LONG-DISTANCE TRADE

In sharp contrast to their neighbours, the Bemba gained considerably from the advent of traders from East Africa. Elsewhere, traders in ivory and slaves frequently became a corrosive influence on the internal affairs of African polities; sometimes, indeed, they uprooted or terrorised whole chiefdoms. Among the Bemba, however, foreign traders never exerted any significant political influence; on the contrary, they served rather to increase the power of the Bemba themselves as against the surrounding peoples. Yet while long-distance trade fortified Bemba hegemony over the plateau, it is also clear that such trade scarcely modified the character of Bemba political organisation; its ultimate effect was perhaps to intensify, rather than weaken, the divisive forces in Bemba politics.

One important, if negative, factor in the continued ascendancy of the Bemba in the later nineteenth century was the decline of Kazembe during this period, and this was due very largely to the impact of

[156] Gann, 'Slave Trade', p. 34

[157] *Last Journals*, I, pp. 186–7, 232; he reported however that the Bisa were engaged in the slave trade by this time (*ibid.*, pp. 168, 170). Mushindo says that Makasa III sold ivory and slaves before the final Ngoni defeat in *c.* 1870 (*History*, s. 65). Kazembe was selling slaves by 1831 (Gamitto, *King Kazembe*, II, p. 99).

[158] Becker, *Vie en Afrique*, II, p. 28; Andreya Masiye, in *Times of Zambia*, 17 February 1971 (from records of the Holy Ghost mission at Bagamoyo); see also below, p. 200, n. 168

[159] Giraud, *Lacs*, pp. 254–61

foreign traders on the Lunda kingdom. In the first part of the century, as we have seen, much territory that had once been tributary to Kazembe was conquered by the Bemba.[160] There was, however, to be no question of a challenge by Kazembe to Bemba expansion, for Bemba encroachment upon his eastern dominions was followed by the encroachment of foreign traders upon his northern and western dominions. Arab, Swahili and Nyamwezi traders settled in Lungu, Tabwa and Bwile country from the 1860s, and despite their own disunity, their access to firearms, trade goods and military support from East Africa meant that they soon became local potentates in their own right. Their importance became brutally clear in 1872, when Kazembe VII Muonga Sunkutu was killed by a force of Nyamwezi under Arab direction, and two Swahili traders installed a rival Lunda prince, Lukwesa.[161] As Cunnison notes, this incident 'started a whole new pattern of political behaviour'—the use of foreign alliances to mount rebellions.[162]

One other group who were soon drawn into this pattern were the Yeke: these were Nyamwezi and Sumbwa who began to settle in Katanga in the 1850s. Their leader, Msiri, soon made himself independent of Kazembe, seized control of the trade route going west to Mwata Yamvo's and Angola, and disputed Kazembe's hegemony over the Lamba and Ushi athwart the middle Luapula. And it was at this same period, in the 1860s, that Kazembe's trade route to the southeast was finally blocked by Ngoni raiders. Within a decade or so, Kazembe had come to be ringed by hostile, or potentially hostile, intruders who were eager to foment strife among the Lunda. It was from the Yeke that Kazembe IX Lukwesa sought help when he in his turn had been deposed by Kazembe X Kanyembo;[163] and after Lukwesa's death his relative Kaindu had Yeke support in a continuing war against Kazembe X. Chitapankwa* claimed in 1883 that Kazembe was his 'vassal' and sent him annual tribute;[164] no doubt such tribute was reciprocated, but it was not until he had obtained Bemba assistance that Kazembe X, in 1893, finally subdued the Lunda rebels and their Yeke allies.[165] Thus in the later years of the nineteenth century foreign traders

[160] See above, pp. 110–16.
[161] Roberts, 'Tippu Tip, Livingstone, and the Chronology of Kazembe', pp. 118–21   [162] Cunnison, 'Kazembe and the Arabs', p. 236
[163] It was not, as Cunnison says, Bemba who helped Kanyembo depose Lukwesa (*ibid.*), but Chishinga (Cunnison, *Historical Traditions*, p. 94).
[164] Giraud, *Lacs*, p. 377
[165] For a résumé of Yeke and Lunda relations see Vansina, *Kingdoms of the Savanna*, pp. 227–34.

enfeebled the kingdom of Kazembe not only by depriving him of much territory and control over trade but also by aggravating and prolonging fundamental internal disputes.[166]

The Bemba suffered no such disturbances. For several reasons, their relations with traders from East Africa were altogether more cordial than Kazembe's. The East Africans made it possible for the Bemba to participate for the first time in long-distance trade; however, for Kazembe the East Africans soon came to represent a real or potential threat to long-established trading interests. Moreover, Bemba country lay near, but not on, the main routes between Katanga and East Africa. There was no occasion for foreign traders to travel through Bemba country except for the purpose of doing business with Bemba chiefs; nor was it to the advantage of either party that the traders should establish their own settlements among the Bemba. The traders had no need to do this, partly because they had bases nearby, among the Lungu and Tabwa, and partly because the Bemba were themselves able to provide them with ivory and slaves. Bemba chiefs did not, as a rule, raise and fit out caravans of their own men for long-distance trading. Perhaps because their traditions (in contrast to the Bisa) were military and predatory rather than commercial, they devoted their energies to organising raids and hunting expeditions. Thus their relations with the East Africans were complementary rather than competitive. East African traders did do business with some of the lesser chiefs on the plateau, including tributaries of the Bemba such as Kafwimbi of the Iwa;[167] but the Bemba were better customers precisely because their chiefs were strong enough to collect ivory and slaves in large quantities, both through channels of tribute and exchange and by organising special hunting and raiding expeditions. And by the same token, the Bemba were dangerous hosts, who were likely, if aroused, to give much more trouble than the Lungu or Tabwa. There is little direct evidence on the point, but it seems that foreign traders rarely settled, hunted or raided in Bemba country.[168] The ivory amassed by Aley, the trader-slave, at

[166] Gann ('Slave Trade', p. 35) has rightly noted that Kazembe was an active partner in the slave trade, but his description is misleading in that it does not take account of Kazembe's steady decline in power in the course of the nineteenth century.

[167] Giraud, *Lacs*, pp. 223–4; they also traded with the Mambwe and Lungu (Carson, journal, 1883, p. 92: LMS/CA/J3; Roberts, 'Abdullah', p. 254).

[168] Though in about 1880 a Bemba slave owned by a Nyamwezi chief reported that she 'had been taken captive in her own country by the slave-hunting Lima people [?traders from the *mrima* coast]' (J. T. Last, *Polyglotta Africana Orientalis*, London 1885, p. 19).

Chitimukulu's in 1883, had indeed been collected by a band of Nyam-wezi mercenaries (*ruga-ruga*) whom he had taken into service as an escort on his way up-country.[169] But the only traders who settled permanently in Bemba country did so for special reasons. A few Nyamwezi were encouraged to stay because they were also crafts-men: their skill as copper smiths will be noted in due course.[170] One Swahili trader, visiting Mwamba's in 1883, had his goods seized in the riots following the death of Mwamba II early in that year; he had to stay on and engage in local trade, and he was later given a village head-manship which his grandson now holds.[171]

The most obvious and sensational result of Bemba trade with East Africans was that the Bemba obtained firearms. In the last years of the nineteenth century, European observers were naturally inclined to lay much stress on the fact that the Bemba, far more than any other people in the region, were armed with guns and had access to supplies of powder and ammunition. It might therefore be supposed that their military achievements were in large part due to their possession of guns. The available evidence, however, suggests that firearms were of rather limited importance for the territorial expansion of the Bemba; they made no more than a subsidiary contribution to the power of the Bemba polity, extensive as this was, in Chitapankwa's* last years.[172]

For the first two-thirds of the nineteenth century, firearms were of little or no military significance on the north-eastern plateau. When Kazembe's Lunda reached the Luapula, perhaps in the early eighteenth century, they terrified the local people by firing guns,[173] but there is no indication that either then or for long afterwards the Lunda had any ammunition. Kazembe probably obtained guns occasionally from Mwata Yamvo, and Kazembe III Lukwesa gave a gun and powder to envoys from a Bemba chief, Mubanga Kashampupo of Ituna.[174] In 1831 Gamitto learned that the Lunda were supplied with guns by Kazembe, but used them only 'to frighten the enemy, since they charge them with powder alone'. As for the Bemba, they fought with bows, axes and spears.[175] There is no good reason to believe that Chileshye Chepela obtained guns from the southeast before his accession as Chitimukulu;[176] on the other hand, Bemba stole two guns from

[169] Giraud, *Lacs*, p. 260   [170] See below, pp. 207–8
[171] Chela Sani, 28 June 1964; for date, see below, p. 217
[172] For a more extended discussion see Andrew Roberts, 'Firearms in North-eastern Zambia before 1900', *Transafrican Journal of History*, 1971, I, ii, pp. 3–21
[173] Cunnison, *Historical Traditions*, p. 42   [174] *Ibid.*, p. 51
[175] Gamitto, *King Kazembe*, II, pp. 115, 159   [176] See above, pp. 103–4

Gamitto's expedition,[177] and either this incident or contact with early traders from the coast could account for the guns which Chileshye* is said by one informant to have given to the Mambwe in exchange for the corpse of his predecessor.[178] In the late 1850s, Kazembe was said to be 'rich in muskets and gunpowder',[179] but it is not clear how much these were used in war. The Bisa ivory traders do not seem to have imported guns, and Livingstone noted none among the Bemba.[180] It is quite possible that throughout the conquests and conflicts of Chileshye's* reign the Bemba not only had virtually no guns but remained ignorant of their proper use.[181]

The decisive change came only with Tippu Tip's defeat of the Tabwa chief Nsama in 1867: this was the first demonstration in the region of the real effectiveness of guns. Livingstone was camped near Nsama's and reported:

> Twenty Arab guns made him flee from his own stockade, and caused a great sensation in the country. . . . The entire population of the country has received a shock from the conquest of Nsama, and their views of the comparative values of bows and arrows and guns have undergone a great change.[182]

Thus for the first time, we may suppose, a local demand for firearms was created. And at just this period the supply was increased by the changeover in Europe to breech-loaders, which threw on to the market a vast number of obsolete muzzle-loaders, both flintlocks and percussion guns.[183] The East African traders, of course, were not eager to sell these indiscriminately and thus undercut their own advantage in firepower, but as the value of ivory continued to rise they were under pressure to meet demands from people such as the Bemba with whom profitable cooperation was both possible and advisable.

Makasa, on the northern marches, appears to have bought guns from 'Arabs' some time before the first Bemba victory over the Ngoni

---

[177] Gamitto, *King Kazembe*, II, p. 142

[178] Chileshye Mukulu, 25 July 1964; see Appendix 2, Note H. Labrecque ('Origines', p. 294) says that Chileshye obtained guns and cloth from Arabs in exchange for Lungu captured in war, perhaps around 1840 (see above, p. 107).

[179] Burton, *Lake Regions*, II, p. 148

[180] There is a report that—at a period which may be dated to around 1860—the Bisa chief Kabanda was protected by Bemba guns against the Ngoni, but this might simply be a storyteller's anachronism and in any case the chronology is uncertain. See Appendix 3, p. 370, n. 23.

[181] Cf. Roberts, 'Firearms', p. 4   [182] *Last Journals*, pp. 258, 231

[183] R. W. Beachey, 'The Arms Trade in East Africa', *JAH*, 1962, 3, iii, p. 452

in Mambwe country, in about 1868.[184] It is also said that the Bemba were sold firearms by Tippu Tip's half-brother 'Kumba-Kumba', who had visited Mwamba's in 1867 and set up a depot at Nsama's in 1869/70.[185] When Chitapankwa* attacked the Ngoni in Mpanda in about 1870, he enlisted the assistance of some traders: according to Young, the 'coastmen' carried guns and also brought a cannon, while the Bemba were armed with spears, bows and arrows.[186] It is not clear how much the traders' guns contributed to the ensuing Bemba victory; other accounts mention only the cannon, and imply that it achieved its main impact by blowing up.[187] But Young relates that Chitimukulu sold to the 'Arabs' most of his captives from this battle, for guns, gunpowder, percussion caps and the cannon.[188] In 1872, Chitapankwa* recruited Swahili for his siege of the Lungu chief Zombe. This time, however, he was ignominiously routed; when the Lungu were relieved, the Swahili fled, and Chitapankwa* 'left nearly all his guns behind him'.[189]

There is no further evidence about the presence or absence of guns among the Bemba until Giraud's visit in 1883. It may well be that the guns used against the Ngoni and Lungu proved a doubtful asset: the muzzle-loaders traded in the African interior were often more dangerous to the user than to his enemy, and of course their efficacy depended upon proper maintenance and access to suitable ammunition as well as powder and caps or flints. And it should not be expected that a people such as the Bemba, whose technology and handicraft traditions were very simple, would be specially quick to adopt unfamiliar and complex weapons. Giraud found that the Iwa chief Kafwimbi had fifty men armed with old guns, but among the Bemba themselves guns seemed to be neither widespread nor important. Nkula had a few old flintlocks, probably obtained from visiting Nyamwezi. Further west, in Ichingo, Sampa was said to have twice as many guns as Nkula, as a result of raiding caravans. Chitapankwa* himself was said not to need powder, since he forbade his people (presumably those in Lubemba) to use guns. The trader Aley had a gunsmith among his followers, but it is not clear

[184] Labrecque, 'Origines', p. 304
[185] R. Young (c. 1900) in Chinsali DNB I, p. 233; see above, p. 195
[186] Young, in Chinsali DNB I, p. 233; Shimulamba (T1) also says that muzzle-loaders were used against the Ngoni. Other Bemba sources say the Arabs had a *munshinga*: this literally means a hollowed-out tree trunk, so could mean a cannon (Chimba, T7; Tanguy, *Imilandu*, p. 55).
[187] Labrecque, 'Origines', p. 310 (this account of the battle differs considerably from Young's); Chimba, T7   [188] Chinsali DNB I, p. 233
[189] Livingstone, Last Journals, II, p. 248; see above, p. 150.

whether he did much, if any, work for the Bemba at the capital.[190] In 1886 an English missionary stationed in Mambwe country heard that the Bemba did not have many guns,[191] and an anonymous Swahili trader who visited Chitimukulu in the 1880s reported that the Bemba fought with spears and small axes: before Chitimukulu went to war, he issued a spear to each of his men.[192]

Only from the 1890s is there clear evidence that guns had become at all common among the Bemba.[193] It is very likely that there was in fact a sharp increase in the African arms traffic in the late 1880s and 1890s. European countries at this time replaced breech-loaders with magazine rifles, so that the market was once again flooded with obsolete weapons, and also with black powder.[194] With easy access now to breech-loaders, long-distance traders in eastern Africa (who included a growing number of Europeans) would have been more ready to sell muzzle-loaders up-country, while powder was a conveniently high-value, low-bulk burden for porters. Besides, the price of ivory rose ever more rapidly at the coast (and presumably in the interior) during this period,[195] as more and more areas were depleted of elephant.[196] This also meant that the export of slaves became increasingly important,[197] which in turn boosted the trade in firearms, since these were much more useful in slave-raiding than in hunting elephant. And for the Bemba there may have been a new stimulus to obtain firearms in the defeat of Mwamba's forces by Swahili and Tabwa in about 1884; indeed, there is a hint that the Swahili used a new type of gun on this occasion which they later introduced to the Bemba.[198]

Thus it is clear that in the last years of the century firearms were a major asset in Bemba raiding. But the last major phase of territorial expansion—the reconquest of Chinama, Ponde's occupation of Lungu country and Mporokoso's settlement in Itabwa—can be dated to the

[190] Giraud, *Lacs*, pp. 223, 238, 242, 261, 269. Giraud vividly describes the melancholy fate of a Nyamwezi hunter who vainly relied on a defective flintlock against an angry elephant (*ibid.*, pp. 268–9).

[191] Carson, journal, 1886, p. 70, LMS/CA/J3

[192] Büttner, *Suaheli-Schriftstücke*, p. 95   [193] See below, chapter 7.

[194] Beachey, 'Arms Trade', pp. 452–3   [195] See above, p. 197, n. 149

[196] Cf. Thomson, *Central African Lakes*, I, p. 302, II, pp. 17, 285–6; F. Stuhlmann, *Mit Emin Pascha ins Herz von Afrika*, Berlin 1894, p. 86; P. Reichard, *Deutsch-Ostafrika*, Berlin 1891, p. 434; see also below, p. 241.

[197] Cf. Crawshay to Johnston, 30 June 1893, enclosure in Johnston to Rosebery, 25 August 1893, FO 2/54. The demand for slaves in the interior rose as they became cheaper, following the increased difficulty of exporting them from the coast.

[198] Shimulamba, T1; see above, p. 159.

years around 1880,[199] before firearms became at all common. It is therefore doubtful whether firearms were an important factor in the growth of Bemba power, as they so clearly were, for example, in the rise of the parvenu Yeke leader Msiri.[200] It is not even certain that firearms were decisive in the expulsion of the Ngoni from Mambwe country: the crucial factors on that occasion would seem rather to have been the resourceful tactics of the Bemba and the massive, if temporary, military alliance of chiefs from all over Bembaland.[201] It may well be that firearms were less important in the relations between the Bemba and their neighbours than in the relations between the Bemba and European intruders in the 1890s.

If firearms were not used in any quantity by the Bemba until the last years of the century, it is unlikely that they stimulated any significant changes in the Bemba practice of the art of war. There is however some evidence that Bemba tactics were influenced by foreign traders. Throughout most of the nineteenth century the main feature of Bemba tactics was the dawn attack, sometimes involving an ambush or the use of decoy parties—as in the final defeat of the Ngoni in Mpanda, or the defeat of Zombe.[202] Gamitto heard that the Bemba 'always procure a surprise attack, but this is put in without discipline and without any particular tactics'.[203] In 1886 a missionary travelling through Mambwe and Lungu country reported that the Bemba chief (perhaps Makasa or Sampa*)

> comes up to a doomed village after dark, builds a platform over-looking the stockade, and at the same time digs a trench underneath it and his men force through the trench in the morning while arrows are poured into the village from the platform above.[204]

But in 1895 a European hunter who had lived for some years near Ponde and Mporokoso wrote that the Bemba had lately

> adopted the Arab mode of warfare—i.e. regularly laying siege to a place. . . . This seems terribly tame work after the mad rush of the

[199] See above, pp. 151, 157, 162.   [200] Cf. Roberts, 'Firearms', pp. 9–10.
[201] See above, p. 145, and sources there cited.
[202] Cf. Milambo, 2 October 1964; Labrecque, 'Origines', pp. 308–10, 315. For a general description, see Sheane, 'Wemba Warpaths', pp. 27–30.
[203] *King Kazembe*, II, .p 159
[204] Carson, journal, 1886, p. 70, LMS/CA/J3. The night march and dawn attack were very common, as a German visitor to the Nyamwezi observed in 1881 (Richard Böhm, *Von Sansibar zum Tanganjika*, Leipzig 1888, p. 86. See also Wallis, *Zambesi Expedition*, I, p. 207.

205

Zulus against a laager or of the Dervishes against a Zariba but one must confess it is infinitely wiser, if losses to the besieging party are to be taken into account.[205]

The first remembered Bemba siege seems to be that against the Mambwe chief Mpande V, soon after the defeat of the Ngoni; this was very successful, though the siege against Zombe a year or two later, in 1872, was a conspicuous failure.[206]

It is likely however that Bemba involvement in long-distance trade contributed to their power less through specific military influence than through the diversification and enlargement of production and exchange in and around Bembaland. This may perhaps seem unduly formal language for an economy which was, as it still is, almost wholly concerned with subsistence, and in which there were no markets. Nonetheless, the evidence does suggest that the presence of alien traders and craftsmen, and the introduction of new commodities, helped to stimulate exchange all over the plateau and thus encouraged the exploitation of local resources.[207] Among the Bemba, much of this increased traffic passed through the capitals of chiefs and thus served to increase their ability to attract and reward supporters. In the relatively loosely structured political system of the Bemba, this could be of considerable significance.[208]

The basis of long-distance trade for the Bemba, as for other peoples in the African interior, consisted of a simple formula: the exchange of firearms, cloth, shells or beads for ivory and slaves. But such exchanges were only made possible by the existence of local networks of exchange, for these were essential to the power by which ivory and slaves were obtained. Conversely, the imports from the coast were not simply amassed by chiefs but were redistributed through the local networks of exchange,[209] thus ultimately increasing their capacity to supply commodities for export. For obvious reasons, firearms were of minor importance in this process, even when they were imported in relatively large quantities; and even when ordinary people did obtain guns a chief could still control the supply of powder and ammunition.

[205] Weatherley to Johnston, 11 October 1895, enclosure in Johnston to Rhodes, 31 December 1895, Rhodes House MSS. Afr. S. 228, 26 (hereafter cited as RH).

[206] See above, pp. 146, 150.

[207] This point can be clearly demonstrated for the Nyamwezi: see Roberts, 'Nyamwezi', pp. 51–63   [208] Cf. above, pp. 169–71

[209] For the same process among the Lozi and Yeke see Max Gluckman, *Economy of the Central Barotse Plain*, Rhodes-Livingstone Paper 7, Livingstone 1941, pp. 79, 92–3

Cloth, however, became a major factor in local exchange. An important chief would distribute cloth as well as hoes among his warriors and favourites.[210] The Chishinga obtained cloth in return for the ironwork they brought as tribute to Mwamba and other Bemba chiefs, and the Lungu smelters who settled near Mwamba's were also paid in cloth.[211] Cotton cloth was always a rare commodity, valued less for its intrinsic utility than for the prestige which it reflected; until the end of the century, Bemba commoners continued to wear bark-cloth,[212] which indeed was more durable than the cheaper imported fabrics. Near Mwaba's, in 1867, Livingstone found that the people were so well clothed from tree-bark that they 'care but little for our cloth'.[213] But in the course of time, cloth came to be used as a form of currency on the plateau: 'four yards of calico, a load of salt, a hoe, and a slave, were all units of equal value'.[214] Imported cloth also came to be used from time to time in marriage payments, at least among the Mambwe,[215] while among the Bemba ornaments made from conus shells (locally called *mpande*) were used for this, as well as being a medium for paying legal compensation and being worn as necklaces; they are also used at the climax of the initiation ceremony for girls (*cisungu*).[216]

Sometimes long-distance traders became directly involved in local patterns of production and exchange. This was especially true of the Nyamwezi (Yeke) who came to Bemba country from Katanga. Their main stock-in-trade was copper, which no less than cloth was much in demand among the Bemba; but their own skills in metalworking were also sought after. In 1867 Livingstone found Chitapankwa's* legs 'loaded with brass and copper leglets', and at Mwamba's he observed:

[210] R. O'Ferrall, 'An old war-song of the Babemba', *Bulletin of the School of Oriental and African Studies*, 1927, 4, p. 840; Richards, 'Bwembya', p. 22; *Land, Labour and Diet*, p. 216

[211] Brelsford, 'Chishinga Ironworkers', p. 29; Songolo, 22 June 1964; Chileshye Mukulu, 15 April 1965. The Bisa exchanged cloth for hoes and axes from the Sukuma in Iwa country (Chiwelewele, 29 April 1965).

[212] Wallace, 'Nyasa-Tanganyika Plateau', p. 613

[213] *Last Journals*, I, p. 180. Gamitto noted that the Bisa continued to wear bark-cloth despite their trade in calico (*King Kazembe*, I, p. 206).

[214] Wallace, 'Nyasa-Tanganyika Plateau', p. 601; cf. Gouldsbury, 'Customary Law', *JAS*, 1915–16, 15, p. 180

[215] *Ibid.*; Watson, *Tribal Cohesion*, p. 37

[216] Dickson Chanda, T2; A. I. Richards, *Bemba Marriage and Present Economic Conditions*, Rhodes-Livingstone Paper 4, Livingstone 1940, p. 70. Among the Lunda of Kazembe, *mpande* were used to open marriage negotiations by 1831 (Gamitto, *King Kazembe*, II, p. 121).

A History of the Bemba

a great deal of copper wire is here made, the wire drawers using for one part of the process a seven-inch cable. They make very fine wire, and it is used chiefly as leglets and anklets; the chief's wives being laden with them, and obliged to walk in a stately style from the weight; the copper comes from Katanga.[217]

The wire-drawers were presumably Yeke: in 1872, towards Tabwa country, Livingstone found 'many Garaganza [Yeke] about; they trade in leglets, ivory, and slaves'.[218] One party of Nyamwezi went to Katanga to buy copper, and under their leader Mundubi set off homewards through Bemba country. They were asked to stay by Mwamba and Chitimukulu, and several of them settled near Mwamba's, where they eventually formed their own village. Some continued to buy copper from Katanga; others worked it at Mwamba's, where they bought slaves, guns and ivory. Mundubi himself settled with a party under Nkula in Ichinga; here they made ironwork and bark boxes and in due course founded their own villages.[219] No doubt these were among the Nyamwezi whom Giraud found at Nkula's in 1883;[220] these latter sold their own products for salt and bark-cloth. Some of the Nyamwezi in the region were porters who had been dismissed by caravan leaders once their loads of cloth had been sold and were then obliged to work for the local people if they were to find the means to return home.[221] Perhaps it was Nyamwezi such as these who were taking salt from Bwile country to Mwamba's in 1872.[222] In any case, the salt trade became intermeshed with long-distance trade. In 1883 a Swahili trader in Itabwa sent his slaves to Chitimukulu's with Bwile salt, and when Mwamba III made peace with the Swahili in 1884, it was salt, not cloth, which he obtained in return for his ivory.[223] In 1889 a group of men from a Swahili trader, Teleka, at Sumbu, were carrying salt from Mweru wa ntipa with which to buy slaves in Lungu and Mambwe country.[224]

[217] Last Journals, I, pp. 186, 198
[218] Ibid., II, p. 254; and see also ibid., p. 331, for an account of Nyamwezi wire-making in Lungu country.
[219] Songolo, 22 August 1964; Kabambaŋombe, T1 and 1 May 1965
[220] Giraud, Lacs, p. 242   [221] Ibid., p. 260
[222] Livingstone, Last Journals, II, p. 256
[223] Giraud, Lacs, p. 420; see above, p. 159.
[224] Trivier, Voyage, pp. 270-1. In 1892 it was reported that Abdullah ibn Suliman levied salt tribute from Kaputa and Mukupa, while he had recently expelled the salt-producing inhabitants of Puta, presumably in an attempt to control their trade (Sharpe to Johnston, 17 December 1892, FO 2/54).

Such growth in the range and volume of local exchange under the impact of long-distance trade may be presumed to have strengthened the bonds between the more powerful chiefs and their subjects. It also seems to have improved Bemba armaments, and more effectively than through the sale of firearms. The greater circulation of trade goods clearly profited local ironworkers and we may suppose that this increased the supply of spears to the Bemba, for using both for warfare and for hunting elephant, for which purpose the available guns were of little use.[225] The evidence on this point is all too slight, but it is worth comparing Gamitto's impression that the Bemba had few spears[226] with Genthe's report from Chikwanda's in 1897: 'I have never come across such fine spears as some of them carried—the blade is very well shaped without a flaw, and much broader than Angoni spears or any others I have seen in British Central Africa.'[227] It may be assumed that by this time the Bemba of Chikwanda had frequent access, whether by raiding, tribute or trade, to the ironwork of their Lala neighbours to the south; further north, the Iwa, Lungu and Chishinga provided alternative sources for Bemba weapons and might even, as we have seen, be rewarded for their services.

The main effect of long-distance trade was thus to multiply transactions both among the Bemba and between them and their neighbours. This enlargement of economic and political scale, and the associated movement of people across the plateau, naturally promoted the spread of customs, techniques and ideas. This process, however, affected the Bemba to a rather limited extent. Since few traders from the coast spent much time in Bemba country, and since Bemba did not, as a rule, venture beyond the plateau, the Bemba were little influenced by the customs of the coast. Islam, the religion of many of the traders from East Africa, made no impression among the Bemba, if only because the traders never sought to proselytise.[228] Nor did literacy make any impact on the Bemba; their chiefs, unlike some in East Africa

[225] Cf. above, p. 204. In the 1890s Chikwanda II used to give the Bisa chief Nkuka gunpowder for hunting elephant, but Nkuka shot nothing 'so got medicine from a Bemba fundi' (Luchembe, 1918 evidence). Cameron and Thomson were impressed by the large elephant spears of the Lungu and Mambwe (*Across Africa*, I, p. 286; *Central African Lakes*, I, p. 302).

[226] *King Kazembe*, II, p. 159

[227] H. Genthe, 'Livingstone's Grave', in *BCAG*, 5 February 1898

[228] Cf. Livingstone, *Last Journals*, I, pp. 233, 279–80. Chitapankwa appeared to Giraud to have adopted some Arab customs, but the evidence is meagre (*Lacs*, p. 263). The traders had, however, contributed to Chitapankwa's appearance: like Nkula, he was covered in red beads from head to foot (*ibid.*, p. 256).

and among the Yao,[229] do not appear to have made any use of traders as scribes. Lunda from Kazembe's seem to have introduced the signal drum (*mondo*) to the Bemba during the nineteenth century,[230] and this was a far from negligible aid to communication, especially when villages were liable to sudden attack. But in general the cultural innovations made at this time by the Bemba were of little political significance.[231]

As elsewhere in Africa, the expansion of trade from the coast led to the introduction of American and other exotic crops in the interior. This tended to increase food production, since the cultivation of the exotic crops did not necessarily reduce the time and labour available for the staple. Maize was available at Kazembe's by 1798, among the Bisa north and east of Lake Bangweulu by 1810, and near the capital of Chikwanda I by 1831.[232] Chitapankwa* gave maize to Livingstone in 1867 and in 1883 impressed Giraud with his abundant maize fields.[233] But in general the soils of Bemba country are ill-suited to the cultivation of maize on a large scale.[234] Sweet potatoes and groundnuts were grown by the Bisa of Kabanda by 1798,[235] but the former at least were little known among the Bemba before the advent of Yeke traders.[236] Groundnuts were common enough by 1867, and sweet potatoes were grown at Chitimukulu's and Mwamba's by 1883.[237] Cassava was

[229] Cf. Andrew Roberts, 'Political change in the nineteenth century', *A History of Tanzania*, eds I. N. Kimambo and A. J. Temu, Nairobi 1969, p. 83; E. A. Alpers, 'Trade, State and Society among the Yao in the nineteenth century', *JAH*, 1969, 10, iii, pp. 419–20

[230] Milambo, 1 October 1964. There was a signal drum at 'Mukulumpe's' before the founding chiefs left 'Kola' (see above, p. 39; see also Appendix 2, Note A). Gamitto described the signal drums at Kazembe's (*King Kazembe*, II, pp. 57, 117); but in the 1940s a Bemba made signal drums for Lunda chiefs (Cunnison, *Luapula Peoples*, pp. 202–3).

[231] The Bemba learned dances from the Ngoni, Namwanga and Bena Mukulu (W. V. Brelsford, *African Dances of Northern Rhodesia*, Rhodes–Livingstone Museum Occasional Papers, new series, 2, Livingstone 1948, pp. 8, 10).

[232] Pinto, in Lacerda, *Travessia*, p. 276; Baptista, 'Exploraçoes', p. 227 (Burton, *Cazembe*, pp. 119, 191, 193); Gamitto, *King Kazembe*, I, p. 166–8; II, p. 149

[233] Livingstone, *Last Journals*, I, pp. 189–90; Giraud, *Lacs*, p. 253. Giraud also noticed maize at Mukuuka Mwilwa's (*ibid.*, p. 228).

[234] Trapnell, *Soils*, p. 35; Richards, *Land, Labour and Diet*, p. 21

[235] Lacerda, *Diários*, p. 247 (Burton, *Cazembe*, p. 92); for the location, see above, p. 87, n. 30. Vansina is thus mistaken in asserting (*Kingdoms*, p. 265) that the Bisa did not cultivate any crop of the American complex at this date.

[236] Kabambaŋombe, 1 May 1965; Milambo, 1 October 1964; Chiwele, 14 July 1964

[237] Livingstone, *Last Journals*, I, pp. 179, 190, 197; Giraud, *Lacs*, pp. 266, 272. The N'umbo or Mumbo' which Livingstone found at Chitimukulu's in 1867

virtually ignored by the Bemba until this century, despite the example of their neighbours. It had become the staple at Kazembe's capital by 1798,[238] and was subsequently adopted by peoples immediately to the east, the north-western Bisa, Tabwa, Bena Mukulu,[239] but it was not reported among the Bemba by Gamitto, Livingstone or Giraud.[240] The first Bemba chief to encourage the cultivation of cassava was apparently Chikwanda II, who presumably adopted it from his Bisa subjects and neighbours; it was also grown at Mwamba's by 1898.[241] Rice was not grown at all in the region, except by the few colonies of foreign traders and by the southernmost Bisa.[242] We may conclude that by 1880 or so maize, sweet potatoes and groundnuts were useful supplements to the food available for distribution at a Bemba chief's village, but none of these were regarded by the Bemba as 'real food'.[243] Millet grain, plundered or levied from the Iwa or Mambwe,[244] would have been a much more important source of supply for the maintenance of a chief's non-cultivating followers.

It is clear that long-distance trade served to increase the power of the Bemba as against their neighbours, and that it did so mainly by increasing the circulation of wealth, in the form of both goods and services. In a very general sense, this brought about a greater cohesion both within Bemba chiefdoms and between them. But it can hardly be said that the political unity of the Bemba was thereby increased. Wrigley remarks of the Ganda that the upward and downward circulation of property, 'most of which was directly or indirectly the product of war . . . created an elaborate nexus of gratitude and expectation, to which in large measure the kingdom owed its remarkable

(*Last Journals*, I, p. 193) was the Livingstone potato (*coleus esculentus*), which is an aboriginal crop (Richards, *Land, Labour and Diet*, p. 20). Livingstone noted bananas for the first time in northern Ituna (*Last Journals*, I, p. 199).

[238] Pinto, in Lacerda, *Travessia*, p. 298 (Burton, *Cazembe*, p. 129).

[239] Gamitto, *King Kazembe*, I, p. 188; Tippu Tip, *Maisha*, p. 45; Livingstone, *Last Journals*, I, pp. 262, 264, 272; II, 256; Giraud, *Lacs*, p. 280

[240] Livingstone first noted it among the Lungu at the south end of Lake Tanganyika (*Last Journals*, I, p. 203).

[241] Chiwele, 14 July 1964: Pineau, *Evêque-Roi des Brigands*, p. 192. In 1900 the Bisa chief Kopa was said to have huge fields of cassava (Molinier to Dupont, 28 December 1900, *CT*, 1901, 89, p. 159).

[242] These last grew a little rice in 1853 (Silva Porto, *Silva Porto e a Travessia*, p. 130), while Kabinga had rice in 1873 (Livingstone, *Last Journals*, II, p. 291).

[243] Richards, *Land, Labour and Diet*, pp. 47, 52, 60

[244] For example, Gouldsbury and Sheane, *Great Plateau*, pp. 24–5; and cf. above, p. 182.

cohesion'.[245] But in Buganda there already existed, in social forms and local economic resources, the basis for a centralised government. Among the Bemba, there was no one predominant 'nexus of gratitude and expectation'; economic change, such as it was, tended to exaggerate, rather than undermine, the centrifugal pressures in their polity. There was no major change in the methods or the scale of food production. Population density remained very low[246]—in itself a major obstacle to control from the centre; and it remained impossible to support anything like a standing army which could serve as the instrument of a paramount's will. Over Bemba country as a whole there was no significant degree of economic interdependence;[247] even the exchange of ironwork, always an essential commodity, was conducted through chiefs' capitals in different parts of the country.

Partly for these reasons, there could be no question of Chitimukulu exercising a monopoly over long-distance trade. Instead, such trade gravitated along the lines of dependence and subordination defined by the various kinship and affinal relationships between the major Bemba chiefs. Makasa III is said to have sold ivory (and slaves) to the Swahili before the final expulsion of the Ngoni in about 1870. Mwamba and Nkula certainly sold ivory before this date; Nkolemfumu did so by 1883; while in the 1890s Ponde and Chikwanda, as well as Mwamba, Nkula and Makasa, were selling ivory or slaves for firearms and cloth.[248] On the one hand, such trade had the effect of tightening these chiefs' control over their own subjects and dependants; the very fact that Bemba chiefs monopolised all ivory within their own territories, and also the sale of slaves,[249] strengthened them against their own people and inhibited the emergence of independent hunter-traders, which happened in parts of East Africa.[250] On the other hand,

[245] C. C. Wrigley, 'The Changing Economic Structure of Buganda', *The King's Men*, ed L. A. Fallers, London 1964, pp. 20–1

[246] See above, p. 166, for the difference in size between the capitals of Chitimukulu and Kazembe—the latter nourished by cassava and plentiful fish nearby.

[247] This point is noted by Gann, *Plural Society*, pp. 25–6.

[248] See above, pp. 137, 161, 195, 202–3; and below, pp. 222–3, 227, 229, 258, 279. Richards is thus mistaken in asserting that Chitimukulu 'controlled the guns provided by the Arabs' ('African Kings', p. 146).

[249] Richards, *Land, Labour and Diet*, p. 145, n. 1

[250] Chiefs of the Nyamwezi and Nyiha—like many others—only demanded one tusk from each pair obtained in their chiefdoms: Roberts, 'Nyamwezi Trade', p. 70; Beverley Brock, 'The Nyiha', in Roberts, *Tanzania before 1900*, pp. 74–5. In the 1880s the Lozi king abolished the previous royal monopoly, allowing the hunter to retain one tusk: Max Gluckman, *Essays on Lozi Land and Royal Property*, Rhodes-Livingstone Paper 10, Livingstone 1943, pp. 85–6.

the growth of long-distance trade gave a new advantage to chiefs on or near the borders of Bemba country. Such chiefs were naturally well placed for slave-hunts; perhaps more important, some of them had access to localised resources, such as the salt of Chinama or the elephant of the Luangwa valley. Chiefs on the western and northern borders were of course close to the trading settlements around Bemba country and to the routes by which foreign traders reached the plateau; and it suited a trader not to penetrate far into Bemba country if he could do business nearer his own base. In this respect, Mwamba, though no longer himself a border chief, was rather better placed than Chitimukulu, in that he was closer to the Swahili between Lakes Tanganyika and Mweru, and lay on the approach route of the Yeke who came east from Katanga through Chishinga country. And since the Bemba had quite recently expanded in these directions, Mwamba had a number of subordinates sufficiently deferential, for the most part, to channel trade towards him. We may suspect the claim that Mwamba's subordinates sent all their ivory to him,[251] but Mporokoso at least may well have traded more as Mwamba's agent than on his own account.[252] At the same time, the new opportunities for external trade tended to diminish the economic dependence of some chiefs on their links with the centre,[253] and even their interest in promotion.[254]

Thus the closing years of Chitapankwa's* reign found the Bemba superficially more united than ever before; but the framework of unity was very fragile. It was based primarily on links between a number of chiefs, each with his own specific economic interests; and no one of them was clearly predominant. Mwamba, however, had within the past two decades become as powerful in secular terms as Chitimukulu, and Bemba political unity depended above all on an understanding between these two chiefs. That such an understanding prevailed during Chitapankwa's* reign was partly due to the fact that the Mwamba title was held by a brother of Chitimukulu who had forsworn any ambition to succeed to the paramountcy. The congruity between the actual power, the genealogical seniority and the political ambitions of Mwamba II helps to explain the entente between himself and Chitapankwa*. This entente survived their occasional differences, but these

[251] Milambo, 2 October 1964; cf. above, p. 181, and below, p. 221

[252] There is no clear evidence that Mporokoso himself traded much with his East African neighbours.

[253] Gluckman makes a similar point in relation to commoners in the Lozi kingdom (*Economy of the Central Barotse Plain*, p. 81).

[254] Cf. above, p. 129; below, pp. 220, 317–18.

served to show how dangerous it was for Chitapankwa* to act alone. In his final campaign against the Ngoni, in about 1870, Chitapankwa* had been careful to obtain the support of Mwamba and many other chiefs.[255] But in 1872, as we have seen, an alliance of Lungu chiefs was able to defeat Chitapankwa* after Mwamba had declined to support him.[256] In any case, the measure of cooperation achieved between Chitapankwa* and Mwamba II was in no way intrinsic to the offices they held. The equilibrium between them was contingent upon their positions as individuals within the whole constellation of alliances among Bemba chiefs. On Sampa's* accession, this was radically upset, and the consequences profoundly affected Bemba reactions to the intrusion of European missionaries and empire-builders.

[255] See above, p. 145, and below, Appendix 3.   [256] See above, p. 150.

Chapter 7

The reign of Sampa*
(1884–1896)

Until about the middle of the nineteenth century, the Bemba were of no great significance in the history of eastern and central Africa, and their horizons were correspondingly limited. For them, the world extended little further than the plateau on which they lived. Unlike the Lunda of Kazembe, the Bemba had maintained no links with the Lunda or Luba states of the upper Congo basin, nor had they developed long-range contacts in any other direction. In the course of Chitapankwa's* reign, however, the Bemba had not only consolidated their position as the most powerful people in north-eastern Zambia; they were drawn into a trading system which extended over much of East Africa and the eastern Congo. Their involvement in this system ultimately brought the Bemba into contact with a still wider world.

The growth of Bemba power under Chitapankwa* was due in part at least to Bemba participation in the trade in ivory and slaves; but another consequence of this trade was European penetration and settlement in the interior of eastern Africa. The enterprise of East African traders had opened up much of the interior to European exploration and missionary activity. The ivory trade (itself greatly stimulated by European demands) and its ancillary, the slave trade, both provoked and facilitated European intrusion, even while it fostered the growth of brigand kingdoms such as those of the Bemba, Nyamwezi or Ganda. Contacts and changes which had evolved over centuries along the coast were compressed in Bembaland into the space of a few decades. When Chitapankwa* became Chitimukulu, the Bemba had only recently begun to trade with the East Africans. Before he died, in 1883, there were European mission stations only just beyond his borders. Six years later, the British were making treaties with chiefs all round the northern fringes of Bemba country. Allowing for all the various other factors in the European partition of Africa,[1] we may nonetheless

[1] It is true that the northward drive of the British South Africa Company, which eventually took over Bembaland, was due to the personal vision, and

215

discern a logic in events whereby the power of the Bemba was likely to be challenged and thwarted just when it seemed to have reached its apogee.

It was certainly not to be expected that the Bemba, at such a point in their history, would readily submit to any foreign power, let alone to one determined to put an end to the slave trade, raiding and local warfare. Yet the 'Bemba question' was solved much more easily than missionaries and British officials had at first anticipated. This warlike people, the terror of their neighbours, eventually offered no more than piecemeal and uncoordinated resistance to the white intruders. The reasons for this seeming paradox are partly to be sought in changes within the Bemba polity following the deaths of Mwamba II and Chitapankwa*. Giraud noted after these events that 'Le plus beau titre de gloire de Kétimkuru était d'avoir assuré l'unité de l'Uemba, divisé récemment encore en une multitude de petites puissances, toujours en guerre les unes avec les autres'.[2] This was an exaggeration, but there was indeed a critical fissure in Bemba politics. Well before 1883, Bemba political ties had polarised around the two leading chieftainships, those of Chitimukulu and Mwamba. In Sampa's* reign, the latter title, though historically junior, ritually inferior, and now held by a nephew of Chitimukulu, became far more powerful. The two chiefs came into open conflict, and this naturally affected the relations between them and other Bemba chiefs. The death of Sampa* in 1896 only intensified the struggle between the two chieftainships, for Mwamba thereupon sought the paramountcy for himself, and when foiled in this he continued to extend his influence into areas formerly dominated by Chitimukulu. These internal divisions influenced Bemba attitudes to the approach of Europeans, who were seen not just as an external threat but as factors to be exploited in the field of internal politics. The pursuit of local rivalries disposed Bemba chiefs to postpone, rather than precipitate, a confrontation with European arms.

Nonetheless, this circumstance might not in itself have precluded the Bemba from making a concerted effort of resistance. They failed to

fortune, of Cecil Rhodes rather than to local factors in the history of east-central Africa. Yet the Company at first 'administered' north-eastern Rhodesia through the agency of the British Central Africa Protectorate, based on Lake Malawi, and it is plain enough that Bembaland had become an area of concern to European, and in particular British, enterprise, quite independently of Rhodes' appetite for empire.

[2] *Lacs*, p. 264: 'Chitimukulu's chief claim to fame was to have unified Bemba country, which has recently broken up again into a number of small powers at war with each other.'

make such an effort partly because there was relatively little pressure upon them to do so: the intruding British officials had their own reasons for avoiding open conflict as long as possible. And this prolonged political uncertainty gave a group of French missionaries both the time and the opportunity to obtain a position of some influence among the northern Bemba. But the ultimate reason why the Bemba did not combine against the Europeans as they had against the Ngoni was the death of the one man who might have led such a combination—Mwamba III. This is not, of course, to say that Bemba deference to British invaders was due to mere chance, but rather that the Bemba political system, lacking centralised institutions of administration, was highly susceptible to the loss of individual leaders, and its dependence on these had been aggravated as much as diminished by such increase in internal cohesion as had been achieved in the later nineteenth century.

INTERNAL CONFLICTS

In the first part of 1883, Mwamba II Chileshye Kapalaula died of smallpox.[3] Chitapankwa* seems to have wished their younger brother Sampa to succeed.[4] Sampa's relations with Chitapankwa* had never been good: Sampa had probably disputed Chitapankwa's* accession and had then given much trouble in Ichinga. But Chitapankwa* may well have hoped that the tension between them would be eased if Sampa, who had already declined to become Nkolemfumu, were given a really powerful post. If so, Chitapankwa* was disappointed. Sampa rejected Ituna contemptuously; he had never been seriously interested in any post but the paramountcy, to which he knew, as Chitapankwa's* brother, he had the best of claims.[5] Thus the Mwamba title went to Nkolemfumu Mubanga Chipoya, whose claim, as a son of the eldest sister of the late Mwamba, was perhaps strengthened by the fact that he was also a son-in-law of both the late Mwamba and of Chitapankwa*. Mubanga Chipoya's claim was not, however, undisputed. Sampa wished the post which he had rejected for himself to go instead to Chyanika, who with Ponde and Chikwanda was the son of a younger sister of the late Mwamba.[6] This may account for the war

---

[3] *Ibid.*, pp. 256, 272; Labrecque, 'Origines', p. 285
[4] Katwamba, T2. Labrecque confirms that Chitapankwa wished Sampa to become Mwamba ('Origines', p. 322; cf. Tanguy, *Imilandu*, p. 63).
[5] Katwamba, T2; Labrecque, 'Origines', pp. 322-3. For Sampa's earlier history, see above, pp. 135-6, 160.   [6] For Chyanika, see below, pp. 221, n. 22; 252, n. 199

which—as Chitapankwa* told Giraud—raged around Mwamba's village in June 1883.[7] It is at least likely that Sampa was already at odds with Mubanga Chipoya, since the two men had recently been neighbours, in Ichingo and Mpuki. And it is fairly certain that by declining the Mwamba title Sampa aroused the wrath of Chitapankwa*. Soon after Giraud's visit, Chitapankwa* became very ill, and there seemed to be nothing to prevent Sampa from at last becoming Chitimukulu. So Chitapankwa* summoned the three leading *bena ŋandu* chiefs— Mwamba III, Nkula I and Chikwanda II—and told them not to obey Sampa.[8]

Chitapankwa* died in October 1883;[9] he would probably have been buried in the following May or June and the rituals of installation would then have gone forward. There is no clear indication that Sampa encountered any actual obstruction to his establishment and investiture as Chitimukulu, but from the first he was gravely handicapped. Owing largely, perhaps, to his own cantankerous pride, he had lacked the advantage of a chiefdom as a base for forming alliances and building up support within and outside the royal clan; instead, he now found himself at odds with all his most important subjects. By contrast, Mwamba III had been Nkolemfumu, and as son-in-law to both the deceased Chitimukulu and Mwamba, he was perhaps likely to stand well with those who had been loyal to them. Certainly, he appears to have inherited much of the territorial influence built up by Mwamba II, which had rivalled that of Chitapankwa* himself. Now that Sampa* had succeeded Chitapankwa*, it was not Chitimukulu but Mwamba, his genealogical junior as well as ritual inferior, who was the most powerful Bemba chief.

There was thus abundant cause for suspicion and hostility between the new occupants of these two positions. It is said by some that Mwamba refused to go and pay homage to Sampa* in the course of his installation.[10] Another version has it that Mwamba did go, but his approach was misconstrued by Sampa* who, significantly, thought

---

[7] Brelsford, *Succession*, p. 7; Giraud, *Lacs*, p. 272. Katwamba (T2) says that Sampa had suggested Mubanga Chipoya, and the 'war' may only have been the usual attack on the dead chief's dependants (cf. Giraud, *Lacs*, pp. 264–5).

[8] Katwamba, T2

[9] Giraud, *Lacs*, p. 377; perhaps Chitapankwa, like Mwamba II, died of smallpox, for in 1895 Mporokoso told a European visitor that 'The Chief [sc. Chitapankwa] died of a great sickness, and so did many of his people' (P. Weatherley in *BCAG*, 15 September 1895). There was certainly smallpox in 1883 among the Ushi, on the upper Luapula (Giraud, *Lacs*, p. 326).

[10] Katwamba, T2; Kachasa, T1

that Mwamba was challenging his accession.[11] In any case, the two chiefs may already have come to blows. A quarrel between some of their respective subjects provoked Sampa* into killing a son-in-law of Mwamba. Mwamba then marched into western Lubemba, killing the *mwina ŋandu* headman Mutale Mukulu and people in two other villages.[12] Sampa then agreed to stop fighting, but it seems that Mwamba probably retained effective control of western Lubemba throughout Sampa's* reign.[13] Certainly, the conflict between them persisted: it is said that Sampa* once razed some villages under Munkonge, a perpetual son of Mwamba,[14] and that Sampa* even attacked Mwamba's own village but was sharply repulsed.[15] Sampa* also sent a present to the Tabwa chief Nsama VI Chimutwe; as the latter was an enemy of Mwamba and Mporokoso, this action may be construed as yet another move directed against Mwamba.[16] Sampa* made further inroads upon Mwamba's sphere of influence by attempting to gain a foothold in country taken from the Lungu of Mukupa Kaoma. On the death of the chief in Lisunga (Mwamba's perpetual son Mukuuka, ShiBwalya Kapila), Sampa* tried to instal his own son, Tente. Tente, however, was so cruel that Mwamba III sent in his own daughter Kasonde NaKabwe and her Lungu consort, Kaliminwa.[17] Sampa* does, however, appear to have achieved some influence at Mwamba's expense in relation to Ponde, part of whose territory bordered on Lubemba. Ponde had been nephew and son-in-law to Mwamba II, but he was perhaps no more likely to defer to Mwamba III, his cousin, than to Sampa*, his uncle. In any case, Sampa* seems to have enforced a measure of deference from Ponde. Sampa* doubtless

[11] Shimulamba, T1, n. 49

[12] Milambo, T16. Brelsford says that Shimumbi I tried to stop the fighting (*Succession*, p. 7). It was probably this war which deterred Giraud from re-entering Bemba country late in 1883: he says that the succession war after Chitapankwa's death lasted a year (*Lacs*, pp. 263, 377).

[13] Milambo, T16, and below, p. 264. Mwamba's encroachments at this time extended about ten miles into Lubemba: as far as the Luchindashi, Mungwi and Chibile rivers (Labrecque, 'Origines', p. 323; Brelsford, *Succession*, p. 7). In the late 1880s Sampa built a village at Tuto, east of the Chibile, in order to pursue his war with Mwamba (Pineau, *Evêque-Roi*, p. 180).

[14] Chitikafula, 28 June 1934 (A. I. Richards, fieldnotes)

[15] Katwamba, T2; Shimulamba, T1, n. 53; they name two different village sites, perhaps because they refer to two different attacks.

[16] Milambo, T10; cf. above, p. 159

[17] Milambo, 2 October 1964; Mwamba, 12 April 1965. Kaliminwa's mother was a Lungu (Mporokoso DNB I, p. 99). Since the late 1940s the chieftainship has once again been held by sons of *bena ŋandu* chiefs, with the title Shibwalya Kapila.

resented Ponde's trade in guns and ivory, and in about 1893, in response to a request from the Lungu chief Chungu, Sampa* attacked some of Ponde's villages. It may be significant that in the following year Ponde consulted Sampa* rather than Mwamba III concerning policy towards European missionaries.[18]

For the most part, however, Sampa's* sphere of influence seems to have been reduced to Lubemba, and not even the whole of that. By contrast, that of Mwamba III Mubanga Chipoya was considerably enlarged during Sampa's* reign. After an uncertain start, Mwamba III retained the influence in the northwest which had been gained by his predecessor. The Swahili defeat of Mwamba III and Mporokoso in about 1884 seems to have resulted in an understanding as to the limits of Bemba and Swahili spheres of influence in Itabwa.[19] Further south, on the western border of Ituna, Mwamba III placed a son, Misengo, in territory formerly occupied by Mukupa Kaoma.[20] And besides encroaching upon Lubemba, Mwamba III also became much more influential than Sampa* in southern Bemba country, where he provided chieftainships for three sons of his sister Chandamukulu Kangwa Chonya. One of these was the Nkolemfumu title, from which Mwamba III himself had been promoted. Mwamba's junior cousin Ponde declined to succeed him as Nkolemfumu, perhaps because Ponde already valued more highly his opportunities for trade and raiding on the Lungu border. Instead, Mwamba III continued for several years to rule Miti himself, and when a new Nkolemfumu was chosen in about 1895 it was Mwamba's own nephew and son-in-law, Kanyanta, who succeeded.[21] Meanwhile, Mwamba III had created a new chiefdom in Mpuki, the country which he himself had once

[18] W. T. [Thomas], in *BCAG*, 12 October 1894; for Ponde's trade, see below, pp. 258, 279. Ponde killed a son of Sampa, Mpapala, though it is not clear when (Labrecque, 'Origines', p. 326).

[19] See above, pp. 159–60.

[20] Goodall, 'Tree'; Kasama DNB III, p. 32

[21] Shimulamba, T1; Brelsford, *Succession*, p. 28; J. E. Thomas, 'Kanyanta and his times', *NRJ*, 1961, 4, v, p. 477; for the date, see below, p. 277. In 1891 a Swahili trader entered Bemba country from the west and heard that the chief was Nkolemfumu (Velten, *Safari*, p. 42), but no doubt the name continued to be attached to the village even when there was no incumbent resident. Werbner suggests that Mwamba made Kanyanta both Nkolemfumu and his own son-in-law in order to create a counterpoise to the rising power of his cousin Ponde ('Federal Administration', p. 39). The small area of Chisansa, which had formed part of Miti when Mubanga Chipoya was Nkolemfumu (see above, p. 160, n. 163) was evidently retained by him as Mwamba, for it has since been part of Ituna.

occupied between the Chambeshi and Lulingila rivers; this chiefdom he gave to Kanyanta's younger brother Mubanga Chisupa, who took the title Mpepo.[22] Both Nkolemfumu and Mpepo sent tribute in ivory to Mwamba.[23] Kanyanta's youngest brother, Mbonkali, was installed in Musoa, between the Mununshi and Lubansenshi rivers, and was given the title Menga.[24]

Further south, Mwamba III extended his influence at the expense of his cousin Chikwanda II. The latter had taken over Chinama not long before Chitapankwa's* death, and he had rapidly become a considerable power. His sister's son Bwalya Changala settled in Chinama during Sampa's* reign, while elsewhere in the area two of Chikwanda's sons, Luenshi and Kapoko, became sub-chiefs.[25] Chikwanda raided far south into Lala and Swaka country,[26] and he developed his own lines of access to coastal imports. In 1886 Portuguese based on Zumbo or Tete made some sort of treaty in Lala country,[27] and Portuguese traders went on to do business with Chikwanda. In 1890 it was reported at Zumbo that Chikwanda could field eight or nine hundred warriors.[28] But during this and the following year Portugal had to

---

[22] Brelsford (*Succession*, p. 28) says that Mubanga Chipoya was still Nkolemfumu when he created a chiefdom for Mpepo, but the evidence is very strong that Mubanga Chipoya himself occupied the area in question until 1883: see above, p. 161. Mpepo I died only in 1945 (*Succession*, p. 24), which also suggests a relatively late date for his installation. It is likely that for some years after 1883, and before Mpepo's appointment, Mpuki was ruled by Chyanika, a brother of Chikwanda II (Mpika DNB II, p. 205). Early in 1883, Chyanika (also called 'Fyani-fyani') occupied the eastern part of Miti (Giraud, *Lacs*, map following p. 220).

[23] Shitantameni 28 June 1965

[24] Brelsford, *Succession*, p. 45; Kasama DNB III, p. 32. In Ichingo, between Miti and Mpuki, the Bisa chief Kabanda seems to have been left in control following Sampa's departure to become Chitimukulu. After the British arrived, Kabanda managed to retain his position as a chief, though much of his country had by then been absorbed by Nkula (cf. Kabanda, T1).

[25] Kalesu, 21 April 1965; Mpika DNB I, pp. 6, 59; II, pp. 99, 201

[26] See above, p. 163.

[27] Eric Axelson, *Portugal and the Scramble for Africa*, Johannesburg 1967, p. 154, n. 113. A treaty was signed on 16 December 1886 in the '*prazo*' 'Chirenga' [sc. Serenje, a Lala chief]; its location is correctly shown on a map reproduced in *ibid.*, following p. 260.

[28] Luiz Ignacio, 'O Zumbo (antes dos ultimos tratados). Relatorio do Governador do Districto de Zumbo, referido ao anno de 1890', *Bol. Soc. Geog. Lisboa*, 1891, 10, vi–vii, p. 315. (Prof. H. W. Langworthy kindly drew my attention to this source.) Ignacio names the *capitao-mor*, Sebastiao Pereira Cardoso, of 'Chirenga'; his stockade (*aringa*) is marked on the map in Axelson, *Portugal and the Scramble* (see note 27 above).

cede by treaty almost all the Luangwa valley to the British, and her agents thus lost any official incentive for cultivating Chikwanda's friendship.[29] And by this time Mwamba III had established his son Chewe Shikasonde as chief, with the title Luchembe, in Bisa country to the west of Chikwanda. Luchembe was originally sent in his early 'teens to live under Chikwanda, and he built on the Lulingila and Lubaleshi rivers.[30] He was then sent by Mwamba 'with an axe and a hoe to call Kawinga [Kabinga, the Bisa chief who had once ruled Mpuki] out of the swamps and to build on the land'.[31] Luchembe soon pushed much further south, for he took over part of Chinama from Chikwanda II, including part of Chibwa salt marsh on the Luitikila.[32] Hitherto, Chikwanda appears to have forwarded tribute in salt only to Chitimukulu;[33] but through Luchembe, Mwamba III now gained a share of this revenue. West of the Mufubushi and north of the Luitikila, salt workers henceforward paid tribute to Luchembe, who in turn forwarded forty cakes of salt each year to Mwamba.[34] Mwamba III did send men to assist Chikwanda in a campaign against the Bisa of Muwele (a headman under chief Chiundaponde)—a campaign in which Mwamba's men claim to have stolen most of the thunder.[35] But Mwamba also encroached upon Chikwanda's southernmost hunting grounds: at Chikwanda's capital in 1897, there were two large parties from Mwamba's who had been raiding in Lala country; all the grown men in them carried guns.[36]

By this time, Mwamba's pre-eminence was of long standing: in

[29] Axelson, *Portugal and the Scramble*, pp. 239–44, 289–97. Such Portuguese agents may well have been of primarily African descent.

[30] Presumably Luchembe settled a short distance west of Masongo, a son of Chitapankwa (see above, p. 162). In 1899 a missionary estimated Luchembe's age at not more than twenty-five (L. Molinier, diary, 23 September 1899, *CT*, 87, July 1900, p. 435).

[31] Mpika DNB II, p. 109; Luchembe, 1918 evidence; and see above, p. 161. Apparently Luchembe took over a largely deserted area and wanted the fugitive Bisa to resettle in it. Neither Kabinga nor 'Kanduchiti' (probably Kopa II Londe) agreed, but Katepela, later Kopa III, quarrelled with his brothers and went to Mwamba shortly before the latter's death in 1898. At Mwamba's request, Katepela did not return to the swamps but settled with another Bisa, Yumba, near Luchembe (Luchembe and Kopa, 1918 evidence). In 1899 Kabinga was still living close to the confluence of the Chambeshi and Lulingila (R. Codrington, 'Journey from Fort Jameson to Old Chitambo', *GJ*, 1900, 15, p. 230).

[32] Luchembe took over all the area between the Chambeshi and Luitikila in which Gamitto had found Bemba headmen in 1831–2 (see above, pp. 114–16).

[33] Cf. above, p. 180.

[34] Luchembe, 1918 evidence; Mpika DNB II, pp. 113, 263

[35] Milambo, T13; cf. Thomas, *Bisa*, p. 52   [36] Genthe, 'Livingstone's Grave'.

11 Chief Mwamba VI Musenga, drawing a diagram to illustrate the division of Bembaland between Mwamba and Chitimukulu. The photograph was taken in May 1965, after the death of Chitimukulu MUSUNGU and before Musenga was chosen to succeed him

12 Police guard outside the post office at Abercorn in 1893; the new
Collector, H. C. Marshall, is in the background. The Sikhs, and probably
also the five uniformed Africans (perhaps Makua), were seconded from the
British Central Africa Protectorate; the other men are probably local
levies. Courtesy of the Livingstone Museum, Zambia

13 The *malaila* war-dance, Chitimukulu's village, 1933. Photograph: Dr.
A. I. Richards

1890, a European travelling around the northern borders of Bemba country gathered that Mwamba 'is now the most powerful of the Awemba chiefs, and has quite superseded Ketunkuru [Chitimukulu]'.[37] It was later said that Mwamba, 'having accumulated a large number of slaves, sent a special caravan to the Unyamwezi country, and purchased guns and powder with which he made his power predominant'.[38] Within Ituna, Mwamba III consolidated his position by appointing many of his relatives to headmanships.[39] And certain leaders outside Bemba country owed their position to Mwamba's support. He sent Chibanda, a nephew of Shimumbi I, to restore Nsumbu Island, which had been seized by alien chiefs, to Matipa II.[40] In about 1890, Mwamba sent troops to help Kazembe X Kanyembo subdue the rebel Lunda aristocrat Kaindu and his Yeke allies.[41] Soon afterwards, Mwamba III sent Luali, a son of Mwamba II, to conquer the Chishinga chief Chama; Luali seized much of Chama's territory, probably including an important iron mine.[42] In 1895 a European hunter near Lake Mweru reported that Mwamba and Mporokoso 'are now not only independent of, but pay no tribute to, their paramount chief'.[43]

[37] Sharpe to Johnston, 26 December 1890, enclosed in Johnston to Salisbury, 3 May 1891, FO 84/2114
[38] Codrington in BSAC, *Reports, 1898-1900*, p. 66. It seems to have been unusual for Bemba chiefs to send their men so far afield: cf. above, p. 200.
[39] Richards, *Land, Labour and Diet*, p. 413
[40] Sheane, 'Wemba Warpaths', p. 24; Milambo, T12. But by 1895 Yombwe, a longstanding rival of Matipa, had reoccupied Chilubi island, which had been under Matipa in 1883 (P. Weatherley, 'The Circumnavigation of Lake Bangweulu', *GJ*, 1898, 12, p. 250; cf. above, p. 142).
[41] Cunnison, *Historical Traditions*, pp. 96-7. Kaindu sought to avenge the death of Kazembe IX Lukwesa, which may have occurred in 1886 (see Roberts, 'Tippu Tip, Livingstone, and the Chronology of Kazembe', pp. 125-8). The Lunda narrative places Kazembe X's visit to Mwamba before the death of Msiri, which was on 20 December 1891.
According to the sources nearest the events, Mwamba mounted an expedition led by four of his sons, and with their help Kazembe X Kanyembo managed to beat off the Yeke attacks and obtain Kaindu's submission. Most of the Bemba went home, suitably rewarded, after Msiri's death in 1891, but Mwamba's sons settled near the Lunda capital, and in about 1893 Kazembe gave one of them, Mwabamukupa, a village of his own (Kawambwa DNB II, p. 155 (before 1914), p. 171; cf. Weatherley to Johnston, 11 October 1895, RH). The Lunda history, however, says that Mwamba's sons came only after the Yeke war, after being driven out of their own countries (Cunnison, *Historical Traditions*, p. 105).
[42] Kawambwa DNB II, pp. 167, 181; cf. above, p. 186, n. 81. In 1900 Luali's village was on the Mwelu river (H. Maître, 'Zwei Forschungsreisen der "Weissen Väter" nach Lobemba und Lobisa', *Petermanns Mitteilungen*, 1902, 48, p. 171).
[43] Weatherley, in BCAG, 15 September 1895

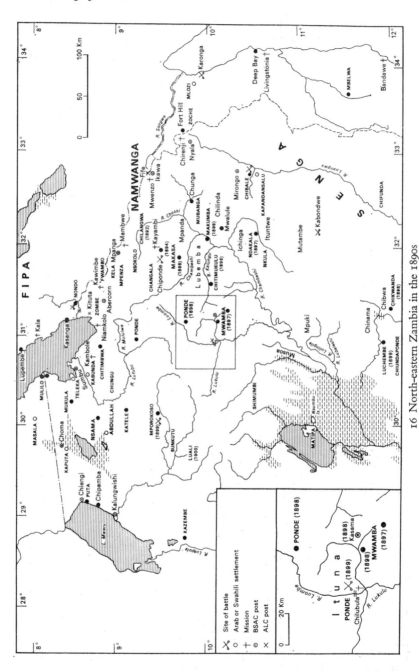

16 North-eastern Zambia in the 1890s

There was one important development early in Sampa's* reign which favoured him rather than Mwamba. This was the opening of a new trade route to the east, by way of Lake Malawi. Hitherto, traders seem only occasionally to have reached the Bemba from Kilwa and the country around the north end of Lake Malawi.[44] By the early 1880s, however, British missionaries were travelling up and down Lake Malawi and across to Lake Tanganyika, and British ivory traders also appeared on the scene.[45] In 1881 the African Lakes Company opened a station at Karonga, near the north end of Lake Malawi, and Arab traders 'soon flocked to the district when they discovered a new market for their ivory'.[46] They had to wait there for their trade goods, and by 1883 one Arab, Mlozi, had settled among the local Ngonde and built a stockaded village a few miles west of Karonga.[47] Mlozi soon became the chief power in the area and in 1887 he clashed with both the Ngonde and the British, but in 1889 he made a truce with the latter which lasted until 1895.[48]

Mlozi's fort became the entrepôt for a trade in slaves as well as ivory which profited especially from the cooperation of the eastern Bemba. Mlozi imported cloth from the British, but also firearms from Kilwa; caravans crossed Lake Malawi from Deep Bay, south of Karonga, and despite the German occupation of the coast between 1888 and 1890 this Kilwa trade continued to flourish.[49] Some of the ivory reached the lake from the country northwest of the Bemba,[50] but most of it, and

---

[44] See above, p. 196.   [45] For details, see below, pp. 231–2, 240.

[46] Fotheringham, *Adventures*, pp. 12, 19; and see H. W. Macmillan, 'Notes on the origin of the Arab War', *The Early History of Malawi*, ed. B. Pachai, London 1972, pp. 265–8.

[47] *Ibid.*, pp. 266, 269 (Moir thought the date was 1886: *After Livingstone*, pp. 133–4).

[48] Macmillan, 'Arab War', pp. 271–6, and see below, p. 255.

[49] 'Other caravans have arrived at Mwera on the opposite side of the Lake. All have varying large quantities of powder and guns. All hail from Kilwa where, without exception, the Senga and Luwemba slave traders do their business . . .' Crawshay (at Deep Bay) to Johnston, 30 June 1893, enclosed in Johnston to Rosebery, 25 August 1893, FO 2/54. A caravan from Kilwa to Bemba country was reported in 1892 (van Oost to a missionary, 4 July 1892, White Fathers Archives (WFA)/c20/304; see also below, pp. 236, 238).

[50] See below, pp. 236, 238. The Arabs of Mlozi seem to have been in regular contact with their counterparts in Tabwa country. Mlozi himself may have traded there for a time: cf. reference to 'Mlozi (of Itawa)' in Fotheringham and Bain to Hawes, enclosed in Hawes to Salisbury, 16 January 1888, FO 84/1883. Katwamba (T3) said that the 'Balungwana' came to Karonga from Kabuta, i.e. the village of Abdullah ibn Suliman near Nsama's. Ramathan, an Arab who fought in Mlozi's battle with the British in 1887, was said to be an agent of

the slaves, came from the region of the Luangwa valley. A colony of Arabs, led by one Salem bin Nasur (also known as Koma Koma) settled among the Senga on the upper Luangwa.[51] One Arab, called 'Kapandansalu', built a village close to that of the Senga chief Chibale. This place became a great slave market, marked by 'the terrible trysting tree where the famed Mlozi . . . held his palavers when he used to meet the Awemba people coming from afar with their human merchandise'.[52]

These Bemba, however, did not necessarily come from Chitimukulu's: chiefs on the eastern borders of Bembaland traded with Mlozi and his colleagues, while the latter visited Bemba country as well as doing business at Kapandansalu's. It is very likely that Nkula's connection with these Arabs was stronger than Sampa's*, if only because Nkula, in Ichinga, was that much closer to the Arab base. Immediately after settling at Karonga, Mlozi formed a plan to ally with the Bemba against the British and the Ngoni of Mbelwa: the Bemba were to move southwards, to the west of the Ngoni, while Mlozi moved down the western shore of Lake Malawi.[53] It is not clear how deeply the Bemba were actually committed to this scheme, but they were almost certainly Nkula's Bemba, for the plan was abandoned after Nkula had suffered a severe reverse. Nkula had put his son Ndakala I in charge of Mutambe, the country taken from the Bisa chief Chibesakunda,[54] but Ndakala's pretensions provoked the Senga chief Chifunda into seeking Ngoni help against the Bemba. Mbelwa sent an army which, with the aid of Senga guns, defeated and killed Ndakala at Kabondwe in October 1887. This evidently caused Mlozi to abandon his plans,[55] though he did send Arab reinforcements to Nkula (after Sampa* had declined to help): Nkula then killed Chifunda.[56]

Chikwanda also profited from the trade with Mlozi. He had already

Kabunda, the Baluchi on Lake Tanganyika (Hawes to Salisbury, 16 January 1888, FO 84/1883).

[51] Cf. Lugard to Ag. Consul, Nyassa District, 10 September 1888, FO 84/1883

[52] Dewar to Smith (from Karonga), 30 October 1889, NLS 7877; cf. Wissmann, *Second Journey*, p. 272: 'The Arabs on Lake Nyasa . . . have their gobetweens in the savage hordes of Uemba.'

[53] Elmslie to Laws, 7 November 1887, NLS 7890; Hawes to Salisbury, 16 January 1888, FO 84/1883   [54] See above, p. 138.

[55] The evidence for this episode is discussed in detail in Appendix 3.

[56] Katwamba, T3; Milambo, 1 October 1964; Peyoni Bwalya, T1. To replace Ndakala in Mutambe, Nkula appointed one Chifumo, or Kolokondwe (Labrecque, 'Origines', pp. 314, 320).

traded with Portuguese from the south, and even after their withdrawal
west of the Luangwa he appears to have obtained guns from Tete,[57]
presumably through the hands of the 'Chikunda' half-caste traders on
the lower Luangwa.[58] But meanwhile he also obtained guns from the
northeast. In 1894 an American journalist passed to the south of
Chinama and heard that Chikwanda

> sells slaves and ivory to the Wangwana [Arab or Swahili] traders,
> some of whom are always in his village. Two caravans left for
> Chiquanda's from Mlozi's stockades, or rather tembe, at Kawali's
> [Chibale's] while we were there. They both had cloth, guns, powder
> and cattle, and said they were going solely for slaves. . . . The
> Walala have but a few old flintlocks; the Awemba unlimited
> supplies of guns and ammunition.[59]

Thus the trade with Mlozi's Arabs provided Sampa* with a very im-
perfect counterpoise to Mwamba's association with traders further west.
How far Sampa* himself profited from trade is not very clear. By
1893 he appears to have had well over a thousand guns at his disposal;[60]
on the other hand, he had been famous before his accession as a
pillager of caravans,[61] and in 1885 he forced a Nyamwezi trader to
sell his cloth for a fifth of its usual value in ivory—hardly an encouragement to other traders.[62] In any case, Mwamba himself was in regular
contact with the 'Senga Arabs' on the Luangwa by 1896, though it is
not clear if he was doing business with them.[63] Besides, Sampa* had

[57] Genthe, 'Livingstone's Grave'. Most of Chikwanda's guns, like those of
Mwamba's men (see above, p. 222), were 'Tower' muzzle-loaders, dated between
1834 and 1866; there were also about a dozen German guns and some French
guns, two of which were double-barrelled. Genthe doubted whether the Bemba
could do much harm with such weapons: 'they are such poor shots'.

[58] Mlozi's trade encompassed the whole of the Luangwa valley: Arabs from
the north end of Lake Malawi bought slaves that had been caught by Kanyemba,
a chief on the south bank of the Zambezi, opposite Zumbo, though Zumbo too
was a source of guns (H. H. Johnston, confidential memo. of 23 March 1893, in
Johnston to Anderson, 23 March 1893, FO 2/54; see also below, p. 229, n. 73).

[59] Glave, 'Livingstone Tree', p. 776

[60] See below, p. 234.   [61] See above, p. 137.

[62] The trader reached Sampa with two hundred men and a hundred loads of
cloth; he left with forty men and 350 lbs. of ivory (Giraud, *Lacs*, p. 532). Aley had
bought ivory from Chitapankwa at 160 metres of white cloth (1–1½ loads) for
every 35 lbs. (*ibid.*, p. 260). An informant confirmed that a large tusk (70–100 lbs.)
might cost three bales (loads) of cloth: Chitichipalo, 31 July 1964.

[63] Bell to Forbes, undated fragment, NAZ/NE/A1/1/1. (For details of this
letter, see below, p. 257, n. 10.)

to reckon with disaffection not only in Mwamba's sphere but also among chiefs who had formerly been dependants of Chitapankwa*. Chikwanda and Nkula, as well as Mwamba, had received Chitapankwa's* death-bed command that they refuse obedience to Sampa. Nkula, as Chitapankwa's* protégé and son-in-law, was especially likely to comply. Chikwanda, to be sure, had small reason to support Mwamba against Sampa*, in view of Mwamba's southward advances, but Chikwanda evidently supported Nkula at Sampa's* expense: Chikwanda seems to have sent an annual tribute of a hundred cakes of salt to Nkula as well as to Sampa*.[64] This, together with the participation of both chiefs in trade with the 'Senga Arabs', was bound to arouse Sampa's* jealousy, and he made war against Nkula in about 1894, though with what result is not clear.[65]

Still more portentous were Sampa's* differences with the border chief closest to Lubemba, Makasa. At the time of Chitapankwa's* death, the Makasa title was held by Chisanga Chipemba, a son of Chitapankwa*.[66] As a son of the deceased paramount, Makasa IV Chisanga took a prominent part in the looting at the capital following his father's death, and he made off with his father's cattle. This annoyed Sampa*, who after his accession attacked Makasa IV at Chiponde, and after failing to defeat him attacked his 'sons' Lombe and Chilangwa. Makasa then returned the cattle.[67] This seems to have ended the dispute, for Labrecque says that Makasa and Mwamba then joined Sampa* in a campaign against the Mambwe; but Makasa IV died soon afterwards, probably in 1891.[68]

This might have been an opportunity for Sampa* to obtain the Makasa title for one of his own sons. But the surviving sons of the

[64] See Appendix 2, Note M (p. 361).

[65] Mukwikile (1913) in Chinsali DNB I, p. 261; the war took place two years before Nkula's death, which occurred in 1896 (see below, p. 254).

[66] See above, p. 146.

[67] Oger, 'Mpanda', 30–33; Kachasa, T1 (Kachasa fought for Sampa on this expedition). Oger says that Lombe was killed; if so, he was clearly not Lombe Shyula of Chilinda (see p. 229, n. 71). Labrecque says that Sampa seized cattle from Lombe and burned his village, but killed another minor chief ('Origines', p. 324; cf. *Ifyabukaya*, p. 107; Tanguy, *Imilandu*, p. 65).

[68] Labrecque, 'Origines', p. 323. Sampa told the Swahili trader Selemani bin Mwenye Chande, who visited him in 1891, that his 'son' had just died (Velten, *Safari*, pp. 42–3; for date, cf. Velten's preface, *ibid.*, vi). It seems quite likely that this 'son' was Makasa IV Chisanga. On the other hand, Selemani's testimony on Bemba relationships is plainly not always reliable, since he was under the impression that Chewe (i.e. Mutale Sichansa) was a 'son' of Chitimukulu (*ibid.*, p. 42).

long-deceased Chileshye* were no less eligible—indeed, they had an arguably better claim—than sons of any later Chitimukulu, for they equally were sons of Chitimukulu, and hence of Sampa*.[69] To be sure, Chitapankwa* had deliberately ignored this in securing the appointment as Makasa of his own son Chisanga.[70] But this can only have served to whet the ambition of Mukuuka Mwilwa, the eldest surviving son of Chileshye*, who had a small area in Chilinda. There may also have been a fear that the spirit of Chileshye* would be angry if his son was passed over again; in any case, Mukuuka succeeded as Makasa V.[71] He was so fearful of Sampa* that he built his new village in the north of Mpanda, on the river Luchewe (where Kayambi mission was later to be built).[72] By 1894, if not earlier, Makasa was trading with Swahili and had armed several of his warriors with guns, which soon became widespread in Mpanda.[73] The hostility between Makasa V and Sampa* was a major reason for Makasa's relatively favourable attitude to the coming of European missionaries.

EUROPEAN APPROACHES, 1883–93

The arrival of Europeans on the edges of Bemba country in the last years of the nineteenth century was but one more factor in this unstable field of political rivalries and alignments. Indeed, it is perhaps misleading to speak thus of one factor, since in reality each European was a factor calling for a policy decision. Just as the Europeans did not invariably think simply of 'the Bemba' but came to distinguish between different Bemba chiefs, so too the latter thought not only of a 'European problem' but also assessed individual Europeans who might

[69] See above, p. 138.   [70] See above, p. 146.

[71] Mukuuka Mwilwa left Chilinda partly under his brother Mutale Musanya and partly under Lombe Shyula, a son of Mwamba I Mutale *wa kabwe*. When Lombe died, his area was taken over by Mwilwa's brother Mubanga Chele, who hitherto had lived to the north, at Chunga. Mubanga died in 1912 and was succeeded by Mutale Musanya, who became Mubanga II (Oger, 'Mpanda', 31–2; Chinsali DNB I, p. 155; Kapinda, T1). Werbner ('Federal Administration', p. 33) wrongly says that Mwamba III appointed his own son to be Makasa; the only son of Mwamba III to become Makasa was Makasa VIII Chileshye (succeeded 1939): Brelsford, *Succession*, p. 35; Makasa VIII, 9 June 1965.

[72] Oger, 'Mpanda', 31

[73] See below, p. 249. In 1897 Edouard Foà noted that the Bemba were armed with guns, and he had only visited the Bemba of eastern Mpanda on a brief excursion from Ikawa (Foà, *Traversée*, p. 118). So too, Grogan and Sharp, who visited Mpanda in 1899, wrote that 'nearly every member of [Bemba] society has a gun imported by Arab traders from the north and by Portuguese from the south' (*From the Cape to Cairo*, p. 78).

or might not seem friendly or useful in a given situation. Bemba attitudes would depend both on the European in question and on the attitudes and actions of other Bemba chiefs in regard to these foreigners. At the same time, one should not overlook the counsels of East African traders as influences on Bemba decision-making. It was they, rather than the Bemba, who were directly at odds with the Europeans; they had more knowledge of Europeans than the Bemba; and as suppliers of wealth they were of ascertained value; that of the Europeans remained to be proved.

The first European travellers in Bemba country—Gamitto, Monteiro, Livingstone and Giraud—had on the whole been well received, despite occasional difficulties due to the apparent obscurity of their intentions.[74] But Giraud's visit to Chitapankwa* in June 1883 was soon followed by that chief's death, and the rumour promptly spread that Giraud had bewitched him.[75] Later travellers in the area reported that for this reason the Bemba did not want to see any more Europeans.[76] At the same time, the Bemba were, for the most part, careful not to pick a quarrel with Europeans, even though these were increasingly no longer only travellers but also neighbours.

The first Europeans to settle near Bemba country were members of the London Missionary Society (LMS), which in 1878 reached Lake Tanganyika from Zanzibar. In 1880 Captain Hore explored the south end of Lake Tanganyika, and in 1883 the LMS built a depot there, at the estuary of the Lufubu river. In 1885, this station was moved eastwards along the southern shores of the lake to Niamkolo: this was evacuated in 1888, but in the previous year the LMS had opened a new mission near the Mambwe chief Fwambo, and in 1889 Niamkolo was reoccupied.[77] Meanwhile, to the northeast of Bemba country, a station had been opened in 1882-3 at Chirenji, at the head of the Luangwa valley, by the Livingstonia Mission of the Free Church of Scotland, then at Bandawe, on Lake Malawi. Chirenji was closed in 1888, but in 1894-5 a station was opened further west at Mwenzo, among the Namwanga.[78] In 1884 the African Lakes Company (ALC) established

[74] Hence Nkula's outburst before Giraud: '"Qu'est-ce que ce Blanc vient faire chez nous?" s'écriait le chef avec des accents d'énergumène. "Une caravane qui n'achète ni vivres ni esclaves ne peut avoir que des intentions de guerre!"' (*Lacs*, p. 239). [75] *Ibid.*, p. 271

[76] Trivier, *Voyage*, p. 343, n. 1; Swann, *Slave-hunters*, pp. 119-20; Gouldsbury and Sheane, *Great Plateau*, p. 17

[77] Hore, *Tanganyika*, pp. 121-4, 233-9, 263, 282, 284, 293.

[78] J. W. Jack, *Daybreak in Livingstonia*, Edinburgh and London, 1901, pp. 169-73, 186-7

its depot at Karonga, on Lake Malawi: this forwarded supplies to the missions further west, and by 1890 there was a regular traffic up and down the 'Stevenson Road' between Lake Malawi and a new ALC post at Kituta, on Lake Tanganyika. From 1891 this traffic was increased by a Catholic missionary society, the White Fathers: in that year, Fr Lechaptois came north from the south end of Lake Malawi, and in July he set up a station in Mambwe country, as part of a plan to link up with the White Fathers already established around Lake Tanganyika.[79] Bemba raiders ranged across the length of the Stevenson Road, but they sought to avoid conflict with white traders and missionaries. Whatever property was clearly European they usually left alone.[80] In 1885 Fred Moir, of the ALC, left a dump of tins at a Mambwe village; in the following year some Bemba visited the place and 'while ruthlessly butchering the inhabitants and carrying off their goods had placed these [tins] carefully aside and left them'.[81] Only within the borders of Bemba country were European goods liable to seizure, as a reminder that white visitors were not wanted.

It was just as well for the Europeans that the Bemba entertained this 'exaggerated dread of and respect for white men'.[82] As yet, the European presence was far from secure. The memory of Livingstone, and the continuing scandal of the slave trade, might attract missionaries to the country south of Lake Tanganyika, but the region had no special appeal for white prospectors, traders or farmers. From a European point of view, it was politically important only because it lay between the rapidly expanding spheres of influence of the Congo Free State, the Germans in East Africa, and the British in southern Africa. In 1889 Cecil Rhodes obtained a royal charter for his newly formed British South Africa Company. To stake out the Company's claims north of the Zambezi, the British consul in Mozambique, Harry Johnston, made a long journey up Lake Malawi and over to Lake Tanganyika, making treaties with chiefs of the Namwanga (Mukoma), Mambwe (Fwambo and Kela), Lungu (Tafuna, Chitimbwa and Chungu) and Tabwa (Mulilo).[83] In 1890 Johnston sent Alfred Sharpe round by this route in a vain attempt to secure Katanga for Rhodes. On the way,

[79] Lechaptois to Lavigerie, 4 August 1891, *CT*, 1892, 54, pp. 242–7
[80] Cf. Swann, *Slave-hunters*, pp. 119–20; Johnston to Salisbury, 17 March 1890, FO 84/2051; also H. H. Johnston, 'British Central Africa', *PRGS*, 1890, n.s. 12, p. 734   [81] Carson, journal, 1886, p. 71, LMS/CA/J3
[82] Johnston to Salisbury, 17 March 1890, FO 84/2051; cf. Jones to Thompson, 23 July 1888, LMS/7/3/D
[83] Johnston to Salisbury, 1 February 1890, FO 84/2051

Sharpe visited the Lunda king Kazembe X Kanyembo and the Tabwa chief Nsama VI Chimutwe; he made treaties with both which purported to put their countries under British protection.[84] The treaties of Johnston and Sharpe provided a basis for agreements on the extent of the British sphere with Germany, in 1890, and with the Congo Free State, in 1894.[85] They ensured that the Bemba would, sooner or later, come under British control, but as yet it was not at all clear when that time would come.

In May 1891 a British protectorate was declared over British Central Africa—the present Malawi. Johnston, the Commissioner, also had responsibility for extending administration to the territory of the British South Africa Company north of the Zambezi.[86] Late in 1891, Johnston sent Richard Crawshay to build a station for the Company at Chiengi, at the north-eastern corner of Lake Mweru. Crawshay left in 1892, but in 1893 another station was built at the mouth of the Kalungwishi river, with a substation, Choma, near the Tabwa chief Kaputa.[87] But with the tiny forces at his disposal, Johnston had no wish

[84] A. Sharpe, 'A Journey to Garenganze', *PRGS*, 1892, n.s. 14, p. 37. For the texts of the treaties, see BSAC to FO, 5 August 1897, FO Print 6337, appendix, p. 343, FO 403/174. The treaty with Nsama called him the 'Paramount Chief' of the 'Itawa branch of the Awemba people': Nsama was then called 'Paramount Chief or King of the Awemba (Babemba) people, and of the Itawa country' in the BSAC's Certificate of Claim to mining rights in the areas 'secured' by Sharpe and his colleague Joseph Thomson (enclosure 2 in Johnston to Rosebery, 14 October 1893, FO 2/55). The Certificate of Claim and the treaties with Kazembe and Nsama are printed in T. W. Baxter, 'The Concessions of Northern Rhodesia' *Occasional Papers of the National Archives of Rhodesia and Nyasaland*, Salisbury 1963, pp. 29, 35-7.

[85] Cf. Johnston to Salisbury, 1 February 1890, FO 84/2051; Hanna, *Beginnings*, pp. 165-6, 220   [86] *Ibid.*, pp. 181-2

[87] Johnston, to Salisbury, 14 December 1891, FO 84/2114; Sharpe to Johnston, 17 December 1892, enclosed in Johnston to Rosebery, 2 January 1893, FO 2/54; see below, pp. 239, 242. In 1893 Dan Crawford, on a visit to Lake Mweru from the Plymouth Brethren mission in Katanga, met 'numbers of rude and as yet unbroken Vemba [?Shila] returning from the Kalungwizi river, where they had been to see the experiments in settled government now to be witnessed there' (G. E. Tilsley, *Dan Crawford of Central Africa*, London 1929, p. 300).

The evidence concerning the early stations of the BSAC in these parts is very inadequate: as Hanna has noted, 'It is impossible in most cases to state precisely when a Collector was appointed to, or took up his duties at a particular post, since Johnston saw no need to report on such matters unless there was some special reasons for doing so' (*Beginnings*, p. 223, n. 3). From 1895 North-Eastern Rhodesia became the direct responsibility of the BSAC, but their administrative records are far from complete. A few scraps of information may be found in H. C. Dann, *Romance of the Posts of Rhodesia, Central Africa and Nyasaland*, London 1940.

to try conclusions with the Bemba as long as they left Europeans alone.[88] The more thoughtful missionaries shared this attitude, even though they had daily evidence of the damage wrought by the Bemba and Swahili.[89]

From 1893 the tempo of European penetration began to quicken. The year before, Adam McCulloch, in charge of the ALC station at Fife (founded in 1890), seems to have entered into friendly relations with 'several of the important Awemba chiefs'.[90] He got them to pay compensation for recent thefts, and they sent in men to work on the Stevenson Road.[91] But in 1893 Johnston had reason to believe that such good will on the part of the Bemba might not last much longer. In June of that year, Sampa*, temporarily at·peace with Makasa, led a joint expedition north into Lungu country.[92] This was apparently an annual raid,[93] which on this occasion was undertaken just after the harvest, when the prospects were best for plunder. This time, however, Sampa* had a most untoward surprise, which profoundly affected his attitude to Europeans.

The Bemba appear to have marched north as far as Lupembe, a Lungu village on the eastern shore of Lake Tanganyika. Sampa* intended to capture Lupembe, but he forbade any attack on whites, and ordered his men to avoid the White Fathers' station at Kala, on the lake shore.[94] Early in July, the Bemba made their way back past Kasanga with a rich haul of slaves and cattle. They then climbed eastward to cross the Kalambo river, above the falls and a little to the

[88] Johnston to Rosebery, 31 August 1893, FO 2/54

[89] Cf. Carson to Thompson, 5 May 1893, 20 July 1893, LMS/CA9/1/B

[90] A. Sharpe, 'A Journey from the Shire River to Lake Mweru and the Upper Luapula', GJ, 1893, 1, p. 534. In 1898 a German visitor noted McCulloch's great influence among the local chiefs, and—significantly—admired his vast capacity for local beer: 'Mac war ein Prachtmensch' (Otto Schloifer, *Bana Uleia: ein Lebenswerk in Afrika*, Berlin 1939, p. 96).

[91] BCAG, 1 January 1894; cf. Johnston to Wissmann, 14 September 1893, enclosed in Johnston to Rosebery, 14 September 1893, FO 2/55

[92] Labrecque says they routed the Mambwe of Chingalaba II, a chief I have not managed to identify ('Origines', p. 325).

[93] In September 1889 some Bemba raiders seized men from Zombe's village on their way north (Trivier, *Voyage*, p. 300), and there was another Bemba raid in the same area late in 1892 (White Fathers' Mambwe diary, 6 November 1892, CT, 59, July 1893, p. 586).

[94] Mambwe diary, 9 March 1895, CT, 68, October 1895, p. 687 (information from a son of Makasa who accompanied the expedition). Two years earlier, Sampa had refused to help the Lungu chief Tafuna IV Kakungu against Europeans, even though Tafuna had sent Sampa ivory (Jones to Thompson, 15 April 1891, LMS/CA 8/3/C).

north of the frontier between the German and British spheres of influence. At this point, the Bemba encountered the Imperial Commissioner for German East Africa, Hermann von Wissmann.[95] Wissmann, who was directing an anti-slavery campaign in the area between Lakes Malawi and Tanganyika, had with him a force of two other officers and sixty trained soldiers; he also had a cannon and a Maxim gun. He could not, of course, deal with the Bemba on their home ground since this was in the British sphere. But in order to assert German authority in the German sphere Wissmann was determined to protect against Bemba attacks both the Lungu and the White Fathers at Kala. To this end, he camped in the stockaded village of a Lungu headman, Nondo,· who had recently moved to the Kalambo from the lake shore.[96] The massive Bemba force, which the Germans estimated at five thousand, now approached Nondo's village.

During the night of 6 July, while the German force kept watch within, the Bemba fired a few shots at Nondo's stockade—an act of provocation from which Makasa vainly tried to dissuade Sampa*.[97] By the following morning, the Bemba had deployed some of their men around ant-hills no more than fifty yards from the stockade. Most of these warriors had guns, and above them flew a motley collection of flags, several from France and others from Zanzibar, England and even Germany. Wissmann then engaged these vanguards in discussion. They explained, through Wissmann's interpreter, that Sampa* had no quarrel with the Germans if they promptly left Nondo's village; otherwise, the Bemba would attack both Lungu and Germans together. Wissmann refused to comply and warned the Bemba that it was a grave matter to do battle with Europeans. Meanwhile, his fellow officers, as also some of the Bemba, began to show signs of impatience with this parley. The delay was well calculated, however; as the great mass of Bemba continued to draw closer, they became ever more vulnerable to Wissmann's firepower. Nondo's councillor fired the first shot from the stockade; Wissmann hurled a grenade into a

[95] This and the next paragraph are based on two eye-witness reports of the encounter. Wissmann's version is given in Wissmann to Anti-Sklaverei Lotterie (Coblenz), 14 July 1893 (National Archives of Tanzania, G1/30, pp. 202–6); this was printed in the *Deutsches Kolonialblatt*, 1893, 4, pp. 492–3, and is the source for Rochus Schmidt's account in C. von Perbandt et al., *Hermann von Wissmann: Deutschlands Grösster Afrikaner*, Berlin 1906, pp. 414–18. The other report is by Selim bin Abakari, one of Wissmann's Swahili N.C.O.s, in his memoirs of this expedition: see Velten, *Safari za Wasuaheli*, pp. 97–101.
[96] Nutt to Thompson, 15 July 1893, LMS/CA 9/1/B; cf. Appendix 2, Note L
[97] Labrecque, 'Origines', p. 325

group of Bemba leaders; and the Germans and Lungu came out of the stockade with two big guns. The Maxim was used with devastating effect. Within a few minutes the Bemba were fleeing in disarray, leaving several dead[98] and wounded. Abandoning their numerous captives and much other booty, the main Bemba force pursued its headlong flight, not halting until it reached the Bemba border—four days' marches distant—the following morning.[99] Sampa* himself got stuck in a marsh (like Chitapankwa* he was evidently too bulky for such exertions), and by the time he got back his people had given him up for dead. The Germans heard that three of his sons had been killed.

This rout of the Bemba was doubtless welcomed by the mission at Kala and by the Lungu, Mambwe and Fipa in the German sphere. The LMS mission at Kawimbe, near the Mambwe chief Fwambo, saw it rather differently.[100] Being in the British sphere, they could not count on German protection,[101] and for this very reason they presented an all too likely target for Bemba reprisals. Carson reported to Johnston that Wissmann had explicitly warned the Bemba that war against the Germans would mean war with all white men. After their crushing defeat, the Bemba were indeed likely to oppose all whites, and it was said that they had sprinkled gunpowder across the path between Kituta and Fwambo as a declaration of war. Thus Carson now asked Johnston

---

[98] It is not clear how many Bemba were killed. Selim bin Abakari, describing how the Germans, while pursuing the main Bemba force, beat off a group of three hundred Bemba who took them in the rear, claimed that 'wherever we went through the woods, there were Bemba corpses' (Velten, *Safari*, p. 99). But Carson, a missionary at nearby Fwambo, reported that twenty Bemba were killed (Carson to Thompson, 20 July 1893, LMS/CA/9/1/B). And in 1895 the White Fathers at Mambwe were told by Makasa's son Kafunga that only three or four hundred Bemba, all under Makasa, came close to Wissmann's force, and that of these only four were killed and one wounded (Mambwe diary, 9 March 1895, *CT*, 68, October 1895, p. 687). Labrecque says ten Bemba were killed ('Origines', p. 325).

[99] This ignominious rout is acknowledged by the Bemba, the more so since it is blamed on Sampa, whose memory is cherished by few (Labrecque, 'Origines', p. 322).

[100] The mission had been moved in 1890–1 from Fwambo's village to Kawimbe, a few miles to the northwest.

[101] Though Wissmann did leave some of his soldiers for a few weeks with the ALC at Kituta, and also lent them his Maxim gun until a German station should be established in the area (Wissmann to Johnston, 14 July 1893, enclosed in Johnston to Rosebery, 31 August 1893, FO 2/54; Wissmann to Johnston, 22 July 1893, enclosed in Johnston to Rosebery, 17 October 1893, FO 2/55).

to ensure that the road to Karonga was kept open.[102] Johnston mistakenly supposed that Wissmann's fight had occurred near Fife, perhaps on British territory, and at any rate on the main line of march from Karonga to Fwambo. He considered that Wissmann was 'a very dangerous person to be travelling about Central Africa' and warned the British Government that as a result of Wissmann's interference the Bemba were gathering their forces together in order to 'attack all the whites on the plateau'. Before the end of July, Johnston had taken steps to make the British presence more unequivocally felt at the south end of Lake Tanganyika. He despatched Hugh Marshall, with a Sikh escort, to open a company station, called Abercorn, at Mbala, near the village of the Lungu chief Zombe above the south-eastern corner of the lake.[103] Johnston encouraged Marshall to engage in friendly relations with Bemba chiefs, but warned him to proceed very carefully.[104]

THE ARABS AND SWAHILI

If Johnston was anxious to avoid conflict with the Bemba, he was no less anxious to postpone a trial of strength with the slave traders on the plateau. He had enough trouble as it was with those in his Protectorate, from Mlozi in the far north to the Yao on the Shire river. For the time being, he could but hope that the truce secured with Mlozi in 1889 would last until the Protectorate's forces were strengthened. Besides, the slaving caravans which came to Bemba country from the north and east traversed German territory, and Johnston looked to the Germans to stop this traffic. The war between the Germans and the coastal peoples in 1888–9, and the subsequent German advances into the East African interior, had admittedly discouraged the traders at Ujiji from forwarding slaves and ivory eastwards. But instead, they and their agents around Lake Mweru increasingly directed their traffic past the south end of Lake Tanganyika to Karonga, across Lake Malawi and through German territory to Kilwa.[105] Until Johnston could be more

[102] Carson to Johnston, 18 July 1893; Nutt to Thompson, 15 July 1893, LMS/CA 9/1/B

[103] Johnston to Rosebery, 31 August 1893, FO 2/54; same to same, 15 September 1893, 17 October 1893, FO 2/55; Marshall to Johnston, 7 August 1894, enclosed in Johnston to Kimberley, 19 November 1894, FO 2/68. There is a photograph of Marshall outside the stockade at Abercorn post office, in about 1894, in Dann, *Romance of the Posts*, pp. 56–7 and see Plate VIII.

[104] Johnston to Marshall, 26 July 1893, enclosed in Wallace to BSAC, 2 November 1912, annex 9, NAR/LO/1/2/75; reprinted in *NRJ*, 1955, 2, v, pp. 47–9

[105] Cf. Sharpe to Johnston, 17 December 1892, enclosed in Johnston to Rosebery, 2 January 1893; Johnston to Anderson, 12 June 1893; Crawshay to Johnston

certain of effective German cooperation, he saw no point in stirring up trouble with which he was ill-equipped to deal.[106] In fact, he was annoyed with Wissmann for provoking not only the Bemba but also their East African allies: towards the end of July 1893, Wissmann had gone with Yule, of the ALC at Kituta, on a hunting trip into Itabwa, had got embroiled near the Tabwa village of Mukula with an Arab called Meso, and had burned his village.[107]

By 1891, indeed, the foreign traders and the Bemba of Mporokoso were the real powers in the country between Lake Tanganyika and Lake Mweru.[108] In July 1889, Abdullah ibn Suliman was visited by the French journalist Emile Trivier, who called Abdullah 'le soultan d'Itaoua' and did not mention Nsama at all.[109] Sharpe noted in 1890 that the Tabwa under Nsama VI Chimutwe 'live on fairly good terms with Abdullah, but occasionally give him trouble by stealing his people and interfering with his caravans; they fight with spears and have few guns'.[110] Chimutwe paid scant regard to his precarious situation, and he soon brought about an alignment fatal to his interests—a Bemba–Swahili alliance. There was trouble between Chimutwe and Abdullah over a woman; moreover, Chimutwe had killed Chilembo, a son of Nsama III's brother Lukwesa. Chilembo's brother, Katele II Makungu, allied with Abdullah; they were joined by Mporokoso, and in 1891, after a six-day siege, Chimutwe was killed at his capital. Chimutwe's sister's son, Chipimbili, fled to the Chishinga, while his mother's

30 June 1893, enclosed in Johnston to Rosebery, 25 August 1893, FO 2/54. In August 1889 Kabunda complained that the war between Mlozi and the ALC was ruining his trade (Trivier, *Voyage*, pp. 283–4).

[106] Cf. Johnston to Rosebery, 25 August 1893, FO 2/54

[107] Wissmann to Johnston, 5 September 1893, enclosed in Johnston to Rosebery, 25 September 1893, FO 2/55. In his official despatch of 5 September 1893, Wissmann wrote that he was attacked at night by a deputy of Rumaliza; Wissmann then sought next day to explain that he had come to hunt, not fight, but he was met by gunfire. In the ensuing fight, six men on the Arab side were killed and eighty slaves released (*Deutsches Kolonialblatt*, 1893, 4, pp. 537–8). Selim bin Abakari recalled that the fight was with Kabunda: Wissmann set out deliberately to threaten Kabunda, at the request of the ALC at Kituta (Velten, *Safari*, p. 101). This is almost certainly wrong: Kabunda's village, at Liendwe, was well to the east of Mukula's, and in any case Wissmann wrote a letter there before the affray with 'Meso' took place (Wissmann to Johnston, 22 July 1893, dated 'Leindwa, Kabunda's', enclosed in Johnston to Rosebery, 17 October 1893, FO 2/55).

[108] Mporokoso doubtless profited from the fact that his perpetual brothers Luali II Mushidi and Sunkutu II Mulenga were at war with each other in the last years of the century (note of 25 January 1914 in Mporokoso DNB, I, 106.

[109] Trivier, *Voyage*, pp. 268–9; and cf. *ibid.*, p. 272

[110] Sharpe, 'Journey to Garenganze', p. 37

sister's daughter's son, Mutuutu, became Nsama VII, evidently with Abdullah's backing.[111] Chimutwe's capital was left in ruins, and Mutuutu did not begin to settle in the area until 1894.[112] When Sharpe returned to Itabwa in 1892, he wrongly took Mukula, a perpetual son of Nsama, to be Chimutwe's successor, and made another treaty with him.[113] As a British official later observed, the Tabwa were 'now broken up by Arab and Babemba oppression into many divisions, some of them still under members of the Nasama [*sic*] family, but not one strong enough to take the lead of the rest'.[114]

For the time being, then, Johnston made no attempt to challenge the East African hegemony to the south and west of Lake Tanganyika. Instead, he was content to increase his revenue by levying duties on the foreign traders' imports, illegal though these mostly were. In 1892, Teleka, the Swahili at Sumbu, took a caravan with ivory and slaves to the country east of Lake Malawi; in 1894 he returned from Kilwa with a large consignment of gunpowder (perhaps as much as 8,000 lbs.). The unlicensed import of guns, powder and ammunition was of course no less illegal than the sale of slaves, but Marshall, at Abercorn, was in no position to enforce the law. Sharpe considered that Marshall had done well to raise from Teleka the full import duty, paid in powder, an exaction to which Teleka cheerfully submitted.[115]

By this time the BSAC had posted an official, W. B. Knight, to

[111] Roberts, 'Abdullah', p. 263; Kasama DNB II, pp. 50–1; Peyala Kapembwa, 21–23 June 1965; Milambo, T11; P. Sikazwe, enclosure in D.C. Abercorn to P.C. Northern Province, 18 May 1944, NAZ/box 6694/NA/26; date from Sharpe, who says the siege lasted three months ('Journey from the Shire River', p. 528).

[112] *BCAG*, 26 September 1894; cf. Watson to Johnston, 8 July 1894, enclosure in Johnston to Kimberley, 19 November 1894, FO 2/68. Chipimbili seems to have returned in 1894: Watson (*ibid.*) reported that 'On the very day I arrived at Nsama's a headman of the old Nsama, who had been living some years in Kissinga, arrived with a few of his people'.

[113] Sharpe to Johnston, 17 December 1892, enclosure in Johnston to Rosebery, 2 January 1893, FO 2/54; cf. Hanna, *Beginnings*, pp. 193–4. There was some excuse for the mistake: Mukula's mud-walled town comprised eight hundred houses (Sharpe, 'Journey from the Shire River', p. 528; cf. *BCAG*, 4 June 1894). In 1896 Europeans still had the impression that Mukula was Nsama (Gibbs in *BCAG*, 15 January 1897).   [114] Wallace, 'Nyasa-Tanganyika Plateau', p. 616

[115] Crawshay to Johnston, 30 June 1893, enclosure in Johnston to Rosebery, 23 August 1893, FO 2/54; Kerr-Cross to Sharpe, 21 May 1894, enclosure in Sharpe to Kimberley, 11 June 1894, FO 2/66 (cf. Glave, 'Heart of Africa', p. 932); Sharpe to Johnston, 17 September 1894, enclosure in Johnston to Anderson, 13 November 1894, FO 2/68; Marshall to Johnston, 7 August 1894, enclosure in Johnston to Kimberley, 19 November 1894, FO 2/68

Sumbu, as much as to be 'in evidence' as for any other purpose; he kept an eye on the 'Arabs' but was said to be on good terms with them.[116] His neighbour, the Baluchi Kabunda at Liendwe in the Lufubu valley, had continued to raid for slaves and export them and to import powder.[117] He was however 'old and feeble, and not being an Arab is not on good terms with Tippu Tip's people [i.e. the Swahili of Abdullah], and had no allies'.[118] In 1894 Kabunda promised Marshall that he would visit the station at Abercorn, but he died in December.[119] In 1896 it was said that his son 'Mlutaluta . . . appears very anxious to keep on friendly terms with the English, and, from time to time, pays a visit to the British South Africa Company's station at Abercorn.'[120] Further west, Watson reported that Kasengere, a 'Makua' ivory hunter who had at one time given the Lungu much trouble from his boma on the Lufubu river, had settled peacefully on the Kalungwishi.[121]

The weakness of these outposts of empire shocked the American journalist E. J. Glave, who passed through the area on his way to the Congo in August and September 1894. Earlier that year, Nsemiwe, a Nyamwezi follower of Abdullah ibn Suliman, destroyed the British flag left by Sharpe with the Tabwa chief Mukula; but Worringham, the official at nearby Choma, was powerless to intervene.[122] Abdullah himself was less provocative. He was evidently unimpressed by Sharpe's warning in 1892 that if he fought Mukula he would be 'making war on the Queen of England'.[123] But when Nsemiwe and a Swahili, Masala, were besieged during August and September 1894 by a Belgian force from the Congo Free State, Abdullah declined to help them and Masala was killed.[124]

[116] Sharpe to Hill, 24 May 1894, FO 2/66

[117] J. A. Moloney, *With Captain Stairs to Katanga*, London 1893, p. 254; Yule to Sharpe, 20 June 1893, enclosure in Johnston to Rosebery, 26 August 1893, FO 2/54

[118] Sharpe to Johnston, 17 December 1892, enclosure in Johnston to Rosebery, 2 January 1893, FO 2/54

[119] Marshall to Johnston, 7 August 1894, enclosure in Johnston to Kimberley, 19 November 1894, FO 2/68; *BCAG*, 7 January 1895; and cf. J. E. S. Moore, *To the Mountains of the Moon*, London 1901, p. 104

[120] *BCAG*, 1 October 1896

[121] Watson to Johnston, 7 August 1894, enclosure in Johnston to Kimberley, 19 November 1894, FO 2/68; *BCAG*, 7 January 1895. Cf. Appendix 2, Note L

[122] Glave, 'Heart of Africa', pp. 927, 932, 930

[123] Sharpe to Johnston, 17 December 1892, enclosure in Johnston to Rosebery, 2 January 1893, FO 2/54

[124] G. Descamps, 'Du Tanganika au Moero', *Mouvement anti-esclavagiste*, 1895, p. 194; Glave, 'Heart of Africa', pp. 930–3; Marshall, 30 July 1895, in *BCAG*, 1 November 1895

Abdullah presumably realised that war with Europeans would only hinder his principal export trade, in ivory, for he was now taking advantage of European transport: in 1895 he sold about a ton of ivory at Kituta, the ALC station on the lake, below Abercorn.[125] Other immigrant traders had for some time been doing the same. In March 1891 Sharpe observed that the Arabs east of Lake Mweru were eager to sell ivory to the ALC who 'of course as usual' could find no cloth to buy it.[126] They bought it nonetheless: later that year, a Swahili caravan from the coast obtained guns and gunpowder in exchange for ivory from a European at the south end of Lake Tanganyika who was presumably an agent of the ALC.[127] In November 1892 Law of the ALC passed Mambwe mission with over a hundred tusks from Kituta, which he had evidently bought from Ujiji traders in exchange for powder; such powder soon found its way to the Bemba.[128] In March 1893 Yule and Swann of the ALC took a huge load of Ujiji ivory from Kituta to Lake Malawi; in April, more Ujiji ivory was taken the same way by Bainbridge, the BSAC official at Kalungwishi; and at least two more ivory caravans from Kituta followed in May.[129]

British officials, as elsewhere in Africa, had hopes of encouraging a 'legitimate' trade which would serve as a peaceful means of transition from the slave trade. And even if it was scarcely legitimate for British subjects to sell firearms for ivory, it was still almost as hard to prevent this as to prevent caravans bringing in their own powder from the coast. From Johnston's point of view, the main thing was that the Swahili and Arabs had promoted the habit of trade and that this habit could gradually be turned to account by a British administration. On his journey to Lake Tanganyika in 1889, Johnston had been greatly taken with the apparent calm and prosperity of Kabunda's settlement.[130] He believed in fact that the immigrant

---

[125] Marshall, *ibid.*

[126] Sharpe to Johnston, 26 December 1890, enclosure in Johnston to Salisbury, 3 May 1891; cf. Johnston to Salisbury, 14 December 1891, FO 84/2114

[127] Velten, *Safari*, p. 32. The Swahili, Selemani bin Mwenye Chande, met the European the day after reaching 'Iyendo', where the chief was 'Kitimbo': this was probably Liendwe, in the territory of the Lungu chief Chitimbwa.

[128] Mambwe diary, 6 November 1892, 9 November 1892, *CT*, 59, July 1893, pp. 586–7; *ibid.*, 23 October 1892, CT, 58, April 1893, p. 410. Lugard complained of the ALC selling guns and powder in 1888 (F. D. Lugard, *The Rise of Our East African Empire*, London 1893, I, pp. 53, 215).

[129] Mambwe diary, 25 March 1893, 27 April 1893, *CT*, 60 (October 1893), 670–1; *ibid.*, 25 May 1893, *CT*, 61, January 1894, p. 222.

[130] Johnston to Salisbury, 17 March 1890, FO 84/2051. Johnston was mistaken

traders might well prove useful allies in the task of civilising Africa. The real obstacle was the African Lakes Company, as yet the only European commercial agency in the area. It was evidently incapable of fruitfully exploiting such opportunities as it had to develop local trade.[131] In view of the ALC's inadequate facilities, Sharpe suggested in 1891 that the BSAC, through Johnston's agency, should itself take the commercial initiative. From a station on Lake Mweru, trade could be started with Msiri and Mwamba.[132] When he returned to the area at the end of 1892, he noted how the troubles between Germans and Arabs had diverted trade southwards from Ujiji and he pointed out that a steamer on Lake Tanganyika would give the British access to ivory markets in the upper Congo and the country north of the lake. 'This enabling the Arabs to sell their ivory on Tanganyika itself will do more to lessen slave transport than much money spent in directly opposing the slave trade.'[133] And if such a trade were to prosper, the prevailing indiscriminate slaughter of elephants would have to stop. In 1879, Joseph Thomson had predicted that 'in twenty years the noble African elephant will be a rare animal', and he could see nothing that might take the place of ivory as a staple export from the interior.[134] In 1893, Crawshay reported (from Deep Bay, on Lake Malawi) that 'ivory is becoming a very scarce commodity in the hitherto much sought districts of Senga and Luwemba'.[135] But as yet there were still great herds of elephant in the Mweru region, and Johnston, with his customary acumen, recommended a Government monopoly of ivory to ensure their survival.[136]

MPOROKOSO AND PONDE

Johnston's cautious advances around the plateau met with equal caution on the part of the Bemba, though they were not uniformly

in supposing that Kabunda had given up slave-raiding: see above, p. 239, and Swann, *Slave-hunters*, p. 192.

[131] Johnston to Anderson, 21 January 1893, FO 2/54

[132] Sharpe to Johnston, 26 December 1890, enclosure in Johnston to Salisbury, 3 May 1891; cf. Johnston to Salisbury, 14 February 1891, FO 84/2114

[133] Sharpe to Johnston, 17 December 1892, enclosure in Johnston to Rosebery, 2 January 1893, FO 2/54   [134] *Central African Lakes*, II, pp. 17, 285–6

[135] Crawshay to Johnston, 30 June 1893, enclosure in Johnston to Rosebery, 25 August 1893, FO 2/54; and see above, p. 204.

[136] Johnston to BSAC, 10 March 1894, in BSAC, *Reports, 1892–4*, pp. 101–2. One of the first acts of the company on taking over administration west of Nyasaland in 1895 was to declare a game reserve around Mweru *wa ntipa*.

well-disposed to European intrusion. The most consistently hostile chief was undoubtedly Sampa*. His defeat by Wissmann must have been a great shock to him; one can well believe that it did induce a fear of white men in general. And by all accounts Sampa* was not disposed by temperament to accept such an affront to his prestige as an argument for conciliation. Perhaps a cooler-headed man would have perceived the value of European support when his power as Chitimukulu was so uncertain. But Sampa* probably had no more precise an idea of how to deal with the British than they had of how to deal with the Bemba. He realised his weakness, inasmuch as he did not attack any European station, but until the last year or so of his life he had no wish to see Europeans in his country.

Sampa's* subordinates were in general less discouraging to Europeans. Soon after his arrival at Abercorn in 1893, Marshall met a Bemba 'chief' (unnamed) near Fife, and reported that 'all the southern and eastern sections of the Awemba evince a strong desire to remain on friendly terms with the English'; he noted that it was only the 'northern Awemba' under Chitimukulu who had been involved in the conflict with Wissmann. In the following year, Marshall received 'friendly messages and a present of ivory' from Changala, the perpetual son of Makasa.[137] In the far west, the Bemba seemed no less accommodating. To be sure, Mporokoso was very much on his guard against Europeans in 1891, the year in which the first BSAC posts were set up between Lakes Mweru and Tanganyika.[138] When a Swahili caravan came to his village from the north in that year, Mporokoso made preparations for war, fearing that his visit might simply be part of a European scheme for a surprise attack.[139] But in 1893 Bainbridge, the official at Kalungwishi, obtained Bemba help in a skirmish with some slave traders. He heard that the 'Arabs' had asked Mwamba to help them drive the English out of Mweru district. 'Mwamba however replied that if anybody was to be "turned out" it should be the Arabs.'[140] In 1892, while at Chiengi, Crawshay had sought to visit Mporokoso; his request was refused, but only, it seemed, because Mporokoso had not yet finished building a new village for himself.[141]

[137] *BCAG*, 1 January 1894, 7 January 1895. This Changala was probably a son of Makasa III Bwalya.
[138] See above, p. 232.
[139] Velten, *Safari*, pp. 34–5. Mporokoso told the Swahili, not very candidly, 'I am poor: all I do is grow millet.'
[140] *BCAG*, 1 February 1894. No 'Arabs' are named; perhaps the Nyamwezi Nsemiwe is meant (cf. above, p. 239).
[141] Weatherley, 30 July 1895, in *BCAG*, 15 September 1895

In July 1895, Poulett Weatherley, a hunter based on a camp near the Lungu chief Chitimbwa, visited Mporokoso and was greatly impressed by him.

About a mile from the boma [stockade] I heard a noise as of a vast crowd approaching, with much singing and beating of drums. Then spears glittered amongst the bushes—louder and louder came the roar of voices, and suddenly four or five hundred Awemba rushed forward and opened out into two long wings on either side of the path. It was a magnificent sight. In the centre of the crowd appeared a tall, very dignified Arab, as I thought but it proved to be The Great Awemba. He was clothed in a spotless white flowing Khansa [long gown], a light blue sort of over shirt, well made and neatly edged with red. He advanced and grasped my hand with both his, saying how pleased he was I had come to visit him. . . . Mporogoso is a tall fine looking, pleasant featured man of about 50 years of age—so quiet— so dignified whilst speaking—no movement—no gesticulation, and such an air of command.[142]

Mporokoso, for his part, evidently took to Weatherley. He emphatically disavowed the common belief that Giraud had brought about the death of Chitapankwa*. Mporokoso also dissociated himself from Sampa*, who had recently surprised Weatherley by asking him to visit him.[143] Mporokoso remarked on this, 'I do not know what to say. Kitiamkulu is not behaving well. The former Chief and I were great friends, but this one and I never visit.' Weatherley concluded:

If there is a friendship worth cultivating amongst the powerful Awemba up here, it is that of Mporogoso. There are only three men—that is to say, three big Chiefs up here—*i.e.* Kitiamkulu, roughly speaking to the N.-E., Mwamba to the S. and Mporogoso to the W. The two latter are of course only headmen of Kitiamkulu's, but their power has so increased as the years have gone by, that they are now not only independent of, but pay no tribute to, their paramount chief.

As long as the present alliance between Mwamba and Mporogoso exists, Kitiamkulu's position must be insecure. Personally, I think

[142] *Ibid.*

[143] *Ibid.* Sampa had heard of, and perhaps was alarmed by, Weatherley's friendship with Chitimbwa and another Lungu chief, Chungu (Weatherley to Johnston, RH, 11 October 1895). Sampa's invitation seems to have been made at the same time or after Ponde's invitation to Weatherley, which was made during the rainy season, and thus not later than April 1895 (*ibid.*). See also below, p. 252.

it would be an excellent thing were Mwamba and Mporogoso to combine and drive out Kitiamkulu, for until something of that sort happens the Awemba country will be to a great extent closed to whites.[144]

Europeans had more reason to be apprehensive of Ponde, the sister's son of Sampa* who occupied country taken from the Lungu of Tafuna.[145] Ponde can probably be credited with most of the Bemba raids reported by LMS missionaries from the time of their first settlement at the south end of Lake Tanganyika. The presence of the Baluchi Kabunda, near the mouth of the Lufubu, and that of the missionaries themselves may have deterred the Bemba to some extent. But the Bemba were emboldened by Kabunda's absence for a time after 1883; they raided on both sides of the Lufubu, and well before 1886 they seem to have driven Kapufi, the Lungu headman near Kabunda's, to seek refuge at Karonga, on Lake Malawi.[146] Kabunda's slave raids, and the depredations of the Bemba, largely depopulated the country between the Lungu chief Chitimbwa and the Mambwe chief Fwambo.[147] In 1894 the Bemba–Lungu boundary was said to run along the Mululwe river, but this does not seem to have been acknowledged by Ponde.[148]

In July 1893, soon after Wissmann's defeat of Sampa*, the LMS mission at Kawimbe, near Fwambo's, vainly sought to make contact with the Bemba through the Lungu chief Chungu.[149] In June 1894, Carson made a long journey from Kawimbe to Kazembe's, but his request to found a mission there was politely refused.[150] Meanwhile, however, a plague of locusts had brought famine to the Bemba, and the LMS missionaries at Niamkolo saw this as a long-awaited opportunity to visit them. In June they despatched messengers to Ponde's village near the Luela stream; these told him that there was plenty of food for

[144] Weatherley, 30 July 1895, in *BCAG*, 15 September 1895

[145] See above, pp. 151, 219.

[146] Hore, *Tanganyika*, pp. 157, 235–7; Swann, *Slave-hunters*, p. 89; Carson, journal, 1886, p. 46, LMS/CA/J3

[147] Moir, *After Livingstone*, pp. 78–9; Fotheringham, *Adventures in Nyassaland*, p. 14; Carson to Thompson, 20 July 1893, LMS/CA 9/1/B; Jones to Thompson, 25 October 1894, LMS/CA 9/2/E

[148] W. Thomas in *BCAG*, 12 October 1894; Weatherley in *BCAG*, 22 April 1895   [149] Carson to Thompson, 20 July 1893, LMS/CA 9/1/B

[150] Watson to Johnston, 8 July 1894, in Johnston to Kimberley, 19 November 1894, FO 2/68; cf. Carson to Thompson, 14 September 1894, LMS/CA 9/2/D. Carson's own account of the expedition does not appear to be in the LMS archives.

hungry Bemba at Niamkolo and sought his permission to approach Chitimukulu. Ponde would not let the embassy go on to Sampa* 'as Kitimkuru had not been well pleased with the white man; but he himself left to show Kitimkuru his new presents and tell him of the white man's wish to visit him'. Ponde was delighted to learn that one of the missionaries, Hemans, was coloured (he came from Jamaica) and he specially asked to see him, sending a small tusk of ivory as a token of good will. The mission failed to make the most of this: they sent Hemans' white superior, Thomas, instead. Hemans was naturally upset at not having been sent to see Ponde: he reported that Ponde's envoys had been most indignant about this, saying that Ponde had no wish to see a white man. Hemans felt that his special value, as a coloured man, was not being fully exploited, and that as a result 'it is very likely that the half-opened door will be closed again against Europeans'.[151]

Whether Hemans was right about this one cannot say. Thomas, not surprisingly, does not mention the subject in his account of his visit to Ponde.[152] But his visit served to show that, while Ponde was cautiously friendly, Sampa* was highly suspicious, if not actively hostile. Ponde had just returned from asking Sampa* if he wanted to see Europeans; Sampa* said he would accept a message, but would not see Thomas himself. Ponde, for his part, wished Thomas to build him a new house, but he did not wish Thomas to settle at his village until Sampa* had been consulted again. Ponde's 'minister' then told Thomas that Sampa* had sent orders to kill Thomas' party, whom he believed to have some evil medicine. Ponde had declined to cooperate, pointing out that a chicken had already survived a poison ordeal designed to test Thomas' bona fides and that anyhow to kill one white man would simply invite massive retribution.[153]

It seems that this early initiative by the LMS was not followed up, even though conditions were unusually propitious: in August 1894 Marshall reported from Abercorn that the Bemba 'have not raided this year on the plateau'—whether in spite of or because of the

[151] Hemans to Thompson, 3 July 1894, LMS 9/2/C

[152] Rotberg's account of this incident is somewhat misleading: he speaks of Ponde as 'the Bemba paramount chief' and says that Thomas 'was refused an audience with the chief' (R. I. Rotberg, *Christian Missionaries and the creation of Northern Rhodesia, 1880–1924*, Princeton 1965, pp. 159–60). We know that Thomas saw Ponde. He was indeed not allowed to see Sampa, but we do not know whether Hemans would have been either, nor can we be sure that Sampa knew that Hemans was coloured.

[153] W. Thomas, *BCAG*, 12 October 1894

famine.[154] In September the LMS opened a new mission, Kambole, close to the village of the Lungu chief Chitimbwa,[155] but for the time being no attempt was made from there to enter Bemba country. Thomas himself had concluded from his visit to Ponde that 'the time had not yet come for the white man to settle near him. He is a small chief to put on such airs. . . . The day of reckoning is coming. We must wait.'[156] In 1895 Poulett Weatherley reported from his hunting camp near Chitimbwa's that Thomas' 'stay amongst the Awemba, owing to his inability to make Ponde respect and protect a white man, did more harm than good'. Weatherley himself never visited Ponde, though he was invited to do so and received friendly messages from a number of Bemba chiefs. He seems to have acquired a certain local prestige as a mediator, and in June 1895 he flattered himself that he had made peace between Ponde and Chitimbwa.[157] But in December Ponde's men captured Chitimbwa's village, killed the chief (Chitimbwa IV Nyente) and carried away rich spoils of cloth, salt and women.[158]

THE WHITE FATHERS, THE MAMBWE AND MAKASA

While the London Missionary Society bided its time, the White Fathers, further east, had begun to make a more sustained attempt to introduce their mission among the Bemba. In July 1891 they had founded a station near the Stevenson Road in the eastern part of Mambwe country. Like the LMS, they were welcomed as protectors against the Bemba.[159] Chitapankwa* had made a pact with the Mambwe chief Kela,[160] but this does not seem to have outlasted Chitapankwa's* death in 1883. Kela and other Mambwe chiefs were repeatedly harassed by Bemba raiders in the 1880s and early 1890s. The Bemba had taken over Mpande's country, in the west,

154 Marshall to Johnston, 7 August 1894, enclosure in Johnston to Salisbury, 19 November 1894, FO 2/68
155 Nutt to Thompson, 29 September 1894, LMS/CA 9/2/D
156 W. Thomas in *BCAG*, 12 October 1894
157 Weatherley to Johnston, RH, 11 October 1895; Weatherley, 6 June 1895, in *BCAG*, 15 August 1895
158 Jones to Thompson, 31 December 1895, LMS/CA 9/3/D; Gouldsbury and Sheane, *Great Plateau*, p. 36. It seems that Nyente had reigned only a year or two: in August 1894, Marshall wrote from Abercorn that Kabunda 'finds he cannot treat the new chief Kitimbwa (Nyente) as he did the old man' (Marshall to Johnston, 7 August 1894, enclosure in Johnston to Kimberley, 19 November 1894, FO 2/68).
159 Van Oost to Lavigerie, 20 April 1892, *CT*, 56, October 1892, p. 574; cf. Swann, *Slave-hunters*, p. 189   160 See above, p. 147

before 1883, and since then they had also encroached upon that of the Mambwe paramount Nsokolo; by 1892, the south-eastern part of Nsokolo's country, athwart the Choshi river, was under Chilangwa, a son of Makasa III.[161] In September 1892 Mpande himself came to settle near the White Fathers, and they gave another group of refugees three guns and some powder with which to defend themselves against the Bemba.[162]

The Mambwe, indeed, suffered like the Lungu and Tabwa from dis-unity in the face of Bemba attacks: it has even been suggested that the British 'may have saved the Mambwe from extinction as a people'.[163] Nonetheless, the Bemba met with determined resistance from both Kela and his relative Fwambo, who by 1885 had supplanted Nsokolo, the nominal paramount, as the most powerful Mambwe chief.[164] Fwambo and Kela beat off repeated Bemba attacks on their stockaded villages.[165] Another Mambwe chief, Mpenza, seems to have made some sort of alliance with the Bemba,[166] but he failed to draw them into a war with Fwambo in September 1889, and two months later Johnston induced Fwambo and Mpenza to make peace.[167] Bemba were repulsed from Fwambo's in 1892 and Fwambo retained his impressive herds of cattle.[168] In April 1893 a group of Sampa's* men were beaten back from Nsokolo's neighbourhood,[169] though not, it seems, through the efforts of Nsokolo himself, who in any case soon fled to the north.[170]

[161] See above, p. 132, and below, p. 248, n. 6.

[162] Mambwe diary, 2 September 1892, WFA; *ibid.*, 26 September 1892, *CT* 58, July 1893, p. 409. In 1888 several Mambwe fought with the ALC forces against Mlozi (Lugard, *Rise of our East African Empire*, I, p. 108).

[163] Watson, *Tribal Cohesion*, p. 75, n. 4

[164] Giraud, *Lacs*, p. 531; Carson, journal, 1886, p. 81, LMS/CA/J3. Fwambo's iron industry was doubtless a factor in his political and military pre-eminence: see above, p. 184.

[165] Carson, Journal, 1886, pp. 78–9; Moir, 'Eastern Route', p. 108. The Mambwe told Giraud that Chitimukulu (i.e. Sampa) had never dared to attack Fwambo (Giraud, *Lacs*, p. 531). In 1891 the White Fathers considered that Kela's village was the Mambwe capital: Lechaptois to Lavigerie, 4 August 1891, *CT*, 54, 1892, p. 245.

[166] Carson, journal, 1886, pp. 82, 84, 92; LMS/CA/J3; Wright to LMS, 15 November 1887, LMS/CA 7/2/D

[167] Trivier, *Voyage*, pp. 300–1, 312, 320; Johnston to Salisbury, 17 March 1890, FO 84/2051

[168] Jones to Thompson, 20 April 1892, 27 August 1892, LMS/CA 8/5/B; Van Oost to Lavigerie, 20 April 1892, *CT*, 56, October 1892, pp. 573–4

[169] Mambwe diary, 8 April 1893, *CT*, 60, October 1893, p. 671

[170] In January 1894, Kosi, brother of the late Nsokolo Chitambi and thus a member of a rival royal lineage, combined with headman Chilundumuzi;

In August 1894 many famine-stricken Bemba came north, not as armed robbers, but to beg food among the Namwanga and Fipa, 'où ils ne sont pas toujours bien reçus. Vieux souvenirs de leurs anciens méfaits.'[171] In the same year, Ponde led another attack on Fwambo, but 'the Bemba died like flies in the cold season'. Fwambo had apparently been sent reinforcements by both Mpenza and David Jones, of the neighbouring LMS mission at Kawimbe.[172] By 1895 the Bemba threat had subsided and the Mambwe were once again making small villages outside the big stockades behind which they had gathered for protection.[173]

The White Fathers, at their mission northeast of Nsokolo's, had from the outset been alert to the challenge presented by the Bemba.[174] For the first three years, Bemba raiding naturally impeded attempts to make contact with them. In December 1891, soon after the Fathers' arrival, a Bemba 'chief' sent men to Mambwe to make friends with them,[175] but this gesture seems to have had no immediate result. In August 1892, Frs Lechaptois and van Oost (the Superior at Mambwe) visited Chilangwa, the Bemba chief nearest to the mission; his village was evidently only a short distance to the south of Mambwe. They parted amicably, and Chilangwa later sent a slave-girl as a present.[176] In March 1893, however, Bemba raiders burned two villages near the mission and in April laid waste one of the Fathers' fields of haricot beans.[177] But the Fathers were hardly less disturbed by the constant

together they took Nsokolo Kamialile prisoner and put out his eyes. Kamialile then fled north into the German sphere. (Mambwe diary, 20 and 22 January 1894, *CT*, 63, July 1894, p. 493; Watson, *Tribal Cohesion*, p, 269; he wrongly gives 1892 as the date of the blinding of Kamialile.)

[171] Van Oost to Lavigerie, 15 August 1894, *CT*, 65, January 1895, p. 196

[172] Silanda, 'Enslavement of Grandmother Mary', LM/IV D9. Presumably this attack took place in the latter part of the year: as late as August, Marshall had reported that there had been no Bemba raids to the north that year (cf. above, p. 245).

[173] Marshall, 30 July 1895, in *BCAG*, 1 November 1895; Carson to Thompson, 3 June 1895, LMS/CA 9/3/C

[174] Lechaptois to Lavigerie, 4 August 1891, *CT*, 54, April 1892, pp. 244–5

[175] Mambwe diary, 4 December 1891, *CT*, 55, July 1892, p. 422

[176] Mambwe diary, 28 August 1892, 3 September 1892, *CT*, 58, April 1893, p. 408. For Chilangwa's location, cf. Mambwe diary, 8 April 1893, *CT*, 60, October 1893, p. 671; and 31 January 1894, *CT*, 63, July 1894, pp. 497–8

[177] Mambwe diary, 19 March 1893, 8 April 1893, *CT*, 60, October 1893, pp. 669–71. One of the villages, Chitene, seems later in the year to have been taken over by a Bemba headman; but tribute was paid to Nsokolo in September 1893 (Mambwe diary, 5 September 1893, 28 January 1894, *CT*, 63, July 1894, pp. 490, 494).

interruptions and distractions caused among the local people by the traffic passing up and down the Stevenson Road.[178] They began to make plans to abandon Mambwe and instead found a new mission in the German sphere; but before moving north they were anxious to do all they could to establish a mission among the Bemba.[179] Early in January 1894, van Oost exchanged presents with Chitika, a Bemba headman who was evidently living just south of the Choshi river. Later in the month, van Oost and Fr Depaillat visited Chitika's village, and on 30 January Chitika directed them a short distance eastwards to the extensive village of Makasa.[180]

On reaching Makasa's, the Fathers were immediately alarmed by indications that he was involved in the slave trade. There were several white-robed Swahili in the village. Makasa's people mostly wore bark-cloth, but in receiving the Fathers Makasa himself wore coloured cloth given him by the Swahili; and some of his assembled warriors fired guns by way of salute. All the same, the Fathers did not fail to appreciate Makasa's high standing as a chief, while he for his part showed himself well enough disposed. He gave them a small Mambwe girl who had been captured recently, and he promised to send them more such captives. He also offered to provide an escort to conduct the Fathers to Chitimukulu's, but to his regret they had not time on this occasion to take up the invitation. They returned, however, well pleased with their first journey among the Bemba;[181] it clearly seemed worthwhile to persevere with the project of a Bemba mission.

During the next fifteen months the Fathers' strength of purpose was abundantly tested, as their hopes were repeatedly raised and lowered. The prospects for a new mission were inevitably contingent upon the Bemba political situation. Makasa, like Ponde, was naturally eager to make the most of his special opportunities, as a border chief, to make contact with strangers, especially wealthy strangers with followers and guns.[182] It has been suggested that Makasa was the more likely to seek new allies in that, as a son of Chitimukulu, he had no prospects of further promotion;[183] but it seems more relevant to note that ever since his accession in 1891/2 Makasa V had regarded Sampa* as an

[178] Mambwe diary, 27 April 1893, *CT*, 60, October 1893, pp. 671–2
[179] Mambwe diary, 19 April 1894, *CT*, 66, April 1895, p. 356; Van Oost to Lavigerie, 7 April 1895, *CT*, 68, October 1895, p. 682
[180] Mambwe diary, 19 January 1894, 28–30 January 1894, *CT*, 63, July 1894, pp. 492, 494–6
[181] Mambwe diary, 30–31 January 1894, *CT*, 63, July 1894, pp. 496–7
[182] Cf. Mpashi, *Abapatili bafika ku Lubemba*, p. 10
[183] Gann, *Plural Society*, p. 25

enemy.[184] And in entering into negotiations himself with white strangers Makasa would have been encouraged both by his own considerable strength, as a conquering marcher lord, and by Sampa's* relative weakness in relation to his other nominal subordinates. At the same time, Sampa* was not so weak that Makasa could afford to ignore him, especially in view of Sampa's* own pronounced aversion to Europeans. Thus while Makasa had good reason to seek closer relations with the White Fathers, he was not in this matter a wholly independent agent, and it was some time before Makasa's dilemma was resolved.

In July and August 1894 Makasa showed his continuing good will towards the Fathers by sending them, as he had promised, some liberated slaves, a woman and three children,[185] who in the current famine may well have been a liability. He exchanged presents with the Fathers at the beginning of 1895,[186] and on 10 January he welcomed a second visit by Fr van Oost. But Makasa had discouraging news concerning Sampa*. At the end of 1894 Palmer, an agent of the African Lakes Company at Fife, had sent four men to Makasa's with a large present for Sampa*; Makasa had provided guides to escort one of them to seek a pact with Sampa* and obtain a wife for Palmer. The impudence of this last request had so infuriated Sampa* that he killed both the ALC envoy and his guides at the Chambeshi river.[187] The Fathers thus doubted whether they would be able to send greetings to Sampa*. But at the end of January Makasa went himself to Sampa*; he delivered the Fathers' greetings, and on his return he informed them that Sampa* was now prepared to exchange gifts with them. On 23 February, Frs van Oost and Guillé obtained an audience with Makasa. They were told that while Sampa* still refused to see any white men, Makasa himself would try to gain Sampa's* permission for the building of a mission in Bemba country. In March, Makasa sent another slave to the Fathers and informed them that he would look for a suitable place for them to build.[188] Early in April he invited van Oost to come and choose the site himself.[189] On 15 April van Oost and Depaillat set out to revisit Makasa; on 20 April, van Oost died, but Depaillat set out once again. Makasa made him an ingenious offer, clearly designed to offend

[184] See above, pp. 228–9.

[185] Mambwe diary, 25 July 1894, 2 August 1894, *CT*, 66, April 1895, p. 360

[186] *Ibid.*, 6 January 1895, *CT*, 68, October 1895, p. 684

[187] *Ibid.*, 10 January 1895, WFA; *BCAG*, 1 April 1895. In July 1895 Mporokoso told Poulett Weatherley that Chitimukulu 'gave muavi (poison drink) to Mr Palmer's boys': *BCAG*, 15 September 1895.

[188] Mambwe diary, 2, 15, 18, 23 February 1895; 13 March 1895, *CT*, 68, October 1895, pp. 685–7   [189] Mambwe diary, 6 April 1895, WFA

Sampa* as little as possible. The Fathers could build within the existing borders of Bemba country, but only in an area which Makasa would return to the Mambwe, while he himself made a new village further south. Depaillat inferred that the Bemba considered the border area already lost to the British.[190]

This offer was quickly accepted. At the end of May, Mambwe mission was taken over by Fr Joseph Dupont, who arrived together with Lechaptois (now Bishop of Tanganyika at Karema). Both men went straight on to Makasa's and confirmed the arrangement. Within a week of their return to the mission, Dupont heard that Sampa*, who apparently had approved Makasa's invitation to the Fathers, had changed his mind and was now preparing to make war on Makasa.[191] Dupont, however, was not to be deterred. Indeed, the very day after receiving this unwelcome news, he made clear in a peculiarly forth-right manner his determination to take up Makasa's offer. He held a meeting of over two hundred Mambwe, distributed beef and beer, and vainly urged them to reoccupy the land which Makasa had promised to vacate.[192] Already, it would seem, Dupont had decided to further the cause of his mission by acting as much like a chief as his calling allowed. Meanwhile, he sent Joseph, an African convert, to enquire at Makasa's into the relations between Makasa and Sampa*. Joseph returned on 29 June; he indicated that Sampa's* threat to attack Makasa was probably due only to excessive drinking, but although Sampa* had few warriors his subordinates had to take note even of his wilder outbursts. Nevertheless, Dupont was confirmed in his belief that Makasa wished to break free from Sampa's* 'tyranny'.[193]

Whatever Dupont's evidence may have been for this conclusion, it is clear enough that he was temperamentally disposed to put the most favourable construction on Joseph's report. He anticipated that Makasa would hold to his agreement with the Fathers even at the risk of provoking war with Sampa*, and he proceeded to act on this assumption. At the request of the British South Africa Company, Dupont had readily assumed full responsibility for all risks and dangers to his mission;[194] he now embarked on the famous strategy of bluff which secured the heart of Bembaland for the White Fathers. On returning to Makasa's, Dupont found the village heavily fortified, and when he eventually managed to see the chief he was not made welcome, since Makasa believed that Sampa* would in fact carry out his

[190] *Ibid.*, 15, 27 April 1895, WFA [191] *Ibid.*, 4, 8, 15 June 1895, WFA
[192] *Ibid.*, 16 June 1895, WFA [193] *Ibid.*, 29 June 1895, WFA
[194] Pineau, *Evêque-Roi*, p. 113

threat. Dupont, however, refused to leave. He may have gained some local support by healing an old woman's ulcerated leg, and his calm persistence made a still greater impression; at all events, Makasa allowed him to stay. News soon came that Sampa* had attacked some of Makasa's villages,[195] but the expected showdown never took place. Sampa* approached Makasa's own village, but apparently he too had been bluffing: he withdrew without launching an attack, and an attempt to have Dupont assassinated miscarried. Meanwhile, Dupont summoned Fr Guillé from Mambwe; he arrived with two hundred liberated slaves, and on 23 July 1895 Dupont founded Kayambi mission.[196]

Faced with this remarkable fait accompli, Sampa* at once asked Dupont to visit him. This invitation may have been made in all good faith. Since he had failed to exclude Europeans from Bemba country, it was reasonable for Sampa* to seek to make them his friends rather than let them ally with his disaffected subordinates. Indeed, it was probably not long before this, and for the same reasons, that Sampa* extended an invitation to the hunter Weatherley, who was in contact with Lungu chiefs and with Mporokoso.[197] Dupont replied to Sampa* by offering to mediate with the ALC concerning Sampa's* murder of their envoy and escort at the end of 1894, and his appropriation of their guns.[198] But a visit to Sampa* seemed premature; Dupont still needed Makasa's support and may have felt that all he had so far gained might be lost if he appeared to be changing horses in midstream. On 29 November the Fathers at Kayambi were visited by people from Chyanika, a brother of Ponde and Chikwanda II Mutale Lwanga, and evidently a subordinate of Mwamba; they brought friendly greetings and were given cloth.[199] On 1 December the *kabilo* Nkolemambwe

[195] One was Musanta (Kayambi diary, 14 July 1895, WFA); another was Masamba (Oger, 'Mpanda', 34). Labrecque says that Sampa killed three of Makasa's warriors: Chipilipili, Kalinda, Mwitaba ('Origines', p. 325).

[196] Kayambi diary, 12, 14, 17 July 1895, WFA; Mpashi, *Abapatili*, p. 15; Pineau, *Evêque-Roi*, pp. 115–18; Oger, 'Mpanda', 34. The first year's diary entries from Kayambi are in fact to be found at the end of the Mambwe diary, which thus continues up to August 1896 as it was only then that the White Fathers formally abandoned the Mambwe station and sold it to the BSAC, though it had been closed since September 1895 (Bell to Forbes, 3 August 1896, NAZ/NE/A1/1/1; Pineau, *Evêque-Roi*, pp. 122, 208). The present Mambwe mission station, further west, was opened in 1938.

[197] See above, p. 243

[198] Kayambi diary, 1 August 1895, WFA. This refers to the BSAC, but clearly this is a mistake.

[199] Kayambi diary, 29 November 1895, WFA (Pineau wrongly says the party

brought a second invitation from Sampa*, but the Fathers were now
concerned not to alienate the BSAC, whom they expected to attack
Sampa* in the following year.²⁰⁰ In March 1896, Sampa* sent again to
Makasa, summoning him to the capital and asking Dupont to come
along as well: he clearly hoped that Dupont would mediate between
him and the British. By now, Dupont was sure that Mwamba, not
Chitimukulu, was the most important chief to deal with; in any case,
he doubted Sampa's* intentions.²⁰¹ Yet these hardly mattered, for
Sampa* was now very ill: towards the end of 1895 he had caught a chill
after leading a raid across the Songwe river into Nyakyusa country.²⁰²
On 20 May 1896, the Fathers at Kayambi heard from Makasa that
Sampa* had died.²⁰³

Sampa's* death put a new complexion on Bemba affairs. There was
the usual commotion at the capital, and many people fled, some to
settle at Mwamba's, some to Mambwe country and some even to work
as porters for the BSAC at Ikawa, their new station near Fife.²⁰⁴
But the death of a Chitimukulu caused a more general confusion and
uncertainty. It involved an interregnum which might last a year or

came from Mwamba (*Evêque-Roi*, p. 150). For Chyanika, see above, p. 221,
n. 22. He was credited with introducing lechwe on the Luena river and stocking
it with fish, but he was also notoriously cruel. He was killed in 1899, probably
by men from Mwamba's (Mpika DNB II, p. 205; D. Campbell, *In the Heart of
Bantuland*, London 1922, p. 126; Kayambi report, October–December 1899, *CT*,
87, July 1900, pp. 427–8.

²⁰⁰ Kayambi diary, 1 December 1895, WFA
²⁰¹ *Ibid.*, 29 November 1895, 31 March 1896, 6 April 1896, WFA
²⁰² Young, in Chinsali DNB I, p. 235; Dewar to Smith, 9 January 1896, NLS
7879. At Chitipa's village, near the abandoned mission at Chirenji, Dewar heard
that the Bemba were at Zoche, ten miles away. Chitipa's people armed themselves
and kept up a great noise all night, and a service was held in which Mrs Dewar
played the violin. The Bemba sacked Chinunka's nearby, but then went home.
They indicated their hostility to the Europeans, however, by blockading the
Stevenson road and strewing it with gunpowder. Later, Dewar heard that
Chitimukulu had instructed a party 'to kill any white people they might meet on
the road' (*ibid.*).
²⁰³ Kayambi diary, 20 May 1896, WFA; cf. Bell to Forbes, 31 May 1896,
NAZ/NE/A1/1/1. Young, and following him Robertson (*Introduction*, xvii) and
Pirie wrongly imply that Sampa died in October 1895 (G. Pirie, 'North-Eastern
Rhodesia', *JAS*, 1905–6, 5, pp. 140–2).
²⁰⁴ *BCAG*, 15 August 1896; Richards, 'Bwembya', pp. 20–1; Annual Report,
Kawimbe, 1896, LMS/Reports (CA); Dewar to Laws, 29 September 1896,
NLS 7879; Bell to Administrator, North-Eastern Rhodesia, 31 August 1896,
NAZ/NE/A1/1/1. As early as 1888 Mambwe from Fwambo's were going to
Lake Malawi in search of work (Jones to Thompson, 25 September 1888,
LMS/7/3/D).

more; and even following the appointment of a successor there would be a 'reshuffle' among chiefly offices throughout the country. And on this occasion the *bakabilo* were unlikely to reach an early decision as to the next Chitimukulu. The new chief could not be installed until after his predecessor had been buried; and this could not take place until after the harvest of a crop sown after his death.[205] Thus Sampa's* successor could not be installed until the following June, so that there was plenty of time in which claims and counter-claims might be discussed and tested, if need be, in battle. And only a few months later, probably in September, Nkula Mutale Sichansa died,[206] so that in Ichinga, too, leadership was in abeyance. When Mwamba III Mubanga Chipoya died in 1898, an always lengthy process of reorganisation was still further prolonged, and the protracted internal crisis coincided with the gravest external threat that the Bemba had yet faced.

[205] Brelsford, *Aspects*, p. 28
[206] Bell to Forbes, 29 September 1896, NAZ/NE/A1/1/1; Dewar to Laws, 2 November 1896, NLS 7879 (both reporting the death of 'Chewe': the contexts indicate that Nkula is meant). See below, p. 279. Brelsford ('Shimwalule', p. 211) reports a story that Sampa and Nkula Mutale Sichansa died on the same day, but this is clearly wrong.

Chapter 8

European occupation
1896–9

By the time of Sampa's* death, there had been important changes in the British presence around the plateau, and in the position of the Arab and Swahili traders. In June 1895 the British South Africa Company took over from the Commissioner of the British Central Africa Protectorate the administrative control of the company's territory north of the Zambezi. Major P. W. Forbes relieved Johnston of this task and as the Company's Deputy Administrator made his temporary headquarters at Blantyre, near Johnston's own headquarters at Zomba.[1] In the latter part of 1895, Forbes toured the company's stations in the far north; he also opened a new station at Ikawa, near Fife, and a substation at Nyala, at the head of the Luangwa valley.[2]

Hitherto, as we have seen, no official action had been taken to antagonise the Bemba. Johnston's policy was simply to 'show the flag' while giving missionaries some sense of security and, like them, keeping a watch for opportunities to obtain Bemba good will. Nor was it Johnston's immediate aim to interfere with the trade in slaves and arms across the plateau. But in October 1894 his grant-in-aid from Britain was more than doubled, and he could now embark on plans for administrative expansion. At the north end of Lake Malawi, this meant depriving Mlozi of his hegemony around Karonga, but the Protectorate now had the troops and guns to achieve this. Early in December 1895, Mlozi's forts were taken and destroyed, and Mlozi himself was hanged.[3] Those who escaped fled to the Arab stockades

[1] Gann, *Plural Society*, pp. 58–9; Hanna, *Beginnings*, pp. 263–4

[2] P. W. Forbes, *Blantyre to Tanganyika*, Reading 1896; Gouldsbury and Sheane, *Great Plateau*, p. 41. Another substation, Mpanga, was opened in March 1896 (Gibbs in *BCAG*, 15 March 1897).

[3] Roland Oliver, *Sir Harry Johnston and the Scramble for Africa*, London 1959, pp. 247–8, 266–8

near Chibale's on the Luangwa, which now became their headquarters under 'Kapandansalu', a relative of Mlozi.[4]

This defeat was clearly of great importance to the Bemba, for much of their trade had gone to Mlozi's. Johnston informed Rhodes—whose company was now responsible for the Bemba—that 'the Awemba raids were, in my opinion, directly due to the instigation and co-operation of the Arabs under Mlozi, and will probably cease of themselves now that Mlozi is hanged'. Johnston allowed that it would be necessary in time to fight 'the obnoxious half-breed Zulus of the south, known as Angoni', but he believed that the Bemba could best be won over by a policy of conciliation, which could be pursued from a line of forts between Lakes Malawi and Tanganyika.[5] Johnston's opinion was fortified by a letter he had received from Poulett Weatherley, which he sent on to Rhodes. Weatherley, writing in October from his hunting camp at Chipamba, near Lake Mweru, had sought to show that 'the Awemba are not so black as they are painted by people who know absolutely nothing about them, save what they have gathered from the stories of boys in their bomas'. Ever since Forbes' tour of the company stations in the far north, Weatherley had 'heard of nothing but rumours of wars, tackling the Awemba etc. at the commencement of next dry season'.

> If fighting is regarded as a necessity—a lesson and a severe one might be struck at the root of all Awemba troubles i.e. Kitiamkulu [Sampa*]. He stands alone, whereas between Mwamba and Mporo- goso there is a strong bond of friendship and their co-operation in deposing Kitiamkulu would be almost a foregone conclusion.[6]

Bemba reactions to Mlozi's defeat did not, in fact, wholly bear out these prognostications. Somewhat ironically, it appears to have made Sampa* more amenable to the British, while Mwamba III became more hostile. Sampa* indeed had already begun to moderate his earlier intransigence towards Europeans, following the White Fathers' establishment of a mission at Makasa's; in the latter part of 1895 Sampa* had twice invited Dupont to visit him and had sought mediation with the African Lakes Company.[7] The defeat of Mlozi did not deter Sampa* from raiding across the Songwe river, not far to the

---

[4] Bell to Forbes, 16 January 1896, NAZ/NE/A1/1/1; Canning to FO, 21 February 1898, FO 403/264. *Kapandansalu* means 'the cloth trader': I do not know his real name.   [5] Johnston to Rhodes, 31 December 1895, RH
[6] Weatherley to Johnston, 11 October 1895, RH
[7] See above, pp. 252–3.

northwest of Karonga, at the end of 1895, but it certainly caused him to reconsider his external relations.[8] Early in 1896 the BSAC official at Ikawa was visited by Mubanga, the nearest Bemba chief, who had himself taken part in the Songwe raid.[9] Mubanga reported that since Mlozi's defeat the Bemba did not trust the Arabs and Sampa* had summoned several chiefs to discuss the 'European question'. These included Mubanga himself, Makasa, Nkula and perhaps Mwamba. It is not known which of these came, but Mwamba annoyed Sampa* by maintaining regular communications with the 'Senga Arabs' on the Luangwa.[10] The defeat of Mlozi had plainly demonstrated the warlike intentions of the British, but Mwamba was doubtless less easily intimidated than his much less powerful paramount. Mwamba was likely in any event to oppose whatever position Sampa* took, both in view of their longstanding enmity and because he stood to gain nothing by supporting Sampa*: in the context of Bemba politics, he had risen as far as he could without actually displacing Sampa*. Besides, Mwamba may well have calculated that if the Arab–British conflict persisted it might be wiser to support the Arabs of Mlozi just because they were militarily weaker: in the event of victory they would be a less overbearing ally. Yet Mwamba was not himself so strong that he could launch a campaign against a largely unknown enemy without assuring himself of support both from other Bemba chiefs and from

[8] Mlozi's defeat may have deterred Sampa from attacking the Livingstonia missionaries at Mwenzo (Jack, *Daybreak in Livingstonia*, pp. 281–2; and cf. above, p. 253, n. 202). James Henderson, writing from Mwenzo on 14 May 1896, reported that Sampa's raid across the Stevenson road at the end of 1895 was part of a joint plan with Mlozi to expel whites, but this account seems to confuse this raid with events of 1887 (M. M. S. Ballantyne and R. H. W. Shepherd, *Forerunners of Modern Malawi: The Early Missionary Adventures of Dr. James Henderson, 1895–8*, Lovedale 1968, p. 160; cf. above, p. 226).

[9] Mubanga's village at this time was near Chunga, well to the north of his present site: cf. Chinsali DNB I, p. 155; R. Young, 'Bobo Young relates his exploits', *NRJ*, 1953, 2, ii, 1953, p. 66; W. V. Brelsford, *Generation of Men*, Salisbury n.d., p. 130.

[10] Bell to Forbes, undated fragment, NAZ/NE/A1/1/1. The reference here is to a page which, as found in the file, is placed after the first page of a letter dated 25 June 1896, though there is no continuity (other than handwriting) between the two pages. Part of this undated page has been published as if it belonged to another letter in the same file, from Bell to Administrator, BSAC, on 16 January 1896, of which there is otherwise only the first page (T. W. Baxter, 'Slave-Raiders in North-Eastern Rhodesia', *NRJ*, 1950, I, i, p. 8). Internal evidence, however, makes it clear that the fragment was written after the letter of 16 January, before Sampa's death in May, and probably before Bell's raids on caravans from April onwards (see below, p. 258).

his own Swahili neighbours. In January, Weatherley heard that Mwamba proposed a 'triple alliance' to expel the Europeans from the whole region, but neither Mporokoso nor Abdullah ibn Suliman would join him.[11] Thus Mwamba's attitude to the British continued to be one of pragmatic distrust rather than open defiance.

This caution was matched by that of the BSAC. It is not clear whether Rhodes or Forbes took any note of Johnston's advice, but they certainly did not flout it. The company did not follow up the defeat of Mlozi by attacking either the Bemba or Mlozi's followers on the upper Luangwa. Instead, it strengthened its posts on the plateau, while seeking to prevent the Bemba from gaining military reinforcements. Such prudence was the more necessary in view of events south of the Zambezi. In March 1896 the Ndebele rebelled, and the Shona rose in June. For the best part of a year, while white lives were in peril in the south, there could be no question of the BSAC undertaking military campaigns eight hundred miles further north. Its agents there might be ready enough to fight, but they could expect no approval, let alone reinforcements, from Blantyre or Salisbury. Rather than intervene directly in Bemba affairs, they used their slender forces only against East African traders in slaves and firearms within easy reach of company stations. During the early months of the dry season of 1896, company officials attacked and routed three Arab or Swahili caravans near Bemba country. In April Bell, from Ikawa, caught a caravan from Unyanyembe (the chiefdom in which Tabora is situated) just as it was crossing the Choshi river into Bemba country; he captured 100 lbs. of powder and 10,000 percussion caps.[12] On 19 June, Bell intercepted a caravan as it left Bemba country at Chunga; he confiscated 1,500 lbs. of ivory and 57 slaves, some of whom had been captured by Ponde from Chitimbwa the previous December.[13] On 26 July Drysdale tracked down a Baluchi-led caravan on the Songwe river and took 1,000 lbs. of ivory and 35 slaves; this caravan was led by an Arab called Feronsa who came from Ponde's.[14]

By this time, Sampa* was dead and no longer a factor in Mwamba's calculations. This in itself may have made Mwamba readier to con-

[11] Weatherley, 4 January 1896, in *BCAG*, 1 April 1896
[12] Bell to Honey, 20 April 1896, 24 April 1896, NAZ/NE/A1/1/1
[13] Bell to Forbes, 25 June 1896, NAZ/NE/A1/1/1; see above, p. 246. One of the slaves released—a baby on his mother's back—was John Chifunda, who became a minister of the LMS at Kambole and was still alive in 1970.
[14] Bell to Forbes, 3 August 1896, NAZ/NE/A1/1/1; Drysdale, 'Report on a Slave Caravan', 21 August 1897 [sc. 96], NAZ/NE/A1/1/2

template closer contacts with Europeans, at the expense of the Arabs. In any case, the company's successes diminished the prospect of an effective anti-European alliance. In May, soon after Sampa's* death, Mwamba asked Makasa to direct the White Fathers to him, and at the end of June he sent a deputation to Kayambi with two tusks of ivory. These were to be forwarded to Ikawa, to meet Bell's demand for Bemba compensation for Sampa's* theft of guns from the ALC at the end of 1894.[15] According to Bell, Mwamba 'also stated that he wished to live on friendly terms with white men and intended to send me more ivory. . . . The Arabs . . . do not seem to stand very high in Mwamba's estimation.' Bell responded to these hopeful signs and sent Mwamba trade goods to the value of the ivory.[16] He also advised Mwamba's men that if Mwamba and Makasa wished to avoid war, they had only to take the advice of the White Fathers. As Dupont wryly noted, this sudden show of good will towards French missionaries on the part of the BSAC had to be understood in the light of its evident inability, as yet, to make war.[17]

MWAMBA AND THE WHITE FATHERS, 1896-7

Dupont, for his part, was now ready to make contact with Mwamba. The news of Sampa's* death in May had not prompted Dupont to take any new initiative. Curiously enough—in view of events at Mwamba's two years later[18]—Sampa* was said by Makasa to have wished to make over his kingdom to the White Fathers, which if true was no doubt meant as a deliberate insult to his hostile relatives. Dupont, however, was still convinced that the British were about to wage war on the Bemba. He decided to bide his time and advised Makasa also to stay at home, for the succession would be arranged by 'messieurs les Anglais'.[19] But by early July, Dupont, as we have seen, had decided that the British were as yet incapable of mounting an invasion. Furthermore, Dupont now had the impression that Mwamba had succeeded Sampa*.[20] In the course of July, Makasa went off to Mwamba's where

[15] Kayambi diary, 31 May 1896, 1 July 1896, 2 July 1896, WFA; see above, p. 250.
[16] Bell to Forbes, 3 August 1896, 12 August 1896, NAZ/NE/A1/1/1
[17] Kayambi diary, 11 July 1896, WFA   [18] See below, pp. 276-83.
[19] Kayambi diary, 20 May 1896, WFA. In fact, as Dupont very likely knew, Makasa plays a part in the accession of a new Chitimukulu: he supplies cattle for the royal burial and has to declare his approval of the royal councillors' choice of a successor (cf. Brelsford, *Succession*, p. 34).
[20] Kayambi diary, 1 July 1896, WFA

several chiefs were gathered in mourning for the death of Makasa's 'official' mother—a sixteen-year-old girl. The Fathers at Kayambi learned, perhaps from Makasa himself, that Ponde had criticised Makasa's hospitality to them. Certainly, Ponde's trade seems to have suffered most from the recent company attacks on caravans and for this reason he may have been specially hostile to Europeans. But Mwamba and Chikwanda came to Makasa's defence and said that they too wished to see Dupont.[21] Encouraged by this news, Dupont sent off a present to Mwamba.[22]

Mwamba appears not to have responded to this overture. In September he was 'said by many Bemba to be anxious for white favour and instruction',[23] but during the latter part of 1896 he was preoccupied with a struggle over the royal succession. Although Dupont was mistaken in supposing that Mwamba had been chosen to be the next Chitimukulu, there is little doubt that Mwamba coveted the position, and as a sister's son of Sampa* he had an excellent claim, for Sampa* had no surviving brothers. Mwamba's chief contender was Chimfwembe Makumba (also known as Mulenga). Makumba was a parallel cousin of Sampa*: their mothers had both been sisters of Bwembya. Makumba was old and infirm, and he appears to have called on Chikwanda II Mutale Lwanga to support his cause. Chikwanda II had his own reasons for opposing the ambitions of Mwamba III, for the latter had already begun to make considerable inroads upon Chikwanda's area of influence in southern Bemba country.[24] Chikwanda thus responded to Makumba's appeal. Some time around the end of 1896, or early in 1897,[25] the two men occupied Chitimukulu's village and seized Sampa's* wives; they thereby ensured that Makumba could perform the ritual intercourse with the dead chief's head wife which is an essential element in Bemba inheritance.[26] By means of this fait accompli, Makumba virtually established himself as Sampa's* successor. At once, however, Mwamba's men fell upon Makumba and Chikwanda. The latter escaped to Chinama, but Makumba was taken

[21] Pineau, *Evêque-Roi*, pp. 153–4; Kayambi diary, 28 July 1896, WFA. Dupont passed the news on to Bell: Bell to Forbes, 31 August 1896, NAZ/NE/A1/1/1.

[22] Pineau, *Evêque-Roi*, p. 154

[23] Dewar to Laws, 29 September 1896, NLS 7879

[24] See above, p. 222.

[25] For dating, see below, pp. 264–5.

[26] Brelsford, *Succession*, pp. 7–8; cf. Richards, 'The Bemba', in Colson and Gluckman, *Seven Tribes*, pp. 181–2; and Bush in Brelsford, *Aspects*, p. 41. For a similar incident in recent Mambwe history see Watson, *Tribal Cohesion*, p. 168.

prisoner by Mwamba, tied up with rope, and beaten.[27] After a while, Mwamba relented, in face of a series of ill omens—attacks on his people by a lion, a crocodile and a snake.[28] These creatures, he believed, embodied the spirit of Bwembya*, whose wrath must have been first provoked when he was deposed to make way for his sister's son Chitapankwa*.[29] Thus it would seem that Bwembya* had special reason to be angry at Mwamba's treatment of Makumba, a son of Bwembya's other sister and thus a member of a line innocent of Chitapankwa's* usurpation. In any case, it was believed that Bwembya* could be appeased if the succession now reverted to Makumba.[30] So Mwamba released Makumba, with the reflection that 'Makumba was very old and would die soon'.[31] Besides, Mwamba appears to have continued, at Makumba's expense, the eastward encroachment upon Lubemba which he had begun in Sampa's* reign: in January 1897 his influence extended far down the Kalungu river.[32]

At the beginning of November 1896, while the dispute between Mwamba and Makumba was still unresolved, Dupont joined Forbes and Bell of the BSAC on an expedition to assess the prospects for penetrating eastern Bembaland.[33] Dupont visited Makumba at his village near the Chambeshi a short distance above its junction with the

[27] Brelsford, *Succession*, p. 8. In March 1897 the White Fathers recorded that Makumba 's'est laissé battré par Mwamba' (Kayambi report, January–April 1897, *CT*, 78, April 1898, p. 240.

[28] Shimulamba, T1, n. 57

[29] See above, pp. 127–9.

[30] Shimulamba, T1, n. 57. Labrecque ('Origines', p. 303) and Mushindo (*History*, s. 64) tell different stories about the harm done by the angry spirit of Bwembya during Chitapankwa's reign. Brelsford was simply told by the *bakabilo* that their predecessors were afraid because it is dangerous to kill a paramount (*Succession*, p. 8). Bwembya's sister's daughter's son, headman Bwembya, who had formally inherited Bwembya's name and spirit, said only that Mwamba was afraid because he had killed a son of Makumba in a raid (Richards, 'Bwembya', pp. 19–20, 26).

[31] Richards, 'Bwembya', p. 26. The Ituna version has it that Mwamba let Makumba become Chitimukulu because Ituna was much more important than Lubemba (Milambo, 26 July 1957: A. I. Richards, fieldnotes; Tanguy, *Imilandu*, p. 74). Elsewhere it is said that Chitapankwa had once burnt Makumba's village, and this was another reason why Mwamba had reason to fear spiritual retaliation (White Fathers, *Ifyabukaya*, p. 109).

[32] See pp. 219, 264. It was later recalled that 'Mwamba annexed most of Kitimkulu's country and was helped by Ponde, who stole Makumba's cattle' (Young, 'Exploits', p. 68). Coxhead asserts that Makumba 'gave a large portion of his territory to Mwamba' ('Native Tribes', p. 6).

[33] Kayambi diary, 2 November 1896, WFA

Kalungu.[34] Dupont was warmly received by Makumba, who seemed to think he was Luchele ŋanga, the white culture hero of Bemba legend.[35] Makumba invited Dupont to stay, but Dupont thought that eastern Lubemba seemed an unpromising area for mission work. He noted that Makumba was at odds with Mwamba—'his suzerain', as Dupont still believed. Many people had left the area to seek shelter with Mwamba; evidently Makumba inspired no great local confidence. Dupont returned to Kayambi convinced that Mwamba was the man to deal with.[36]

Meanwhile, Mwamba had renewed his attempts to make contact with Europeans and learn more about them. While Dupont returned to Kayambi, Bell went on to Mwalule, where he met a messenger from Mwamba. As yet, Mwamba still hoped to succeed Sampa*: Bell gathered that after Sampa's* burial Mwamba would 'assume control of affairs and reside at Ngwena, the residence of the big chief'. Mwamba extended 'friendly assurances' to Bell,[37] although a few weeks earlier he had refused to allow Bell to visit him: Bell was 'associated with all the fighting that has been going on, so Mwamba not unnaturally thinks Bell has come to make war and seize him hence his refusal'.[38] Mwamba's suspicions were further aroused by news of Dupont's visit to his rival Makumba, and he sent some men to Kayambi to learn the reason for it.[39] But in December he sent out another party to visit both Kayambi and the stations of the ALC and BSAC. These envoys asked for a white doctor to come and heal Mwamba's sick people.[40] They also

[34] Chileshye Mukulu, 28 November 1964; cf. Velten, *Safari*, p. 42

[35] Kayambi diary, 5 March 1897, WFA; cf. Labrecque, 'Origines', p. 261, and pp. 40–2 above. In Ankole, west of Lake Victoria, Stanley's expedition in relief of Emin Pasha, in 1889, was at first mistaken for the Bachwezi, legendary early rulers, returned miraculously to earth (H. M. Stanley, *In Darkest Africa*, London 1890, II, pp. 335–6).

[36] Kayambi diary, 11 November 1896, WFA; Pineau, *Evêque-Roi*, p. 154. Other White Fathers sources say that Dupont was rebuffed by Makumba, but they are clearly confusing this with a later occasion (*Ifyabukaya*, p. 109; Tanguy, *Imilandu*, p. 75; see below, p. 276).

[37] Bell to Forbes, 24 November 1896, NAZ/NE/A1/1/1. Bell evidently warned the people at Mwalule against providing Chitimukulu with the customary companions in the grave. Labrecque says that in fact only eight people were killed to accompany Sampa, and he gives the credit for this to McKinnon, Bell's successor at Ikawa ('Origines', p. 325).

[38] Dewar to Laws, 2 November 1896, NLS 7879

[39] Kayambi diary, 18 November 1896, WFA

[40] Dewar to Smith, 8 January 1897, NLS 7880; cf. Dewar, letter of 31 December 1896, in *Aurora*, 1 April 1897

brought gifts of ivory. They produced one tusk for Dupont, in gratitude for his part in establishing good relations between Mwamba and the BSAC the previous July.[41] A second tusk was for McCulloch, the ALC agent at Fife, while the third was for Bell, the BSAC official at Ikawa. Dupont shrewdly noted that these presents might mean more than a general wish on Mwamba's part to be friendly with Europeans; they might be intended to find out who would respond most generously. Unless the British made quite exorbitant presents in return, Dupont was determined to excel them. Just after Christmas, Mwamba's men returned from Fife and Ikawa, laden with cloth, and Dupont gave them another large present. It appeared that Mwamba was indeed holding a competition, and Dupont, like Bell and McCulloch, despatched a few men, including the catechist Joseph, to report on Mwamba's decision.[42]

On 2 January 1897, Joseph came back to Kayambi with news of a most encouraging interview. The British envoys, he said, had not been well received: like Sampa* two years before, Mwamba was angered to be asked to provide their masters with women. Dupont, on the other hand, was welcome to visit Mwamba, and to this end Mwamba had despatched an escort to conduct Dupont to Ituna. Dupont still regarded Mwamba as Sampa's* successor, and Mwamba's predominance was attested by the fact that the escort was led by Chikutwe, a *kabilo* of Chitimukulu.[43] This seemed to be the opportunity Dupont had been waiting for. Nonetheless, he decided to wait and see how things looked after Sampa's* burial, which he guessed would be followed by further complications[44] and which anyway would not take place for a few more months.

Other Europeans were less cautious. Around the end of 1896 an artisan at Ikawa called Spencer made a vain attempt to reach Lubemba and Ituna by way of Mwalule.[45] On 24 January 1897, Robert Young, a trooper in the BSAC police, set out from Ikawa for Mwamba's. Young took a different route from Spencer; he approached by way of Kayambi and then struck directly southeast through Mpanda and Lubemba. At Chikutwe's village, Young heard that Makumba had taken Sampa's* place, though he would still have been living on the eastern borders of

[41] See above, p. 259.
[42] Kayambi diary, 16, 26, 27 December 1896, WFA
[43] Kayambi diary, 2 January 1897, WFA
[44] Kayambi diary, 19 January 1897, WFA
[45] Kayambi diary, 26 December 1896, WFA. Spencer was employed at Ikawa to superintend house-building (Bell to Forbes, 31 August 1896, NAZ/NE/A1/1/1).

Lubemba.[46] Young continued by way of 'Mkarui's' (i.e. Akalweo, a site once occupied by Sampa*), where skulls still hung on poles. A little further on, Young came to the village of the *kabilo* Kashinge, which was said to belong to Mwamba, who thus seemed to have taken over much of western Lubemba.[47] Young heard from the local people that Mwamba wanted to become Chitimukulu, 'but the other chiefs won't have it'. Mwamba intended after the harvest (i.e. May–June) to subdue Makumba, Ponde and other chiefs; and two headmen in Lubemba said that they would seek help against Mwamba from the BSAC at Ikawa.[48]

Despite a previous warning from Spencer that Mwamba would offer armed resistance, Young was allowed to reach Mwamba's village. (This was on the Mabula stream, and thus near the eastern borders of Ituna.)[49] But when Young was admitted to Mwamba's presence, he refused to sit on the ground, and Mwamba would not listen to him. One of Mwamba's followers later recalled that Young

> stood up in front of Mwamba and spoke his business. We were all staring at his face. He was not still, after the manner of a chief, but he stood there twirling his moustaches and looking quickly about him from left to right. But Mwamba was silent, and he looked straight in front with his eyes.[50]

Young found the people 'civil enough' and he was allowed to stay the night, but when it became clear that he had come empty-handed he was asked to leave. Young gathered that there had been a large number of Arabs at Mwamba's,

> but he has cleared them out of his village because he has found out a lot of the lies they had told about the White Men. He told them they were liars and that they had told many lies to keep the White Men out of his country but now White Men could come to the country if they brought Chuma [wealth].[51]

[46] There could be no question of the paramount-elect building a new capital before his predecessor had been buried; and it is not at all clear that Makumba had as yet been formally chosen as the next Chitimukulu.

[47] Cf. above, p. 219

[48] R. Young, 'Report on a Patrol to Mwamba's', enclosure in McKinnon to Forbes, 1 March 1897, NAZ/NE/A1/1/2

[49] The village was called *Nyama lya mwana umo* (Milambo, 13 April 1965).

[50] Richards, 'Bwembya', pp. 35–6

[51] Young, 'Report on a Patrol to Mwamba's', enclosure in McKinnon to Forbes 1 March 1897, NAZ/NE/A1/1/2

Young's visit brought no immediate advantage to the BSAC. It had indeed served to confirm that Mwamba was by no means committed to war with Europeans; it had also revealed that Mwamba's ambitions confronted much Bemba opposition. Charles McKinnon, who took over from Bell at Ikawa at the beginning of 1897, considered that the company should exploit this division. He apparently expected that a military force would soon be sent into Bembaland, and in forwarding Young's report to Forbes, the Deputy Administrator at Blantyre, McKinnon stressed that 'Mwamba wants to make himself Chief but the other factions don't want him . . . when you go there I don't think you will have much trouble as one or other factions will be sure to join us'.[52] Forbes, however, had never authorised Young's visit to Mwamba, and in any case he was still thinking in terms of supporting Mwamba's bid for supremacy.[53] Meanwhile, Forbes was quite ready to see the White Fathers establish stations at both Chitimukulu's and Mwamba's. Already, in January, he had sent Dupont a letter to this effect, coupled with a reminder that the company was not yet strong enough to do battle with all the Bemba if Dupont got into difficulties.[54] Dupont made no move during March—the worst of the rainy season—but meanwhile he heard from the *mwina yandu* headman Mutale Mukulu that although Mwamba had beaten Makumba, he would no longer oppose his accession as Chitimukulu.[55] Thus the prospects for beginning mission work in the heart of Bemba country seemed much improved.

The White Fathers had the more reason to be hopeful in that they already enjoyed a certain prestige among the Bemba in and around Mpanda. They had brought some of their followers and pupils with them from Mambwe, and the new school at Kayambi soon attracted children from the neighbourhood.[56] Makasa, who was still living near Kayambi,[57] continued to hold the Fathers in much respect. To be sure,

---

[52] McKinnon to Forbes, 1 March 1897, NAZ/NE/A1/1/2

[53] Kayambi diary, 13 February 1897, *CT*, 78, April 1898, p. 239; see below, p. 270

[54] Forbes to Dupont, 17 January 1897, LM/G57; Kayambi diary, 13 February 1897 *CT*, 78, April 1898, p. 239

[55] Kayambi diary, 5 March 1897, WFA; cf. above, p. 261

[56] The school at Kayambi began with 57 pupils; at the end of 1897 there were over 200 (Mpashi, *Abapatili*, p. 19; Kayambi report, 1897, *CT*, 78, April 1898, p. 244). Mpashi's father was one of the first pupils at Kayambi (*Abapatili*, p. 19).

[57] Makasa moved his village about fifteen miles south of Kayambi in February 1898 (Kayambi report, January–June 1898, *CT*, 80, October 1898, p. 492; Molinier to Mgr. (? Dupont), 26 May 1899, *CT*, 84, October 1899, p. 489

he showed little desire for Christian instruction,[58] nor indeed did he or other Bemba chiefs seem to value pioneer missionaries as educators and technical innovators. Their limited experience of contact with a literate culture and more advanced technology may largely account for the difference in this respect between Bemba chiefs and certain leaders among the Lozi, Tswana or Ganda.[59] Nonetheless, Makasa displayed a taste for intellectual discussion with Dupont,[60] and he kept himself informed about the Fathers' work, for their catechumens included at least one of his sons, Kapoko, and also a niece.[61] And in December 1896 Makasa brought a number of people to Kayambi with seeds to be blessed by the Fathers, as he was much impressed by their good harvests.[62] One woman came to Kayambi for medical treatment from Chimba's village, over forty miles away; Dupont later heard that since her return she had continued to say her prayers.[63] Dupont himself had the somewhat double-edged reputation of being *'un sorcier sans pareil'*, and his local name was *'Moto moto'*, the man of fire.[64] One day, women came from Makasa's to Kayambi and sang Dupont's praises:

> This man is our chief.
> What parent loved his children as he does,
> *Moto moto*, who helps poor people?
> If you have seen another like him, tell us!
>
> He treats our children,
> He gives them life.
> If you have seen another like him, tell us!
>
> He kills lions,
> He cures the sick.
> If you have seen another like him, tell us![65]

[58] 'Makasa est un homme superstitieux qui se laisse conduire par ce qu'il appelle ses dieux' (Kayambi report, January–June 1898, *CT*, 80, October 1898, p. 492. [59] See above, pp. 203, 209.

[60] 'Makasa nous fait une longue et amicale visite. Nous parlons un peu de tout—religion, géographie, astronomie. Ces Wabembas ont vraiment une intelligence extraordinaire: ils abordent avec aisance les problèmes les plus relevés' (Kayambi diary, 28 July 1895, WFA).

[61] L. Molinier, diary, 24 September 1899, *CT*, 87, July 1900, p. 436. I do not know if Kapoko was the same as Kafunga, a son of Makasa who was a pupil of the White Fathers up to 1896 (Kayambi diary, 12 February 1897, WFA).

[62] Kayambi diary, 26 December 1896, WFA

[63] J. Dupont, 'Voyage de cinq semaines dans l'Ubemba', *CT*, 78, April 1898, p. 258 [64] Pineau, *Evêque-Roi*, pp. 60, 124

[65] Mpashi, *Abapatili*, pp. 17–18; Pineau, *Evêque-Roi*, pp. 133–4

Dupont had impressed Makasa by his obstinacy and Mwamba by his diplomacy. The men sent out by Sampa* to kill Dupont in July 1895 had retreated in awe of his marksmanship; they had seen him kill a guinea-fowl for supper with his first shot.[66] And in March 1897 Dupont scored a triumph over the locusts which once again ravaged the country.

Le Père Supérieur fait alors des exorcismes, et en quelques instants les sauterelles disparaissent. Nos indigènes et enfants en sont tout étonnés et glorifient la puissance de notre Dieu. La protection du ciel s'est aussi montrée très visiblement à l'égard du bon nombre d'indigènes non chrétiens qui étaient venus faire bénir leurs semences. Jusqu'à ce moment les sauterelles ont épargné ces récoltes et les nègres crient bien haut qu'il n'y a rien de puissant comme les remèdes du bon Dieu.[67]

By early April of 1897, it was clear to Dupont that he must visit Mwamba very soon if he was to have any chance of success. The reputation of Europeans had not been enhanced by the intrepid Spencer, who had eventually reached Mwamba's and tried to pass himself off as a son of Queen Victoria: he was bundled up in a cowskin and thrown out of the village.[68] Dupont was also anxious to forestall any advance by the Scottish Protestants who had recently settled at Mwenzo and were said by Young and Makasa to be planning missions in Lubemba and Chilinda.[69] This seems unlikely, as in fact the Livingstonia mission had no immediate designs on the Bemba,[70] and it is possible that the Protestant threat was largely of Makasa's own making.

[66] Pineau, *Evêque-Roi*, pp. 118–19

[67] Kayambi report, 1897, *CT*, 78, April 1898, p. 240: 'The Father Superior then pronounced exorcisms, and in a few minutes the locusts vanished. This astonished our natives and children, who glorified the power of our God. Heavenly protection has also been very clearly displayed in regard to the large number of non-Christian natives who had come to have their seeds blessed. Up till now, the locusts have spared these crops, and the negroes cry loudly that nothing is so powerful as God's medicine.'

[68] Kayambi diary, 2 April 1897, *CT*, 78, April 1898, p. 240; Milambo, 13 April 1965. Spencer was known as 'Chinondo' ('the hammer').

[69] Kayambi report, 1897, *CT*, 78, April 1898, pp. 239–40

[70] After Sampa's death, Dewar, at Mwenzo, was keen to visit the Bemba, but Laws at Livingstonia discouraged expansion in this direction. In any case, in November 1896 Dewar's carriers refused to enter Bemba country, and there is no evidence in the Livingstonia records that Dewar made contact with Makasa (Dewar to Laws, 29 September 1896; Laws to Smith, November 1896, NLS 7879; Dewar, letter of 31 December 1896 in *Aurora*, 1 April 1897; Dewar to Smith, 8 January 1897, NLS 7880; Laws to Smith, 10 March 1898, NLS 7881).

To be sure, Makasa consulted Dupont and undertook to tell the Protestants to stay away.[71] But there is not a wholly implausible story that Makasa feared Dupont as a rival and invited the Protestants to come and do battle with him.[72] After all, people had apparently been calling Dupont a chief, if only by artistic licence: perhaps Dupont had been rather too successful. Be this as it may, Dupont set off from Kayambi on 12 April armed with large presents but no weapons. He had had some difficulty in recruiting porters, since Makasa was certainly reluctant to let Dupont take his cloth to other chiefs, but after various delays he reached Mwamba's a week later. Since Young's visit, the chief had moved westwards to the Lukupa river, where he was building a new village.[73]

Dupont was soon given an audience. He found Mwamba sitting on skins of lion and leopard on top of an ant-hill; he wore a headdress of parrot feathers and smoked hemp through a hubble-bubble. (Coastal influence was further attested by a headdress of cowries which he wore a few days later.) Around him were gathered a vast crowd of people: 'three or four thousand' armed warriors, drummers, minstrels and medicine-men. Dupont himself was by no means an unworthy member of this imposing assembly. Clothed in a white burnous and preceded by four pages bearing a carpet, he cut a much grander figure than Young had done in January. Dupont was not, however, much more successful. Mwamba's councillors had been divided over the reception of Dupont; the war-leader Kalimanshila wished to send him away. Mwamba played cat-and-mouse with Dupont for nearly two weeks. At first he affected to believe, like Makumba, that Dupont was Luchele ŋanga. He welcomed 'Moto Moto', 'a true Mubemba who has done much good at our friend Makasa's', though he declared that, after Spencer's visit, he had no wish to see the British again. But Dupont's bona fides was not yet beyond question, despite his presents. And on 3 May an Arab caravan arrived with news of a raid by the British, Dupont's 'brothers', who had stolen their guns, powder and cloth. Surely, the Arab leader said, this proved that the Europeans' avowals of friendship simply masked a determination to 'eat up the country'. Mwamba was swayed by this and at once told Dupont to leave.[74]

[71] Kayambi report, 1897, *CT*, 78, April 1898, p. 240

[72] Mpashi, *Abapatili*, p. 16; there is, however, no hint of this in the Livingstonia records.

[73] The village was close to the Milungu stream (see below, p. 277); it was named *Amafula* (Milambo, 30 April 1964).

[74] Dupont, 'Voyage de cinq semaines', pp. 246–258; cf. Pineau, *Evêque-Roi*, pp. 157–74, 195

The mission seemed to have failed. Yet the very fact that Dupont had been kept so long under observation might eventually tell in his favour. And from Mwamba's point of view time was needed to ponder and discuss Dupont and the European question in general. Besides, as we have seen, he had plans for a campaign against Makumba, Ponde and others.[75] It may well be that he wanted to assure his supremacy before coming to any irrevocable decision about the Europeans. For the next year or so, Mwamba seems to have suspended contacts with the Europeans, but he gave them no cause for intervention.

MWAMBA, THE BSAC AND THE EASTERN FRONTIER, 1897

Meanwhile, the BSAC continued to eschew any direct intervention in Bemba affairs. Early in 1897 Forbes reported on the company's position in north-eastern Rhodesia. The stations around the northern borders of Bemba country were evidently armed primarily for defence. At Ikawa, in the newly-declared 'Chambezi district', the Collector, McKinnon, had a white policeman (Young) in charge of forty African police. To the east, at Nyala, there were two Assistant Collectors with twenty police; there was another post with a Makua sergeant and eight police. Between them all, they could muster one seven-pounder gun, a one-pounder Hotchkiss, 10 Martini–Henry rifles, 25 Sniders and about 70 muzzle-loaders. The Tanganyika district, which comprised Abercorn, Sumbu and Mpanga stations, had no big guns but was better equipped with rifles and it had about a hundred policemen.[76] These forces hardly made the company's stockades impregnable, but Bell and his successor at Ikawa, McKinnon, had both asked—though in vain—for a Maxim.[77] The main purpose of these stations was simply to keep the 'open part' of the country between Lakes Mweru and Malawi in a quiet state, for which purpose Forbes, at Blantyre, thought their armaments quite adequate.[78]

There were still no definite plans for the occupation of Bemba country: well into 1897 the company's resources were stretched to the limit by the African revolt in Southern Rhodesia. At the same time, there seemed every likelihood of a civil war in Bembaland, from

[75] Cf. pp. 264 and 271–2. Ponde was angry with Mwamba for not becoming Chitimukulu, since he himself wanted to become Mwamba (Kapanda, in Willis Enquiry, 1924).   [76] BSAC, *Reports, 1896–7*, p. 43

[77] Bell to Forbes, 24 April 1896, NAZ/NE/A1/1/1; McKinnon to Forbes, 8 February 1897, NAZ/NE/A1/1/2

[78] Forbes, in BSAC, *Reports, 1896–7*, p. 44

which the company could scarcely stand aside. McKinnon, at Ikawa, evidently favoured a policy of supporting Makumba and other opponents of Mwamba III.[79] In this, at least in the first part of 1897, he was opposed by Forbes, who was probably influenced by Weatherley's earlier reports and advocated using the company's forces 'to place the Nowamba [Mwamba] at the head of the tribe as a friendly chief'.[80] But Bemba rivalries, and the company's relations with Bemba chiefs, were complicated by a factor of which Forbes took too little account— the continued presence of Arabs on the Luangwa. In January 1896 Bell had predicted that 'these Luangwa Arabs will require attention before the Bemba'.[81] Forbes expected no trouble from the Arabs, as he believed that most of them had left the country.[82] In the event, however, Bell was proved right. In September 1897 the Luangwa Arabs provoked Forbes' subordinates at Ikawa into taking action against them, and this in turn made it much harder to reach an understanding with Mwamba than Forbes had anticipated.

Early in 1896, perhaps in February, Bell had despatched Young from Ikawa to visit Kapandansalu's on the upper Luangwa. The place seemed peaceful enough, which was hardly surprising so soon after Mlozi's crushing defeat. But the Arabs were only biding their time. And the Bemba in the neighbourhood were decidedly hostile: a party from Nkula's had even attacked the Arabs (without success) because they had 'let the white men into the country'.[83] In September 1896 Nkula I Mutale Sichansa died.[84] No successor could be installed until May or June 1897, at the earliest, and probably not until the larger question of the Chitimukulu succession had been resolved; besides, there was the likelihood of claims being made by the former ruling house in Ichinga, most of whom were now in exile.[85] But a year or two before his death, Nkula had 'divided the country' between Mukwikile I and Ndakala II Kasonde.[86] The latter, a son of Nkula Mutale Sichansa and a younger

79 See pp. 265 and 274

80 Forbes, in BSAC, *Reports, 1896–7*, p. 44

81 Bell to Forbes, 16 January 1896, NAZ/NE/A1/1/1.

82 Forbes, in BSAC, *Reports, 1896–7*, p. 44

83 Bell to Forbes, undated fragment, NAZ/NE/A1/1/1 (see above, p. 257, n. 3). Young later wrote that he visited the Senga Arabs 'in the beginning of 1896' (Chinsali DNB I, p. 236).

84 See above, p. 254.   85 See above, p. 135.

86 Mukwikile I (1913) (Chinsali DNB I, p. 261); Mukwikile thus extended his authority as far south as the river Manshya (*ibid.*). In 1946 his area reverted to Nkula, and Mukwikile took over Mukumbi, his present area south of the Manshya.

brother of the Ndakala killed by the Ngoni in1887, [87] quickly emerged as the dominant power in Ichinga.[88] He seems to have shown no wish to make contact with Europeans, and Bemba and Arab raids persisted in the Luangwa valley. It is likely that firearms continued to filter through into Bembaland both from the northeast and from the half-caste Chikunda slave-raiders lower down the Luangwa.[89] In September 1897 there was an Arab caravan from German territory near Kapandan-salu's, and early that month a large supply of ivory came in there from the Bemba.[90]

It is clear that Ndakala Kasonde was by no means an independent agent: he was an ally and subordinate of Mwamba.[91] The deaths of Sampa* and Nkula Mutale Sichansa had opened the way for Mwamba to extend his influence into eastern Bembaland. As we have noted, Mwamba seems by March 1897 to have renounced his claim to succeed Sampa*, but he had demonstrated his superiority over Makumba by capturing and humiliating him, and by taking from him, at least temporarily, much of Lubemba.[92] If Mwamba could not become Chitimukulu, he could still hope to dominate the Bemba scene if the paramount was to be the feeble Makumba. And whether or not Mwamba chose to resist European intrusion by force, a well-stocked armoury was essential both for negotiating with the Europeans and for furthering his political ambitions within Bembaland. We have already seen that Mwamba had angered Sampa* in 1895/6 by maintaining contact with the Arabs on the upper Luangwa.[93] We may suppose that after Sampa's* death this traffic increased. Once the BSAC began to obstruct the import of firearms from the northeast, Mwamba must have been still more anxious to do business with the traders on the Luangwa.

[87] See above, p. 226; Oger, 'Mpanda', 36; Chinsali DNB I, p. 135; informants at Makasa's, 9 June 1965. Kasonde took the name Ndakala on the death of his brother. He had a second personal name, Chansa: hence his father's teknonym, Sichansa (Mubanga, 20 May 1965). Young's account is confused by his occasional references to Ndakala as 'Nkula' and as a son of Mwamba (R. Young, 'Bobo Young relates his exploits', *NRJ*, 1953, 2, ii, p. 67; Chinsali DNB I, pp. 241–2). Mwamba III Mubanga Chipoya called Ndakala 'son' because Ndakala's father, Nkula Mutale Sichansa, was a brother of Mwamba III.

[88] He built a village beside the Luvu river, near the site of Chinsali (cf. Young to Magistrate, Kasama, 12 January 1914, Chinsali DNB III/KL).

[89] Cf. above, pp. 225–7

[90] Young to McKinnon, n.d. (20 September 1897), NAZ/NE/A1/1/2; cf. Young, Chinsali DNB I, p. 237

[91] The White Fathers later called him a 'créature de Mwamba' (Kayambi report, 1897, *CT*, 78, April 1898, p. 244.

[92] See above, p. 261.   [93] See above, p. 257.

It was doubtless partly this consideration which prompted Mwamba to interfere in the affairs of Mwalule, the royal burial grove east of the Chambeshi. On 15 June the White Fathers heard that Sampa* had at long last been buried.[94] Shortly before, a group of Mwamba's men invaded Mwalule and expelled the then Shimwalule, Chimbwi; Chimbwi was replaced by his nephew Nsofu *ya mutembo*, and it was Nsofu who buried Sampa*.[95] According to McKinnon, Shimwalule Chimbwi had opposed Mwamba's earlier ambition to succeed Sampa*.[96] We may certainly suppose that Mwamba was anxious to see a man of his own choice occupy this post, which was not only of supreme religious importance but commanded a measure of secular authority[97] near the eastern borders of Bembaland, now of very great strategic significance.[98]

Meanwhile, however, local agents of the BSAC were also extending the range of their operations. They had had no orders to do so, but McKinnon and Young, at Ikawa, were clearly impatient with the circumspection of their superiors. In January 1897, as we have seen, Young visited Mwamba without any authorisation from Forbes, and in April McKinnon went so far as to hold what was probably the company's first trial of a Bemba: 'Papeua', a 'son' of Chitimukulu, was sentenced to five years' hard labour for grossly mutilating people.[99]

---

[94] Kayambi diary, 15 June 1897, WFA

[95] Brelsford, 'Shimwalule', p. 211; cf. Shimwalule, 18 May 1965; Chifumo, T1; Chibingo, T3 (these informants, however, were not clear as to whom Chimbwi buried, or who buried Sampa).

[96] C. McKinnon, 'Journey from Domira Bay, Lake Nyasa, to Fife, on the Tanganyika Plateau', *GJ*, 1902, 19, p. 604

[97] 'In the past the Shimwalule used to receive ivory, cattle and salt, not only from Chitimukulu but also from Nkula, Mwamba and Nkweto' (Brelsford, 'Shimwalule', p. 209).

[98] It was probably the custom of succession at Mwalule which gave Mwamba an opportunity to intervene. No Shimwalule could bury more than one Chitimukulu: if a Shimwalule who had buried one Chitimukulu lived on until the death of another, he had to be replaced. Thus it could often happen that a new Shimwalule had to succeed before Chitimukulu could be buried. A White Fathers source says that 'Shinta' (evidently to be identified with Chimbwi) had buried both Chitapankwa and Mwamba II (*Ifyabukaya*, p. 110), though Brelsford says that it was Chimbwi's predecessor Chishiki who buried Chitapankwa ('Shimwalule', p. 211). My informants at Mwalule were not clear about this.

[99] McKinnon to Forbes, 5 April 1897, NAZ/NE/A1/1/2: Forbes' reaction is not known. I am not sure of the identity of 'Papeua': he may in fact have been the *mwina ŋandu* Chyanika, whose atrocities were reported by Dupont to the BSAC, though he escaped to Makasa's (Kayambi report, October–December 1899, *CT*, 87, July 1900, pp. 427–8; and see above, p. 252, n. 199).

And in August McKinnon sent Young to open a new station in the Luangwa valley, from which he could deal with the slavers there. Young built his station at Mirongo, a few miles north of Kapandansalu's.[100] Chibale, the nearby Senga chief, naturally welcomed the prospect of deliverance from the Arab yoke: his people had had to grow grain and hunt elephant for the Arabs.[101] Ndakala was less encouraging. Chibale told Young that men had come to him from Mwamba and Ndakala threatening to cut off his head unless he went to Mwamba to explain why he had let the Europeans into his country. Young thereupon sent Chibale some ammunition from Mirongo.[102] On 15 September Chibale's village was attacked by Kapandansalu and other Arabs, together with a number of Bemba. Hearing of this, Young at once made his way there with fifteen policemen; as they entered the village, the Arabs and the Bemba left it, but they then laid it under siege. After five days, on 21 September, Young was relieved by McKinnon and Drysdale, and the company forces inflicted a crushing defeat. The Arab stockades were burned, Kapandansalu and other Arabs were taken prisoner, and several hundred slaves were released. Ndakala escaped and made a stand in Ichinga, but 'the ever victorious Army with its Nordenfeldt chased him across the Chambeze via Maruli and he took refuge with Makasa'. McKinnon now 'burnt all villages belonging to Dakara and Nkulu'.[103]

It may be presumed that Mwamba was greatly perturbed at this striking victory by the BSAC. The European ring round northern and eastern Bembaland was closing in fast, and Mwamba's freedom to manœuvre was now critically curtailed. It is not clear how far he himself was implicated in the attack on Chibale's. According to both McKinnon and Young, Bemba from both Ndakala's and Mwamba's

---

[100] Young, Chinsali DNB I, pp. 235, 240; cf. Young, 'Exploits', p. 67

[101] McKinnon to Daly, 10 October 1897, NAZ/NE/A1/1/2 (FO Print 7074, no. 15, FO 403/264).

[102] Young to McKinnon, n.d. (?8 September 1897); same to same, n.d. (?9 September 1897), NAZ/NE/A1/1/2

[103] McKinnon to Daly, 10 October 1897; Young to McKinnon, n.d. (20 September 1897), NAZ/NE/A1/1/2; Young, Chinsali DNB I, pp. 235–7, 241–2; Young, 'Exploits', p. 67. It was perhaps in Mpanda that Ndakala, in November 1897, seized and blinded Chifwasa, a former councillor of Sampa's who had escaped being buried with him and had fled to Kayambi. The Fathers then sent Chifwasa south to open relations with Bisa chiefs, but he died after being caught and blinded by Ndakala (Kayambi report, 1897, *CT*, 78, April 1898, p. 244. In January, Mwamba sent Dupont three tusks by way of compensation (Kayambi report, 1898, *CT*, 80, October 1898, p. 491).

took part in it.[104] There is an undocumented report that after the fighting at Chibale's Mwamba was so furious that he embarked upon 'an orgy of murder and mutilation'.[105] On the other hand, Young heard during the siege, or shortly before it, that Mwamba sought the friendship of the BSAC.[106] And some time after the siege Mwamba sent his war-leader Kalimanshila to Mirongo with presents of ivory, saying that Ndakala was a fool: he should have obeyed Mwamba's orders to live at peace with the white man.[107] It is at least clear that Mwamba now sought to dissociate himself from the siege of Chibale's, while Young's spirited defence of the village greatly increased his local prestige.

By this time, however, McKinnon and Young had clearly come to see Mwamba as an opponent, and they were prepared to risk battle with him to demonstrate who were the real masters of the plateau. Despite Ndakala's expulsion from Ichinga, Mwamba still retained some influence east of the Chambeshi, at Mwalule, and the officials at Ikawa were disinclined to tolerate this. In October 1897 Frs Dupont and Boisselier visited Mwalule and found it occupied by a 'former minister' of Mwamba; they were told that they could not settle there without Mwamba's permission. They also learned that the previous Shimwalule, carrying certain relics, had gone to the British.[108] As Young later recalled, the fugitive Chimbwi came to Mirongo while Young was building the station there, and he asked Young to help him

[104] McKinnon to Daly, 10 October 1897, NAZ/NE/A1/1/2; Young, Chinsali DNB I, p. 240

[105] K. Bradley, 'Adventurers Still', *NRJ*, 1959, 4, i, p. 3

[106] Young to McKinnon, n.d. (20 September 1897), NAZ/NE/A1/1/2. Young thought that the reason for Mwamba's friendly disposition was that Worringham (the BSAC official at Fort Jameson) had attacked Chikwanda, burning his villages and taking Chikwanda himself prisoner. But this story is almost certainly an exaggerated rumour, probably based on the adventurer Hugo Genthe's visit to Chikwanda. Genthe travelled west via Fort Jameson and spent some time at Chikwanda's in September and October 1897. In a fit of exasperation he set fire to the chief's old village while Chikwanda was away building a new one, but his behaviour on finally meeting Chikwanda was civil enough (Genthe, 'Livingstone's Grave'). The first white man to visit Chikwanda appears to have been F. Smitheman, of the Rhodesia Concessions Expedition; he travelled from Zomba to the Bisa chief Kopa, reaching Livingstone's grave at Chitambo on 1 August 1897. Smitheman reported that Chikwanda was very friendly and provided many bearers (*African Review*, Bulawayo, 7 January 1899).

[107] Young, Chinsali DNB I, p. 237; 'Exploits', pp. 66–7. It would be most interesting to know whether the risings in Southern Rhodesia, and their suppression by the Company in 1897, became a factor in Mwamba's calculations.

[108] Kayambi report, 1897, *CT*, 78, April 1898, p. 243; White Fathers, *Ifyabukaya*, p. 110

regain possession of Mwalule. Young agreed, and Mwamba's men were driven back across the Chambeshi.[109] This presumably took place in the latter part of October or November.[110] According to Young, Mwamba sent a force under Kalimanshila to avenge this defeat. 'They had been served out with 14 kegs of gunpowder, percussion caps and bullets, and came as far as the Chambeshi river but never crossed it.'[111]

Makumba's fears were not allayed by Mwamba's reverses. He too sent ivory to Mirongo, asking for support against Mwamba should he challenge his succession as Chitimukulu. The embassy was sent on to Ikawa; McKinnon agreed to back Makumba, who proceeded to take up his new position.[112] For the time being, the company took no further action concerning the Bemba,[113] and Dupont (now Apostolic Vicar of Nyasa) resumed the initiative. In May 1898 he received an invitation to settle from Chikwanda, who had lately moved to Ichinga in a bid to succeed as Nkula.[114] Dupont went off to Ichinga and was warmly received, but he thought the population too sparse to justify a mission. He returned to Kayambi by way of Makumba*, who had moved up the Kalungu to make a new capital. Makumba* welcomed the prospect of a mission; indeed, he had already sent an invitation to the Protestants

---

[109] Young, Chinsali DNB I, pp. 235, 241. Mwamba's appointee, Nsofu ya Mutembo, fled to Makasa's (as Ndakala had also done): Brelsford, 'Shimwalule', p. 211; Chifumo, T1; Chibingo, T3.

[110] This is the inference to be drawn from the White Fathers' testimony, although Young's account, in which the chronology is very blurred, suggests that the reinstatement of Chimbwi took place before the defeat of Kapandansalu. His compressed narrative also implies, probably quite wrongly, that Chimbwi's expulsion, visit to Mirongo and reinstatement happened within a few days.

[111] Young, Chinsali DNB I, p. 235. Some time after the death of Mwamba III, Young allowed Nsofu ya Mutembo to replace Chimbwi once again (Brelsford, 'Shimwalule', p. 211; cf. Chifumo, T1; Chibingo, T3). Bemba informants are presumably the source for the story that 'Shinta's' (i.e. Chimbwi's) removal of the relics from Mwalule alarmed Mwamba, who sought 'Shinta's' return by sending tusks to him and to Young. After Mwamba's envoys had reported that the British had more powerful guns than the Arabs, Mwamba himself got Shinta to return to Mwalule (White Fathers, *Ifyabukaya*, pp. 10–11).

[112] Young, Chinsali DNB I, p. 237. In a later account of these events, Young wrote that Mwamba's mission to Mirongo followed that of Makumba ('Exploits', pp. 66–7).

[113] But in May 1898 soldiers of the BSAC were sent to Makasa to fetch men for work at Mambwe; Makasa sent the soldiers on to Kayambi, where only a few men followed Dupont's advice to go with the soldiers: the Bemba did not yet feel 'conquered' (Kayambi diary, May 1898, WFA).

[114] See below, p. 279.

at Mwenzo.[115] In fact, these last were in no position to accept it,[116] but Dupont was determined to forestall the 'heretics'. He hurried on with preparations, only to be turned away on his return to Makumba* in September.[117]

THE LAST PHASE, 1898–9

It is very likely that Makumba* was acting under pressure from Mwamba, who may well not have been eager to see Europeans installed elsewhere than at his own village. In any case, Dupont's disconsolate party soon had their spirits raised by a summons from Mwamba, to whom Dupont returned on 11 October.[118] He found the chief gravely ill and shockingly emaciated, though mentally alert.[119] Mwamba was clearly not going to live long, and it was for this very reason that his advisers had urged him to summon Dupont. When a royal chief died, other royals would invade his capital and kill those commoners who had gained power through his favour; their authority was resented, and besides, the chief had to be provided with an escort in death. Perhaps the fearless Dupont could protect Mwamba's people from the ferocity of the *bena ŋandu*. Mwamba agreed: 'Bwana Moto Moto' was the only man who had ever dared look him straight in the face. When Dupont arrived, Mwamba expressed concern that his intentions should be so much distrusted at Mirongo; it was not true, he said, that he wished to kill the English. Mwamba asked Dupont to build at his village and thereby testify to his good will. Moreover, said Mwamba, if Dupont could cure him, the two of them would share

[115] Kayambi report, January–June 1898, *CT*, 80, October 1898, pp. 492–3. While visiting Makumba, Dupont camped on a hill above the site of the present Malole mission, only a few miles from the royal capital sites along the Kalungu (Pineau, *Evêque-Roi*, p. 175).

[116] See above, p. 267, n. 70.

[117] Kayambi diary, 20 September 1898, *CT*, 82, April 1899, p. 245. Makasa and Chipukula sought to prevent Dupont from settling at Makumba's by discouraging people from enrolling as porters (Kayambi diary, 8 October 1898, *CT*, 82, April 1899, p. 246).

[118] Kayambi diary, 20 September 1898, 5 October 1898, *CT*, 82, April 1899, pp. 245–6; Pineau, *Evêque-Roi*, p. 181

[119] This and the following paragraph are based on Pineau, *Evêque-Roi*, pp. 178–200. According to Pineau, 'La principale source d'information de cette periode est un petit carnet où Mgr Dupont crayonnait les faits au jour le jour dans la fièvre même des évènements' (*ibid.*, p. 178, n. 1). I have not been able to locate this notebook. Dupont does not appear to have written any other extended account, public or private, of this crucial visit to Mwamba.

Ituna; if he died, Dupont would become 'master of the country' and take care of his people. Dupont built a camp and chapel three miles away, on the Milungu stream. Here he received daily requests from Mwamba for more presents, despite the mounting piles of cloth inside Mwamba's huts. Mwamba became rapidly weaker, and Dupont alleviated his pain with morphine. He heard cases until the very end; noblesse oblige, and, as an old man remarked to Dupont, the *bena ŋandu* die at their posts.

On the night of 23 October Mwamba died. There was a rush or women and children to Dupont's camp, while the men took to the bush, leaving the capital to Kalula,[120] a nephew of Mwamba, and to Mwamba's sister Chandamukulu Kangwa Chonya. These two soon came to avow obedience to Dupont, since Mwamba himself had entrusted the country to him; indeed, Mwamba had specifically commended Kangwa Chonya's children to Dupont's care.[121] Later on the 24th, Kalimanshila and other warriors, who had at first doubted Dupont's authority, arrived and also declared their loyalty to him. They soon compelled the submission of Kanyanta, Chandamukulu's eldest son, who had become Nkolemfumu three years before and was a likely successor to Mwamba.[122] At sunset, Mpepo, another son of Chandamukulu, forced his way in through a hostile crowd to see Dupont. Perhaps it was only Dupont's presence which prevented Kalimanshila from killing Mpepo; as it was, the latter withdrew. The *bena ŋandu* were unwilling to be cheated of their accustomed prey: Chandamukulu, her sister Chilobelobe,[123] and Mpepo all begged Dupont to permit them at least a few victims, but Dupont adamantly refused. During the next few days he received further affirmations of 'homage' from the environs.[124] Disputes were brought before him, and he settled them with the aid of Chandalila, an old man who had induced Mwamba to receive Dupont the previous year.

Thus Dupont seemed to be well on the way towards exercising something of the extensive authority enjoyed by Mwamba Mubanga Chipoya. But the Bemba can have viewed him only as a regent, not as a chief, and in any case Dupont was aware that the secular power of

[120] I have not been able to identify this man in other sources.

[121] Milambo, 13 April 1965

[122] Mwamba IV Kanyanta, in Willis Enquiry (1924). Pineau calls him 'Mfupa'; this was one of Kanyanta's names (cf. African Elders, *History of the Bena ŋoma*, pp. 66–7).

[123] I.e. Chimbabantu, who became Chandamukulu in 1905

[124] Pineau mentions one 'Youba, chef puissant sur le Loukoulou'; he does not seem to have held any chiefly title (*Evêque-Roi*, p. 195).

the British would soon intervene to take over this bloodless conquest. He made this clear to a meeting of headmen on 26 October, and they agreed to follow Dupont in submitting to the British, only asking that they send a force quickly to make sure that there was no massacre. Dupont reported this to the company,[125] but already McKinnon and Young were on their way to Mwamba's. Earlier in the year (it is not clear when), they had been asked by Makumba* for help against Mwamba. It is not clear whether they received a further invitation; at all events, they went to Chitimukulu's in October 1898, with their joint 'army' of about fifty Nyasa police and Iwa and Senga auxiliaries. On their way, they heard of Mwamba's death; they stopped briefly at Chitimukulu's and arrived at Mwamba's on 4 November.[126]

Complications arose at once, for McKinnon seems to have wanted Dupont to leave.[127] But the officials' most pressing concern was the behaviour of Ponde, who wanted to succeed Mubanga Chipoya as Mwamba. Shortly before, Ponde had come south[128] and advanced on Mwamba's; Dupont contrived to keep him at bay,[129] partly, no doubt, because Ponde had no support from the *bena yandu* at Mwamba's. Chandamukulu strongly opposed his claims; in fact, she and others at Mwamba's thought that Ponde had bewitched Mwamba.[130] Ponde, after all, was the son of a sister of the mother of the late Mwamba and Chandamukulu: he belonged to a rival line of descent, and conflict over succession to so senior a title was inevitable. When McKinnon arrived, Ponde informed him of his intention to become Mwamba, but McKinnon told him to go home and wait until the question of the succession had been properly discussed. At first, Ponde was inclined to

[125] Letter dated 26 October 1898 in Pineau, *Evêque-Roi*, pp. 196–7

[126] Young, Chinsali DNB I, p. 237; cf. 'Exploits', p. 66; Pineau, *Evêque-Roi*, p. 209

[127] See below, p. 282.

[128] Ponde's own village at this time was about thirty miles north of Mwamba's, between the Luombe and Vibwe rivers (Abercorn DNB I, p. 91).

[129] Pineau, *Evêque-Roi*, p. 199; Dupont to Codrington, 4 September 1899, enclosure in Codrington to BSAC, Salisbury, 19 September 1899, NAR/LO/1/2/1. According to Brelsford, 'Ponde and his followers seized Mwamba's village and began to fortify it' (*Generation of Men*, p. 55). But there is no reference to this in what appears to be Brelsford's source—an account obtained from McKinnon by F. H. Melland in *Eastern Africa Today*, ed F. S. Joelson, London 1928, p. 306.

[130] When Mutale, daughter of Ponde's sister Mandechanda, reached puberty and was thus due for initiation (*cisungu*), Ponde told her brother, Bwalya Changala, to send *mpemba*, the white powder used in ritual, to Mwamba, who rubbed it on his body. This was thought to have caused his illness. (Nkula Bwalya Changala, in Willis Enquiry, 1924; Richards, 'Bwembya', pp. 36–7).

give battle, but he withdrew when the company forces not only displayed fixed bayonets but demonstrated the Nordenfeldt gun. McKinnon and Young then set up Kasama station on the Milima stream, a few miles east of Mwamba's.[131] For a few months, Ponde kept the peace, but by March 1899 he had lost patience. He moved back into Ituna, fortified a village on a rocky outcrop above the Luombe river, and ignored official requests to leave it. Young and McKinnon were no doubt spoiling for a fight; so far, they owed their position in the heart of Bembaland more to Dupont than to their own efforts. Together with officials from Abercorn, they stormed Ponde's stockade with a large force just before dawn; inside, they found plenty of ivory, cloth and brass wire. Ponde himself escaped and for a few weeks lay in hiding but he then emerged and submitted.[132]

During the six months between Mwamba's death and the defeat of Ponde, the rest of Bemba country remained very quiet; throughout this period, the advent of the British occasioned no other resistance. Chikwanda II Mutale Lwanga had accepted British overrule early in 1898. A few months after Ndakala had been defeated at Chibale's and fled from Ichinga to Mpanda, Chikwanda came north to Ichinga and sought permission from the officials at Mirongo or Ikawa 'to take over Dakara's [Ndakala's] old place'.[133] In fact, Chikwanda sought to become Nkula. In this, Chikwanda had the support of the dying Mwamba,[134] but Chikwanda's independent negotiation with the British suggests that he had made a decision to ally with them and Makumba* against Mwamba: this would certainly be consistent with their earlier relations.[135] McKinnon 'appointed' Chikwanda chief of the 'Chewe country', disallowing a belated claim by the old lineage expelled by Chitapankwa*. The latter were now irrevocably excluded from the succession in Ichinga, but those who had settled in Fungwe country were allowed to return, and one of them, Mulenga *wa cilaka*, was assigned a territorial chieftainship over Ituntwe, east of the river Luvu.[136] Moreover, another member of the old lineage, Chimbuka Chewe, managed to obtain the relics of Nkula I Mutale Sichansa, so

[131] Young, 'Exploits', pp. 67–8; McKinnon's version of Ponde's withdrawal is given in Joelson, *Eastern Africa Today*, p. 306. In 1901 Kasama station was moved a few miles south to its present site (Kasama DNB I, pp. 150, 153; II, p. 1).

[132] Young, 'Exploits', p. 68; Chinsali DNB I, p. 238; Nkula in Willis Enquiry (1924)

[133] McKinnon to Daly, 14 March 1898, NAZ/NE/A1/1/2; see above, p. 273.

[134] Nkula in Willis Enquiry (1924)   [135] See pp. 222, 260, 286.

[136] Chinsali DNB I, p. 230; Brelsford, *Aspects*, p. 40; see above, p. 135. For the later history of this lineage see Appendix 2, Note N (p. 361).

that Chikwanda was never properly installed as Nkula, even though he continued to be recognised as such by the administration.[137]

As for Mporokoso's attitudes and activities in 1897 and 1898, nothing seems to be known. In December 1896 he was still on good terms with Poulett Weatherley, now encamped at Chipamba on Lake Mweru, but he was evidently not prepared to cooperate with Europeans in general. Watson, the Collector at Kalungwishi, had fallen out with Kazembe and wanted the Bemba to help him defeat Kazembe. Mwamba and Mporokoso sent messages to say that they were prepared to co-operate if Weatherley was entrusted with making a peace settlement. Watson would not allow this, so the Bemba chiefs withdrew their offer, saying that 'they did not know the white man at Kalungwishi'.[138]

In February 1899, shortly before the engagement with Ponde, McKinnon made a tour of the country west of Ituna and went some distance down the Kalungwishi: this may have taken him into the country of Mporokoso and Sunkutu. McKinnon reported:

> The people who were originally under Mwamba are of course all very friendly indeed and the fact of us turning out Ponde will have a great effect to the good because they know now we can help and defend them. . . . The Awemba will never fight to my belief.[139]

Ponde was soon to prove McKinnon wrong, but it is probably true enough that by this time the other chiefs in western Bemba country had acknowledged British supremacy. The trouble was that there were still some East Africans in the area who did not yield so soon. Despite the British victories at Mlozi's and Chibale's, some foreign traders still hoped to cut their losses and set up a Muslim state around the Luapula.[140] Many of Mlozi's followers had taken refuge at Kazembe's,[141] and one

[137] Chinsali DNB I, pp. 278–9 (Entry by McKinnon, 25 May 1899); Brelsford, *Succession*, p. 29; *Aspects*, pp. 40, 44. Chikwanda left his nephew Bwalya Changala in charge of part of his country, while other minor chiefs in his territories were also recognised by the British: his sons Kapoko and Luenshi, and two Bisa chiefs, Chitembo (in part of Mukumbi) and Nkuka (who had returned to Kasenga) (Mpika DNB II, pp. 25, 99, 101, 147–8, 179–81; Mpika annual reports, 1905–6, 1907–8, NAZ/KSD/4/1/1). Chikwanda returned to Chinama in 1908 and became Chitimukulu in 1911; in the previous year, Bwalya Changala formally succeeded as Nkula (Chinsali DNB I, p. 279).

[138] Weatherley to Forbes, 14 December 1896, NAZ/NE/A1/5/1

[139] McKinnon to Codrington, February 1899, NAZ/NE/A1/1/2

[140] H. T. Harrington, 'The Taming of North-eastern Rhodesia', *NRJ*, 1954, 2, iii, p. 12

[141] Sharpe to FO, 29 September 1899, FO 2/210; cf. Tilsley, *Crawford*, pp. 271, 294

man from Mlozi's, a Muscat Arab called Nasoro bin Suliman ('Chisesa')
settled near Mporokoso.[142] After Mwamba's death in October 1898
the Swahili at his village also retreated to Mporokoso,[143] who as we
have seen was ill-disposed to the officials at Kalungwishi. Besides, these
had suffered a severe loss of face in 1895, when Kazembe obliged
Watson, with a force of armed police, to withdraw from his capital,
and he may have repelled another British advance in 1897.[144] In April
1899 Law, the Collector at Abercorn, went with other officials to
Mporokoso, to negotiate for the westward extension of the telegraph
from Zomba, but was turned away. Law summoned help from Harrington, now the Collector at Kalungwishi, and together they broke
into Mporokoso's stockade. Mporokoso fled, but returned in due course
and submitted. The British learned that 'the Awemba themselves had
taken no part in the fighting and that it had been done by Nasoro bin
Suliman and his followers'.[145] Nasoro fled to Abdullah bin Suliman,
who handed him over to the British in June.[146]

The extension of British control over North-Eastern Rhodesia was
completed a few months later. Impressed, no doubt, by news of
Young's exploits, Kazembe sought to negotiate with him; after Young
established a company station in Ituna, Kazembe sent him ivory, with
a request that he come and build a station in Lunda country. Young,
however, was obliged to refer Kazembe to Watson, his old enemy at
Kalungwishi. And Codrington, the new Administrator of North-
Eastern Rhodesia, was determined to 'punish' Kazembe for rebuffing
Watson's force in 1895.[147] On 27 October company police, reinforced
by troops from the British Central Africa Protectorate, marched on
Kazembe's capital. They encountered no resistance; Kazembe had fled
across the Luapula, and the Swahili in the neighbourhood had either
fled with him or had gone far to the south. Kazembe finally negotiated

[142] Harrington, 'Taming of North-eastern Rhodesia', p. 9
[143] Codrington in BSAC, *Reports, 1898–1900*, p. 67
[144] Codrington to BSAC, Salisbury, 19 September 1899, NAZ/NE/A2/1;
Weatherley, 4 January 1896, in *BCAG*, 1 April 1896. Dan Crawford, of the
Plymouth Brethren, visited Kazembe in June 1897, and his diary suggests that
Kazembe had just been attacked by the British (Tilsley, *Crawford*, pp. 396–7).
Crawford later wrote a melodramatic account of his visit, according to which he
and his wife had to be protected by Kazembe from British gunfire (*Back to the
Long Grass*, p. 163).
[145] Harrington, 'Taming of North-eastern Rhodesia', pp. 9–10. This may not
be strictly true, as one Bemba, wounded in the fighting, says he was fighting for
Mporokoso against the Europeans (Chinyumba, 17 June 1965).
[146] Harrington, in *Livingstone Mail*, 21 June 1928; cf. 'Taming of North-
eastern Rhodesia', p. 11   [147] Young, 'Exploits', p. 69

his submission through the mediation of Plymouth Brethren missionaries, and he returned to his capital in 1900.[148]

After the submission of Mporokoso, the most pressing question
facing the British in Bemba country was that of succession to the
Mwamba title. Ponde was not the only claimant to make difficulties
for the company; there was also Bishop Dupont. When McKinnon
arrived at Mwamba's in November 1898, he lost no time in telling
Dupont to leave.[149] For this, McKinnon had no authority; indeed, he
had no authority from Codrington to be at Mwamba's at all. It is true
that McKinnon did not know that Forbes had authorised Dupont's
mission to Mwamba. It is also apparent that McKinnon was impulsive
and arrogant,[150] while the contemporary Fashoda crisis did not
contribute to friendly relations between Frenchmen and Britons. But
McKinnon may have been understandably annoyed by Dupont's
patent authority among Mwamba's people and his claims to be
Mwamba's heir: here indeed was a missionary meddling with
politics.[151] Dupont was alarmed and hurt by the officials' reaction: had
he not enabled them to occupy the heart of Bembaland without
bloodshed? His main concern was to secure a large grant of land on
which to build a mission near Mwamba's, but he felt that the company
had need to be reminded of his unique right to favourable treatment.
So on 15 January 1899, he obtained from various notables an attestation
that on 12 October 1898 Mwamba had publicly appointed him,
Dupont, as Mwamba's successor and heir, giving him:

> the whole of his country with the rights of the soil, all his goods
> movable and immovable, real and personal . . . both the right of
> sovereignty over the whole country and territory and the special
> protection of his women and children.[152]

Whether or not Mwamba had done this was, of course, strictly beside
the point. The only people entitled to appoint and instal his successor

[148] Sharpe to FO, 29 December 1899, FO 2/210; Harrington, in *Livingstone
Mail*, 21 June 1928   [149] Pineau, *Evêque-Roi*, p. 209

[150] See above, pp. 272–3. In June 1899 his ideas of rough justice and his
methods of labour recruitment provoked a severe reprimand from Codrington
(Codrington to McKinnon, 28 June 1899, NAZ/NE/A/2/1).

[151] McKinnon to Codrington, 28 November 1898, NAZ/NE/A1/1/2

[152] Codrington to BSAC, Salisbury, 6 March 1899, NAZ/NE/A2/1; this is
quoted by Rotberg (*Christian Missionaries*, p. 35) from a copy in NAR/LO
5/4/13. The attestation is described in similar terms in a summary of events at the
beginning of the Chilubula mission diary (WFA). The original document was lost
in 1906 (Pineau, *Evêque-Roi*, p. 215, n. 1).

were the *bakabilo* in Lubemba; they would doubtless take note of views at Mwamba's, but their choice would be limited to a few closely related *bena ŋandu*. Indeed, Pineau's account implies that Dupont was perfectly aware who the potential heirs were.[153] The views of chiefs in matters of succession are demonstrably unreliable, if law rather than force is the criterion. In so far as Dupont claimed to be Mwamba's heir, the situation had other parallels in central Africa,[154] but no Bemba chief has power to appoint a successor other than the power of his 'appointee' to bend the law by force of arms.

Lacking this option, Dupont had to give ground. In any case, Codrington visited Bembaland in May 1899 and proved much more sympathetic than his subordinates to Dupont's legitimate concern for his mission. Codrington was not best pleased at the way in which McKinnon and Young had set up a station and fought a battle with Ponde without consulting him; he may well have been disposed to accept Dupont's criticism of their behaviour.[155] Dupont's fears were allayed; Codrington recommended a grant to his mission of five square miles and in September was able to report on 'the good feeling at present existing between the mission and the Administration'.[156]

Meanwhile, Codrington sounded out Bemba opinion on the Mwamba succession, and Chandamukulu recommended to him her son Nkolemfumu Kanyanta. Dupont seems to have had a candidate of his own at the mission, but he bowed to Codrington's views, and Kanyanta's claims were approved at a meeting of headmen at Kasama

---

[153] Pineau, *Evêque-Roi*, pp. 193, 195. Elsewhere, the White Fathers relate that Mwamba specifically told Dupont that Kanyanta was to succeed him, and they say nothing of any bequest to Dupont (*Ifyabukaya*, p. 113; Tanguy, *Imilandu*, p. 76).

[154] There is a legend that the Yeke chief Msiri became chief in Katanga after being given the bracelet of chieftainship by the Sanga chief Mpande as he lay on his deathbed (F. S. Arnot, *Garenganze*, London 1889, p. 232; Cunnison, *Historical Traditions*, p. 83). When Kazembe IX Lukwesa sought help from Msiri in regaining his kingdom from Kazembe X Kanyembo, he promised that Msiri should have it when he died (Vansina, *Kingdoms of the Savanna*, p. 230). Msiri, in his turn, declared before his death that Dan Crawford, the missionary at his court, was to have his country (Tilsley, *Crawford*, p. 151). The Nyamwezi leader Mirambo appointed the missionary Southon 'chief of the Kwikuru [capital]': Southon declined the honour (Southon to LMS, 1 June 1880, LMS/CA/3/2/A).

[155] Cf. Young, 'Exploits', pp. 69–70

[156] Codrington to BSAC, Salisbury, 15 June 1899; same to same, 19 September 1899, NAZ/NE/A2/1. Codrington also allowed the new mission (called 'Chilubula', the place of escape) to exercise the powers of a chief (as now restricted by the BSAC) over not more than ten square miles, in an area to be defined by the local chief (Chilubula diary, 8 July 1899, WFA).

village, near Mwamba's, on 29 May .[157] No doubt the officials had yet to learn of the correct procedures for selection and installation, but they had given their backing to the right man. On 5 September, after Mwamba III Mubanga Chipoya had been buried, Kanyanta was 'officially' installed as Mwamba in the presence of Ponde, Luchembe and Sunkutu.[158]

AFTERMATH

After so many doubts and hesitations, the British had finally subdued the Bemba with astonishing ease. The crucial test of Bemba submission came in 1901, when taxation (at first in kind) was introduced. The Bemba complied with a readiness which surprised and delighted their new overlords: in that first year 'the Awemba in Awemba district alone [northern and western Bemba country] paid without any bother or trouble over 14,000 taxes'.[159] Young and Codrington considered that the Bemba welcomed British rule as a deliverance from the cruelties of the ancien régime; the gradual occupation of the surrounding country had inhibited Bemba chiefs from raiding other tribes, so they took to raiding and selling their own people.[160] How far this was really true is not easy to determine, and in any case raiding to the north continued until at least 1895, while it lasted on the southern borders until 1898. But there can be no doubt that Bemba chiefs felt themselves increasingly insecure in face of both European intrusion and the internal crises following Sampa's* death, and it would not be remarkable if this insecurity had accentuated the customary harshness of Bemba rule.[161] To contemporary Europeans at least, there seemed to be a popular reaction against the *bena ŋandu*. According to Pineau, Mwamba's war-leader Kalimanshila quite renounced his former hostility to Europeans: in a vain attempt to retain his position when his master was no longer there to protect him, Kalimanshila made a stirring address in Dupont's presence: 'We don't know the *bena ŋandu*

---

[157] Nkula Bwalya, in Willis Enquiry (1924); Codrington to BSAC, Salisbury, 15 June 1899, NAZ/NE/A2/1. Chikwanda II Mutale Lwanga (the Nkula *fainéant*) may also have sought to become Mwamba (Brelsford, *Succession*, p. 8).

[158] Codrington to BSAC, Salisbury, 19 September 1899, NAZ/NE/A2/1

[159] Young, Chinsali DNB I, p. 238; cf. Codrington to BSAC, Salisbury, 24 August 1901, NAZ/NE/A2/4/1/4; BSAC, *Reports, 1900–02* (for N. Loangwa and Awemba districts).

[160] Young in Chinsali DNB I, pp. 238–9; cf. Codrington in BSAC, *Reports, 1898–1900*, p. 67; also Gouldsbury and Sheane, *Great Plateau*, p. 21

[161] See above, pp. 167–8.

any more; we're not afraid of them. If they try to kill us we'll wipe them out.' (Applause.) 'Our masters are the white men; we know no others.'[162] Fr Molinier, on his way south to found a mission near Luchembe's in 1899, remarked upon

> la révolution qui a soulevé le peuple contre ses chefs, aussitôt que Mwamba a disparu. Sa grande autorité n'est plus là pour maintenir l'ancien ordre, et les Bena-Gandu (chefs de la famille régnante) sont partout détestés et abandonnés. C'est le châtiment bien mérité de toutes les cruautés et de toutes les injustices du passé, car les Bena-Gandu sont les pires des tyrans.[163]

This was hardly the first time, of course, that a group of invaders had claimed to rescue the invaded from injustice and oppression. And it would be quite wrong to suppose from such evidence that the Bemba simply transferred their obedience from their chiefs to their new rulers; as always, the imposition of colonial rule was a much more complex process. But the control exercised by Bemba chiefs clearly diminished very sharply well before the company's administration became at all effective. The Bemba took the first opportunity to disperse from their chiefs' large stockaded villages: by October 1899 the section-heads (*bafilolo*) of Mwamba's village were forming their own villages, and the same process took place elsewhere.[164] As Richards later observed, the company gained prestige from the very fact of having overcome the powerful Bemba chiefs, and it attracted to itself much of the deference which the Bemba had always shown to their rulers.[165]

There may, in any case, have been a further reason for Bemba compliance with British rule. The fights at Chibale's, Ponde's and Mporokoso's had indeed shown that the company was, in a military sense, more powerful than the most powerful chief. Yet the Bemba had not, as a people, been defeated. Their reaction might have been different if European occupation had come about after a massive confrontation,

[162] Pineau, *Evêque-Roi*, p. 193
[163] L. Molinier, diary, 19 September 1899, *CT*, 87, July 1900, p. 432: 'the revolution which raised up the people against their chiefs as soon as Mwamba was gone. No longer can his great authority uphold the old order, and the *bena ŋandu* (chiefs of the ruling dynasty) are everywhere hated and deserted. This is their well-deserved punishment for all the cruelty and injustice of the past, for the *bena ŋandu* are the worst of tyrants.'
[164] *Ibid.*; anonymous letter of 1 October 1899 in *CT*, 86, April 1900, p. 266; Codrington in BSAC, *Reports, 1898–1900*, p. 67
[165] Richards, 'Political System', p. 114

such as some Europeans had feared was only too likely, between a European force and a grand alliance of Bemba chiefs. Defeat in such circumstances might have been more than Bemba pride could well accept. But in 1898 Codrington—mindful, no doubt, of the Ndebele rising two years before—assured his superiors that there was no likelihood of a Bemba rising.[166] Such assurances have all too often proved disastrously wrong. And it is easy, with the advantage of hindsight, to assume that because no rising in fact took place, it was never likely. But there may nonetheless be good reason to suppose that the Bemba were not disposed to rebel, just because they had not suffered the indignity of defeat. Instead, they could reasonably feel that they had themselves taken the decision to allow a European presence. Individual chiefs—Ndakala or Ponde—might have misjudged the situation, though their very foolhardiness saved something of Bemba military honour. But at the central points in the Bemba polity, at Chitimukulu's and Mwamba's, a test of strength was rejected.

In part, as we have seen, this was due to a rational reluctance to make irrevocable commitments for or against Europeans. In Bembaland, as in most other parts of Africa, the strength of European intruders lay less in their often fragile local forces than in their extended lines of communication and reinforcement. While it took time for Bemba leaders to assess this factor, its importance became steadily more apparent during the 1890s. And if growing knowledge of the world far beyond Bembaland provided reasons for delay, so too did the situation within Bembaland. The Bemba were united neither for warfare nor diplomacy, and it must have seemed no easy task to muster an effective anti-European alliance, especially after Sampa's* defeat by Wissmann in 1893. And this very lack of political unity meant that Bemba capacity to resist was severely handicapped by the deaths of their three most important chiefs between 1896 and 1898. Since Bemba military power depended, not upon a specific military organisation, but upon alliances between chiefdoms, the loss of these chiefs affected the situation quite as much as the individual attitudes of these chiefs. There is thus a significant contrast between Bemba reaction to European intrusion and that of Mpezeni's Ngoni, who despite their internal divisions mobilised against the company in January 1898.[167] It is even possible that news of Mpezeni's defeat was a factor in Chikwanda's submission to the British not long afterwards, and in Mwamba's continuing reluctance to fight them.

[166] Codrington to BSAC, Salisbury, 25 August 1899, NAZ/NE/A2/1
[167] Barnes, *Politics in a Changing Society*, pp. 85–93

At the same time, Bemba chiefs were able to procrastinate just because British officials were equally disinclined to provoke a massive confrontation. The forces at the disposal of the company's local agents were indeed very limited, but this was due partly to the fact that there was no special pressure upon them to hasten the occupation of Bembaland: on the contrary, during the revolt of 1896–7 in Southern Rhodesia, there was every reason to delay. The company's wars with the Ndebele in 1893, and with Mpezeni's Ngoni in 1898, came about largely because in both cases African land and labour were wanted immediately by Europeans. By contrast, there was little European demand for the modest economic resources of Bemba country and its environs. After the region had been subdued, it was visited by European rubber collectors, and later labour recruiters,[168] but neither exerted any pressure for its early subjugation. And once the Belgians, Germans and British had gained the upper hand in their respective spheres around Lake Mweru, the Stevenson Road and Lake Malawi, the British occupation of Bembaland could only be a matter of time. The company therefore had every reason to watch and wait for an opportunity to exploit the political weakness of the Bemba rather than precipitate a test of their military strength.

This caution on the part of both Bemba and British made it possible for a third group, the White Fathers, to play a significant, if minor, role in the submission of the Bemba to alien rule. During the six years following their establishment in Mambwe country, the Fathers took advantage of the protracted political uncertainty to make their own approaches to Bemba chiefs. Local political rivalries enabled them to gain a foothold among the northern Bemba, under the aegis of Makasa. They had neither the time nor, perhaps, the opportunity, to make any political impact through their work of proselytisation. But their conduct at Makasa's made a favourable impression among the northern Bemba. And as white men who seemed in some way independent of the company officials, yet were evidently allied to them, the Fathers

---

[168] For the rubber-collectors, see Sharpe to FO, 29 September 1899, FO 2/210; G. M. Rabinek, 'Report on the Trade of the Country to the south of Lake Tanganyika', enclosure in Codrington to BSAC, Salisbury, 15 June 1899, NAZ/NE/A2/1; and also R. H. Hobson, *Rubber: a Footnote to Northern Rhodesian History*, Rhodes-Livingstone Museum Occasional Papers 13, Livingstone 1960. Early labour migration is noted in the annual reports for Mpika district from 1903/4. In June 1899 the African Lakes Corporation (successor to the African Lakes Company) asked that the four thousand acres supposedly due them on Lake Malawi be marked off instead in Bemba country, but Codrington replied that the claim was invalid (Codrington to Sharpe, 22 August 1899, NAZ/NE/A2/1).

were of considerable political interest to the Bemba. They served to extend the possibilities for gathering political intelligence and for the practice of diplomacy. The White Fathers made it easier for both Bemba and British to learn more of each other while holding back from actions such as might cause widespread conflict. Moreover, Dupont's success in this role, coupled with his personal prestige, enabled him to prevent conflict among the Bemba themselves: when Mwamba III died, this redoubtable outsider was available to fill the immediate, if temporary, vacuum in leadership. This plainly smoothed the entry of British officialdom into the heart of Bembaland, though it should perhaps be stressed that Dupont's performance as a 'white chief' was made possible, not simply by Mwamba's death, but by the overall context of political relations during the past few years both within Bembaland and between the Bemba and the British.[169]

It is clear that Bemba reactions to European intrusion largely bear out recent analyses of the imposition of colonial rule elsewhere in Africa. The aims of Bemba rulers were very different in important respects from those of European missionaries and administrators. By comparison with some other ruling groups in East and central Africa, Bemba chiefs were not much interested in literary education or technical change. They saw Europeans in general as a threat to their present way of life, which was largely based on plunder and conquest. It may well be that in the end the Bemba would have offered substantial resistance to the British, had it not been for the death of Mwamba III. There was in any case fighting at Chibale's, at Ponde's, and at Mporokoso's; and this might seem to bear out the suggestion by Robinson and Gallagher that the more an African polity 'hung together on the luxuries of slave-raiding, plunder and migration, the less its aristocracy had to lose by struggling against the Europeans'.[170]

Yet this alone is clearly too crude an equation to do justice to the great variety of African responses. And in fact the same writers note that 'at a time of down-turn [African] rulers would have strong reasons for striking a bargain with the new invaders'.[171] This remark might seem no less apposite to the Bemba. In their case, indeed, the

[169] The availability of Pineau's adulatory biography of Dupont has led historians to place a disproportionate emphasis on the dramatic events at Mwamba's in October 1898: cf. Gann, *History of Northern Rhodesia*, pp. 84–5; Rea, 'The Bemba's White Chief'.

[170] R. E. Robinson and J. Gallagher, 'The Partition of Africa', *The New Cambridge Modern History*, ed F. H. Hinsley, XI, Cambridge 1962, p. 618

[171] *Ibid.*

'down-turn'—the decline in power relative to the outside world—was a matter of internal rather than external relations, and could itself be seen as due largely to dependence on 'the luxuries of slave-raiding, plunder and migration'.[172] It is certainly evident that among the Bemba, as among other powerful and predatory African peoples, there were leaders who did not consider that immediate and uncompromising resistance was the only alternative to abject submission.[173] Their most powerful leader, Mwamba III, was also the most anxious to exploit every possibility for advantageous accommodation to the fact of white military power on the borders of Bembaland. He had no wish to invite white retribution before he had made the most of his opportunities to increase his own power in relation both to the British and to other Bemba chiefs. And if such a policy of restraint was especially advisable in view of the political divisions among the Bemba, it was made possible by the relative weakness of the local agents of European empire, which in turn was largely due to the limited purposes of Europeans in this particular part of Africa. Whatever the differences in outlook between the Bemba and the British, they shared a common interest in gaining time for political manœuvre. And, as so often, it was the senior leaders, on both sides, who, seeing the wider issues involved, best appreciated this interest; on the whole, it was among the subordinates, on both sides, that the hotheads were to be found.

The limited concerns of the white intruders in Bemba country also permitted a large measure of political continuity to be carried on into the colonial period. The Bemba retained their system of chieftainship, and even if British rule divested Bemba chiefs of much power, control over chiefly succession remained in Bemba hands. As for their extensive conquests during the past half-century and more, these were almost all left under Bemba chiefs. The only important exceptions were Mutambe and Chingoli, which were reoccupied by Chibesakunda and Chinkumba,[174] and some areas taken within the past decade or so

---

[172] See above, pp. 212–13.

[173] Cf. Stokes and Brown, *The Zambesian Past*, p. xxxi; also J. D. Hargreaves, 'West African States and the European conquest' (pp. 206–14) and T. O. Ranger, 'African reactions to the imposition of colonial rule in East and Central Africa', (pp. 304–6) *Colonialism in Africa*, eds L. H. Gann and Peter Duignan, Cambridge 1969, I

[174] Nkula, 1917 statement, Chinsali district files. Chibesakunda was presumably prompted to seek Young's support for his return by Ndakala II's flight to Mpanda in 1897. Mukwikile I, who had previously occupied Chingoli, stayed in country that had once been under Chibesakunda (Nkula, *loc. cit.*). This area extended down the eastern bank of the Chimanabwe river to the Manshya

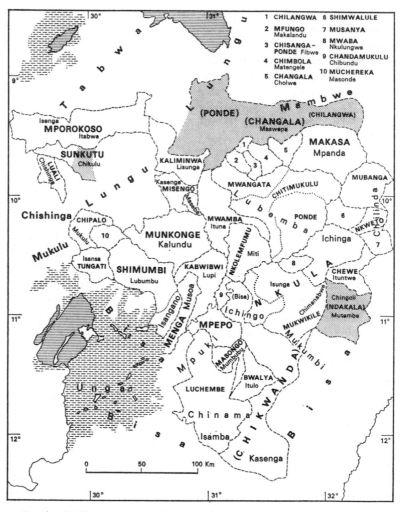

17 Bemba chiefdoms, *c.* 1905. The shaded portions represent areas retroceded by the Bemba

from the Mambwe and Lungu. Makasa himself appears to have returned his conquests north of Kayambi to the Mambwe of Nsokolo.[175] Makasa's 'son' Chilangwa, who in 1892 had occupied country athwart the Choshi river, moved west to Ponde's country, athwart the upper Luombe.[176] In the early 1900s the Mambwe chief Mpande had regained authority over his people at the expense of Makasa's 'son' Changala, who withdrew to the western part of Mpanda.[177] And during the same period the Bemba–Lungu border was redefined to run along the upper reaches of the Luombe river, thus retroceding to the Lungu part of the territory once occupied by Ponde.[178] Chilangwa moved south, to a small area west of Chimbola which was part of his original territory. Ponde himself seems to have been easily induced to leave his country, which no longer had any special strategic or economic value: instead, soon after 1903, he took over the southern part of Lubemba from the increasingly senile Makumba*; he valued the access he now had to the fish of the Chambeshi.[179]

Colonial rule brought far-reaching economic and social changes which were not, for the most part, to the advantage of the Bemba as a group. But for this very reason, it was of great importance that their

(Chinsali DNB I, p. 261) and is variously listed as Chimanabwe and Mukumbi (cf. Northern Rhodesia Government, *General List of Chiefs*, 1930, 1940, etc.). Chingoli was amalgamated with Mutambe in 1946. In 1911 Kasenga, under the Bisa chief Nkuka, was detached from Chikwanda's chiefdom, but this decision was reversed in 1914 (1918 evidence, p. 18).

[175] This is indicated by his remarks when allowing the White Fathers to settle at Kayambi, by his withdrawal to the south in 1898 (see above, p. 265, n. 57, and by the absence of any official record that part of Mpanda was ceded to the Mambwe after 1899.

[176] Abercorn DNB I, p. 5; see above, p. 248.

[177] Abercorn DNB I, pp. 5, 86, 91; cf. Molinier to Dupont, 26 May 1899, *CT*, 84, October 1899, p. 489. Another 'son' of Makasa, Chipukula, appears to have lost his former authority athwart the Choshi river by 1897, when it was said that his people had deserted him (Kayambi diary, February 1897, *CT*, 78, April 1898, p. 239). This Chipukula was presumably not the first holder of the title, who was the father of Makumba.

[178] Minor retrocessions to the Lungu were later made from the chiefdoms of Mporokoso and Kaliminwa (Gibson Hall, 'Notes'; Mporokoso DNB I, 103). In the far west, Sunkutu lost control of his Lungu subjects in the early 1900s (Mporokoso DNB I, p. 104), and Lwali's small chiefdom was retroceded to the Chishinga in 1941 (Brelsford, *Aspects*, p. 5).

[179] Abercorn DNB I, pp. 5, 88; Mporokoso DNB I, p. 99; Shimulamba, 12 October 1964; Kasama DNB II, pp. 173, 214; List of Chiefs and Headmen, Kasama District (1918), NAZ/ZA/1/9/27/1A. Several villages in north-western Lubemba were placed under a *kabilo*, Mwangata, in the early 1900s (cf. Appendix 1(c) and Kasama DNB II, pp. 136, 209).

pre-colonial system of chieftainship should have been preserved, albeit in a diminished and circumscribed form. Amid the upheavals of the twentieth century, the Bemba have retained a sense of corporate continuity and communal pride through the survival of their political structure, a living testimony to their imperial past.

Chapter 9

Conclusions

This study of Bemba history has revealed a political system in the process of growth and change over a period of more than a hundred years before the imposition of European rule. It seems appropriate to conclude by considering how far this historical study may further understanding of pre-colonial African political organisation in general, and that of the Bemba in particular. For the history of the Bemba is not only of local interest to the historian of central Africa: potentially, it is also of theoretical interest to historians and anthropologists concerned with the study of political change in pre-colonial Africa.

This concern is a relatively recent phenomenon. The first attempt to collect and compare studies of pre-colonial African political systems was published in 1940,[1] but thereafter, with a few notable exceptions,[2] the subject was somewhat neglected for a time, and in any case it remained the preserve of social anthropologists who were mainly concerned with conditions under colonial rule. Within the past decade, however, both historians and anthropologists have paid increasing attention to African state systems, while the latter have become more interested in history per se. In line with a growing interest in social processes as opposed to social structures, several anthropologists have sought to substitute a dynamic, diachronic perspective for the static, synchronic perspectives of formal structural–functional analysis.[3]

[1] Fortes and Evans-Pritchard, *African Political Systems*

[2] E.g. A. Southall, *Alur Society*, Cambridge n.d. (1956); J. H. M. Beattie, 'Checks on the Abuse of Political Power in some African States: a preliminary framework for analysis', *Sociologus*, 1959, n.s. 9, pp. 97–114

[3] Cf. E. E. Evans-Pritchard, *Anthropology and History*, Manchester 1961, reprinted in his *Essays in Social Anthropology*, London 1962), pp. 46–65; Max Gluckman, *Order and Rebellion in Tribal Africa*, London 1963, p. 41; Peter C. Lloyd, 'The Political Structure of African Kingdoms', and Aidan Southall, 'A Critique of the Typology of States and Political Systems', in *Political Systems and*

Indeed, it is precisely a more refined approach to the analysis of how social structures function that has prompted some anthropologists to look to history for guidance. It is considered that social structures must be studied in action through time in order to assess the relative inter-dependence of their components. Political systems, and kingdoms in particular, lend themselves well to such analysis since they tend to preserve more evidence of their past than smaller-scale structures. It is also argued that sociological understanding may be advanced by comparing divergences within related and similar systems; as was suggested in chapter 1, north-eastern Zambia comprises a fruitful field for such comparison, which could prompt inferences about social change of much interest to the historian.[4] The latter may take note of South-all's warning that 'it would be fatal if it should be thought that ethno-historians naïve in the theory of social anthropology can supply the dimension of time and change';[5] it is equally true that this dimension cannot be supplied by the anthropologist naïve in historical methodology. And in fact, while some anthropologists have continued to produce essentially synchronic studies of African states at some undated point in the pre-colonial past, others have engaged in genuinely historical enquiries, while historians are improving their ability to interpret evidence from and about African societies. There is thus a growing body of insights into the indigenous processes shaping the pre-colonial history of Africa, to which a study of Bemba history may make some small contribution.

In this chapter, then, I summarise earlier chapters in order to show how it was that the Bemba developed a more cohesive and powerful political organisation than most other peoples of the central African savanna. I then compare this account with previous assessments of Bemba political structure. Next, I compare the Bemba to some other African polities in respect of both internal organisation and ecology. Finally, I consider how far a cyclical model of African political development, in terms of recurrent processes of division or secession, is appropriate to Bemba history.

The most striking fact about Bemba history is that in a region characterised by small-scale polities prone to fission the Bemba developed an extensive and relatively unified political organisation, in which

the Distribution of Power, A.S.A. Monographs 2, London 1965, pp. 63–112, 113–40
[4] Cf. Lloyd, 'Political Structure', p. 107; Southall, 'Critique', pp. 130–4; and above, p. 37   [5] Southall, 'Critique', p. 133

membership of a widely dispersed ethnic group was more or less synonymous with allegiance to a common paramount. Throughout the savanna and woodland of eastern Katanga and north-eastern Zambia, a multitude of small chiefdoms had been formed between, at latest, the sixteenth and eighteenth centuries. These chiefdoms drew upon traditions of government which derived from the Luba and Lunda. Among these two groups of peoples, there emerged a few fairly extensive states, in which a king exercised power through a number of subordinate territorial rulers. By 1800 or so, in the main Luba kingdom and in the Lunda kingdoms of Mwata Yamvo and of Kazembe on the Luapula, royal dynasties controlled some areas beyond a central heart-land through appointed or hereditary overseers of hereditary local chiefs.[6] But such imperial structures were exceptional. The type of polity common to the region as a whole as the small chiefdom, within which a hereditary ruler exercised judicial and fiscal authority over hereditary village headmen. The clan to which the chief belonged enjoyed special esteem as a clan of rulers: in general, chieftainships could only be held by members of such a ruling clan. Thus a number of contiguous chiefdoms might be ruled by members of one clan, and some of these might be able to trace descent to a common ancestor, or might even be close kin. And some chieftainships might be linked with each other, or with village headmanships, in relations of perpetual kin-ship. Thus some chiefdoms were acknowledged as senior in rank to certain others, and hence were entitled to certain rights over them. But in practice the ties between chiefdoms were rather limited; it was unusual for any one chiefdom to assert much authority over its neighbours for any length of time. And within a chiefdom, discord was likely to arise from the ambitions of members of the chiefly clan who had not inherited chieftainships. To any one title there might be a number of claimants, since whether succession was patrilineal or matrilineal it was usually adelphic: all the children of a ruler's brothers, or his sisters, might be competing with his own brothers and cousins. For the most part, the history of such small-scale polities appears to be characterised by ephemeral hegemonies, occasional military co-operation, and repeated fission and secession. All these phenomena may be discerned, in the course of the eighteenth and nineteenth centuries, among most of the peoples of north-eastern Zambia: the Tabwa, Lungu, Mambwe, Bisa, Lala, and the various groups around Lake Bangweulu.

[6] Vansina, *Kingdoms*, pp. 74–5, 80–2, 157, 171; Cunnison, *Luapula Peoples*, p. 158

This type of polity is extremely common in eastern and southern Africa. It has been distinguished in two recent typologies of African states: by Vansina, who calls it a 'regal kingdom', and by Lloyd, who calls it a 'royal aristocracy'.[7] Vansina observes: 'In this type of state stresses within the royal clan or lineage and wars of succession are frequent and often lead to splits and secessions, as with the Xhosa, Pedi, Venda, Letswalo, Sukuma, Haya, Zande and Alur.'[8] Such fission frequently results in the emergence of clusters of states, each ruled by members of the same clan and perhaps uniting against enemies outside the cluster, but acknowledging no one head over all the cluster. Vansina cites the Alur, Zande and Sukuma as examples of such clusters, which correspond to the 'multi-kingdom tribes' noted by Richards.[9] The Mambwe provide an example of a cluster in process of being formed: the paramountcy achieved by Nsokolo over the chiefdoms held by his agnates was breaking down by the end of the nineteenth century.[10] The history of the more numerous Bisa chiefdoms is much less clear, but since the earlier nineteenth century at least the Bisa have certainly been a 'multi-kingdom tribe' in which fissiparous forces have prevailed. The oldest chieftainships belonged to long separate lineages and were independent of each other, and though they exercised some influence over more junior titles related to them, these too became attached to particular lineages and seem to have been largely autonomous.[11]

Since the small-scale 'regal kingdom' was long the most characteristic form of polity over much of Africa, it is important to ask how far the Bemba polity differed from it, and for what reasons. The Bemba, after all, shared with many peoples between the Lualaba and Luangwa a common cultural background and traditions of chieftainship, and inhabited much the same sort of environment. Nevertheless, by the late nineteenth century they had developed a political organisation which for military efficacy and territorial extent surpassed the kingdom of Kazembe and rivalled those of Msiri's Yeke or Mpezeni's Ngoni. The explanation suggested by the present study is that, while Bemba politics remained rooted in kinship, the bonds of kinship were so manipulated and diversified as to give Bemba chiefs an interest in

---

[7] Jan Vansina, 'A Comparison of African Kingdoms', *Africa*, 1962, 32, iv, pp. 324–35; Lloyd, 'Political Structure', pp. 99–106. Vansina's classification anticipates Lloyd's more fully than the latter seems to realise ('Political Structure', p. 65).   [8] Vansina, 'Comparison', pp. 332–3

[9] *Ibid.*, p. 332; Richards, 'African Kings', p. 144

[10] Cf. above, pp. 144–7, 246–7   [11] Cf. above, pp. 108–9

continued subordination to a common paramount. In themselves, such kinship links would not alone have held Bemba chiefs together in a common polity, but their geographical position facilitated trade and conquest, and in a society permeated by the idiom of kinship it was through the network of royal kinship that material and territorial gains were distributed.

The earlier history of the Chitimukulu dynasty remains obscure; we still know very little about the foundation of the oldest Bemba chiefdoms and their relationships with each other and with the paramountcy. It is, however, apparent that by the middle of the eighteenth century there were several distinct lineages within the royal clan, established in control of different chiefdoms. It also seems that succession to the paramountcy itself was not reserved to any one lineage. Perhaps the earliest Chitimukulus were in fact all members of a single shallow matrilineage. We do not know, but if they were, the field of choice for the royal succession gradually widened. The paramountcy was successively occupied by men from a number of different lineages in the royal clan, and these lineages, whatever their genealogical distance from each other, dominated different parts of Bembaland on either side of the Chambeshi.[12] Such competition for the paramountcy evidently distinguishes the Chitimukuluship from other long-established chieftainships in the region. The genealogies for the dynasties of Mwansabamba (Bisa), Matipa (Bisa) and Nsokolo (Mambwe) are by no means firmly established, but they do appear to be more continuous than that of Chitimukulu; throughout the pre-colonial past, chiefly succession was confined in these cases to two or three lineages, and it was unusual for any one of these to be identified with a particular subordinate title.[13] If, by contrast, succession to the Chitimukuluship was open to the holders of lesser Bemba chieftainships, more or less distantly related but located within a fairly compact area, this could well have promoted a common interest in continued subordination. It is doubtful whether the Bemba evolved any regular system of alternation or rotation between lineages, as in the Luba chiefdom of Kalundwe.[14] But in general, any form of circulating succession is likely to have an integrative effect, as Goody has noted for

[12] See above, chapter 3.
[13] See tables 2 and 3.
[14] Verhulpen, *Baluba*, pp. 287–8; see also below, p. 322. Alternating succession has been attributed to the Lwembe kingship among the Nyakyusa, but this appears not to be supported by the available genealogical evidence: Simon Charsley, *The Princes of Nyakyusa*, Nairobi 1969, p. 29.

the Gonja kingdom in northern Ghana.[15] At all events, throughout the eighteenth century Chitimukulu continued to be acknowledged as paramount among the numerous small chiefdoms ruled by *bena ŋandu* on the plateau of north-eastern Zambia.

As a people, then, the Bemba were already more unified politically than their Bisa neighbours to the south and west. By the latter part of the eighteenth century, the older Bisa chieftainships, such as Mwansabamba, Matipa[16] and Mukungule, were independent of one another, and the lines of succession to each remained distinct. This is not to say that the Bemba were already the most important polity on the plateau. At least one Bisa dynasty—that of Matipa in Lubumbu—appears to have exercised a paramountcy over subordinate chiefdoms no less extensive than that of Chitimukulu.[17] It is very likely that, for a time, geography favoured the chiefs in Lubumbu: their role as collectors and distributors of wealth would have been enhanced by their position between the woodland of the plateau and the very different economies on the margin of Lake Bangweulu.[18] Nevertheless, these western Bisa came under the sway of a power greater than any on the plateau—Kazembe's kingdom on the Luapula. The Bisa became active in trade between Kazembe's and the east coast, but this probably contributed more to Kazembe's power than to that of Bisa chiefs. And meanwhile the cohesion of the Bemba polity was significantly increased: a single lineage not only retained control of the paramountcy but established new chiefdoms for its own members and agnatic kin in newly conquered areas. Thus when, in the first half of the nineteenth century, Kazembe developed new trading contacts with East Africa at the expense of the route to the southeast, Bemba chiefs moved southwards to replace him as overlord of the western Bisa.

It was the reigns of Mukuuka* and Chiliamafwa*, around the end of the eighteenth century, which marked the first stages in the rise of the Bemba polity to pre-eminence.[19] Mukuuka*, from the lineage in Iyaya, created a new chiefdom, Ituna, in western Bembaland for his brother Chitundu. Mukuuka* was succeeded by his sister's son Chiliamafwa*, whose brother Mubanga succeeded Chitundu in Ituna. Chiliamafwa seized Mpanda from the Mambwe and assigned it to his

[15] Jack Goody, 'Circulating Succession among the Gonja', *Succession to High Office*, ed Jack Goody, Cambridge 1966, pp. 150, 161–3
[16] I use this name for convenience, though it was not adopted by the dynasty in Lubumbu until the mid-nineteenth century.
[17] See above, pp. 108–9.   [18] See above, p. 188.
[19] This paragraph summarises the narrative content of chapters 4 and 5.

son Makasa, while Mubanga's son Munkonge took over a small area from a subordinate of the Bisa chief of Lubumbu. Chiliamafwa* was succeeded by Chinchinta*, probably his nephew, and when Chinchinta* was deposed in about 1827 he made way for Chileshye*, son of a daughter of a younger sister of Chiliamafwa*. Chileshye's* brother Mutale soon succeeded as chief in Ituna, taking the title Mwamba, and he also took over the old Miti chiefdom; while in the east Chileshye's* perpetual son Makasa seized territory from another old Bemba chiefdom, that of Nkweto. In the far south, the Bemba overran the Bisa in Chinama, where Chikwanda, a nephew of Chileshye*, became chief; in the west, they invaded the Bisa in Lubumbu, and the Bena Mukulu. The Bemba failed to hold these conquests, but in the 1860s many of Matipa's Bisa and the Lungu of Mukupa Kaoma were conquered by Mwamba II (another nephew of Chileshye*), who carved out new chiefdoms for his sons. Meanwhile, royal power was extended eastwards by Chileshye's* successor, his nephew Chitapankwa*. Ngoni depredations in the 1850s left the southeastern Bisa chiefs unable to offer resistance to the Bemba, and much of their country was assigned by Chitapankwa* to a nephew who had replaced the old lineage in Ichinga. Further south, the Bemba regained Chinama; a nephew of Chitapankwa* became Chikwanda II, while another became chief in Miti. Meanwhile, in the northwest, Mwamba II took more country from the Lungu and Tabwa and assigned it to his sons.

Thus, during the century or so before Chitapankwa's* death in 1883, significant changes had taken place both in the pattern of succession to the paramountcy and in the relations between the paramount and his subordinates. Four members of a single shallow lineage within the royal clan, from the same part of Bembaland, had successively become Chitimukulu. The right of other lineages to succeed was thereby eroded. But in itself this development might not necessarily have bound the Bemba polity more closely together: indeed, the pattern of Bemba royal succession now came to resemble that of neighbouring dynasties, such as that of Mwansabamba, which achieved no comparable cohesion. What now sharply differentiated the Bemba polity from its neighbours was the fact that the newly dominant lineage not only gained control over the paramountcy but also provided new chiefdoms both for its members and for their sons—a radical innovation in this matrilineal society. As this process continued, the paramountcy once again became open to a number of subordinate chiefs, despite the ascendancy of one royal lineage. For whereas in the eighteenth century the subordinate chiefs had belonged to a number of more or less distantly related lineages, during the nineteenth century an increasing number came from the same lineage which had in effect established a monopoly of the paramountcy. Furthermore, Bemba history in the nineteenth century bears out Lloyd's observation:

> It would be a rare kingdom in which the political elite was drawn exclusively from the royal lineage. Faced by the perpetual rivalry from other members of the royal lineage, the king tries to buttress his own power by granting political office to those who depend on him alone for this favour and not on their membership of the royal lineage—to affinal and maternal [for the Bemba, read paternal] relatives, to loyal supporters from other groups within the ruling class, to slaves and lowly commoners.[20]

It was not simply the triumph of one royal lineage but the diversification and multiplication of the sources of political power, and hence of the links between chiefs, which made the Bemba polity in the late nineteenth century so much more coherent, despite its greater extent, than it had been a hundred years earlier.

These changes in political structure were both effect and cause of territorial expansion. New conquests made possible the creation of chieftainships for a widening circle of men related in one way or another to the most senior chiefs. It was primarily by subduing neighbouring peoples that one group of *bena ŋandu*, together with their agnates and affines, secured their ascendancy over all other Bemba families. But if territorial expansion made possible the distribution of chieftainships not only among royals but also among their sons and affines, it can also be said to have made this necessary. There were opportunities to distribute many new chieftainships, but if these had all been given to royals, some of the new chiefs would have been too remotely related to the paramount to have had much prospect of promotion to senior posts. They might thus have valued leadership of a locally dominant lineage more highly than their association with Chitimukulu. From the latter's point of view, the risks of secession might be lessened if new chieftainships were denied to all royals except those few who, as brothers or nephews of the paramount, were sufficiently closely related to him, and sufficiently junior in years, to be able to look forward to promotion within the Bemba system. And as often as not there was a shortage, rather than an excess, of such men

[20] Lloyd, 'Political Structure', p. 105; he assumes here that the royal lineage is patrilineal.

who were also qualified for office by age and proved ability.[21] Such a situation, indeed, is characteristic of a matrilineal dynasty: however polyandrous the royal women, they cannot produce potential heirs in anything like the numbers possible for a polygynous patrilineal dynasty. This deficiency may partly account for the distribution of chieftainships among sons of Chitimukulu or Mwamba, even if this was also prompted on occasion by the desire to provide checks on the power of royal chiefs. In any case, appointment to chieftainship provided a new answer to the problem of what to do with sons of Chitimukulu: the creation for them of new titles as *bakabilo* inevitably brought diminishing returns. It may be significant that Chiliamafwa*, the last chief to have made a son (Lumpombwe) a *kabilo*,[22] was also the first to appoint a son (Makasa) to a chieftainship.[23] And once the principle was established of granting chiefdoms to the sons of royals, their ambitions increased the competition for power and hence pressures for further expansion.

Bemba history thus illustrates a theme familiar to historians of institutions everywhere: expansion both promoting and promoted by increasing concentration of power within a particular group. But this reciprocal effect cannot alone, of course, account for the growth of Bemba power at the expense of their neighbours. We must consider what special advantages may have favoured the rise to prominence of a particular royal lineage, the conquest of more and more territory, and the continued adherence of Bemba chiefs to a common polity.

We know too little about the reigns of Mukuuka* and Chiliamafwa* to be able to explain satisfactorily why their lineage succeeded both in retaining control of the paramountcy and in founding new subordinate chiefdoms. Goody indeed has remarked of the Gonja kingdom that attempts by one lineage to end a system of circulating succession are likely to be inhibited by alliances among rival lineages, and by the very fact that rotation is part of the political ideology.[24] But among the Bemba royal succession had apparently followed a less regular and accepted pattern of rotation, so that there was probably no very clear break with convention when first Chiliamafwa* and then his presumed

---

[21] See above, pp. 179–80.

[22] Tanguy, *Imilandu*, p. 26. Lumpombwe himself said that it was 'Chitimuluba' who made his ancestor a *kabilo* (18 September 1964), but I do not know of any *bakabilo* who owe their titles to Chitimukulus more recent than Chiliamafwa.

[23] We may also recall that Makasa came to play a minor part in the rituals of royal burial and installation: cf. Brelsford, *Succession*, p. 34; and below, p. 311, n. 63.

[24] Goody, 'Circulating Succession', p. 164

nephew Chinchinta* became Chitimukulu. And meanwhile their close kin had begun to extend their influence well beyond Iyaya around the northern borders of Bemba country; not only into Lubemba but into the Mambwe country of Mpanda and into Ituna, further west. Perhaps the latter move was a response to the settlement of Leopard clan chiefs among the Lungu, or else to the eastward expansion of Kazembe's kingdom; in any case, Chiliamafwa's* brother Mubanga was able to divert an eastward campaign by the powerful Kazembe III Kanyembo.[25] The conquest of Mpanda, in the reign of Chiliamafwa*, may have contributed significantly to the resources of Chitimukulu. Through Makasa, his real (and henceforth perpetual) son, Chitimukulu could hope to profit from an enlarged field of tribute, while the borders for raiding further north into the cattle country of the Mambwe had been considerably extended.

If it remains somewhat difficult to account for the rise of the Iyaya lineage of Mukuuka* and his successors, we can clearly distinguish certain very general factors favouring the expansion of Bemba power once a particular group of royals had made itself pre-eminent. It has been suggested that the Bemba were predisposed to raiding and warfare by their geographical situation. They themselves occupied tsetseinfested and relatively infertile woodland, while surrounding areas yielded cattle, ironwork, salt and abundant fish.[26] The warlike character of the Bemba was attested by Lacerda in 1798, and by 1832, as we have noted, they were said to be 'powerful and feared by all for their fierceness, which their territorial position helps them to exercise'.[27] In the course of the nineteenth century, the central position of the Bemba proved both an economic and strategic advantage: they had plenty of room to expand while driving their neighbours into environments that compelled more specialised modes of life or impeded rapid combination.

During the reign of Chileshye* (1826/7–c. 1860), the Bemba also began to profit from major changes in the pattern of long-distance trade.[28] Hitherto, they had taken no part in the trade conducted by Lunda and Bisa between Kazembe's, the lower Zambezi, and the east coast. In the late 1820s, Bemba pushed south into Bisa country, mainly in order to secure direct access to imported cloth. In this objective, the venture seems to have had little success, but it was followed by numerous Bemba conquests to the south and east. This was in fact partly due

[25] See above, p. 96.   [26] See above, pp. 125–6, 182–9.
[27] See above, pp. 97, 126.
[28] The next four paragraphs summarise the arguments of chapter 6.

to the decline of the southern trade route. During the 1830s and 1840s, Kazembe was visited by a growing number of Arab or Swahili traders who had come from the east coast opposite Zanzibar by way of Lake Tanganyika. Owing to these new contacts, Kazembe's interest in the southern route appears to have diminished. At all events, he made no effort to defend his Bisa and Lungu tributaries when their territories were conquered by Bemba invaders during Chileshye's* reign. The Bisa trade finally collapsed under the pressure of Ngoni raids during the 1850s and 1860s, and thereafter Bemba conquest and raiding extended southwards through Bisa country and as far as the country of the Lala.

The growth of the new, northern trade route pioneered by the East Africans was to the advantage of the Bemba inasmuch as it diverted Kazembe's energies away from his former dominions around the northern and eastern fringes of Lake Bangweulu. But it was also of much more positive value to the Bemba because it gave them their first regular access to overseas imports. For whereas they failed to gain any significant share in the Bisa trade, they soon came to play an important part in the East African trade. The Bemba were well placed to make contact with traders approaching Kazembe's and Katanga from Lake Tanganyika or the southern highlands of what is now Tanzania. From the 1850s, Bemba country was visited by East Africans, who were as ready to buy ivory (and later slaves) from the Bemba as from the Lunda of Kazembe. Bemba chiefs were sufficiently powerful to organise the supply of large quantities of ivory and slaves; yet they had no ambition to compete in the carrying trade. These circumstances made for relatively harmonious relations between the Bemba and the East Africans. The latter had no occasion to provoke Bemba hostility by establishing permanent settlements in Bemba country, for they were able to do business with them from bases among the less organised Lungu, Tabwa, Bwile and (after 1885) Senga. Indeed, the Bemba soon came to derive far more advantage from the East Africans than did Kazembe, whose capital had first attracted them to the region. Whereas Bemba country lay to one side of the main line of East African trade, the direct route to Katanga and its copper lay through Kazembe's kingdom. Thus Bemba encroachment on his eastern dominions was followed by East African encroachment to the north and west. With access to firearms, trade goods, and military support from East Africa, Arabs, Swahili and Nyamwezi traders became local potentates between Lakes Tanganyika and Mweru, while Msiri in Katanga seized control of the trade running west from the Luapula to the western Lunda and

Angola. And from 1872 onwards Kazembe's kingdom was further enfeebled by succession disputes in which the foreigners intervened to further their own interests at Kazembe's expense.

The participation of the Bemba in the East African ivory and slave trade both promoted the expansion of the Bemba polity and facilitated a growing measure of cohesion. Access to firearms was probably of minor importance until the late 1880s, but the import of beads, shells and mass-produced cloth greatly increased the ability of chiefs to attract and reward supporters. Not only was there a marked increase in the variety and quantity of goods for exchange; the introduction of new commodities, and the arrival of alien traders and craftsmen, stimulated the exchange of local products as well, thus encouraging the more intensive exploitation of local resources. The exchange of ivory for cloth at the courts of Bemba chiefs in the middle of the plateau meant that they imported and redistributed products from surrounding areas. The very fact that this was achieved, not so much through unconstrained trade as through raids, tribute levies and reciprocal payments meant that the growth of long-distance trade served to strengthen the bonds between a chief and his subordinates. Not only were Bemba chiefdoms drawn into a closely-knit pattern of kinship and affinal relationships: these relationships were underpinned by the growing volume and extent of exchanges among chiefs and subjects in terms of material goods, labour and military support.

In this way, the advent of long-distance trade improved the capacity of Bemba chiefs to cooperate in raiding and warfare, and so to increase yet further the goods and services at their disposal. It was such cooperation which largely accounts for the military supremacy of the Bemba. No doubt this owed something to an increased use of spears, made possible by the general growth of trade and exchange; but on their own, Bemba chiefs, including Chitimukulu himself, were by no means invincible.[29] What distinguished the Bemba from their neighbours was their ability on occasion to come together from considerable distances and join in concerted military action, as in the final victory over Mperembe's Ngoni in about 1870. It is also noteworthy that extensive campaigns of conquest, such as those to the south, southeast and northwest during the 1870s and early 1880s, were not just the haphazard achievements of restless nephews and sons of the major chiefs: they enlarged the spheres of influence centred on Chitimukulu and Mwamba, and reflected a considerable degree of direction and

[29] Cf. above, pp. 116–19, 145, 146, n. 91, 150, 159, 226

overall control. All this was made possible by the multiplication of incentives for cooperation and subordination. The concentration of chieftainships within a small group of royals, their agnates and affines, created new possibilities for promotion and thus enhanced the value of belonging to a single polity under Chitimukulu. And the growth of trade increased the material, and thus also political, fruits of patronage, dependence and alliance.

So far, I have tried to show to what extent, and by what means, the Bemba polity took a different form from those of neighbouring peoples. It may now be useful to compare the resulting picture of Bemba political organisation with the assessments made by earlier writers. The undoubted military achievements of the Bemba have prompted several writers to overemphasise the 'centralised' nature of Bemba government, and this tendency has probably been reinforced by nostalgic exaggeration on the part of informants around the paramount's capital. To be sure, Codrington in 1901 gave too little weight to the factors making for cohesion among the Bemba: writing just after the death of Mwamba III had revealed the Bemba polity at its weakest, he considered that among the peoples of the north-eastern plateau groupings under one chief, such as Mwamba, Chitimukulu or Kazembe, were ephemeral, and due only to 'vague ideas of combination and co-operation for self-defence and the raiding of weaker tribes. Every village is more or less a republic.'[30] Yet Codrington also believed that the Bemba had formed a 'military organisation' after the repulse of the Ngoni,[31] and in 1910 Gouldsbury and Sheane described numerous officials doing the bidding of the paramount throughout Bemba country.[32] These accounts seemed to have influenced some later writers: in 1954, Gann wrote of the Bemba's 'centralised, military organisation',[33] and in 1958 Watson wrote that the Mambwe paramount 'had no centralized administrative machinery, such as that operated by the Bemba paramount chief'.[34]

This persistent emphasis on the 'centralised' character of Bemba government may also have owed something to Richards' accounts of her field studies in the 1930s—a period when social anthropologists were less familiar with state systems than with small-scale organisation

[30] *B.S.A.C. Report, 1898–1900*, p. 70
[31] *Ibid.*, p. 66.   [32] *Great Plateau*, pp. 24–6
[33] 'Slave Trade', p. 34; Gann cites Wissmann's hearsay report (cf. above, p. 169, n. 25).
[34] *Tribal Cohesion*, p. 171

at the level of the band or lineage. It was implicitly by comparison with such forms of organisation that Richards credited the Bemba, in *Land, Labour and Diet*, with a 'centralised form of government' and a 'highly centralised political system'. Yet both this study and her contribution to *African Political Systems* (1940) made it clear that the component chiefdoms were 'self-contained units' under the 'overlordship' of a paramount; Richards also noted that 'there was no general military organisation', nor any regular general meeting of chiefs.[35] And if the power and cohesion of the Bemba were not to be attributed to any system of centralised administration, it remained to provide some alternative explanation. Richards noted, of course, the diverse bonds of kinship linking chieftainships; she also tended to exaggerate the paramount's control over ivory and guns.[36] But she laid particular stress on the unique ritual importance of the paramount, and in recent papers she has examined in some detail the force of Bemba belief in the mystical power of the paramountcy, and the complex means by which this supposed power is maintained.[37]

There can of course be no simple answer to the question of how far political action in pre-literate societies is constrained by mystical beliefs rather than by mundane considerations of economic and military power. The role of Chitimukulu's priest-councillors (*bakabilo*) in maintaining belief in his supremacy may well have been considerable, and I discuss it further below. But the historical evidence is too meagre to enable us to assess with any confidence the actual importance of ritual and religious factors in Bemba political history.[38] To the historian, at least, it would seem prudent to assess and account for the political cohesion of the Bemba in secular terms as far as possible. And two social anthropologists have drawn attention to the actual distribution of political power among the Bemba as a major factor for integration. Gluckman, mainly on the basis of Brelsford's *Succession of Bemba Chiefs* (1944), argued that the Bemba polity achieved a measure of unity and cohesion through the very fact that chiefs competed for succession to the paramountcy: 'the tendency of the Bemba territorial chieftainships to separatism is here canalised in a struggle to make the chief into the king'.[39] This develops Gluckman's earlier

35 *Land, Labour and Diet*, pp. 25, 355; 'Political System', pp. 107–8, 111–12
36 Cf. above, p. 212
37 'Social Mechanisms'; 'Keeping the King Divine'
38 See above, p. 172 and n. 36, and below, pp. 310–13.
39 Gluckman, 'Succession and Civil War', p. 22; this paper was written in 1947.

suggestion that the ritual value of a paramount chief 'arises from the conflicts aroused by his power over subordinate groupings'.[40]

Other points in Gluckman's arresting, but somewhat formalistic, analysis are given further consideration below; here we need only note that it has prompted a critique by Werbner, who argues that Bemba cohesion arose not simply from competition for the paramountcy but from competition for succession to, and control over, a variety of subordinate posts. Secession was inhibited by a web of kinship and affinal ties between different territorial chiefs, and by the very fact that these chiefs were drawn from different 'strata' of the kingdom— some from the close matrikin of the paramount, others from more distant branches of the royal clan, and others again from the sons of the senior royal chiefs.[41] Werbner considers that 'the unity and inter-dependence which developed in the kingdom was federal in nature'; this is surely misleading, since a federation requires a central power with clearly defined rights over the whole federal structure such as Chitimukulu never seems to have possessed.[42] Nonetheless, Werbner's analysis is a useful contribution to our understanding of the Bemba polity in the later nineteenth century, and its main points are borne out by the present study (which was largely completed before his work became known to me). The main limitation of Werbner's analysis is that despite the emphasis on instability and fluctuating relationships and on the role of long-distance trade, it remains primarily a structural analysis, in which the element of time is given too little place. It was not, indeed, Werbner's concern to explain just what made possible the relationships he discusses, but it is clear that this question can only be answered by investigating the timing and causes of Bemba expansion during the nineteenth century. And while Werbner notes that there was some 'diversification in trade and perhaps in tribute', a close examination of the historical evidence has indicated that patterns of economic interdependence were more significant than Werbner was able to demonstrate.[43]

[40] *Order and Rebellion*, p. 51: this is from an article written in 1945 or 1946 (the original source is not given).

[41] Werbner, 'Federal Administration'. The purpose of Werbner's arguments is unnecessarily obscured by his failure to cite Gluckman's article, the chief object of his criticism.

[42] Werbner, 'Federal Administration', p. 22. Vansina ('Comparison', p. 333) and Lloyd ('Political Structure', p. 82) agree that few, if any, true federations are to be found among pre-colonial African states.

[43] 'Federal Administration', p. 30. It may be noted in passing that Werbner's use of historical evidence is sometimes insufficiently critical; moreover, by

We may now turn to consider Bemba history and politics in the context of political growth and change elsewhere in pre-colonial Africa. We do not as yet have any comprehensive typologies of such African state systems in terms of processual as well as structural models, though Lloyd has made a useful beginning.[44] At present, any systematic comparison of this kind would itself be a considerable task of research. It may nonetheless be helpful to compare the Bemba with some other African polities in respect of the distribution of political power; the relationship between royals and commoners; the means by which royal succession was determined; and the underlying ecological base.

It has already been noted that in one respect the Bemba belong to a very large category of African polities: those 'regal kingdoms' or 'royal aristocracies' in which executive political power is mainly distributed among members of the clan to which the king himself belongs.[45] We have also seen that in the course of the eighteenth and nineteenth centuries the Bemba polity was transformed from a congeries of chiefdoms ruled by different branches of the royal clan into the hegemony of one such branch, in which an increasing number of chiefs belonged to a single shallow lineage. This latter basis for the distribution of power appears to be rather uncommon, though our impression may well be due only to ignorance. Vansina cites two examples of such polities: Burundi, and the Kede on the middle Niger. The Kede polity differed from the Bemba in one important respect: while members of the dominant lineage were promoted through a series of titles, these were not tied to particular areas as among the Bemba.[46] The rise and decline of Burundi affords greater opportunities for contrast with Bemba history, and I discuss this below in the context of fission and secession.[47]

We may, however, recall here that in the Bemba case chiefdoms were

accepting the conventional date for Chileshye's accession (*c.* 1850), he presents the process of Bemba expansion as still more rapid than in fact it was.

[44] Cf. Vansina, 'Comparison', pp. 333–4; Lloyd, 'Political Structure', pp. 94–101; Southall, 'Critique', p. 132   [45] See above, pp. 295–6.

[46] Vansina, 'Comparison', p. 332; Nadel, 'The Kede', Fortes and Evans-Pritchard, *African Political Systems*, pp. 178–9

[47] See below, p. 318. Developments under colonial rule are not strictly relevant here, but we may note that during this century the structure of the eastern Lunda kingdom of Kazembe came to approximate to that of late-nineteenth-century Bembaland: the governors, drawn from different lineages of Lunda aristocrats, gave way to chiefs selected by Kazembe from his own family: Cunnison, *Luapula Peoples*, pp. 167, 185.

distributed not only to a particular group of royals but also to their non-royal kin. As Lloyd has observed, this is probably a frequent corollary of the pre-eminence of one lineage, since it provides a counterweight to the ambitions of those chiefs eligible for the highest posts.[48] It would clearly be of much interest to note other examples of these developments. We know that political offices were given to the matrikin of the Luapula Kazembe and the Ganda *kabaka*,[49] but these rulers did not have to contend with subordinate chiefs among their close patrikin. And in any case, for purposes of comparison with the Bemba, the most relevant polities would be those under matrilineal dynasties, where sons were ineligible for the highest offices. There seem to have been no titles for the sons of royals in Ashanti, though certain administrative posts became hereditary in patrilineages.[50] The Kuba provide an example of overcompensation: from the seventeenth century the matrikin of the Bushoong king were progressively excluded from subordinate political office in favour of his sons, and the kingdom was eventually torn by rivalry between kings and heirs apparent, supported by their respective sons.[51] There do not seem to have been any chieftainships for sons of Bisa chiefs, though sons of Chibesakunda might become priest-councillors (*bantungwa*).[52] Among the Lungu the Chitoshi chieftainship, founded by the mid-nineteenth century, was reserved for sons of Mukupa Kaoma; and among the Tabwa there was, by the late nineteenth century, at least one chieftainship, Katele, for real or classificatory sons of Nsama.[53] In both these polities there was also at least one subordinate chieftainship for the ruler's matrikin,[54] so that the principle of diversifying the bases of executive power appears to have taken root, if on a very small scale.

Two further aspects of the Bemba polity which invite comparison are the relationship between royals and commoners, and the means by which the succession was determined. On the face of it, these are likely

[48] See above, p. 300.

[49] Cf. the *bacanuma* in Kazembe's kingdom (Cunnison, *Luapula Peoples*, pp. 164–6), and for Buganda, Martin Southwold, 'Succession to the Throne in Buganda', in Goody, *Succession to High Office*, p. 87

[50] Ivor Wilks, 'Ashanti Government', *West African Kingdoms*, eds Daryll Forde and Phyllis Kaberry, London 1967, p. 214

[51] J. Vansina, 'Recording the oral history of the Bakuba: II. Results', *JAH*, 1960, 1, ii, pp. 267–8

[52] Kapandansalu, 28 April 1965

[53] Cf. above, pp. 106, 139, 153–4; and below, p. 311, n. 63

[54] Lunshinga, perpetual 'nephew' to Mukupa Kaoma; Kaputa, 'brother' to Nsama

to be important factors in the stability and cohesion of any polity. In the Bemba case, they are closely linked and most conveniently discussed together. Succession to the paramountcy and the more senior subordinate chieftainships was controlled by a group of hereditary commoner priest-councillors (*bakabilo*),[55] who decided the appointments, organised the rituals of burial and installation, supervised other rituals of paramountcy and guarded the paramount's relics.

The importance of 'counter-balancing institutions' was briefly acknowledged by Fortes and Evans-Pritchard, who noted that the distribution of ritual duties may serve as a sanction on the abuse of political power.[56] In fact, groups of 'stake-holders', to use Goody's term,[57] may be found in many African polities. In the wide field of West African kingdoms we may refer to Kom, Gonja and Jukun.[58] Examples in central Africa are the *ibaam* council of the Kuba; the *olusenje* council in Mbailundu (Angola); the Ndembu *ayilolu*; the Lamba *bena milenda*; the Bisa *bantungwa* or *bamushika*; the Namwanga *amalongwe*; the Fipa *ataambikwa*; and the Nyiha *awahombe*. Cunnison's remarks on the *bakaLunda* of Kazembe are also appropriate to the *bakabilo* of Chitimukulu:

> They are the owners (*bene*) of the kingship but yet they are under the authority of the king. . . . If the king errs, then the aristocrats fear for the kingship because of the king in office. . . . The final sanction is in a sort of alliance between the living aristocrats and the spirits of the dead Kazembes, who have a considerable power over the king. . . . [59]

In all these cases the 'stake-holders' are commoners, or at least ineligible for the kingship. At the same time, several of the polities cited, including of course that of the Bemba, are what Lloyd has called royal aristocracies. In his discussion of such systems, Lloyd assumes that royals not only occupy most political offices but also have 'control of rituals' as well as control over the appointment of rulers. He thus predicates a basis antithesis between an all-powerful 'ruling class' and a 'dominated commoner class' which may even reject the ideology of its rulers.[60]

[55] These remarks on the *bakabilo* apply also to the Chimba title, and to some extent to the royal undertaker, Shimwalule: see above, pp. 15–16.

[56] *African Political Systems*, pp. 11, 19

[57] Goody, *Succession to High Office*, pp. 10–12

[58] Forde and Kaberry, *West African Kingdoms*, pp. 135, 201; Michael W. Young 'The Divine Kingship of the Jukun', *Africa*, 1966, 36, ii, pp. 135–53 (especially pp. 146–7).　　　[59] Cunnison, *Luapula Peoples*, pp. 169, 173

[60] Lloyd, 'Political Structure', p. 106

But this is clearly not necessarily a characteristic of royal aristocracies. For when their stake-holders are commoners, the integrity of the kingdom is promoted: commoners are given a particular interest in the kingship, for they can arbitrate and manipulate the rivalries of different royals. And as Richards has observed, a group of 'neutral arbitrators' to determine royal succession is of special value wherever there are likely to be several potential heirs.[61] This point is clearly illustrated by Garbett's study of spirit-mediums among the Kore-Kore of Rhodesia.[62] Furthermore, for a matrilineal dynasty, such as that of Chitimukulu, the 'neutral arbitrators' may have an additional value: for a period, at least, increasing their ranks can be one way of giving authority and prestige to the sons of paramounts who could not succeed their fathers.

Not only, however, were the Bemba *bakabilo* neutral arbitrators, ineligible for the kingship; they also stood somewhat apart from the political structure as a whole. For unlike the Lunda aristocrats, who were territorial governors, and unlike the councillors who chose the Lozi kings, the *bakabilo* had no special executive roles, and thus no special power bases, other than those of village headmen. They were not themselves chiefs, but advisers of chiefs and guardians of chieftainship.[63] Their very lack of executive power enhanced their political influence, in that it increased their capacity for disinterested judgement. And while their positions were closely associated with the sources of Bemba power, they were not appointees of Chitimukulu but hereditary titleholders whose predecessors had occupied the same villages in the Bemba heartland since their titles had been created. Thus the senior *bakabilo* had good reason to speak of themselves as 'we, the Bemba'.[64]

In these respects, to be sure, the *bakabilo* are probably not unusual. But there is a further point which does perhaps distinguish them from their counterparts in many other African polities. They regulate succession not only to the paramountcy but also to the more senior

[61] Richards, 'African Kings', pp. 139–40

[62] G. Kingsley Garbett, 'Religious Aspects of Political Succession among the Valley Korekore (N. Shona)', in Stokes and Brown, *The Zambesian Past*, pp. 137–70 (especially pp. 152–6)

[63] It has been said that Makasa's 'power at the appointment [of Chitimukulu] is greater than that of the *Bakabilo*' (Brelsford, *Succession*, p. 34). This is not supported by any evidence from the nineteenth century, and I doubt whether Makasa could ever do more than publicly approve the choice made by the *bakabilo*. It is probable, however, that among the Tabwa Nsama's perpetual son Katele takes a leading part in the choice of a new Nsama (note of 1936 in Mporokoso DNB I, p. 120).   [64] Cf. Richards, 'Political System', p. 108

chieftainships for members of the royal clan. Thus not only do they constitute a corporate group of commoners counterposed to the kingship; they are counterposed to the exercise of power by the royal clan in general. They form a central, enduring and relatively disinterested source of political legitimation, not only for Lubemba, the royal domain, but for Bemba country as a whole. We may conclude that the continuity of the kingship, and the integrity of the kingdom, was promoted by thus articulating a clear distinction between an abiding *source* of political authority and the transience of all individual *use* of it. The integrative force of such a distinction may also be seen in the relationship between spirit-mediums and the Kore-Kore chiefdoms (whose organisation differs considerably from that of the Bemba).[65]

In theory, then, the *bakabilo* of Chitimukulu would appear to be an unusually strong force for stability and continuity in a kingdom strained by dynastic disputes and rapid expansion. It is, however, virtually impossible to show how far this was actually true in practice. The numbers and the prestige of these *bakabilo* were obviously effects as well as causes of political developments, though we know too little of the history of even the most important titles among them to demonstrate this in any detail. Over the past century the growing physical, secular power of Chitimukulu has undoubtedly intensified the inherent conflict between him and his *bakabilo*. A praise for Chitapankwa* asserts that he had no respect for ancestral shrines.[66] Richards heard that during the later nineteenth century one *kabilo*, a holder of the Munuca title, was blinded; another Munuca was deposed; and holders of the Chimba and Chitikafula titles were also humiliated.[67] But except for occasional references to *bakabilo* in connection with disputes over succession to the paramountcy,[68] there is little evidence as to the part they have played in determining relations between Bemba chiefs. And as Goody has observed, a succession dispute may well be resolved by a fait accompli rather than by formal election: this was

[65] Garbett, 'Religious Aspects'. Compare also the opposed but complementary roles of emperor and pope, or king and archbishop, in medieval Europe: the work of Prof. Walter Ullmann is especially relevant, e.g. *A History of Political Thought in the Middle Ages*, Penguin Books 1965.

[66] *Mukungula mfuba*: literally, 'who sweeps away the ancestral spirit-huts': Labrecque, 'Origines', p. 278

[67] Richards, 'Keeping the King Divine', p. 33. Labrecque says that Chitapankwa actually killed a Chimba ('Origines', p. 321), but this may be an exaggeration arising from the hostility between Chimba and Chitimukulu in the 1920s.

[68] See above, pp. 102–4 and 128–9, for the coups of Chileshye and Chitapankwa.

evidently true of the accession of Makumba*.[69] For want of adequate evidence, the role of the *bakabilo* in maintaining the integrity of the Bemba polity must remain something of an enigma.[70]

Whatever their actual influence, the *bakabilo* of Chitimukulu were the only Bemba corporate group functioning at a tribal or national, and not merely local, level. There was no group of executive officials directly under Chitimukulu, drawn from all over Bembaland and enforcing his will throughout the country; nor was there any council of chiefs or their deputies representing different parts of the country. Where such centralised institutions arose in pre-colonial Africa, the circumstances seem in one way or another to have varied considerably from those obtaining among the Bemba. Either the ecological base of the political structure was very different, or else the political structure owed its form not to endogenous development so much as to the implantation—whether through conquest or imitation—of a type of organisation which had originally evolved elsewhere.

The most striking examples of centralised and quasi-bureaucratic political systems in East and central Africa during the nineteenth century are the kingdoms of the Ganda and Lozi.[71] In Buganda, most of the territorial chiefs were not hereditary; they were chosen by the king on the basis of ability and loyalty rather than birth, and if they fell from favour they were liable to instant dismissal. The same was largely true of the numerous state officials without special territorial responsibilities—the prime minister, the treasurer, the military leaders, the roving inspectorate. The king was no mere *primus inter pares*; he stood at the apex of an administrative structure for the kingdom as a whole, which permeated and dominated the local administrations. The Lozi kingdom was unified on a non-territorial basis by a council composed largely of non-hereditary titleholders. Some were political and judicial officials; others organised the levy of tribute, in labour and kind. Some were overseers to hereditary chiefs in outlying parts of the kingdom, but in general their territorial spheres of action were dispersed and overlapped. As a rule, they were not associated with any one part of the kingdom, and their peregrinations enabled them to keep a check on each other.

[69] Goody, *Succession to High Office*, p. 12; see above, p. 260.

[70] Richards describes two meetings of *bakabilo* in the 1930s: 'Conciliar System', pp. 115–25.

[71] Cf. Martin Southwold, *Bureaucracy and Chiefship in Buganda*, Kampala 1961); L. A. Fallers, 'Social Stratification in Traditional Buganda', in Fallers, *The King's Men*, pp. 64–116; Gluckman, 'The Lozi', in Colson and Gluckman, *Seven Tribes*, especially pp. 1–14, 31–55

In both Buganda and the Lozi kingdom, political structure was closely related to the local ecology. In both cases, the environment facilitated the production of a sizeable food surplus, enough to sustain a relatively large group of non-food-producing specialists in government and war. The key factor in Buganda was the banana, which in various forms thrives around the western shores of Lake Victoria. The prosperity and coherence of the Lozi kingdom was founded on the alluvial soils of a flood plain on the upper Zambezi, which made possible stable, intensive cereal agriculture and thus also a busy trade with the surrounding woodland. Furthermore, as Colson has noted, the fertility of land in Buganda and the Lozi kingdom meant that land was valued as a good in itself. A given area might be productive, not just for two or three years out of ten, but for many years in succession. At the same time, land had scarcity value: in Buganda, because the ecology supported an unusually dense population in relation to the cultivable land; in the Lozi kingdom, because the fertile flood plain constituted a limited part of the kingdom as a whole.

> It was possible for the king to reward his followers with the grant of landed estates without at the same time transferring to them full political rights over the occupants of the land. It was also possible for him to set aside estates as permanent endowments for the support of national offices. The grading of offices in the administrative hierarchy could be maintained over the years since it was supported by the allocation of stable units of land rather than the loyalties of subjects. Estates could be scattered throughout the kingdom rather than concentrated in a single area. Thus the risk of creating a territorial focus for the power of any great official based on a body of localized supporters was minimized. Officials remained bound to the service of the state.[72]

Thus among both the Ganda and Lozi the local ecology made possible the emergence of centralised state structures based on appointive rather than hereditary office. These developments were clearly exceptional. But in a few other parts of East and central Africa a variety of special circumstances favoured at least a tendency towards more centralised government and away from recruitment to office on the basis of kinship. In the uplands of what is now eastern Zambia, the Ngoni of

[72] Elizabeth Colson, 'The role of bureaucratic norms in African political structures', in *Systems of political control and bureaucracy in human societies*, ed V. F. Ray, Proceedings of the . . . American Ethnological Society, Seattle, 1958, pp. 45–6

Mpezeni maintained during the later nineteenth century a territorial organisation in which there was much scope for promotion on the basis of merit rather than birth. The Ngoni political system, like that of the Bemba, was segmentary in structure: territory was distributed among royals, and conquest tended ultimately to increase their power at the expense of the paramount. But though the political system was prone to fission, this weakness was partly offset by the quasi-national basis of Ngoni military organisation, derived from the Zulu, whereby age-regiments recruited members from all over the country and promoted them on the basis of military skill.[73] And while the local ecology afforded no such special advantages as were present in Buganda and the Lozi kingdom, it was certainly more favourable than in many other parts of central Africa. In the first place, Mpezeni's Ngoni had chosen to settle in country that was fairly free of tsetse-fly, so that they were able to breed and keep cattle. In theory, all cattle belonged to the paramount, and though in practice cattle were dispersed throughout the state, political office carried with it rights to the control of cattle; they constituted wealth which could be used by the paramount's subordinates to further his own interests.[74] Moreover, the heartland of Mpezeni's kingdom was relatively fertile. Maize flourished there and had probably been the staple since the early nineteenth century. The average carrying capacity of Mpezeni's country was between 25 and 30 persons per square mile as against between a mere 5 and 10 on the north-eastern plateau. For a time, this made possible a high density of population. And while many were mobile and non-cultivating warriors, these were supported by levies on local maize surpluses as well as plunder further afield.[75]

Yet another type of political centralisation was achieved in an environment much more similar to that of the Bemba than those of the Ganda, Lozi or Ngoni. In the woodland of western Tanzania, the scattered and semi-nomadic Kimbu were for long organised in a multitude of small chiefdoms. Upon these, in the later nineteenth century, the Nyamwezi warlord Nyungu ya Mawe imposed a relatively unified and durable structure of appointed territorial deputies.[76] This achievement, as also the more fragile military hegemony of Nyungu's contemporary Mirambo, owed something to the example of the northernmost Ngoni, while Mirambo at least appears to have

---

[73] Barnes, *Politics in a Changing Society*, pp. 62–3   [74] *Ibid.*, pp. 31, 132–4
[75] Trapnell, *Soils*, pp. 35, 99–100; Barnes, *Politics in a Changing Society*, p. 232
[76] A. E. M. Shorter, 'Nyungu-ya-Mawe and the "Empire of the Ruga-Rugas"', *JAH*, 1968, 9, pp. 235–59; idem, *Chiefship in Western Tanzania*, Oxford 1972

benefited from the spread of American crops.[77] But the rise of both leaders was made possible by the very fact that the conquered chiefdoms were so small and disunited. In both these cases, centralisation can be seen as the result, not of internal political change, but of action by an external imperial power more or less free of the constraints of local traditions.

Among the Bemba, neither internal economic conditions nor external influence and interference were such as to induce radical political change. By contrast with the Kimbu, or indeed with their own neighbours, the Bemba had gradually evolved a relatively large-scale political organisation or a hereditary basis, and this enabled them to withstand the Ngoni. Thus there was no question of change through conquest; yet there is no evidence that the Bemba experience of the Ngoni provoked them to imitate Ngoni military organisation.[78] And despite the enlargement of Bemba horizons in the nineteenth century, economic change was not so extensive as to bring about a radical restructuring of Bemba political organisation. We may indeed discern the beginnings of a trend towards appointive rather than hereditary office, among the Bemba as among other African societies whose economic and military capacity was diversified through increased contact with the outside world.[79] War-leaders and the commanders of sections in the large capitals of the later nineteenth century were chosen by their chiefs on the basis of merit and loyalty rather than birth. And there was increasing need of 'specialists' such as ivory-hunters and store-house keepers.[80] But while this trend could be observed in the capitals of the more powerful chiefs, it did not involve the creation of truly central institutions or agents of government. Long-distance trade reinforced rather than transformed traditional political ties. New food crops were adopted, but millet remained the only staple, and food surpluses were obtained by raiding rather than by cultivation. The overall population density remained very low, probably between 5 and 10 persons per square mile. Much of the population might be concentrated around the capitals of chiefs, but a village of a thousand people was exceptional.[81] The subjects of Chitimukulu were unevenly dispersed over a very large area, which impeded communication. It was difficult to mobilise large numbers of

---

[77] Roberts, 'Nyamwezi Trade', pp. 62–3   [78] Cf. below, Appendix 3

[79] Cf. Roberts, 'Political Change in the Nineteenth Century' in Kimambo and Temu, *History of Tanzania*; Forde and Kaberry, *West African Kingdoms*.

[80] See above, pp. 166, 168, 170; Richards, *Land, Labour and Diet*, p. 148.

[81] Cf. above, pp. 165–6, 211–12

men for war, or to support very many specialists in war and government. Transferable wealth remained very limited, for land had little intrinsic value while it was difficult to maintain cattle in any quantity. It thus seems impossible to accept Stevenson's contention that the Bemba developed a 'state' during the nineteenth century and that this was in part due to a marked rise in population.[82] If a positive correlation, such as Stevenson attempts, is to be made between high population density and centralised government, the Bemba would seem to support it in a quite opposite fashion to his argument. All the evidence suggests that, in an area of rather low population density, the Bemba polity remained fundamentally decentralised and exhibited few of the characteristics of a 'state'.

There is, indeed, some reason to suppose that the Bemba polity had reached the limits of territorial extent and internal cohesion possible in a physical and cultural environment such as theirs. And it may well be asked whether the Bemba polity would have maintained for long such cohesion as it developed during the nineteenth century. The question is not merely hypothetical: major internal conflicts dominated Bemba politics for more than a decade before British arms became a factor. The measure of unity achieved under Chitapankwa* did not outlast his death. Sampa's* sphere of influence was much more limited, and he was more or less constantly at war with one or other of his close kin among the *bena ŋandu*.[83] While this was partly due to Sampa's* personality, there were also structural pressures making for decentralisation. It might be argued that although, in the short run, conquest and long-distance trade increased political integration among the Bemba, in the long run they exerted a divisive influence. The rapid expansion of the polity inevitably strained its capacity for long-distance communication: the elaboration of kinship links between chiefs could not indefinitely compensate for the very limited technology at their disposal. Moreover, in the Bemba situation, long-distance trade tended to favour chiefs in border areas at the expense of those nearer the centre, since the latter were unable to prevent other chiefs from sharing in such trade. Chiefs with access to long-distance trade might even prefer to forgo the prestige which promotion to a more senior post

[82] Robert F. Stevenson, *Population and political systems in tropical Africa*, New York, 1968, pp. 88–114. Stevenson's demographic speculations are based on an uncritical use of very meagre evidence, while his political typology takes no account of work in this field since *African Political Systems*; indeed, he appears to concede its inadequacy in a footnote (*op. cit.*, p. 244).

[83] See above, pp. 216–29.

might carry. This may have been one factor in the refusal of Mwamba II Chileshye Kapalaula to become Chitimukulu when Bwembya* was deposed (in the early 1860s); more certainly, it accounts for the refusal of Ponde, in the far north, to succeed as Nkolemfumu in 1883/4, while it may be significant that Ponde's elder brother Chikwanda II was equally eligible for this post, yet did not leave his newly-won territory in the far south.[84]

The increasing power of subordinate chiefs in relation to Chitimukulu did not, of course, result in more or less uncoordinated struggles between autonomous rulers. Such a development may indeed be observed in the dynastic history of Burundi, which bears some resemblance to that of the Bemba. In the earlier nineteenth century, the Rundi king Ntare II made many conquests and ceded some of them to his sons, some of whom also took over areas formerly ruled by chiefs of non-royal descent. But Ntare did not develop other means of binding together his greatly enlarged kingdom, while his own territorial base continued to consist only of dispersed estates. He died in about 1850 and was succeeded by one of his younger sons, Mweezi II, only after a succession war and a regency. Some of Mweezi's brothers became virtually independent, and the discrepancy between their large territories and Mweezi's own scattered and much smaller domains resulted in intermittent warfare which lasted into the present century.[85]

Among the Bemba, by contrast, the distribution of conquered territory among close relatives of the paramount resulted in the emergence of one chieftainship in particular—that of Mwamba—as a rival to the paramountcy. This development can partly be explained by the fact that the rise to power of a single royal lineage among the Bemba took place more gradually than the achievement of territorial power by Rundi royals. Mwamba's chiefdom, Ituna, was the first to be created for close relatives of Chitimukulu, and from the outset the post was almost invariably held by a brother of the reigning Chitimukulu. This both reflected and confirmed its pre-eminence over all older chieftainships other than the paramountcy itself. The position of Ituna on the western borders of Bembaland enabled its chief to profit from the declining power of Kazembe and from the establishment

---

[84] See above, pp. 129, 220. We may also note that after the British occupation, which deprived border areas of such special value, Ponde moved to Lubemba (above, p. 291).

[85] J. Vansina, 'Notes sur l'histoire de Burundi', *Aequatoria*, 1961, 24, pp. 1–10; J. Vansina, *La Légende du Passé* (1972), ch. 6. Arab raids and Hutu revolts were also factors in the disintegration of Burundi in the late nineteenth century.

of East African traders between Lakes Tanganyika and Mweru. As a result, Mwamba II already enjoyed an extensive sphere of influence by the time other royals closely related to Chitimukulu (e.g. Nkula Mutale Sichansa and Chikwanda II) began to obtain chiefdoms for themselves in the 1870s. Thus when, in the reigns of Sampa* and Makumba*, the sphere of Chitimukulu's influence contracted, the result was not simply to make outlying chiefs more independent; this decline was partly due to Mwamba's pre-eminence, and it also increased his scope for extending it still further.

It has been suggested, in view of Mwamba's great power in the late nineteenth century, that the Bemba polity may have been in danger of breaking up: indeed Richards has remarked that Mwamba III was showing signs of secession.[86] But there seems no good evidence for this; on the contrary, it is clear that Mwamba III not only tried to succeed Sampa* but that, even when frustrated in this ambition, he sought to make his influence paramount throughout eastern as well as western Bembaland, nominating a new Shimwalule in the process.[87] These efforts were, of course, cut short by the death of Mwamba III in 1898, but they testify strongly to a continuing interest in remaining within the polity. As Werbner points out

> First, Mwamba III had a stake in exercising control in his own office and in not only wielding but also extending his own and his bonded men's power over territories, men and resources. Second, he had a stake in king-making and in wielding influence over the ruler of Chitimukulu's dominions.[88]

These considerations, as much as reverence for the authority of the *bakabilo*, would have restrained Mwamba from secession. A somewhat analogous situation may be observed in the Shambaa kingdom of north-eastern Tanzania: there, in the late 1860s, the most powerful chief was a king's son, Semboja, whose base was at the foot of the Usambara hills, on a trade route to the coast. Semboja defeated and killed a king, but he declined to take the kingship himself, since this would have meant leaving the trade route for the royal capital in the hills. Yet he had no wish to break away from the old kingdom; instead, he sought to

---

[86] 'African Kings', p. 147

[87] See above, pp. 271–2. Richards cites the story that Mwamba III 'refused to succeed to the Chitimukuluship because he said his own post was equal in authority' ('African Kings', p. 147); as we have seen, this is derived from Mwamba's chief councillor, Milambo (see above, p. 261, n. 31).

[88] Werbner, 'Federal Administration', p. 39

exercise control over its affairs by having his own son made king.[89]

If there was never likely to be secession from the Bemba polity, there were nonetheless tensions within it which would undoubtedly have provoked continuing internal change. To be sure, we cannot say just what course this would have taken had British rule not put an end to wars of succession and conquest. But the dynastic history of the Bemba in the present century indicates the kind of change which might have taken place, and it helps to bring the events of the nineteenth century into clearer focus. The continuing hold on the paramountcy by descendants of the sister of Mukuuka* created as many problems as it solved. As this group multiplied in the course of time, it comprised an increasing number of royals who all had better claims to the paramountcy than members of any other royal line. Competition between rival branches of this dominant line supplanted the competition between rival lineages which characterised the eighteenth century. This ever-growing field of competition had to be restricted if there was not to be a return to the extensive dynastic rivalry of the eighteenth century. Thus throughout the nineteenth and twentieth centuries the descendants of all but a few royal women have been progressively excluded from succession to the paramountcy. On the other hand, among the descendants of Mukuuka's* sister, succession has not been confined to the male offspring of a single line of royal women. Thus Chileshye* became Chitimukulu even though his mother's mother was a sister of his predecessor's mother. During the next three reigns, the paramountcy was held by descendants of Chileshye's* elder sister. Makumba*, a son of his younger sister, succeeded in 1898, but when he died in 1911 there was no question of allowing the paramountcy to continue in this junior line; instead, it reverted to Chikwanda*, a descendant of Chileshye's* elder sister—thus traversing the same genealogical distance as at Chileshye's* own accession. Thereafter, the paramountcy has been confined to descendants of two sisters of Chitapankwa* and Sampa.*

This has also, of course, affected appointments to other chieftainships. The details are given by Brelsford;[90] only a summary is needed here. In the present century, royal chieftainships have largely been in the hands of two lines within the dominant branch of the royal clan. Members of one line—the descendants of Mukukamfumu II Kasonde —have monopolised succession to the posts of Chandamukulu, Mwamba and Nkolemfumu, while the first four Mpepos also came

---

[89] Steven Feierman, 'The Shambaa', in Roberts, *Tanzania before 1900*, p. 11
[90] *Succession*

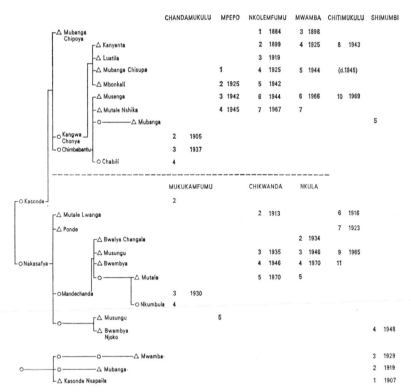

Fig. 17 Bemba royal chieftainships, twentieth century. Dates on the right of each column are those of death or transfer. Chitimukulus numbered from Chileshye; Nkulas from Mutale Sichansa; Chandamukulus from Chilufya Mulenga.

from this line. Members of the other line—the descendants of Nakasafya—have monopolised succession to the posts of Mukukamfumu, Nkula and Chikwanda. They obtained the Shimumbi title from the remote line which produced the first three Shimumbis, and though this title then passed to the rival line, the latter lost the Mpepo title to the line of Nakasafya. As for the paramountcy, this has twice been obtained by holders of the Mwamba title (Kanyanta*, Musenga*), and four times by members of the other line (Chikwanda*, Ponde*, Musungu*, Bwembya*).

We may thus observe the emergence in the present century of two distinct groups of royals. Not only have they both competed successfully for the paramountcy; they have gained and retained control of certain subordinate chieftainships. To this extent, they have both developed identifiable local ties: the line of Mukukamfumu I (and

321

Mwamba) has entrenched itself north of the Chambeshi (on its right bank), while the line of Nakasafya (and Nkula) has similarly entrenched itself south of the Chambeshi (on its left bank). In recent disputes over succession to the paramountcy the two groups have clearly exhibited a sense of corporate identity and common interest against one another.[91] It is true that the integrity of Bembaland has been promoted by the possibility of promotion from one royal chieftainship to another. It is also true that 'the circulation of princes prevented the development of localised descent lines'.[92] Such circulation is in fact essentially a phenomenon of the twentieth century. But it should be noted that in so far as Bembaland as a whole has been united by competition for office this has only taken place at the highest level, that is, competition for the paramountcy. In all other respects, there have been not one but two major fields for promotion, in two distinct royal lines. And though indeed this has still inhibited the emergence of localised descent lines, the two main groups of royals do have specific geographical ties and interests.

These developments, of course, have taken place under the constraints of colonial and post-colonial rule. If Bemba raiding and conquest had continued, and if force had continued to be a factor in internal politics, there might well have been quite other results. Nonetheless, this glimpse into recent history serves to illuminate the problems which would have continued to face Bemba rulers even had they remained independent. And though we can only guess at the solutions which they might have reached, we can see that they might well have involved, if not secession, then perhaps civil war on a territorial as well as dynastic basis. There might have been some return to competition for the paramountcy among a number of more or less distant lines. One means of accommodating such competition would be a regular order of alternation or rotation: indeed, the last four appointments to the paramountcy are evidence of alternation in practice, if not in principle.[93] The reasons for these particular decisions, recent though they are, are not wholly clear to me, but they were not directly

[91] *Succession*, pp. 24–5; NAZ/Sec/Nat 184–5

[92] Richards, 'African Kings', p. 147

[93] Alternating succession in the Namwanga chieftainship, and in those both of the southern Mambwe (Nsokolo) and the northern Mambwe in Tanzania, seems also to be essentially a phenomenon of the twentieth century, due perhaps to common external constraints. Cf. Willis, *Fipa*, p. 34; Aaron Sichivula, 13 June 1965; W. B. Tripe, 'A curious form of chiefly succession in Mambwe-Nyanda, Ufipa District', *Tanganyika Notes and Records*, 1939, 7, pp. 88–91.

influenced by the wishes of the government,[94] and they appear to reflect not simply genealogical seniority but also the distribution of power within the royal clan. The very fact that many chiefdoms have come to be identified with one or other of two distinct lines of royals has rendered it politic to allow both lines a continuing right at least to the highest office of all.

This review of dynastic tensions among the Bemba invites the question how far their history bears out interpretations of African political history in terms of repetitive, cyclical development. It has been suggested by two historians that much African history 'runs through very short-term cycles of expansion and contraction, like the heaving of a diaphragm'.[95] This impression may appear to be supported by the observations of anthropologists. Most African kingdoms were based on hereditary but indeterminate succession. Social systems of this kind are susceptible to recurrent crises as the number of potential heirs increases in the course of time and competition for office intensifies. In such systems there is an inherent predisposition to enact a repetitive cycle of conflict. Gluckman, indeed, has argued that any institution has a specific time scale built into it: it requires a certain period of time, which Barnes has called its 'structural duration', to work out the implications of its rules and customs in their local setting.[96] In the case of many African polities where dynastic conflict was usually resolved by secession, the structural duration was often very short, sometimes no more than two generations.[97]

The Bemba polity, based as it was on hereditary but indeterminate succession, was clearly subject to the same kind of recurrent tensions

[94] For the succession 1944–6 see Willis Enquiry (1924); Brelsford, *Succession*, pp. 24–6. In 1966 President Kaunda had to remind local officials of the United National Independence Party that the choice of a new Chitimukulu should be left to the traditional Bemba authorities (cf. *Times of Zambia*, 15 September 1966). See also R. P. Werbner, 'Constitutional Ambiguities and the British Administration of Royal Careers among the Bemba of Zambia', *Studies in the Anthropology of Law*, ed L. Nalder (forthcoming).

[95] Robinson and Gallagher, 'The Partition of Africa', p. 618

[96] Max Gluckman, 'The Utility of the Equilibrium Model in the Study of Social Change', *American Anthropologist*, 1968, 70, ii, pp. 220–1

[97] Cf. above, p. 296. For clear examples of repetitive cycles of secession see E. E. Evans-Pritchard, 'The Zande State', *JRAI*, 1963, 93, i, pp. 134–54; I. Schapera, 'Kinship and Politics in Tswana History', *JRAI*, 1963, 93, ii, pp. 159–73. Schapera takes exception (*ibid.*, p. 165) to Richards' remark that 'the survival rate of African kingdoms is inevitably low' ('African Kings', p. 136): Richards evidently had in mind their structural duration rather than their historical duration.

as other, less successful polities. And though these tensions did not split the Bemba polity apart, Gluckman at one time argued that they did provoke a recurrent cycle of events in Bemba history:

> At the beginning of the rule of a new lineage, the chiefs are close relatives of the king and in the direct legal line of succession to the kingship. Within three or four generations one junior branch . . . drifts away from the main line, and loses the legal right of succession, by genealogical position, to the kingship. They then assert that they have the right—on one or other alternative 'legal' ground—and are prepared to fight for the throne with their people's support. If the senior branch wins, presumably it would depose the junior branch from all its seats of power; if the junior branch wins, the senior man in it presumably becomes king and gives his close relatives the big subordinate posts. All the main seats of power are now again held by one small family, and all the sub-chiefs are again in the direct line of succession to the throne. I am prepared to assert that the process now begins again as a repetitive cycle in Bemba history.[98]

The present study, however, indicates that Bemba history followed a rather different course from that depicted in the literature available to Gluckman. Gluckman explicitly says:

> We have assumed on the evidence of the chart [Goodall's genealogy as abbreviated by Brelsford], that when Chileshe seized the kingship, he expelled the close relatives of his predecessor from the big territorial chieftainships, and placed there his own close relatives . . . all the big titles were held by men who clearly had the right of succession to the kingship.[99]

But this assumption involves telescoping what in fact appears to have been the sequence of events, as well as misapprehending the situation under Chileshye's* predecessor Chinchinta*. Only one close relative of Chinchinta* had a chiefdom of any size (Ituna); besides, there was no comprehensive reassignment of chiefdoms under Chileshye* but only the beginning of a process continued by Chitapankwa*. As figure 7 shows, at the time of Chileshye's* death Mwamba was the only chief who was a close matrilineal relative of Chitimukulu. (Shimumbi was the son of a female parallel cousin.) Mwamba had displaced the old Nkolemfumu lineage, but no new chief was appointed to that post. By the death of Chitapankwa*, both Nkula and Nkolemfumu

[98] Gluckman, 'Succession and Civil War', pp. 22–3   [99] *Ibid.*, p. 20

had been taken over by nephews of Chitimukulu, while two other nephews, Chikwanda II and Ponde, had taken over newly conquered territory; and early in Sampa's* reign a small area was given to Mpepo I, the son of a niece of Sampa*. But even at this late date Nkweto and Mwaba remained under the control of lineages long distinct from the dominant line. Thus it was only towards the end of the nineteenth century that one lineage began to hold enough posts to make possible the kind of recurrent crisis envisaged by Gluckman.

It must also be recalled that the preponderance of a single royal lineage was achieved not simply by displacing older lines but by extending Bemba territory, creating new chiefdoms, and assigning some to sons of Chitimukulu and Mwamba. In the long view, the most significant phase in Bemba dynastic history is not (as several writers have assumed) the accession of Chileshye*, but the reigns of Chileshye's* predecessors Mukuuka* and Chiliamafwa*, for these rulers consolidated the hold of a single royal lineage on the paramountcy while creating one new chiefdom for royals (Ituna) and another (Mpanda) for sons of Chitimukulu. The fact that so little now is known about these developments should not be allowed to obscure their great importance as innovations, which were followed up by Chileshye*, his brother Mwamba I and their successors. As Werbner has pointed out, if one concentrates, as Gluckman did, on the distribution of power within the royal clan alone, 'one is tempted to fit into "the developmental cycle of a lineage" what are political processes within a bilateral kinship group'.[100] This wider distribution of power was, as we have seen, intimately related to the involvement of the Bemba in a particular historical process—the irruption of the East African ivory trade and slave trade during the middle and later nineteenth century. Finally, it was only in the present century, in the context of this new political structure, and in the unprecedented conditions of subordination to an external power, that there eventually emerged two distinct and opposed groups of royals, identified with different parts of Bemba country.

Bemba history, in short, is not, so far as we can tell, any more cyclical in character than the history of better known kingdoms; it exhibits instead a non-repetitive development, a series of different responses to ever-changing internal and external conditions. It is, to be sure, clear enough that in a closed system, and given the conditions (rules of succession etc.) postulated by Gluckman, there might well have been a recurrent crisis. In reality, however, political systems are never closed, and in so far as there are repetitive features these tend to

[100] Werbner, 'Federal Administration', p. 40

325

produce spiral rather than cyclical patterns of change.[101] Any form of endogenous change within a system is likely to affect its susceptibility to influence by external factors. And in the case of large-scale political systems, such as kingdoms, factors external to the system are especially likely to induce change, since there are few or no larger systems within which such external influences can be regulated and moderated. It is the kingdom itself which is most susceptible to external change, since by definition it represents one social system against the outside world. Hence the histories of kingdoms in Africa, no less than elsewhere, are likely to display not cyclical but cumulative and irregular change. In a recent work, Gluckman has suggested that 'Regions of Africa have probably displayed what can be called an oscillating equilibrium between a large state holding together a while and a number of smaller states'; he adds that only economic exchange—whether in the form of external trade or internal differentiation—can promote a more permanent kind of authority.[102] It is noteworthy that Gluckman speaks of an equilibrium with respect to regions rather than to societies or states: in this statement at least there is no claim that the history of particular social structures displays equilibrium.[103] And in any case, the proviso regarding the effects of economic exchange would seem to apply to many places and periods in African history. The task of the historian, if not also the anthropologist, must be to analyse the interaction of non-repetitive processes of economic or political change with the pressures for repetitive change within political systems; he will then appreciate the means by which some dynasties contrived to transcend their inherent tendencies to short-term cyclical development. The history of the Bemba shows clearly how in practice a polity based on principles of kinship could nonetheless undergo continuous, non-repetitive structural change over a period of at least two centuries.

[101] Discussing the limitations of 'equilibrium models', Lloyd writes: 'The *status quo ante* can never be fully restored, for at the very least, each series of events creates new precedents which will influence future events': 'Conflict Theory and Yoruba Kingdoms', *History and Social Anthropology*, ed I. M. Lewis, London 1968, p. 57.

[102] Max Gluckman, *Politics, Law and Ritual in Tribal Society*, Oxford 1965, pp. 143–4

[103] Thus with reference to Zulu history Gluckman writes, 'The political field from at least 1400 until about 1800 can be analysed as being an actual state of stable equilibrium (in stasis). It was composed of many tribes . . .' ('Equilibrium Model', pp. 232–3). That is to say, the equilibrium is to be found in the underlying, long-enduring patterns of relationships within a large-scale system comprising individually unstable and transient small-scale components.

Appendices

1 Tables (a) Outline Chronology   328
            (b) Bemba chiefs, showing areas occupied and former
                rulers   338
            (c) Census figures for Bemba country, early twentieth
                century; Note on Labour Migration   342

2 Supplementary Notes   344
            A. Insignia of Bemba chieftainship   344
            B. Clichés in legends of 'tribal' origin   346
            C. The crossing at Matanda's   347
            D. The 'Bemba' north of Lake Mweru   348
            E. The early history of Makasa   349
            F. Chileshye Chepela's visit to Kazembe 351
            G. The displacement of Chimbola   352
            H. The burial of Chinchinta   353
            J. The Bemba, Kamanga and Ngonde   354
            K. Chileshye* and Chewe   356
            L. The Bemba and the Lungu of Tafuna 357
            M. The Chibwa salt industry   359
            N. The later history of the displaced Chewe lineage 361

3 The Bemba and the Ngoni   363

4 Select Historical Texts   377
            (i) Chief Nkweto Mulenga: The foundation of chief-
                tainships   378
            (ii) Chileshye Mukulu: The accession of Chileshye* 381
            (iii) Njalamimba: Mwamba II and the Tabwa 382

5 List of Informants   384

6 List of Written Sources   390

Appendix 1 (a) OUTLINE CHRONOLOGY OF BEMBA HISTORY AND RELATED EVENTS

(N.B. The dating and sequence of some incidents is conjectural, based on arguments presented in the text.)

Date	Internal Bemba politics	Bemba external relations	Events elsewhere	Date
?mid-17th cent.	Chilufya* est. as Chitimukulu on Kalungu river *Bena yandu* achieve predominance in Lubemba, Chilinda, Ichinga		Kazembe II founds kingdom on lower Luapula	c. 1740
later 18th cent.	fl. Katongo*; Mukuuka* Ituna chiefdom created Bemba still confined N. and E. of Lukulu/Chambeshi confluence Mubanga Kashampupo succeeds in Ituna	Mubanga Kashampupo receives gun from Kazembe III	Bisa trading between Kazembe's and lower Zambezi region Extensive Bisa chiefdoms in Lubumbu and under Mukungule Eastward campaigns by Kazembe III	later 18th cent.
?c. 1790	Accession of Chiliamafwa*		Lacerda's expedition to Kazembe	1798
early 19th cent.	Mpanda chiefdom created for Makasa	Bemba treaty with Mukupa Kaoma I of Malaila Lungu Munkonge I occupies Bisa country W. of Lukulu river Bemba seize country from Mambwe of Mpande	Kazembe IV campaigns against Chishinga, Mukulu and Bisa in Lubumbu	early 19th cent.

Date		Date	
?c. 1820	Accession of Chinchinta*		
c. 1827	Chinchinta* deposed by Chileshye*		Plague of locusts
1826–30	Bemba wars with Bisa of Kabanda, Kabinga and Mwansabamba Chikwanda I occupies Chinama; Kabwibwi I occupies Lupi		
		1831–2	Monteiro and Gamito's expedition to Kazembe
			Swahili traders at Kazembe's
?c. 1830	Mutale *wa kabwe* succeeds in Ituna and takes over Miti (he later becomes Mwamba I)		
1831–c. 1840	Bemba temporarily overrun or displace Bisa in Lubumbu, and Bena Mukulu, but then partly withdraw		
		1835	Zwangendaba's Ngoni cross Zambezi
?1830s	Lukonde Mwaba becomes Mukukamfumu I		
	Mukupa Kaoma II (Lungu) invades Ituna, but is repulsed and killed by Mwamba I and Chileshye*		
		1841/2	Nsama III (Tabwa) routs Arabs from Ujiji; they settle at Kazembe's
		c. 1845	Zwangendaba dies; Ngoni disperse from Ufipa
c. 1850	Bisa kill Chikwanda I; Bemba withdraw from Chinama		
	Ngoni (of Mpezeni and Mperembe kill Makasa I in Chilinda		
		1850s	Mpezeni moves south
	Makasa III occupies N. Chilinda		

Date	Internal Bemba politics	Bemba external relations	Events elsewhere	Date
1850		Mperembe invades Lubemba; repulsed by Chileshye*, he moves south and settles on Manshya river, whence Ngoni raid eastern Bemba, and Bisa in Chinama		1850s
		Bemba sell ivory to traders from Tabora	?Mpezeni raids Chinama	
			Msiri settles in Katanga	
late 1850s	Mwamba I dies in Iwa country			
c. 1860	Chileshye* dies	Munkonge II seizes country from Lungu of Chitoshi	Mpezeni crosses Luangwa and harasses Nsenga	c. 1860
early 1860s	Bwembya* deposed by Chitapankwa*	Mwamba II defeats alliance of Matipa I (Lubumbu) and Mukupa Kaoma III; Matipa retreats to L. Bangweulu Tungati I and other Bemba occupy Isansa, Masonde, Mukulu	Mperembe's Ngoni break up Bisa trade route to Kazembe's; move north from Manshya to Lungu, and briefly invade Itabwa	early 1860s
		Chitapankwa* seizes Chibundu from Kabanda	Nsama III defeats alliance between Kazembe VII and Arabs	
	Chitapankwa* gives Chibundu to his mother, who takes Chanda-mukulu title from Iyaya lineage			
1863/4		Tippu Tip first visits Bemba Bemba seize Isunga from Mungulube		
1866/7		Tippu Tip returns; visits Mwamba with Kumba-Kumba		

?c. 1867	Bemba conquer Munshimbwe (Lungu) and begin to settle west of Luombe river		
February 1867	Livingstone visits Chitapankwa* and Mwamba II	May 1867	Tippu Tip defeats Nsama III
?late 1860s	Succession disputes in Ichinga; Chitapankwa* kills Mwaba and instals Mande	?late 1860s	Mperembe's Ngoni settle at Ititini, among Mambwe
	Some Bemba flee north from Ichinga to Nyala		
	Sampa briefly occupies Ichinga but then moves to Ibwe		
	Mutale Sichansa becomes Nkula		
1869/70	Tippu Tip visits Chitapankwa*, Mwamba II, Nkula	1869/70	Tippu Tip goes west to Manyema, leaving Kumba-Kumba at depot in Itabwa
c. 1870	Chitapankwa* and Makasa III defeat Ngoni of Mperembe at Ititini, but he then seizes Makasa's capital Chitapankwa* and several other Bemba chiefs combine to expel Ngoni of Mperembe, who go east to Mbelwa's	c. 1870	
early 1870s	Bemba kill Mambwe chief Mpande, whose country is given to Changala		
	Mwamba II expels Matipa I from shore of Lake Bangweulu to islands; Shimumbi I takes over Lubumbu		
	Mukwikile I and Ndakala I displace Chinkumba and Chibesakunda		

Date	Internal Bemba politics	Bemba external relations	Events elsewhere	Date
1871/2	Makasa III dies			
September 1872		Chitapankwa* and Makasa IV besiege Zombe, but Lungu alliance routs Bemba	Kazembe VII Muonga killed by E. African traders	1872
		Mwamba II helps Kumba Kumba to defeat and kill Nsama IV, and Nsama V to succeed.		
c. 1875		Mporokoso I occupies S. Itabwa; Sunkutu invades Chishinga of Chama	Mukupa Katandula est. independent Tabwa chiefdom	1870s
1870s	Miti assigned to Mubanga Chipoya, who as Nkolemfumu	expels Kabinga from Mpuki	Nsama V killed by E. Africans	
?1870s		Mporokoso helps establish Nsama VI	Abdullah ibn Suliman stays briefly in Itabwa	
		Bemba begin to trade heavily in slaves		
1877		Chitapankwa* and Makasa IV repulsed by Namwanga		
		Chitapankwa* defeats Namwanga		
		Bemba ally with Kela and Mpenza (Mambwe)		
c. 1880		Bemba regain Chinama from Bisa; Chikwanda II installed	Mwansabamba (Kopa I) withdraws to Luangwa valley	early 1880s
		Chitapankwa* defeats (and kills?) Zombe. Ponde est. in Lungu country		

Date	Bemba events	Northeast Zambia events	Date	Regional events
1883 June October	Mwamba II dies Giraud visits Chitapankwa* Chitapankwa* dies	Smallpox epidemic in Northeast Zambia	1883	LMS build station at S. end of Lake Tanganyika
			1882–3	Livingstonia est. mission at Chirenji (closed 1888)
			1883/4	Abdullah ibn Suliman comes from Tabora and settles with Nyamwezi at Kabuta in Itabwa
1884	Sampa* succeeds Mwamba III occupies W. Lubemba and continues to rule Miti			
c. 1884	Matengele given to Chimbola	Mporokoso I and Mwamba III defeated by Nsama VI and Abdullah		
		Chikwanda I harasses Chitambo (Lala)	1884	ALC open trading post at Karonga
1880s	Mwamba III appoints Mpepo I in Mpuki; Menga I in Musoa		1886	Portuguese treaty with Lala Mlozi moves (from Itabwa?) to Karonga
May 1887		Nkula and Mwilwa defeated by Iwa	1887	LMS open mission at Fwambo's
October 1887		Ndakala I defeated by Senga and Mbelwa's Ngoni at Kabondwe		
late 1880s		Bemba begin to adopt guns on large scale Arabs settle on upper Luangwa for trade with E. Bemba Traders from Zambezi visit Chikwanda	1887–9	Mlozi at war with ALC

Date	Internal Bemba politics	Bemba external relations	Events elsewhere	Date
			Johnston's treaties between Lake Malawi and Lake Tanganyika	1889
?c. 1890	Mwamba III sends Luchembe I to Chinama	Bemba encroach on Nsokolo's (Mambwe) country		
			Sharpe makes treaties with Kazembe X, Nsama VI	1890
			ALC est. at Fife and Kituta	
c. 1890		Mwamba III's men help Kazembe X defeat Kaindu and Yeke; some Bemba settle near Kazembe's		
c. 1891		Mporokoso I and Abdullah kill Nsama VI		
		Luali conquers Chama (Chishinga)		
			Br. C. Africa Protectorate created	May 1891
			White Fathers settle at Mambwe	July 1891/2
			BSAC post est. on Lake Mweru	
July 1893		Sampa* and Makasa V routed by von Wissmann on the Kalambo		July 1893
			BSAC post est. at Abercorn	August
January 1894		White Fathers first visit Makasa V		January 1894
		Plague of locusts in eastern Africa		
June			LMS open Kambole mission	June
			Belgians defeat Nsemiwe and Masala	September
		Thomas (LMS) visits Ponde		
			Livingstonia est. mission at Mwenzo	1894–5

Date			Date	
1895		Sampa kills ALC messenger	1895	
c. 1895	Kanyanta becomes Nkolemfumu		June	BSAC takes over admin. of North-Eastern Rhodesia
		White Fathers found Kayambi mission	July	
				BSAC est. at Ikawa
		Ponde raids Chitimbwa (Lungu)	December	Johnston defeats Mlozi
		Sampa* raids across Songwe river	March–June 1896	Ndebele and Shona rebel in Southern Rhodesia
1896 May June	Sampa* dies	Mwamba III exchanges gifts with BSAC, Ikawa	April–July	BSAC intercept E. African caravans N. of Bemba
September	Nkula dies			
November		Dupont (W.F.) visits Makumba; Bell (BSAC) visits Mwalule	November	
December		Mwamba III invites visits from WFs, BSAC, ALC	December	
late 1896–early 1897	Mwamba III fights Makumba over Chitimukulu succession			
January 1897		Young (BSAC) visits Mwamba III	January 1897	
?March	Mwamba III allows accession of Makumba*			
April		Dupont (WF) visits Mwamba III	April	
?June–October June	Mwamba III occupies Mwalule Sampa* buried			
			August	BSAC est. post at Mirongo

Date	Internal Bemba politics	Bemba external relations	Events elsewhere	Date
1897 September		BSAC defeat Luangwa Arabs and Ndakala II		September
early 1898	Makumba* est. new capital			1898
May–June		Dupont visits Chikwanda II in Ichinga, and Makumba*		May–June
October	Mwamba III dies	Dupont visits Mwamba III		October
November		BSAC est. station near Mwamba's		November
March 1899		BSAC defeat Ponde		March 1899
		BSAC defeat Mporokoso and Arabs		April–May September
September	Kanyanta becomes Mwamba IV		BSAC occupy Kazembe's	October

Appendix 1(b) BEMBA CHIEFS, SHOWING AREAS OCCUPIED, AND FORMER RULERS

Bemba chief	Territory	Date of installation	Former ruler	Tribe	Later history of territory[1]
BWALYA	Itulo	1898	Chikwanda II		To Chikwanda, 1911
CHANDAMUKULU	Chibundu	1870s?	Kabanda	Bisa	To Nkolemfumu, c. 1941
CHANGALA	Cholwe (part of Mpanda)	?late 1860s	Makasa	Mambwe	To Makasa, 1944
	Maswepa	1870s	Mpande		Retroceded early 1900s
CHEWE	Ituntwe	c. 1900	?Nkula		To Nkula, 1935
CHIBANDA	Lubumbu (part)	?1870s	Shimumbi I		To Shimumbi, 1930
CHIKWANDA	Chinama	(i) c. 1830	Mwansabamba	Bisa	Part to Luchembe, early 1890s
		(ii) c. 1880			To Luchembe, 1890s
	Isamba		?Mwansabamba	Bisa	
	Itulo	1880s	Nkuka		To Bwalya, 1898
	Kasenga		Chitembo (under Mukungule)		To Lukaka, 1920s
	Chipindo (part of Mukumbi)				
CHILANGWA	Matengele	1870s	Mvula	Mambwe	To Chimbola, ?c. 1885
	Mambwe (part)	?late 1880s	Nsokolo	Mambwe	Retroceded, c. 1900
	Fibwe (part)	c. 1900	Ponde		To Makasa, 1944
CHIMBOLA	Matengele	?c. 1885	Chilangwa		
CHIPALO	Mukulu	1860s	Chikumbi	Mukulu	
CHIPUKULA	?	1870s	Mpande (and Nsokolo?)	Mambwe	Retroceded, c. 1897
CHISANGAPONDE	Fibwe (part)	?c. 1900	?Mfungo		To Chitimukulu, 1944
CHISANGULA	Maseba	late 19th cent.	Mwamba?		To Mwamba, late 1920s

Chiefdom	Area	Date	Chief	People	Disposition
FWANGILA	Tupempe (part of Mpanda)	?1840s	Makasa		To Makasa, 1930s
KABWIBWI	Lupi	1830s	Nkaka Kasela	Bisa	To Nkolemfumu, 1944
KALIMINWA	Lisunga	?c. 1890	Shibwalya Kapila		
KALULU	Lubumbu (part)	later 19th cent.	Shimumbi I		To Shimumbi, 1930
KASONKA	Mukulu	later 19th cent.	Chipalo		To Chipalo, 1937
LOMBE	Chilinda (part)	c. 1891	Mwilwa		To Mubanga, ?c. 1900
LUALI	Chishinga	c. 1890	Chama		Retroduced, 1941
LUCHEMBE	Mpuki (part)	c. 1890	Chyanika (under Nkolemfumu)		
	Chinama (part)	early 1890s	Chikwanda		
	Isamba	1890s			
LUKAKA[2]	Chipindo	1920s			To Mukwikile, 1946
MAKASA	Mpanda	early 19th cent.	Mwine Nsanso, Kavwinta	Mambwe	To Mwilwa, early 1870s
			Mwine Chilanga, Nkweto	Namwanga	To Mpepo, 1943
MASONGO	Chilinda (part)	?late 1840s	?		
MBIDIA[3]	Munbubu	c. 1880			
MENGA	Isangano	1910	Shimumbi		To Shimumbi, 1930
MFUNGO	Musoa	1890s	?Nkolemfumu		To Nkolemfumu, 1944
	Makalandu	?late 1880s		Mambwe	To Chisangaponde, c. 1941
MISENGO	Kasenga	?1880s	Mukupa Kaoma	Lungu	To Munkonge, 1946
MPEPO	Mpuki (part)	?c. 1890	Chyanika (under Nkolemfumu)		
MPOROKOSO	Maseba	1860s	Munshimbwe	Lungu	To Mwamba, 1880s
	Itabwa	c. 1875	Nsama	Tabwa	
	Isenga				

Bemba chief	Territory	Date of installation	Former ruler	Tribe	Later history of territory[1]
MUBANGA	Chunga Chilinda (part)	c. 1880 ?c. 1900	? Lombe	Namwanga	
MUCHEREKA	Masonde	1860s	Chinyimba	Bisa	To Chipalo, 1944
MUKWIKILE[4]	Chingoli Chimanabwe (part of Mutambe?) Chipindo (part of Mukumbi)	1870s c. 1900 1946	Chinkumba ?Nkula Lukaka	Bisa	Retroceded, c. 1900 To Nkula, 1946
MUNKONGE	Kalundu Bulungu (part)	?c. 1820 ?c. 1860	Muma Chalwe Chitoshi	Bisa Lungu	
MUSANYA	Chilinda (part)	?c. 1891	Mwilwa		To Nkweto, 1944
MWABA	Nkulungwe	?18th cent.	?		To Nkula, 1944
MWAMBA	Ituna Maseba	late 18th cent. 1880s	? Mporokoso		
MWILWA	Chilinda (part)	early 1870s	Makasa		To Lombe and Musanya, c. 1891
NDAKALA	Mutambe	1870s	Chibesakunda	Bisa	To Chifumo (and Nkula?), 1887; mostly retroceded, c. 1900
NKOLEMFUMU	Miti Mpuki (part)	? 1870s	? Kabinga	Bisa	To Chyanika; then to Mpepo and Luchembe, c. 190c
	Musoa	?1870s	Mubenshi	Bisa	To Mengai n 1890s

NKULA	Ichinga Isunga	? 1870s (occupied by Benba in 1860s)	? Mungulube	Bisa	To Mukwikile, c. 1900
	Chimanabwe Ichingo (part)	?1887 1890s	Ndakala Kabanda		Part to Makasa, late 1840s
NKWETO	Chilinda	?	?		Retroceded, early 1900s
PONDE* 1880s			Kasonso?	Lungu	To Kaliminwa, c. 1890
SHIBWALYA KAPILA	Lisunga	1870s	Mulumbwa	Lungu	
SHIMUMBI	Lubumbu Isangano	early 1870s ?	Matipa ?	Bisa Bisa	To Mbidia, 1910
SHIMWALULE	Mwalule	?	?		To Nkweto, 1944
SUNKUTU	Chikulu	?1870	Lushinga Chama	Lungu Chishinga	Retroceded, early 1900s To Mporokoso 1937
TUNGATI	Isansa	1860s	Chama	Bisa	

[1] The sources for amalgamations not mentioned in the text are Brelsford, *Aspects*, p. 5, and *Succession*, pp. 30, 32, 36–8, 40, 42–5.

[2] Lukaka, a son of Chikwanda II, was living in Itulo, under Bwalya, in about 1905 (Mpika DNB, II, p. 147). By 1930 he was a sub-chief in Chipindo (Northern Rhodesia Government, *General List of Chiefs*, 1930).

[3] Mbidia, a brother of Shimumbi I, was given charge of Isangano in 1910, in succession to Mubanga, a nephew of Shimumbi I, who had become Shimumbi II in 1907 (Shinakasa Chitolo, 29 June 1965; Luena DNB I, p. 65).

[4] In addition to evidence cited in the text, see NAZ/Sec/Nat/27 (N. Province), items 52/5 of 15 July, 1938, and 68 of 30 December 1944; also Government Notice no. 301 of 1946.

Appendix 1 (c) CENSUS FIGURES FROM BEMBA COUNTRY, EARLY TWENTIETH CENTURY

District	Chief	Villages	Huts	Population
KASAMA		1914[1]	1908	1926
Huts: DNB II, pp. 164–74	Chitimukulu	12	687	16,668
Pop.: DNB I, p. 24	Ponde	19	1,084	
	Mwangata	16	1,003	
	Mwamba	16	844	7,953
	Chisangula	4		
	Munkonge	14		5,161
	Nkolemfumu	9	436	2,085
	Kabwibwi	6	631	1,904
	Menga	4		1,129
	Misengo	4	333	942
	Chandamukulu	2	173	815
CHINSALI				1916–17
Pop.: DNB I, p. 112	Nkula	57		7,735
	Chewe	14		1,409
	Shimwalule	13		1,143
	Nkweto	11		875
	Musanya	9		652
	Mukwikile	4		649
	Mwaba	5		522
MPIKA			1910	1910
Huts and pop.:	Chikwanda	18	1,141	3,034
Annual report, 1911,	Luenshi		71	197
NAZ/KSD 4/1/1	Kapoko	5		
	Bwalya	7[2]	341	805
	Lukaka	5	243	648
	Luchembe	23	1,006	2,622
	Mpepo	6	240	532
	Masongo	6	289	617
LUENA (LUWINGU)			1907	1910
Huts: Luena DNB I,	Shimumbi	18	907	
62, 70, 76, 82	Tungati	11	579	
Pop.: *ibid.* II, 45	Chipalo	5	710	6,500
	Kasonka	4		
	Muchereka	3	243	

Notes: [1] NAZ/ZA 3/1/1   [2] Mpika DNB II, 147 (before 1910)

District	Chief	Villages	Huts	Population
MPOROKOSO		1913	1913	1913
All figures from DNB I, 81	Mporokoso	33	2,667	7,351
	Kaliminwa	19	1,944	5,904
	Sunkutu	3	184	521
ABERCORN				1914
Pop.: DNB I, 130	Makasa and others			9,686
ISOKA	Mubanga	?	?	?

Note on labour migration
To use these early census figures as a guide to Bemba demography in the late nineteenth century, it is necessary to have some idea as to how far they may be affected by labour migration. It must first be noted that up to at least 1914 most officials only counted huts, estimating population on an average of 2·5 or more persons per hut.[1] For the first decade at least of this century, while labour migration from North-Eastern Rhodesia may often have been for periods of a year or less at a time, the number of huts in a village may not have been greatly affected by the absence of migrants. The actual scale of migration is difficult to assess, since the available records are incomplete and sometimes ambiguous. But it had certainly reached a high level well before 1914. In Kasama sub-district in 1911–12 there were thought to be 7,290 taxable males; it is not clear whether these were reckoned to include absentees, but 3,957 men were registered for work, and most such men would have worked outside the 'Awemba district' (equivalent to most of the present Northern Province). In 1913–14, one chiefdom (apparently Bisa) in Mpika sub-district, comprising 354 'taxable' huts, lost 104 men to the mines; presumably others left for other places of employment. With migration on this scale, it is fairly clear that the available figures tend to under-represent the total population whose villages of origin were in north-eastern Northern Rhodesia.[2]

[1] Cf. Kasama DNB II, p. 14; Mporokoso annual report, 1909–10 (NAZ/KSU 4/1/1); Awemba district annual report, 1914–14 (NAZ/ZA7/1/1/1). The Mporokoso figures of 1913 were based on a count of names, but it is not clear whether absentees were included (Mporokoso DNB I, 81).
[2] Kasama DNB II, pp. 15, 361; Mpika annual report, 1913–14 (NAZ/ZA 7/1/1/1).

Appendix 2

Supplementary Notes

A. INSIGNIA OF BEMBA CHIEFTAINSHIP (p. 42, n. 5)

The insignia of Bemba and other chiefs in north-eastern Zambia are primarily of interest to the historian as testimony to contacts, past or present, with the Luba of eastern Katanga. Chief Mwamba has a hardwood staff carved with figures of a man and woman who are identified locally with Mwase and Chilimbulu, characters in the Bemba legend of migration.[1] It is said to have been made for the early chief Nkole *wa mapembwe*, and to have been given by Chileshye* to his brother Mutale, the first Mwamba. The staff used to be taken into battle; the chief would thrust it into the ground and stay by it until the battle was over.[2] In recent times, Mwamba has taken the staff with him on journeys, though when I visited a new Mwamba, Mutale Nshika, in 1969 I found that it had been placed among his relics. So far as I know, there are no other staffs of this kind among the Bemba, and rather than credit it with high antiquity it seems reasonable to suppose that it is either an import or the work of a migrant Luba craftsman. It closely resembles a staff said to come from Chilubi Island, on Lake Bangweulu,[3] but both are very similar to the Luba staff illustrated by Olbrechts.[4] In the latter, the cicatrisation on the stomach of the seated woman is similar to that on the Bemba staff, as is the simulated basketwork decoration of the plaque on which she sits. Unfortunately, Olbrechts could not give the provenance of his staff, but such objects are widely found in Luba and Lunda country. In 1899 a British South

[1] See above, p. 41.
[2] Mwamba VI Musenga, 1 July 1964, 9 October 1964; see above, p. 85.
[3] F. H. Melland, 'Some Ethnographic Notes on the Awemba Tribe', *JAS*, 1904–5, 4, p. 337
[4] F. M. Olbrechts, *Les Arts Plastiques du Congo Belge*, Brussels 1959, plates 192, 197, 200

Africa Company expedition seized several from Kazembe's; these are now in the National Museum of Rhodesia, Bulawayo.

The relics of the more senior Bemba chiefs include, or have included, iron bowstands, which have also been owned by a few royal councillors. These bowstands are said to have been brought from Luba country; they are not identified with particular chiefs.[5] There is a close resemblance between Bemba bowstands and Luba (?Hemba) specimens recorded by Colle.[6] A few Bemba chiefs and priests still have skinless slit signal drums: Tungati has one of the large type (*lunkumbi*), while Chimba and Shimwalule have the small one (*mondo*). Tungati's was made in Lubumbu early this century,[7] but the origin of the others is not known. One informant said that such drums were introduced from Kazembe's during the nineteenth century.[8] The Bwile chief Puta, at the north end of Lake Mweru, has a *lunkumbi* which he says was made for him by Luba of Mwenge (northwest of Pweto, on the Luvua river).[9] Bemba chiefs do not seem to have possessed either single or double iron bells, which are common emblems of chieftainship elsewhere in the Congo basin.[10] Gamitto, however, observed a double iron bell being sounded at the grave of Kazembe III; in 1892 Sharpe obtained one from Kazembe's and gave it to the British Museum; and Kazembe II is said, on first reaching the Luapula, to have given one to the Bena Mukulo chief Matanda.[11] The Shila chief Mununga, on Lake Mweru, owns a double bell; he says that 'we came from Luba with them' and that they are made only by Luba, for example at Kalamata (below Mwenge on the Luvua).[12]

---

[5] Cf. A. I. Richards, 'Bow-Stand or Trident?' *Man*, 1935, 35, pp. 30–32; W. V. Brelsford, 'The Bemba Tridents', *NADA* (Salisbury), 1935, 13, pp. 18–21; *idem*, 'Notes on some Northern Rhodesian bowstands', *Man*, 1940, 40, pp. 39–40

[6] *Ibid.*, also B. M. Fagan, 'A Collection of Nineteenth-Century Soli Ironwork', *JRAI*, 1961, 91, p. 236

[7] Shitantameni, 28 June 1965

[8] See above, p. 210. Gamitto describes and illustrates a *mondo* and *cinkumbi* seen at Kazembe's in 1831 (*King Kazembe*, II, 56–8).

[9] Puta, T1

[10] Jan Vansina, 'The Bells of Kings', *JAH*, 1969, 10, ii, pp. 187–97. Vansina includes the Bemba in his distribution list, but only on the basis of the White Fathers' *Bemba-English Dictionary*, which incorporates much material from outside the area of Bemba chiefdoms.

[11] Gamitto, *King Kazembe*, II, p. 14; A. Sharpe, 'A Carved Stool and other objects from British East Africa', *Man*, 1901, 1, p. 49; Cunnison, *Historical Traditions*, p. 39

[12] Mununga, T1

B. CLICHÉS IN LEGENDS OF 'TRIBAL' ORIGIN (p. 45, n. 12)

The tower motif (perhaps akin to the Babel story) occurs in the legends of origin of Lubunda, the Rat clan leader on the Luapula,[13] the Lamba, Ushi,[14] Tabwa (Zaïre),[15] Luvale (the Kaposhi clan),[16] Luba,[17] Rozwi.[18] Baumann gives other examples from central Africa.[19] Other motifs in the Bemba legend of migration may be similarly documented: the concealed pit as a mantrap (Luba, Tabwa of Zaïre, Luapula peoples);[20] the menial work (eastern Lunda, Bisa, Senga, Tumbuka);[21] seeds carried in the hair (Lamba, Senga, Tabwa of Zaïre, Hemba);[22] Luchele as the name of a benevolent person or deity (Lala, Ambo, Lamba, Ila);[23] incest as the origin of a new people or dynasty (Bisa, Lala, Lamba, Luba, Tumbwe, Lozi, Lovedu).[24] The motif of seeds in

[13] Cunnison, *Luapula Peoples*, pp. 37, 70

[14] C. M. Doke, *Lamba Folk-Lore*, Memoirs of the American Folk-Lore Society, 20, New York 1927, pp. 277–8; Munday, *Kankomba*, p. 8

[15] J. Weghsteen, 'Origines et dispersion des hommes d'après les légendes tabwa', *Annali del Pontificio Museo Missionario Etnologico* (formerly *Annali Lateranensi*), 1962, 26, pp. 216–18

[16] White, 'Clan, Chieftainship and Slavery', p. 62

[17] Roland, 'Résumé de l'histoire ancienne de Katanga', p. 18

[18] Livingstone, *African Journal*, pp. 313–14; Sister M. Aquina, 'The Tribes in Chilamanzi Reserve and their relation to the Rozvi', *NADA* (Salisbury), 1965, 9, ii, p. 41

[19] H. Baumann, *Schöpfung und Urzeit*, Berlin 1936, pp. 256–60. The tower motif also occurs in legends of the Rwanda, Rundi and Kuba (J. Vansina, personal communication).

[20] Weghsteen, 'Origine et histoire des Watabwa', p. 366; Cunnison, *Historical Traditions*, pp. 52, 132

[21] *Ibid.*, p. 7 (referring to Luba followers of Chibinda Ilunga); Thomas, *Bisa*, p. 5; Miracle, 'Aboriginal Trade among the Senga and Nsenga', p. 214; T. Cullen Young, *Notes on the History of the Tumbuka-Kamanga Peoples*, London 1932, p. 160

[22] C. M. Doke, *The Lambas*, London 1931, p. 31; M. P. Miracle, 'Ivory Trade and the Migration of the Northern Rhodesian Senga', *Cahiers d'études africaines*, 1963, 3, iii, p. 431; Weghsteen, 'Origines et dispersion des hommes', p. 218; P. Colle, *Les Baluba*, Brussels 1913, I, p. 205

[23] Munday, *Kankomba*, p. 2; J. T. Munday, 'The Creation Myth amongst the Lala of Northern Rhodesia', *African Studies*, 1942, I, pp. 50–1; B. Stefaniszyn, *Social and Ritual Life of the Ambo of Northern Rhodesia*, London 1964, pp. 135–6; Doke, *Lambas*, p. 30; E. W. Smith and A. M. Dale, *The Ila-Speaking Peoples of Northern Rhodesia*, London 1920, p. 203

[24] Munsoma, T1; W. V. Brelsford, *The Tribes of Zambia*, Lusaka n.d., p. 41; Munday, *Kankomba*, p. 1; F. Grevisse, 'Salines et Salinières indigènes du Haut-Katanga', *Bulletin du C.E.P.S.I.*, 1950, 11, p. 69; Burton, *Luba Religion*, p. 5; Colle, *Baluba*, I, p. 51; M. Mainga, 'The Origin of the Lozi', in Stokes and Brown, *The Zambesian Past*, pp. 245–6

the hair is characteristic of claims—as in the Lamba case—to have introduced agriculture, and thus civilisation in general. Some Bemba claim that Chiti and his followers brought the seeds of finger-millet, kaffir-corn and other Bemba crops,[25] but this is in keeping with the function of the legend as a tribal charter that accounts for the Bemba way of life: there is reason to suppose that in fact such crops had been cultivated in north-eastern Zambia since long before the establishment of the Chitimukulu dynasty.[26]

There is one version of the Bemba legend of migration which says that in the beginning both black and white people lived in Luba; they went together to the sea and the whites went to Europe while the blacks went east again and came to Bemba country. This version was given by chief Mwamba in 1897; it was probably a story current at the time to explain the recent arrival of Europeans in Bemba country.[27] Another version of this legend was recorded among the Yeke of Katanga in 1896,[28] and Baumann quotes still more from central Africa.[29]

C. THE CROSSING AT MATANDA'S (p. 49, n. 21)

I have only two versions of the Bemba migration legend which say just where the migrants crossed the Luapula,[30] but these agree that they were ferried across by Matanda, and this was confirmed by a Bisa informant.[31] Labrecque's map of the migration route locates the crossing to the north of the Luapula/Luongo confluence, and thus to the north of Matanda.[32] But an in earlier version of his history, Labrecque relates that when Chiti had crossed the river he gave himself the praise-name *ntalasha matanda*, 'I slide across on mats';[33] and according to Chileshye Mukulu, Matanda was so named because there were no boats, but only mats, with which to ferry the migrants across. Eastern Lunda traditions—at least as recorded by Labrecque—say that it was

[25] Richards, *Land, Labour and Diet*, p. 20
[26] See above, p. 72
[27] Dupont, 'Voyage de cinq semaines dans l'Ubemba', p. 252 (this is retold by Colle, *Baluba*, I, pp. 46–7, but he gives the wrong date). There seems to be an echo of this story in a note by R. Young, 'Kitimkuru's Awemba', Chinsali DNB I, p. 231.
[28] D. Crawford, *Thinking Black*, London 1913, pp. 269–70
[29] Baumann, *Schöpfung und Urzeit*, pp. 330–3
[30] Mushindo, *History*, s. 8, and Chileshye Mukulu, T1, T7
[31] Munsoma, T1; cf. Thomas, *Bisa*, p. 10; Cunnison, *Luapula Peoples*, p. 34
[32] Labrecque, 'Origines', p. 264   [33] Labrecque, 'Tribu', p. 636

Matanda's country that Kazembe II entered when he first crossed the Luapula.[34] About twelve miles north of Matanda's village (as of 1960), there is a fortified site known as Yombe, with a circular ditch 110 yards long,[35] but I do not know what local traditions have to say about it.

D.   THE 'BEMBA' NORTH OF LAKE MWERU (p. 69, n. 94)

Several early European travellers heard of 'Babemba' or 'Wawemba' north and west of Tabwa country,[36] and even in recent years 'Bemba' have been recorded in this area.[37] Such Bemba probably include, or included, the people of Kasanga and Tumbwe, and the Bena Marungu.[38] Colle mentions a Tumbwe chieftainship on the Marungu plateau called 'Mukulu wa Babemba'. He considered that this was derived from the Tabwa, who themselves (in his view) owed their chiefs to a north-westward migration by Bemba of Chitimukulu. Colle gives no source for the stories he quotes to this effect, for which the traditions of the Bemba and Tabwa of Zambia offer no support.[39] Labrecque heard somewhere that some of the pre-Chitimukulu Bemba fled to 'Kabuta' on Lake Mweru, but this may be an echo of the tradition of the Shila chief Mununga, on Lake Mweru, whose ancestor is said to have come from Bembaland with Nkuba.[40]

Colle is evidently the authority for Verhulpen's view that the Kasanga, Tumbwe and Tabwa represent northward migrations by the Bemba of Chitimukulu,[41] and Verhulpen frequently refers to these

[34] Cunnison, *Historical Traditions*, pp. 36–9

[35] J. H. Chaplin, in Northern Rhodesia Monuments Commission Tour Report 4, 1960

[36] Livingstone, *Last Journals*, I, p. 353; H. M. Stanley, *Through the Dark Continent*, London 1880, p. 315 and map; Thomson, *Central African Lakes*, II, pp. 28–9; H. Glauning, 'Die Fortschritte der Pendelexpedition', *Mitteilungen . . . aus den deutschen Schutzgebieten*, 1900, 13, p. 27

[37] J. Maes and O. Boone, *Les Peuplades du Congo Belge*, Brussels 1935, I, p. 39. The name also appears in this area on some modern maps. An early Belgian observer applied the term Bemba to the Tabwa of chief Mulilo: C. G. F. Delhaise, 'Chez les Wabemba', *Bull. soc. roy. belge. geog.*, 32, 1908, pp. 173–227, 261–83.

[38] It is worth remarking here that Arab informants of Richard Burton called the Bena Marungu 'Mbozwa', a name which Livingstone recorded for what are now mostly Bena Chishinga, east of Kazembe's (Burton, *Lake Regions*, II, p. 152; Livingstone, *Last Journals*, I, pp. 310, 315, 331, 333, 349–50).

[39] Colle, *Baluba*, I, pp. 49–52, 64–5

[40] Labrecque, 'Origines', p. 263; Chisanga, T1

[41] Verhulpen, *Baluba*, pp. 84, 118, 375

groups as Bemba.[42] It was perhaps by confusing these 'Bemba' with those of Chitimukulu that Lechaptois was led to suppose that the 'Wabemba du Nyassa', recoiling from Ngoni attacks, conquered Itabwa and forced people there to go north.[43] And it may well be that it is these 'Bemba' of the Marungu plateau who are referred to in the 'saying, well known throughout Lubaland, which attributes a common parentage to the Luba and the Bemba, in the chieftainship of Ntumb-we'.[44] Colle concludes that 'les Babemba du Nyassa [presumably those of Chitimukulu], et ceux d'Itabwa ou Batabwa, ont avec les Baluba des liens d'une commune origine', but he scarcely demonstrates this.[45] The point is worth making, since Mary Douglas (apparently following Colle) has remarked that 'the Bemba are said to have shared a common origin with the Luba, especially the Luba Hemba of Warua district'.[46] On the strength of this, Douglas proceeds to an argument about the Bemba of Chitimukulu. It may well indeed be right to connect their customs with those of the Luba–Hemba, but there appears to be no evidence for such an association in the oral traditions of either group.

There are small groups of people called Bemba, including a few chiefs of the *bena ŋandu*, to the west of Lake Mweru and the Luapula estuary. In 1959 the Bemba population in the Mweru and Luapula *secteurs* of Katanga was reckoned to be about 20,000.[47] I know nothing about the history of these Bemba, but some are probably descended from Bemba who settled in Kazembe's kingdom in the late nineteenth century.[48]

E.   THE EARLY HISTORY OF MAKASA (p. 98, n. 22, and Fig. 11, p. 147)

There is some confusion about the first holders of this title. Oger, the leading authority on Mpanda traditions, says that the first two Makasas were both sons of Chiliamafwa*: their names were Kalulu and Chansa *wa mbala*. The next one was Bwalya, a son of Chileshye*.[49] Goodall shows both Kalulu and Bwalya as sons of Chileshye*.[50] He does not

[42] *Ibid.*, pp. 47, 66, 69, 108, 126
[43] A. Lechaptois, *Aux Rives du Tanganika*, Algiers 1913, pp. 28–9; this passage is mentioned by Colle, *Baluba*, I, p. 49.
[44] Burton, *Luba Religion*, p. 3   [45] Colle, *Baluba*, I, p. 52
[46] M. Douglas, 'Matriliny and Pawnship in Central Africa', *Africa*, 1964, 34, iv, p. 308
[47] O. Boone, *Carte Ethnique du Congo (Quart Sud-Est)*, Tervuren 1961, p. 12
[48] See above, p. 223, n. 41.
[49] Oger, 'Mpanda', 12, 22   [50] Goodall, 'Tree'

mention Chansa *wa mbala*; an entry in the Mporokoso District Note-book agrees that this man was a son of Chiliamafwa* but does not say whether he was Makasa.[51] Sheane agrees with Goodall that the first two Makasas were sons of Chileshye*, but he may simply have been following Goodall or using a common source.[52] My informants at Makasa's said that the first Makasa was either Chikompe or Chansa *wa mbala*, both of whom were sons of Chinchinta*; but they also said that 'Chiliamafwa' was a praise for Chinchinta*, so they need not perhaps be taken very literally on this point. They mentioned a third Makasa, Kusula, also a son of Chinchinta*, who is not mentioned by any other source. Kusula was followed by 'Kalulu Kangwa Bwalya', a son of Chileshye*.[53] Lastly, Labrecque says that Chiliamafwa* had a son called Nondo Mpya (the new hammer) who became Makasa I.[54] Chikunga says that Nondo Mpya's mother was Kasuba *montelwa* (wife of Chileshye* and then Chitapankwa*;[55] but this is probably a faulty recollection of Labrecque, who says that Kasuba *montelwa* was the mother of Makasa Bwalya.[56]

I think it is possible to reconcile these different lists. The name Chikompe given at Makasa's for Makasa I may be accounted for by Oger's report that his Makasa I (Kalulu) originally held a headman's title, Chikompe. 'Kalulu Kangwa Bwalya' is evidently the Bwalya mentioned by the other sources as Makasa II or III. My informants at Makasa's mentioned no other Makasas called Bwalya, and said that 'Kalulu Kangwa Bwalya' was succeeded by Chisanga, whom Oger says succeeded Bwalya: thereafter, these lists correspond. (My informants at Nkweto's also spoke of Makasa 'Bwalya Kalulu',[57] but it is common enough for Bemba chiefs to be credited with the personal names of their predecessors, since through positional succession they assume their identities.) Since both Oger and my informants at Makasa's agree that Bwalya was the first Makasa appointed by Chileshye*, I think it is fair to suppose that Goodall was mistaken in giving Kalulu as a son of Chileshye*. As for Labrecque's report that Makasa I, son of Chiliamafwa*, was originally called Nondo Mpya, this is explicitly contradicted by Oger, who says that Nondo Mpya was the son of a sister of

[51] Mporokoso DNB, I, p. 268   [52] Chinsali DNB, I, p. 155
[53] Makofi and Chituba, 9 June 1965.
[54] Labrecque, 'Origines', p. 286. Labrecque adds three names between Makasa I and Makasa *wa cisenga*, but there is no reason to suppose that they are more than praise-names, or additional personal names.
[55] Chikunga, T3   [56] 'Origines', p. 277
[57] Makwaya, 16 May 1965

Chinchinta* who lived in Mpanda under Makasa but, being a royal, was specially honoured.[58]

It thus seems probable that the first Makasa was Kalulu, formerly Chikompe, a son of Chiliamafwa*. Kalulu is given by all sources the praise *wa cisenga*. This refers to Chisenga, the site close to Nkweto's present village near which the Bemba under Makasa fought the Ngoni. It is universally reported that Makasa was killed at Chisenga; Oger specifically says that this was Makasa Kalulu, and there is no reason to doubt that he is right.[59] The battle at Chisenga took place around 1850, and if, as is likely, Chiliamafwa* (who died some time around 1820)[60] appointed Makasa I himself, the latter would have been well advanced in years when he fought the Ngoni, but not necessarily implausibly so. Oger says that the next Makasa was Chansa *wa mbala*, another son of Chiliamafwa*, and that he was succeeded by Bwalya, a son of Chileshye*. (At Nkweto's, Makasa 'Bwalya' was said to have fought the Ngoni at Chisenga, but evidently there has been confusion with Kalulu: as we have noted, they also spoke at Nkweto's of one 'Bwalya Kalulu.) Oger says that Bwalya died after the Bemba finally expelled the Ngoni (that is, *c.* 1870) but before Chitapankwa* was defeated by the Lungu chief Zombe, which happened in 1872.[61] Thereafter, the succession to the Makasa chieftainship is clear enough.[62]

F. CHILESHYE CHEPELA'S VISIT TO KAZEMBE (p. 100, n. 37)

The most plausible version of this episode seems to be that of Chikunga, who says Chileshye was sent to Kazembe's by Chiliamafwa* to obtain a war charm (*ilamfya*).[63] Chileshye Mukulu says that after his quarrel at Nkolemfumu's Chileshye went to Kazembe's but found no *mucinshi* (manners, etiquette) there, so he came back.[64] The Lunda agree that Chileshye visited them, and was given materials for an *ilamfya*, but they say that this happened after the Portuguese visit in 1831–2 and that Chileshye was Chitimukulu at the time.[65] ·The weight of the Bemba evidence supports the view that Chileshye had indeed become

[58] Labrecque, 'Origines', p. 286; Oger, 'Mpanda', 14–19; also A. I. Richards, fieldnotes at Makasa's, 20 April 1933

[59] Oger, 'Mpanda', 14; see also below, Appendix 3.

[60] See above, p. 104.   [61] Oger, 'Mpanda', 29; and see above, p. 150.

[62] See above, pp. 228–9.

[63] Chikunga, 11 September 1964; cf. Tanguy, *Imilandu*, p. 26

[64] Chileshye Mukulu, T1 (see Appendix 4/ii)

[65] Cunnison, *Historical Traditions*, pp. 71–2

Chitimukulu by 1831,[66] but only Milambo says that Chileshye was Chitimukulu when he visited Kazembe, and he says that Chileshye went simply to get craftsmen and singers.[67] Perhaps Chileshye paid two visits to Kazembe's, both before and after becoming Chitimukulu. But it is very unusual, even nowadays, for Chitimukulu to leave Bemba country, and special rituals are necessary.[68] Since Kazembe is regarded as a close kinsman by Chitimukulu, a personal visit might have been thought in order, at least in time of great stress such as the Lunda describe; but this might equally have been an argument against his leaving the country. One would expect the Bemba to claim that Chileshye was only a young man, not yet a chief, at the time of his visit, and the Lunda to claim that he was a chief, and Chitimukulu at that: they clearly relish their account of how Chileshye is supposed to have grovelled before Kazembe. But the reference in the Lunda story to Chileshye complaining of the capture of Mukukamfumu strongly suggests that his visit took place before his accession: see Note K, below.

G. THE DISPLACEMENT OF CHIMBOLA (p. 104, n. 54)

As there is some difference between the account of this episode given in chapter 4 and the story current at Chimbola's, I discuss the latter here. Significantly, it hardly mentions Chinchinta* and lays most stress on the old line's loss of power throughout Lubemba. As it names Chitapankwa, and not Chileshye, as the leader in the *Miti* line, the story might appear to be about a quite different incident. But the genealogical evidence makes it very unlikely that Chitapankwa is really meant, and in one account there is some uncertainty as to whether Chileshye* or Chitapankwa* ruled first.[69] And on another occasion this same informant said that it was Chileshye who expelled Chimbola *wa museshi*, otherwise Chinchinta.*[70]

The story goes that Chilufya, a brother of Chimbola *wa museshi*, objected when their mother Namungoli sent Chimbola to succeed as Chitimukulu. Chilufya attacked the village of Namungoli, who got Chitapankwa (?Chileshye) to come and help her. Chitapankwa found Chilufya sitting on an ant-hill and killed him. But then Chitapankwa drove Chimbola away, and 'those who were previously chiefs ran

[66] See above, p. 104. [67] Milambo, 9 October 1964

[68] Cf. Richards, *Land, Labour and Diet*, p. 248

[69] Chibwe, T1 [70] Chibwe, 9 September 1964

away, to this place and that'.[71] This story, as one would expect, is also known at Chandaweyaya's. Chandaweyaya herself told the story about Chilufya's death, though her version was not at all clear. She did not seem to connect it with the expulsion of Chinchinta*, but she did cap it by remarking, 'They took this country, destroyed and buried it, and people couldn't tell that this is an important place.'[72]

Mushindo relates a quite different story from all my informants. He says that when Chanda (Chandamukulu) was about to die, during the reign of her brother Chiliamafwa*, she excluded her own sons from the royal succession, as they did not care for her. Instead, she transferred the succession to Mukukamfumu's family, gave them a calabash of kaffir-corn, and said, 'As these seeds shall be multiplied, so shall your blessings and power as great rulers of Bembaland.' Before Chiliamafwa* died, he repeated the words of his sister Chanda, because her children 'did not give him his place as their king'.[73] This version probably reflects the rivalry in the 1930s between the houses of the then Chandamukulu and Mukukamfumu. Mushindo, in Ichinga, is likely to have leaned towards the latter party, since all Nkulas in the first half of this century were sons of one Mukukamfumu.

H. THE BURIAL OF CHINCHINTA (p. 104, n. 55)

Since Chileshye* had forcibly deposed Chinchinta*, he was bound to fear his spirit as a potentially malign influence, and he could not afford to alienate Chinchinta further by leaving his body in a foreign country. So a Bemba force went off to wrest the corpse from the Mambwe. They were repulsed, and the Bemba decided instead to placate the Mambwe paramount, Nsokolo. Milambo says that the Bemba gave Nsokolo large presents of cloth, obtained from traders from the coast (*balungwana*). In return, Nsokolo gave up Chinchinta's body and the Bemba took it back to be properly buried at Mwalule.[74] Labrecque's brief reference to the incident is broadly similar; he adds that the Bemba were scared into recovering the body by the first raids of the Ngoni, whom they believed to embody Chinchinta's angry spirit.[75] Mushindo agrees that the Bemba failed in their attempt to obtain Chinchinta's body by force, but he says that Nsokolo eventually handed it over to Chewe, the chief in Ichinga.[76] According to two other

[71] Chibwe, T1 [72] Chandaweyaya, T1 [73] Mushindo, *History*, s. 36
[74] Milambo, T2 [75] Labrecque, 'Origines', p. 273
[76] Mushindo, *History*, s. 43

versions, Nsokolo did not relent; instead, the Bemba obtained the corpse from a Mambwe called Sumbi. Chileshye Mukulu says that the Bemba bribed Sumbi to steal Chinchinta's body, by giving him presents of both cloth and guns.[77] It is possible that the Bemba did have cloth from the coast, and at least two guns, to give the Mambwe on this occasion.[78] But the Bemba author Stephen Mpashi implies that Sumbi seized the body on his own initiative; he was then rewarded by Chileshye* with food, and with a chieftainship over a small area near the Luchewe river. Sumbi was later killed in revenge by the Mambwe.[79]

J. THE BEMBA, KAMANGA AND NGONDE (p. 121, n. 137)

Mushindo relates that after Chileshye* defeated Chewe, many Bemba fled from Ichinga, and together with some Bisa and Sukuma went east across the Luangwa valley to the upper reaches of the Hewe river, in Kamanga country. Here they built a village, Mawuwo, and boasted to the Kamanga chief, Chikulamayembe, that they had been sent by Chileshye* to conquer the Kamanga and Henga. But Chikulamayembe allied with the Ngonde chiefs Kyungu and Muyombe; they besieged the Bemba village, and eventually burned it down.[80]

The main points in this story are borne out by Kamanga and Ngonde traditions, as recorded by Cullen Young. According to the Kamanga, the Bemba, led by 'Chepere', made conquests as far east as the Senga chief Chibale before reaching the Hewe river. Then the Bemba were defeated by Chikulamayembe VI Bamantha, aided by Kyungu. The reference here to 'Chepere' probably arises from the fact—if Mushindo is right—that the intruding Bemba claimed to have been sent by Chileshye* *cepela*. Cullen Young argued, on the basis of Kamanga and Ngoni traditions, that this war must have taken place after the northward trek of the Ngoni (c. 1840).[81] Ngonde tradition points to a *terminus ante quem* for the war: it relates that a Bemba leader called 'Chepere' or 'Chepera' attacked an Ngonde sub-chief, Muyombe, but was then defeated by Mwakasangula, son of the reigning Ngonde chief, Kyungu Mwangonde.[82] This suggests a date in the early 1840s, since Mwakasangula had succeeded Mwangonde as Kyungu by the time

---

[77] Chileshye Mukulu, T4 and n. 23   [78] See above, pp. 194, 201–2.
[79] Mpashi, *Abapatili bafika ku Lubemba*, pp. 2–3
[80] Mushindo, *History*, s. 45
[81] Cullen Young, *Tumbuka-Kamanga Peoples*, pp. 102–4, 106, 168, 170–1
[82] *Ibid.*, p. 72

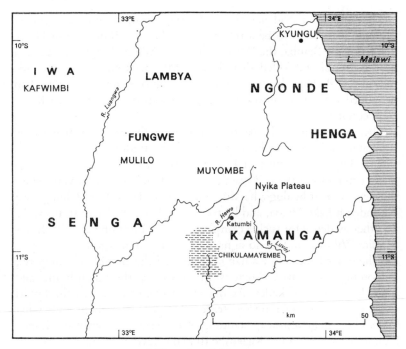

18 Ngonde and Kamanga

the Ngoni first reached Ngonde country,[83] which probably happened some time during the 1840s, when the Ngoni were still based on Ufipa.[84] But Bemba traditions suggest a date in the 1850s.[85]

Godfrey Wilson, who also recorded this Ngonde tradition, appears to have put questions about the Bemba–Ngonde war to Mwamba V Mubanga Chisupa, who said that it took place in the reign of Chileshye* *cepela*, and that the Bemba were led by Mwamba (i.e. Mwamba I Mutale), who was defeated and died of his wounds on the way home.[86] This version is almost certainly not a genuine Bemba tradition, but the result of conflating Wilson's own knowledge of Ngonde tradition with the well-known Bemba tradition that Mwamba I Mutale died in the course of a campaign against the Iwa. This appears the more likely when we recall that Mwamba died some time around 1860, whereas we have just seen that there is some reason to suppose that the war took place in the 1840s.

[83] Wilson, *Constitution of Ngonde*, pp. 28–9
[84] Cf. Elmslie, *Wild Ngoni*, p. 25   [85] See above, pp. 121–2.
[86] Wilson, *Constitution of Ngonde*, pp. 26–7

The only other evidence clearly bearing on the Bemba–Kamanga–Ngonde war seems to be a report that, when the Kamanga of Hewe fled from the Bemba, the 'Muyombe' chief Winga fought the Bemba near Katumbi and killed their leader 'Mwenenkonde, son of Chitimukulu'.[87] Perhaps this was Nsunge, the son of Chinchinta* who had provoked Chileshye* into causing the exodus from Ichinga to Kamanga country.[88]

There is a slight possibility that rumours of the Bemba war with the Kamanga and Ngonde have influenced the traditions of Kazembe's Lunda. The latter claim that Kazembe III Lukwesa Ilunga (d. 1804/5) made conquests as far as 'Nyasa', 'and the whole land is covered with the trenches that he dug'; he 'dug a ditch in order to fight Chungu wa Nkonde on Lake Nyasa, and he too surrendered'.[89] There seems to be no other evidence for such a campaign by any Kazembe, and Professor Monica Wilson could see no signs of such a trench in Ngonde country.[90] On the other hand, the Kamanga relate that the Bemba of 'Chepere', on coming east, 'settled down as if they were at their own home' and built three large stockades. At the site of one of these, on the Luviri river, Cullen Young reported traces of a perimeter ditch and 'what looks like a huge ash-heap standing in the centre'.[91] Since the Lunda look back to the reign of Kazembe III as the heyday of Lunda power, it would not be very surprising if they had (perhaps with Labrecque's assistance) included in the story of his achievements some details of a campaign which had in fact been executed somewhat later by a Bemba leader.

K.   CHILESHYE* AND CHEWE (p. 121, n. 137)

The conflict between Chileshye* and Chewe is perhaps to be identified with the 'rebellion' against Chileshye* which is mentioned in the history of Kazembe's Lunda. This relates that when Chileshye* and Mutale came to Kazembe IV Keleka, they told him, 'At our place there is no peace. There are many disobedient people who trouble us and they have captured our princess Mukukamfumu and many people have been killed in the war against the rebels.'[92] There is, so far as I know,

---

[87] Isoka DNB, p. 500   [88] See above, p. 121.
[89] Cunnison, *Historical Traditions*, pp. 50, 52
[90] Cunnison, *Luapula Peoples*, p. 154, n. 2
[91] Cullen Young, *Tumbuka-Kamanga Peoples*, pp. 168, 170, 102–3
[92] Cunnison, *Historical Traditions*, p. 71

only one reference in Bemba traditions to the capture of a Mukukam-fumu: this occurs in the story of the war between Munkonge and Mulenga Mwimba. The Lungu of Mukupa Kaoma, in alliance with Munkonge I or his sons, killed Mulenga Mwimba and captured his wife Lukonde Mwaba, who was the mother of Chileshye* and is generally said to have been Mukukamfumu I. This incident occurred when Mubanga Kashampupo was chief in Ituna, and probably when Chiliamafwa* was Chitimukulu.[93] Thus it cannot safely be identified with an event which (if the Lunda are right) occurred after Chileshye's* accession. If we accept the Lunda chronology (and this is questioned in Note F above), we might well suppose that Mukukamfumu (either Lukonde Mwaba or her successor, who was later killed by the Ngoni)[94] was captured a second time, in the course of Chileshye's* war with Chewe.

L. THE BEMBA AND THE LUNGU OF TAFUNA (p. 151, n. 110)

The chronology for Lungu-Bemba relations presented in the text is based on inferences concerning the movements of Tafuna IV Kakungu and the date of the destruction of Zombe's village. It is not in fact clear when Kakungu was expelled from Isoko. In 1872 Livingstone passed through Zombe's village on the Lucheche river but evidently by-passed Isoko, and he does not mention either Tafuna or Kakungu.[95] In 1876 Stanley noted 'Kakungu village' near the mouth of the river Kawa (i.e. in the neighbourhood of Kasanga),[96] but Kakungu may have been the name of a headmanship then held by a successor to the man who became Tafuna IV. Thomson passed through Zombe's in 1879 and 1880, but on both occasions, like Livingstone, he travelled well to the north, and well below, Isoko, and he does not mention Kakungu or Tafuna except in a very garbled summary of Lungu history.[97] In May 1880, Kakungu was reported by a missionary to be near the mouth of the Lunzua river (i.e. a short way north of Isoko), while Tafuna was said to be a neighbour of Zombe's.[98] There is thus some reason to suppose that Tafuna IV Kakungu was not expelled from Isoko until

---

[93] See above, pp, 98, 131.   [94] See below, Appendix 3.

[95] *Last Journals*, II, pp. 248–9

[96] Stanley, *Dark Continent* (1880 ed.), p. 346

[97] Thomson, *Central African Lakes*, I, pp. 304, 317–18; II, p. 212

[98] Stewart's map in Wookey to Whitehouse, 31 May 1880, LMS/CA 3/2/A; Hore to Thompson, 8 May 1880, LMS/CA 3/1/D (Wolf, *Tanganyika*, pp. 120–1)

the early 1880s. It is however likely that he was expelled some time before Zombe's town was destroyed by the Bemba, since it was later reported that after Kakungu's expulsion from Isoko 'he went to the Bemba; they attacked in force and laid waste the country'.[99]

There is no doubt that Zombe's village was destroyed some time between 1880 and 1883. In 1880 Hore described Zombe's 'large and fortified town' as a flourishing place, and Zombe had guns and powder.[100] The London Missionary Society decided to build a station there, but in 1883 Griffith heard at Liendwe, at the mouth of the Lufubu river, that 'the town of Zombe . . . has been completely destroyed and that no people any longer live in that neighbourhood'.[101] Fred Moir, coming from Lake Malawi and intending to meet LMS missionaries at Zombe's, found the place deserted.[102] In 1886 Carson passed 'the remains of what used to be the large village of Zombe'; apparently the chief there had wanted to build again on the same site if he had some hope of European support, so the village had presumably not been abandoned voluntarily in the ordinary course of village movements.[103]

It remains, however, uncertain whether this destruction was the work of the Bemba, and if so, whether it is to be identified with the destruction of Zombe's recorded in Bemba traditions. According to both Labrecque and Gouldsbury and Sheane, Chitapankwa* crushed Zombe in the year following the Bemba rout, while Mushindo and Milambo conflate both actions into a single victorious campaign.[104] But if these accounts are correct, we must either attribute the destruction of Zombe's in 1880–3 to people other than the Bemba, or else explain why the Bemba should not appear to recall a second devastating victory over Zombe. It might be conjectured that Zombe's was destroyed in 1880–3 by the Baluchi trader Kabunda: in the first part of 1883 Kabunda appears to have devastated the country around Liendwe,[105] and Moir and Fotheringham thought it was he who had ruined Lungu country further east.[106] But Hore implies that Bemba raiders had also

[99] Jones to Thompson, 15 April 1891, LMS/CA 8/3/C

[100] Wolf, *Tanganyika*, pp. 116, 118; Hore to LMS, 8 May 1880, LMS/CA 3/1/D

[101] Griffiths to LMS, 14 September 1883, LMS/CA 5/3/A

[102] Moir, 'Eastern Route', p. 109

[103] Carson, journal, pp. 85, 92, LMS/CA/J3

[104] Labrecque, 'Origines', p. 315; Gouldsbury and Sheane, *Great Plateau*, p. 36; Mushindo, *History*, s. 77; Milambo, T15

[105] Giraud, *Lacs*, pp. 429–30; cf. Swann, *Slave-hunters*, p. 98; Fotheringham, *Adventures*, pp. 14–16; Hore to LMS, 14 September 1883, LMS/CA 5/3/A

[106] Moir, *After Livingstone*, p. 82; Fotheringham, *Adventures*, p. 14

been active recently in the region,[107] and Giraud indicates that the Bemba devastated the Lungu/Mambwe border area in or before 1884.[108] It may be that in 1880-3 Zombe's was destroyed by Ponde rather than by Chitapankwa*, in which case the action might well not have been remembered in the Bemba heartland. On the other hand, there seems to be no indication from the Lungu side that Zombe's was destroyed twice within ten years or so. Instead, we have already noted evidence that the Bemba helped Kakungu to retaliate against Zombe after the latter had been expelled from Isoko, probably after 1880. And in any case it would seem quite reasonable to suppose that the Bemba have in fact telescoped their initial defeat and subsequent victory into a rapid succession of events: such telescoping is a common feature of oral reminiscence, let alone tradition, and a story of swift retaliation would reflect much more credit on the Bemba than a delay of ten years.

M. THE CHIBWA SALT INDUSTRY (p. 187)

Output

A very crude estimate of the scale of production at Chibwa salt marsh in pre-colonial days can be made on the basis of information about operations there during the colonial period. It is clear that during October 1900 a large number of people were making salt at Chibwa,[109] and in October 1904 540 'families' were counted there, excluding subjects of chiefs Kopa and Kapoko.[110] In the 1930s, 'as many as 35 villages, some from as much as 50 miles away, used to migrate to the Chibwe [*sic*] in September of each year': this might be taken to represent at least 500 people.[111] By 1904, of course, there was the new incentive of selling salt to the government offices at Mpika, but this would seem to have affected, not the number of people who came to make salt, so much as the amount they found it worth while to produce.

The output of a visiting family depended on their prospects for selling part of their output locally, and on their capacity for carrying the rest away. It does not appear that there was any significant local market in salt before the colonial government and the White Fathers at Chilonga began buying salt in the 1900s. Thus in earlier days a small

---

[107] *Tanganyika*, p. 235   [108] *Lacs*, p. 531
[109] Molinier to Dupont, 28 October 1900, *CT*, 89, January 1901, p. 161
[110] Mpika DNB (1905), I, p. 30
[111] Mpika Tour Report 8 (1952) (copy in Mpika DNB II, p. 262)

family group would probably have been content with an output of about 80 lbs. For this, they might spend a week or two at Chibwa: a family including two adults could cut enough grass in one day to produce about 40 lbs. of salt,[112] but several days would be needed for the process of extracting the salt. If we estimate that 500 such groups might be found at Chibwa at any one time, we might well suppose that in the course of a four or five week season there might be at least twice that number. It would therefore seem that 50,000 lbs. would be a very conservative estimate of annual output at Chibwa in pre-colonial days.[113]

This conjecture can at least be compared with inferences from early figures for government purchases at Mpika of salt produced at Chibwa and a less important source on the Chalwi stream. In 1904–5, 20,000 lbs. was sold to the Boma, and in 1906 almost twice this amount. It was estimated in the latter year that the total output from the Mpika area might be between 55,000 and 60,000 lbs.[114] Since the White Fathers also bought salt, this estimate would imply that at most 15,000 lbs. was produced for exchange and consumption in African villages. This seems an unduly low figure, in view of the conjecture in the last paragraph. It is possible that, as the government demand increased, people tended, not so much to increase their total output as to sell much of it at Mpika rather than carry full loads home. But in 1906 an official reported that the salt workers 'retain enough for their own use; the surplus bought by the Administration they have to be encouraged to produce'.[115] Probably the total amount produced for African demands remained fairly constant, while the amount produced for sale to Europeans varied rather closely with their often erratic demands. Thus in 1906 the total output may well have been considerably greater than the official estimate.

Tribute

Each salt-worker at Chibwa paid tribute of one ball of salt: such balls were formed when brine was evaporated in pots, and each ball weighed about 3 lbs. So much is clear from Gamitto, Brelsford and the reports of

[112] Report on Chibwa Salt Industry by Supervisor of Co-operative Societies, Kasama, 29 October 1953 (NAZ/Box 6737, file 24/10).

[113] For details of salt production elsewhere in East and central Africa see J. E. G. Sutton and A. D. Roberts, 'Uvinza and its Salt Industry', *Azania*, 1968, 3, p. 69.

[114] Mpika annual reports, 1904–5, 1906–7, NAZ/KSD 4/1/1. In 1905 labour recruiters from the Witwatersrand Native Labour Association visited the district during the salt-working season, and consequently had very little success (*ibid.*, 1905–6).

[115] Mpika annual report, 1905–6, NAZ/KSD 4/1/1; and cf. *ibid.*, 1909–10

officials at Mpika.[116] If, as suggested above, a man and woman could usually produce about 80 lbs., each adult would be due to pay tribute on about 40 lbs. Thus a tribute payment of one ball would represent rather less than one-tenth of output. This figure seems quite plausible, since tribute of one-tenth of output was levied from salt-workers at Uvinza in western Tanzania.[117]

It is not clear whether the tribute exacted by senior chiefs from chiefs at Chibwa also approximated to the same fraction. If 300 nuclear families visited Chibwa in a season, as much as 1,000 balls of salt might be paid in tribute, and probably much more than this was often in fact forthcoming. In the 1890s, Luchembe, whose rights extended over a good deal less than half the salt-producing area, forwarded 40 cakes to Mwamba.[118] Chikwanda is said to have forwarded a hundred balls to Chitimukulu, and a hundred to Nkula;[119] this arrangement is much more likely to have obtained in Sampa's* reign than in Chitapankwa's*[120] but it is not clear whether it continued after Luchembe's arrival in the area in about 1890. In any case, these last figures should probably not be taken very seriously.

N.   THE LATER HISTORY OF THE DISPLACED CHEWE LINEAGE (p. 279)

Mulenga *wa cilaka* died in 1912, and as no successor could be found in his lineage, the Chewe title was taken in 1919 by Bwembya, a younger brother of Nkula II Bwalya Changala. Nkula II died in 1934; he was succeeded by Chikwanda III Musungu, who in his turn was succeeded as Chikwanda by Chewe Bwembya. A nephew of Chewe Mulenga *wa cilaka* claimed the now vacant Chewe title, but the chieftainship was of little practical importance and the Government amalgamated it with that of Nkula.[121]

When Bwembya became Chewe in 1919, he gave the relics of Chewe Mulenga *wa cilaka* to Nkula II Bwalya, and they are still at

[116] Gamitto, *King Kazembe*, II, p. 148; Brelsford, *Aspects*, p. 23; Mpika DNB II, p. 263; Mpika Tour Report 8 (1952)

[117] Sutton and Roberts, 'Uvinza and its Salt Industry', p. 70. In south-eastern Zambia, tribute in iron was exacted at one-ninth of output: 'The Story of Rashid bin Hassani', in Perham (ed.), *Ten Africans*, p. 86.

[118] Luchembe I (1918 evidence); Mpika DNB II, pp. 113, 263

[119] Kalesu, 21 April 1965

[120] Nkula received salt from Chibwa in 1883, but there is no suggestion that it came as tribute (see above, p. 188).

[121] Chinsali DNB I, p. 279; II, 10; Mbutuka, 14 May 1965; Brelsford, *Succession*, p. 30; Brelsford, *Aspects*, pp. 40, 44; Chief Secretary to Provincial Commissioner, Kasama, 7 October 1935, NAZ/Sec/Nat 416

Nkula's.[122] I am not quite sure if these relics include those of the displaced 'Ngoshye' lineage, to which the Chewe and Nkula titles had originally belonged.[123]

In 1970 the Chewe title was claimed by Mr Julius Sekwila, of Kitwe, who gained public notice by also claiming the Chitimukuluship in the course of a prolonged succession dispute.[124]

---

[122] Nkula Bwembya, 10 May 1965   [123] Cf. Brelsford, *Aspects*, pp. 3–4
[124] *Zambia News*, 27 September 1970; *Times of Zambia*, 31 May 1971, 4 June 1971

Appendix 3

The Bemba and the Ngoni

In the course of chapters 4, 5 and 7, I referred in passing to conflict between Bemba and Ngoni. Here I examine in greater detail the record of this conflict, which was one of the most notable features of nineteenth century history on the north-eastern plateau: the Bemba offered the most decisive resistance encountered by the Ngoni in the course of their spectacularly successful migrations.

The importance of this resistance can be overemphasised. It did not really determine the pattern of Ngoni settlement: the relatively fertile uplands east of the Luangwa valley were obviously more desirable (and less unlike the Ngoni homeland in Natal) than the woodland of the plateau west of the valley. In any case, the main thrust of Ngoni settlement in Zambia appears to have taken place more or less independently of the Ngoni–Bemba wars. Nor does there seem to be any evidence to support the suggestion that under the impact of Ngoni attacks the Bemba developed a 'military organisation'.[1] The Ngoni did indeed have this effect on certain other peoples with whom they came into conflict.[2] And it is clear that the danger presented to the Bemba by the Ngoni put a high premium on strong leadership: as we have seen, Bwembya* is said to have been replaced as Chitimukulu because he was half-witted and incapable of coping with the Ngoni.[3] But there is no evidence that the Bemba underwent any demonstrable social or political change under Ngoni pressure.

Nonetheless, the fact that the Bemba were able to repel the Ngoni war-bands meant that the Bemba survived as a single polity, instead of fragmenting like other people who had stood in the path of the Ngoni. Until the arrival of the Europeans, the Bemba continued to dominate the whole north-eastern plateau, enjoying as formidable a reputation

[1] See above, p. 169, n. 25.
[2] E.g. the Sangu and Nyamwezi: cf. Roberts, *Tanzania before 1900*, pp. 43–44, 133   [3] See above, p. 128.

for rapine and slaughter as did the Ngoni themselves in the southeast. Just as the Lunda of Kazembe pride themselves on defending the peoples of the plateau from the menace of the Yeke,[4] so the Bemba boast of their achievement in driving away the Ngoni. (I have even heard a Bemba speak of a Bemba expedition to 'protect' a Bisa chiefdom against the Ngoni, much as the European colonial powers took it upon themselves to 'protect' vast areas of Africa against one another.) When work on the Copperbelt brought Bemba and Ngoni face to face again, they evolved a joking relationship based on their historic enmity and its corollary: respect for a worthy opponent.[5]

In view of this continuing consciousness of a shared history, it is disappointing, and a little surprising, that the incidents of Bemba–Ngoni warfare are not more clearly remembered on either side. The most detailed and coherent testimony is to be found in written records of traditions compiled thirty years ago or more. Collating these presents considerable problems, and though it is possible to reconstruct a fairly comprehensive picture of Ngoni activities west of the Luangwa much in this picture remains somewhat conjectural. One difficulty is that while evidence from the Ngoni contributes usefully to that from the Bemba, the two groups of evidence overlap very little, so that there are few common points of reference. For this reason, it will be convenient to begin by examining the Ngoni evidence, and providing it with a chronology where possible, before considering the relevant Bemba evidence.

Ngoni traditions, as reported by Chibambo, Cullen Young and Elmslie, agree that after their crossing of the Zambezi (dated by an eclipse to 1835) the Ngoni under Zwangendaba moved northwards, east of the Luangwa, until they reached Ufipa, east of the south end of Lake Tanganyika.[6] Fraser says that on the way the Ngoni spent six years in Senga country, gathering recruits, but there is no clear indication that the Ngoni encountered the Bemba at this stage.[7] Soon after the Ngoni

---

4 Cunnison, *Historical Traditions*, p. 104

5 Cf. J. Clyde Mitchell, *The Kalela Dance*, Rhodes-Livingstone Paper 27, Manchester 1956, pp. 38–40; A. L. Epstein, *Politics in an Urban African Community*, Manchester 1958, p. 6

6 Y. M. Chibambo (tr. C. Stuart), *My Ngoni of Nyasaland*, London n.d. [1942]; Cullen Young, *History of the Tumbuka-Kamanga Peoples*; W. A. Elmslie, *Among the Wild Ngoni*, London and Edinburgh 1901; cf. Burton, *Lake Regions*, II, pp. 75, 153

7 D. Fraser, *Winning a Primitive People*, London 1914, p. 312; cf. Elmslie, *Wild Ngoni*, p. 25; W. H. J. Rangeley, 'Mtwalo', *Nyasaland Journal*, 1952, 5, p. 57. In a

arrived in Ufipa, Zwangendaba died. There was a bitter struggle over the succession, and several groups split off and migrated in different directions. This breakup may be dated to about 1845.[8] One Ngoni *nduna*, Chiwerewere Ndhlovu, led a group eastwards to the north end of Lake Malawi, while another group, led by most of Zwangendaba's sons, subdued the Tumbuka chief Chikulamayembe in about 1855.[9] These Ngoni then elected Mbelwa as paramount chief.

Meanwhile, two other sons of Zwangendaba, Mperembe and Mpezeni, had formed followings of their own and had moved south of Lake Tanganyika into Bemba and Bisa country. It is not clear at what stage this further fission took place. Wiese, whose brief account of Ngoni migrations is the earliest record from the Ngoni now in Zambia, says that when Mpezeni came of age he and the late regent, Ngai, made an expedition against some people near Lake Bangweulu. Mpezeni's brother, 'M'chaxo', took advantage of his absence to break away to the east and set up his own kingdom, later known as 'M'pambera' (sc. Mbelwa).[10] Elmslie says that the secession of Mpezeni and Mperembe took place after Mbelwa's Ngoni had moved east and south to Lake Malawi; Chibambo says Mpezeni parted from Mbelwa near Lake Malawi.[11] There is obviously a disagreement rooted in the rival attempts of Mpezeni's and Mbelwa's Ngoni to substantiate their claims to universal hegemony over all Ngoni.[12] For present purposes, it is enough to say that Mpezeni seems to have led away his Ngoni to the south round about 1850.

According to Chibambo, Mpezeni and Mperembe crossed the upper

paper published some time before his book, Fraser wrote that 'From the Zambesi they [the Ngoni] fought their way to Nyasaland, then striking west, they passed through the Senga and Wemba populations till they reached Lake Tanganyika' (D. Fraser, 'The Zulu of Nyasaland: their Manners and Customs', *Proceedings of the Philosophical Society of Glasgow*, 1900–1, 32, p. 61). This reference to the Bemba does not recur in *Winning a Primitive People*.

[8] Stanley, *Through the Dark Continent*, p. 319. Burton describes the progress of one such group through the country east of Lake Tanganyika, evidently in the early 1850s (*Lake Regions*, II, pp. 75–6).

[9] Cullen Young, *Tumbuka-Kamanga Peoples*, p. 115. One or other of these groups must have been the 'Mazitu' (a common name for Ngoni) whom Livingstone encountered to the north of the Chewa chief Mwase wa Kasungu in 1863 (Livingstone, *Narrative*, pp. 526–41; cf. Fraser, *Primitive People*, p. 314).

[10] Carl Wiese, 'Em M'Pesene', *Bol. Soc. Geog. Lisboa*, 1891, 10, p. 468. Wiese was at Mpezeni's from 1889 to 1891.

[11] Elmslie, *Wild Ngoni*, p. 28; Chibambo, *My Ngoni*, p. 35

[12] Elmslie, Fraser and Chibambo report Mbelwa's tradition. See Barnes, *Politics in a Changing Society*, pp. 22–3, for a discussion of this problem.

Luangwa at Kapinga and went away to Bisa country. They tried to settle in Bemba country, and Mperembe became a 'chief' there, but he was forced to move on.[13] Lancaster says that Mpezeni skirted Bemba country, raiding the Bisa and Lala, and for a time settled at 'Cherongo' (sc. Chilonga?) on the Muchinga escarpment, where crops were harvested.[14] The other versions of Ngoni history say only that Mpezeni left Mperembe to move south through Bisa country and then crossed the Luangwa. This probably took place before 1861: in that year, it was reported at Zumbo that the Nsenga were harassed by 'Mupesene',[15] while Livingstone, at the south end of Lake Malawi, heard that Ngoni had been raiding near the Luangwa and that 'Mpzene' was a Zulu chief.[16] By 1866, Ngoni were crossing the Luangwa from the east bank to raid the Bisa on the lower Munyamadzi river.[17] As for Mperembe, he continued for a while to raid the country west of the Luangwa and to fight the Bemba, but then, 'war after war proving too much', he too left the north-eastern plateau, settling in Tumbuka country under Mbelwa.[18] There is a cryptic note on Mperembe by Crawshay, a British official who visited the old chief late in 1893: 'Formerly Perembi lived in Luwemba, and on friendly terms with Mwamba (Moamba), but through disagreement which led to fighting in which he was worsted, he ultimately had to leave. He told me he was friendly with Mwamba now, but not with Kitimkulu.'[19]

The main evidence from the Bemba on Bemba–Ngoni relations is to

[13] Chibambo, *My Ngoni*, pp. 35–8

[14] D. G. Lancaster, 'Tentative Chronology of the Ngoni', *JRAI*, 1937, 67, p. 86. This is very poorly documented and no reliance can be placed on it.

[15] Pacheco, 'Voyage de Tête à Zumbo', p. 315

[16] Wallis, *Zambezi Expedition*, I, p. 195. Livingstone does not say where 'Mpzene' was at this time. He calls the Ngoni 'Mabibele or Mazuite of Binda'.

[17] Livingstone, *Last Journals*, I, pp. 159, 163. This may be the basis for Lancaster's assertion that in 1865 Mpezeni's Ngoni were at Mkoma at Mbangombe hills, and in 1868 at Mpinduka hill on the 'Matambadzi' river ('Tentative Chronology', p. 81), and for Winterbottom's assertion that Mpezeni crossed the Luangwa to the east in 1865 (J. M. Winterbottom, 'Outline Histories of Two Northern Rhodesian Tribes', *RLJ* 1950, 8, p. 18). Lancaster simply says that this had happened by 1873: 'Chronology', p. 81.

[18] Fraser, *Primitive People*, p. 315; cf. Cullen Young, *Tumbuka-Kamanga Peoples*, p. 130; Chibambo, *My Ngoni*, p. 38; Elmslie, *Wild Ngoni*, p. 28. Winterbottom says this happened in 1869, but he gives no evidence for this ('Outline Histories', p. 18). Lancaster says that Mperembe's Ngoni were defeated by Arabs and Bemba near Chikumbo, in 'Lake Bangweulu District' in 1868, and that this was the occasion of Mperembe's migration to Mbelwa's ('Chronology', p. 81). This seems to be a misrepresentation of Livingstone's testimony, which I cite below.

[19] BCAG, 4 June 1894

be found in the histories by Mushindo and Labrecque;[20] I was not myself able to obtain much oral testimony on this subject. As there are some points of difference in these two written sources, I present parallel summaries of their narratives: the sections placed in the centre contain those episodes which both writers describe in much the same way, and in the same order.

section	MUSHINDO	LABRECQUE	page
52	Ngoni under Zwangendaba march from Zambezi to Chewa, Tumbuka, Namwanga, Iwa.		
		Ngoni under Zwangendaba build Chibungu, on Kanchibia river.	298
	Chileshye* is Chitimukulu.		
		Mperembe leads away group who help Lungu of Munshimbwe against Bemba.	294–5
		Ngoni attack Mwaba; kill his brother Chibamba, but are repulsed,	298
52	Ngoni defeat and kill Makasa at Chisenga.		299–300
		and also kill Changala.	
53	Ngoni cross Chambeshi river at Ilonga	Ngoni march through Mpanda into Lubemba.	300
53	Ngoni attack Chitimukulu's village, Kasansama; repulsed, but kill his daughter, NaKatongo Chifita, on Katuba stream, and proceed to Kalungu/Chibile confluence.		301–2
53	Ngoni burn Mwangata's village; move west into Ituna and then south.	Ngoni move north to source of Chambeshi and build Buningi.	302
	Chileshye* is Chitimukulu.		
53	Ngoni kill Kamfwa, grandson of Chileshye*, in Musoa.	Mperembe's Ngoni kill Kamfwa, son of Makasa, near W. border of Ituna, but are repulsed by Chitapankwa.	295
	Ngoni kill chief Mbulu on Lake Bangweulu.		

[20] Mushindo, *History*, s. 52–5, 65–74; Labrecque, 'Origines', pp. 298–314 (this is followed by Tanguy, *Imilandu*, pp. 33–8, 45–55)

section	MUSHINDO	LABRECQUE	page
54	Ngoni march east through Ichingo; build Chibungu near confluence of Manshya and Mwaleshi; raid Bisa in Chinama, and Lala;		
55	kill Chibamba, brother of Mwaba, but fail to defeat Mwaba; burn Mwalule village; march north via Safwa rapids and Ituna.		
	Chileshye* dies.		
		Mperembe's Ngoni rejoin main body at Buningi.	302
55		Ngoni halt on Saisi/Chambeshi watershed; build Ititini.	302
65	Mapupo rebels against Zwangendaba; flees to Makasa.		
65	Makasa lives at Manga, at confluence of R. Kabishya and Mombo river. Ngoni invade Mpanda. Mapupo, an Ngoni, spies on Ngoni for Bemba;		303
66	Makasa kills Mperembe and is then joined by Chitapankwa*; they expel Ngoni from Ititini, and burn it.		305
67	Chitapankwa* returns home; Ngoni then attack and capture Makasa's capital; kill Mukukamfumu; and capture Chimbabantu. Makasa flees west to Chilukutu.		306
68	Ngoni then build Chipekeni, near Makasa's capital.		307
69	Makasa and Mwamba ready to submit, but Chitapankwa* refuses.		
70	Bemba envoys to Ngoni feign submission but are exposed by poison ordeal.		
71	Chitapankwa* and Mwamba join Makasa at Chipekeni; Nkula, Shimumbi and lesser chiefs also come.		308
71	Chitapankwa* independently skirmishes with Ngoni, and	Ngoni attack Mwamba, but are repulsed.	309
72	narrowly escapes.		
73	Chitapankwa*, smoking hemp, entices Ngoni to bridge across Mombo stream. Bemba ambush Ngoni there and storm Ngoni camp. Bemba have two cannon, which misfire.		310
	Two cannon, overfilled with powder, swing round and kill some Bemba.	One cannon blows up and kills a Swahili.	
74	Zwangendaba dies of grief and anger. Ngoni flee to south-east.		311

There is clearly a broad agreement between Mushindo and Labrecque on the nature and sequence of most of the individual events in this story. The most important difference concerns the order of events up to the settlement of the Ngoni in Mambwe country. But there is a major difference between both these Bemba-derived accounts and all the Ngoni sources. Neither Mushindo nor Labrecque mention the original Ngoni settlement in Ufipa[21]—an event which incontrovertibly took place, and which as we have seen can be dated to around 1840. And related to this omission by Mushindo and Labrecque is their common supposition that Zwangendaba, so far from dying in Ufipa in about 1835, remained the Ngoni leader right up until their final defeat by Chitapankwa*.[22] In fact, it is likely that all the incidents of Bemba–Ngoni conflict related by Mushindo and Labrecque took place after the Ngoni diaspora from Ufipa. The Ngoni accounts strongly support this view, and there seems more reason to credit their picture of the overall sequence of events than that from the Bemba side. The Ngoni, after all, have had good reason to remember the main outline of their great migrations, since this helps to explain the subsequent relations between different Ngoni groups. The Bemba, on the other hand, have naturally been more concerned to remember individual episodes of conflict with the Ngoni inasmuch as these affected particular Bemba leaders and are associated with particular parts of Bemba country. The synoptic accounts by Mushindo and Labrecque are probably to some extent the result of incorporating a series of separately remembered events in an overall narrative in which the order of events is partly based on conjecture.

We may thus conclude that Mushindo and Labrecque are mistaken in presenting the initial conflict between Bemba and Ngoni as taking place in the course of the Ngoni advance northwards from the Zambezi. But if such conflict took place, instead, when Ngoni were moving southwards from Ufipa, Mushindo's description of the sequence of events is probably more accurate than Labrecque's. Ngoni moving southwards would have been more likely to collide first with Bemba in Chilinda, as Mushindo says, than further south or west, on the Kanchibia or at Mwaba's, as Labrecque says. There is further evidence

[21] This is also omitted in Young's very brief reference to Ngoni movements: he says the Ngoni first came to Bemba country after 'smashing' the Bisa and Senga (Chinsali DNB I, p. 233).

[22] Kabanda, the Bisa chief, also said (T1) that 'Sungandaba' was the leader of the Ngoni against the Bemba: the plateau peoples in general tend to call all Ngoni chiefs Zwangendaba. See also above, p. 25.

to support this conclusion. Mushindo's sequence of events here agrees with a statement by chief Luchembe in 1918: the Ngoni built at Chibungu, on the river Manshya, after killing Makasa and then being defeated by Chitimukulu.[23] Thus Labrecque must be mistaken in saying that the Ngoni moved north to Ititini immediately after their campaign in Lubemba. He is also mistaken in placing Chibungu on the Kanchibia river.

For most of the individual episodes mentioned by Mushindo and Labrecque, there is confirmation from various other sources. It is well known that Makasa and Changala were killed in Chilinda, and the site of the battle, Chisenga, is still remembered.[24] The death of Nakatongo Chifita near the Katuba stream, not far from the site of Malole mission, is also remembered.[25] Thomas' history of the Bisa relates that the Ngoni raided the Bisa of Mwansabamba from Chibungu, on the Mwaleshi river.[26] Concerning the northward march of the Ngoni through Bembaland, Mushindo's account might at first seem to conflict with evidence from Shimulamba. This informant said that the Ngoni killed one of his ancestors, a son of Nkolemfumu, on the east bank of the Chambeshi, near Mwaba's; he insisted that the Ngoni did not then cross the Chambeshi but continued up the east (left) bank.[27] This may well be strictly true: Mushindo says that the Ngoni went on to Mwalule after leaving Mwaba's, but Shimulamba may simply be diverting attention from a crossing of the Chambeshi by the Ngoni *after* their visit to Mwalule, such as Mushindo relates.

As for the settlement of the Ngoni in Mambwe country, it is known there that the Ngoni allied with the Mambwe chief Mpande,[28] and it was Mpande V Chitongwa who advised the Ngoni to administer a poison ordeal to Bemba who came suing for peace after the Ngoni had captured Makasa's capital.[29] Several sources confirm details of the battles

[23] Luchembe, 1918 evidence. Kabanda says that one of his predecessors withstood an attack by Ngoni and also helped the Bemba drive the Ngoni away to the north, but the order of events is not clear (Kabanda, T1 and n. 9). Thomas says that Kabanda repelled the Ngoni with the aid of Bemba guns (*Bisa*, p. 41). Grant, in writing of the Ngoni near Lake Victoria, appears to record a garbled impression of Bisa and/or Bemba resistance to the Ngoni: 'The only race in the south that ever mastered them, and can pass through them, are the Wabeesa, living to their west' (J. A. Grant, *A Walk across Africa*, London 1864, p. 119).

[24] Chikunga, T3; Milambo, T1; Chinsali DNB II, pp. 50, 54
[25] Katenda, 31 May 1965   [26] Thomas, *Bisa*, p. 41
[27] Shimulamba, T1, n. 39
[28] Watson, *Tribal Cohesion*, p. 152; Abercorn DNB I, p. 100 (1906–07); see also above, pp. 143–4.
[29] Labrecque, 'Origines', p. 307; Chikunga, T1

between Bemba and Ngoni on the northern borders of Bembaland, and Young adds some information about Bemba armaments.[30] The Ngoni sources, as we have seen, concede that Mperembe was eventually defeated by the Bemba, though Mushindo, Labrecque and Young are clearly mistaken in claiming that Mperembe was killed by the Bemba; this same Mperembe was alive and well in 1893.[31]

It remains to provide a chronology for Bemba–Ngoni relations. The Ngoni defeat of Makasa at Chisenga probably occurred in the early 1850s. It must have happened after the initial Ngoni diaspora from Ufipa, which took place around 1845,[32] and in any case Bemba informants indicate that Makasa was killed in the latter part of Chileshye's reign.[33] The Ngoni passage through Lubemba, and their subsequent settlement at Chibungu, may also be dated to the 1850s, but it was evidently later than the Bisa rebellion in Chinama: there is no indication that Bemba encountered Ngoni in Chinama, though Ngoni are said by Bisa to have raided Chinama from the Mwaleshi. It was in any case presumably these Ngoni who broke up the Bisa trade route through Chinama in the early 1860s.[34] The final expulsion of the Ngoni from Mambwe country can be dated to about 1870. It clearly took place after Livingstone's journey through Bembaland in 1867, since he implies that the Ngoni then still menaced the Bemba, though he gives no details of any battles.[35] According to both Mushindo and Labrecque, the expulsion of the Ngoni was soon followed by Chitapankwa's* unsuccessful campaign against the Lungu chief Zombe, which took place in 1872.[36]

[30] Chinsali DNB I, pp. 233–4; see also above, p. 203.

[31] See above, p. 366. Labrecque mistakenly says that Mpezeni led the Ngoni march to the south-east after their final defeat ('Origines', p. 311).

[32] See above, p. 365.

[33] Chikunga, T3; Milambo, T1; Shimulamba, T1. The date 1856 for the first Bemba–Ngoni conflict, which is cited in such recent works as Gann, *History of Northern Rhodesia*, p. 20, may be traced back through Lane-Poole (*Native Tribes of the Eastern Province*, p. 9) and Gouldsbury and Sheane (*Great Plateau*, p. 29) to Robertson (*Introductory Handbook*, p. xx); there is no good authority for it.

[34] See above, pp. 119–21, 192–3.

[35] *Last Journals*, I, p. 199; cf. above, p. 143. Lane Poole (*Native Tribes of the Eastern Province*, p. 9) says that Livingstone speaks of the Bemba, under 'Mapupo', defeating Ngoni under 'Malalami'. There is no such story in the *Last Journals*. As for these names, Mapupo occurs as an Ngoni spy who misled the Bemba before their major defeat by the Ngoni at Manga (Labrecque, 'Origines', p. 303); for Malalami, or Mulalami, see below, p. 373.

[36] Mushindo, *History*, s. 75; Labrecque, 'Origines', p. 314; see above, p. 150. It was presumably for this reason that Labrecque gave 'about 1869' as the date of the Ngoni capture of Makasa's capital ('Origines', p. 305).

This chronology helps us to collate the Bemba-derived accounts with the Ngoni sources. As we have seen, the latter all agree that Mpezeni left the plateau west of the Luangwa some time before Mperembe, who wielded much power there for a time before being obliged to move eastwards. We have also seen that Mpezeni had probably crossed the Luangwa by 1860.[37] Thus, while Mpezeni may have taken part in the defeat of Makasa in Chilinda, he had probably split off from Mperembe before the Ngoni invasion of Lubemba, their southward migration to Chibungu, and their subsequent move north into Mambwe country.

There is one phase in Ngoni wanderings, following their earlier wars with the Bemba, to which neither Bemba nor Ngoni sources explicitly refer: this is the Ngoni invasion of the country around the south end of Lake Tanganyika. According to a tradition in this area, Mperembe and another Ngoni leader, 'Mwamboshi', led a group into the country of the Lungu chief Chitimbwa; he

> gave them all they asked for, and the Alungu were unmolested. It was against the Watawa [Tabwa] the Angoni were intending warfare. . . . [They] crossed the Lovu [Lufubu] and continued as far as Moliro [Mulilo] before they returned. . . . The Angoni proceeded through Zombe's country and camped on the Mashyete stream—near the present Anglo-German boundary. The Alungu worked for them. . . .[38]

From other sources, we gather that these Ngoni were repelled by the Tabwa of Nsama some time before 1867.[39] Some years later, a 'Zulu javelin' was displayed by Tabwa near Cameron's Bay, south of Mulilo's,[40] and it was presumably a reference to this same expedition which gave Stewart, in 1879, the mistaken impression that one Ngoni group had actually settled to the west of Lake Tanganyika.[41] There is

[37] See above, p. 366.

[38] Mporokoso DNB I, p. 245. 'Mwamboshi' was presumably Mhambose, wife of Zwangendaba, from whom Mperembe inherited his segment (Barnes, *Politics in a Changing Society*, pp. 14, 218). Labrecque says that 'Mamboshi' was killed in the final Bemba victory ('Origines', p. 310); he calls her the mother of Zwangendaba.

[39] Tippu Tip, *Maisha*, p. 19; notes from Nsama's, 21–23 June 1965.

[40] E. C. Hore, journal, May 1880, LMS/CA/J3 (Wolf, *Tanganyika*, p. 121); he was told that the javelin had been captured 'at Katanga', but there is no other indication that any Ngoni went so far west.

[41] Stewart, 'Lake Nyasa', p. 270; he is followed in this detail by Elmslie and Lane-Poole. Barnes notes that Stewart was probably misinformed on this; he

no mention by Livingstone of the Ngoni invasion of Itabwa, but while at the south end of the lake, in March and April 1867, he attested to the presence of Ngoni in Lungu country. He heard that 'Mazitu' (i.e. Ngoni) were living in hills south of Mbete, on the lake, and that they had recently raided along the lake shore to the north-west.[42] One group, somewhere to the east, was said not to plunder, but already the Lungu had been 'greatly reduced in numbers by the Mazitu, who carried off very large numbers of the women, boys, girls, and children. They train or like to see the young men arrayed as Mazitu but it would be more profitable if they kept them to agriculture.'[43]

A somewhat garbled impression of the Ngoni impact on the Lungu was later recorded by Joseph Thomson, who visited the south end of Lake Tanganyika in 1879: he wrote that 'about twenty years ago' the Lungu, under a chief called Kakungu, were harassed by the raids of 'Mazitu' or 'Watuta' under Tafuna. The latter captured Kakungu's eldest son, Mulalami; he learned the customs and mode of warfare of the Mazitu, and in due course came back to train his own people along the same lines. These 'counterfeit Watuta' terrorised their neighbours no less effectively than their exemplars. Kakungu then gave Mulalami that part of his kingdom between Zombe's and Ufipa, but when Mulalami died his military system collapsed, and his people discarded both the name and the practices of the 'Watuta'.[44] It is conceivable that these 'counterfeit Watuta' are to be identified with the 'Mazitu' of whom Livingstone heard, but the latter nowhere hints at this, and the obvious mistakes in Thomson's references to Lungu leaders do not encourage one to take this account very literally. The name 'Watuta' seems to have been adopted quite generally by or for the Lungu of Tafuna, rather than being confined to any particular section of them. Cameron, when sailing round the south end of Lake Tanganyika in 1874, gathered that the Lungu chief Chitimbwa was 'chief of all the Watuta'.[45] When Stanley made the same voyage two years later, he recorded the presence of 'Watuta strangers' a little to the north of Kasanga, while he had earlier been informed of 'the Watuta in the

does not, however, take account of the evidence that there was at least a temporary movement of Ngoni around the south-western corner of the lake (*Politics in a Changing Society*, p. 22). At the same time, it should be noted that Mulilo, after his defeat by Nsama, is said to have spent a year on the east shore of the lake, to the north of Kala, and to have made an alliance there with Ngoni; this probably occurred in the early 1860s. Delhaise, 'Chez les Wabemba', p. 274; cf. above p. 153.   [42] *Last Journals*, I, pp. 213, 226

[43] *Last Journals*, I, p. 205   [44] Thomson, *Central African Lakes*, I, pp. 317–18
[45] Cameron, *Across Africa*, I, p. 287

neighbourhood of Zombe', at the southeast end of Lake Tanganyika'.[46]

By 1868 some Ngoni appear to have penetrated also west of Lake Bangweulu. In that year, Livingstone reported that Ngoni had fought with some success against the Chishinga of Chikumbi until a group of Nyamwezi intervened, who 'beat off the Mazitu with their guns, while all the country people fled'.[47] There is no indication as to whether these Ngoni were those of Mperembe or a quite separate group.[48] Since Livingstone indicates that Kazembe was much concerned at this attack on one of his subject peoples, it is a little surprising that there should be no mention of Ngoni attacks in the official Lunda history.[49] But it is unlikely that Livingstone, who was so close to the event, should have been mistaken in reporting the invaders as Ngoni. At all events, it does not seem that there were any Ngoni living west of the Luangwa valley after their final defeat by the Bemba in about 1870.

Both oral traditions and contemporary written records point to only one notable conflict between Bemba and Ngoni after Mperembe's defeat at Chipekeni. Late in October 1887 there were Scottish missionaries from Livingstonia at the village of the Ngoni chief Mbelwa when one of his armies returned from an expedition west of the Luangwa:

> The Angoni army joined the Basenga and Babisa against the Awemba who were preparing for a second attack on these tribes. The Angoni were thoroughly victorious and routed the main village and killed all the people as well as the chief who was being carried off on a machilla. The Angoni wanted to spare and capture the women and children but the others were bent on revenge for past wrongs and spared none.[50]

This battle can conclusively be identified with one that is clearly remembered by both Bemba and Bisa informants, who agreed on the essentials.[51] Nkula Mutale Sichansa put his son Ndakala in charge of country taken from the Bisa chief Chibesakunda.[52] Then a Senga

[46] Stanley, *Dark Continent* (1880 ed.), pp. 322, 346

[47] Livingstone, *Last Journals*, I, p. 308

[48] Lancaster gives no authority for his statement that they were Mperembe's ('Tentative Chronology', p. 81).

[49] Livingstone, *Last Journals*, I, pp. 293, 330; Cunnison, *Historical Traditions*.

[50] Elmslie to Laws, 7 November 1887, NLS 7890; cf. W. P. Livingstone, *Laws of Livingstonia*, London 1921, p. 237; Elmslie, *Wild Ngoni*, p. 245

[51] Milambo, 1 October 1964; Mbutuka, 14 May 1965; Kapandansalu, T1; Peyoni Bwalya, T1; cf. Mushindo, *History*, s. 81–2; Chinsali DNB II, p. 50 (statement by chief Nkula in 1917); Labrecque, 'Origines', pp. 311–13

[52] See above, p. 138. One informant spoke euphemistically of the Bemba 'protecting' Chibesakunda's country against the Ngoni.

chief, Chifunda, got help from the Ngoni and together they killed Ndakala at Kabondwe, near the site of Mulanga mission.[53] Winterbottom mentions the battle in a history derived from Ngoni sources: he says that when Mbelwa was asked for help by a Bisa [*sic*] chief, Chifundo, an Ngoni force went and defeated the Bemba, who were led by 'Chandalala'.[54] In a Senga account of the battle, the Bemba leader is called 'Chandalala', while Mushindo calls him 'Ndakala Chandala'.[55] Labrecque adds that reinforcements from Nkula arrived just after Ndakala's death and obliged the Ngoni to return home.[56]

The defeat of Ndakala had a larger importance than that simply of an incident in Bemba–Ngoni relations: it seems to have checked the Bemba from giving aid to Mlozi's attack on the African Lakes' Company's station at Karonga in November 1887.[57] The missionary Elmslie reported that Mbelwa's Ngoni had heard the Bemba were 'in league with the Arabs. This [the Bemba] chief's plan was to work down the Loangwa and neighbouring country and the Arabs were to work on this side [near the lake]. This is the Angoni story and you will see it corresponds with what we already know.'[58] Nothing came of this scheme; no Bemba force joined Mlozi; and Europeans in the area considered that this was directly due to the Ngoni victory in October.[59] Indeed, this victory encouraged Laws of the Livingstonia mission to press for a military campaign against Mlozi which would put paid to his imperial ambitions.[60] There appears to be no record, written or oral, of any later Bemba–Ngoni conflict, though Ngoni probably continued to raid west of the Luangwa.[61]

[53] Nkula then killed Chifunda: see above, p. 226.

[54] Winterbottom, 'Outline Histories', p. 18; he relates the story to the account in Livingstone's *Laws*, but errs twice in dating it to Laws' first visit to Mbelwa in 1877. In fact, Laws' first visit was in 1879 (Livingstone, *Laws*, pp. 161–2), and he heard of the Bemba defeat after his third visit (*ibid.*, p. 237).

[55] Information from the Senga of Kambombo, kindly supplied by Dr H. W. Langworthy; Mushindo, *History*, s. 81–2

[56] Labrecque is clearly wrong in saying that Ndakala was killed shortly before Chitapankwa's death. He says that it was Mperembe who helped Chifunda, and that both were assisted by an Englishman called Jameson who used a machine-gun ('Origines', 312–14). I have not managed to clarify either of these points.

[57] See above, p. 226.   [58] Elmslie to Laws, 7 November 1887, NLS 7890

[59] Cf. Hawes to Salisbury, 16 January 1888, FO 84/1883; Livingstone, *Laws*, p. 239

[60] Hanna, *Beginnings of Nyasaland and North-eastern Rhodesia*, p. 94

[61] In 1889 Elmslie reported the return of some of Mbelwa's Ngoni from an expedition to the Bisa (Elmslie to Laws, 10 October 1889, NLS 7892). In 1894 it was reported that 'the Marambo [Senga country] is a favourite place for Ngoni

SUMMARY

After crossing the Zambezi in 1835, the Ngoni under Zwangendaba moved northwards, east of the Luangwa, and settled in Ufipa. When Zwangendaba died, in about 1845, the Ngoni split up under different leaders. Mbelwa went east and then south to Tumbuka country. Another group, probably led by both Mpezeni and Mperembe, moved southwards around the eastern borders of Bemba country. In about 1850 these Ngoni defeated the Bemba at Chisenga, in Chilinda, killing Makasa I and Changala I. Mpezeni then went further south and perhaps settled for a while near Chinama but did not encounter Bemba there. By 1860 he had moved on to the southeast, across the Luangwa. Mperembe's Ngoni followed up the defeat of Makasa by entering Lubemba, but they were repulsed by Chileshye* and moved south through Ituna and across the Chambeshi into Bisa country, where they built a camp called Chibungu, near the Manshya/Mwaleshi confluence. From there, during the years around 1860, they attacked the Bisa in Chinama and the Bemba at Mwaba's and Mwalule. They then recrossed the Chambeshi and went north through Ituna into Lungu country. Some Ngoni then went west as far as Itabwa but returned to settle for a time among the Lungu. The Ngoni then built a new base at Ititini, on the Saisi/Chambeshi watershed, and allied with the neighbouring Mambwe chief Mpande. After invading Makasa's country, Mpanda, the Ngoni were expelled from Ititini by Makasa and Chitapankwa*, but they then returned to Makasa's village, Manga, killed Mukukamfumu, captured Chimbabantu, and expelled Makasa himself. The Ngoni then built a new camp, Chipekeni, near Manga, but in about 1870 they were expelled by a large force under Chitapankwa* and other leading Bemba chiefs. This time, the Ngoni fled eastwards to the Namwanga and then went south: Mperembe eventually settled near the Ngoni of Mbelwa. In 1887 Mbelwa sent an army across the Luangwa to assist the Senga chief Chifunda against the Bemba of Ndakala; the Ngoni and Senga defeated the Bemba at Kabondwe.

impis' (Stewart to Smith, 15 August 1894, NLS 7877); and in the same year Glave heard that Ngoni of Mpezeni and Mbelwa raided through Bisa and Lala country to the Luapula (*BCAG*, 1 January 1897).

Appendix 4

Select Historical Texts

NOTE

The three texts which follow have been chosen as examples of different kinds of historical narrative. The first is a typical legend of origin, explaining how certain chiefly titles were founded, and their subsequent relationships. Various episodes in the story, such as the settlement of Mfungo, Chimbola and Mwamba, have the character of aetiological inventions, and this impression is confirmed when they are compared with other evidence bearing specifically on these subjects.[1] The story about Mumena's dogs (of which Mushindo gives a slightly different version)[2] may well be a more or less standardised cliché, in view of the importance of dogs in other stories explaining political relationships.[3] As for the reference to Mumena's invitation to Nkweto, this may well be an elaboration arising from the informant's own career as a holder of both titles in succession.[4]

The second text relates how Chinchinta* was deposed in favour of Chileshye*, from whose sisters all later Chitimukulus traced their descent. For this reason,[5] it is perhaps the earliest episode in Bemba history, subsequent to the foundation of the dynasty, which is still remembered in a number of traditions in different chiefdoms. The version given here is not as full as others which I recorded, and in certain respects it contradicts them: contrast this account of Chinchita's* expulsion with the traditions which describe a large-scale assault on the royal capital.[6] Nonetheless, the basic elements of the story correspond to those in other versions, and it is clear that the protagonists are actual historical characters.

[1] Cf. above, pp. 94–6, 104–5, 130–2, 132, n. 24; and see map 9.

[2] Mushindo, History, s. 28

[3] Cf. J. van Velsen, 'Notes on the History of the Lakeside Tonga of Nyasaland', African Studies, 1959, 18, iii, p. 109, n. 23

[4] Cf. p. 83, n. 20   [5] Cf. pp. 26–7   [6] Cf. pp. 102–4.

The third text concerns events in the later nineteenth century for which much evidence can be adduced from different sources.[7] It relates how Mporokoso's country was obtained from the Tabwa (in about 1875) and is thus of much more local significance than the second text: it concerns an episode in the history of subordinate chiefdoms on a frontier rather than that of the royal dynasty as a whole. The story represents oral reminiscence in process of becoming oral tradition: the informant did not himself take part in the events, but he learned about them from participants, such as his own mother's brother Mporokoso I.

THE FOUNDATION OF MUMENA, NKWETO AND OTHER CHIEFTAINSHIPS
(from tape-recording by chief Nkweto Mulenga (T1), 17 May 1965)

I talk of our chieftainship. I am chief Nkweto, and I live in Chinsali district. I have ruled people in three places: first of all at Binda; then [Chitimukulu] Kanyanta removed me from there, and I went to Mumena; and from there I went to Nkweto. David Shyula was sent away from this chieftainship: he didn't listen to people; he was removed in 1951.

All the chiefs came from Kola. Those who came to spy out the land were Mutale Mukulu, Mumena, Chimbola and his nephew Mfungo. When they came with their nephew, he carried fruit seeds. They came to the hill called 'Mushimwa and Namukonda' [the latter is a hunting goddess]. They said, 'There is salt there, nephew; you must break the salt and bring it to where we, your uncles, are living.' So Mfungo stayed there. But soldier ants invaded his house, and he said, 'My uncles have left me in distress [*makalandu*].' So they called Mfungo's place Makalandu, because his house was invaded by ants when he was left there.

At that hill, the three chiefs found a grove. Mutale Mukulu said 'I will stay here'; then all three slept there, Mutale Mukulu, Chimbola and Mumena. Then they began to share out the country. Mumena said, 'I am going this way.' Chimbola said, 'I am going this way.' So Mutale Mukulu said, 'You are leaving me where disagreement started [*pe tumba milandu*].' So that place is called Katumba.

Mumena and Chimbola set off. Chimbola stopped in a thick bush and said to his brother Mumena, 'You go on and leave me here in the thick bush [*matengele*].' So Mumena replied, 'Stay here, my friend, this

---

7 Cf. pp. 155–7

is Matengele.' So now people call Chimbola's country Matengele. Mumena set off with two dogs and crossed the Kalungu river. By sundown he felt really thirsty. He wanted to sleep at the foot of a tree, but he could find no water at all. While he slept under the tree, his two dogs went over the plain and made a hole from which water came out. The chief arose and went to drink water at this spring. He exclaimed, 'Ah! this is at the puddle [*kasembo*].' So that is why people call Mumena's country Kasembo.

So that was where Mumena lived. Then Chitimukulu set off from Kola. He said, 'Let me follow my uncle and brothers.' So he followed Chimbola and Mutale and Mumena. He arrived with his soldiers, and he fought Mutale Mukulu and Mumena. The soldiers fought until they killed people of Mutale Mukulu, who then surrendered, saying, 'It is no good killing people like this. If you kill people, whom will we have to give orders to?' So Chitimukulu said, 'That man has surrendered.' Then he went to find Chimbola, and he fought him too. Chimbola said, 'My friend, do not kill people. If you do, whom will we have to give orders to?' So Chitimukulu said, 'This man too has surrendered.' Now he went to Mumena's, and again he killed people. Mumena said, 'I do not want to lose all my people in battle, for then there would be no one to give orders to.' So Chitimukulu said, 'This man also has surrendered.'

Then Chitimukulu turned back and found his way with his soldiers to the Kalungu river. Then he said, 'My people, put up your shelters here; the sun is going down.' So he slept there. At six o'clock he said to his soldiers, 'Go and draw water from the river.' The soldiers went to the river and found there a dead crocodile. It stank very badly, and they said, 'What a terrible smell.' One of them looked at the sandbank and saw the crocodile lying there. He said, 'What creature has died here?' They looked closely at it, but could not say what it was. Then Chitimukulu got up from where he was sitting; he came to the river and said, 'Men, is this the animal whose name you don't know?' They said, 'Yes, your Majesty.' The chief said, 'It is a crocodile. Let us build at this very place. This is *ŋwena*.' So the chief built there, and they called the place *ŋwena*, because of the crocodile which had died on the sandbank.

After some time, Chitimukulu sent for Mumena, so that they could share the country. Mumena came, and they sat by the Milando stream, which goes into the Kalungu river. They stretched their legs in the river, to wash the bracelets which they wore round their ankles. Chitimukulu said, 'Mumena, the country across the Kalungu is all yours. The country on this side is all mine. Chimbola and Mutale Mukulu are in my country.' That is what Chitimukulu did.

In the evening, he summoned his soldiers and said, 'Men, come and call me Conqueror of Countries [*mpalakashya twalo*]. We took their countries from them because we are men of firm purpose.' He fought Mutale Mukulu, Chimbola and Mumena; that is why they praised him as Mpalakashya. He would not have taken the country if he had not been firm.

This is what I was told by the old men. Chitimukulu and Mumena shared the country between them; Mumena lived in his country across the Kalungu. Then Chitimukulu said, 'Mumena's country is very large. Men, go back to Kola and summon my younger brother, and I will give him part of Mumena's country.' It used to be Mumena's on this side of the river. So the soldiers brought Mwamba from Kola, and he came to Chitimukulu who said to him, 'My brother, go to the west, because the country of Mumena is very big.' Then Mwamba said, 'You brought me here, and I thought I would stay with you in the same village, but now you send me elsewhere.' Chitimukulu replied, 'Go away; it's where you missed your aim [*ni kwituna*—perhaps also 'where you were sent on your way'].' That is why they call Mwamba's place Ituna.

Then Mumena heard that Chitimukulu had sent for his younger brother, and had given him part of his [Mumena's] country. So Mumena sent soldiers, saying, 'I too will fetch my younger brother, Nkweto.' The soldiers brought Nkweto from Kola. When they arrived back at Mumena's village, he said, 'My brother, Chitimukulu shared the country with me. But now he says my country is too big. So he fetched his brother and cut off part of my country. He must watch out, because he came here through fighting. I will be very happy if you go across the Chambeshi.' So Nkweto said, 'So you are sending me elsewhere to wait for the country.' Mumena replied, 'Go; it is a place for waiting [*cilinda*].' That is how these names began: Ituna for Mwamba's, and the other name for this place.

That is what I know. Nkweto came to live on this side of the river. He waited here in the country of Mumena, so it is called Chilinda. Nkweto lived here and died; who then was to succeed him? Then came Chileshye Mwaba, David Shyula, and then myself, Mulenga. That is all, sir.

THE ACCESSION OF CHILESHYE*
(from tape-recording by Chileshye Mukulu, T1, 30 May 1964)

. . . Mutale *wa munkobwe* died; the next was Salala. Salala *bana bonke* died; the next was Katongo *ncilamalilo*. Katongo died; the next was Mukuuka *wa malekano*. Mukuuka *wa malekano* died; the next was Chiliamafwa. Chiliamafwa died; the next was Susula, whom they called Chinchinta.

Chinchinta made a great mistake when he went to Chitimukulu's. He called people to come and work for him. If they didn't come, he would send people from his capital to destroy their granaries. So they disliked Chinchinta and brought a message to Mulenga—that is the same man as Mutale Mukulu—saying, 'We want you to succeed here in Lubemba.' Mulenga refused and said, 'Chinchinta is my nephew; I can't succeed my nephew; no, no. I am going to appoint someone here', and the man he appointed was Chileshye Chepela.

Now Chileshye Chepela's father was Mulenga Mwimba, and Mulenga Mwimba had married two wives. One was Mwimba Nsangwa, the mother of Kabwibwi; the other was Mukukamfumu. They were both pregnant. Mwimba Nsangwa's child was Kabwibwi, and that of Mukukamfumu was Chepela—Chileshye Chepela. Chileshye Chepela was born without fingers on one hand. His mother then said, 'This is my child, but I do not like it; I want to throw him away.' But Mwimba Nsangwa said, 'No, you mustn't throw this child away. We can't choose a baby, indeed; we choose kaffir corn [a proverb]. So you had better give him to me, my friend, and I can look after him.' Mukukamfumu gave her Chileshye Chepela, and she began to look after him, so Chepela grew up with his friend Kabwibwi.

When they had grown up, they were playing a ball-game when Chileshye Chepela missed the ball. His cousin, a son of Nkolemfumu, began to laugh at him, saying, 'You missed the ball, and you have only one arm.' Chepela took a small stick and beat Nkolemfumu's son on the neck; then Chepela ran away. He went to Kazembe's, in Lunda country, and stayed there for a time. But he found there were no proper manners there, so he said, 'I will go back home to Lubemba.' On his return, he went to see his mother, in Ituna. She said to him, 'Don't stay here in Ituna; you left here after a quarrel. Go away to your "grandfather" in Lubemba, Mutale Mukulu.' Chileshye Chepela agreed to this and came to Sanga [a river], in Mulenga's country. Mulenga received him, and he explained why he had come. Then the chief said, 'Very well, grandson, stay here.' So Chepela stayed there.

One day, Mutale Mukulu sent Chepela to Chitimukulu—it was Chiliamafwa at that time. Chepela went to chief Chiliamafwa and stayed at the capital, and they looked after him. Chiliamafwa gave Chepela a village, and he built it near the Mfinshe stream. Then he moved, and built 'Chitila Muto' [the leftovers]; and then he built yet another village by the Chibile river, near the forest of Changa.

It was when Chepela went to build there that Mulenga was chosen to be Chitimukulu. Mulenga refused to succeed and said, 'No; my nephew became Chitimukulu before me. You had originally chosen me, but then you talked against me [and chose Chinchinta instead]. I myself will make the appointment.' And he appointed Chileshye Chepela, telling him that he was now to succeed as Chitimukulu. Chepela said, 'Very well; but what about Chinchinta? what shall we do about him?' Then Mulenga said, 'Well then, we will send Chinchinta away.'

Mulenga and Chepela now went to see Kashinge [a *kabilo*]. They sent a man to ask Kashinge if Chinchinta was at the capital. Kashinge said, 'No; he is right here. He must go and see Chileshye Chepela. I invited him here and gave him two calabashes of beer.' Chinchinta drank his beer, but meanwhile Mulenga made preparations, and when Chinchinta began to say, 'I will leave now', they began to fight him, there at Kashinge's. Mulenga drove him away, and Susula went back home to the capital. There he told his wife, 'Boil some water so that I can wash my legs.' His wife put water on to boil, and as it came to the boil Chinchinta heard shouting from people coming near. He went into the relic-house with Shilukula [a *kabilo*]. Mulenga and Mutale Mukulu [*sic*] arrived and asked, 'Where is your husband?' Chinchinta's wife answered, 'He is in the relic-house.' So in they went and fetched out both chief Susula and Shilukula. They killed Shilukula on the spot, but they let the chief have his wife and said to him, 'Go away, wherever you please.' So Chinchinta left, and went to Nsokolo's country, and Chileshye Chepela succeeded as Chitimukulu.

MWAMBA II HELPS KAFWIMBI TO DEFEAT HIS TABWA RIVALS AND BECOME NSAMA V (from tape-recording by Njalamimba, T1 19 June 1965)

My name is Njalamimba. My grandfather Chiteba did not live here [i.e. near Mporokoso's]; he lived in Ituna; that is where his home was. Kafwimbi, the great chief of the Tabwa, came and surrendered in Bembaland, saying, 'Mwamba, I want you [to help me]; my nephews have taken my country.' But Mwamba refused, saying, "Shall I set out on an expedition just on account of these Tabwa? No, I won't go myself; but I will give you my sons. They will go and kill them with their spears.' He [Kafwimbi] said, 'Ah! you are cheating me. They have been annoying me.' Mwamba said, 'My two sons will go with you.'

So Mulume Nshimba, called Lombe [i.e. Mporokoso I] came here, and so did Kaoma, who was the stronger of the two. They set off from the Luombe river . . . with their friend Sunkutu. These were the men whom Mwamba gave to Kafwimbi. He said to him, 'Go with these men, Sunkutu and Mulume Nshimba, Lombe. They will fight them; they will not be defeated.' Kafwimbi said, 'Ha! so they won't give in?' Mwamba said, 'Go away and see for yourself.'

So off they went with chief Kafwimbi, ruler of the Tabwa. They began to fight, and fought again and again. Then they said, 'This place is too far away.' So they went and built [a village] at the source of the Kabwafya. Again they fought, and chased them down the hills into Tabwa country. They chased them to Chibubo, where they surrendered. But Kafwimbi said, 'No; they will soon rise again and kill me; they are still too near me.' They sent the heads of the people they killed to Milenge [Mwamba's village].

They pursued them relentlessly until they came to a place where they asked some [other] people to come and fight; these were some of Kafwimbi's own Tabwa. With their help, they drove the enemy down to Chulu, on the Mofwe river, and across the Kalungwishi river. They came back and chased [another group] across the Kalungwishi. They found chief Puta at Katete, among the salt-makers, and they killed him. They found chief Kabelenga [i.e. Kalembwe, a nephew of Puta], and they killed him too. It was he whom they chased to the Mofwe, which runs into the Kalungwishi . . .

So they killed them and brought their heads to Mwamba, at Milenge; they came and paid tribute to 'Mushipe Shinte' ['the strong tree-stump'—a praise-name]. Chief Kafwimbi said, 'Well done, Mwamba.' And Mwamba said, 'Now you have seen [what my sons can do]. And you said they would be too strong for you. But can I be beaten by such people? You have seen what I have done. Now reward me as you promised.' So Kafwimbi gave Mwamba this country where we are now; he said, 'The boundary is the Luangwa river, as far as its junction with the Kalungwishi, which is on the other side—that is what I give you.'

Mwamba said, 'Indeed! I already have this big country; how can

o

you offer me this tiny area on the Kalungwishi? Will they still take ivory to you? Is it your country? No, no; this area is too small.' So Kafwimbi said, 'We will add on country west of the Luangwa, to the Kalungwishi, as far as Pasa, and then right up to Lake Tanganyika.' But he and Mununga [the Shila chief] refused to give Mwamba the land across the Kalungwishi [i.e. Mununga's country].

Appendix 5

List of Informants

Abbreviations: C, Chitimukulu; H, Headman; L, Literate; P, Predecessor; B, Brother; D, Daughter; F, Father; M, Mother; S, Son; Z, Sister

Names (title in capitals)	Position and year of appt.	Authority for information and his kin relation to informant	Periods mostly away at work outside N. Province
AARON SICHIVULA	former court (member, Nsokolo's)	elders at Zumbi	1924, 1948–63 (L)
CHABUKILA	perpetual son of Chibesakunda	singers for C'kunda Mwelwa	2 yrs. before 1914
CHANDAWEYAYA Mwamba	*namfumu*, Lubemba 1958	MM	—
CHEWE KALUBILA Mwamba	*ŋandu* H, Lubemba ?1933	P(MB)	—
CHIBINGO Chileshye	*kabilo* for Shimwalule 1956	F (Shimwalule Kangwa); P(MB)	1939–53
CHIBWE Agostino Kalengule	priest for Chimbola	F	?
CHIFUMO John Chipwepwe	*kabilo* for Shimwalule 1964	F (Shimwalule Chipwepwe)	—

Names (title in capitals)	Position and year of appt.	Authority for information and his kin relation to informant	Periods mostly away at work outside N. Province
CHIKUNGA Joseph Muma	*kabilo* for C 1951	P(MMB)	— (L)
CHILESHYE MUKULU Sampa	*ŋandu* H, Lubemba 1954	P(MMB)	1920–32, 1949–54
CHIMBA Kangwa	priest for C 1947	P(MB)	1914–18, 1925–41
CHIMBOLA Mutale	CHIEF ?*c.* 1930	?	1 yr. before 1911
Chimpamba	elder, Mutale Mukulu's	Mafuta Katongo (H)	?
Chinyumba	villager, Mporokoso's	—	?
CHIPASHA Chileshye	*kabilo* for C 1943	P(MMB)	6 yrs. before 1943
CHISANGA Paulo	elder, chief Mununga's (Shila)	P(MB)	1939 (L)
CHISUTULA Chileshye	priest for Mwamba	MM	1911–25 (L)
Chitichipalo Chanda	villager, Lubemba	—	—
CHITIKAFULA Kabungo	*kabilo* for C 1962	—	1941–68
CHITUBA Mutale	*kabilo* for Makasa	Makasa V (d. 1920)	1918–22
CHIWELE	*kabilo* for Chewe Kalubila *c.* 1948	P(MB)	—
CHIWELEWELE Chiwala	'grandson' of Chibesakunda Chimba Tata		?
Dickson Chanda	H, court assessor, Kabanda's 1961	P(MB)	1927–41 (L

Names (title in capitals)	Position and year of appt.	Authority for information and his kin relation to informant	Periods mostly away at work outside N. Province
KABAMBA ŊOMBE Chisupa	Yeke H, Ichinga 1941	F	1930s
KABANDA Mulenga	Bisa chief 1946	P(MMB)	?
KABWA Braimu	*kabilo* for C 1949	—	1914–18 (L)
KABWELA Mulembo	priest for Bisa chief Chinkumba	—	?
Kachasa Lazaro	villager, Lubemba (F of Kapasa Mwenya)	—	?
KAKWELA Edward	keeper of royal graves, Lubemba 1954	P(MB)	1914–45
Kalesu	elder, Chiŋandu's (near Chikwanda's)	?	?
KAMIMA Mutale	priest for Mwamba 1947	P(MMMZS)	1911–14
KAPANDANSALU Kabungo	Bisa H (S of Chibesakunda Mwelwa)	F, B	?
KAPASA Mwenya	H, Lubemba	P(MB)	—
Kapasa Matumbo	elder at Mwaba's	MMB (S of a former Mwaba)	before 1914
Kapeso Chipe	villager near Kabanda's	F	1941–6
Kapinda	elder at Mubanga's	?	?
Kapoka	court assessor, Mubanga's	MMB (S of Chileshye*)	—
KAPUKUMA Mwaba	*kabilo* for C 1964	—	1924–62

Names (title in capitals)	Position and year of appt.	Authority for information and his kin relation to informant	Periods mostly away at work outside N. Province
KASHITU Chimfwembe	*kabilo* for Shimwalule 1946	other *bakabilo* at Mwalule	before 1928
KATENDA Chokwe	*kabilo* for C 1927	P(MB); P of Chitikafula; P of Munuca	1914–18
KATWAMBA Mubanga	B of H. Mulilo, Lubemba	P of Mulilo (MMB)	?
Luchembe	villager, Mulenga wa Chibungu's	?	?
LUMPOMBWE Mwamba	*kabilo* for C 1927	P(MMB)	?1920
MAKOFI Agostino	*kabilo* for Makasa	Makasa V (d. 1920)	?1920–?30
MAKUMBO Joseph	*kabilo* for Mukupa Kaoma 1935	F	2 yrs. before 1935
MAKWAYA Mulenga	*kabilo* for Nkweto	P(B)	—
MBUTUKA Chishika	ɲandu H, Ichinga	Kabungo IV (MMZS)	3 yrs., *c.* 1920
MILAMBO Chileshye	*kabilo* for Mwamba 1944 (DS of Mwamba I)	P(MB); Mwamba IV	early 1900s (L)
Molo Makungo	elder at Mukupa Kaoma's	F	11 yrs. before 1930 (L)
MPYANA BWALYA Chanda	H, Ichinga 1924	MZS; M	*c.* 1910–24
MUBANGA Mutale Ponde	chief 1951	MB of Mukwikile II	—
MUKUUKA MULEYA	H, Ichinga	?	before 1914
MULENGA WA CHIBUNGU Chisanga	ɲandu H, Lubemba 1958	?	1920s
MULOMBELWA Bwalya	*kabilo* for C 1946 +	P(MB)	?*c.* 1925

387

Names (title in capitals)	Position and year of appt.	Authority for information and his kin relation to informant	Periods mostly away at work outside N. Province
MUMBA ŊOMBE Sampa	*kabilo* for C 1957	?	?4 years
MUMENA Chewe	*ŋandu* H, Lubemba 1955	?	?
MUNGULUBE Mutale	Bisa H (former chief)	M, MB	2 yrs.
MUNKONGE Chilekwa	chief (S of Mwamba V) 1931	—	—
MUNSOMA Munungalelwe	elder at Matipa's	F	—
MUNUCA Kangwa	*kabilo* for C 1959	P of Chitikafula	1931–59
Mutale Musonko	elder at Mwamba's	?	?
MWABA WA NKULUNGWE Mwansa	*ŋandu* H (former chief) 1964	P(MB)	before 1935
MWAMBA Musenga	chief 1945	—	*c.* 1914–17
Mwango Mwela	head messenger, Kabanda's	F	1925–31
NJALAMIMBA Kabungo	H, near Mporo- koso; early 1900s	MB (Mporokoso I)	—
NKOLEMAMBWE Mulenga	*kabilo* of C 1927	P	—
NKOLEMFUMU Mutale Nshika	chief 1946	Kanyanta*	—
NKWETO Mulenga	chief 1951	*bakabilo* of Kanyanta*, 1920s	—
NSEMIWE Hamed	Swahili H, Itabwa 1952	P(F)	1940–3
NSENSHI Mutale	*kabilo* for C 1963	—	1929–63
Nshilika Mwenya Chiyanse	B. of H. Kashoki, in Lupi	Kabwibwi Kayula	1921–44

Names (title in capitals)	Position and year of appt.	Authority for information and his kin relation to informant	Periods mostly away at work outside N. Province
Peyala Kapembwa	elder at Nsama's	F (son-in-law of Katele II)	1914–18, 1924–7 1937–40
PEYONI BWALYA Sakeo	elder at Chimwala's, Ichinga	F	? (L)
PUTA Hilya Kasoma	chief (Bwile) 1937	M	1935–7
Sampa Kalambwe	villager near Chandaweyaya's	?	?
SANI Chela	Swahili H near Kasama	Ps (F, FF)	—
Sewuka	villager at Kabungo's, Ichinga (BS of Chewe Mulenga *wa cilaka*)	FZS (Kabungo IV)	5 yrs.
SHIMAKASA Chitolo	*kabilo* for Shimumbi 1949	P(MB)	1927–33
SHIMULAMBA Yumba	*kabilo* for Nkolem-fumu 1924?	P(MB)	—
SHIMWALULE Chipwepwe	senior keeper of Bemba royal graves 1961	—	?
Shitantameni	court assessor, Tungati's 1961	MMB; F (P of Chitikafula)	— (L)
SONGOLO Kazyoba	Yeke H near Kasama	F	?
TUNGATI Kangwa	chief (S of Mwamba VI) 1946	—	? (L)

Appendix 6

List of Written Sources

1. Manuscripts
2. Printed material:
    (a) Primary sources for central and eastern Africa before 1900
    (b) Works relating primarily to the Bemba
    (c) Works relating to east and central Africa
    (d) Other works

I. MANUSCRIPTS

FO   Foreign Office files at the Public Record Office, London

LM   Manuscript collection of the Livingstone Museum, Livingstone, Zambia

LMS Archives of the London Missionary Society, Congregational Council for World Mission, London

NAR National Archives of Rhodesia, Salisbury

NAT National Archives of Tanzania, Dar es Salaam

NAZ National Archives of Zambia, Lusaka

NLS Manuscript collection of the National Library of Scotland, Edinburgh

RH   Letter from Johnston to Rhodes, 31 December 1895, with enclosure from Weatherley to Johnston, 11 October 1895, in Mss. Afr. S. 228, 26, Rhodes House, Oxford

WF   Archives of the Generalate of the White Fathers (Padri Bianchi), Via Aurelia 269, Rome

The abbreviation DNB refers to District Notebooks: all the District Notebooks of Northern Rhodesia are housed in the National Archives of Zambia. I have also used these further abbreviations in referring to unpublished materials:

1918 evidence: evidence submitted in the Chikwanda–Nkuka dispute, 1918. NAZ/ZA/1/9/27/6/1

Goodall, 'Tree': 'Tree of the House of the Wemba Chiefs' by E. B. H. Goodall (Kasama, 1910; revised at Luwingu up to 1912, with additions). NAZ/KSZ 4/1

Willis Enquiry: Enquiry into the dispute on the succession of Chitimukulu, 1924 (enclosure in Mporokoso DNB)

Individual references are also given for the following items:

GIBSON HALL, J., 'Notes on Lungu royal family extracted from Notes by J. Gibson Hall', in H. C. Marshall, 'Notes on African Genealogies', n.d. (?*c.* 1905), LM/G 69/5/7

MARSHALL, H. C., 'The Awemba under chiefs Mporokoso, Kalimilwa and Sunkutu. A review of their History, Laws and Customs with additional notes on the Alungu and Watabwa', n.d. (?*c.* 1905), LM/G 69/5/6

CHIEF MUSHYOTA VII, 'History wa Bena Chishinga' (1941, MS in possession of the author (P. O. Kawambwa)

OGER, L., 'History of Mpanda' (tr. Ann Tweedie from 'Calo ca Mpanda', n.d. (?*c.* 1960). TS in Library of the University of Zambia

SILANDA, H. E., 'The Enslavement of Grandmother Mary' (tr. L. M. A. Simukonda), TS biography of a Mambwe ex-slave captured by Ponde, n.d. LM/IV/D 19.

SIMTALA, P. M., 'History of Kafwimbi', MS dictated by P. M. Simtala, with advice from elders at Kafwimbi's; tape-recorded on 19 May 1965

VIBETI, Simon, 'History of the Bisa', n.d. (?*c.* 1936–50). MS in possession of Mr Medard Kasese

2. PRINTED MATERIAL

This bibliography lists only works cited more than once in the footnotes. I use the following abbreviations:

BCAG *British Central Africa Gazette*, Zomba, 1894–1902, filed by the Public Record Office as CO 541/1–2

BSAC British South Africa Company

CT   *Chroniques Trimestrielles de la Société des Missionaires d'Afrique* (*Pères Blancs*), Lille, 1879–1909
        There is one complete set of this periodical in the archives of the White Fathers' Generalate, Rome, and another at Kata-gondo Seminary, Masaka, Uganda; there is also a complete microfilm copy in the Library of the University of Zambia, and a very incomplete set at the White Fathers' St Edward's College, Totteridge, Hertfordshire
GJ   *Geographical Journal*
JAH   *Journal of African History*
J(R)AS   *Journal of the (Royal) African Society*
J(R)AI   *Journal of the (Royal) Anthropological Institute*
JRGS   *Journal of the Royal Geographical Society*
NRJ   *Northern Rhodesia Journal*
PRGS   *Proceedings of the Royal Geographical Society*
RLJ   *Rhodes–Livingstone Journal (Human Problems in Central Africa)*

Note: The first five volumes of *Aurora*, a journal published by the Free Church of Scotland mission (Livingstonia, 1897–; subsequently *The Livingstonia News*) are to be found in the Manuscripts Room of the University Library, Edinburgh; they are missing from the British Museum file.

(a) *Primary sources for central and eastern Africa before 1900*
BAPTISTA, P. J., 'Exploraçoes dos Portuguezes no interior d'Africa meridional', *Annaes maritimos e coloniaes* 1843, 3, v, pp. 162–90, 223–40, 278–97, 423–39, 493–506 (translated by B. A. Beadle in Burton, *Lands of Cazembe*, pp. 167–244).
BECKER, Jerôme, *La Vie en Afrique*, Paris 1887
British South Africa Company, *Reports on the Administration of Rhodesia* (title varies), London 1889–1903
BURTON, R. F., *The Lake Regions of Central Africa*, London 1860; *The Lands of Cazembe*, London 1873.
BÜTTNER, C. G., (ed. and tr.), *Suaheli-Schriftstücke*, Stuttgart and Berlin 1892 (see Anon., 'Beschreibung von Usango, Ruemba und andern Reichen im südwestlichen Theile von Deutsch-Ost-afrika', pp. 91–102)
CAMERON, V. L., *Across Africa*, London 1877
CARVALHO, H. Dias de, *Ethnographia a historia tradicional dos Povos da Lunda*, Lisbon 1890
CRAWFORD, Daniel, *Back to the Long Grass*, London n.d. (?1924)

DUPONT, Joseph, 'Voyage de cinq semaines dans l'Ubemba,' *CT*, 78, April 1898, pp. 246–58

ELMSLIE, W. A., *Among the Wild Ngoni*, London 1901

FOÀ, Edouard, *La Traversée de l'Afrique*, Paris 1900

FOTHERINGHAM, L. M., *Adventures in Nyassaland: A Two Years' Struggle with Arab Slave-Dealers in Central Africa*, London 1891

FRASER, Donald, *Winning a Primitive People*, London 1922

GAMITTO, A. C. P. (tr. Ian Cunnison) *King Kazembe and the Marave, Cheva, Bisa, Bemba, Lunda, and other peoples of Southern Africa* . . . Lisbon 1960

GENTHE, Hugo, 'Livingstone's Grave' (letter of 22 October 1897), *BCAG*, 5 February 1898

GIRAUD, Victor, *Les Lacs de l'Afrique Equatoriale*, Paris 1890

'Lieut. Giraud's attempt to cross Africa via Lake Bangweulu and the Upper Congo' (tr. and ed. anon.), *PRGS*, 1885, n.s. 6, pp. 332–7

GLAVE, E. J., 'Glave in Nyassaland'; 'Glave's Journey to the Livingstone Tree'; 'Glave in the Heart of Africa', *Century Magazine* (New York), 1896, n.s. 30, pp. 589–606, 765–81, 918–33

GROGAN, E. S., and SHARP, A. H. *From the Cape to Cairo*, London 1900

HARRINGTON, H. C., 'The Taming of North-Eastern Rhodesia' *NRJ*, 1954, 2, iii, pp. 3–20

HORE, E. C., *Tanganyika*, London 1892

'Lake Tanganyika', *PRGS*, 1882, n.s. 4, pp. 1–28

JOHNSON, Harry, *Night and Morning in Dark Africa*, London 1903

KIRK, John, *The Zambesi Journal and Letters of Dr John Kirk*, ed. R. Foskett, Edinburgh 1965

KOOTZ-KRETSCHMER, Elise, *Die Safwa*, Berlin 1926–9 (II, pp. 321–31: reminiscences of 'Xisi-Nguririje-Sixyujunga', a Bisa woman; abridged translation in E. Kootz-Kretschmer, *Stories of Old Times*, London 1932, pp. 1–18)

de LACERDA e ALMEIDA, F. J. M., *Diários de Viagem*, ed S. B. de Holanda (Bibliotheca popular brasileira, 18), Rio de Janeiro 1944
Travessia da Africa, Lisbon 1936

LIVINGSTONE, David, *African Journal 1853–1856*, ed I. Schapera, London 1963
The Last Journals of David Livingstone . . . , ed H. Waller, London 1874
Private Journals 1851–1853, ed I. Schapera, London 1960

LIVINGSTONE, David and Charles, *Narrative of an Expedition to the Zambesi and its Tributaries* . . . *1858–1864*, London 1865

MAITRE, Henri, 'Zwei Forschungsreisen der "Weissen Väter" nach Lobemba und Lobisa', *Petermanns Mitteilungen*, 1902, 48, 1902, pp. 169–72

MOIR, F. L. M., *After Livingstone: an African Trade Romance*, London 1923

'The Eastern Route to Central Africa', *Scottish Geographical Magazine*, 1885, 1, pp. 95–112

PACHECO, A. M., 'Voyage de Tête à Zumbo' (tr. C. Millot), in P. Guyot, *Voyage au Zambèse*, Paris 1895, pp. 225–325

RICHARDS, Audrey I., 'The Story of Bwembya', *Ten Africans*. ed M. Perham, London 1936 (reprinted 1963), pp. 17–40

SELIM bin Abakari' 'Safari yangu ya Nyassa', *Safari za Wasuaheli*, ed Carl Velten, pp. 50–105

SHARPE, Alfred, 'A Journey to Garenganze', *PRGS*, 1892, n.s. 14, pp. 36–47

SILVA PORTO, A. F. da S., *Silva Porto e a travessia do continente Africano*, Lisbon 1938

SLEMAN bin Mwenye Tshande, 'Safari yangu ya barra Afrika', *Safari za Wasuaheli*, ed Carl Velten, pp. 1–49

STANLEY, H. M., *Through the Dark Continent*, London, 1880 (second edition)

STEWART, James, 'Lake Nyasa and the water route to the lake region of Africa', *PRGS*, 1881, n.s. 3, pp. 257–74

SWANN, A. J., *Fighting the Slave-hunters in Central Africa*, London 1910

THOMAS, W. ['W.T.'], Letter in *BCAG*, 12 October 1894

THOMSON, Joseph, *To the Central African Lakes and Back*, London 1881

TILSLEY, G. E., *Dan Crawford of Central Africa*, London 1929 (includes extracts from Crawford's diaries)

TIPPU TIP, *Maisha ya Hamed bin Muhammed el Murjebi, yaani Tippu Tip* (Swahili text with translation by W. H. Whiteley), East African Literature Bureau, Nairobi 1966

TRIVIER, Emile, *Mon Voyage au continent noir: la 'Gironde' en Afrique*, Paris and Bordeaux 1891

VELTEN, Carl (ed.), *Safari za Wasuaheli*. Göttingen 1901 (translated by Carl Velten as *Schilderungen der Suaheli*, Göttingen 1901)

WALLACE, L. A., 'The Nyasa–Tanganyika Plateau', *GJ*, 1899, 13, pp. 595–622

WALLIS, J. P. R. (ed.), *The Zambezi Expedition of David Livingstone, 1858 to 1863*, London 1956

WEATHERLEY, Poulett, Letters in *BCAG*, 15 August 1895, 15 September 1895, 1 April 1896, 1 January 1897, 15 January 1897, 1 March 1897, 1 June 1897, 15 June 1897, 30 April 1898, 24 December 1898, 24 August 1899

WISSMANN, H. von, *My Second Journey through Equatorial Africa from the Congo to the Zambesi in the years 1886 and 1887* (tr. M. Bergmann), London 1891

    Despatches dated 14 July 1893 and 5 September 1893 in *Deutsches Kolonialblatt*, 1893, 4, pp. 492–3, 537–8

WOLF, James B. (ed.), *Missionary to Tanganyika 1877–1888: the writings of Edward Coode Hore, Master Mariner*, London 1971

YOUNG, Robert, 'Bobo Young relates his Exploits', *NRJ*, 1953, 2, ii, pp. 65–71 (letter of 20 July 1914 from Young to Lt.-Col. S. Gore-Browne)

(b) *Works relating primarily to the Bemba*

BRELSFORD, W. V. *Aspects of Bemba Chieftainship*, Rhodes-Livingstone Communication 2), Livingstone 1944

    'Shimwalule: a Study of a Bemba Chief and Priest', *African Studies*, 1942, 1, iii, pp. 207–23

    The Succession of Bemba Chiefs, Lusaka 1944 (second ed. 1948)

GLUCKMAN, Max, 'Succession and civil war among the Bemba', *RLJ*, 1954, 16, pp. 6–25

GOULDSBURY, Cullen, 'Notes on the Customary Law of the Awemba', *JAS* July 1915, 14, 56, pp. 366–85; October 1915, 15, 57, pp. 36–85; January 1916, 15, 58, pp. 157–84

    and SHEANE, Hubert, *The Great Plateau of Northern Rhodesia*, London 1911

LABRECQUE, Edouard, 'La Tribu des Babemba: I, les Origines des Babemba', *Anthropos*, 1933, 28, pp. 633–48

    'Les Origines des Babemba de la Rhodésie du Nord (Zambia)', *Annali del Pontificio Museo Missionario Etnologico* (formerly *Annali Lateranensi*), 1968, 32, pp. 249–329

MPASHI, Stephen A., *Abapatili bafika ku Lubemba*, Cape Town 1956, Lusaka 1966, 1968

MUSHINDO, P. B., *A Short History of the Bemba*, Lusaka (in press)

PINEAU, Henry, *Evêque-Roi des Brigands: Monseigneur Dupont*, 4th edition, n.p. (Montreal?), n.d. (1960?)

REA, W. F., *The Bemba's White Chief*, Historical Association of Rhodesia and Nyasaland, Local Series 13, Salisbury 1964

RICHARDS, Audrey I., 'African Kings and their Royal Relatives', *JRAI*, 1961, 91, ii, pp. 135–50

    'The Bemba of North-Eastern Rhodesia', *Seven Tribes of British Central Africa*, eds E. Colson and M. Gluckman, London 1951, pp. 164–93

RICHARDS, Audrey I.—*cont.*
  Chisungu, London 1956
  'The Conciliar System of the Bemba of Northern Zambia', *Councils in Action*, eds A. I. Richards and Adam Kuper, Cambridge 1971, pp. 100–29
  'Keeping the King Divine', Henry Myers Lecture 1968, *Proceedings of the Royal Anthropological Institute*, 1968, pp. 23–35
  Land, Labour and Diet in Northern Rhodesia, London 1939 (second edition 1961)
  'The Political System of the Bemba Tribe—North-Eastern Rhodesia', *African Political Systems*, eds M. Fortes and E. E. Evans-Pritchard, London 1940, pp. 83–120
  'Social Mechanisms for the Transfer of Political Rights in Some African Tribes', *JRAI*, 1960, 90, ii, pp. 175–90
ROBERTS, Andrew D., 'Chronology of the Bemba', *JAH*, 1970, 11, ii, pp. 221–40
ROBERTSON, W. G., *An Introductory Handbook to the Language of the Bemba People*, London 1904 (Historical part reprinted in 'Kasembe and the Bemba nation', *JAS*, 3, 10, January 1904, pp. 183–93)
SHEANE, J. H. West, 'Some Aspects of Awemba Religion and Superstitious Observances', *JAI*, 1906, 36, pp. 150–8
  'Wemba Warpaths', *JAS*, 11, 41, October 1911, pp. 21–34
TANGUY, F., *Imilandu ya Babemba*, London 1948, 1963
TWEEDIE, Ann, 'Towards a History of the Bemba from Oral Tradition', in Stokes and Brown, *The Zambesian Past*, pp. 197–225
WERBNER, Richard P., 'Federal Administration, Rank, and Civil Strife among Bemba Royals and Nobles', *Africa*, 1967, 37, i, pp. 22–48
WERNER, Douglas, 'Some Developments in Bemba Religious History', *Journal of Religion in Africa*, 1971, 4, i, pp. 1–24
WHITE FATHERS, *Bemba-English Dictionary*, London 1954
  Ifyabukaya: Fourth Bemba Reader, Chilubula n.d. (1932)
WHITELEY, W. H., *The Bemba and Related Peoples of Northern Rhodesia*, London 1951 (International African Institute, Ethnographic Survey of Africa, East Central Africa, part 2)

(c) *Works relating to East and central Africa*
AFRICAN ELDERS (assisted by E. Labrecque), *History of the Bena-Ŋoma (Ba-Chungu wa Mukulu)*, London 1949
APTHORPE, R. J., 'Problems of African History: the Nsenga of Northern Rhodesia', *RLJ*, 1960, 28, pp. 47–67

BARNES, J. A., *Politics in a Changing Society*, Cape Town, 1954; Manchester 1967

BEACHEY, R. W., 'The Arms Trade in East Africa', *JAH*, 1962, 3, iii, pp. 451–67

BEIDELMAN, T. O., 'Myth, Legend and Oral History: a Kaguru Traditional Text', *Anthropos*, 1970, 65, pp. 74–97

BIRMINGHAM, David, *Trade and Conflict in Angola*, Oxford 1966

BRELSFORD, W. V., *Generation of Men. The European Pioneers of Northern Rhodesia*, Salisbury n.d. (1966)

'Rituals and Medicines of Chishinga Ironworkers', *Man*, 1949, 49, pp. 27–9

BURTON, W. F. B., *Luba Religion and Magic in Custom and Belief*, Tervuren 1961

CHIBAMBO, Y. M., *My Ngoni of Nyasaland* (tr. C. Stuart), London n.d. (1942)

COLLE, P., *Les Baluba*, Brussels 1913

COLSON, Elizabeth, and GLUCKMAN, Max (eds), *Seven Tribes of British Central Africa*, London 1951

COXHEAD, J. C. C., *The Native Tribes of North-Eastern Rhodesia: their laws and customs*, Royal Anthropological Institute Occasional Paper 5, London 1914

CULLEN YOUNG, T., *Notes on the History of the Tumbuka-Kamanga Peoples*, London 1932 (reprinted 1970)

CUNNISON, Ian G., 'History and Genealogies in a Conquest State', *American Anthropologist*, 1957, 59, i, pp. 20–31

History on the Luapula, Rhodes-Livingstone Paper 21, Cape Town, 1951; Manchester 1969

'Kazembe and the Arabs to 1870' in Stokes and Brown, *The Zambesian Past*, pp. 226–37

'Kazembe and the Portuguese, 1798–1832', *JAH*, 1961, 2, i, pp. 61–76

The Luapula Peoples of Northern Rhodesia, Manchester 1959

'Perpetual Kinship: a political institution of the Luapula Peoples', *RLJ*, 1956, 20, pp. 28–48

'The Reigns of the Kazembes', *NRJ*, 1956, 3, ii, pp. 131–8

(ed and tr.), *Historical Traditions of the Eastern Lunda: Central Bantu Historical Texts II*, Rhodes-Livingstone Communication 23, Lusaka 1962

DANN, H. C., *Romance of the Posts of Rhodesia, British Central Africa, and Nyasaland*, London 1940

DELHAISE, C. G. F., 'Chez les Wabemba' [Tabwa of Mulilo], *Bull. soc. roy. belge geog.*, 1908, 32, pp. 173–227, 261–83

FALLERS, L. A. (ed), *The King's Men: Leadership and Status in Buganda on the eve of Independence*, London 1964

GANN, L. H., *The Birth of a Plural Society*, Manchester 1958
'The End of the Slave Trade in British Central Africa, 1889–1912', *RLJ*, 1954, 16, pp. 27–51
A History of Northern Rhodesia, London 1964

GARBETT, G. Kingsley, 'Religious Aspects of Political Succession among the Valley Korekore (N. Shona)' in Stokes and Brown, *The Zambesian Past*, pp. 137–70

GLUCKMAN, Max, *Economy of the Central Barotse Plain*, Rhodes-Livingstone Paper 7, Livingstone 1941

GRAY, Richard, and BIRMINGHAM, David (eds), *Pre-Colonial African Trade*, London 1970

HANNA, A. J., *The Beginnings of Nyasaland and North-Eastern Rhodesia, 1859–95*, Oxford 1956

HUGHES, J. E., *Eighteen Years on Lake Bangweulu*, London n.d. (1933)

JACK, J. W., *Daybreak in Livingstonia*, Edinburgh and London 1901

KAPFERER, Bruce, *Co-operation, Leadership and Village Structure*, Zambian Paper 1, Manchester and Lusaka 1967

LANCASTER, D. G., 'Tentative Chronology of the Ngoni', *JRAI*, 1937, 67, pp. 77–90

LANE-POOLE, E. H., *The Native Tribes of the Eastern Province of Northern Rhodesia* (*Notes on their Migrations and History*), Lusaka 1949 (third edition)

LIVINGSTONE, W. P., *Laws of Livingstonia*, London 1921

MACMILLAN, H. W., 'Notes on the origin of the Arab War', *The Early History of Malawi*, ed. B. Pachai, London 1972, pp. 263–82

MIRACLE, M. P., 'Aboriginal Trade among the Senga and Nsenga of Northern Rhodesia', *Ethnology*, 1962, 1, ii, pp. 212–22

MUNDAY, J. T., 'Kankomba', in *Central Bantu Historical Texts I*, Rhodes-Livingstone Communication 22, Lusaka 1961

PHILLIPSON, D. W., 'The Early Iron Age in Zambia: regional variants and some tentative conclusions', *JAH*, 1968, 9, ii, pp. 191–211
Prehistoric Rock Paintings and Engravings of Zambia, Livingstone 1972

RICHARDS, Audrey I., 'Some Types of Family Structure amongst the Central Bantu', *African Systems of Kinship and Marriage*, eds A. R. Radcliffe-Brown and D. Forde, London 1950, pp. 207–51

ROBERTS, Andrew D., 'Firearms in North-eastern Zambia before 1900', *Transafrican Journal of History*, 1971, I, ii, pp. 3–21
'The History of Abdullah ibn Suliman', *African Social Research*, 1967, 4, pp. 241–70

ROBERTS, Andrew D.—*cont.*
'Nyamwezi Trade', in Gray and Birmingham, *Pre-Colonial African Trade*, pp. 39–74
'Political change in the nineteenth century', *A History of Tanzania*, eds I. N. Kimambo and A. J. Temu, Nairobi 1969, pp. 57–84
'Pre-Colonial Trade in Zambia', *African Social Research*, 1970, 10, pp. 715–46
'Tippu Tip, Livingstone, and the Chronology of Kazembe', *Azania*, 1967, 2, pp. 115–31
(ed.), *Tanzania before 1900: seven area histories*, Nairobi 1968
ROLAND, H., 'Résumé de l'histoire ancienne de Katanga', *Problèmes sociaux congolais*, 61, June 1963, pp. 3–41
ROTBERG, Robert I., *Christian Missionaries and the creation of Northern Rhodesia, 1880–1924*, Princeton 1965
ST JOHN, Christopher, 'Kazembe and the Tanganyika-Nyasa Corridor, 1800–1890', in Gray and Birmingham, *Pre-Colonial African Trade*, pp. 202–28
STOKES, Eric, and BROWN, Richard (ed), *The Zambesian Past*, Manchester 1966
STRUYF, Y., 'Kahemba: envahisseurs Badjok et conquérants Balunda', *Zaïre*, 1948, 2, iv, pp. 351–90
THOMAS, F. M., *Historical Notes on the Bisa Tribe, Northern Rhodesia*, Rhodes-Livingstone Communication 8, Lusaka 1958
TRAPNELL, C. G., *The Soils, Vegetation and Agriculture of North-Eastern Rhodesia*, Lusaka 1953
VANSINA, Jan, *Kingdoms of the Savanna*, Madison 1966
'Notes sur l'histoire de Burundi', *Aequatoria* (Coquilhatville), 1961, 24, pp. 1–10
VERHULPEN, E., *Baluba et Balubaïsés*, Antwerp 1936
WATSON, William, *Tribal Cohesion in a Money Economy*, Manchester 1958
WEGHSTEEN, J., 'Origine et histoire des Watabwa (Haut-Congo)', *Annali lateranensi*, 1960, 24, pp. 364–75
'Origines et dispersion des hommes d'après les legendes tabwa', *Annali del Pontificio Museo Missionario Etnologico* (formerly *Annali Lateranensi*), 1962, 26, pp. 213–19
WHITE, C. M. N., 'Clan, Chieftainship and Slavery in Luvale Political Organisation', *Africa*, 1957, 27, i, pp. 59–73
WILLIS, Roy G., *The Fipa and Related Peoples of South-West Tanzania and North-East Zambia* (International African Institute, Ethnographic Survey of Africa, East Central Africa, London 1966, part 15

WILSON, Godfrey, *The Constitution of Ngonde*, Rhodes-Livingstone Paper 2, Livingstone 1939

WILSON, Monica, *Peoples of the Nyasa-Tanganyika Corridor*, Cape Town 1958

WINTERBOTTOM, J. M., 'Outline Histories of Two Northern Rhodesian Tribes', *RLJ*, 1950, 9, pp. 14–25

(d) *Other works*

ALLAN, William, *The African Husbandman*, Edinburgh 1965

BAUMANN, Hermann, *Schöpfung und Urzeit des Menschen im Mythus der afrikanischen Völker*, Berlin 1936 (reprinted 1965)

BOHANNAN, Laura, 'A Genealogical Charter', *Africa*, 1952, 22, iv, pp. 301–15

FINLEY, M. I., 'Myth, Memory and History', *The Listener*, 23 and 30 September 1965

FORDE, Daryll, and KABERRY, Phyllis (eds), *West African Kingdoms*, London 1967

FORTES, Meyer, and EVANS-PRITCHARD, E. E. (eds), *African Political Systems*, London 1940

GLUCKMAN, Max, *Order and Rebellion in Tribal Africa*, London 1963
'The Utility of the Equilibrium Model in the Study of Social Change', *American Anthropologist*, 1968, 70, pp. 219–37

GOODY, Jack, 'Circulating Succession among the Gonja', in Goody, *Succession to High Office*, pp. 141–76
(ed.), *Succession to High Office*, Cambridge 1966

LEACH, Edmund, *Genesis as Myth and other Essays*, London 1969

LLOYD, P. C., 'The Political Structure of African Kingdoms: An Exploratory Model', *Political Systems and the Distribution of Power*, A.S.A. Monographs 2, London 1965, pp. 63–112

NADEL, S. F., 'The Kede', in Fortes and Evans-Pritchard, *African Political Systems*, pp. 164–95

ROBINSON, R. E., and GALLAGHER, J., 'The Partition of Africa', *The New Cambridge Modern History*, ed F. H. Hinsley, 11, Cambridge 1962, pp. 593–640

SOUTHALL, Aidan, 'A Critique of the Typology of States and Political Systems', *Political Systems and the Distribution of Power*, A.S.A. Monographs 2, London 1965, pp. 113–40

VANSINA, Jan, 'A Comparison of African Kingdoms', *Africa*, 1962, 32, iv, pp. 324–35
De La Tradition Orale, Tervuren 1961

Index

Abdullah ibn Suliman, trader, 5, 158–60, 208n, 225n, 237–40, 258, 281

Abercorn (Mbala), 4, 20n, 143n, 187n, 236, 238–9, 242, 245, 269, 279, 281; *and see* Plate VIII

aetiology, 45, 47, 49, 55, 61, 64, 73, 377

affines, xxix, 129n, 172, 177–9, 300, 307

African Lakes Company, 4, 225, 230–1, 233, 237, 240–1, 247n, 250, 252, 256, 259, 262, 287n, 375

agriculture, xxvii–xxviii, 183–4, 210–11, 273, 314–15, 347, 366, 373; *see also citemene*, crops

Aley, trader, 197–8, 200, 203, 227n

Ambo people, 346

Amer ibn Said, trader, 195

Angola, 2, 50n, 57, 107, 191, 199, 310

anthropology, xxiii, xxiv, 37, 44, 65, 293–4, 306, 323, 326

Arabs, 104n, 192n, 193, 348n
and ALC, 240; and Bemba, 103n, 195–6, 202, 212n, 229n, 258, 281; influence on Bemba, 205, 209n, 268; and Chitapankwa, 150, 170n, 203; and Germans, 241; and Kazembe, 191n, 194, 199; and Mwamba III, 242, 259, 264, 268; and Tabwa, 152–3, 155, 198–9, 202, 237; *see also* Kumba-Kumba, Tippu Tip. 'Senga Arabs' on upper Luangwa, 225–8, 255–8, 270–1, 273, 275n; *see also* Kapandansalu, Mlozi

arbitration, 158–9, 181

archaeology, 36, 65–7

Ashanti, 309

assimilation, cultural and political, 20–2, 32, 46, 74, 99

bafingo, see undertakers

Bagamoyo, 194, 196, 198

Bainbridge, F. G., 240, 242

bakabilo (priest-councillors of Chitimukulu), 18, 43, 58, 71, 83, 171–2, 174, 306, 319
appointment of Chitimukulus, 79, 90n, 101–4, 129, 171–2, 254, 259n, 310, 382; appointment of other chiefs, 88, 132, 171–2, 283, 310; conflict with Chitimukulu, xxxi, 15, 19, 29, 312; creation of titles for b., 78–80, 301; functions, xxxi, 13–16, 310–11; 'house of Katongo', 16, 80, 91–2; source of political cohesion, 311–13

bamukabenye, see relics, wives of

banamfumu, see 'mothers of chiefs'

Bangweulu, Lake, 3, 66, 109, 121, 127, 140, 188–9, 192, 222, 298, 365

Bantu language family, 38, 66

bark cloth, xxvii, 98n, 188, 207–8, 249

Barnes, J. A., xxiii, 365n, 372n

bashilubemba (senior councillors of Chitimukulu), 15–16, 19, 30

bazimba, see Leopard Clan

beads, 113, 137, 150, 192, 206, 209n

beer, xxviii, xxx, 14, 88, 107, 137, 169–70, 233n, 251, 382

Bell, J. M., 258–9, 261–3, 265, 269–70

Bemba:
definition of B. people, xxvii; extent of country, xxvii, 78, 87, 92, 123, 164, 318; history sum-

Bemba—*cont.*
  marised, 297–9, 301–5, 324–5;
  language, xxviin, xxxi, 15, 45,
  51, 54n, 66, 74; name, 42, 68;
  people north of Lake Mweru,
  348–9; *see also* borders
bena bowa, see Mushroom Clan
Bena Marungu, 348
Bena Mukulo, 40; *see also* Matanda
Bena Mukulu, 10, 19, 20, 79n, 110,
  116, 119n, 139n, 141, 210n, 211;
  iron-working, 186, 189
bena ŋandu, see Crocodile Clan
bena ŋoma, see Drum Clan
bena ŋona, see Mushroom Clan
bena tembwe, see pall-bearers
Bisa, xxviii, xxxi, 2, 60, 65, 73, 87,
  174n
  and Bemba, 50, 173–4, 354, 364;
  as 'owners of the land', 16, 20, 42,
  133n, 163n; assimilation with
  Bemba, 21, 99; and Mwaba, 84;
  and Munkonge, 97, 110–11; first
  loss of Chinama, 111–14; of
  Lubumbu, 114–17; recovery of
  Chinama, 117–18; second loss of
  Lubumbu, 139–42, 180; B. and
  Chitapankwa, 133; and Nkula,
  87, 88n; 137–9, 226, 374; and
  Sampa, 136; second loss of Mpuki
  and Chinama, 160–3; and Mwamba III, 222; under British rule,
  133n, 221n, 280n, 289, 291n
  and Ngoni, 119, 121, 128, 133,
  162n, 192–3, 371
  origins of B. Chieftainship, 41, 45,
  49, 55, 64; political organisation,
  78, 93, 108–9, 295–6, 298, 309–10;
  production, 183–4, 186–7, 210–11;
  slave trade, 198; trade, 12n, 17,
  42, 183, 200, 202; trade with
  Kazembe, 107–10, 114, 121, 189–90,
  192–4; 298; B. traders on east
  coast, 190, 195; local trade, 186,
  188, 298; traditions, 9, 12, 34, 346;
  see also firearms, Kabanda, Kopa,
  Lubumbu, Matipa, Mukungule,
  Mwansabamba
Boisselier, Fr, 274

borders; of Bemba country, xxx,
  87, 96, 98, 102, 106, 113–14, 116,
  143, 157, 162n, 165, 181, 213, 220,
  235, 244, 251, 291, 383–4; Bisa,
  133n, 162; Kazembe's, 109–10,
  114, 116
bowstands, 345
Brelsford, W. V., xxiii, xxiv, 8, 11,
  58, 160n, 306, 320, 324
bride-wealth, *see* marriage payments
British Central Africa Protectorate,
  6, 216n, 232, 236, 255, 281
British South Africa Company, 6, 7,
  215, 231–2; first stations around
  Bemba country, 236, 238–42, 253,
  255, 258–9, 261, 282n; armaments,
  269, 279; armed forces, 269, 278,
  281, 287; and Kazembe, 281, 345;
  and Mporokoso, 242; and Mwamba III, 259, 262–5, 270, 273–5; and
  Ngoni, 286; and 'Senga Arabs',
  270–3; and White Fathers, 251,
  252n, 253, 265, 278–9, 282–3,
  287–8; administration of Bemba,
  82n, 85n, 133n, 221n, 262n, 272,
  279, 284–5, 289, 291, 342–3, 359–
  60; *see also* Abercorn, Codrington,
  Marshall, McKinnon, R. Young
Bulombwa, 42, 64, 72–4
burial, 32, 75–6; of Bemba chiefs,
  14–16, 75–6, 83, 172, 254, 259n,
  272, 301n, 310; and killing of
  retinue, 262n, 273n, 276; of
  Chewe Chimfwembe, 134; Chinchinta, 353–4; Chitapankwa, 218;
  Chiti, 42, 73, 78; Kapampa, 79;
  Makasa, 174n; Sampa, 262–3, 272
  among Bisa, 75–6, 162n; Lungu,
  97n
Burundi, 60, 74n, 76n, 308, 318
Bwalya, Makasa III, 98n, 107, 121,
  128–9, 138n, 143–6, 196, 198n,
  202–3, 212, 242n, 247, 349–51
Bwalya, Mukwikile I, 135, 138
Bwalya Chabala, burial grove, 16,
  123n, 172
Bwalya Chabala, name for Chilufya
  Mulenga, daughter of Muku-
  lumpe, 40n, 87n

Bwalya Changala, Nkula (d. 1934), 221, 278n, 280n, 361–2

Bwembya I, Chitimukulu, 11, 105, 118n, 123, 127–30, 180, 261, 318, 363

Bwembya II, Chitimukulu (succ. 1970), 321, 361

Bwembya, headman near Kasama, 6, 166n, 261n

Bwile people, xxxi n, 158n, 159, 187, 199, 208; *see also* Puta

capital of Chitimukulu, xxxi, 29, 42, 78, 80, 98, 99n, 103–4, 119, 123, 166, 184n, 198, 201, 210, 219n, 253, 264n, 275, 276n; *see also* Ŋwena

Carson, Alexander, 235, 244, 358

Carvalho, H. Dias de, 52

carving, xxvii, 14, 42, 50n, 54n, 344

cassava, xxvii, 21, 51, 115, 210–11, 212n

cattle, 39, 162n, 227
among Bemba, xxvii, 97, 189, 317; in Bulombwa, 42, 72–4; at Chitimukulu's, 75n, 228, 261n; and Makasa, 259n; as tribute, 146, 189; among Mambwe, 247; among Ngoni, 315

cattle raiding: by Bemba, among 'Fipa', 42, 49, 73, 75, 78; Lala, 163; Lungu, 233; Mambwe, 98, 189; by Kazembe, among Lungu, 110; Mambwe, 96

cattle skins, 42, 73, 75, 76n, 82, 174n, 267

centralisation, among Bemba, 92–3, 165, 171–3, 212–14, 305–6, 313, 316–17; among Ganda, Lozi, Ngoni, Kimbu, 313–16

Chaba, 140–2

Chabukila, Bisa headman, 133

Chama, Bisa chief, 108, 109n, 115, 141

Chama, Chishinga chief, 157, 186, 223

Chambeshi river, 16, 17, 32n, 41–2, 56, 87, 91–2, 109–10, 118–19, 137, 161–2, 182, 250, 275, 291, 297, 322

Chandalala, Bemba leader, 375

Chandalala, trader, 157n, 158n

Chandalila, elder at Mwamba's, 277

Chandamukulu, of Chibundu, 84, 131, 220, 277–8, 283, 320

Chandaweyaya, 80, 84, 98, 101–2, 105, 129–31, 353

Changala, Mambwe chief, 64

Changala, son of Makasa, 119, 145–6, 169n, 242, 291, 370

Chansa, Makasa II, 121, 184n, 349–51

charters, *see* mythical charters

Chewa people, 55, 57, 111, 174n, 193, 195n, 365n

Chewe, chief in Ichinga, 87–8, 90–1, 92n, 101n, 122–3, 134, 353–4, 356–7, 361–2; exiled lineage, 135, 145, 146n, 270, 279, 361–2

Chewe Kalubila, chief of Bemba royal clan, xxx, 69–70, 80, 82, 84, 90, 92

Chibale, Senga chief, 226–7, 256, 273–4, 279–80, 285, 288, 354

Chibamba Manshi, 79, 84n, 88, 90–1

Chibanda, 142n, 223

Chibengele, 79

Chibesakunda, Bisa chief, 133n, 138–9, 188, 226, 289, 309, 374

Chibinda Ilunga, 51–2, 57, 346n

Chibundu, 131

Chibungu, Ngoni camp, 119, 128, 133, 142, 143n, 370–1

Chibwa salt marsh, 114, 187–8, 222, 359–61; *and see* Plate V

Chibwe, Lungu headman, 148, 157n

chieftainship, and *bakabilo*, 15, 19; growth of, xxv, 39, 67–8; and oral tradition, xxvi, 12–13, 18–19, 28–9, 46; rights and duties, xxx–xxxi, 165–71

Chiengi, B.S.A.C. post, 232, 242

Chifunda, Senga chief, 55, 226, 375

Chifwasa, 273n

Chikanamulilo, Namwanga chief, 146–7, 196n

Chikompe, 350–1

Chikuku Mwela, early ruler in Ituna, 95

Chikumbi, Bena Mukulu or Chishinga chief, 116, 141, 374
Chikunda traders, 227, 271
Chikunga, *kabilo*, 16, 42; as informant, 9, 30, 51, 58, 69, 350–1
Chikutwe, *kabilo*, 16, 263
Chikwanda, chief of Bemba royal
clan, 321; Chikwanda I Nkumbula, 104, 113, 117–18, 162, 180,
192, 210
Chikwanda II Mutale Lwanga
(d. 1918), 118n, 173, 186, 209, 284n,
291n, 318–19, 325, 361; settles in
Chinama, 162–3; and cassava, 211;
tribute, 169, 209, 222, 361; trade,
212, 221–2, 226–7; and Sampa,
218, 228; and Mwamba III, 221–3,
228, 260, 279; and Europeans, 5,
260, 274n, 275, 279, 286; moves
to Ichinga, 275, 279–80
Chilando Chipala, Bisa chief, 109,
115n, 141n
Chilangwa, Bemba chief, 132, 150,
169n, 180, 247–8, 291
Chileshya, Mambwe chief, 146
Chileshye Chepela, Chitimukulu (d.
c. 1860), 11–12, 27, 70, 84n, 91,
98n, 107, 127–8, 130, 134, 138,
146, 161n, 179–80, 194, 229, 324–5,
349–51, 355, 357
upbringing, 100; visit to Kazembe,
100–1, 351–2, 356; replaces Chinchinta as Chitimukulu, 103–4,
353–4, 381–2; gives Miti to
brother, 105–6; and staff, 344;
gives Lupi to half-brother, 111;
and Chikwanda I, 117–18; and
Ngoni, 119, 121; and Nkweto,
Chewe, Kafwimbi, 121–3, 354–7;
and E. African traders, 103n,
201–2, 353; death, 123
Chileshye Kapalaula Malama,
Mwamba II (d. 1883), 25n, 75n,
105n, 124, 127–9, 136, 167, 173,
178, 180–1, 189n, 219, 223, 318–19,
324; sent to Chinama, 118;
becomes Mwamba II, 123; and
agriculture, 210–11; and Bisa of
Lubumbu, 140–2; and S. Bisa,

160, 162; and Chitapankwa, 15
155, 180–1, 213–14; and S. Lungu,
139–40, 143; and Mambwe, 145–6;
and Ngoni, 145–6, 366; and
Swahili, 129, 151–2, 155–6, 158–9,
203, 212–13; and Tabwa, 151–2,
155–6, 158–9, 382–4; and Tippu
Tip, 136, 195; and Yeke, 208;
death, 159, 161, 201, 216–17
Chileshye Mukulu, chief of Bemba
royal clan, xxx, 69, 80, 85, 107n,
173, 184; as informant, 17, 24, 26n,
50, 54, 91, 107n, 347, 351, 354,
381–2
Chiliamafwa, Chitimukulu, 26, 102,
110, 117n, 179, 301, 325, 349–51,
353, 357, 382; reign, 95–101
Chilimbulu, 41–2, 344; *and see* Plate III
Chilinda, chiefdom, 83, 119–21, 146,
180, 196, 228–9, 267, 380
Chilobelobe, *see* Chimbabantu
Chilubi Island, 109, 115, 117, 142,
223n, 344
Chilubula, 9, 282, 283n
Chilufya *ca mata yabili*, Chitimu-
kulu, 26, 42–3, 57, 77, 83, 88
Chilufya Mulenga, sister of Chiti,
39–40, 42, 44
Chilufya Mulenga, mother of Chita-
pankwa, 131, 132n
Chilundumuzi, Mambwe headman,
146, 247n
Chimanabwe, 291n
Chimba, priest and regent, 15–16,
30, 40, 42–3, 51, 266, 310n, 312, 345
Chimbabantu, 145, 277
Chimbala, 42
Chimbola, chief of Bemba royal clan,
xxix, xxx, 69, 80, 84–5, 92, 95,
98n, 102, 104n, 130–2, 174, 291,
352–3, 378–80
Chimpili hills, 111, 116–17
Chimpolonge, 90
Chinama, chiefdom, 103n, 108, 111–
114, 116–21, 162–3, 179, 186–8,
192, 204, 213, 221, 371; *see also*
Chikwanda, Mwansabamba
Chinama, Tabwa chief, 155–6
Chinchinta, Susula, Chitimukulu, 11,

Chinchinta—*cont.*
  27, 58, 92n, 105, 111, 122, 131n,
  183, 194, 202, 324–5, 350–4, 356,
  381–2; reign, 101–4
Chindo, 72–3
Chingoli, 138, 289
Chinkalanga, Bisa headman, 84
Chinkumba, Bisa chief, 25n, 138,
  184, 289
Chinsali, xxvi, 8, 10, 134–5, 271
Chintu Kapenda, 111, 114
Chinyimba, Bisa chief, 109, 115,
  141
Chipalo, Bemba chief, 117, 141,
  152n, 181
Chipasha, *kabilo*, 16
Chipasha *wa makani*, early ruler in
  Ituna, 95
Chipekeni, Ngoni camp, 145
Chipukula, 146, 276n, 291n
Chisanga, early Nkolemfumu, 85n,
  105
Chisanga Chipemba, Makasa IV,
  146–8, 150–1, 178, 205, 228–9
Chisangula, 157n
Chisansa, 97, 100, 103, 106n, 107n,
  160n, 220
Chisenga, battle-site, 119, 351, 370–1
Chishika, *kabilo*, 16
Chishimba Falls, 71, 98n, 136
Chishinga people, xxviii, xxxi, 5,
  12, 19, 20n, 76, 116n, 139n, 144n,
  155, 157, 190, 199n, 207, 213, 223,
  237, 238n, 291n, 348n, 374;
  iron-working, 184, 186, 188, 209,
  223
Chishisa, 79, 90
Chisoka, 79, 88, 90–1
Chisutula, priest, 98n, 103
Chitambo, Lala headman, 163, 192–3,
  274n
Chitapankwa, Mutale Mutuka, Chitimukulu (d. 1883), 11, 25, 57, 70,
  75n, 87n, 121, 123n, 131–2, 137,
  139, 164, 165n, 171, 173–4,
  178–81, 198, 201, 215, 229, 317,
  324, 352, 361
  early career, 128–9; becomes Chitimukulu, 129, 261; and E. Bemba,

Bisa, 133–6, 138; and S. Bisa, 160,
  162; and E. African traders, 155,
  195, 209n; and Kazembe, 199;
  and Livingstone, 171, 210; and
  N. Lungu, 148–51, 203, 214, 351,
  358–9; and S. Lungu, 143; and
  Mambwe, 146–7, 246; and Mwamba II, 150, 155, 180–1, 213–14; and
  Namwanga, 146–7; and Ngoni,
  143, 145, 203, 214; and Sampa,
  217–18; and shrines of ancestors,
  312; and Tabwa, 155; death, 218,
  221, 230, 243
Chitembo, 280n
Chiti *muluba*, 39–44, 52–4, 61, 65, 71,
  73, 75, 77, 80, 83n, 88, 90n, 347,
  378–80
Chitika, 249
Chitikafula, *kabilo*, 10, 15, 30, 80,
  312
Chitimbwa, Lungu chief, 148, 150,
  231, 240n, 243–4, 246, 258, 372–3
Chitimukulu:
  paramountcy over all Bemba,
  xxvii, xxix, xxxiv, 19, 34, 39, 43,
  46–7, 78, 92–3, 171–3, 181, 184,
  298
  and *bakabilo*, xxxi, 15–16, 29, 172,
  177; as 'divine king', xxx, 171;
  early history, 24, ch. 2 *passim*;
  first visited by European, 3;
  genealogy, 25–7, 57–8, 60, 90;
  lists of, 7–8, 11, 26, 53, 58–61,
  90–1; and long-distance trade,
  196; and Mwamba, 150, 155, 180–
  1, 213–14, 216; positional succession, xxviii; and Shimwalule, 16,
  58, 88, 272; *see also* succession;
  *and entries for individual Chiti-
  mukulus*
Chitoshi, Lungu chief, 106, 139,
  141n, 309
Chitundu, 95
Chivuta, Mambwe chief, 146
Chokwe people, 52, 75n
Choma, B.S.A.C. post, 232, 239
chronology, 3, 11–12, 25, 34, 56–65,
  91, 104, 113, 116n, 117n, 122–3,
  123n, 143n, 151n, 275n, 357, 371

Chunga, 229n, 257n, 258
Chungu, Bena Mukulu chief, 10, 110, 116, 155
Chungu, Lungu chief, 148, 158, 220, 231, 243n, 244
Church of Scotland, *see* Livingstonia Mission
Chyanika, 'Fyani fyani', 217, 221n, 252, 253n, 272n
citemene, xxvii, xxviii, 14, 39, 72, 100n, 183
clans, xxix, 18, 20, 37, 46, 67–8; *see also clans by name*
clichés, 23, 26, 45, 52n, 79n, 80n, 98n, 107n, 346–7, 377
cloth, imported; among Bemba, 113, 192, 206–7, 212, 252, 353–4; and Chileshye, 103n, 194; Chitapankwa, 150; Kabungo, 116; Makasa V, 249, 268; Mporokoso, 243; Mwamba III, 263, 277; Nkula, 137
and A.L.C., 240; Bisa, 113, 142n, 190; E. African traders, 208, 225, 227, 268; Kazembe, 190, 193n; Yao, 191
Codrington, Robert, 169n, 281–4, 286, 287n
Colle, P., 345, 348–9
communication, 210, 316–17
Cookson, P., 58n, 85n, 107n
copper, 107, 189, 190, 192, 207; copper-working, 207–8; brass wire, 279
Copperbelt, xxvii, 28–9, 32, 364
councillors, 29, 40, 82, 87, 100, 121, 165n, 268, 273n, 276, 309, 345; *see also bakabilo*
crafts, craftsmen, 99n, 198, 201, 203–4, 206, 267, 352; basketwork, xxvii, 182, 188, 344; *see also* carving, copper, iron-working, weaving
Crawford, Dan, 61n, 232n, 281n, 283n
Crawshay, Richard, 232, 241–2, 366
Crocodile Clan (*bena ŋandu*), 16, 39, 72, 95, 98, 176n, 218, 278; political importance, xxix, 19–20, 42–3,

78, 80, 82–8, 91–2, 177–8, 283, 298; and commoners, 19, 276–7, 284–5, 309–12; former chiefs of, xxx, 17, 24, 33, 69–70, 80, 82–7, 173; among other peoples, 19n, 54, 61, 69, 349
crops, xxvii, 210–11, 248, 267, 314–16, 347
Cunnison, Ian, xix, xxiii, xxiv, 22, 24, 65, 199, 310
cyclical development, 323–6

dancing, 118, 129, 210n
diviners, 119n, 134, 268; *see also* magic, poison ordeal
Drum Clan (*bena ŋoma*), 19
drums, 137, 159, 268; *see also* signal drums
Drysdale, J., 258, 273
Dupont, Joseph, 4, 251–3, 259–63, 265–9, 273n, 274–9, 282–3, 288

Early Iron Age, 38, 65–7
East African traders, 151–2, 155, 157, 160, 183, 190, 194, 198, 200, 202, 209, 215, 230, 280, 319; *see also* Arabs, Swahili
eclipses, 35–6, 364
elders (*filolo*), 166, 168
Elephant Clan, 100
elephant hunters, xxx, 17, 33, 134, 136–7, 158, 163, 170, 197, 200, 204, 209, 239, 241, 273, 316
environment, xxvii, 20–1, 36, 66, 125–6, 182, 298, 302, 314–15
Evans-Pritchard, E. E., 310

famine, xxviii, 170, 244, 246, 250
federations, 307
Fife, ALC post, 233, 236, 242, 250, 253, 255, 263
Fipa people and country, 20, 42, 49–50, 71n, 72–3, 74n, 78, 100, 118, 149–50, 195, 235, 248, 310, 355, 364–5
firearms, 201–5, 209
among Arabs and Swahili, 145, 153, 195, 199, 202–4, 225, 227, 238, 240, 258, 268

firearms—*cont.*
   among Bemba, 97, 201, 212, 227,
   240, 271, 354, 370n; chiefs' control
   of, 203, 206, 306; Chikwanda II,
   227; Chileshye, 103n, 202; Chitapankwa, 150, 203; Makasa, 202,
   229, 249; Mwamba, 208, 222, 275;
   Nkula, 137, 180n, 203; Sampa,
   203, 234, 252
   among Bisa, 119, 142n; Europeans,
   180n, 201, 235, 240, 252, 269, 279,
   375n; Iwa, 203; Lala, 227; Lunda,
   97, 101–2; Lungu, 358; Mambwe,
   247; Nyamwezi, 137, 203, 374;
   Senga, 226, 273; Tabwa, 237
fish, xxvii, 17, 21, 32n, 99, 115, 169,
   182, 188, 212n, 253n, 291; fish-
   trade, 28
Foà, Edouard, 5, 229n
Forbes, P. W., 255–6, 258, 261, 265,
   269–70, 272, 282
Fort Jameson (Chipata), 5
Fortes, M., 310
fortification: ditches, 85, 99, 166, 348,
   356; stockades, Bemba, 99n, 113,
   116, 143, 166, 243, 251, 264, 279,
   281; Bisa, 116; East Africans', 155,
   159, 255, 273; Lungu, 234–5, 358;
   Mambwe, 205, 247–8; Tabwa, 153
Fox, Robin, 44n
Freud, Sigmund, 44
Fungwe people, 135, 139, 145n
Fwambo, Mambwe chief, 184, 230–1,
   235, 244, 247
Fwangila, 100

Gamitto, A. C. P., xv, 2–3, 33, 55n,
   109, 191, 194, 210n, 211, 222n, 345;
   among Bisa and S. Bemba, 111–16,
   187, 201–2, 209, 230; quoted on
   Bemba, 113–16, 126, 205, 302;
   on Bisa, 109n, 111, 113–15; on
   Bena Mukulu, 116; on Lunda, 201
Ganda people, xxvi, xxx, 211–12, 215,
   266, 309, 313–15
Gann, L. H., xxiv, 200n, 371n
genealogy, 8, 19, 25–7, 57–8, 60,
   64–5, 83n, 84n, 90–1, 94–7, 116n,
   144n, 152n, 180

Genthe, Hugo, 5, 209, 227n, 274n
Germans, 168n, 225, 231, 233n, 234–7,
   287
gift-exchange, 97, 116, 159, 170–1,
   182–3, 187, 250, 259, 263
Giraud, Victor, 3, 25n, 165, 211,
   219n; quoted on Bemba politics,
   162, 216; on upper Luangwa, 189;
   among Iwa, 203; at Mwilwa's,
   146n, 180; at Nkula's, 137, 161n,
   162, 180n, 208; at Chitimukulu's,
   166–8, 171, 196, 210, 218, 230, 243;
   at Shimumbi's, 142n, 181; in
   Itabwa, 159n; among Mambwe,
   184, 359
Glave, E. J., 5, 227, 239, 376n
Gluckman, Max, xxiv, 306–7, 323–6
Gonja kingdom, West Africa, 298,
   301, 310
Goodall, E. B. H., 8, 349–50
Goody, J. R., 297, 301, 310, 312
Gouldsbury, Cullen, 8, 181, 358
granaries, xxviii, 102, 310
graves, 17, 60; *see also* burial;
   'owners of the land'
groundnuts, xxvii, 210–11
Guillé, Fr, 250, 252

Hanna, A. J., xxiv, 232n
Harrington, H. T., 281
headmen, *see* village headmen
Hehe people, 196
Hemans, James, 245
Hemba people, 39, 69, 72, 345–6,
   349
hemp-smoking, 268
Heusch, Luc de, 44
history: Bemba and Luapula histories
   compared, 21–4, 48–9, 52–3; *see
   also* aetiology; mythical charter;
   oral tradition; time, concepts of
Hore, E. C., 230, 358
hunting, 51, 70; *see also* elephant
   hunters

Ichinga chiefdom, xxx, 16, 21, 24,
   87–8, 90–2, 122, 129, 134–8, 160n,
   165n, 173, 217, 273–4, 279, 353–4

Ichingo, Bisa chiefdom, 119, 160, 174, 203, 218, 221n; *see also* Kabanda
Ikawa, BSAC post, 229n, 253, 255, 257–9, 262n, 263–5, 269–70, 272, 274–5, 279
Ila, 346
ilamfya, see war-charm
incest, 40, 44–5, 47–8, 346
insignia, xxviii, 174, 344–5; *see also* relics
iron, iron-working, xxvii, 66, 74–5, 79, 163, 182–6, 188–9, 207–8, 212, 247n; iron mines, 85, 183–5, 223
Isangano, 142n
Isansa chiefdom, 108, 115, 141
Isenga, 156–7, 159
Islam, 209, 280
Isunga, Bisa chiefdom, 133–4, 138, 162n; *see also* Mungulube
Ititini, Ngoni camp, 143, 145
Ituna chiefdom, xxx, 14, 24, 123, 173, 217, 277, 279, 281, 318, 325; meaning of name, 380; chiefdom created, 95; and Chileshye, 103; headmen in, 165n, 223; and Lubemba, 71, 95, 219–20, 261; and Lungu, 88n, 96–7, 106–7, 143, 184; and Miti, 87, 96, 105–6, 160; and Ngoni, 119, 128, 142–3; and Shimumbi, 119n
Ituntwe, 279
ivory, 182; chiefs' control of, xxx, 142, 169–70, 212, 306; presents, 128, 131n, 149, 158–9, 171, 233n, 242, 245, 259, 263, 273n, 274–5, 281; prices, 196–7, 202, 204, 227
ivory trade, xxvi, 127, 155, 198, 206, 225, 236, 238, 240; among Bemba, 103, 114, 134, 136–7, 191–2, 194–7, 200, 208, 212–13, 215, 220, 227, 258, 271, 279; among Bisa, 109, 114, 142n, 189–93, 195
Ivuna salt pans, 187
Iwa people, xxxi, 12, 49–50, 72, 145, 146n, 207, 211, 355; cattle, 42, 76, 189; iron-working, 75, 184, 209; and E. African traders, 200, 203;

as BSAC auxiliaries, 278; *see also* Kafwimbi
Iyaya, 84, 88, 94, 103, 130–1, 132n, 174; *see also* Chandaweyaya, Chimbola

Johnston, H. H., xv, 231–2, 235–8, 240–1, 247, 255
Jones, David, 248
Jones, G. I., 23
Joseph, African Christian, 251, 263
justice, administration of, xxx, 165–8, 272, 277, 282n

Kabanda, Bisa chief, 55, 87n, 103–4, 111, 119, 131, 136, 160–2, 174, 202n, 210, 221n, 370n
Kabemba, 51
Kabinga, Bisa chief, 104n, 161, 186, 211n, 222
Kabondwe, battle-site, 226, 375
Kabotwe, 42
Kabumba, 131
'Kabunda', trader, 158n, 237–8, 240, 241n, 244, 246n, 358
Kabungo, Bemba headman among Bena Mukulu, 116–17
Kabungo, Bemba headman in Ichinga, 134–5
Kabwa, *kabilo*, 16, 42, 80
Kabwibwi, Bemba chief, 100, 111, 119, 181, 381
kaffir-corn, xxvii, 72, 347, 353, 381
Kafunga, son of Makasa, 235n
Kafwimbi, Iwa chief, 42, 64, 72, 99n, 123, 138, 178, 184, 188, 200, 203
Kaindu, Lunda aristocrat, 199, 223
Kakungu, Lungu chief (Tafuna IV), 149–51, 357–9, 373
Kakwela, 16
Kalambo Falls, 66–7, 233
Kalelelya, 42, 68, 70
Kalemba, 80
Kalimanshila, war-leader, 268, 274–5, 277, 284
Kaliminwa, 219, 291n
Kalulu, Makasa I, 98–100, 119, 121, 195n, 349–51, 370–1
Kalulu, chief in Lubumbu, 142n
Kalundu chiefdom, 97, 108, 110, 123, 139

Kalundwe, Luba kingdom, 39, 54, 91n, 297
Kalungu river, 16, 39, 42–3, 45, 56, 64, 77–8, 80, 83, 85, 98, 261–2, 275, 276n, 379
Kalungwishi river, 232, 239, 280; BSAC post, 232, 242, 280–1
Kamanga people, 122, 354, 356
Kambi, 87n
Kambole mission, 246, 258n
Kambwili, Bisa chief, 104n
Kamenge, *kabilo*, 16
Kamfwa, 115, 143
Kamima, 70–1, 79
Kamponge, 90–1, 120, 134
Kanabesa, 70, 72n, 90
Kangwa *wa mpumpa*, *kabilo*, 9, 16
Kankomba, 41, 55, 57
Kanyanta, Chitimukulu (d. 1943), 29n, 181n, 321; as Nkolemfumu, 220, 277, 283; appointed Mwamba IV, 284
Kaonde people, 53
Kapampa *mubanshi*, 79, 102n
'Kapandansalu', trader, 226, 256, 270–1, 273, 275n
Kapasa, 40, 42, 44, 72
Kapoko, son of Chikwanda II, 221, 280n, 359
Kapoko, son of Makasa V, 266
Kapolyo Mfumu, 84, 90n
Kapoma, 158n
Kapopo, 50–1, 54
Kapukuma, 15, 30, 80
Kaputa, Tabwa chief, 153, 187, 208n, 232, 309n
Kapuufi, Fipa chief, 149
Karonga, 6, 225–6, 231, 236, 244, 255, 257, 375
Kasama, xxvi, 6, 9, 65, 70–1, 85n, 95n, 279, 283
Kasanga, on east shore of Lake Tanganyika, 151, 233, 357, 373
Kasanga, people in S.E. Zaïre, 348
Kasansu, 79, 90
Kasembo, 83, 379
Kasenga (Bisa country), 118, 162, 280n, 291n
Kasenga (Lungu country), 157n

Kasenge, *kabilo*, 16
Kasengere, hunter, 158n, 239
Kashinda, 157, 159
Kashinge, *kabilo*, 264, 382
Kasonka, 141n
Kasonso, 148, 150
Kasuba *montelwa*, 129n, 350
Katanga (Shaba), xxv, 8, 28, 38–9, 67, 107, 151, 193n, 194, 195n, 199–200, 207–8, 213, 231, 232n, 283n, 295
'Katanga', trader, 161
Katele, Tabwa chief, 153, 158, 237, 309, 311n
Katenda, *kabilo*, 15, 30, 80
Katonga, 85
Katonga, chiefly title, 87–8, 90
Katongo *ncilamalilo*, Chitimukulu, 16, 80, 90–2
Katongo, son of Mukulumpe, 39–40, 88
Katumba, 84, 88, 91, 94, 102–3, 378
Katwamba, 32n
Kavwinta, 100, 145n
Kawambwa, 5
Kawimbe mission, 235, 244, 248
Kayambi mission, 4, 229, 252–3, 259–60, 262–3, 265–8, 273n, 275, 291n
Kazembe, king of eastern Lunda: kingdom, xxiv, xxvi, 2, 28, 47, 50–4, 61, 75n, 100, 123, 129, 166n, 169n, 190, 198–200, 207n, 296; capital, 2, 53n, 96, 107, 111, 151, 166n, 186, 190–1, 194, 210–11, 223n, 280–1, 345; and firearms, 201–2; long-distance trade, 107 109–10, 121, 189–94, 199; military organisation, 169n, 191n; political organisation, 199–200, 308n, 309–311; traditions, 10, 21–2, 48, 52–3, 346–7, 351, 356, 364, 374
and Bemba, 95–6, 100, 116, 199, 223, 280, 318, 351–2; Bemba settlers at Kazembe's, 61n, 223n, 349; and Bena Mukulu, 110, 116, 374; and Bisa, 107–10, 114, 189–90, 192–4, 298; and Ngoni, 374; and Tabwa, 96, 110, 152; *see also* Arabs, British South Africa Company, Swahili

Kazembe II Kanyembo Mpemba, 345, 348

Kazembe III Lukwesa Ilunga (d. *c.* 1805), 61, 96–7, 102n, 109–10, 190–1, 193n, 201, 356

Kazembe IV Keleka, 110, 191, 356

Kazembe VII Muonga, 152, 153n, 155n, 157n, 199

Kazembe IX Lukwesa, 199, 223n, 283n

Kazembe X Kanyembo, 199, 223, 232, 244, 280–1, 283n

Kazembe, brother of Chiti, 40, 49

Kazembe Mushidi, 52–3

Kede people of N. Nigeria, 23–4, 308

Kela, Mambwe chief, 147, 231, 246–7

Kilwa, 192, 195–7, 225, 236, 238

Kimbu people, 315–16

kinship and politics, 53, 171–3, 295–7, 299–301, 307–9, 317–26; *see also* lineage, marriage, matriliny, patriliny, perpetual kinship, succession

Kituta, ALC post, 231, 235, 237, 240

Knight, W. B., 238–9

'Kola', 39, 49–50, 64, 76–7, 80, 83, 88, 378, 380

'Koma Koma', trader, 226

Kombo-Kombo, Bemba headman, 142

Kopa, Bisa chief, 9, 55, 162, 222n, 274n, 359

Kuba, 45n, 309

'Kumba-Kumba', trader, 155–6, 158, 195, 203

labour migration, xv, xxvii, 20n, 28–30, 32, 165n, 168n, 233, 253n, 275n, 287n, 343; *see also* porters

Labrecque, E., 9–11, 51, 52n, 58, 73, 79, 96n, 141n, 143n, 156n, 347–8, 350, 353, 358, 367, 369–71, 375

Lacerda e Almeida, F. J. M. de, 2, 73, 87n, 96–7, 191

Lala people, xxviii, 41, 45, 49–50, 55, 57, 65, 163, 193, 221–2, 227, 346, 366, 376n; iron-working, 184, 186, 209

Lamba people, 45, 193, 199, 310, 346–7

land, supernatural control over, xxx, xxxi, 14, 20, 169–70; *see also* 'owners of the land'

language, xxvii n; *see also* Bemba l., Luba l.

Late Stone Age people, 38, 65

Law, Andrew, 240, 281

Lechaptois, A., 231, 248, 251, 349

legends of origin, 346–7; Bemba legend, xvi, 9, 19, 23, 26, 38, 77, 80, 171, 344, 347; summary, 39–43; analysis, 43–76

Leopard Clan (*bazimba*), 19, 95, 97n, 148, 152

Lettow-Vorbeck, P. E. von, 6

lineage, Bemba concept of, xxix, xxxiii; lineage history, 24; royal lineages, 26–7, 78, 88, 90, 94, 102–3; *see also Miti* branch; succession

Lisunga, 157

literacy, 209, 266, 288

Livingstone, David, xv, 2–3, 5, 11, 25, 165, 189n, 202, 211, 230–1, 274n, 371; on upper Zambezi, 191n, 194; near Lake Malawi, 192, 366; in Mukumbi, 163n, 183; in Isunga, 133; at Mwaba's, 134n, 207; at Chitimukulu's, 171, 196, 198, 210; in Ituna, 143, 167; at Nsama's, 153, 202; among Lungu, 148n, 150, 357, 373; among Chishinga, 374; at Matipa's, 142

Livingstonia mission of Free Church of Scotland, 3, 4, 135n, 146n, 147n, 230, 253n, 257n, 267–8, 275–6, 374–5

Lloyd, P. C., 296, 300, 308–10, 326n

locusts, 104, 244, 267

Lombe Shyula, 147n, 178–9, 196n, 228n, 229n

London Missionary Society, 3, 7, 230, 235, 244–6, 248, 358

Lozi people and kingdom, 53n, 189n, 198, 206n, 212n, 213n, 266, 311, 313–15, 346

Lualaba river, 68–9

Luali, Bemba chief, 223, 237n, 291n

Luangwa river and valley, 41, 49, 55–6, 104n, 111, 126, 135, 137, 139, 153n, 162, 189, 191, 197, 213, 222, 226–7, 255, 271, 273, 366
Luapula peoples, xxiv, xxviii, 21–4, 28–9, 48, 65, 346; *see also* Kazembe; Lunda
Luapula river, 17, 39, 40, 45, 47–50, 55–6, 61, 67, 69, 193n, 199, 280, 347, 376n
Luba kingdoms, xxv, 48, 75, 215, 295; *see also* Kalundwe, Kola
Luba language, 14–15, 51, 66, 68, 74
Luba peoples, 45, 66, 68–9, 71, 344–7, 349; *see also* Hemba
Lubansenshi river, 73, 221
Lubemba, 24, 36, 49, 84, 91–2, 100, 267, 283; Chitimukulu's power in, xxx, 88, 166, 173, 203; elephant in, 197, 241; and Ituna, 71, 95, 219–20, 261, 263, 271; and Mambwe, 79, 98; and Ngoni, 119, 124; royal headmen in, 17, 33, 69–70, 80–5, 173, 351; reorganised by BSAC, 82n, 85n, 291
Lubumbu chiefdom, 108–10, 115, 117–18, 140–2, 162n, 180, 345
Luchele Ŋanga, 40–2, 45, 55n, 262, 268, 346
Luchembe, 222, 284–5, 361
Luchindashi river, 41
Luena river, 56, 141, 253n
Luenshi, 221, 280n
Lufubu river, 148, 158n, 230, 239, 358
Lukonde Mwaba, 98, 100, 103, 106, 127n, 130–1, 357
Lukulu river (tributary of Chambeshi), 87, 97, 111, 131, 140, 187n, 277n
Lukutu river, 109, 114
Lukwesa, Tabwa chief, 153, 237
Lumpombwe, 16, 80, 103, 301
Lunda kingdoms, xxv, 21, 75, 190n, 215, 295; influence on Bemba, 54, 210; on Bena Mukulu, 116; *see also* Kazembe, Mwata Yamvo
Lunda people, 20, 45, 57, 97, 188, 344

Lungu people, and cattle, 110, 189; cloth-working, 188; iron-working, 75, 184, 207, 209
northern Lungu, of Tafuna, 3, 5, 12, 19, 34, 97n; internal politics, 95, 148–9, 295, 357–8; and Bemba, 149, 157–8, 291, 358–9; and Chitapankwa, 128, 150–1; and E. African traders, 153, 198–200, 208; and Europeans, 231, 234–5, 252; and Kasengere, 239; and Kazembe, 110; and Ngoni, 143, 145, 372–3; and Ponde, 151, 173, 204, 244, 246; and Sampa, 219–20, 233–5; *see also* Chitimbwa, Chungu, Kakungu, Tafuna, Zombe
southern or 'Malaila' Lungu of Mukupa Kaoma, xxviii, xxxi, 5, 12, 19, 20, 34, 72, 75–6, 87n, 88n, 95, 110, 127n, 148, 152, 157, 180–1, 202n, 357; *see also* Mukupa Kaoma
Lunshinga, Lungu chief, 309n
Lupi chiefdom, 108, 111, 119n, 123; *see also* Kabwibwi
lupwa, xxix, 177, 326
Luvale people, 46n, 53, 346
Luvu river, 88, 90n, 133–4, 279
Luwingu, xxvii
Lwao river, 157
Lweeji, 51, 57
Lyangalile, 78, 149

magic, 17, 21n, 40–1, 140, 170; *see also* war-charm, witchcraft
maize, xxvii, 210–11, 315
Makalandu, 132n, 378
Makasa, chieftainship for sons of Chitimukulu, xxx, 9, 103, 121, 123n, 132, 169n, 174, 180, 228, 259n, 311n, 349–51; created, 98–100, 301; relics and burial, 174n; *see also* Makasa I, Kalulu; II, Chansa; III, Bwalya; IV, Chisanga Chipemba; V, Mukuuka Mwilwa
Makua, 158n, 239, 269
Makumba, Chimfwembe Mulenga, Chitimukulu (d. 1911), 174, 260–5, 269–71, 275–6, 278–9, 291, 313, 319

Malawi, Lake, 3, 4, 6, 30n, 67n, 107, 190, 193, 196, 216n, 225–6, 230–1, 236, 241, 365

Malenga, Bisa chief, 192

Mambwe people, xxviii, xxxi, 3, 4, 12, 18, 20, 65, 72–3, 88n, 96, 102, 129, 148n, 151, 166n, 170n, 182, 194, 202–3, 211, 235, 253, 295; cattle, 76, 98, 189; iron-working, 75, 184, 247n; political disintegration, 144–7, 246–7, 296; royal succession, 322n; wars with Bemba, 79, 98–100, 132, 144, 146–8, 233n, 246–8, 353–4; raided by Bemba, 98, 182, 189, 231, 248; regain land from Bemba, 251, 291; and E. African traders, 200, 208; and LMS, 230,; and Ngoni, 133, 142–5; and White Fathers, 246–7, 251; see also Fwambo, Mpande, Nsokolo

Mambwe mission, 4, 231, 235n, 240, 246, 248–9, 251–2, 265, 275n

Manda, Tabwa chief, 152n

Mande Namusenge, 134–6, 138

Manga, village of Makasa III, 144–5

Manganja people, 193

manioc, see cassava

Mann, W. M., 68n, 69n

Mapupo, 144, 371

marriage, xxix, 32, 122; between Bemba and other peoples, 20, 97, 100, 145n, 147, 156, 159n, 162n, 178–9, 219; cross-cousin marriage, 44n, 128, 136, 177–8; daughter-exchange between Bemba chiefs, 181n; marriage payments, 121n, 186n, 188–9, 207; see also wife-inheritance

Marshall, H. C., 236, 238–9, 242, 245; and see Plate VIII

Masala, trader, 239

Masaye, 90–1, 120

Maseba, 152, 157

Masonde, 109, 115, 141

Masongo, 162, 180–1, 222n

Matamba, 50n

Matanda, chief of Bena Mukulo, 40, 49, 345, 347–8

Matengele, 84n, 132, 150

Matipa, Bisa chief, 55, 64, 76n, 180, 188, 297–8; Matipa I Muma, 117, 140–2; Matipa II Kabamba, 223

Matipa, Tabwa chief, 155–6

matriliny, xxviii, xxix, 20, 42, 69, 80n, 148, 174n, 301, 309

Mbala, see Abercorn

Mbelwa, Ngoni chief, 136n, 145, 226, 365–6, 374–5, 376n

Mbete, 143n, 150, 373

'Mbozwa', 348n

Mbutuka, 24, 88

McCulloch, Adam, 233, 263

McKinnon, Charles, 262n, 265, 269–70, 272–5, 278–80, 282–3

Menga, 221

Mfungo, 69n, 132n, 378

Mhambose, 372n,

Milambo, informant, 17, 122, 352–3, 358

military organisation, 88, 168–9, 205, 286, 306, 316, 363, 373; see also war

millet, xxvii, xxviii, 184, 211, 242n, 316

minstrels, 18, 54, 268, 352

Mirambo, Nyamwezi chief, 167, 283n, 315

Mirongo, BSAC post, 7, 273–6, 279

Misengo, 220

missionaries, xxvi, 3–4, 50n, 147, 214–15, 220, 225, 229, 231, 255, 282, 283n; see also Livingstonia, London Missionary Society, White Fathers

Miti chiefdom, 85, 87, 96, 100, 103, 105–6, 124, 142, 160, 173, 220

Miti branch of royal lineage, 104n, 105–6, 118, 124–5, 130–1, 132n, 164, 173–4, 299, 352

Mlozi, trader, 225–7, 236, 237n, 247n, 255–8, 270, 280–1, 375

Moir, Fred, 231, 358

Molinier, Fr, 285

Monteiro, J. M. C., xv, 111, 191, 230

'Morungabambara', 87n

'mothers of chiefs,' xxix, 80, 84, 178; see also Chandamukulu, Chandaweyaya, Mukukamfumu

Mozambique, 2, 6, 36, 190–1, 194n, 231
Mpanda chiefdom, 98–100, 103, 107, 121, 123, 145, 184, 229, 263, 265, 279, 289n, 325; *see also* Makasa
Mpande, Mambwe chief, 99, 143–4, 146, 206, 246–7, 291, 370
Mpanga, 147, 255n, 269
Mpashi, Stephen A., 10, 265n, 354
Mpenza, 147, 247–8
Mpepo, chief, 221, 320–1; *see also* Mubanga Chisupa
Mperembe, Ngoni chief, 119, 136n, 143–6, 153, 365–6, 371–2, 374, 375n
Mpezeni, Ngoni chief, xxiii, 119, 136n, 286–7, 296, 315, 365–6, 372, 376n
Mpika, xxvi, 359, 361
Mporokoso, chieftainship, 7, 18, 291n; Mporokoso I Mulume *wa nshimba* (d. 1909), 173, 181, 204–5, 218n, 244; in Maseba, 152; settles in Itabwa, 157–9, 383; defeated by Swahili, 159, 220; allies with Arabs, 281; allies with Swahili, 237; trade, 196, 213, 242n; and Sampa, 223, 243–4; and BSAC, 242, 258, 280–2, 285, 288; and P. Weatherley, 243, 252, 280; burial, 174n
Mpuki chiefdom, 104n, 161–2, 218, 220, 222
Msiri, Yeke chief, 167, 199, 205, 223n, 241, 283n
Msomani, 186
Mubanga Chele, chief in Chilinda, 147, 196n, 229n, 257
Mubanga Chipoya (Chisala), Mwamba III (d. 1898), 4, 167, 173n, 229n, 319, 361; as Nkolemfumu, 85, 136n, 160–1, 173, 178, 212, 218; becomes Mwamba III, 217; his capital, 166, 211, 264, 268, 276, 279, 284–5; and Swahili and Tabwa, 159, 204, 208, 220, 227, 258; and Miti, 220; and Sampa, 218–19, 223, 225, 243, 257; and Chikwanda II, 221–2, 260, 279; his

caravan, 223; and Kazembe, 223; and Ngoni, 366; and 'Senga Arabs', 227, 257, 271; and Ndakala II, 271, 273–4; and Mwalule, 262, 272, 274–5; and Makumba, 260–5, 269–71, 276, 278; and White Fathers, 253, 259–60, 262–3, 267–9, 273n, 276–7; as historian, 347; and BSAC, 241, 256, 258–9, 262–5, 268–9, 273–6, 280, 286, 289; death, 277–8, 281, 285, 288; burial, 284
Mubanga Chisupa, Mwamba V (d. 1945): as Mpepo I, 221, 277, 325; as Mwamba V, 355
Mubanga Kashampupo, chief of Ituna, 95–8, 100, 103–6, 110, 139n, 201, 357
Mubenshi, 161
Muchereka, 117, 141, 146n
Muchilingwa, 17
Muchinga escarpment and hills, 20, 73, 109, 111, 127, 162n, 186, 366
Muchinka, Lala chief, 163
mucinshi, xx, 351, 381
Muhammed ibn Saleh, 152–3, 194
Mukoma, 64n,
Mukukamfumu, title for 'mothers of chiefs', 131, 145, 320–1, 352–3, 356–7, 381
Mukula, Tabwa chief, 153, 155, 158, 237–9
Mukulika, 64
Mukulu, *see* Bena Mukulu
Mukulumpe, 25, 39–40, 44, 50–1, 54–5
Mukumbi, 162–3, 270n, 280n, 291n
Mukungule, Bisa chief, 109, 110, 138, 162, 163n, 183, 298
Mukupa Kaoma, Lungu chief, 309; and Bemba, 96–8, 106–7, 110, 116, 139–43, 219–20; and Tippu Tip, 195
Mukupa Katandula, Tabwa chief, 156–8, 208n
Mukuuka Mwilwa, 146–7, 174, 180, 210n; as Makasa V, 166n, 188n, 212, 273, 275n, 291; and Sampa, 229, 233–4, 235n, 249–53, 257; trade, 249; and White Fathers,

Mukuuka Mwilwa—*cont.*
249–53, 259–60, 265–8, 276n, 291n;
and BSAC, 275n
Mukuuka *wa malekano*, Chitimukulu,
26–7, 57, 79, 88, 90–1, 101, 325;
reign, 94–5
Mukwikile, Bemba chief, 135, 138,
146n, 177, 180, 270, 289n
Mulambalala, 42, 56
Mulema, 17
Mulenga, Tabwa chief, 155, 158
Mulenga Mwimba, 97–8, 100, 103,
127n, 160n, 357, 381
Mulenga Pokili, 78, 82, 87n, 90
Mulenga wa Chibungu, chief of
Bemba royal clan, 80, 82–3, 90
Mulewa Chimfwembe, *kabilo*, 10,
16; *and see* Plate III
Mulilo, headman, 17, 32n, 79n
Mulilo, Fungwe chief, 139n
Mulilo, Tabwa chief, 152–3, 231,
372, 373n
Mulombelwa, 16
Mulopwe, 39, 68, 73
Mulumbwa, Lungu chief, 157
Muma Chalwe, Bisa chief, 110
Mumba Ɲombe, *kabilo*, 16, 80
Mumbi Mukasa, 39, 44
Mumena, 69n, 80, 82, 88, 90–2, 173,
377–80
Mumpuku, Bisa chief, 115
Mundubi, trader, 208
Mungulube, 55, 87, 119, 133, 138
Munkonge, Bemba chief, 97–8, 100,
103, 110, 127n, 139, 141, 145, 152,
173, 174n, 181, 219, 357
Munshimbwe, 143, 152
Munuca, *kabilo*, 15, 30, 79, 80,
312
Mununga, Shila chief, 61, 345, 348,
384
Mupundu, 105n
Musanya, 184, 229
Musenga, Chitimukulu (d. 1969), 29n,
32n, 181n, 321; as Mwamba VI,
see Plate VII
Mushindo, P. B., xx, 10, 27, 58, 74,
91, 121, 122, 143n, 353–4, 358,
367, 369–71, 375, 377

Mushroom Clan: *bena bowa*, 16;
bena ŋona, 41, 108
Mushyota, Chishinga chief, 139n, 155
Musoa, 143n, 161, 221
Musukwa, 42, 66, 68, 70, 98n
Musungu, Chitimukulu (d. 1965), 29,
32n, 321, 361
Mutale Mukulu, chief of Bemba
royal clan, 69, 80, 84–5, 88, 90, 92,
94, 101–2, 103n, 105, 173n, 184,
219, 265, 378–82
Mutale Sichansa, Nkula (d. 1896),
162n, 173–4, 279, 319, 324; helps
to depose Bwembya, 129; as
Mwaba, 135; becomes Nkula, 136;
and Bisa, 138; and Chitapankwa,
135–6; and E. African traders,
136–7, 195, 203, 208, 212, 226;
and Giraud, 180n, 230n; and Iwa,
146n; and Lungu, 151; and
Mwamba II, 178; and Ngoni, 136,
145, 226, 374–5; and Sampa, 177,
218, 228; death, 254, 270–1
Mutale *wa kabwe*, Mwamba I: early
career, 100–1, 103; Mwamba I,
105–7, 117–18, 123, 139n, 140, 160,
180, 229n, 325, 344, 355
Mutambe, 138, 162n, 226, 289, 291n
Mvula, Mambwe chief, 132
Mwaba, chief of Bemba royal clan,
xxix, 10, 82, 84, 87, 90, 92, 119,
134–5, 138, 174, 177, 179, 189n,
207, 325
Mwabamukupa, 223n
Mwala, 109, 117, 140n
Mwaleshi river, 87n, 119, 136
Mwalula, 85, 105n
Mwalule, royal burial grove, 16, 42,
49, 56, 79, 88, 123, 134, 172, 262–3,
272–5, 353; *and see* Plate II
Mwamba, chief of Bemba royal clan,
xxix, xxx, xxxi, 11, 17, 20, 24, 42n,
96, 119, 169, 177, 196, 207–8, 272n,
282–3, 320–1, 344, 380; origin of
title, 105; *see also* Mwamba I,
Mutale *wa kabwe*; II, Chileshye
Kapalaula; III, Mubanga Chipoya,
IV, Kanyanta; V, Mubanga Chis-
upa

Mwamba, Mambwe chief, 105
Mwana Bwalya, *kabilo*, 16
Mwangata, *kabilo*, 80, 103, 291n
Mwansabamba, Bisa chief, 9, 64, 108, 111, 117n, 118–21, 142, 162, 297–9
Mwase, 41–2, 55, 195n, 344, 365n
Mwata Yamvo, 48, 50–4, 64n, 75n, 80, 107, 190, 199, 201, 295
Mwela Rocks, 65–6, 70
Mwenzo mission, 230, 257n, 267, 276
Mweru, Lake, 5, 61n, 187, 232, 236, 241, 256, 345
Mweru wa ntipa, Lake, 187, 197, 208, 241n
Mwimba Nsangwa, 97, 100, 381
Mwine Chilanga, 99
Mwine Nsanso, 100
Mwinempanda, 109, 114
mythical charters, 22–4, 43–4, 47, 56–7, 347

Nadel, S. F., 23
Nakapapula, 65, 67
Nakasafya, 178, 321–2
Namwanga people, 64n, 67n, 72, 75–6, 145–7, 195, 196n, 210n, 231, 248, 310, 322n
Nasoro bin Suliman, 281
Ndakala I, 138, 226, 271, 374–5
Ndakala II Kasonde, 270–1, 273–4, 279, 286, 289n
Ngalagansa, 42, 73
Ngonde, 55n, 99n, 225, 354–6
Ngoni, 64n, 127–8, 132–3, 146, 151, 153, 162n, 198, 209, 256, 296, 354–5; political organisation, 286, 315–16
and Bemba, 363–76; first wars with Bemba, 119–24, 136, 138, 351, 353, 369–71; wars with Bemba in north, 142–5, 149–50, 160, 169n, 202–3, 205–6, 212, 304, 357, 370–1; battle with Ndakala I, 226, 271, 374–5; influence on Bemba, 169n, 210n, 363
and Bisa, 119–21, 192–3, 199, 366, 370–1, 376n; and BSAC, 286–7; and Lungu, 143, 145, 372–3; and Tabwa, 143, 153, 349, 372, 373n;

see also Mbelwa, Mperembe, Mpezeni, Zwangendaba
ngulu, 17, 33, 71, 98
Ŋwena, Bemba royal capital site, 42, 70, 80, 83, 166, 262, 379
Niamkolo mission, 230, 244–5
Nkaka Kasela, 111n
Nkalamo, Bisa chief, 115, 117
Nkanka, 87n
Nkansi, 149
Nkole, brother of Chiti *muluba*, 39–43, 51, 54, 65, 72, 83n, 85, 88, 90n
Nkolemambwe, *kabilo*, 15, 30, 252
Nkolemfumu, chief of Bemba royal clan, xxix, 16, 33, 85, 87, 95–6, 100, 105, 106n, 124, 136n, 160, 173, 178, 217, 220–1, 277, 283, 318, 320, 324, 351; *see also* Mubanga Chipoya
Nkole *wa mapembwe*, 85, 87n, 344
Nkondo, group of Mambwe, 99–100
Nkuba, Shila chief, 61, 69
Nkuka, Bisa chief, 162, 209n, 280n, 291n
Nkula, chief of Bemba royal clan, xxix, xxx, 24, 29, 87–8, 90, 119–20, 122, 134–8, 173, 179, 272n, 275, 279–80, 321–2; *see also* Chewe; Ichinga; Mutale Sichansa
Nkulungwe, 84, 90, 134–5, 138; *see also* Mwaba
Nkweto, chief of Bemba royal clan, xxix, xxx, 82–3, 87, 92, 119, 121, 174, 177, 272n, 325, 350–1, 378, 380
Nkweto wa Chisungu, 80, 90
Northern Rhodesia Government, 7, 29n, 82n, 83n, 323
Nsama, Tabwa chief, 152, 158n, 203, 309, 311n; Nsama III Chipili Chipioka, 152–3, 195, 202; IV Katandula, 153, 155–7; V Kafwimbi, 153, 155–8, 382–4; VI Chimutwe, 158–60, 219, 232, 237–8; VII Mutuutu, 238
Nsemiwe, trader, 159, 239, 242n
Nsenga people, 41, 49, 55, 96, 192n, 366

A History of the Bemba

Nsenshi, *kabilo*, 79n, 80
Nsokolo, Mambwe paramount chief,
64, 73, 99, 104, 131n, 144–7, 247,
248n, 291, 297, 353–4
Nsumbu Island, 117, 142, 223
Nsunge, 122, 134
Ntamba Lukuta, 79
Ntasu, 98–9
Ntuka, Bemba headman, 114
Nyakyusa people, 76, 253
Nyala, 135, 255, 269
Nyamwanga, *see* Namwanga
Nyamwezi people and traders, xxvi,
69n, 73, 75n, 137, 158n, 159, 162n,
183, 193, 196n, 199, 200n, 201, 203,
204n, 205n, 206n, 208, 212n, 215,
227, 283n, 315; *see also* Mirambo,
Nsemiwe, Yeke
Nyiha people, 76, 196, 212n, 310

Oger, L., 9, 99, 349–51
Oost, Fr van, 248–50
oral traditions, 23–4, 36, 137, 179,
369–70; analysis of, 1, 31, 34–5,
377–8; social basis of, xxvi, 12–22,
77, 94, 369; records of, 7–12, 53n,
364; transmission of, 7, 12–13, 18,
28–32, 35; *see also* legends of origin,
mythical charters
Otter Clan (*bena mbao*), 97n
'owners of the land', 16, 20, 71, 99,
110n, 121, 163n

pages, 168, 170, 268
pall-bearers, 16, 80
Palmer, C. R., 250
patriliny, 21, 39, 45, 54, 69, 74, 80n,
99, 148, 301, 309
'Pembamoto', trader, 139n, 155n
Pernambuco: cotton from, 188n; a
person from, 191n
'perpetual behaviour', 13, 16, 82,
100n
perpetual kinship, xxviii–xxx, xxxiii,
25, 28, 65, 80, 82, 84, 138, 176,
295; *see also* sons of chiefs
'Pilula', 42, 78
Pinto, F. J., 2n, 61n, 96, 193
Pirie, G., 7–8
poisoning, 41, 132, 146n, 159n

poison ordeal (*mwavi*), 100, 132, 167,
245, 250, 370
pombeiros, 2, 110n, 191
Ponde, Bemba chief of royal clan,
173, 181, 204–5, 217, 243n, 318,
321, 325; and Lungu, 151, 244,
246, 258, 359; trade, 212, 220,
249, 258, 260, 279; and Sampa,
219–20; and LMS, 220, 244–6;
and Mambwe, 248; and Mwamba
III, 260, 261n, 264, 269; and
BSAC, 278–80, 282–6, 288;
occupies S. Lubemba, 291
population: decline, 163, 244; density,
212, 275, 314–17; estimates of
Bemba population, xxvii, 165–6,
168n, 342–3; growth, 43, 46, 85
porters, 197–8, 204, 208, 267n, 268,
276n
Portuguese: records, 2, 36, 57;
traders, 190–1, 221, 227, 229n;
see also Gamitto; Lacerda
positional succession, xxviii, 25, 27–8,
350; *see also* perpetual kinship
pottery, 65–7, 98–9
praise-names, 18, 26, 28, 55, 58, 60,
79, 85, 87n, 95, 128n, 152, 312,
347, 350–1, 380, 383
praise-poems (*mishikakulo*), 14–15,
35, 51, 54, 74, 137, 266
priests, 14, 17, 18, 29, 33, 71, 84, 121,
345; *see also* bakabilo
'proto-Bemba', 67–75, 82
Pumbwe, *kabilo*, 80n
Puta, Bwile chief, 187, 208n, 345,
383

Quelimane, 190, 191n

raiding, 107, 126, 170, 181–3, 189,
284, 316
Bemba raiding: among Bisa, 117,
191; E. African traders, 137, 203;
Lungu, 148, 233; Mambwe, 128,
146, 231; Nyakyusa, 253, 256;
seasonal raiding, 168n, 233, 245
Ngoni raiding among Bisa, 119,
128, 163, 192, 375n, 376n; among
Lungu, 373

416

raiding—*cont.*
see also cattle-raiding, slave-raiding
rainfall, xxvii
regency, 15–16, 42, 277
reign-lengths, 60
relics of chiefs, 14, 16, 26, 42–3, 50n, 80, 91, 105, 118, 129, 134, 171, 174n, 274, 279, 310, 344–5, 362; see also 'wives of the relics'
resistance to colonial invasion, 216–17, 285–9
Rhodes, C. J., 216n, 231, 256, 258
Rhodes–Livingstone Institute, xix, xxiii–xxiv
Rhodesia, revolt in Southern, 258, 269, 274n, 286–7; Kore-Kore, people in, 311–12
Richards, A. I., xv, xix, xxiii, xxiv, 6, 8, 13, 23, 26, 29, 177, 186, 285, 296, 306, 311–12, 319, 323n
ritual, xxx, xxxi, 13–15, 20, 29, 30, 71–2, 75–6, 80, 88, 92, 121, 165, 168–9, 171–2, 260, 266, 278n, 306, 310, 352
Robertson, W. Govan, 7–8
rubber collectors, 287
'Rumaliza', 237n
Rwanda, 12, 32, 74n, 76n

Safwa people, 76, 196
Safwa rapids, 41
Said ibn Habib, 194
Salala *bana bonke*, 78n
salt, 114, 143n, 159, 163, 169, 180, 186–8, 207–8, 213, 222, 228, 246, 359–61, 378; *and see* Plates V and VI
Sambeek, J. van, 9
Sampa, Mulenda Kapalakashya, Chitimukulu (d. 1896), 57–8, 131n, 165n, 244, 273n, 317, 319, 325, 361
earlier career: in Ichinga, 87n, 129, 134n, 135–6; in Ichingo, 136, 160, 174, 203; quarrels with Bwembya, 129, Chitapankwa, 129, 136; Mande, 136; Mwamba II, 136; Nkula, 137, 176–7, 228
becomes Chitimukulu, 217–18; and E. African traders, 137, 226–7;

attitudes to Europeans, 233, 242–3, 245, 250, 252–3, 256–7, 259, 286; and Germans, 233–5, 286; and Lungu, 233, 235; and Makasa, 228–9, 233, 249–53; and Mambwe, 247; and Mporokoso, 223, 243; and Mwamba III, 218–19, 225, 228, 243, 257–8; and Ngoni, 366; and Nkula, 176–7, 228; his sons, 219, 220n, 235; and Tabwa, 219; village sites, 99n, 219n, 264; and White Fathers, 233, 250, 252–3, 267; death, 253–5, 271, 284; burial, 262–3, 272
Sangu people, 196
secession, 118, 157, 295–6, 300, 306–7, 319, 322
Selemani bin Mwenye Chande, trader, 5, 228n, 240n
Selim bin Abakari, 4, 234n, 235n
Sena, 191
Senga people, 20n, 41, 49–50, 55, 133, 135, 137–8, 188, 226, 241, 273, 278, 346, 374, 375n; see also Chibale, Chifunda
Serenje, 221n
Sewuka, 87
Shambaa kingdom, Tanzania, 319
Sharpe, Alfred, 223, 231–2, 237–41, 345
Sheane, J. Hubert West, 8, 181, 350, 358
shells, 207, 268
Shibwalya Kapila, Bemba chief, 157, 181, 219
Shila people, xxxi n, 19, 53, 61, 69; see also Mununga
Shimulamba, informant, 17, 87, 370
Shimumbi, chief of Bemba royal clan, 117, 321; Shimumbi I Nsapaila Nkumbula (d. c. 1905), 8, 118, 119n, 142, 145, 174, 177, 180–1, 219n, 223, 324
Shimwalule, 16, 20n, 42, 58, 88, 119, 272, 310n, 319, 345; *and see* Plates II and VI
Shiwa Ŋandu, 87n, 162n
shrines for deceased chiefs, 14, 79, 95n, 110n, 312; *see also ngulu*, spirits

Shula Malindi, 79
sieges, 146, 150, 205–6, 237, 239, 273
signal-drums ('talking-drums'), 39, 210, 345; *and see* Plates V and VI
Silva, J. B. Abreu da, 191n
Silwamba, 100, 145
slave-raiding, 137, 200, 204, 213, 233, 239, 241n, 246, 258, 284, 288
slavery, among Bemba, 197
slaves, xxvi, 103, 131, 137, 167, 300; liberated, 250, 252, 258, 273; as presents, 248–50; value of, 207
slave-trade, 189, 196, 204, 208, 231, 236, 238, 240–1, 255; among Bemba, 167, 196–8, 200, 206, 212, 215, 223, 225–7, 258
smallpox, 145n, 165n, 217, 218n
Smitheman, F., 274n
Sompe, *kabilo*, 16, 80
songs, 14, 137, 266
Songwe river, 67n, 253, 256–8
sons of chiefs, as title-holders, xxx, 79–80, 94, 98, 103, 106, 138, 145–6, 153, 173–4, 176, 180–1, 219, 228–9 238, 299, 301, 309, 311, 325; *see also* Makasa, Mporokoso, Munkonge
Spencer, 263–4, 267–8
spirits, ancestral, 14, 133, 163n, 310; and retribution, 129, 131, 173, 229, 261, 353; other spirits, 70–1; *see also ngulu*; shrines
spirit-mediums, 311–12
spirit possession, 71
'stake-holders', 310–11; *see also bakabilo*, councillors
'Stevenson Road', 231, 233, 236, 246, 249, 257n, 287
Stewart, James, engineer, 3, 184, 372
'structural duration', 323
succession, 296; adelphic, 60, 295; alternating, 297n, 322; indeterminate, 13, 323; rotational, 91, 297, 301, 322
 within Bemba royal clan, xxix, 180, 213, 306–7; of early Chitimukulus, 27, 78, 88–9, 91–2, 297, 320; in 19th century, 299–300, 312, 320, 324–5; in 20th century, 289, 320–3, 362

of Chiliamafwa, 95; Chinchinta, 101–2; Chileshye, 103–4, 353; Bwembya, 128; Chitapankwa, 129; Sampa, 218; Makumba, 260–1, 265, 275, 313
 in Ichinga, 90–1, 134–6, 270, 279–80; in Ituna, 95, 104–5, 123, 217–18, 278, 282–3; in Miti, 105–6, 160, 220, 277; at Mwalule, 272n
 among Bisa, 297–9; of Kazembe, 199–200, 304; among Mambwe, 297; among Ngoni, 365; among Tabwa, 153, 156–8, 238, 311n
 see also bakabilo, matriliny, positional succession, sons of chiefs, wife-inheritance
Sukuma people, 20, 42, 73–5, 78, 87, 97, 110, 354; iron-working, 184, 186, 188, 207n
Sukwa people, 67n
Sumbu, 238–9, 269
Sunkutu, 157–8, 181, 237n, 280, 284, 291n, 383
Susula, *see* Chinchinta
Suumba Kasuumba, Fipa chief, 78, 149
Swahili people and traders, 25, 137n, 193, 212–13, 233, 255, 353
 among Bemba at Chikwanda's, 227; Chitimukulu's, 196, 204; Makasa's, 249; Mwamba's, 201, 281; Nkolemfumu's, 161; fighting for Bemba, 145, 150, 203, 237; settlers in Bemba country, 17, 201
 and Chishinga, 139n, 155n; and Kazembe, 94, 199; and Matipa, 142n; among Tabwa, 153, 158–9, 208, 220, 239, 242; *see also* Abdullah ibn Suliman; Teleka
Swaka people, 221
Swann, Alfred, 240
sweet potatoes, xxvii, 210–11

Tabora, 73, 150, 158–9, 194–6, 198, 258
Tabwa people, xxviii, xxxi, 5, 12, 19, 76, 95, 181, 187, 199, 211, 295, 346, 348–9; and Bemba,

Tabwa people—*cont.*
151–3, 155–60, 204, 220, 247,
382–4; and E. African traders,
152–3, 155–60, 195, 198, 200, 202,
208, 220, 225n, 237–8; and
Kazembe, 96, 110, 152; and Ngoni,
143, 153, 349, 372, 373n; *see also*
Kaputa; Mukupa Katandula;
Mulilo; Nsama
Tafuna, Lungu chief, 148–51, 157,
170n, 231, 233n, 357, 373
Tambo people, 188
Tanganyika, Lake, 3–5, 66, 143, 148,
150–2, 193–4, 196, 225, 230–1, 233,
236, 240
Tanguy, F., 9, 11, 30, 58
taxation, 284
Teleka, trader, 208, 238
Tente, 219
terror, 167
Tete, 190–1, 227
Thomas, F. M., 9, 121n
Thomas, William, 245–6
Thomson, Joseph, 25n, 171n, 197,
241, 357, 373
time, concepts of, xxvi, 19, 22–6,
69–70, 77, 82
'Tippu Tip' (Hamed bin Muhammed
el Murjebi), trader, 2, 25, 136,
148n, 149, 153, 155, 159, 162n,
195–6, 202–3, 239
'Tituna', 135n
Tonga people (of S. Zambia), xxvi
trade, xxvii, 12n, 307, 326; in local
products, 182–9, 206–9; long-distance trade, 183, 189–214, 316–17,
325; *see also* Arabs; Bisa; firearms;
ivory; slaves; tribute; Swahili
trade routes, 2, 107, 110, 113, 129,
151, 190–1, 193, 196, 199–200, 213,
225–7, 298, 319, 371
treaties, 97–8, 147, 151n, 215, 221–2,
246; with Europeans, 231–2, 238
tribe, xxvii, 20–1, 23, 37, 39, 43,
45–6, 56, 68
tribute, xxx, 29, 165, 169–71, 182,
184, 187–9, 200, 207, 208n, 307,
361; for Chikwanda, 163, 180,
361; Chitimukulu, 61n, 78, 88, 98,

117, 180, 184, 189, 199, 222–3, 228,
243, 361; Kazembe, 97, 107, 110,
190; Makasa, 99, 146, 195n;
Mwamba, 118, 152, 158, 181, 207,
221–2, 361; Nkula, 188n, 228, 361;
Nsokolo, 248n; Shimwalule, 16,
272n; *see also* cattle; ivory
Trivier, E., 4, 237
tsetse fly, xxvii, 74, 189
Tumbuka people, 145, 346, 365–6
Tumbwe people, 346, 348–9
Tungati, Bemba chief, 117, 141,
152n, 181, 345
Tweedie, Ann, xix, xxiv, 9n, 70n,
90n, 91n
typologies, 296, 308, 317n

Ujiji, 159, 193–4, 196, 236, 240–1
Umuonga, 70
undertakers (*bafingo*): 83–4, 107n;
for Chitimukulu, 16, 19; *see also*
Kakwela; Shimwalule
Unga, 20n, 188
Uningi, 143n, 187n
Unyanyembe, 159, 258
Ushi, 20n, 45, 189n, 199, 218n, 346

Vansina, Jan, xix, xxv, 32, 35, 51–2,
60, 75, 296, 308, 345n
Velten, Carl, 4–5
Verhulpen, E., xxv, 8, 11–12, 52, 54,
57, 348
villages: administration of chiefs',
166, 168n, 285, 316; village
histories, 31–3; movement of
villages, xxviii–xxix, 17, 36–7;
size of villages, xxvii, 116, 165–6
village headmen, xxviii, xxx, 16–17,
80, 82, 88, 95, 165, 169–70, 223,
285, 295
village-sites (*fibolya*), 14, 33, 36–7, 56,
70, 87n, 90n, 95n, 98–9, 103, 121,
140; *see also* capital
Vinza people of Tanzania, 76n, 361

warfare, 113, 126, 145–6, 150–1, 168,
183, 203, 205–6, 234, 237, 304,
344, 373; *see also* firearms, fortification; military organisation;

warfare—*cont.*
sieges; war-charm; war-leaders; weapons
war-charm (*ilamfya*), 100, 159, 351; *and see* Plate IV
war-leaders, 78, 118n, 145n, 168, 268, 274, 284, 316
Watson, A. B., 280–1
Watson, William, xxiii, 65
weapons, 79, 137, 153, 183, 202–4, 237, 243, 372; *see also* firearms
Weatherley, Poulett, 5, 205, 218n, 223, 243, 246, 252, 256, 258, 270, 280
weaving, xxvii
Werbner, R. P., xix, xxiv, 172, 177, 179, 195n, 307, 319, 325
White Fathers: records of, 4, 9, 10, 30; found Mambwe mission, 231, 246; at Kala mission, 233–5; visit Chilangwa, 248; and Makasa, 249–53, 256, 259–60, 265–8, 276n, 287, 291n; found Kayambi mission, 252; and Makumba, 261–2, 275–6; and Mwamba III, 253, 259–60, 262–3, 267–9, 273n, 276–7; and BSAC, 251, 253, 265, 278–9, 282–3, 287–8; school, 265; and Bisa, 273; found Chilubula, 283; found Chilonga, 285; buy Chibwa salt, 359–60
wife-inheritance, 129n, 260
Wissmann, Hermann von, 4, 234–7, 242, 244, 286

witchcraft, 167, 230, 245, 266, 278
'wives of the relics' (*bamukabenye*), 16–17, 131n
women, xxviii, 137n, 246, 252, 266, 277, 282, 382; as occasions of conflict, 41–2, 107n, 122, 140, 143, 167, 237, 250, 263; as political authorities, xxix, 111n, 113, 119, 134; *see also* gift-exchange; marriage; 'mothers of chiefs'; wife-inheritance; 'wives of the relics'
Worringham, F. C., 239, 274n

Yao people, 107, 191, 210n, 236
Yeke people, 17, 73, 111n, 199, 205, 206n, 207–8, 213, 223, 296, 347, 364; *see also* Msiri
Yombwe people, 142, 223n
Young, Robert, 7, 12, 27, 58, 196n, 263–5, 267–70, 271n, 272–5, 278–9 281, 283–4, 371
Young, T. Cullen, 354, 364
Yule, James B., 240

Zambezi river, 2, 36, 52, 119, 190, 193–4, 227n, 364
Zanzibar, 2, 159, 191, 194–6, 198, 230
Zombe, Lungu chief, 146n, 147n, 148n, 149–51, 203, 205–6, 233n, 236, 351, 357–9, 372–4
Zulu people, 128n, 206, 315, 326n
Zumbo, 190, 192n, 221, 227n, 366
Zwangendaba, 119, 364–5, 369